WHEN COINS WERE KING

The Coins, Power Struggles, and Personalities That Defined a Nation

MICHAEL F. MORAN

4001 Helton Dr., Florence, AL 35630
whitman.com

Correspondence concerning this book may be directed to the publisher,

Attn: *When Coins Were King*, at the address above.

ISBN: 978-07948-51002 / ZT1947 09/25 / Ebook ISBN: 978-07948-50937
Printed in China

Dedication

This book is for Dee Dee, who has been by my side for fifty-five years and more.

I also want to acknowledge Congressman Andy Barr (KY 6) and retired Congressman Jimmy Hayes (LA 7) for their friendship and belief in my "quixotic adventure." Without their efforts, there would be no reissue of the Morgan and Peace dollars.

CONTENTS

Foreword, by Jeff Garrett ... vii
Prologue ... ix

Part 1. King of the Hill

1. How to Move a Mountain ... 2
2. A Mess from the Gitgo ... 7
3. That Midas Touch ... 12
4. Promontory Point ... 20
5. The Great Gold Heist ... 26
6. Billy Ralston's Sweet Setup ... 32
7. A Bright Shiny New Mint ... 38

Part 2. The Crime of Seventy-Three

8. A Hodgepodge Affair ... 47
9. Flirting with a Quixotic Idea ... 53
10. Rollout ... 58
11. Kelley v. Hooper ... 64
12. Fruits of Victory ... 69

Part 3. House of Cards

13. No Common Muckers ... 76
14. Too Many Rotten Apples for the Barrel ... 82
15. Linderman to the Fore ... 90
16. Humpty Dumpty Sat on a Wall ... 99
17. Humpty Dumpty Had a Great Fall ... 106

Part 4. John Sherman

18. Resumption ... 115
19. No Redemption for the Double Dime ... 119
20. Dogfight ... 124
21. Turning Point ... 133
22. Art Breaches the American Consciousness ... 138
23. A Gathering of Scoundrels ... 148
24. Dollar of Our Daddies ... 160
25. Linderman's Demise ... 173
26. Grasping the Golden Ring ... 182
27. Changing of the Guard ... 188
28. We Want Garfield! ... 193

Part 5. Rising Giants

29. Triumph and Tragedy ... 198
30. The Pendleton Act ... 208
31. Stirrings of Controversy and Conflict ... 217
32. In Death's Shadow ... 225

33. Change but No Change 237
34. The Sherman Clan 248
35. A Rooseveltian Return 255
36. Pandora's Box 266
37. Barber's Masterpiece 273

Part 6. An Affair for the Ages

38. The Greatest Show on Earth 282
39. A Breach of Faith 289
40. The Sum of All Evils 294
41. Pride and Prejudice 301
42. Seeking to Best the Mint 307
43. And All Hell Broke Loose 312
44. A Tale of Two Men 322
45. A Cross of Gold 329
46. A Glorious Retreat 333

Part 7. Victory in Hand

47. Laying the Foundation 341
48. Barber's Revenge 348
49. In the Bright Sunlight of Morning 352
50. To Buffalo and Beyond 358
51. The Art of Governance 367
52. In His Own Right 376
53. A Medal as Millard Fillmore and More 381
54. An Unwanted Interference 392
55. Trial by Fire 402
56. Racing Against Death 414
57. Twice a Failure 422
58. Chaos Reigns 430
59. A Bad Time for a Bear Hunt 435

Part 8. Beauty Is Truth, Truth Beauty

60. Frank Leach 449
61. The Last Word 460
62. The Golden Era Begins 464
63. Fixing an International Nuisance 476
64. The Great War and the Return of the Silver Dollar 483
65. The Nicest Birthday Present Ever 488
66. The Bitter End 494

Epilogue 497
Acknowledgments 505
About the Author 506
Notes 506
Bibliography 506
Index 507

FOREWORD

Jeff Garrett

I have known the Mike Moran for twenty years. I doubt anyone else possesses the unique qualifications to tell this story about our money. Mike has an engineering degree, which enables him to understand the process of coin production. Serving his fourth four-year term on the Mint's design review board, the Citizens Coinage Advisory Committee, Mike is a "greybeard," knowledgeable in coin designs and in the ways of the Mint. In addition, he has a master's degree in business, which, coupled with his extensive business experience, enables him to understand and explain the financial policies that drove American coinage in its heyday.

The story begins with the discovery of the Comstock Lode on the western edge of what was then the Utah Territory. William McKendree Gwin, California's "first senator," was successful in slicing this barren land away to form a new territory, called Nevada. His action gave the financiers in San Francisco the upper hand in developing this discovery, which would eclipse the Gold Rush of 1849. Thus, Billy Ralston and his Bank of California crowd ruthlessly muscled out would-be competitors.

Ralston's reign came to an ignominious end when his bank failed in 1875. The subsequent scandals would reach all the way to the director of the Mint in Washington, D.C. Yet the silver from the Comstock Lode was not to be denied. Mined in never-before-seen quantities, it would flood the world's markets and create a political movement in the United States.

Mike details the story of John Sherman, first as the powerful chairman of the Senate Committee on Finance and then as Treasury secretary, as he fought to stem the demand for unlimited silver coinage while maintaining a de facto gold standard for the international markets. This story is rich in detail, including the fact that senators were well into their cups—in fact, embarrassingly drunk—in the early-morning voting that restored the silver dollar as legal tender currency in 1878.

Mike also serves as an officer of the congressionally chartered Theodore Roosevelt Association. He has in-depth knowledge of the rise of the twenty-sixth president. Roosevelt, serving on the Civil Service Commission, ran head into John G. Carlisle, the Democratic secretary of the Treasury. In anger over Carlisle's blatant political appointments, Roosevelt recommended that the Treasury Department, including the mints, come under the jurisdiction of the commission. Initially, President Cleveland tabled Roosevelt's recommendation, but politics would force him to take that action in May 1896. With a stroke of Cleveland's pen, the machine politics that had riddled each of the mints and assay offices came to an abrupt end.

The presidential election of 1896 proved an inflection point in the struggle of gold versus silver in American politics. The flamboyant William Jennings Bryan led Silver Democrats against William McKinley and the Republicans. Theodore Roosevelt was in the thick of this campaign, delegated to follow Bryan through the swing state of Michigan, giving speeches supporting gold. In a little-remembered speech in Detroit, Roosevelt proclaimed, "We are citizens of a republic ever brightened by the rays of the morning." This is the genesis of what would become the design for the spectacular obverse of the Saint-Gaudens twenty-dollar gold piece.

Mike, working from his past research, gives us both the genius and the flaws of Augustus Saint-Gaudens, America's premier sculptor at the end of the nineteenth century. From the ashes of the Morgan tomb fire to his disastrous Columbian World's Fair Award Medal, Saint-Gaudens rises to create the *Shaw Memorial* and the *Sherman Monument.* Thus Theodore Roosevelt, recognizing William Jennings Bryan as the probable Democratic candidate in 1908 with silver a likely campaign issue, turned to Saint-Gaudens to provide fresh designs for our gold coinage. In this manner, Roosevelt sought to make gold coins tangible objects in the lives of everyday Americans. He never anticipated the delays he would have to surmount in the bureaucracy of the Mint Service. Nor did he realize that Saint-Gaudens was fighting a losing battle with cancer.

Mike presents the ensuing struggle in easily understood terms. He points out that Saint-Gaudens missed a golden opportunity in March 1907 to do an end run around engraver Charles Barber at the Philadelphia Mint. He also highlights a last revision made by Saint-Gaudens but never provided to Roosevelt as the sculptor sought a marriage of obverse and reverse designs that would strike up effectively when placed into mass production.

Mike also brings to focus a little-recognized fact: While Roosevelt and Saint-Gaudens struggled over the design for the twenty-dollar gold piece in the spring and summer of 1907, the director of the Mint paused the striking of these coins with the old design in Philadelphia. He compounded his error by not moving the vast hoard of gold coinage stored at the San Francisco Mint due to the cost of transportation. Thus, when the Panic of 1907 hit, efforts to quell the run on the New York banks and trust companies were severely hampered by a shortage of gold coins. Roosevelt's drive for fresh designs on the gold coinage almost caused a blot on his presidency.

There are fresh insights on the origin of the Peace dollar design as the story progresses through the recall of gold in 1934 and the withdrawal of silver coins from circulation in 1965. However, Mike does not stop there, but adds the story of the legislation reauthorizing the Mint to strike silver dollars in 2021. He and Tom Uram were the visionaries behind this legislation.

While this book covers a broad time span, it doesn't overlook the forgotten details that give life to the story. The use of the term "the one percent" to describe the rich and powerful was not invented by the current generation. And Franklin Roosevelt's "best birthday present ever," the Gold Reserve Act of 1934, was far from it.

Mike has married numismatics with American history in this story of the golden age of coinage in an engaging manner. It was a time when coins drove American politics—a time when coins truly were king.

PROLOGUE

It is gone now; a time when what jingled in our pockets had value, mattered to us. It was a golden era and a silver one, too. Those coins drove politics in the last half of the nineteenth and early years of the twentieth centuries. They still exist in the hearts and minds of those who collect coins. This is a story of how those coins came to be, and how they drove our politics in ways that still affect our nation today.

Our story starts with the great Comstock Lode, a discovery of gold and silver that outshone the California Gold Rush and fueled a rebound in our nation's shaky paper-driven economy after the Civil War. You will read about the outsized personalities who fought life-and-death struggles to control the vast wealth of the Comstock. Against this backdrop are the political shenanigans that fed off the Comstock Lode's great wealth and the shockingly widespread corruption at the San Francisco Mint.

Next we shift to the national stage as the size of the Comstock strike impacts the market for silver, already saturated with excess quantities from the move by European countries away from silver to the gold standard. Enter John Sherman, a man every bit as pivotal in the nation's history as his more famous brother, the Civil War general. From his powerful position as chairman of the Senate's Committee on Finance, Sherman leads the effort to address the impact of a growing silver supply on the nation's monetary structure. His actions will fuel a split within the major political parties and lead to William Jennings Bryan's famous "Cross of Gold" speech in 1896.

Into this political cauldron comes a young, idealistic politician, Theodore Roosevelt. He plays an outsized role in attacking the vast political-spoils system that had so thoroughly undermined government, including the United States Mint Service. In combating the silver movement in the 1896 presidential race, Roosevelt speaks of his vision of America, "a Republic ever brightened by the rays of the morning [sun]."

When Roosevelt ascends in meteoric fashion to the presidency, he brings with him a cast of characters that includes Augustus Saint-Gaudens, America's most famous sculptor, a rock star of his time. The two men team up in an artistic collaboration to replace the designs of America's gold coinage. The result is the most stunning coin design ever to grace American coinage—the Saint-Gaudens twenty-dollar gold piece. But Roosevelt's purpose was deeper than creating objects of beauty. He wanted gold coinage to be an everyday element in the lives of Americans. Thus the people would embrace these gold coins through their spectacular art and silver would truly become the subsidiary metal and its politics sidelined.

Roosevelt is almost thwarted in this endeavor by passive resistance within the Mint. The resulting delays are driven, for the most part, by a long-standing personal feud between Saint-Gaudens and the engraver. With Saint-Gaudens dying from cancer, completion of his designs becomes a race against death. Finally, the delay in issuing the new gold coins exacerbates the Financial Panic of 1907. Theodore Roosevelt then must align himself with his adversary, Pierpont Morgan, to prevail.

What transpires will usher in a period of economic stability that provides the financial foundation for the United States to assume a position of leadership among the nations of the world.

For two decades coins enjoyed a glorious ride. Yet there were fissures in this foundation of wealth. The Federal Reserve, established in 1913 to prevent future financial panics like those that had plagued the country every 20 years, reigned but did not rule in the 1920s. Required gold reserves to support the nation's paper currency were too lenient. Speculation was rampant. Meanwhile, gold accumulated as the result of favorable trade balances, pushing gold coinage to record highs. That was like pouring accelerant upon a raging fire.

Economists will long argue about the causes of the Crash of 1929 and the Great Depression that reached seemingly bottomless depths in 1933. Another Roosevelt president, Franklin, was faced with a need to counter the deflation sweeping the country. The recall of gold coinage, followed by a devaluation of the dollar, was a first major step. It was the beginning of the end of the reign of coins.

The end for coins came quietly to a final resting place with the elimination of silver from our subsidiary coinage in 1965. The link between face value and intrinsic value was permanently broken. Our coinage was now no different from our paper currency. In fact, without the legal tender status conferred by law, these new metal discs were little more than tokens. Over the subsequent years ongoing inflation has eroded their purchasing power, relegating the minor coins to a point of insignificance.

Still, for coins the story ends on a better note. In 2021 a law was passed that provided for the coinage again of Morgan and Peace silver dollars. While now being struck as numismatic items, the law allows for striking these coins annually; there is no sunset provision. The face value of these two silver dollars is meaningless, but the concept of a legal tender coin with intrinsic value has returned. Though gold and silver coinage are never to reign again as they once did, there is a future role for these silver dollars.

Part 1

King of the Hill

Chapter 1
How to Move a Mountain

California Senator William McKendree Gwin settled into his chair on the floor of the new Senate chamber in the nation's capital. It was February 26, 1861. In a week his second term would end and he would be swept away by the winds of war. As opulent as this theater-like chamber was, everyone complained. It was cold and drafty.

At least it wasn't raining. Rain on the glass-paneled ceiling coupled with the room's terrible acoustics would have made doing business today nearly impossible. And the business of the day had major implications. It concerned control of silver and gold just across the California state border in Utah Territory.

By the beginning of 1860 rumors were afloat all over San Francisco about this silver strike in Utah Territory. Gwin could not ignore it. One of his neighbors on Rincon Hill, a young banker and political supporter, Billy Ralston, was already involved and making loans to the mining companies.[1] A twitch of the pencil was all it would have taken to put this discovery in California.

Gwin had been involved in setting the state's eastern border prior to statehood—an arbitrary border at best. Now, if allowed to stand, control of this mineral wealth would go to Salt Lake City and not San Francisco. Gwin was not about to let that happen.

The saga begins on a bleak-looking peak called Mount Davidson, at 7,868 feet the highest in Nevada's Virginia Range. Its surface was home to a lot of sagebrush, a few scattered juniper trees, and not much else. Rough little gullies cut into its eastern slope. The Forty-Niners drawn overland by the lure of gold in California passed by without a second thought. If anyone stopped, it was to rest the horses in the Carson River Valley before the final push over the Sierra Nevada Range to the goldfields.

Early in 1850 Mormons on their way to California camped on the Carson River to wait for the snow to melt in the Sierra Nevadas. Whiling away the time, they prospected on the eastern and southern sides of Mount Davidson at the southern end in an area that would be known as Gold Canyon. While they found some gold, it was not the bonanza they felt sure of striking in California, and they moved on.

It was only when the easy pickings of placer mining gave out in California that a few derelict prospectors backtracked east looking for the next big gold strike. Even then there was nothing. By the winter of 1858–1859, only the toughest of the lot remained. Then word came of gold discovered at the head of Gold Canyon in an area known as Gold Hill. This was the southern outcrop of the ore body.

At the same time two prospectors were working at Six Mile Canyon, the head of which was two miles from that of Gold Canyon. They were digging a pit to capture water for their primitive rocker boxes used to separate the gold from the extraneous material when they discovered a strange-looking layer of blue-black sand about four feet from the surface. When they washed this material, they found gold in abundance. At this point Henry "Old Pancake" Comstock bulled his way in, claiming grazing rights in the area. A partnership of convenience was formed. The date assigned to this discovery was June 11, 1859.

The men at first ignored the black sand that clogged their rockers, casting it aside as they recovered their gold. However, as they dug deeper, the oxidized sand gave way to a solid vein of rock that could not be worked in their rockers. They had to crush this rock, using sledgehammers to recover the gold. Only with the aid of two *arrastras*, primitive mills for grinding and pulverizing gold or silver ore, could they keep mining.[2]

They were working a *lode*, mining terminology for what geologists call a vein. It is a deposit of ore that fills or is embedded in a fissure in a rock formation or between two layers of rock. *Ledge* is the term for the entire ore deposit. This ledge would in places spread out within cavernous pockets to yield an amazing amount of ore. When a mine reveals such a pocket, it is said to be "in bonanza."

Some two weeks after the discovery, a rancher took the cast-off material to Nevada City, where it assayed out at $3,000 per ton in gold and silver. In August 1859 the first ore reached San Francisco, where 38 tons yielded gold and silver worth $112,000. Refined bars of silver were exhibited in the windows of one of the banking houses. The rush was on.

J. Ross Browne, a sometime Treasury investigator, was a writer and traveler who had come west to California in 1849. In early 1860 he visited Virginia City, a town on the eastern slope of Mount Davidson. What he described was anything but a bonanza.

> On a slope of mountains speckled with snow, sagebushes and mounds of upturned earth, without any apparent beginning or end, congruity or regard for the eternal fitness of things lay outspread the wondrous city of Virginia. Frame shanties, pitched together as if by accident; tents of canvass, of blankets, or brush, of potato-sacks and old shirts, with empty whiskey-barrels for chimneys; smoky hovels of mud and stone; coyote holes in the mountain side forcibly seized and held by men; pits and shafts with smoke issuing from every crevice; piles of goods and rubbish on craggy points, in the hollows, on the rocks, in the mud, in the snow, everywhere, scattered broadcast in pell-mell confusion, as if the clouds had suddenly burst overhead and rained down the dregs of all the flimsy, rickety, filthy little hovels and rubbish of merchandise that had ever undergone the process of evaporation from the earth since the days of Noah.[3]

The first prospectors to arrive laid claims but lacked the expertise and capital to evaluate and develop their holdings. Comstock and the others sold out for pittances and left in search of easier pickings. Development would come through stock corporations, distributing risk across the shareholders. These corporations, in addition to paying dividends, would also levy assessments or cash calls when capital expenditures exceeded cash flows from the mining operations. These shares would find a ready outlet for trading when the San Francisco stock exchange was established in 1862.

One of the first with the potential to exploit the Comstock was Billy Ralston. His banking firm, Donohoe, Ralston & Company, had the money. Also one of the partners, Eugene Kelly, resided in New York City and provided access to Eastern financial markets. The Union had resorted to printing greenbacks to finance the Civil War while California banks, forbidden by its constitution from issuing paper currency, aided by plentiful gold, stayed on the gold standard. Shipments of gold and silver went east, and all kinds of goods priced in greenbacks came west. It was profitable to buy in the East where gold brought an added premium in greenback spending power. It took $113 of greenbacks to buy $100 of gold in 1862, $145 in 1863, and $203 in 1864. Thus, profits came to the California merchants, the San Francisco banks, and the speculators. Profits came seemingly effortlessly to Donohoe, Ralston & Company.[4]

On April 28, 1860, the Ophir Gold & Silver Mining Company was incorporated with Ralston as treasurer. One of the other incorporators was Louis Garnett, the melter and refiner at the San Francisco Branch Mint

The mining was not easy, even with capital. Ore veins were encased in large masses of unstable rock consisting of partially decomposed porphyry, a coarse-grained rock and sheets of clay that swelled when exposed to air. As mining progressed at the Ophir Mine, heavy machinery became necessary, including a steam-powered lift to move men and materials in and out of the mine. Supporting the cavernous mining areas were honeycombs of timbering. In addition, the raw ore had to be pulverized in a stamping mill, requiring water, before transportation to San Francisco for smelting and refining.[5]

To make matters worse for Ralston and the other Ophir investors, a title dispute arose in December 1861. At issue was whether the Comstock Lode was one continuous ledge, as the Ophir Mine owners claimed, or multiple ledges. The newer Burning Moscoe miners argued that the Comstock Lode consisted of many discrete, unlinked ore bodies and they were working distinct, separate pockets of gold and silver.

The resulting court case ended in a hung jury. With so much money riding on the outcome of title lawsuits, ruthless tactics by the attorneys were the order of the day. It was common knowledge that witnesses, jurors, and judges were bribed. Both sides would use any defense necessary to win. It was a situation made to order for Ophir's lawyer, Bill Stewart.[6]

William "Bill" Morris Stewart had come to California seeking gold with the other Forty-Niners and found the law instead. He was part of the original movement among California miners to establish a body of mining laws to regulate title. He also had a reputation as an intelligent, aggressive lawyer who would use any technicality, trick, or threat to win a case. He could win exceptionally complex cases against able opponents. He was Billy Ralston's man.

Ultimately the case would go before the territorial Supreme Court to be ruled a single ledge. Then in the face of public opinion favoring the small miner, the ruling justice resigned, and his replacement reversed the decision. Stewart tried an end-run through a proposed constitution for the new state that would allow appointing judges friendly to the single-ledge theory. In the end, he succeeded.[7] Ultimately, geologists concluded the Comstock was one large ore body running along a single fault line. The way was clear for Billy Ralston to make major investments in the Comstock Lode.

Now seated in the elegant new Senate chamber, Sen. Gwin was alert this February day of 1861. How things had changed since he first took his seat as California's newly minted senator in September 1850. At the height of his power, he had been the unchallenged leader of the southern wing of the Democratic Party in California, known as the "Chivalry." Opposing Gwin had been the leader of the northern wing of the party, Senator David Broderick, who learned his trade with Tammany

David Broderick, upon arriving in California became a principal in the Pacific Company, a San Francisco private mint operating before the establishment of a federal branch mint and issuing five- and ten-dollar gold pieces in 1849. Ultimately the pieces were found to be notoriously short in the gold content compared to their face value. By the time this fact became known, Broderick had moved on to politics.

Democrats in New York City. After Broderick was killed in a duel by a member of the Chivalry, his party faction affiliated with the Republicans in the Presidential election of 1860. As a result, the Republicans narrowly carried California, leaving the state Democratic Party in disarray. Gwin not only could not gain re-election, he was finished politically.

This was Gwin's last gasp. A new bill, S.563, carving out the western counties of Utah into a new territory named Nevada was finally going to the Senate floor. Efforts had been made over the last two weeks to get it on the calendar while there was still time to get it passed in the House before this Congress adjourned. There was initial debate as to whether a window for slavery to exist would be provided, consistent with that contained in the Kansas-Nebraska Act of 1854. Gwin voted with his southern colleagues on that issue, knowing full well it would be defeated. Too many southern states had already left the Union. Gwin just could not let go of his southern roots.

And now the way was clear. No more debate, the bill was read a required third time and passed.[8] Wresting control of this mineral wealth from Utah was Gwin's parting gift to his adopted home, California. The House passed S.563 on March 1, 1861.[9] The territory would become a state in 1864 with Bill Stewart going to Washington as one of its senators. The gold and silver strike, known as the Comstock Lode, would prove to be gargantuan. Its silver would ignite a storm of populist politics that would rage for the remainder of the 19th century and beyond.

Chapter 2
A Mess from the Gitgo

The San Francisco Branch Mint that came into operation in April 1854 was a makeshift operation of the first order. Its very authorization had been touch and go. Despite the need for a mint to monetize California's gold production, there were forces in Congress arrayed against it. A branch mint was a political plum. In the end San Francisco got its mint and New York City's financial interests received the consolation price of an assay office. The downside for San Francisco was that Congress cut the appropriation for establishment of this mint to the bone.

When Joseph "Jos" Harmstead learned that San Francisco was to get a branch mint, he picked up stakes and headed for California. By his own admission, mint work was in his blood. As a new machinist, he had helped set up the first steam coin press in Philadelphia in March 1836. He had gone to New Orleans to take a similar position when that branch mint opened in 1838. Over time he learned that employment at the New Orleans Branch Mint relied far too much upon the whims of the political party in control.[1] Once in San Francisco, he quickly discovered that he had not escaped politics. Jobs at the mint came through California Senator William Gwin.

Harmstead would remember the date well; it was September 17, 1853. Up Rincon Hill to Harrison Street he climbed. When he reached Gwin's address, he found more

The first San Francisco branch mint.

steps to climb to reach the home. He was thoroughly out of breath as he knocked on the door. The meeting went well enough, but he left with nothing firm. That came in November in a letter from Mint Director James Ross Snowden appointing him as a machinist at the new branch mint.

Just as the branch mint was a product of compromise, so was its initial management. The superintendent, Lewis Aiken Birdsall was Senator Gwin's man. The two most important operative officers, John Eckfeldt as coiner and John Hewston as the melter and refiner came from the Philadelphia Mint. They bore the responsibility of making the mint actually work. The assayer, Agostin Haraszthy, knew almost nothing about his job.

Hewston quickly assessed Birdsall as potential trouble. This "short, jolly, imperious man with the grey mustachios," was anxious to have as much patronage as possible. Some of Birdsall's appointments were purely political and outrageous … telling a handsome widow desperate for a job that it was hers, if she became his mistress.[2] And as cramped as the mint was, he wanted the fourth floor for his personal apartment.[3]

John Eckfeldt was the scion of a family that had been a fixture at the Philadelphia Mint from its inception. His father was foreman of the coining room there. His great uncle had been the coiner at Philadelphia for a generation. While knowledgeable, this Eckfeldt was hard to please, alienating about everyone in the coining room. It was not

This double eagle was the first struck at San Francisco and resides in the National Numismatic Collection.

long before Harmstead, the glow of the first double eagle struck from his coin press having long worn off, wrote to the California governor in an attempt to have Eckfeldt removed. That complaint got J. Ross Browne, representing the Treasury Department, to the mint for an investigation. Browne concluded that John Eckfeldt was a gentleman of talent and integrity and highly qualified to be coiner.[4]

Eckfeldt seemed not to be deterred by the investigation. In October 1856, William Bein, an employee in his coining department, was accused of stealing gold and silver clippings. He slipped them out of the mint by adhering them with a sticky substance to the inside of his boots. In the trial, testimony revealed that both Eckfeldt and his assistant coiner gave coin blanks to the men in the coining department in violation of mint regulations, a fact that both men at first denied.

A grand jury, responding to bills of indictment, indicted Eckfeldt and his assistant coiner. However, due to absences and illness, the membership of the grand jury changed. The reconstituted grand jury unanimously ignored the bills of indictment.[5] Browne was again called in to investigate. While the assistant coiner was dismissed, Eckfeldt, like a cat with nine lives, survived. This time Harmstead appealed to Gwin's rival in the Senate, David Broderick only to be met with silence.

By now the wear and tear of continuous coin operations had made a bad situation worse for the mint structure. As part of his investigation into Eckfeldt, Browne found that the building could not long stand the strain of the volume of coinage being produced. Acid leakage and the weight of machinery on the upper floors that displaced rafters made future expenditures to repair the building inexpedient. The interior of the building was dark in most spaces. With poor ventilation, it was hot, particularly in summer. Acid fumes from the refinery permeated everywhere. In short, it was a miserable place to work.

John Hewston had lasted only a year at the branch mint before he resigned, moving into private sector assay work; it only added to the turmoil. Much to Hewston's disgust, in a musical chairs affair, Agostin Hasaszthy assumed the melter and refiner's position. However, there was poetic justice here. When Haraszthy resigned his position in April 1857, his accounts came up short for the final seven months. He was out of balance by more than $201,000, of which $51,000 was allowable as wastage. Some of the bullion had volatilized during the refining process as was evidenced by gold found on the rooftops surrounding the mint. Yet that explanation was not a complete answer. Had all the missing gold been volatilized, the roofs around the mint would have had a golden glow in the bright California sunshine. This case would drag for years with Haraszthy finally being acquitted. (In 1891, house movers working on Eckfeldt's former residence, while excavating the basement floor discovered a wooden box filled with small gold ingots and granules worth $143,000. This evidence strongly argues that Eckfeldt stole the gold and then set Haraszthy up to take the fall.)

When Charles Hempstead was appointed superintendent of this branch mint, he walked into this position with full knowledge of Eckfeldt's shortcomings. Working under an interim appointment, his hands were tied without the full force of a formal nomination and Senate approval. Nevertheless, Hempstead sent a letter to President James Buchanan praising Jos Harmstead as a gentleman of intelligence, fully conversant with the scientific and practical operations of the coining department. Harmstead's experience suited him for any position in that department.[6] It was a subtle way of asking that Eckfeldt be removed.

After the Mint, John Hewston went to work for the private assay firm of Kellogg and Humbert. Shown is one of their gold ingots recovered from the SS *Central America* shipwreck.

Hempstead's nomination was approved in the Senate May 11, 1858.[7] From here on, Eckfeldt was on borrowed time. It seemed as if Harmstead's time had come. Rumors concerning Eckfeldt's imminent removal reached the newspapers in December 1858. On January 7, 1859, President Buchanan named a new coiner to the San Francisco Branch Mint, it was not Harmstead but one Riley Slocum.[8] This man, while employed in the coining department, had also served as president of the Board of Aldermen in San Francisco. Plus, he traveled to Washington to advocate for his own appointment.

The *Daily Alta* had more to say on the subject. It seemed that Slocum had served on the original grand jury in the trial of William Bein and that he, in collusion with another juror, had managed to get Eckfeldt presented for perjury in the case. The motive of course was to obtain Eckfeldt's position.[9] Jos Harmstead never had a chance in this game of hardball.

The fruits of Slocum's victory were short-lived. With a national victory for the young Republican Party in the presidential election of 1860, the Democrats at the mint were out. Robert Stevens was the new superintendent. He was the son-in-law of the fiery Edward Baker, Lincoln's close friend. William Schmolz was the new coiner. Eckfeldt returned as the assistant melter and refiner. Harmstead was going to need the patience of Job if he ever expected to gain appointment as coiner at the San Francisco Branch Mint.

Stevens got off to an embarrassing start in a very public spat with the new mint treasurer and assistant U. S. treasurer for the San Francisco Sub-Treasury, David W. Cheeseman. This Nevada man had a reputation for being poor but honest, a rare combination among office seekers for San Francisco. Opposition was raised against his appointment in Washington, and again a still greater fight in San Francisco. However, he had Secretary of the Treasury Salmon Chase in his corner to carry the day.[10] Not surprising, given the lack of local support, Cheeseman had trouble raising the bond required for his dual position, further delaying his official commission.

When Cheeseman arrived the second week of June 1861 under an interim appointment, the treasurer in place, Jacob Snyder, refused to turn over the keys. Rumors flew to the effect that Snyder was going to turn the money in the vaults over to secessionists. The next morning Cheeseman returned, backed by a group of tough-looking friends, and Snyder capitulated.

The mint treasurer had two or three clerks under him that the superintendent upon consultation appointed upon his nomination. Cheeseman had promised these positions to friends in order to gain the necessary signatures on his performance bond. Meanwhile Stevens, unaware of the protocol, promised these positions to friends of his father-in-law. The result was that both sets of clerks reported for duty. Cheeseman's men held the keys to the vault while Stevens's men had bonds in place for their positions. Cheeseman also appointed a cashier and assistant clerk associated with his position as assistant treasurer. He carried the day, but now had two men with grudges to bear.[11]

Greed caught up with Stevens in January 1863. He had riddled the mint with incompetent workers. Some did not bother to even show up except on paydays. The going "rate" to secure a position at Stevens's mint was a payment of $500 in gold.[12] J. Ross Browne, called in by Treasury for yet another investigation, reported that Stevens had regularly purchased supplies at 50 percent above market rates from selected merchants. Also, he had hired his mentally ill brother to a position of importance. Stevens was removed May 9, 1863.[13]

Stevens's replacement was Robert Swain. Swain would occupy the superintendent's chair for six years, somehow holding the place together and giving it a bit of stability.

Chapter 3

That Midas Touch

Luck rode on the shoulders of Billy Ralston. On June 27, 1867, he moved the Bank of California into its palatial new headquarters in San Francisco. Ralston had cut no corners, spared no expense. He had driven countless pilings down to bedrock to ensure a stable foundation. The exterior with its 42 columns was of polished blue stone quarried at Angel Island in the Bay. A great bronze door guarded the main entrance on California Street. The financial district coalesced around the bank, becoming known as the Wall Street of the West.

The interior exuded an opulence not seen heretofore in San Francisco. The floors consisted of alternate squares of black and white marble. The ceilings of the main banking area were 19 feet high, frescoed by competent artists. At each teller's elbow were stacks of gold and silver coins that could be scooped up with little trowels as needed. From where the patrons stood, they could also see a large coin table piled high with even rows of gold coins. To the rear of everything was the directors' room, marble paneled with frescoed scenes of Bridal Veil Falls and the floor of Yosemite Valley.[1]

The opulent headquarters of the Bank of California, as seen in 1868, were located at the corner of California and Sansome Streets.

The bank owed its magnificence to the Ophir Gold & Silver Mining Company. A shaft had been sunk to exploit the mine's quartz ledge at the point of the original discovery. This ledge quickly widened from four feet to 20 and then to 30 feet.[2] The Ophir Mine was in bonanza. Money flowed in amazing fashion. In a few short weeks the company was able to pay off the cost of its stamping mill. Bill Stewart's legal charges were a minor nuisance. Ophir had been incorporated with capital of $5,042,000 with16,800 shares issued at a par value of $300 each. In April 1862 those shares were selling for $1,225. In October they peaked at $3,000.

The story of the Gould and Curry Mine was much the same. An ore lead turned into a bonanza, the stock spiraled, and Ralston exited just before the production began to tail off.[3] This was not a game for amateurs. Still for those in touch with mine operations, investing could reap large dividends. For Ralston, the issue was how to control this veritable gusher of gold and silver.

Ralston's string of luck in the Comstock was rudely interrupted in January 1863. The Ophir Mine hit water at the 400-foot level. A miner plunged his pick into a clay seam and out shot a stream of hot water, scalding one workman and knocking others down. When it was over, a hot, steaming, foul-smelling lake of water 100 feet long, 30 feet wide, and 21 feet deep existed. Hardly had that lake been drained than another water pocket was tapped. Everywhere in the Lode the story repeated itself.

Ralston's solution was to install an 80-horsepower engine and pump from Vulcan Iron Works in the Gould and Curry, the wettest mine. Eight months later, water ripped the engine from its foundation. Ralston responded by ordering a massive 120-horsepower engine with a bigger pump. However, it would take a year for this behemoth to be installed and operational. Meanwhile the Comstock Lode and, therefore, San Francisco depended on dewatering the mines.[4]

Ralston had a second problem as well, a disagreement with his banking partners over their future business strategy. Seen from Ralston's eyes, California was a cornucopia of investing opportunities fueled by a rapid increase in its agricultural and industrial output. With the burgeoning Comstock Lode providing the capital, what more could a banker desire?

His partners, Eugene Kelly and Joseph Donohoe, had doubts. They were content to manage a conservative loan portfolio to established businesses in San Francisco. They were not comfortable with the high-risk stakes of the Comstock Lode. Kelly, in particular, wanted more of the firm's money sent east to invest in the New York financial markets. He also believed that some of Ralston's loans were not adequately secured.

When matters reached an impasse, Ralston bolted.

California had modified its corporate charter laws in 1863 to permit savings banks to make commercial loans. On June 24, 1864, the Bank of California's certificate of incorporation was filed in the county clerk's office. This would be just the second joint-stock corporation empowered to do commercial lending in the state.

Ralston had created a powerhouse. The bank opened for business in the former offices of Donohoe, Ralston & Company. Ogden Mills, the oldest and strongest banker on the Pacific Coast, would be the bank's president. Ralston would serve as cashier, the chief operating officer, making all of the day-to-day decisions. James Lees of Lees and Waller, an old friend of Ralston's from his earliest days, would handle the bank's New York transactions.[5] With an initial capitalization of $2 million, only two of New York's 55 banks were larger.[6]

This image presents Billy Ralston at the height of his power, a leading citizen of San Francisco and ruler of the Comstock Lode.

Billy Ralston now had his hands on the wheel of his own ship. His institution would be a source of ample credit for the economic development of the Pacific Coast. California would become self-supporting, an entity unto itself. To accomplish these goals, he brought his book of business with him. This made an enemy of Ralston's partner, Eugene Kelly in New York City.

To fuel his bank, Ralston knew he had to control the Comstock Lode. Into this equation entered William Sharon. Sharon had lost heavily in a shady stock bet on a Comstock mine. Concurrently, Ralston's corresponding bank in Virginia City had failed as word leaked out that unmanageable quantities of water were being encountered in the mines, causing stock pledged on loans to nose-dive.

Ralston needed someone to salvage as much of the Bank of California's money as possible from the fiasco. J. D. Fry, Ralston's father-in-law, convinced Ralston to take Sharon on as his agent for the location. Fry would guarantee the $15,000 performance bond the bank required for the position.[7] Ralston, in turn, loaned Sharon money and gave him $500 to feed his family.[8] However, Billy hedged his bet, sending his brother, James Alpheus Ralston, to be Sharon's assistant.

Sharon was a small, dark, nervous man. He sported a dangling mustache and a small lip beard. He dressed in plain black.[9] His only display was a gold-headed cane. He was a legendary poker player. When told of Sharon's habit, Ralston asked, "Does Sharon win or lose?" Told that his agent most generally won, Ralston replied, "Then I didn't misjudge him."[10]

Sharon went right to work, regaining much of the Bank of California's lost capital. Then Sharon visited the mines, actually going to the working faces. He made two recommendations to Ralston. First, the Bank of California must monopolize the Comstock Lode both on and below the surface. It must control the supplies, the timber needs, and the haulage. But above all, the bank must control every mine and mill on the Comstock. By control, Sharon meant holding only enough stock in an entity to dictate management decisions. Second, the water from the offending rock strata must be drained off the Lode. Before anything else, they must solve this problem. With the bank's capital committed to the Comstock, Billy Ralston really had no choice in the matter.[11]

Bill Sharon was placed in Virginia City by Billy Ralston to act as the representative of the Bank of California. Sharon rapidly consolidated the bank's power over the Comstock mines and mills.

On September 6, 1864, the Virginia City branch of the Bank of California opened with Sharon as manager and Ralston's brother as cashier.[12] Sharon's first initiative was to undercut competing banks by offering interest rates on loans that seemed cheap by comparison. The end result was that five competing banks in Virginia City and three in nearby Gold Hill either failed or exited the market. Sharon also absorbed the two best-established banks. He now had the Bank of California in a dominant position with loans to the most important mines and stamping mills, requiring the pledge of stock certificates and assets as security.[13]

Not only was Sharon tough; he was lucky. A few months after arriving, he gained control of the Yellow Jacket Mine for the Bank of California. Supposedly worthless, it went immediately into bonanza. Then as the Yellow Jacket's profits began to slip, Hale & Norcross and its neighbor to the north, the Savage, boomed into prominence.[14] By 1866 he had added control of the Chollar, Potosi, and Crown Point mines. In addition, Ralston helped in the control of the Kentuck Mine. All these came into bonanza that year.[15] For Sharon there were profits on the side purchasing a mine's stock, "bulling" it to new highs with selected positive rumors, and then selling.

At this stage, businessman Adolph Sutro met with Ralston in San Francisco. He had a dewatering solution: Drive a tunnel from the mines on Mount Davidson down to the Carson River. In this manner both ore and water could be removed from the workings. In exchange there would be a $2 per ton royalty for ore thus transported. Ralston jumped at it but then suffered buyer's remorse. The royalty from the mine owners' viewpoint was really a tax. Ralston withdrew his support, resulting in the two men being at each other's throats. Eventually, Sutro built his tunnel, but it was not completed in time to make any significant impact on the Comstock Lode.

While the Sutro affair was playing out in San Francisco, Sharon was flexing the bank's muscles with the stamping mills. These mills were built to make money by processing ore. Not only did they gain a fee from the mines for the ore processed but they also gained the rights to the tailings. Typically, 70 percent of the assay value of the ore was recovered for the mines. Of the other 30 percent within the tailings, about half could be recovered through reprocessing for the benefit of the mill owners.[16] Given adequate feedstock, it was like having a mine without all the headaches of mining. As long as these mills had ore to process, they could repay their loans. If a mine hit a "dry spell," the mills quickly found themselves in trouble, unable to service their loans.

Sharon was merciless if a mill was in default; he foreclosed. Worse, he was not above squeezing a mill by diverting ore from a mine that the Bank of California controlled to another mill. One by one the mills fell, with their water rights, to the bank. By the end of 1865, some of the best mills were under the control of the Bank of California.[17]

In August 1866, Billy was hit with the unexpected death of his brother, James, at the age of 31 after a two-week illness. James was an honest and religious soul held in high regard in Virginia City.[18] Ralston had lost his check on Sharon, but after two years of dealing with the man, he now held him in high esteem.

By 1867 Ralston and the bank controlled seven stamping mills. Sharon fed the mills belonging to what was now termed the "Bank Crowd" and starved the few remaining independent mills. Their owners offered to reduce processing fees by one-half, but no mines took advantage of the reduction, fearing to offend the bank. By 1869 they would control 17 mills, consolidated under the Union Mill and Mining Company.

In another Sharon move, the superintendents of the mines under bank control were notified that the interests of Union Mill and Mining Company were paramount to their own. Sometimes when a rich ore body was discovered, the superintendent was told to mix rock with the ore. In that way the mills could extract a larger fee than justified from the mine, thus transferring profits from the mine's stockholders to Union Mill and Mining.[19]

Meanwhile investment fever reached new heights on the San Francisco exchanges for the shares of the mining companies not controlled by the Bank of California or the Bank Crowd. Reports of a find would drive a stock to fantastic highs. Then in a few days or weeks, news would trickle out that the ore was petering out, and the stock would crater. In this game, Bill Sharon was the consummate player.

On March 5, 1868, the Bank Crowd incorporated the Virginia and Truckee Railroad. It was a bold move done with other people's money. The counties of Washoe and Ormsby contributed $500,000 under their bonding authority with the understanding that property taxes would service the bonds and generate revenue to boot. Somehow that added tax revenue never quite seemed to materialize. The mines that had originally volunteered to fund a portion of Sutro's tunnel were made to contribute that amount, $887,374, to the railroad. That was enough to fund the initial construction.

As president of the Bank of California, Ogden Mills served as a check against Ralston's more risky business ventures.

This was not an easy track to construct. Ground was broken on February 19, 1869, and eight months later service was established between Virginia City and Carson City. From the mines to the mills, the track was a continuous decline, dropping 1,600 feet in 13-1/2 miles with a maximum grade of 2.2 percent. The total curvature of the line was equal to going in a circle 17 times. There were six tunnels totaling 2,400 feet, all lined with zinc to prevent fires.

The line was eventually extended another 31 miles along the Truckee River to Reno where it joined with the Central Pacific on August 24, 1872. In all, the line stretched 52 miles while covering a total distance as the crow flies of only 16-1/2 miles. It was known as the crookedest railroad in America. In the end Ralston, bank president Ogden Mills, and Sharon owned the railroad in equal amounts.[20]

For the Bank Crowd, this was not a one-way haul. On the back haul, the line brought timber from the Tahoe Basin. Here the Carson and Tahoe Lumber and Fluming Company, under their control, owned 50,000 acres of timber. Added to that were the machinery and supplies coming from San Francisco.

Ralston and his associates now controlled the Comstock Lode. If that were not enough, they also set up a water distribution system under the name of the Virginia and Gold Hill Water Company.[21] Ralston had funded Sharon's vision, and they could now squeeze the Comstock like a lemon.

Billy Ralston's grand vision was to harness the wealth of the Comstock Lode to fund the development of San Francisco. He saw the city rising to be a greater port than New Orleans. With its relative isolation from the rest of the nation, Ralston wanted the region to develop its own industries, to be self-supporting and independent. He wanted a cosmopolitan city as the centerpiece of this empire. And in this vision, the tentacles of Billy Ralston and the Bank of California would be everywhere.[22]

In less than three years Ralston had nearly $1 million invested in Pacific Woolen Mills, another $2 million in New Montgomery Real Estate, and $600,000 loaned to Kimball Manufacturing, which produced rolling stock for the railroads. He organized the Union Silk Manufacturing Company with capital of $250,000. He built a large dry dock at Hunter's Point, near the city to service ocean going vessels. He was an investor in the Culp Consolidated Tobacco Company, using imported seed from Havana. He even bought and transported from Illinois the Cornell Watch Factory.[23]

There were other ways that Ralston exerted his influence in the business community. When the Central Pacific Railroad broke ground on the western end of the transcontinental railway, the toughest going was in the early construction. The initial capital put up by the founders of the railroad was insufficient to carry them to the point of receiving bonding aid from the federal government. Leland Stanford, the railroad's president, went to the Pacific Insurance Corporation seeking a personal loan of $100,000. Ralston told the board that the Bank of California would backstop the loan if it went delinquent. The loan was approved.[24] No project was too daunting if it furthered his vision of California.

At the same time Bank of California was moving into its new headquarters, Ralston was spending $1 million on a summer residence 22 miles south of the city on the peninsula. The property was flanked on one side by the coastal mountain range and on the other by foothills. He "upgraded" the home on the property, christened Belmont, expanding it to 55,000 square feet over four stories with some 50 guest rooms.[25]

While the San Francisco and San José Railroad passed near the entrance to Belmont with daily train service, Ralston almost always used a coach-and-four. His passion was horses. His ivy-covered stable nearly always had 60 to 100 of the best horseflesh on hand. Blacks were his favorites. Characteristic of the man, his drives to Belmont were races against the steam locomotive, and he most always won. He had two prearranged stops along the way to change out the teams. He even had a long stretch of the road resurfaced with pulverized rock so that he could make better time.[26]

For the uncrowned king of San Francisco, a voice in Washington was an increasing need. In the summer of 1865 an amalgamation of the Republicans and Northern Democrats, called the Union Party would decide on California's next senator. Ralston's man was Charles Felton. A lawyer by training, he was active in the mercantile business and banking. Felton started early, wrapping up votes among the state legislators with news reports making indirect allusions to money changing hands.[27] Felton

Belmont, Billy Ralston's extravagant country home, served as a weekend retreat for Ralston and his favored guests. Here, amidst lavish entertainment, business relationships were cemented.

had serious competition. F. F. Low, a former governor, and Aaron Sargent, a former Congressman, were in the running. However the winner was Cornelius Cole, Secretary of State William Seward's friend.[28] When Low saw he could not win, he threw his support to Cole. No one seemed to want Sargent.

Unfazed, Ralston had an alternative home for Felton. No one knew who wanted David Cheeseman out as treasurer of the mint and assistant treasurer at the Sub-Treasury, but a betting man would have put his money on Ralston. President Andrew Johnson nominated Felton on July 20, 1868, to replace Cheeseman, and the Senate approved the nomination in spite of a move by California's other senator, John Conness, to reconsider.[29,30]

One of Felton's first acts was to request the secretary of the Treasury to increase temporarily the bullion fund at the mint by $1 million. The pretext was to better accommodate the bullion depositors during the annual settlement of accounts of the mint at the June 30 fiscal-year end when all coining operations ceased. The secretary consented, and Felton kept these funds in the Sub-Treasury. Somehow Treasury lost sight of the money and their temporary nature became permanent.[31]

In the end, Charles Felton would serve Billy Ralston much better in this position.

Charles Felton would prove invaluable as Ralston's man at the San Francisco Branch Mint.

Chapter 4

PROMONTORY POINT

A transcontinental railroad should have happened long before May 10, 1869. However, the politics of slavery stymied all efforts to designate a primary route in the 1850s. Only after the South seceded from the Union did efforts start to make real progress. In 1861 the Central Pacific Railroad was organized to build east from Sacramento. The Union Pacific Railroad was organized in 1862 to build west from Omaha. To aid the financing, the federal government provided land grants and construction subsidies. But no dirt was moved until the end of the Civil War.

The initial going was tough for the Central Pacific. It had to breach the Sierra Nevada Range where land grants added little of value and subsidies were inadequate for rugged terrain. Once construction was solidly underway, the Bank of California was instrumental in helping the railroad place the necessary bonds in Europe to fund this construction.

On the other hand, the Union Pacific raced across the prairies west of Omaha. Subsidies for this terrain proved generous, and land grants had value. The going got tough when construction reached the east slope of the Rocky Mountains. Finally, the Union Pacific used Mormon financing over the last leg.

The two lines met at Promontory Point in northwest Utah. At this point, the elevation is about 5,000 feet—800 feet above the nearby Great Salt Lake. Looking east from the meeting point, there was a clear view of the crystal-blue waters of the lake with the snow-capped Wasatch Range on the horizon. West, beyond the Great Salt Lake, was nothing but desert.

The morning of the ceremony dawned cold and misty. There was ice on the puddles. But with the rising sun, the mist burned off to reveal a beautiful clear day. Just before noon the two engines were drawn up to face one another at the gap between the two rail lines."

Ogden Mills's son, Edgar, representing the Bank of California, would be the master of ceremonies at the event. Fred Tritle, also part of the party as well as a candidate for governor of Nevada, carried with him a silver spike from the Comstock Lode. Tritle was the superintendent of the Yellow Jacket Mine and an initial shareholder in the Virginia & Truckee Railroad. A second spike made of iron, gold, and silver was carried by Anson Safford, the recently appointed governor of Arizona Territory.[1]

At Promontory Point the rails of the Central Pacific and Union Pacific met, linking California to the nation and, more importantly, opening the state's markets to competition from Eastern manufacturers.

Here the telegraph operator sent to the nation at large: "Keep quiet. When the last spike is driven at Promontory Point, we will say 'Done!' Don't break the circuit but watch for the signals of the blows of the hammer." With all in place, heads bowed and the invocation was given. With the "amen," the telegrapher operator sent a message east: "We have got done with the praying. The spike is about to be presented."

Indeed, two golden ceremonial spikes were handed to Leland Stanford of the Central Pacific. One was smaller, was clearly a memento of the famous event. The other spike, made from twenty-dollar gold pieces, more commonly called double eagles, weighed 14.13 ounces and was 5-5/8 inches long. There were great details engraved on the side of the spike. However, on its head was simply: "The Last Spike." As the spikes were presented, they were placed in auger holes prepared in advance in the ceremonial tie. More speeches were required. Meanwhile, Thomas Durant from the Union Pacific returned to his railcar complaining of a headache.

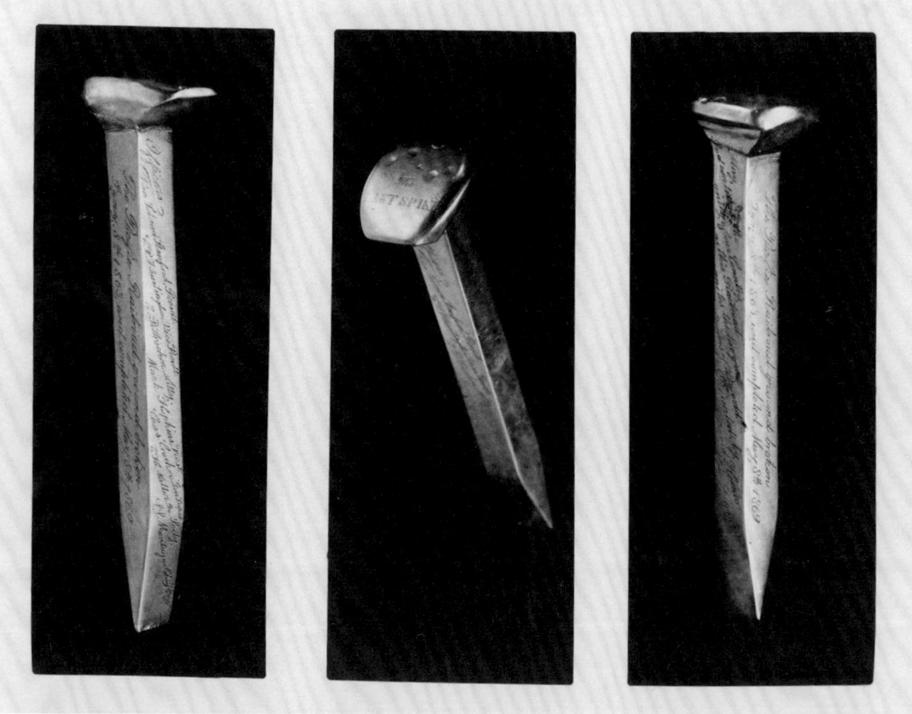

This is the ceremonial golden "last spike" from Promontory Point. Note the indentations on the head of the spike made by the spike maul during the ceremonial striking.

The real last spike was made of iron, its head polished and wired to one side of the national telegraph hookup. In this way the actual blows driving the spike could be recorded as they happened. The spike had already been partially driven into a regular tie adjacent the ceremonial laurel tie.

What the celebration at Promontory Point lacked in size—fewer than 1,000 people came from all corners of North America—San Francisco easily made up for that morning.

About 11 o'clock the bells rang and the steam whistles at all the foundries and machine shops, the vessels in the harbor, and the branch mint let loose a deafening scream, continuing for what seemed an hour. Then the parade commenced, involving troops and military bands, fraternal organizations, and detachments of firemen.

Judge Nathaniel Bennett, a respected attorney of long standing in the city, gave the oration of the day. The *Sacramento Daily Union* quoted part of his speech:

> Now travel and commerce on the beneficent errands, outstrip the wind in its progress. Boundless space has, for the purposes of business and pleasure, become contracted almost to a mathematical point. The far distant has been brought near. The remote has been made present. The lightning only outstrips the steam-impelled cars.[2]

It was as if the speech had been aimed at Billy Ralston. And with each blow, that last spike went deeper into his empire.

While the nation saluted the singular event of the joining of the rails at Promontory Point, Billy Ralston had less reason to celebrate. The year 1869 was shaping up to be a difficult period for him and the bank.

Actually, the problem had started the previous year. Comstock production fell that year by $5 million from the $13.7 million achieved in the flush times of 1867.[3] Compounding the problem, the miners' union had exacted a wage increase from $3 to $4 per day for all underground workers that was cemented when 300 of their members demonstrated in September 1867 at the Savage Mine, the last holdout.

Then the unthinkable happened. Ralston and William Sharon lost control of the Hale & Norcross. John Mackay, superintendent of the Kentuck, and Jim Fair, superintendent of the Ophir, had determined to have a go at the Bank Crowd. As superintendents, they had access to any of the other mines. An inspection of the Hale & Norcross led the two men to believe that more ore was yet to be discovered there. In January 1868 they began to accumulate shares. However, their funds were quickly expended, requiring them to turn to two men they knew in San Francisco, James Flood and William O'Brien. As partners, Flood and O'Brien had invested in some of the leading Comstock mines in 1862. While they were now running a saloon in the city, they had the capital to keep Mackay and Fair in the game.[4] Still the four men came up short.

Ralston had been forced to go to financier Alvinza Hayward for help to fend off the four upstarts and retain control of the Hale & Norcross. In return, Hayward gained acceptance as one of the Bank Crowd. Still Sharon could not help himself; he was both arrogant and foolish in victory. He called the four men muckers and bartenders worth $4 a day.

Meanwhile the Hale & Norcross went "dry." No dividends were declared, and the stock plummeted from its peak during the confrontation of $2,925 per share to $11.50 per share.[5]

The four men saw their opening and began to buy again. In mid-February, word leaked to the *Gold Hill Daily News* that prospects were very good for encountering more good ore bodies in the Hale & Norcross in the lower level.[6] Then two days later the same paper announced that Fair and Mackay had more than 4,000 shares of the

Hale & Norcross, a controlling interest.[7] Flood and O'Brien were still in the background but equally involved.

Actually, it was more dramatic than that. Control came down to 100 shares held by a widow in San Francisco. Sharon sent a coded message to Ralston that was intercepted by Flood, allowing him to get there first. The widow received $8,000 per share for her holdings, and Ralston and Sharon were shown the door.[8] The four men quickly bought the Bacon Mill at Gold Hill. They would add two more in quick succession.[9] The Bank Crowd's monopoly was dented but hardly broken.

Even though the Hale & Norcross went into bonanza, total production from the Comstock Lode would drop another $1.3 million in 1869. Ralston revealed to Sharon the tight position he and the bank were in. Unless there was a new bonanza, Ralston would not be able to liquidate his large, indebted position with the Bank of California, and the bank would have to suspend.

Sharon insisted the Comstock Lode was not played out. Work was progressing in the deeper levels of the Crown Point Mine. There was also a promising lead in Yellow Jacket. Yet while comforting Ralston, Sharon made a mental decision. For the last two years, the men had invested 50-50 together in a partnership. Sharon would now start to back away, investing strictly for himself.

It got worse. On the morning of April 7, the Yellow Jacket Mine caught fire. It happened at shift change. The daylight shift was headed down in the cage to replace the graveyard shift as smoke began to billow out the shaft. The fire was at the 800-foot level, allowing the day-shift men to be retrieved. However, the men coming off shift at the 900-foot level were trapped. The Yellow Jacket steam whistle began to shriek the alarm, summoning the fire department. Smoke went through the inter-connecting drifts to the Kentuck and Crown Point Mines, forcing their evacuation.[10] All the firemen could do was pour water down the shaft in an attempt to suppress the flames.

The superintendent of the Crown Point Mine, John Percival Jones, was the unlikely hero of the day. Born in Herefordshire, England, Jones had come to America as a toddler and at age 20, drawn by the lure of gold, had journeyed to California. His politics had caught the attention of Sharon and Ralston resulting in their offering him first the superintendent's position at Kentuck and then at Crown Point. Nothing in this background revealed the streak of steel that drove Jones that day.

Jones, observing the futile efforts, took over in the evening. He made several attempts to breech the 800-foot level to reach the trapped miners. However, each time he was driven back by the gases emitted from the fire. Finally he penned a note, placed it in a cage with a lantern, and dropped it to the 900-foot level. After what seemed an eternity, the cage was retrieved. The lantern was extinguished, and the note, untouched.

Rescue now was pretty much out of the question. Still the fire must be extinguished. Jones with a volunteer went down one more time. The goal was to attach a steam line to the mine's blower. By injecting steam, the fire could be put out. They made it to the blower but failed to attach the line. Jones just barely made it out with his companion unconscious.[11]

The fire would burn for weeks, devouring the timber roof supports. Without these supports, the roof collapsed, forcing the mining in the impacted gallery to be abandoned. In all, 42 bodies were recovered and 3 were left entombed. Accidents killing and maiming men were common in the mines, but there never was a catastrophe to equal the fire at the Yellow Jacket.

Ralston would ultimately donate $5,000 to the widows and orphans of the Yellow Jacket fire.[12] He would also make a capital call in July on the Yellow Jacket shareholders of $10 per share.[13]

It was reflective of Ralston's now tight situation that he wrote Mark Hopkins, treasurer of the Central Pacific, on May 8, 1869, the original day scheduled for the joining of rails at Promontory Point. He bluntly stated: "We must ask you people not to lean on us for a while—You know it is our pleasure to do all your wants when in our power."[14]

Whether Ralston needed more bad news or not, he got it. All that summer of 1869, traveling salesmen poured over the new rail link from Chicago and St. Louis, flooding California and Nevada with an avalanche of goods. The markets for woolen, silk and cotton goods, tobacco, furniture and more were quickly glutted.

There was no way Ralston's fledgling companies, once protected by the high cost of transportation into Pacific Coast markets, could compete. They lacked the size to gain economies of scale. Eastern manufacturers had large established markets allowing them to use incremental cost-based pricing for their California-bound products. With the collapse in business activity, rents dropped and, with them, real estate values for commercial properties.[15]

Many firms failed, others consolidated, and some just quit. Ralston was hit everywhere at once. He did what he could, auctioning off his real estate holdings.[16] However, in many cases there was no ready buyer. His capital and the bank's nonperforming loans were simply frozen assets of indeterminate value. Throughout this ordeal Ralston was faced with the necessity of maintaining the bank's one percent per month dividend.

Ralston was not alone in his predicament. The whole San Francisco region went into a mini recession.

Chapter 5

The Great Gold Heist

It was July 1869, and Billy Ralston needed $1 million in gold coin before the Bank of California opened the next day. How he raided the Sub-Treasury, walking out with sacks of gold coins, is the stuff of legend, hardly believable generations after it took place. The root causes of this brazen act lay within the American financial system.

To describe the monetary structure of the United States in 1869 as chaotic would be an overstatement. But descriptive terms such as "cobbled together," "inflexible" and "antigrowth" would certainly fit. At the onset of the Civil War, the country had not had a national currency for some 25 years, not since Andrew Jackson vetoed the charter extension of the Second Bank of the United States. The national currency structure that evolved during the Civil War was driven by the need to finance the Union's war effort. It yielded a financial system that could and would be manipulated.

The initial move to finance war expenditures involved $50 million of 7.3% interest bonds in August 1861, followed by two more $50-million issues later in the year. Funding was in gold, which drained the banks. However, this gold was recycled into the economy in payment for war materials, allowing the banks to re-accumulate gold to participate in the subsequent bond issues.

Then Union setbacks on the battlefield, deteriorating relations with England and France, and a Treasury projection of a large budget deficit sparked widespread specie hoarding. On December 30, 1861, banks across the country ceased paying coin against their obligations. The Treasury Department followed suit the next day. For all intents and purposes, the United States had abandoned the gold standard.[1]

In reaction, Congress was forced to authorize the first of three issues of United States Notes in February 1862. These notes were legal tender for all debts, public and private, except customs duties. By the end of the war, Congress had authorized some $450 million of these notes, soon called "greenbacks" for their distinctive reverse. The first notes were issued in April 1862 and immediately passed at a discount to gold coin. As the war expanded and the Union suffered more military setbacks, the discount to gold of these notes escalated, resulting in severe inflation.

A second funding of the war came from a profusion of federal debt instruments. The most important and ultimately the most controversial were the so-called 5-20s. These were tax-exempt bonds bearing a 6% interest payable in coin that the government could call in as little as five years but must call in 20 years. These bonds were sold for greenbacks but the law was silent on the principal repayment, currency or specie.[2]

At war's end there was a problem: To resume specie payments, greenbacks had to be convertible on a one-to-one basis with gold coin. To accomplish this resumption in the short term, the Treasury had to retire a substantial amount of these United States Notes. This would mean a drastic contraction of the currency, resulting in deflation with unacceptable economic consequences.

The third element in the war-driven financial system was the National Banking Act of 1863. This act called for a system of national banks under federal charter that, upon the deposit of federal bonds purchased in the open market with the controller of the currency, could issue new National Bank Notes equal in amount to 90 percent of the value of the bonds on deposit. These new notes were to be receivable for all public debts except customs duties, and payable for all government obligations except interest on the national debt. Congress placed a cap on the total amount of these notes issued at $300 million and subsequently amended that amount, increasing it by $54 million.[3] Although not legal tender they were redeemable in greenbacks and hence virtually equivalent.[4]

In April 1866 Treasury Secretary Hugh McCulloch was successful in passing the Contraction Act that allowed him to withdraw greenbacks from circulation. However, political resistance mounted, and the Contraction Act was repealed in February 1868. At that point $44 million in greenbacks had been retired.[5]

The 5-20 bonds became an issue in the 1868 presidential campaign. Soft-money men wanted the bond principal repayable in greenbacks. The argument was that these bonds had been originally purchased in greenbacks and the holder was not entitled to a windfall. Ulysses Grant's victory gave the hard-money men an upper hand, and in March 1869 Congress passed the Public Credit Act requiring payment of bond principal in coin. In July 1870 Congress would return to amend the act, requiring repayment in gold coins or the standard silver dollar.[6]

There were three major problems with this currency-driven financial system. Because greenbacks were not at par with specie, gold and silver coins would not

Greenbacks and National Bank Notes issued during the Civil War

circulate—they were still hoarded. Second the system was inelastic. Monetary supply could not be expanded or contracted to meet seasonal demand, critical for the post-Civil War agricultural economy. In spring and summer cash piled up in the rural or country banks. These funds were transferred to New York for short-term investment—call loans for brokers and stock market speculators. Stock prices boomed. In the fall these funds moved back to the rural areas for harvest. Times would then get proportionately tough on Wall Street.[7] The third problem was that the capital needed to create a national bank largely resided in New England where the economy was mature and its capital needs limited and stable. In other regions with economies in early-stage growth, capital needs outstripped availability restricting investment for national bank startups.

It was into this delicate balance of currency matters that railroad magnate Jay Gould and stockbroker Jim Fisk, with easy money available from the interior areas, attempted to throw a monkey wrench in the late summer of 1869. The use of gold by merchants for hedging and for paying customs duties (payable in gold coin only) and foreign balances put the commercial community at the mercy of New York speculators. Foreign traders were frequently "short" of gold—that is, they borrowed gold to be sold as a hedge against a falling premium, pledging greenbacks as security.

This situation offered Gould and Fisk an opportunity to plunder the import/export merchants. If they could win control of the gold supply, they could squeeze the foreign traders who needed gold to meet short contracts or to pay customs duties. To be successful, they needed the Treasury with $100 million in gold in its vaults to sit on the sidelines. Otherwise their attempted corner would be smashed.

By Thursday, September 23, 1869, gold contracts had been pushed up 12 points to 144. Commerce through New York was paralyzed since foreign traders refused to buy gold for customs remittances. Bankers and merchants showered Treasury Secretary George Boutwell with demands that he sell coin. At noon on the 24th (Black Friday) gold contracts hit 160, and Boutwell ordered the sale of $4 million of coin. The premium on gold contracts collapsed, falling in 15 minutes to 133. The crisis was over quickly.[8]

In San Francisco, Billy Ralston, already in a tight financial position personally, was backed into a corner. The mini recession in California had now worked its way through the system to the Bank of California. He was short gold coin.

President Grant was determined to make wholesale changes in the federal workforce in San Francisco. Among others, he removed the branch-mint superintendent and the operative officers. As a result, the mint would be closed to depositors for at least a month to close out the books of the former officers. Worse, Grant wanted San Francisco Mint Treasurer Charles Felton replaced by David Cheeseman. There were those in power in Washington who believed Felton would use government money to help out that "damned Bank of California" if it was in a tight place.[9]

Ralston wired California's congressional delegation asking that the proposed new branch mint officers not be confirmed. There was a large amount of gold bullion on hand waiting to be coined and the existing officers were fully capable of overseeing the branch mint.[10] He even had the banking firm of Lees and Waller apply pressure as agents for the Bank of California in New York.

Unfazed by this opposition, President Grant on April 16 proceeded to nominate Jos Harmstead as coiner along with Joe Cochran for melter and refiner and Oscar Munson, brought over from the Denver Branch Mint, for assayer.[11] Jos Harmstead had achieved his life's dream. On April 19 Grant nominated Cheeseman as treasurer of the mint and assistant treasurer for the Sub-Treasury.[12]

The issue came to a head on April 21. The Senate Committee on Finance recommended tabling the nomination of Cheeseman. However, with Senator John Sherman's support, the three operative officers were approved.[13] Two days later, Bill Stewart wrote Ralston that Treasury Secretary George Boutwell, newly installed under Grant, promised to withhold the commissions of the three operative officers until the gold coin shortage had safely passed. However, Boutwell made clear that any further conversation should be directly with Grant.[14]

The timing of what happened next is open to some uncertainty. That the events in question even happened are based upon the 1913 memoirs of Asbury Harpending, a business associate of Billy Ralston.

It was July 1869, just as Gould and Fisk were starting to corner the gold market in the East. Their actions caused gold coin to drain out of California making Ralston's situation even worse. Meanwhile Secretary Boutwell had been true to his word, holding back the commissions of the three operative officers until the end of June.[15] The branch mint went down on July 10 for the settlement of accounts, and no bullion would be received or coined until the reopening on August 14.[16]

All the banks in San Francisco were short of coin. Then Ralston learned through the rumor mill that there would be a run on his bank the next morning. He had bullion available but not nearly enough coin beyond the normal daily needs.

The mint was still closed for the changeover so exchanging bullion for coin there was not an option. In reaction to the run-up in gold prices in the East, President Grant had forbidden the issuance of any gold coin out of any Treasury vaults, to prevent profiteering. Ralston was seemingly trapped. He needed $1 million in gold coin before the bank opened the next day to survive the anticipated run.

In a panic, Ralston recruited Harpending and Maurice Dore. He told the two men to meet him at the bank at one that night. At the appointed hour, they walked the few steps to the United States Sub-Treasury located on Montgomery between Sacramento and California Streets. In Harpending's own words what transpired next left him in utter astonishment.

> A dim light was burning within. Mr. Ralston asked us to halt a few paces from the entrance; then to our great surprise he opened the door of the Sub-Treasury, without challenge of any kind, and closed it after him as he stepped inside. Presently he emerged with several sacks of coin. "Take that back to the bank," he said. "The gentleman there will give you something to bring back." The party at the bank received the cash, tallied it and handed us gold bars for the same value. These we took to the Sub-Treasury, where we found Mr. Ralston smilingly awaiting us with a new cargo of sacks on the sidewalk. We turned over the bars and made another journey to the bank.

So in the dead of the night the two men transferred nearly five tons of gold in Harpending's recollection. They kept at it until daybreak. During this time not a person passed to interrupt the two men. Harpending suspected that Ralston had had an arrangement with the beat cop.

The next morning, true to the rumors, there was a crowd at the door of the bank. The large working table had gold coins in stacks. Tellers brought more trays from the vaults. The crowd melted away. That was not the case at one of the other banks. Ralston hurried over and told the waiting customers that the bank was absolutely sound. However, if they were still desirous of obtaining their savings, they should bring their passbooks to the Bank of California where they would be honored. Ralston came out looking like a hero. He never told his partners, Ogden Mills or Bill Sharon how he had escaped a catastrophe.[17]

Ralston was not out of the woods yet. As Gould and Fisk ramped up their operation in August and early September, Lees and Waller, agent for the Bank of California in New York was now feeling the squeeze. Another midnight transfer at the Sub-Treasury was out of the question. This time Henry Linderman, in San Francisco now as a special agent inspecting the mint for the Treasury Department, came to Ralston's aid. He urged Secretary Boutwell to authorize gold transfers from the East Coast to the West Coast by telegraph through the Sub-Treasury system. A businessman on the East Coast who owed money or wished to transfer money to the West Coast could deposit gold coin at an East Coast Sub-Treasury. That would allow Ralston to lean on the Central Pacific, the bank's largest debtor, to start depositing gold for the benefit of the bank in the East.

As the gold conspiracy in the East escalated in September, Lees and Waller hit the wall. They wired Ralston for $500,000 immediately at any cost. The Bank of California and Lees and Waller stayed afloat just barely until Black Friday hit. Ralston's friend, James Lees, called it a severe squeeze—one that he hoped neither of them would ever experience again.

The gold game was only half of Ralston's funds problem in 1869. That fall California farmers had a record grain harvest. Ralston took advances from Lees and Waller to the tune of $1 million to fund the needs of the farmers. James Lees began objecting strenuously. At the same time, Ralston drew down £500,000 against a £250,000 line of credit with his London agent, Oriental Bank. The Oriental Bank went up in arms making Ralston put up personal assets as security for the overdraft. The Bank of California failed to meet the February 1870 deadline for repayment of the overdraft but made enough progress to buy more time. By summer of 1870, the crunch was over, and Ralston was released from his obligations.[18]

It had been very, very close. Billy Ralston still had his bank but left unanswered was how he pulled off the bullion-for-coin exchange at the Sub-Treasury. And, from where did the refined bullion originate that the Bank of California used in the exchange?

Chapter 6
Billy Ralston's Sweet Setup

Billy Ralston may not have understood the term "vertical integration with value added at each step in the chain of supply." However, he certainly practiced its principles. He controlled the mines of the Comstock. He controlled the processing mills. He controlled the railroad used to move the bullion on its first leg to San Francisco. The last piece in this chain was a refinery. The former melter and refiner at the San Francisco Branch Mint and fellow investor in the Comstock, Louis Garnett, was his man.

In 1865 Ralston, working with the Oriental Bank of London to develop new markets for his Comstock mines, shipped several consignments of silver bars to China and India. Soon the total reached $7 million per year.[1] To render this ore into silver bars of acceptable fineness, Ralston joined with his former partner, Joseph Donohoe, Garnett and two others to form San Francisco Assaying and Refining Works on April 27, 1866. One of their first acts was to acquire the assaying business of Kellogg and Stearns at 416 Montgomery Street. This gave them a physical location and the services of John Hewston Jr., who was employed by the assayers. Garnett would be the manager, and Hewston would be the assayer and superintendent.[2]

With Garnett and Hewston working under the same roof, it wasn't long before Ralston set his sights on capturing a substantial share of the branch mint's refining business. The San Francisco Assaying and Refining Works used the sulfuric acid method for parting gold from silver, much cheaper with a higher metal recovery than the mint's nitric acid process. Specifically, the process refined the bullion to a higher purity than the nitric system and allowed for recovery of trace metals. So the refiner gained the advantage of adding back silver to dilute his refined gold bars to the mint-specified 900 fineness and the revenue from the sale of the byproduct.

In Ralston's thinking, they needed the mint's refining volumes to gain economies of scale. About one-third of the value of the bullion mined in Nevada was gold and the remainder, silver. About half the product was refined in San Francisco. The gold went to coinage, and the silver went to the China market. The other half was exported, unrefined, to Europe.[3] Ralston wanted all the business.

Ralston's first order was to undercut the branch mint's price for refining. In turn, Superintendent Robert Swain responded by cutting the refining price at the mint, suffering a loss. Garnett estimated that the government was losing four or five cents an ounce in its refining activity.[4] At this point Joseph Donohoe could see that the refining works were going to be run for Ralston's advantage, putting him and his partner, Eugene Kelly, in New York in a subservient relationship. As a result, Donohoe withdrew from the partnership with Ralston.

Learning that one should not cut prices against a competitor that has no incentive to earn a profit, Ralston turned to Washington for the solution. He encountered resistance there in March 1867 when California Senator John Conness submitted a resolution requesting that the secretary of the Treasury disclose any information relative to proposed changes in laws on the refining of gold and silver.[5] There were two applicable laws concerning refining. An 1853 act required the secretary of the Treasury to limit the amount of refining at the Philadelphia Mint whenever private establishments were capable of refining bullion. The second act, passed in 1861, extended this requirement to the branch mints and the assay office in New York City.[6]

Conness had shined a bright light on Ralston's intentions. More importantly, Eugene Kelly now took an active stance against allowing contract refining in San Francisco. He enlisted California's other senator, Cornelius Cole, to request of the Treasury Department that no contract refining be done. He also engaged the services of Robert Stevens, the disgraced San Francisco Branch Mint superintendent, now employed as clerk to the House Appropriations Committee in Washington.[7]

To oppose Kelly and Stevens, Ralston sent Hewston east. The former melter and refiner tried first to get Treasury Secretary Hugh McCulloch to give a contract to the refining works under the existing laws. Contrary to logic, the secretary decided he lacked authority. That forced Hewston to turn to the House Committee on Coinage, Weights and Measures to seek legislation for the necessary authorization. Delays ensued giving Stevens and Kelly time to enlist enough House members to oppose contract refining, stalling the bill until adjournment.

In exasperation, Hewston wrote Ralston that he did not like living in Washington and transacting business with the "set one finds here." So he started over, traveling to Philadelphia to meet with Henry Linderman, newly in his first term as mint director. Hewston's visit put Linderman in a difficult position. He had previously opposed contract refining. However, he was President Johnson's appointee and Johnson had been impeached on March 3. Simply put, Linderman needed politically powerful friends. Hewston told Ralston that it was not easy, but he had convinced Linderman to change his mind.

In addition, Hewston now had Senator Cole on his side. But Cole had a price; he had a friend back in San Francisco who wanted an arrangement with the refining works or part of the business. Hewston told Ralston that he promised nothing and became affected with a dullness of hearing. However, Hewston was extremely concerned that Kelly would learn of his plans to end-run the legislative process and thwart him once again.[8]

On June 25, Hewston met with Secretary McCulloch and struck a deal. McCulloch would in a few days give orders to Swain to contract with such parties that could do the work. In fact, McCulloch did just that. Superintendent Swain was entirely receptive. He believed private parties could do the refining cheaper; they did not have the government red tape to hinder them.[9] Also, removing the function took away a great deal of the opportunity to steal bullion when it was in a transition state in the refining department. The contract called for the mint to exchange unparted bullion for refined bullion on an equivalent basis at a cost of eight cents per ounce, a savings of three cents to the government.[10]

However, before the effective date of the order, Stevens moved to block it. Introduced in July 1868, joint resolution, HR. 337, provided that the mint and its branches would continue to refine gold and silver bullion and that no contract to exchange crude or unparted bullion for refined bars should be made without authorization by law. The joint resolution also repealed the acts of 1853 and 1861 that permitted contract refining. The resolution easily passed the House.[10] Concurrently the issue was resolved in a Committee of Conference; buried in appropriations for sundry civil expense in fiscal 1869 was a provision that no contract to exchange unparted bullion for refined bars could be made in the coming year unless authorized by law.[11,12] Senator Stewart had advocated for the provision with a one-year cap. For once, Billy Ralston had been bested, temporarily.

Matters were in flux at the start of 1869. The incoming Grant Administration was intent on pushing Johnson appointees out the door. There would be a new Treasury secretary, requiring education on contract refining. Finally, there would be a new Congress with new faces requiring renewed lobbying efforts.

Eugene Kelly wasted no time in firing the first shot to get in front of Grant and the new Congress. He submitted a very detailed petition against contract refining to the House Committee on Coinage, Weights and Measures. He questioned the motive of the San Francisco Assaying and Refining Works. In spite of the immediate benefits to taxpayers, contract refining would eventually result in a monopoly.[13]

Kelly's lobbying then took a blow in February when Robert Stevens disengaged from the effort. He wanted to return to San Francisco and replace Swain in his old job as mint superintendent. He needed Ralston's "home endorsement," calling the banker an old acquaintance and one whose influence and importance Stevens always acknowledged while at the branch mint.[14]

Ralston was certainly not going to support Stevens after Stevens had opposed him in Washington.[15] However, he put Stevens on the payroll to lobby for the Bank of California on Capitol Hill. Billy Ralston was not giving up. There was some $50 million of unrefined gold and $10 million of unrefined silver coming from the West Coast into San Francisco to be refined. The mint refined $6 to 7 million, San Francisco Assaying and Refining Works refined about $15 million, and the rest was exported.

The gold bullion refined by Ralston was then bought by the San Francisco banks and forced into the mint for coining.[16] The reward from displacing the mint's refining was simply too great not to keep trying.

Ralston turned to Nevada Senator Bill Stewart. On January 22, 1869, Stewart introduced a simple bill authorizing the mint and its branches to exchange unparted bars for refined bullion. Accompanying the legislation were letters from the secretary of the Treasury and Mint Director Linderman in support of the legislation.[17] On that same day, William Kelley, chair of the House Committee on Coinage Weights and Measures, introduced an identical bill.[18]

Eugene Kelly countered, getting the Senate bill discharged from the Committee on Appropriations and ordering it to the Committee on Finance.[19] There he used Senator Edwin Morgan, a longtime associate from New York City, to oppose Stewart's bill.[20] With adjournment of this Congress looming, Ralston was blocked again.

Stewart wasted no time introducing the same legislation in the following Congress on March 5, 1869.[21] The bill was referred to the Committee on Finance and for 11 months sat dormant. To add fuel to the fire, Kelly apparently spread rumors in New York and Washington that the Bank of California management was corrupt and its condition unsound.[22] With the problems that Ralston was facing at that time, these observations had merit.

Senator George Williams from Oregon, broke the logjam when he asked Treasury for reports on refining at the New York Assay Office and the San Francisco Branch Mint.[23] The disclosure of the mint's refining costs was enough to break the bill out of committee without amendments.[24]

The fireworks commenced in the Senate on May 13, 1870, when Williams moved in Committee of the Whole to amend the sundry appropriations bill to permit the exchange of unparted bars at the mint and its branches for refined bullion. Senator Cole immediately proposed to amend the amendment to remove the charge to outside bullion depositors for coinage. Removal of that charge had strong support from western senators but in this case was a deliberate distraction designed to derail contract refining. The debate turned chaotic and pretty much stayed that way.

Williams regained the floor in an attempt to restore some order to the debate. He reminded the senators that the secretary of the Treasury and the director of the mint had reviewed this issue favorably. The Committee on Finance had examined it—all winter long, Stewart added sarcastically. Yet there was reluctance to consider this amendment in an appropriations bill.

Now James Nye, the other senator from Nevada, took the floor, advocating for removal of the coinage charge. His lack of support would have been troublesome enough but then he took it to a personal level with Bill Stewart. Nye reminded Stewart that he had helped put in the 1869 provision in the sundry-civil-expenses appropriation a prohibition against contract refining. Stewart denied it. Stewart was in a box. To admit his complicity was to leave himself open to revealing his objective of saving Ralston to fight another day. Nye stated that Stewart most certainly had, and Nye wanted to know just what had changed in the meantime. Nye answered his own question; nothing had changed since 1869 except the persistence of those who desired this change.

Then Nye went off the deep end. If separating metal could not be done as cheaply in government offices as it was done in private establishments, there was a degree of imbecility attendant in their management that demanded investigation and reform.

He stated:

Sir, if I should go personally to the manager of the mint at San Francisco and charge him with that I should get a specimen of western justice administered to me between the eyes at once.

By embarrassing Bill Stewart, thereby crossing Billy Ralston, James Nye had just shot himself in the foot. The battle to replace him in the Senate promised to be a catfight.

Stewart made a valiant effort to counteract Nye's impact. Refining was manufacturing, not coining. Refining was not done in any other established mint in the world. Throwing every argument against the opposition that he could think of, Stewart correctly pointed out that contract refining took away the risk for excessive refinery wastage that had bedeviled the mint in San Francisco in the early years.

The debate wound down on the light side. Senator Samuel Pomeroy of Kansas noted that the English had discussed the coinage charge for 200 years before removing it. The Senate had just commenced it. John Sherman, chair of the Committee on Finance, exasperatingly observed that it would take another two days if the Senate delved into it further. Pomeroy replied that if it had taken the English 200 years, they would all be dead in the Senate before they got through with the discussion. Williams, to a chorus of laughter, said they might as well die in this way as any other.

As the opposition intended, the issue of contract refining had gotten hopelessly intertwined with the controversial coinage charge. Williams's amendment was then voted down with only six in favor and the nays not counted.[25] The bill was dead—or so it seemed.

The bill in fact was not dead. It was enacted in modified form on July 15, 1870, as part of the appropriations for sundry civil expenses of the government for the fiscal year ending on June 30, 1871. It was part of continuing appropriations for a new mint in San Francisco. The compromise gave the San Francisco Assaying and Refining Works the right to contract for refining until the new mint facility was placed in service.[26] It gave Ralston time and potentially a victory as the refining method for the new mint had not yet been determined.

How in the world did this happen? In the heat of a debate on the House floor on April 9, 1872, Fernando Wood of New York City made the accusation that the conference committee had added the provision. Eugene Kelly's hand was visible when Wood called it a legislative fraud. Aaron Sargent, now back in the House after his failed senate bid in California, could not let Woods's accusation stand. This amendment came over from the Senate in the version they passed. The House did not concur on all the Senate amendments. Then in conference, the House receded from this particular objection, and it became part of the final enacted legislation.[27] The problem with Sargent's version of the events was that the official record of House debate on the conference report did not back him up.

Sargent's hands were clearly dirty. In later years Mint Director Linderman would get the blame and deservedly so, as his subsequent dealings with Ralston would reveal.[28] But one culprit overlooked was Robert Stevens as secretary to the House Committee on Appropriations. He had access to all parties and was the most logical one to craft the compromise.

On August 10, 1870, the superintendent of the San Francisco Branch Mint made a contract with the San Francisco Assaying and Refining Works at eight cents per refined ounce for a net benefit to the government of three cents. Either party could terminate with thirty days' notice. However, that was a meaningless clause as the superintendent conveniently dismantled the mint refinery, tearing out the refining apparatus and selling it to junk dealers at a fraction of its value.[29]

After the fact, there was speculation. For example, an amount of raw bullion is brought to the mint for coinage. It is melted and assayed to determine its value, and a warrant is issued for payment. The warrant is presented to Mint Treasurer Charles Felton. He determines to pay the bullion depositor from that portion of the bullion fund at the Sub-Treasury. This crude bullion is received at the San Francisco Assaying and Refining Works in exchange for a voucher for an equivalent amount of refined bullion. Ralston then borrows from the refining works the refined bullion from this exchange and presents it to the mint in exchange for coins. In effect the mint through the bullion fund at the Sub-Treasury has made an unsecured loan to the Bank of California for which there is no record.[30]

As long as the refining contract was in place, the mint was Billy Ralston's private banker, providing him with an unsecured line of credit against which he could draw down interest-free loans. With this sweet setup, what could go wrong?

Chapter 7

A Bright Shiny New Mint

It wasn't just that Jos Harmstead was the new coiner at the San Francisco Branch Mint. Barring unforeseen difficulties, he would be the coiner when the new mint at San Francisco was placed in service. It would be the best that the United States could construct, far outshining the mother mint at Philadelphia. He had been involved from the very start. When A. B. Mullett, then assistant supervising architect, arrived at the mint to examine future sites for the new building, he had questions about the coining machinery. Superintendent Robert Swain called Harmstead instead of the coiner to answer the man's more detailed queries. If Harmstead found fault with the layout as planned of the coining process, he would have only himself to blame.

The new building had been authorized on July 2, 1864. Output at that time far exceeded original expectations, with more increases expected. The first mint was situated on Commercial Street, one of the narrowest streets in the city. The building was exceedingly warm no matter the season of the year. There was no storage capacity for bulk purchases, such as coal, requiring these items to be acquired inefficiently on an as-needed basis. A warehouse had been rented for items constantly in use. The superintendent's office was located across the street, and the operative officers did not even have decent desks. Put simply, the San Francisco Branch Mint was a disgrace to the government.[1]

The paltry sum of $300,000 was appropriated to purchase a site and erect the building.[2] Worse, the appropriation was in greenbacks and must be reduced by 40 percent when expressed in coin, required on the Pacific Coast. Part of the reason for the low number was that vacant land already owned by the federal government, next to San Francisco's post office and customs house, was considered more than ample for a new mint building. That tract, situated in the lower part of the city on land reclaimed from the Bay, would require extensive pilings. California Sen. John Conness wondered if there would be any true savings after the expense of the pilings. That decision would have to be made by the government's architect.[3]

Another factor would enter into the location of the new mint building. Harmstead recalled that, at the beginning of the first mint's second year of operation, a weak tremor had struck the city. An agitated John Hewston asked that he check out the coin presses for excessive vibrations. Harmstead then explained to Hewston that it was only a small tremor, frequent for the area, and to think nothing of it.[4]

The same could not be said for the earthquake of January 9, 1857, that centered along the San Andreas Fault in central and southern California. Yet its notoriety was slight, having occurred at a time when economic development in the area was still in its infant stage. Smaller events centering on San Francisco followed later in the year but with little serious damage or loss of life. Tremors and small earthquakes were turning out to be an everyday fact of life in San Francisco.

Architect Mullett reviewed the situation carefully from a practical engineering viewpoint. He found the site in the block with the customs house "utterly unsuitable," as 80-foot pilings had been driven for that building yet failed to achieve a firm foundation. The whole appropriation for the mint would be absorbed driving suitable pilings for the building. Instead Mullett recommended purchasing land in an area where a deep bed of compact sand rested upon a substrata of rock that would yield a firm and reliable foundation. This sand deposit was 26 feet thick with the first 12 feet being dry and the remaining 14 permeated with water. The yielding nature of the sand would diminish the vibrations from any earthquake and protect the building from any possible cracks in the substrata. A floating foundation of concrete would be required, adding slightly to the project expense.[5]

Superintendent Swain endorsed Mullett's decision in favor of the sand foundation. He wanted the lot to be 275 feet square to provide space for the proper storage of coal and acids. The building itself should be five times the footprint of the existing mint, which was only 70 feet square. With increased facilities, Swain believed the deposits, particularly of raw silver bullion, would be much larger.[6] Director of the Mint James Pollock endorsed the plans as well in July 1865. However, he thought the appropriation totally insufficient, believing the cost would ultimately reach $1 million. Perhaps spurred by that assessment, he recommended that San Francisco provide the land for the mint.[7]

In February 1867 the lot at the corner of Fifth Street and Mission was purchased for $100,000 in coin.[8] There would be no gifts of land from this city.

If anyone had doubts about the need for a sturdy building, the earthquake of October 21, 1868, erased that idea. At about 8 that morning, Jos Harmstead was in the machine shop repairing a vertical tube from one of the milling machines. He heard a low rumble. Tools began to slowly roll to his right. Then his stool began to rock. The next thing he knew, he was on the floor. The structure began to sway from east to west. Harmstead picked himself up and exited the building as quickly as he could.

Coming into the street he saw the pavement littered with debris.[9] The earthquake registered a magnitude of 6.3 to 6.7 on the Richter scale. The main arch over the treasurer's room was cracked open about 1-1/2 inches. Also, the top 25 feet of the chimney was loose and ready to tumble down.

Several days later, to ensure the safety of the mint's customers, a large amount of money was sent over to the Bank of California for disbursement there. Customers could take their bullion directly to the San Francisco Assaying and Refining Works and then go to the Sub-Treasury to redeem their warrants from Charles Felton.

A. B. Mullett, now the supervising architect of the Treasury Department, came to San Francisco in September 1869 to oversee the start of work. The trenches were dug, the top five feet of sand removed, and a massive four-to-six-foot–thick concrete floating foundation set.[10] Now it would be up to Congress to keep the supplemental appropriations flowing.

Robert Swain left the mint a bitter, depressed man. In congressional hearings on Pacific Coast retrenchment of the federal government, held in San Francisco in the fall of 1869, he would testify negatively on the ability of Harmstead and the other new operative officers. He would point out that his replacement as superintendent was an Oakland lawyer who knew absolutely nothing about running a mint. Swain glossed over the fact that William Schmolz, the coiner Harmstead replaced, had a shortfall in his accounts at the changeover of $13,000.[11] In fact, 700 ounces of gold supposedly went missing during the July settlement of accounts and was swept out of sight as it fell within the limits of the liberal wastage allowance.[12] Swain would die two years later from an overdose of laudanum. The *San Francisco Chronicle* later said of the man that he was strong but dishonest.[13]

Swain had one thing right. When Oscar Hugh LaGrange took the helm of the mint on August 27, 1869, all he knew about coins was how to make change.[14] His claim to fame was his command first of a volunteer Wisconsin cavalry regiment and then a full cavalry brigade in the Army of the Cumberland during the Civil War. His personal courage at the head of his brigade amounted almost to rashness. He thrived on headlong cavalry charges in which he could be found in the front rank. In September 1863 he was sent in pursuit of Joe Wheeler's Confederate cavalrymen. He caught Wheeler's men by surprise looting supplies from a captured wagon train and gave them a rare bruising.

Months later in a vicious charge, he and a number of his men were captured by Wheeler. His men would go to the notorious Andersonville prison camp while he, under protest of being separated from them, ultimately was exchanged. Back in action he drove his men so hard in a futile pursuit of Nathan Bedford Forrest on a raid into Kentucky in the winter of 1864–65 that 10% of his force ended up in the hospital with frostbite. In all, the man had five horses shot out from under him. At the end of the war, with Congress in a victorious mood, handing out "political stars" to further entrench the Republican Party, he received a promotion to brevet brigadier general of volunteers.[15]

In 1866 Hugh LaGrange received his law degree and eventually went to San Francisco, where, as a former Wisconsin abolitionist, he immediately affiliated with the Bay Area Republicans. He had one problem when he arrived: He had no money. Falling back on his original profession, he taught school for one year. After working in the political trenches for an increasingly powerful Republican political ring, he was elected district attorney for Alameda County in 1868.[16] This position gave him the party visibility necessary to successfully seek the appointment to the mint.

The most striking feature of Hugh LaGrange's appearance was his luxurious mustache. While brave in battle during the Civil War, he lacked the moral fiber to withstand the demands of Ralston and the Republican political ring.

Harmstead got along well enough during the initial months with LaGrange. The superintendent, serving under an interim appointment, was receptive to his advice. John Cochran, the new melter and refiner was a friend and a colleague, another plus. Also, LaGrange allowed Harmstead to name his brother-in-law as the assistant coiner and to add his stepson as a workman in his department. They would have his back among the political appointees under him. That was a good thing because almost immediately Harmstead was accused of seeking payments for men to retain their jobs at the mint. It would be investigated, and Harmstead would be exonerated, with LaGrange asking only that the affair be kept out of the newspapers.[17]

Still there were quirks about LaGrange. He rarely left his office, communicating with his officers by letter. When he did visit the operating departments, he cut quite the figure, dressed in black knee boots and carrying a pointing stick.[18] He just could not leave his military past behind him. He also had a temper, threatening violence to anyone who crossed him personally.[19] Yet underneath this prickly hedgehog defense, people soon learned, was a weak man hiding behind the trappings of his office.

LaGrange's affairs took a serious turn for the worse in November 1869. His nomination for superintendent would need to be confirmed with the opening of the second session of the 41st Congress on December 6, or his interim appointment would terminate. Just before the opening of the session a sordid story originating in Wisconsin questioning his character and suitability for his position reached the Senate. It was so bad LaGrange was forced to take a leave of absence to go to Washington to save his nomination.

LaGrange had been a schoolteacher at Ripon, Wisconsin, prior to 1855. During this time, he became infatuated with one of his students, Jennie Stowell. Their acquaintance continued after she and her parents moved to Hastings, Minnesota. The relationship never quite matured until LaGrange was ready to leave with his regiment for the war front. He invited Jennie to the encampment, where they were married by the regimental chaplain. The next day, the regiment shipped out with Jennie following along until it reached Harrisburg, Pennsylvania, when she decided to return home. Pining for her after she had departed, LaGrange proclaimed she had a pure soul that confirmed his belief in angels. He spoke of her low, soft voice, the pale little face, and the little feet, whose coming he used to watch for from the window of the little red schoolhouse.

As the war progressed Jennie received an allotment from his salary that she managed carefully so that moneys would be available for him to go to law school. However, LaGrange was not so loyal to her. While posted at Macon, Georgia, he met and fell for Lizzie Andrews, a divorcee with a young son. At the end of the war, Lizzie followed LaGrange north to Albany, New York, where he entered law school. On the other hand, he told Jennie that he was too poor to afford her joining him, and she should stay home until he graduated.

Once LaGrange graduated, he was on the spot. He met Jennie on June 6, 1866, and proceeded to weave a story of lies and deceit. Lizzie was an innocent girl that he had gotten into trouble, and she could not return to her friends. Jennie offered to take the child as her own. LaGrange held Jennie in limbo until July 19, when he wrote her that he was leaving the state and that she should get a divorce. Jennie returned home a rejected woman with only the solace that LaGrange and Lizzie deserved each other. Jennie even learned that LaGrange asked his mother to persuade her to grant a divorce. With that, LaGrange with his Southern belle left for California on money from a diamond she sold.[20]

Once in Washington, LaGrange went to his friend, Associate Justice of the Supreme Court Stephen Field. Field combined with Secretary of the Senate George Gorham, a stalwart of the California Republican Party, to persuade the opposed senators to muffle their complaints about LaGrange's nomination.[21] There was a divorce decree that would subsequently turn out to have forged signatures that would explain Field and Gorham being able to carry the day for LaGrange.[22] Whatever did transpire was sufficient. LaGrange was nominated and confirmed in the Senate on December 22, 1869.[23] The ex-schoolteacher now had a free hand.

Over the winter of 1869–70, work on the foundation of the new mint seemed to crawl. Finally in May plans were initiated for the laying of the cornerstone. Of primary importance were the contents of the casket, as a time capsule was then called, to be placed in a cavity in the stone. In addition to typical material one might expect to be included, LaGrange wanted one each of all the coins struck at the mint.

Up to that point in 1870 Jos Harmstead had struck only half dollars and double eagles. He had taken delivery the past December of 80 working dies that were locked in his vault. However, he did not have any dies for the silver dollar. LaGrange had a solution; he had the Carson City Branch Mint loan an obverse die for the occasion.[24] In addition to placing the coins in the casket, he decided that some 11 or so silver dollars would be given to dignitaries privately as a memento.

While Harmstead had the other dies, he had not closely examined them. In early May, Harmstead received an order to strike 2,000 one-dollar gold pieces. But a pressman discovered an oversight, a missing "S" mintmark, showing it to Harmstead on May 16. The coiner then inspected the other dies and found the same problem with the three-dollar gold piece. As these two coins were only sporadically struck at the San Francisco mint, it would not normally have been an issue. In addition, there was not the usual workaround, using a reverse die from 1869, as these were the two coins that had both the date and the mintmark on the reverse.

LaGrange was not happy, issuing a long sigh in front of Harmstead. He would have to telegraph Director Pollock for instructions. Pollock refused to allow the issuance of the coins without a mintmark; he would send new dies. In a classic foul-up, Pollock sent reverse dies for both the silver and gold dollar coins and the three-dollar coin. Yet surprisingly, the three-dollar gold coin reverse die still lacked the S mintmark.[25]

On May 23, with the dedication of the cornerstone two days away, Harmstead executed a workaround for the three-dollar gold piece. He had an S punch of just the right size. To place the mintmark, the coiner had to heat the three-dollar die and then run the risk that the act of punching the S into the die would cause it to crack. It was the first time Harmstead had performed this operation.

With the successfully punched die in hand, Harmstead and his assistant coiner went to the pressroom to see how his handiwork actually looked on the coin. They were using raw gold that had assayed at 893 fine. It had come from a recent discovery on the Feather River in the lower Sierra Nevada Range. Jos liked the results. He hesitated, wanting one of his own when his brother-in-law, reading his mind, urged him to go ahead. Harmstead for once in his life did something not quite right, slipping another blank planchet into the coining chamber. It came out and went right into his pocket. Afterwards he gave it to his wife, Francis, and it spent its early years in a bezel suspended from a chain as a necklace. As it turned out, there were no more orders that year for the unpopular three-dollar gold pieces, so Harmstead's coin turned out to be unique. Later that day they struck the remaining coins using polished coin blanks. The work was tedious, having to fit, remove, and refit each set of dies. Apparently, Jos struck an extra half dime as well, as it surfaced in the numismatic community in 1978.[26, 27]

The cornerstone ceremony took place on the afternoon of May 25, 1870. The site had been carefully prepared with part of the foundation walls bridged over, floored, and furnished with seats for the dignitaries. Also, rows of bleachers occupied the northern and eastern walls of the quadrangle facing the cornerstone. The space immediately around the stone was reserved for the officers and choir of the Masonic Order. There was an abundance of bunting and flags of all nations, including one with a harp on a green background.

At one o'clock, the ceremonies commenced as the dignitaries accompanied by bands left the Masonic Temple. Members of the Knights Templar complete with drawn swords escorted the entourage. Harmstead recalled seeing an inebriated group stumble out of Tom Sawyer's Saloon to give an unruly applause to the procession.[28] What the drunks thought of the Knights Templar in their short mantles of black velvet with the Templar's Cross on the left shoulder, plumed hats, sashes, aprons,

This three-dollar gold piece was stuck by coiner Jos Harmstead for himself while he was preparing the San Francisco coinage to be placed within the cornerstone of the new mint building. The marks on the reverse above the wreath are those of an assayer, placed at a later date to verify the gold content.

gauntlets accentuated by the swords, and small daggers at the waist was not reported in the next day's newspapers.

It was an hour before the crowd of several thousand could hear the approach of the procession. As the officials took their assigned seats, the implements for the ceremony were spread before them on a small table near the stone. These were the silver square, level, and plummet. There was a Bible, candlesticks, and small pillars representing the different orders of architecture. Gold and silver vases contained corn, oil, and wine for the consecration of the stone.

First LaGrange addressed the grand master. There could be nothing more appropriate than that the Order should lay the foundations of all public buildings. Within these walls the government would exercise one of the distinguished attributes of authority by placing marks of coinage upon one of the most glittering and fascinating productions of the Pacific Coast—gold. In the name of the government, he extended an invitation to the grand master to lay the cornerstone. The grand master accepted with pride and pleasure.

In addition to the coins, which were not even mentioned in the *San Francisco Chronicle* report of the ceremony, the casket contained various governmental reports from the Treasury Department, the state of California, and the city of San Francisco and a listing of names of persons connected with the erection of the new mint. There were photographs of some of the prominent buildings of San Francisco and examples of silk produced in California. Lastly was an example of Continental paper currency from 1776. These were all placed in the copper casket and deposited in the cavity prepared in the cornerstone.

Next the grand master, assisted by a workman, spread cement on the lower stone, and the cornerstone, a handsome piece of gray granite, was lowered into place. The deputy grand master and other Masons tested the stone with their respective implements and pronounced the work well done. The grand master proclaimed the foundation stone to be well formed, true, and trusty. Then he distributed the vessels of corn, oil, and wine that were in turn ceremoniously poured on the stone. Orations defining the role of this mint within the fabric of government followed.

"The power to coin money is the essence of authority. It is the source of power and the means of its use. By this power the ocean is covered with the white-winged messengers of commerce, and the stimulus to industry, thrift, and enterprise is maintained and by its art, science and literature are cultivated and supported. The sovereignty which coins the money of a commonwealth is the paramount of authority."

The speeches completed, the procession returned to the Masonic Temple.[29]

The next day the *Chronicle* described the new mint's planned appearance. The main frontage would be on Fifth Street. The upper two stories would be faced with fine blue sandstone from British Columbia. The facing of the basement would be Folsom granite. The basement would be used for storage and the boilers and engine that would power the mint. The operating machinery would be on the two floors above. Not a word was said about the refinery.

The inner foundation walls were built with the best-quality brick. The intent was to use the best engineering and construction materials to make the building both fire- and earthquake-proof. The girders for the first floor were nearly all in place, having been supplied by the Phoenix Iron Works of Philadelphia. A set of massive granite steps was to lead from the street to the first-floor entrance. The roof would be copper. The paper speculated that the building would be completed by July 1871 and cost about $1 million.[30] That was wrong on both counts. It would be reported in 1875 when the new mint had been in operation only a matter of months that the all-in cost of the building plus furnishings and machinery was $2,201,198.32.

The new mint would cast a long shadow, totally eclipsing the mother mint at Philadelphia. Yet all would not be well. Within a few years the *San Francisco Chronicle* would derisively call it the temple of Mammon on Fifth Street where General LaGrange reigned as presiding deity.

Part 2

The Crime of Seventy-Three

Chapter 8
A Hodgepodge Affair

The widespread coin hoarding that resulted from the suspension of specie payment by first the federal government and then the banks early in the Civil War had a profoundly negative impact on daily commerce. It was the absence of even the smallest denominations that were at the root of the problem. Merchants and customers alike were in a bind to make change. In the spring of 1862, Congress legalized postage stamps for use as currency. These quickly became nasty and were replaced by mica-encased postage stamps, known as postal currency. Fractional currency, at first in a form that resembled enlarged postage stamps, then followed. However, these notes, while addressing the shortage of silver coins, were largely an unsatisfactory substitute for the missing one-cent piece. Merchants began issuing store tokens in place of the penny in 1862 and the practice became widespread in 1863.

Mint Director Pollock was aware of the acute cent shortage, having minted almost unprecedented quantities of one-cent pieces in both 1862 and 1863 to no avail. These pennies, 88% copper and 12 % nickel were trading at 120% of face in 1863. Pollock had a problem with these coins; the nickel cost too much. It was also difficult to work in the melting pot, even alloyed with copper, and its inherently hard nature was destructive of dies. He saw no need to be concerned with intrinsic value for a coin that in reality was a mere token. It's worth was not its intrinsic value but that it's legal tender status, though limited, would make it redeemable and therefore tied to the silver coinage. The public would be accepting of a cheaper metal, making the nickel wasted money in the alloy. In addition, the nickel had to be imported with payment in gold or its equivalent.[1]

Pollock had a solution: He recommended bronze one- and two-cent pieces composed of 95% copper and 5% tin and zinc in suitable proportions. He would retain the existing Indian Head design on the one-cent piece and directed new designs for the two-cent piece from his engraver, James Longacre. For the two-cent piece Longacre provided two obverse designs. One featured his favorite motif, a shield. The second featured a bust of George Washington, a radical departure from previous American coin designs.

James Pollock, a deeply devout man, would serve as director of the mint in the administrations of Lincoln and Grant.

The two-cent piece designs were distinctive for another reason; both included a variation of a religious motto. The idea had come from Mark Watkins, a Baptist minister in Pennsylvania, in a letter to Treasury Secretary Chase in late 1861. Watkins regretted the absence of the Almighty God in some form upon our coins. Chase had passed the letter with his endorsement to Pollock, an intensely religious man.[2] The issue drifted with some pattern pieces struck incorporating the motto into existing coin designs. Now the larger two-cent piece offered the perfect vehicle to introduce a new motto. Secretary Chase gave Pollock his choice between the two designs and Pollock took the shield and with it, the

Pattern two-cent-piece obverses (J-309 and J-315) showing possible design alternatives for the proposed coins.

motto "In God We Trust." At the beginning of 1864 as Pollock sought Congressional authorization to issue the new coin and change the metallic content of the one-cent piece, he encountered another obstacle.

Joseph Wharton had just purchased the Gap Nickel Mine with a smelting works in Lancaster County, Pennsylvania. He also had invested in a refinery or finishing works in Camden across the Delaware River from Philadelphia. With the proposed switch out to a bronze penny, he faced losing a major market in which he enjoyed an unchallenged competitive advantage for his nickel. Having political connections, the mine was in the congressional district of the Radical Republican Thaddeus Stevens: he would not go down without a fight.

In the face of opposition, Chase procrastinated. Pollock, attempting to force the issue, pressed the secretary, stating it would be impossible to meet the enormous demand for pennies using the present copper-nickel alloy.[3] Still gaining no action, Pollock sounded the alarm; he was running out of nickel and foreign sources could not resupply him for some months. He had used nickel from Wharton but Wharton could not supply nearly enough to meet the mint's needs.

Suddenly on March 18th Chase's procrastination ended in an uncharacteristically blunt letter to Senator William Fessenden, chair of the Committee on Finance. Immediate action was needed. Chase supported Pollock's recommendation to use bronze and noted that the director feared outside opposition from private sources might defeat this bill. The Senate promptly responded passing the needed legislation. The House would be another matter.

In April Joseph Wharton took his best shot at retaining nickel as an alloy for coins. He issued a pamphlet that advocated American coins should not pretend to intrinsic value but should be a system of tokens. These tokens should be redeemable into larger money. The alloy of nickel and copper was the proper material for these tokens because of its beauty, durability and competitive cost. Several nations had already applied this alloy to their minor coinage. Our token coinage should be for denominations of ten cents and less.

The new two-cent piece bearing the motto "In God We Trust."

In the House debate, Stevens put up a spirited fight. However the chairman of the Committee on Coinage, Weights and Measures, John Kasson, was having none of it. Kasson argued that it did not bode well to have the government tied to one producer to supply metal critical to the nation's coinage. He carried the day.[4] Pollock had his bronze coins and his motto.[5]

That was not the last word on nickel coinage. Chase left the Treasury Department on June 30, 1864 in an unsuccessful effort to challenge Abraham Lincoln for the Republican Presidential nomination. Lincoln chose a reluctant William Fessenden to replace Chase at Treasury. Fessenden was merely a placeholder, serving only through the end of the 38th Congress before returning to the Senate on March 4, 1865. So in the waning days of the 38th Congress, Wharton and his nickel operation made a return appearance.

In an apparent change of colors, Director Pollock submitted draft legislation to Kasson calling for three-, five- and ten-cent pieces composed of 75% nickel and 25% copper. The mint director had met with Fessenden to recommend the three-cent piece. The five-cent piece was not objectionable but beyond that denomination, he could not recommend the copper-nickel alloy. Pollock did speculate that if approved, the coins would be a good substitute for the three- and five- cent fractional notes. Public dislike of fractional currency had manifested itself in the common slang term for them, shinplasters.[6]

March 3rd, the last day of the 38th Congress was hectic with pressing legislation facing life or death in those closing hours. To have a completely new bill introduced and expect it to pass both houses seemed the height of folly. However, the rails were greased but only for a three-cent piece. Included in the "one-day wonder" legislation that passed both houses was permission for the director of the mint to add the motto "In God We Trust" to such gold and silver coins that would admit of such a legend.[7] Wharton got his nickel coin and Pollock got his motto.

Persistence was a virtue of Wharton's. After President Lincoln's assassination, Hugh McCulloch, became the new secretary of the treasury under Andrew Johnson. Wharton actively lobbied McCulloch to replace the small fractional notes with his copper-nickel coins. He wanted a five- and a ten-cent piece of as much as 33% nickel to compliment the three-cent piece. He called for the two-cent piece to be discontinued. He argued further that these copper-nickel coins were the best solution for the minor coinage. With little intrinsic value, they would not be withdrawn from circulation as had happened with the small silver coinage during the Civil War.[8]

Presented with Wharton's positions, Pollock took offense at the proposal to remove the two-cent piece, the first to bear the motto that he so strongly supported.[9] However again he hedged, calling in his annual report of June 30, 1865 for a five-cent piece of copper-nickel alloy as a substitute for the five-cent fractional note. This coin should only be issued for a set length of time, assuming that silver would begin to circulate with the ending of the Civil War.[10] The way was now clear politically for a nickel five-cent piece.

The legislation easily passed the House. Senator John Sherman now chair of the Committee on Finance brought the bill to the floor with one amendment. The weight of the coin was increased slightly to 77.16 grains. No one paid much attention that this weight in grains was equivalent to five grams on the metric system. The amended bill passed the Senate and the House accepted the change. The nickel, as it would be called, became an American coin.

On May 28th Pollock went to Washington with pattern pieces prepared by Longacre. One, prepared by the engraver the previous year, recycled the obverse from the two-cent piece.[11] In this version the shield rested on tied arrows with the motto "In God We Trust" arched above. The reverse had the numeral 5 surrounded by thirteen stars set in rays. There were other designs using the discarded bust of Washington from the two-cent piece as well as reverses that inserted a wreath in place of the stars and rays. Longacre also prepared an obverse with the bust of Lincoln but Pollock discarded that one without showing it to Secretary McCulloch.

Pattern pieces (J-464 and J-488) bearing the images of Washington and Lincoln proposed by Engraver Longacre for the new nickel pieces.

Pollock's favorite was the shield design paired with the stars and rays reverse. He recommended its acceptance, calling it a neat and unique design, standing above the other patterns in artistic beauty. McCulloch concurred.[12]

One person was not pleased with the new coin—Joseph Wharton. He called the coin's diameter too small for its weight; the alloy was entirely devoid of resonance. The obverse shield suggested a tombstone surmounted by a cross and overhung by weeping willows, reinforced by the religious motto above it. He called it a curiously ugly device.[13]

Just as political winds were shaping American coinage in a haphazard fashion so it was with the establishing of branch mints. At the beginning of the Civil War the Mint Service consisted of the three large mints at Philadelphia, New Orleans and San Francisco and two small mints located in the southern goldfields. After the war the two small southern mints were discontinued and New Orleans mothballed. However the number of mints in service was far from rationalized.

The shield nickel issued in 1866 and much criticized by Joseph Wharton. Curiously, the United States now had both nickel and silver three- and five-cent pieces.

In 1862 Thaddeus Stevens introduced legislation to establish a mint in Denver. In the ensuing debate in the Senate, William Fessenden spelled out the previously implied policy of establishing branch mints wherever they were needed based upon significant gold deposits and the distance of those deposits from existing mints. The bill passed. Denver would only strike gold coins. In January 1863, California Congressman Aaron Sargent introduced HR. 663 to place a branch mint to coin gold and silver at Carson City, Nevada Territory to service the Comstock Lode.[14] It passed the House one day before adjournment. In the Senate the proposed mint at Carson City was questioned, much of the silver and gold coming from the Comstock was being exported as bullion. Coinage would find its way out of the territory only through payments for wages and supplies. Fessenden complained that he did not "see the necessity of this railroad speed on legislation." It passed anyway.

Second thoughts about branch mints began to erode support by early 1864. Meanwhile a move was afoot to establish a branch mint in Oregon. Pollock argued that Philadelphia and San Francisco were adequate for meeting the nation's needs. It was not good policy for refining and coining in locations that lacked access to the necessary chemicals and a skilled workforce. Second, the cost of coinage at such a remote location would exceed the cost of transportation of bullion. As a result, this bullion would soon find its way to the cheapest point of conversion to coinage. What he did not say here was in most cases, given the coinage charge at the mint, the bullion would be exported to London where there was no such charge. Pollock could not carry the day. Dalles City in Oregon was authorized and Carson City was saved.[15]

Dalles City would be abandoned when the gold discovery gave out. Denver would be relegated to an assay office operation, retaining its status as a mint in name only. Carson City would continue toward completion, surviving a last-ditch effort to close the mint by not providing an appropriation for its operation. Bill Stewart saved the day arguing that the completed mint deserved a fair trial given that the money had been spent for its erection.[16]

Chapter 9
Flirting with a Quixotic Idea

Director James Pollock had been a Lincoln man through and through, having served in Congress with the late President. When Andrew Johnson opposed the 14th Amendment giving citizenship to formerly enslaved peoples, Pollock resigned.[1] On January 2, 1867, President Johnson nominated William Millward to be the director.[2] Twelve days later the Senate Committee on Finance refused to recommend this nomination. On second try, Johnson nominated Henry Linderman and the Senate approved on April 1, 1867.[3]

Henry Linderman was a Democrat. The odds of his retaining this position beyond Johnson's term in office were not good. Yet he took the job. He had become chief clerk at the Philadelphia Mint in 1853, owing this position to the influence of his uncle, Pennsylvania Senator William Brodhead. He had departed in 1864 for a job as a banker and broker. Linderman knew the mint's operations while having a good background in banking and finance. It should have been a good appointment. Yet there were two standards of conduct for Henry Linderman, one for himself and another for everybody else. He would take credit for uncovering irregularities in the New York Assay Office that had developed from a too cozy relationship with bullion dealers.[4] On the other hand, Billy Ralston, who would come to know Linderman intimately, called him "an old hog!"[5] That was later. Now, perceived as a short-timer working for a President with no political base, Linderman was going to have a difficult time establishing his authority.

At the same moment, an international monetary conference organized by France and consisting of seventeen nations was convened in Paris in conjunction with the Paris Exposition of 1867. Driven by the increase in trade and the lack of uniformity of the various European coinages, France had entered into a treaty with Switzerland, Italy and Belgium, known as the Latin Monetary Union, effective August 1, 1866. The intent now was to pattern a broader agreement that included among others, Great Britain and the United States.

There was good reason for the United States to participate in these talks. America was a trading nation. Settlement of deficits that arose from this activity was made in gold coin. These coins were then transferred to the creditor nation's mint to be melted and recoined according to that nation's monetary specifications and unit of value. What resulted was a useless round robin expense associated with this recoinage. The timing was also right for this country. Essentially no gold and silver circulated domestically yet.

The Latin Monetary Union mandated the four countries strike fully exchangeable gold and silver coins of a uniform fineness and weight based upon a fixed silver to gold ratio of 15-1/2 to 1. But there were quirks. It limited the silver coinage in each country to six francs per person. Also it prohibited the issue of any intermediate gold coin denominations between ten and twenty francs and twenty and fifty francs. The rub here was that the British sovereign and the American half eagle most closely equated to a 25-franc coin.

Samuel Ruggles was a scientific commissioner to the Paris Exposition and the American representative to this monetary conference.[6] Importantly he had the backing of the powerful Chamber of Commerce of New York State and the confidence of Secretary of State Seward. He had come to the exposition as an advocate of international coinage and was personally in favor of the French twenty-five-franc piece as the common unit.

Here entered John Sherman, newly minted chair of the Senate Committee on Finance. He traveled to Europe intent upon adding gravitas to his résumé by meeting the political class of London, Paris and Berlin. Disraeli, Gladstone, Bismarck and Prince Louis Napoleon were all on his dance card. As the brother of the famous American general, they in turn were interested in him. He traveled to Paris twice, once to visit the exposition and the second time strictly for business.

On this second visit he received a communication from Ruggles. Opinion at the conference was running strongly in favor of adopting the French five-franc gold coin as the standard unit of money. Ruggles wanted Sherman's opinion of the probability that Congress would agree to reduce the weight of the dollar gold coin to correspond to the French coin. Ruggles even pushed farther, could he present Sherman's opinion to the conference.

Sherman told Ruggles there had been so little discussion in Congress on the topic that Sherman could not say how an international currency might be received. However, he believed that Congress would adopt any practical measure that would give the commercial world a uniform standard of value. This would put an end to the intricacies of exchange and discount and eliminate the considerable loss upon exchange that accrued as profit to the brokers and bankers.

Sherman supported the use of the gold five-franc piece as the standard measure of value. Gold, on the basis of convenience through value, was the medium of exchange in international trade, not silver. That would leave each nation to regulate divisions of this unit into silver coins or tokens. A "common gold standard" would regulate silver coinage of which the United States would furnish the greater part, especially for the Chinese trade. Likewise, Sherman believed the change so slight to bring a British sovereign into line with a new 25-franc piece that they should do it, particularly if the United States made equivalent adjustments.

The conference closed with a set of recommendations including adoption of the French five-franc piece and its multiples to be the unit of measure. Thus an American half eagle would be reduced in value by about 17-1/2 cents and a British sovereign, by four cents to achieve a value equivalent to 25 francs.

As good as these recommendations sounded, they still rang hollow. While Great Britain's representative agreed to the proposition, the leaders of the country balked. The objection was that it would disrupt the value of the shilling and farthing in the smaller purchases of life. But in Sherman's opinion it was simply a matter of British pride.[7]

Ruggles submitted his report but was frustrated when the New York papers defended the British reluctance to join an international agreement when the great monetary struggle of the future must lie between the British pound and the American dollar.[8] More frustrating for Ruggles, he personally presented his report to President Johnson who "did not seem quite to understand the matter."[9]

John Sherman could be determined and, at times, bull-headed. He plowed ahead despite Ruggles' note of caution. His bill, to provide a uniform currency among nations, was detailed, carefully thought out. Input from Linderman was likely. It was read and reported to his Committee on Finance. Overlooked within the bill the standard silver dollar weighing 412-1/2 grains would be eliminated. The weight of two half dollars would be equivalent to a silver French five-franc piece. This bill was called the French plan.

The bill had two questionable provisions. It did not mandate that existing public and private debts be adjusted to reflect the reduction in intrinsic value of one dollar in gold to the value of five gold francs, about 3.5 cents. In other words, the dollar would be devalued by 3.5%. Only government bonds repayable in coin were exempt. Without this exemption the value of government bonds, a substantial portion held in Europe, would drop and the United States' credit rating would take a beating. Furthermore, the mints would receive all silver and gold coins under the old standards beginning on October 1, 1868, to be exchanged for certificates payable in new coins beginning January 1, 1869. The windfall in the form of gold from this exchange went to the government. If enacted, these two clauses would greatly assist in the resumption of specie payments, suspended since the first year of the Civil War.

John Sherman had overreached. Head bowed, he reported back to the Senate that he could not carry his own committee. Specifically, Senator Edwin Morgan was threatening to submit a written minority report. Morgan was not to be fooled with.

Senator Edwin Morgan's opposition would doom the move to an international currency in the United States.

William Kelley as chair of the House Committee on Coinage Weights and Measures would play an important role in the nation's coinage until derailed by the Crédit Mobilier scandal.

He had been one of Lincoln's "war governors." His opposition guaranteed this bill had no chance in open debate.[10]

Morgan's point was simple; the standard value of gold coins should be brought to that of the half eagle. While unification was desirable, it must be universal. To do so unilaterally would be of little benefit to the United States. Morgan jumped on the lack of an adjustment to account for the reduced value of a dollar in repayment of the existing public debt, saying it would cause the government embarrassment.

The committee directed Sherman to postpone the bill until the next session. In bitterness Sherman would later write that Morgan opposed the bill because it would hurt the profits of the New York brokers and bullion dealers. In that period of postponement, the bill took another hit; the British government formally refused to consider adjusting its gold coins.[11]

On the House side Judge William Kelley was now chair of the Committee on Coinage, Weights and Measures. He had earned his moniker by having served previously in a minor judgeship in Philadelphia. Kelley introduced his version of an international coinage that varied slightly from Sherman's. He carried over the elimination of the standard silver dollar and adjusted weight of two half dollars to one five-franc piece. However, his bill called for a standard gold dollar weighing 1-2/3 grams. Thus a double eagle would have the weight of three German crowns. This measure, called the German bill, also went nowhere.

Kelley was not done. He convened his coinage committee, which in turn produced instructions for Mint Director Linderman to draft a bill authorizing copper-nickel minor coins in denominations up to ten cents. Weights would be in grams with uniform designs employed.[12] He would go after a metric-based system of minor coins. This was right out of Wharton's playbook.

The bill he introduced on February 21, 1868, called for copper-nickel one-, three-, five- and ten-cent pieces. Weights were specified proportionately, starting with the ten-cent piece at 10 grams. The exception was the one-cent piece at one-and-a-half grams.[13] The need for a larger one-cent piece stemmed from the fact, as determined by coiner Snowden in experiments at Philadelphia, that a one-gram piece was too small.[14] Existing coinage in bronze, silver, or copper-nickel in these denominations would cease. Kelley forced this bill out of his committee and with amendments it passed and went to the Senate. Sherman sat on it until two days before adjournment, effectively killing it.

With the opening of the 41st Congress in early December 1869 and Morgan gone from the Senate, Sherman wasted no time in introducing another bill on international coinage. This bill was a mirror image of his first bill with the exception that it included a coinage charge of 1/4% for all deposits of gold for coinage, a reduction from the existing rate of 0.5%.[15] This was a nod to the California delegation but not what they wanted. Billy Ralston wanted free coinage of gold. Whether or not the coinage charge was involved, the bill never came out of Sherman's committee.

Kelley would try again for copper-nickel minor coinage in the House only stir up a stink. In a heated exchange, Benjamin Butler wanted a specific amendment requiring the mint director to purchase the lowest cost and best bid. Kelley stated that Wharton produced the best nickel. However, the richest nickel ore came from a mine in Missouri. Butler testily rebutted that in his opinion the wording in the bill would give the contract to Wharton. At this point the hour was late and the House abruptly adjourned.[16]

Debate picked up the next day. In Butler's view as the bill now stood, Wharton received a preference in the bidding. With millions of dollars involved, Butler wanted a transparent purchasing process. Kelley stated that his legislation was an official bill. It came from the secretary of the treasury at the request of the mint director. Butler sharply noted that it came from McCulloch and Linderman. Trouble was, both men were out in the incoming Grant Administration. Butler moved that the bill be recommitted, which carried.[17] In fact James Pollock was back in as director of the mint in Linderman's place.

Afterwards circumstances seemed to point to Linderman trying to lock in the business for Wharton after he left. There was no record of a quid pro quo for this act. However, Linderman on unofficial business often used the letterhead stationery of his brother's coal business. The ethics of the day would not have looked askance had Wharton given Linderman's brother a coal contract for his smelter operation in Lancaster County.

There would be additional efforts in the House and Senate to gain an international coinage that would likewise meet with failure. The golden opportunity when coins were not circulating in the country had been stymied by Senator Morgan. In the end, it was nothing more than a quixotic adventure.

Chapter 10
ROLLOUT

It was Treasury Secretary George Boutwell's first report on the state of the country's finances. He had been a member of the three preceding Congresses in the House, voting with the nickel interests to restructure the minor coinage. He understood the factors bubbling just below the surface concerning an international coinage. In addition, there were issues with each of the branch mints.

Boutwell had held onto Henry Linderman after the Grant Administration removed the mint director from his post, teaming him with Deputy Comptroller of the Currency John Jay Knox Jr. to investigate all the mints and assay offices in 1869. Subsequently the two men uncovered a scheme involving loans of bullion and unauthorized certificates of deposit to favored bullion dealers at the New York Assay Office.[1] While Knox took the lead on this issue, Linderman took the credit in his personal correspondence.[2]

Now, Boutwell set pen to paper. The mining and coining of the precious metals was so large a national interest that it deserved more attention. He called for a bureau or officer in the Treasury Department in Washington charged specifically with the management of this sprawling operation.[3] Once Boutwell's report was delivered to Congress, he set Knox, consulting with Linderman, in motion to draft a bill accomplishing his proposed reorganization.[4]

This first draft established the mint and its branches and assay offices as a bureau of the Treasury Department with its chief officer, the director of the mint, serving a

A youthful Henry Linderman sat for this photograph while in San Francisco in 1869.

John Jay Knox Jr. began his government service in the Treasury Department in 1863, eventually rising to comptroller of the currency.

five-year term. It defined the duties of the various mint officers, empowered the superintendents to appoint clerks and workmen and set salaries. It set the weights of the gold and silver coinage, identical to the existing standards with one exception. The dollar was reduced from its standard weight from 412-1/2 grains to 384 grains, proportional to the half dollar. Thus, it would be treated as a subsidiary silver coin with legal tender capped. The gold dollar would be the sole unit of value.

There were changes for the minor coins as well. This draft called for copper-nickel coins of one, three and five cents. Continuing existing practice, only Philadelphia would strike these coins, giving Joseph Wharton's nickel interests the advantage of proximity. Thus, the two-cent piece, silver three-cent piece and the half dime would be abolished. Likewise, a bronze penny would be no more.

One element of change in the bill was subtle; the engraver's role in new designs was reined in. The engraver at Philadelphia was authorized to prepare all working dies for use in coinage at the various mints. When new coins or devices were authorized, the director, at his discretion and with the approval of the secretary of the Treasury, was empowered to engage the services of one or more artists for this purpose. Design requirements were unchanged: the obverse must feature an image emblematic of Liberty and the reverse, an eagle. The motto "E Pluribus Unum" was restored, having been removed in the Mint Act of 1837. The director might also include the motto, "In God We Trust" with the approval of the secretary of the Treasury and space permitting on gold and silver coins. Finally, there was a slam at the Philadelphia Mint. Each mint was now to be known as the mint at a specific location. The term, branch mint, was done away with.

Next Knox submitted the draft legislation to a virtual who's who of past Philadelphia mint officers. Director of the Mint Pollock disapproved of the move of the director to Washington. Pollock also stated that the problems and difficulties in the mint system had their origin in the disregard of provisions, rules and regulations already in place. Pollock was in favor of the reduction in the weight of the silver dollar. He wasn't happy about the minor coins proposed. It made no sense to strike a copper-nickel cent that was and would always be more expensive than a bronze cent. He supported elimination of the coinage charge for gold coins.[5]

One by one they weighed in. Most agreed with the move to Washington. Linderman took exception to the provision retaining the silver dollar. He believed it would be better to discontinue the coin. Having a higher intrinsic value than its face amount, the standard silver dollar had long ceased to circulate and the denomination as a subsidiary silver coin served no practical purpose. Its weight and size would restrict its use in daily commerce.

The officers at the San Francisco Branch Mint answered as one. The coinage and refining charges should be repealed. The policy of the government should be to retain bullion at home rather than allow the difference between mint charges of our own and foreign countries to operate as a premium to encourage shipment aboard. There was also a note of discord from San Francisco. The operative officers wanted control of the hiring subject to the approval of Superintendent La Grangc. La Grange was just as adamant about retaining that control.

Surprisingly the duties of the engraver came in for some spirited comment. To ex-coiner Franklin Peale, the term engraver was a misnomer. The mint service really required a diesinker. The highest grade of artistic ability should be made subservient to the production and issue of coins. Liberty on the obverse should be a classic design. A full-length figure was inappropriate on such a small palette. The eagle should be eliminated from the reverse. A simple wreath around the denomination in low relief would allow for a better, higher relief on the obverse.[6] Others went a step further. The office should be abolished and the director empowered to employ competent outside artists to prepare designs and dies. The office was useless and a hindrance to improved art.[7]

One clause came in for absolutely no comment. Silver bullion deposited by private holders would be paid in silver bars or discs only. No deposit for silver coinage would be received. Thus, the Treasury Department would control the amount of silver coinage, matching it to the needs of commerce.

In his report accompanying the final draft of his bill, Knox did an about face on the silver dollar. The existing statutes had two units of value, a silver dollar and a gold dollar. The standard silver dollar currently enjoyed a premium compared to the gold dollar of a little over 3%. The country could not have two differing units of value. Therefore, Knox recommended dropping the dollar coin entirely. If such a coin would be authorized, it should be issued only as a commercial dollar, not as a standard unit of account, to circulate in competition with the Mexican dollar in the orient as advocated by Billy Ralston and Louis Garnett.[8]

Knox left the copper-nickel minor coinage provisions intact but complained the cost of this coinage to date was more than one-half its nominal value. "If the manufacture of this coinage had been under the supervision of an officer not influenced by the clamor for patronage, and independent of all local pressure, its cost would not probably have been more than one third of its nominal value."[9] Knox was indirectly accusing Henry Linderman.

There were also technical fixes. The deviation from standard fineness allowed on gold coins was tightened. The allowance for wastage was reduced for silver and gold.

Secretary Boutwell sent the proposed mint legislation to the Hill on April 25, 1870. In this final version, it was duly referred to Sherman's Senate Committee on Finance and Kelley's House Committee on Coinage Weights and Measures. Here the bill sat until December when Sherman's committee finally reported the bill back to the Senate with amendments.

The Committee on Finance agreed to the elimination of the standard silver dollar with no replacement at a reduced silver content. The gold dollar would be the unit of value. The committee bought into the concept of copper nickel minor coinage and hence the elimination of the two-cent piece and the half dime. The committee rejected the elimination of the coinage charge on coins, bars and ingots, calling for a reduction from 0.5% to 0.3%. S.859 left the clause allowing the exchange of unparted bullion for fine bars unchanged. In Boutwell's submittal the sections authorizing the disposal of the southern branch mints and dropping the terminology of branch mint had been eliminated. Sherman reinserted these clauses.[10]

Debate in the Senate, sitting as a Committee of the Whole, began in earnest on January 9, 1871. Action immediately stalled as debate over the coinage charge swirled. Senator Cornelius Cole from California was adamant that the charge be entirely removed. He estimated that as much as $12 million in bullion was driven into the export market annually, mainly to London, for coinage as a result of the charge.

Sherman seemed obtuse to this issue of bullion retention. He argued the business of the coinage charge involved a matter of detail over which it was somewhat difficult to secure the attention of the Senate. Condescendingly, he said he hoped to secure that attention long enough to show that the amendment was necessary. He then launched into a long-winded discussion that was futilely countered by the western senators, led by Bill Stewart. The amendment inserting the coinage charge survived in a close vote.

The next day the bill was reported to the Senate as amended. Debate again centered on the coinage charge. Cole gained the floor. He had a letter from Ralston that he asked the chief clerk to read.

> The effect of this [coinage] charge is to promote the expropriation of the precious metals to other countries where no such charge exists. The charge acts as a premium in their favor and against the enlargement of our coin base which at the present time especially needs all the help we can give it, looking to the resumption of specie payments.

On the debate dragged until finally the presiding officer called the question. Robert Stevens told Ralston that Bill Stewart dragged Henry Wilson of Massachusetts to the floor for the vote.[11] This time the coinage charge was removed.

It was time to vote on S.859. In amended form it passed easily. The elimination of the standard silver dollar had not been addressed in the debate. Piqued over losing the debate on the coinage charge, Sherman voted against his committee's bill.[12]

Next S.859 went to the House and was referred to the Committee on Coinage, Weights and Measures. Judge Kelley sat on the bill for six weeks. On February 28th, he reported out of committee a substitute. No silver dollar coin reappeared. The coinage charge was back in at 0.2%. It made no difference, only six days left before the 41st Congress adjourned. By delaying, Kelley had killed the bill.

There was more to this story and Billy Ralston had the details. Knox and Linderman while in San Francisco on their inspection trip the prior year had been guests of Ralston at Belmont—a glorious, alcohol infused time according to Linderman.[13] Afterwards, Ralston agreed to leave the issue of the coinage charge and all other such matters in Linderman's hands.[14] Ralston now had both Linderman and Robert Stevens working for him in Washington.

In his first letter to Ralston, Linderman used a code name: "Guyescutes." Linderman would fall back on code names and letters in code when he knew he was on thin ice. Linderman feared that an amendment critical to Ralston retaining the position of treasurer of the mint would possibly endanger the bill. He also observed that there was general apathy toward the bill in the House and a quiet opposition from Philadelphia, represented by Judge Kelley.[15]

After Congress adjourned, Linderman gave Ralston his postmortem on the situation. There was no doubt that Kelley procrastinated due to Philadelphia pressure and the influence of Senators Sherman, Morrill and Fenton. Also, Kelley was a candidate for the chair of Ways and Means and did not want the responsibility for this bill to get in the way. Finally, either Seligman or one of the bullion dealers in New York claimed that the Bank of California would gain unfair advantage from the removal of the coinage charge. Linderman and Secretary Boutwell had applied pressure just to get Kelley to bring the bill out of committee. Had the session been ten days longer, the bill would have passed.

Linderman expected success in the next Congress provided they continued their efforts in a quiet and prudent way. It would be important to put the bill through the House with Sherman's coinage-charge amendment omitted. Kelley lately was for free coinage of gold and Boutwell certainly was in their corner. Linderman reminded Ralston that the new bill would keep the proviso in the 1870 contract refining law in place, limiting that activity at San Francisco to the interval before completion of the new mint. He did not want to fight that matter over again.

Linderman observed: "Things make haste slowly here." Money would not be required and would in fact defeat the bill. Their best argument was to urge the necessities of cheap refining and a free gold coinage for the financial and industrial good of the country. There was talk that the former mint director might be kept employed by Boutwell while the coinage legislation was under consideration. However, Linderman was not willing to enter into any such service if it interfered with his independence.

Linderman billed Ralston $3,500 for expenses associated with his work to date which Ralston would promptly pay.[16] He assumed that Ralston would want him to continue his efforts in the upcoming 42nd Congress, working to maintain the current contract refining arrangement in San Francisco and resolving the coinage charge satisfactorily. He would do this for $5,000. In a fit of conscience, Linderman stated he would not have undertaken this effort if not for the fact that he had advocated for contract refining and free coinage before this bill was drafted. Linderman was strongly convinced of their necessity, and it was a labor of love! Unfortunately, he could not afford to give his services without compensation.[17]

Chapter 11
Kelley v. Hooper

John Sherman had pinned the tail on the donkey. The donkey was Judge Kelley who was being blamed by Boutwell for the failure to pass the coin bill in the last Congress. Four days into the 1st Session of the 42nd Congress, Kelley responded by introducing HR.5.

The coin bill sat in his committee for a month until January 9, 1872.[1] Kelley had picked a day when two of the minority members of his committee were absent, hoping to slide the bill through to approval after a reading by the clerk. Fernando Wood immediately called his hand, asking Kelley if he intended to call the question after the reading. Kelley, caught, could only answer in the negative, saying he wanted the bill to be fairly considered.

Clarkson Potter from New York quickly gained control of the discussion and put Kelley on the spot. Was there any change in the value from the coins now issued? Potter's question was in regard to international coinage. No. Were there any new denominations? No. Did this bill preserve the gold and silver devices now in use? Yes. Potter objected to the expanded use of copper-nickel in the coinage. To Potter it was made for no earthly purpose except to enrich certain gentlemen who had a monopoly on nickel in Pennsylvania. Potter did not see the urgency of this legislation when specie did not freely circulate, had not, and would not for years to come. Yet not one word from Potter concerned the elimination of the standard silver dollar.

Samuel Hooper, the veteran congressman from Massachusetts, stepped into Kelley's place to help shepherd the coin bill to enactment. Conveniently, he would die in 1874, leaving questions about the bill's passage forever unanswered.

The judge observed that Potter was "a little rabid about Pennsylvania." If he were so opposed to copper-nickel, Kelley would drop it from the bill. Potter told him to strike out the clause. Kelley, his bluff called, could only stammer that the bill was symmetrical and that he did not have another clause to insert in its place.

With so much verbal jousting, Kelley asked that the House in a Committee of the Whole take up the bill. He got the unanimous consent needed. Judge Kelley preceded to a real a shellacking. The bill came up again the next day during the morning hour and after much debate was recommitted.[2] HR.5 was dead, and Kelley was in real trouble.

Rumors were swirling about Judge Kelley's involvement in a growing scandal involving Crédit Mobilier of America. This sham company had been structured to provide a screen through which the officers of the Union Pacific Railroad could line their pockets by overcharging the railroad for its services that were reimbursed by the U. S. government on a mileage basis through Congressional appropriations. To ensure that there would be inadequate oversight, Congressman Oakes Ames, whose brother Oliver was president of the Union Pacific, gave Crédit Mobilier stock, paying exorbitant dividends at favorable prices and terms, to selected Congressmen, including Kelley. He argued that the transaction was really a loan and tried to give the money back to Ames in repayment. Nobody was having that excuse. Kelley even asked his wife to come down from Philadelphia to stand by his side. She refused.[3] In the end Kelley's leadership role in the House was put on a long pause.

With HR.5 in shambles, Judge Kelley stepped aside as chair of the Committee on Coinage, Weights and Measures and Samuel Hooper became the acting chair.[4] Hooper made the decision to start fresh rather than amend the original bill. Even so when Hooper reported the bill out of committee on February 13, 1872, Congressman McNeely, a Democratic member of the committee, expressed surprise. He had attended every meeting of the committee and yet had no idea what was in the bill or that it was being reported to the House. With that the speaker postponed discussion.[5] Lost in this cutoff was the first appearance of a provision for a trade dollar of 420 grains.

Hooper gained the House floor again on April 9, 1872, for a make-or-break session for this bill, now termed HR.1427. Consistent with all previous versions of the proposed legislation, the bill declared the gold dollar as the unit of value. The trade dollar contained in the February bill was gone. In its place was a subsidiary silver dollar with a standard weight of 384 grains. Hooper explained that the standard silver dollar of 412½ grains did not circulate. Only in follow up discussion was the fact revealed that this new dollar was lumped with the other subsidiary silver coins, restricted to a legal tender value of $5 in any one transaction. Also, the copper-nickel minor coins survived the redraft and their bronze counterparts would be dropped.

The coinage charge was back in at 0.2%. There was also a suspicious clause that kept the existing practice of receiving silver bullion by weight and paying out the same on an intrinsic basis in subsidiary silver coins to be continued at New York and Philadelphia for two years. Bullion dealers had been clearing about 5 cents in face value for each ounce of silver by transferring these coins in bulk to certain South American countries, a real gravy train. Given that this bill provided that only the secretary of the Treasury be empowered to purchase silver bullion in the future for coinage, this clause was a sop to the bullion dealers to quiet their opposition.

The reading done, Hooper circled back to the silver dollar. The standard silver dollar had rarely circulated in this country because of the difficulty of making silver coins conform intrinsically to the gold standard. When undervalued against gold, as was the present condition, these coins went to the melting pot for their bullion. The purpose of the subsidiary silver coins with an intrinsic value below their face amount was to supply the public need for small change. They were tokens of value, not the value itself, for exchange and circulation domestically. In addition, holding their intrinsic value below their face amount, generated seigniorage to the government and prevented their being exported.

Hooper next turned to the section providing for the exchange of unparted bullion for refined bullion. He believed that the business of government was to coin money, not refine bullion. Private enterprise could do it better and ought to be encouraged.

At this point, Clarkson Potter had had enough. He had in his hand Pollock's critique to Knox questioning the need for the bill. This revision in the statues made him suspicious. The change in the weight and value of the silver dollar needed to be seriously considered. He had not been able to resist the conviction that the bill was designed to make a place for a particular person. The purpose of the bill had been stated to be uniformity. It occurred to Potter that the real motive was to increase demand for nickel as the new minor coinage. The cost of recoining the existing minor coins to conform to the new weights would be an extravagance. Potter did not give the refining clause a pass either. He thought it was intended to protect the system of private refining that existed in San Francisco.

After some heated exchanges, Fernando Wood, former leader of the Tammany Democrats in New York City, took the floor to reinforce Potter's attack on the refining arrangement in San Francisco. Wood made a telling observation about that refining. The arrangement rendered the bullion insecure in the process of exchange. Wood also observed that someone out there had enough influence to ensure the continuance of private refining and this dependence would expose the government to exorbitant charges. This was too much information for Wood to have at his command. There was one person in New York City, no friend of Ralston and Linderman, who did—Eugene Kelly.

At length, Hooper attempted to regain control of the process. He would entertain amendments to the bill within specific sections. Wood objected. He wanted the bill to be read section by section with amendments made as the sections were read. Hooper, overwhelmed, could only agree to proceed in this manner in a Committee of the Whole.

When Hooper came to the enacting clause, James Brooks moved to strike it out, killing the bill. His argument, tongue in cheek, was to the point.

"No member of this House has seen a silver dollar or a golden eagle except as a curiosity in a museum for some four, five or six years, nor is likely to for a like period into the future. It is a farce to consider these regulations at this time."

Brooks withdrew his amendment and the clerk continued to read each section. When he reached the seventh, it was late afternoon, and the House adjourned. Hooper had fared no better than Judge Kelley.[6]

Throughout late winter and spring of 1872 Linderman was operating from the Metropolitan Hotel in Washington. He had had his hands full with Eugene Kelly and the New York Chamber of Commerce over the coin bill and in particular, the refining clause. On May 19th Linderman told Ralston that he had kept the opposition down, but he could not let up until the bill passed the House. "A rod is in the soak for those fellows and will have it laid on unmercifully when the Bill again comes up as it will as soon as the tariff bill is disposed of." While he would not bother Ralston with the details, he needed $1,500 right away. Most of it had already been spent. That was way too much for dinners and entertainment. Linderman wasn't saying but something needed fixing.

Linderman also warned Ralston of an expected weakening of silver prices. Those countries maintaining a bimetallic standard would be overrun with silver unless additional markets could be found for the metal. If those markets did not materialize, a serious decline in price was inevitable. He believed the demonetization of the silver dollar and placing silver purchases firmly in the hands of the secretary of the Treasury were timely for the country.[7]

It was Monday, May 27, 1872. Hooper rose in the House to offer a substitute for HR.1427. This third iteration of the coin bill would be known as HR.2934. Brooks immediately asked for a postponement. The leader of the opposition, Potter, was absent and it was Brooks' impression that Potter disagreed with the substitute. Hooper declined, saying it was too late in the session. The speaker instructed that the bill be read and would not budge.

As the clerk read the bill, questions arose. Then McNeely stated that as a member of the committee he was satisfied that the bill ought to pass. Without Potter present that undercut opposition. Aaron Sargent called for the vote; the bill passed. No one asked for a division of the vote so individual votes were not recorded. [8]

What had Hooper and Linderman done? It was easier to understand using a scorecard of the changes.

1. The superintendent at each mint and assay office retained the power to appoint all clerks and workmen and set their wages subject to the disapproval of the director of the mint.
2. The silver dollar made its appearance with a reduced weight of 384 grains with legal tender capper at five dollars in any single transaction. Because of its almost identical silver content with the French five-franc piece it quickly became known as the French or franc dollar.[9]
3. Copper-nickel one-, three- ,and five-cent pieces were retained although existing minor coinage would not be recoined.
4. The cost to the depositor of converting gold bullion into coin would be 0.2%.
5. The bullion dealers in Philadelphia and New York City would be able for two years to receive silver coin in payment for silver bullion.
6. The bill retained the ability to exchange unparted bullion for refined bullion. The refining charge at a mint was capped at the contract rate.[10]
7. The treasurer at each mint moved over as assistant treasurer for the respective sub-treasury.

The only question unanswered was why Neely closed off Democratic opposition, eliminating the chance to thoroughly review the bill. Now HR.2934 went back to the Senate and John Sherman's Committee on Finance.

Chapter 12
FRUITS OF VICTORY

With the adjournment of the 2nd Session of the 42nd Congress on June 10, 1872, Boutwell sent Henry Linderman on a tour of European mints to study the latest minting processes. The Europe that Linderman experienced was undergoing a cataclysmic change in its power structure. The Franco-Prussian War of 1870 had not only put an end to the Second Empire of France's Louis Napoleon, it gave birth to a unification of the various German states with Prussia to form the German Empire. Subsequently, the coinage law of November 23, 1871 called for the introduction of the gold mark on July 9, 1873 replacing the silver coins of the previous German states. Concurrently $350 million of silver would be demonetized, casting an instant cloud over this metal's market price.

Linderman issued a special report in November. The facts indicated the gradual but inevitable adoption of the gold standard and consequent demonetization of silver by all commercial nations. Paper money redeemable in gold would serve as the primary circulating medium.

The policy of the United States under these circumstances must be to seek out a market in China for its silver bullion in a form that gave advantages over the Mexican dollar that currently enjoyed wide acceptance in the Far East. After consulting with some of the leading businessmen in San Francisco, meaning Louis Garnett and Billy Ralston, Linderman recommended a new coin slightly more valuable than the Mexican dollar.[1] This new American dollar would only be minted at the request of the owner of the bullion and at his expense. This coin would not be legal tender for any domestic payments but simply stamped with its weight and fineness, making it strictly a bullion piece.

Secretary of the Treasury Boutwell in his annual report of December 2, 1872 addressed the silver issue in a negative fashion. Internationally silver coinage should be designed exclusively for commercial uses with other nations. Domestically silver should be used for the coinage of tokens redeemable by government at their nominal value. Addressing the market overhang of German surplus silver holdings, silver prices were likely to continue to decline making it impossible to issue silver coin redeemable in gold without ultimate loss to the government when presented for redemption. That was a roundabout way of saying that Boutwell, at a minimum, wanted the legal tender status of the standard silver dollar limited in nature.

To dissemble is defined in Webster's dictionary as the act of concealing facts, intentions or feelings under some pretense. John Sherman was a master of the art of dissembling.

Shortly after the 3rd congressional session opened in December 1872, he brought HR.2934 out of the Finance Committee. Sherman was at his best here. He informed his colleagues that this bill in substance had passed the Senate in the last Congress. In its somewhat modified form, it had passed the House again in this Congress. So for all intents and purposes, this bill had passed both houses. His committee proposed the modification of only a single section from the House version. Just what that modification was, Sherman did not say. In typical Sherman fashion, he wasn't volunteering anything.

Sherman supposed it would have to go through the formal full reading unless the Senate was willing to accept in good faith the statement of the Committee on Finance that this action was not necessary. One could almost see Sherman crossing his fingers in hope that HR.2934 would slide by with this nonchalant recommendation. It did not. California Senator Cole insisted it be printed so that he could carefully see the amendments.[2]

On January 17, 1873 Sherman rose to move that the Senate sitting as a Committee of the Whole consider the coinage bill now amended by his committee. He had been told it was a matter of vital importance to the government. Amendments from the Committee on Finance represented points of difference between the two Houses and could go to a committee of conference without a controversy there in the Senate. Once again Sherman was attempting to speed through the bill's deliberation.

The first two amendments were technical corrections, quickly approved. The next two amendments dealt with weight loss tolerances for gold coins. Both passed causing California Senator Eugene Casserly to observe sarcastically that very few senators were paying attention. By now it should have been apparent to everyone in the Senate chamber that Sherman had the votes in hand for passage of this bill.

Sherman came to the silver coinage section and passed right by without comment that a trade dollar had been added. In the minor coinage section, the committee dropped the copper-nickel one-cent piece in favor of the existing bronze composition.

The next amendment dealt with a change in the reverse design requirements. The eagle was omitted on the silver dollar, half dollar and quarter and on the reverse of these three coins plus the dime and in its place the weight and fineness was to be added. Casserly asked how strong Sherman felt about this change. Sherman replied that the eagle was preserved on the gold coins in "a size large enough to be caged." Casserly pointed out that the quarter and half dollar were the money of the people and he hated to see the eagle removed.

Sherman argued that the preceding section [on silver coinage] called for a coin [the reduced weight subsidiary silver dollar] exactly equivalent in value to the English shilling and French five-franc piece. Sherman was proposing that these silver pieces be accepted worldwide. Incorporating their weight and fineness would better enable that acceptance than an eagle that foreigners might mistake for a buzzard. Then Sherman backed off confessing that he did not think it very important and let slip that it was Linderman promoting an international coinage.

Casserly continued his cross-examination. Responding, Sherman divulged that the bill adopted the international gram instead of the grain for our silver coins. Not wanting to wade into details, Sherman did not explain that the weight of the subsidiary dollar coin was increased from 384 grains to 385.8 grains or twenty-five grams with pro rata adjustments for the other silver coins. Sherman did disclose for the first time that a trade dollar had been included in the amended bill mainly for the benefit of the people of California and others engaged in trade with China.

Casserly, stating that his only point was to retain the eagle on the silver dollar, half dollar and quarter, called the question and defeated Sherman's amendment. Smarting from this defeat, Sherman tartly hoped that the Senate that was so patriotic as to retain the eagle would now hurry along with the bill.

There were more fixes to incorporate the new trade dollar. The owner of silver bullion could exchange it at the mint for bars or trade dollars, paying the mint's actual cost for the conversion.

Sherman now gathered up steam and began to move quickly through the amendments. He worked his way to the end before Casserly stopped him. The fight was now on to remove the gold coinage charge of 0.2%. All the old talking points about retention of bullion were rehashed. This time it wasn't even close. Casserly lost.

As it had in the House, HR.2934 as amended passed the Senate with no division of the vote.[3] Thus both representatives and senators were not on record as supporting or opposing this bill. As Senator Stewart lamented later, the Pacific Coast senators were swayed to let the standard silver dollar with its unlimited legal tender status go in favor of the trade dollar that had such potential in the China market. They swallowed the coinage charge, though reduced, and voted in favor.

Now the bill went to the Committee on Conference to hammer out the differences in the two versions. On the committee from the House were Hooper, Stoughton and McNeely. From the Senate it was Sherman, Scott and Bayard. On February 6, 1873 Sherman and Hooper submitted the report of the committee in their respective chambers. The report while accurate could not have been any more opaque. The changes agreed to in conference dealt with the Senate amendments to HR.2934.

Worse the bill's sections did not correspond because the Senate had deleted a full section in their amended version. Still the cold hard facts were there. Amendment 8 in Section 15 after the word silver inserted the word trade. The French dollar, or franc dollar or just plain subsidiary silver dollar was no more.[4]

By inserting the trade dollar into the silver coinage of this section, it became legal tender up to five dollars as with the other silver coins, allowing it to circulate in domestic commerce. There was one rub. While the subsidiary silver coinage was controlled through silver purchases by the Treasury Department, trade dollars were not. Any one could bring silver to the mint for conversion to trade dollars as long as they paid the cost of coinage. Thus if the price of silver declined such that the bullion cost plus coinage was below face, the brokers would have a heyday floating trade dollars in the domestic economy. Sherman should have known better; he had been told from more than one source that silver prices were expected to decline.

Both the Senate and the House of Representatives agreed to the conference report. Not a question had been asked in either chamber. The president signed the Coinage Act into law on February 12, 1873.[5]

Upon passage of the Coinage Act of 1873, Henry Linderman immediately gained a recess appointment to be director of the mint. The formal nomination would come the following December 2nd.[6]

Barely settled in his new position, Linderman took time to write Ralston on March 9. With the exception of the very small gold coinage charge, he believed they achieved all they set out to accomplish. The ability to exchange parted bullion for unparted bullion was settled. For Linderman, the implementation of the trade dollar coinage was of first importance. Then Linderman indulged himself with a victory lap. "Was a measure more carefully and persistently guarded than this coinage bill by me?" Linderman did acknowledge the mining interests owed the reduction of the coinage charge primarily to Ralston. Linderman was thankful for Ralston's steady support.

In closing, Linderman stated that he had not the least ambition to be director of the mint. However it was incumbent upon him to see that the measures in the law were properly put into operation. He would give his full attention to the trade dollar and try to get it out in acceptable form.

Already heavy on self-congratulation, Linderman's postscript was a step too far.

'The last thing on this earth that you would have me do is to come to you in the shape either of a mendicant or official shyster but such is not my purpose. I simply desire to say that now that my work is done, I leave the matter of any extra compensation entirely to you & whether you may do much, little or nothing at all, I shall be content. 'I have fought a good fight,' 'have kept the faith' and leave the rest with you. In your own time & in your own way dispose of it. I should not now have mentioned the subject but that I desire 'the deck cleared for action' and all matters off my mind before commencing my new work.

I shall put my oar in things here quietly but deeply & in the various contingencies that may arise in the next few years, will always remember & try to serve my friend R always depend on that no matter what ever may turn up."[7]

John Sherman in his autobiography had an entirely different view.

"There never was a bill proposed in the Congress of the United States which was so publicly and openly presented and agitated. I know of no bill in my experience which was printed, as this was, thirteen times, in order to invite attention to it. I know of no bill which was freer from any immoral or wrong influence than this act of 1873."[8]

There was a short postscript to this story. The following year, Congress embarked on an effort to clean up outright errors in the statute books in a massive revision. It was with understanding there would be no legislative fixes embedded in the revision. When the body of work came up for approval in both houses, there was only a cursory review. However there were two changes that impacted the Bureau of the Mint. The standard 412 ½-grain silver dollars issued before the Coinage Act of 1873 were restricted in legal tender status to five dollars in any one transaction, the same as the subsidiary silver coins. In addition the motto "In God We Trust" was not addressed in the required inscriptions for coinage.[9] Only two men had the knowledge to make these changes, former mint director and now superintendent of the Philadelphia Mint, James Pollock, and Henry Linderman. Pollock would never have dropped the motto. "In God We Trust" is on his gravestone.[10] These two backdoor maneuvers had all the earmarks of Linderman.

The Coinage Act of 1873 was perceived as an innocuous law. The average American citizen could not have cared less about mint regulations, the coinage charge, or contract refining. Implementation of a trade dollar not intended to circulate domestically would have been a mere curiosity. The only tangible impact was the demonetization and therefore effective removal of the standard silver dollar from everyday commerce. Yet that should not have had a galvanizing impact as very few of these coins actually circulated.

The coinage Act of 1873 might have slipped into history as an arcane law of little significance if not for the unfortunate timing of its enactment.

By the time the financial collapse hit the United States, it was a full-blown worldwide depression. The German Empire, flush with capital from French war reparations payable in funds convertible into gold, embarked on a program of broad industrialization. This in turn led to stock market speculations that were unsustainable. The inevitable failure came with the crash of the Vienna Stock Exchange on May 9, 1873. When the bubble burst, the string of failures and bankruptcies quickly spread from Austria Hungary into the German Empire and on through continental Europe and Great Britain. Where there was overinvestment, the results were brutal.

For the United States the Achilles heel was railroad overexpansion. The trigger for the collapse was the sell off in Northern Pacific Railway bonds. First to go was the investment house of Jay Cooke & Company handling those bonds in September 1873.[11] This set off a string of bank failures closing the New York Stock Exchange on September 20th for ten days.[12] With demand for rails down, the iron industry died.

Then the coal industry faded. They fell like cascading dominoes. Money went into hiding. The Panic of 1873 had arrived.

The commercial nations of Europe should have expanded their monetary supply to counteract the recession. They did not, following instead the lead of the Latin Monetary Union that limited and subsequently extended indefinitely free conversion of silver into coin at their mints. While their laws permitted payment of debts in silver, custom demanded gold. That placed the Latin Monetary Union, and particularly the French, on a de facto gold standard. By 1879 the rest of Northern Europe and Scandinavia had followed.[13]

In the United States there was a very limited expansion of the money supply. However the political leadership had been educated prior to the Civil War when clerical influences pervaded American higher education at most colleges. A minister often taught political economy as a branch of "moral philosophy." So phrases like "sound money" used to promote the gold standard carried gravitas. Hard money equated with virtue and resumption of specie payments was a question of common honesty.[14]

As more nations went to the gold standard, demand for gold outstripped supply. The great discoveries in California and Australia were depleting with no replacement in sight. In this system, the value of gold was fixed. Therefore the value of other commodities must decline to reflect gold's increased purchasing power. Sound money now came with a price, deflation. In this scenario, creditors gained, being repaid in increasingly valuable gold. Debtors on the other hand lost for exactly the same reason.

For the American farmers of the South, Midwest and Great Plains, the combination of debt plus falling crop prices gradually became an intolerable burden and a rallying point for political change. Gradually the demonetization of the standard silver dollar began to stand out like a sore thumb; it was the cause for all their miseries suffered in the ensuing financial panic. Thus, the Coinage Act of 1873 became known as the "Crime of '73." It would give birth to a silver movement that caught fire, expanding beyond the mere re-monetization and coinage of a standard silver dollar. It would roil American politics for the remainder of the 19th and early 20th Centuries.

For John Sherman the Coinage Act of 1873 would cost him the one prize he most eagerly sought, the Presidency. For Billy Ralston the price would be far dearer.

Part 3

House of Cards

Chapter 13
No Common Muckers

When John Percival Jones took over as superintendent at Crown Point, he inherited a rundown, washed-up mine with worn out machinery. In addition, he needed cash to drive a shaft to the lower levels in hopes of discovering a new ore ledge. Jones was not without reason for wanting to go deeper. The fire that took out the neighboring Yellow Jacket Mine in April 1869—in fact the fire that had given him hero status—had squelched a promising ore lead. There was hope the possible ore body might be found again and developed through the Crown Point Mine.

Jones pressed his search at the 1,000- and 1,100-foot levels, the bottom of his mine. He convinced Ralston and his partner Sharon, who owned a controlling interest in Crown Point, to levy assessments upon the shareholders amounting to $240,000 or $20 per share.[1] All through the spring and summer of 1870, Jones burned through the money in a futile search for the elusive bonanza. First from the base of the mine-shaft, he took a horizontal or drift cut 800 feet to the east at an acute angle to the Yellow Jacket Mine boundary. It should have picked up the Yellow Jacket lead, but it didn't—nothing but hard, gray porphyry. Then Jones backed up and cut a perpendicular drift and then a second one – nothing. In December an additional assessment of $1 per share was levied.[2] Worse for the shareholders, the price of Crown Point stock had tanked from $100 per share in June 1868, in the face of continued assessments, to a rock bottom $2 per share in November.[3] With 12,000 shares outstanding, the property had a market value of $24,000; it had hit junk status. At this point, there was a real question whether the proposed assessment would fail.

Despite his futile efforts, Jones had faith in the mine's potential for a bonanza; he had been buying all the Crown Point stock he could. When his money ran out, he had borrowed from friends. Then he had persuaded San Francisco brokers to carry large blocks of Crown Point stock in his account in a deal that required him to protect them on the downside and share on the upside.

Alvinza Hayward had been named president of Crown Point at the shareholders' meeting in June 1870. Ralston had felt obligated to bring Hayward into the Bank Crowd due to his financial support during the crunch at the Bank of California. However, with production in the Comstock sagging, the spoils were thin, and the presidency of Crown Point looked like a dead-end position.[4]

When the most recent drift began showing pockets of ore, Jones felt optimistic enough to approach Hayward. Infected by Jones's enthusiasm, Hayward began purchasing shares at the $2 mark and agreed to carry a large block of the stock for Jones's account.[5] Neither man felt inclined to tell Ralston and Sharon of their suspicion that a bonanza was in the making. Hayward picked up 5,000 shares at an average cost of less than $5 per share.

Not until Jones had gone through a bout of cold feet did the ore pockets coalesce. As news of the strike began to leak, the stock started climbing. Brokers for Hayward and Jones first bought shares at prices ranging from $90 to $120 per share. When Crown Point reached $180, they picked up another large block.[6]

On March 11, 1871, the local Gold Hill Daily News told the world that the ore body in Crown Point was assaying better and proving more extensive as development work progressed.[7] By May, the main shaft had reached the 1,200-foot level with a drift driven south toward the Belcher Mine that ran into the same ore body. The stock jumped again, and Sharon now found himself on the outside looking in. However, he wasn't caught empty-handed; he held 4,100 shares of Crown Point.

Sharon assumed with his nucleus of shares he could retain some form of control at the company's annual meeting in June. Hayward, on the other hand, wanted his slate of officers and directors elected free of any such encumbrance, setting the stage for a fight. As The Daily State Register at Carson City put it, a common friend, considered by some to be the financial Napoleon of the Comstock Lode, prevailed to prevent the fight. Ralston wanted no messy public airing of the dispute.

Negotiations were opened, and Hayward agreed to certain stipulations concerning where the ore would be crushed. Sharon agreed to sell his holdings to Hayward for $300 per share, giving Jones and Hayward control of more than 10,000 Crown Point shares in total. In return Hayward sold Sharon his holdings in neighboring Belcher.[8] Sharon, believing the extent of the ore deposit limited, felt sure that he had gotten the better end of the deal. It was the largest financial transaction to date in the Comstock Lode.[9]

By late summer, Alvinza Hayward knew who had gotten the better deal as the ore body had proven to be literally a mountain within the mountain. The base of the deposit extended to the 1500-foot level with a substantial portion within the confines of the Belcher Mine. Possibly this was the most important ore body yet discovered in the Comstock Lode.[10] Yet for Sharon the discovery left a bitter taste; it wasn't enough that he shared in the bonanza as it extended into Belcher. Hayward had betrayed the Bank Crowd and bested Sharon personally.

In July, Jones and Hayward purchased the idle Yellow Jacket Mill on the Carson River. That shut Ralston and Sharon completely out from any derivative profits from the Crown Point ore. Shortly afterward, the two men ordered new machinery, driven exclusively by steam, to upgrade capacity at Crown Point.[11]

All through the fall, prices for the key mining stocks on the Comstock rose on the San Francisco Stock and Exchange Board. The working people of the city were rolling their savings into these stocks with seemingly no end in sight as Crown Point topped $400 per share in December and never looked back.[12] When, on May 4, 1872, Crown Point closed at $1,740 per share, it seemed too good to be true.[13] The paper profits of Jones and Hayward at Crown Point and Ralston and Sharon at Belcher were staggering. Then Jones and Hayward wrested control of the Savage Mine from Sharon and subsequently discovered a lead that promised another bonanza.[14] The bad blood between Sharon and the Crown Point owners only got worse.

Riding high, John P. Jones now set his sights even higher. The political bug had bitten Jones hard in California. He had run unsuccessfully on the George Gorham ticket for lieutenant governor. Given his favorable standing in Virginia City with the miners after the Yellow Jacket fire, Jones was avidly cultivated by the Nevada Republican Party. Better yet, the 1872 race for James Nye's seat in the Senate was wide open after the senator opposed Ralston on the contract refining issue.

Jones was no neophyte here. He set up political clubs throughout the state aimed at electing a slate of Republican legislators who would vote for him. However, Jones was not without competition, as Bill Sharon wanted the seat. It promised to be a bitter struggle.

In early May, rumors began to circulate that Jones had been involved in starting the fire at the Yellow Jacket Mine. The informant, Isaac Hubbell, was a foreman there at the time of the fire. The alleged motive was to short Yellow Jacket stock in order to make a killing after the fire. Hubbell had been telling the story to others for several months before it reached Sharon's ears. He claimed Sharon was willing to pay for his testimony - $50,000 to $100,000 with another million to be spent, blackening the name of Jones. Yet push as Sharon might, Hubbell would not place Jones in the Yellow Jacket Mine before the fire. It was said that Hubbell then took the story of his dealings with Sharon to Jones.[15]

Next, the story leaked to the newspapers. Motives were questioned. Sharon was forced to disclaim any purpose to do Jones harm in the affair. No one believed a word of the accusation regarding Jones while most readers attributed the part allegedly played by Sharon as true to character.[16]

Two subsequent facts cannot be disputed in the affair: Hayward promptly closed all his accounts at the Bank of California, and the market for Comstock mining stocks crashed on May 15, 1872.[17] Crown Point had hit a high of $1,825 per share just before the fall.[18] Perhaps the bubble started to burst when the Savage Mine lead failed to produce anything substantial in late April.[19] Regardless, Sharon in early May decided to take his $5 million invested in Comstock mining shares off the table. Belcher, Savage, and Crown Point, the biggest beneficiaries of the market run-up, were hard-hit. As Sharon raked in his money, Jones and Hayward were hurt the most with huge paper losses from the ensuing market crash. However, these did not compare in pain to that suffered by the small investors in San Francisco who lost their savings in the speculative frenzy.[20]

In August 1872, after the fireworks were over, a Storey County grand jury investigated accusations against Jones in the mine fire and exonerated him.[21] Sharon, now in an untenable position, was done. On August 16, claiming illness, he withdrew from the Senate contest.[22]

Jones was not yet home free in his quest for the Senate seat. In September the *San Francisco Chronicle* set its sights on Jones, deploring that he lacked the needed education, reading, and training to sit in the Senate. The contest itself was criminal, as bribery was open, beginning a year in advance of the election. Jones funded the

James Fair moved to California and began his mining career prospecting for gold in California's Feather River district. With the strikes on Davidson Mountain, he moved to the Virginia City area, operating a stamp mill on the Carson River. Eventually he became superintendent of the Hale and Norcross Mine. Here he formed a partnership with John Mackay, James Flood, and William O'Brien. Their subsequent exploits would earn them the title of Silver Kings.

Born dirt poor in Dublin Ireland, John Mackay migrated with his family to New York City where, as a young boy, he earned money for the family selling newspapers. He came to California in 1851 and eventually worked his way to the Comstock Lode. Here he labored for wages by day and worked small claims in his spare time. Gradually becoming successful, he constantly rolled his earnings into mining investments that ultimately led to his partnership with the other Silver Kings.

clubs he had organized for conducting his campaign, subsidized brothels, and bought and packed the state legislature primaries. A more specific allegation involved the withholding of dividends to the Crown Point shareholders in order to fund the Jones campaign from the company's coffers.[23] This accusation was without merit as a large pocket of water had been encountered and dewatering had proceeded slowly.[24]

Jones virtually swept into office on January 21, 1873.[25] In a speech delivered in the state Assembly Chamber shortly after his election, he declared that in all future issues that might arise between capital and the people, he would be found steadfast and faithful to the interests of the people.[26] Jones had just declared for silver.

The activity around the Crown Point Mine could not have provided a better cover for John Mackay and Jim Fair if they had arranged it themselves. From the boundary of Hale & Norcross, the mine that gave them their first success against Ralston and Sharon, they could look across a seemingly barren stretch of property 1,300 feet to the once equally lucrative but now depleted Ophir Mine. Yet that tract had returned nothing despite its being honeycombed with shafts and drifts down to the 500-foot level. The majority of the block was organized as the Consolidated Virginia. The remainder was held in the neighboring California Mining Company, itself struggling to stay solvent.

In 1871 Mackay and Fair brought their San Francisco partners, Flood and O'Brien, into their plan to control the Consolidated Virginia and explore the deeper levels. From December 1870 to April 1871, the Consolidated Virginia shares doubled from $5 to $10 on 11,600 shares outstanding, but this activity was totally overshadowed by the concurrent run-up of Crown Point shares.[27] Once the four men had control, they levied assessments against the shareholders that kept the stock at depressed prices.

James Flood and William O'Brien were the money men behind James Fair and John Mackay. Flood, more than the other three Silver Kings saw to the investments from the proceeds of the Consolidated Virginia and California Mines.

When the four men had increased their control of Consolidated Virginia to 75 percent, they announced their desire to punch a drift north from the neighboring Gould & Curry Mine, controlled by Sharon through Best & Belcher, into the Consolidated Virginia. Sharon was cooperative, saying, arrogantly, that he was helping those Irishmen blow their profits from the Hale & Norcross.

Jim Fair commenced the drift in May 1872. In mid-September as affairs reached a critical stage, the drift encountered a stringer of knife-thin ore in the Best & Belcher. Fair followed the lead foot by foot for 100 feet into the Consolidated Virginia before he took ill for a month, and others turned the drift east without success. By now $200,000 had been spent in a futile search for what seemed the Holy Grail and the checking account of the Consolidated Virginia was nearly empty. Worse, the worth of the four men controlling the mine could hardly stand another extended dry spell of "exploration by pick and shovel."

Fair returned and backtracked to the point of departure from the apparently endless thread of a lead. In February 1873, eleven feet beyond where he renewed his work, Fair cut into a seam of ore seven feet wide, assaying at $60 per ton. Two smaller ore bodies were then found in close succession. On March 1 the main ore body widened to 12 feet. However, production was hampered as the air in the long prospecting drift was becoming unbearably foul and hot from the lack of adequate ventilation.

Efforts were now redoubled to drive the shaft, now at a depth of 710 feet and needed for the full development of the mine, down as quickly as possible.[28] By mid-October 1873, the shaft had broken through, accessing an ore body 50 feet wide. This entire time the four men had managed to keep the news from the public, restricting access to the lower levels because of the excessive heat and bad air.[29]

This ore body was rich beyond expectations, assaying from $93 to $632 per ton. The shaft first hit the bonanza at the 1,167-foot mark. The deeper they pushed the shaft, the more ore they found. When the 1,500-foot level was reached, the ore was richer still, and no end seemed in sight.[30] There was no telling how much silver had been discovered here.

Billy Ralston had just lost his ironclad grip on the Comstock Lode. But there was more. Ogden Mills had had enough of Ralston's near scrapes with bank failure and resigned the presidency of Bank of California in July 1873, selling his shares in the bank as well. Then in September 1873 James Lees died unexpectedly. The checks and balances to restrain Ralston were suddenly gone.

Chapter 14

Too Many Rotten Apples for the Barrel

Once confirmed by the Senate, San Francisco Branch Mint Superintendent Hugh LaGrange could do as he pleased. There was virtually no oversight from the mint director in Philadelphia. His involvement with the Bay Area Republican Party bosses carried right over to his mint administration with virtually no accountability other than his own conscience that was sorely lacking.

When Thomas Fitch ran for re-election to the House of Representatives from Nevada in 1870, LaGrange collected $2,000 from the branch mint employees for his campaign. He did this through a subscription that was perfectly legal at the time. Then he blatantly failed to forward the money to Fitch. That such an action was easily discovered by disgruntled employees bothered LaGrange not at all.

LaGrange quickly dispensed with a key internal control that required operative officers to inspect supplies purchased by the superintendent or his clerk and to countersign the invoices before processing for payment. His stated reasons were the need to obtain the best prices by purchasing in bulk for such items as wood and coal and then keep these supplies with the vendor until needed due to the lack of storage area at the mint. LaGrange would also fall back on the lame reasoning that he took these actions from force of habit acquired in his military command and never for the purpose of defrauding the government.[1]

LaGrange's motive here was suspect. With his office across the street from the mint itself due to lack of space, LaGrange took no real interest in the operations. He found it an inconvenience to consult regarding anything, much less his purchases, with the operative officers—Jos Harmstead, the coiner, John Cochran, the melter and refiner, and Oscar Munson, the assayer. His relationship with them had become querulous, and they often delayed examining the billings.[2] Besides, Charles Felton, the mint treasurer, was LaGrange's political colleague and would pay any bills approved by him.[3]

The purchase of coal and wood became a virtual revolving door when it came to vendors. One supplier, John Middleton, had maintained good relations with the mint, supplying coal, charcoal, and wood at competitive prices. Suddenly LaGrange gave the business to George Hoag. When Middleton complained, the superintendent dodged him.[4] Felton was involved, either loaning Hoag money or investing as a partner, depending upon who was pressing him for answers.[5] Trouble quickly developed as all bills paid by the treasurer went to the Treasury Department in Washington for review. Jos Harmstead would recall two of Hoag's bills being questioned and returned for his verification. Investigating, the first was for wood paid for but never delivered. The second involved coal priced substantially over market. Harmstead refused to certify either billing.[6]

In a move that would ultimately haunt him, Hugh LaGrange in September 1870 engaged the services of an old acquaintance, George Pinney. Pinney had just arrived in Oakland, destitute, and came to LaGrange seeking money to feed his family. The superintendent employed him on an informal basis for the first two months before placing him in the warehouse as a clerk. The two men had met briefly in Wisconsin in the 1850s when Pinney was an unordained Baptist minister conducting fiery revivals. Pinney subsequently separated from the Baptists to become U.S. marshal, first for Dakota Territory and then for Montana Territory where he also published a partisan newspaper. As a stump speaker and general promoter, Pinney proved quite successful in politics while his speculations in mining properties were less so. His personal life appeared undisciplined when, after the death of his first wife, he met and married Flora Bray, a 16-year-old actress. And his reputation took a turn for the worse when a bitter political feud with an ex-governor of Wisconsin terminated with Pinney killing the man in self-defense.[7]

George Pinney was an exceptional con artist and chronic wife abuser. He fit right in at the San Francisco Branch Mint where his side deals helped bring down the superintendent, Hugh LaGrange.

Pinney's arrival at the San Francisco Branch Mint coincided with the termination of its refining operations as the result of the contract with the San Francisco Assaying and Refining Works. LaGrange delegated the disposal of the resulting surplus zinc to Pinney, instructing him to approach Thomas Selby who ran a large smelting operation. Pinney extracted a $200 commission from Selby on top of a $2,800 sale of the zinc. He then gave the proceeds to LaGrange who forgave $300 in advances that he had made to Pinney.[8] However when Pinney made a written report of the transaction, LaGrange told him not to do that again. There was a second zinc transaction with Selby in May 1871. In this case, Selby was told to treat the zinc as a loan of material because the mint was not authorized to sell it.[9]

When it came to coal, Harmstead had only caught the tip of the iceberg. Pinney would insist the bill be made out for the full amount of the purchase even though the mint physically could only take a partial delivery. Pinney would expect a kickback for the undelivered portion that might or might not ever make it to the mint.[10]

Borax was another source of cash for LaGrange. This material had been sitting in the warehouse at the time LaGrange took over. Again, he used Pinney to dispose of it. In this case, LaGrange took the money and used it to fund his bloated payroll that exceeded the branch mint's appropriation.[11]

Yet another source of cash came from copper ingots delivered in barrels for use as the alloy in gold and silver coins. In this instance, two barrels were ordered but only one appeared at the mint. The bill was kicked back from Washington, and Felton went to the melter and refiner, Cochran, who refused to certify the bill. The problem stuck out like a sore thumb because Pinney was the payee on the invoice for the copper. Ultimately, LaGrange was called to account and made Pinney replace the undelivered barrel of copper.[12] In another instance, a barrel left the warehouse and was recorded as a loan to the Carson City Branch Mint. When asked to account for the missing barrel, LaGrange said that it must have happened while he was away fishing with Henry Linderman.[13]

Pinney quickly reached the status of knowing too much about LaGrange's dealings at the branch mint. He was very aggressive, making good money through commissions on his transactions. That the vendors upped the prices of their goods to cover those commissions bothered him not one bit.

LaGrange, on the other hand, was skimming cash either into his own pocket or to cover his excess payroll through the sale of surplus goods and kickbacks from overbilling. Only once in his first years did LaGrange forward any sale proceeds to the mint treasurer for deposit to the government.[14]

It did not take long for LaGrange to get cold feet over Pinney's activity; it was far too blatant. In addition, the man drank heavily and was a womanizer.[15] The issue was how to ease Pinney out of the mint. There was an opening for chief deputy in the office of Dr. L. M. Care, director of internal revenue for California. LaGrange described Pinney to Dr. Care as a shrewd, active, and moneymaking man, and Dr. Care could save money with Pinney in his office. Just how, LaGrange did not say. Care did not take the bait.[16]

Next LaGrange turned to Rufus C. Spalding, the recently appointed paymaster at the Mare Island Navy Yard. LaGrange reached out to Spalding while the man was on a fishing excursion at Pescadero, a small village well south of San Francisco. LaGrange knew two clerkships would be available and said it would please the "administration" if Spalding would allow them to fill one of those slots. In the face of this onslaught, Spalding folded, provided the man was trustworthy.

Working both sides of this deal, LaGrange told Pinney that while there would be a reduction in pay, the job was important due to the political influence associated with the Navy Pay Office. All went smoothly and Pinney started his new position as second clerk on July 1, 1871.[17]

If Hugh LaGrange felt relieved for having rid himself of George Pinney, he was mistaken. Unbeknownst to the superintendent, Pinney upon leaving the mint prepared a ledger book detailing all the transactions that he had made for LaGrange during his short stay there.

It was the inexperienced and extra people that LaGrange forced on Jos Harmstead that thoroughly upset the man. As the coiner, he was responsible for his costs and his wastage, the loss of gold and silver in the coining process. The wastage was easily minimized by constant vigilance. The costs were composed of two elements—labor and equipment operating and maintenance expense. Having lived and breathed coins for a lifetime, he instinctively knew and trusted his machinery.

Harmstead could harden the coin dies provided by the engraver at Philadelphia and deliver a well-struck specimen within the weight tolerances every time. With the exception of power from the steam boilers, his coining apparatus really required very little in the nature of supplies. The reality was that coining was a labor-intensive business. He needed a few good men, such as George Parkinson, whom he brought back into the mint in 1869 as foreman of the rolls (which converted bars of bullion into strips of metal for coining).[18] There were others, whose work he respected, that he was careful to retain. LaGrange, much to Harmstead's consternation, upset all of this.

If Harmstead were to have looked back, he would have said LaGrange's interference in his operations started in April 1870. In typical fashion, LaGrange initiated it by letter, asking if reductions could be made in the coiner's workforce. Harmstead did not think the letter out of place; the general came onto the floor only every few weeks. He replied that he was correctly staffed except in the adjusting department where coin blank weights were checked. Staffed by women, thought particularly adapted to this finite work, Harmstead believed he had two more than needed.

Two days later, Harmstead was answering LaGrange's concern that the turnover of employees in his department, when the coiner assumed office, had adversely affected production. Then, LaGrange's chief clerk asked if the wages paid were competitive with the private sector with Harmstead answering in the affirmative. Finally in a change in LaGrange's activity within the mint, he began showing up in the various departments on a regular basis. He would sit and watch the activity, rarely asking questions.[19] At this point LaGrange suspended a few individuals with little impact to the operations.[20]

In early September, Harmstead, as well as Cochran and Munson, received another missive from LaGrange asking for more reductions. Harmstead replied in the negative. LaGrange overrode him, terminating his chief adjuster, John Collison, a reliable employee of ten years standing. Harmstead, enraged and unable to replace the man's skills, protested in writing and was, likewise, denied in writing. LaGrange stated that he was in charge and would make the decisions on cutting employees. Undeterred, Harmstead went to LaGrange's office the next day. In Harmstead's words: "General Oscar Hugh LaGrange didn't yield, just like he was back on his horse at the front lines, commanding his troops instead of running a federal mint."

LaGrange's visits to the operating departments were now a daily affair. More removals of experienced employees came in October. In particular, LaGrange had removed Lewis Henry, a "skillful noteworthy engineer," without any charge being made against him. This time Harmstead protested to special Treasury Agent Ross Browne whose investigation had led to the removal of Robert Stevens as superintendent in 1863. LaGrange stood firm against the threat, and Harmstead found it difficult to control his temper. Yet, the coiner was disappointed with Browne who listened to his complaints but lacked any sympathy for his plight.

What frustrated Harmstead most was that LaGrange, after removing experienced employees, would then bring in replacements with no knowledge whatsoever of mint operations. And it seemed that every one of them had ties to the Bay Area Republican political bosses. Harmstead termed them "friends of LaGrange" but that was a gross understatement.

Harmstead reached the end of his rope when he received a letter from LaGrange proposing to increase the number of women adjusters from 15 to 20 on November 30, 1870. His existing force only worked five hours per day. He needed no more adjusters. Besides, he had no room in the already cramped quarters where the women worked. Most were single, widows or spinsters, needing the job as a means of support. However, others were girlfriends of the politicians, paid from the public treasury and kept out of sight.[21] Once hired, they were not fired.

All this got Harmstead a second letter giving notice that LaGrange had appointed four additional adjusters and instructing him to assign them to duty. The superintendent addressed the space issue by proposing to remodel the adjacent room used for storage, a room little bigger than a closet. Harmstead refused to sign the payroll that included these women. In response the general insisted that the number of hours required for the adjusting of coin blanks in these working conditions was certain to impair the women's health. LaGrange was exercising the power vested in him by law to remedy this evil by reducing the hours each adjuster was to work under these difficult conditions.

The next morning, when the four new adjusters reported for duty, Harmstead stated he had no work, apologizing for any inconvenience he may have caused them. He next sent a note to LaGrange requesting that the superintendent send his order from the day before, justifying the additional adjusters, to the secretary of the Treasury for resolution. One hour later Harmstead received a not unexpected blast of the general's temper. LaGrange would cheerfully send that letter to Treasury Secretary George Boutwell and, furthermore, he deemed Harmstead's refusal, his third in this affair, to employ the women an act of insubordination and destruction of the superintendent's authority. He would report Harmstead's actions to the president.

Harmstead had support from Cochran who told the coiner that it took a "lotta guts" to defy the general and hoped it would blow over soon. In fact, Harmstead expected to be removed. However, he had not thought that one through, as a fifth adjuster's identity was now known—Jane LaGrange, the general's mother.

Nevertheless, it was a stressful two months waiting for a reply from the authorities back east. LaGrange had forwarded letters from three doctors attesting to the bad ventilation in the adjusting room to strengthen his case. The reply from Secretary Boutwell came in a letter written on January 17, 1871, directly to Harmstead. The coiner's conduct was an act of insubordination. The action of the superintendent was approved, and Harmstead was ordered to assign the women to duty.

Harmstead had lived to fight another day. In fact, that Boutwell had not removed him was hardly a ringing endorsement for LaGrange. From that point forward, theirs was a strictly business relationship, and Harmstead never disobeyed LaGrange's orders again.[22]

What Harmstead did not know was that LaGrange was in an increasingly tight spot politically. The mint superintendent was obligated to support Senator Cornelius Cole in his 1871 re-election bid. Cole had nominal control over the customs house, mint, and navy yard, providing him a political base in San Francisco. His opponent once again was Aaron Sargent, from the House of Representatives. After his defeat by Cole in 1865, Sargent had quietly gathered support among the powerful elite of California.

Sargent was a diligent and skilled operative. He indirectly attacked Cole at any point of weakness. Thus, LaGrange quickly came into his sights with his blatant dealings at the mint. On April 17, 1870, Sargent brought complaints of LaGrange's padding of the mint payroll into the open; operations at the mint were disgraceful. His informants had told him that the necessity for an increased appropriation of operating funds for the branch mint had arisen because LaGrange had terminated experienced, efficient employees for unskilled men and that there were more on the payroll than could possibly be employed.

Changes were continually being made without consulting the department heads with the operative officers having "utterly worthless and untrustworthy subordinates" forced upon them, bringing the mint in some instances to a standstill. Expenses had suddenly increased on an annual basis under LaGrange by $40,000. It was for this reason that Sargent had successfully combated an increase in appropriations for the branch mint in the next fiscal year.[23]

Sargent's informant was most likely Cochran who had sought the congressman's support in his effort to gain his appointment as melter and refiner. LaGrange, while obligated to Cole, would be in a perilous spot if Sargent prevailed, particularly in dealing with those who supported the congressman.

Indeed, Sargent had the support of the Republican ring, consisting at that point of George Gorham, his ally in Washington, and Bill Carr. Carr, a former railroad construction contractor, spoke for the Southern Pacific, successor to the Central Pacific, in the affairs of the Bay Area. It was rumored that the railroad did not want Cole reelected. Thus, Carr had gone to Sargent for a deal. Sargent got the railroad's support for the Senate seat, and Carr got the patronage that would come to Sargent as a result.[24] Substance to the rumors of the Southern Pacific involvement came from the active support for Sargent provided by William Whitney Stow. He was the attorney and political strong arm for the railroad. In addition, Sargent offered his allegiance to Billy Ralston. With the Bank Crowd and railroad on his side, Sargent seemed assured to gain the senate seat. The campaign played out over the summer and fall of 1871.[25]

Yet there was resistance within the Republican Party. Sargent's opponents jeeringly called him the candidate of the Gorham-Stow-Carr railroad ring. They called a meeting of "straight" Republicans on August 24, 1871, that some 3,000 attended at the Pacific Hall in San Francisco. Frank Pixley, former California attorney general and U. S. attorney for California, addressed the crowd, calling the slate headed by Sargent a mongrel ticket and a corrupt job put up by Gorham, Stow, and Carr. After Sargent, Gorham would surely follow into the Senate, taking democrat Eugene Casserly's place.[26]

When the meeting adjourned, Carr and Stow, incensed over being called out in such a negative way, followed Pixley to the upscale Lick House. Stow put a pistol to Pixley's chest and demanded a retraction. Pixley dared Stow to murder him. Knives came out of nowhere, and a chair-bashing brawl ensued.[27]

Sargent easily carried the Republican caucus in December, defeating Cole handily. The Placer Herald summed it up nicely. The customs house, mint, navy yard, and the federal host fought well, but it was no go. Now there would be a new deal in federal appointments on the Pacific Coast. "Well, let her rip she's a rotten hulk anyhow."[28]

As if to reinforce this observation, 26 of the 55 Republican legislators that voted for Sargent in the caucus would gain government positions.[29]

LaGrange was now on thin ice, expecting to be purged any day. In an understanding through a mutual friend, Sargent was persuaded that LaGrange was of more use to the party in office than out of it. An agreement was reached that LaGrange could continue at his post, "patronizing rather than persecuting the

As senator, Aaron Sargent served both Billy Ralston and the people of California. In matters of national importance, he could be counted upon to represent the people well. In matters of politics and personal power, he could be absolutely ruthless.

lesser members of the reigning political dynasty." In exchange LaGrange would be given timely notice to resign should his position be required. He described himself as a sort of political prisoner on parole inside the party."[30] Whomever Carr, Gorham, or Sargent wanted hired, LaGrange was going to comply.

Meanwhile, George Pinney found himself in hog heaven in the Navy Pay Office at the Mare Island Yard. He was working with many of the same vendors as served the mint. There would be no interruption in the commissions and kickbacks flowing his way. In the Senate race, Pinney backed Sargent and quickly earned Sargent's recognition and praise as a good speechwriter.[31] When Sargent wrote Pinney requesting that a certain state senator be given a lumber contract through the pay office in exchange for his vote in the Republican caucus, Pinney was only too happy to oblige.[32]

The job was not taxing, giving Pinney time to actively deal in mining stocks. Alvinza Hayward gave him the tip to take a position in Crown Point. Pinney even brought LaGrange into this investment. At one point LaGrange was ahead by $1,000 and Pinney by $10,000. When the market for Crown Point and the other mining stocks collapsed on May 15, 1872, the two men lost all their paper profits and more. Hayward, perhaps in awe of the general's war record, made up most of LaGrange's losses.[33]

Hayward provided no such backstop for Pinney's stock losses. The man was on his own. Pinney had good days and bad days on the market. When he had bad days, he went home and beat his wife. He would punch her, kick her, and drag her by her hair. He did it openly in front of others without remorse. She was frequently with either a swollen face or a black eye.[34]

Chapter 15

Linderman to the Fore

Albeit an interim appointment, Henry Linderman had his old job back as director of the U.S. Mint. He would build the new D.C. bureau on his own terms. For the nucleus of his staff, he chose first Martin Davis, the assistant coiner at Philadelphia and a relative of Linderman's wife, and Edward Leech from the Treasury Department in Washington. Linderman also wanted Robert Preston from the auditing department of Treasury, but the man at first turned him down. He would come aboard a year later.[1] Linderman's management style would best be described as overbearing with an obsession for complete adherence to the newly formulated regulations of the bureau. Even postage stamps were dispensed from his headquarters; in short, he was a micromanager.

Linderman's first task was to get the trade dollar, authorized in the Coinage Act of 1873, out the door and into the channels of international commerce. Fortunately, his predecessor, James Pollock, had already ordered engraver William Barber to begin design work in 1871. Initially Barber had not overly pushed the envelope on his designs, borrowing the Indian Princess design of his predecessor, James Longacre, for one version of the obverse. For another, he simply replicated the Seated Liberty of the current circulating coinage. The reverse had a distinctly international look with the denomination, weight, and fineness encircled by an olive wreath. The following year Barber prepared additional pattern designs, transitioning to an eagle on the reverse in place of the wreath.

With the legislation approaching final form, matters grew urgent in early 1873. Pollock, not satisfied with Barber's work, hired Joseph Bailly, an École des Beaux-Arts–trained artist and Philadelphia engraver of some renown, as an assistant engraver.[2] His specific assignment was to provide two obverses for the new trade dollar. One was a bust of a young but stern neo-Roman Liberty. It went nowhere. The second had more potential. Liberty was seated with a hand laid upon the globe and surrounded on each side by two primary trade goods, wheat and cotton. The concept was good, but the modeling of Liberty's legs was out of proportion to her torso.

William Barber, an assistant engraver at the Philadelphia Mint, took over the engraver's position after the death of James Longacre on January 1, 1869.

William Barber went to school on this design, placing a properly proportioned seated Liberty upon a bale of cotton. A shock of wheat was positioned to the backside of the cotton. Liberty offered an olive branch in her right hand and held a ribbon bearing the inscription "Liberty" in her left while looking to the ocean's horizon. For the reverse, the international style was augmented by several variants of eagles from one of defiance to a standing eagle slightly modified from the standard circulating coinage with the shield removed from its breast. The coin was

The first pattern piece (J-1154) for the proposed trade dollar, then known as a commercial dollar, was designed by William Barber in 1871.

large enough that Barber was able to incorporate both “In God We Trust” and “E Pluribus Unum” in the obverse and reverse designs in anticipation of the inscription requirements of the new coin law.

In late April, Linderman put the heat on Pollock, now reduced to the position of superintendent at the Philadelphia Mint, to wrap up the design phase on the trade dollar. In his words, for commercial reasons it was desirable that the trade dollar be issued as soon as possible.[3] What he did not say was that the Comstock mines badly needed a new home for their silver. It was another month before Pollock had pattern pieces in hand from Barber for Linderman to review and make a recommendation to

This pattern trade dollar (J-1281) employed the obverse design by Joseph Bailly with a reverse prepared by William Barber.

One of several other 1873 trade dollar pattern (J-1322) by William Barber. Those in this group (J-1287, J-1300, J-1304, J-1308 and J-1310) show little variation in the designs.

the new secretary of the Treasury, William Richardson. Even before receiving these pattern pieces, Linderman ordered Pollock to begin steps for coinage as soon as possible, reminding the superintendent that working dies would have to be provided to the San Francisco and Carson City mints as well.[4]

On May 31 Linderman received seven sets of obverse and reverse patterns from which to choose. He picked Barber's most advanced obverse design of Liberty seated upon the bale of cotton. Barber had placed "In God We Trust" along the plinth at the base of the figure. However, in a move that generated more work for the engraver, Linderman chose for the reverse the standing eagle that included both mottos on scrolls above and below the national bird. Linderman wanted the scroll across the base that replicated the religious motto dropped and the eagle enlarged to fill the resulting void. There were also two stars on the reverse that separated the rim inscriptions that he wanted omitted. Then, in typical fashion, he stated, "the secretary desires the coin issued as early as possible."

The adopted design for the 1873 trade dollar used modifications of the obverse of J-1322 and the reverse of J-1304.

Linderman also requested that Pollock return the specimens sent back to illustrate his points after Barber had understood the changes to be made.[5] This action would become standard as Linderman built his own unique coin collection. In a nod to the collecting community, he authorized Pollock to make available the rejected patterns to the public and officers and employees of the mint at three dollars each.[6]

On June 10 Linderman complained to Pollock that six days should have been sufficient for Barber and his assistants with the aid of a reducing machine to make the "minor" alterations required. Peevishly, he said he must report the delay to the secretary.[7] It would be July before the mints began putting out significant quantities of trade dollars. Even so, Linderman was not happy with the finished product. The design was not striking up well enough. Reductions were made in the relief of the troubled spots that Linderman thought an improvement, and he authorized new dies incorporating these changes be sent to the other mints if Pollock thought it desirable.[8]

In addition, Linderman complained that the figure of Liberty on the obverse was defective in grace, being somewhat stiff, unnatural, and not finely finished. He wondered if it could be improved and whether he should let Barber try or bring in an outside artist.[9] This dissatisfaction was going to eat at Linderman

Linderman, in changing the reverse and enlarging the eagle, had changed the striking characteristics of the coin. By rushing the refinement of the design, he omitted the final review. In addition, he did not take into account the fact that designs placed into full production in most cases did not coin as well as single pattern pieces.

The trade dollar design wasn't Linderman's only challenge in his new post. From day one, he inherited a situation with the potential to blow up his confirmation. San Francisco coiner Jos Harmstead was at the heart of it. This was not a simple squabble over adding useless employees to his department. It involved the bullion fund.

In February 1872 a small San Francisco paper published by a man named Bennett alleged that Charles Felton was improperly using public funds as treasurer at the branch mint. The newspaper went out of business shortly thereafter. Over the spring, Hugh LaGrange tried and failed to tamp down the controversy. As a result, Treasury Secretary George Boutwell sent Linderman west to team up with John Torrey, a local botanist of some renown, in late summer to investigate the situation. Heads of the various departments, including Jos Harmstead, gave written, notarized statements.

Linderman did not really take the effort seriously, as this was the trip when he and LaGrange took off to go fishing. Besides, at the time Linderman was on Billy Ralston's payroll. His main concern seemed to be whether melter and refiner John Cochran or Harmstead had divulged any details of the shortfall outside the San Francisco Branch Mint.

Harmstead stated that he had no knowledge of any irregular or unlawful use of public funds belonging to the branch mint. He did relate that the cashier in one or two instances pressed him for a delivery of coin, saying that he was $60,000 short of cash on hand to pay depositors. Harmstead knew how much bullion was in his possession. After conferring with Cochran, he could place a ballpark figure to the total bullion on hand, and it was way short of what it should have been.

Cochran would recall that he and Harmstead, after four distinct examinations of the bullion vaults, came up each time with bullion on hand of $1.5 million. The bullion fund total was supposed to be $2.8 million.[10] Cochran did not keep quiet about the shortfall, speculating that the missing funds must be invested in mining stocks. The implication was that either LaGrange or Felton had lost the money.[11]

The most likely cause of the shortfall was extractions made through the San Francisco Assaying and Refining Works. The raw bullion purchased through the bullion fund and refined there on contract would be taken by Ralston and the Bank of California rather than returned to the mint. Ralston and the bank would then present the refined bullion to be coined at the mint. In effect, Ralston and the bank were borrowing from the bullion fund with no record at the mint.[12]

Torrey and Linderman completed their investigation, finding nothing. LaGrange's story was that he had removed the unaccounted bullion funds from the mint because the security of the building was inadequate, and the vaults could not accommodate the additional gold coins.[13] LaGrange's explanation was hogwash. The vaults at the mint regularly held far more coinage. But the investigation was relegated to the dustbin with LaGrange's explanation leaked to the newspapers.[14]

Yet after assuming office Linderman, empowered under the Coinage Act of 1873 with the ability to terminate the San Francisco Assaying and Refining Works contract with the San Francisco Mint, did just that on April 8, 1873. He communicated to LaGrange that he had no problem embracing a new contract containing a provision authorizing the value of the unrefined bullion to be deposited in gold coin by the contract refiner with that deposit held by the superintendent until the completion of the refining and exchange.[15] In this manner the mint would be covered against loss while the bullion was out of its control. In addition, he cut the amount of the bullion fund back to $2 million.[16] If there were any truth to the allegations of Cochran and Harmstead, these actions would prevent any further abuses.

Even with the change in contract refining, Linderman found himself in another box. The San Francisco Mint would be a key player to meet the full demand for gold coins and the added burden of the new trade dollars. When LaGrange sought permission to establish a silver bullion fund of $500,000 in addition to his gold bullion fund, Linderman had no choice but to seek authorization. However, he was able to circumvent LaGrange by insisting that only fine silver be purchased for trade dollars, thus cutting out the need for contract refining.

As for Ralston and the Bank of California, they were tight on funds again in spite of the Belcher Mine being in bonanza. In December 1872 Ralston was writing an abject apology to the head of the Oriental Bank in London for having overdrawn for an extended period on the bank's line of credit.[17] When the rumors of shortages in the bullion fund brought on the investigation, Ralston had drawn sufficient funds from the Oriental Bank to ensure that Felton appeared clean as a whistle. Subvert the investigation and fix the problem later.

Ralston waited patiently for Ulysses Grant's re-election. A second term starting March 4, 1873, would give the president the authority to suspend government officers without cause while Congress was not in session. Harmstead and Cochran had come too close for comfort in the impromptu investigation.

Ralston turned to George Gorham, a gatekeeper of sorts in his position as secretary of the Senate, in a tirade in two letters on February 3, 1873. Gorham in response called Cochran and Harmstead incompetent and personally and politically offensive. They were Senator Cornelius Cole's men and their appointments had been made in the face of Gorham's opposition. Gorham would do all in his power to see that they did not remain "to obstruct and confuse the legitimate operations of the mint."[18]

Harmstead quickly heard rumors that LaGrange had submitted his name in a list of officers to be replaced at the mint. On March 14, 1873, he telegraphed Attorney General George Williams, who had been a senator from Oregon at the time of Harmstead's confirmation, asking him to intercede on his behalf with President Grant. Williams passed the buck on this one to Boutwell. The problem there was that

Boutwell resigned his position as secretary of the Treasury on March 16 to take his seat as the newly elected senator from Massachusetts, terminating any recourse for Harmstead.

Harmstead hung on in April, hoping against all hope that he might survive. In desperation he even went to see Aaron Sargent when the senator was in San Francisco. Harmstead could not get beyond introducing himself before Sargent interrupted him. He acknowledged Harmstead's thirty years of service to the mint and that he had nothing against him, but he wanted his place for a friend.[19]

After a failed run for governor of California, George Gorham was appointed secretary of the Senate in 1868, a job he held until 1879. In this position he held strong influence over federal appointments in California. When Billy Ralston needed something done in Washington, Gorham was one of his main contacts.

The hammer officially dropped on May 12, 1873. It came in the form of a letter from LaGrange announcing Harmstead's suspension and asking that the coiner deliver the keys to his vault and office to the chief clerk. There was no recognition of Harmstead's dedication and service to the mint. LaGrange did not even have the decency to deliver the letter personally, entrusting that chore to his chief clerk. Just a month shy of his 60th birthday, Harmstead would be out of a job. Worse, mint work was all that Harmstead knew. The man went home on that May evening devastated. He had lost the job of his dreams after just four short years.

The new coiner was Jefferson Babcox. He at least knew the job, as LaGrange did not. Babcox had worked at the mint in the 1860s with Harmstead and then came back in 1870 as supervisor of deposit melting. The tipoff to his allegiance came with the individuals that went on his bond. One was W.T. Garratt, a buyer of copper and surplus supplies from the mint through George Pinney. The other was Charles Felton. There would be no more trouble over the bullion fund for Ralston; Babcox was his man.[20]

Harmstead, in true fashion, pledged to work with Babcox to smooth the transition. As the two men worked out the details of the handover, Babcox told Harmstead that LaGrange had seemed a bit too pleased that he was rid of his coiner. Nevertheless, Harmstead swallowed his pride a couple days later and asked LaGrange if there were any other positions available. LaGrange said no but he would contact Harmstead should the situation change.[21] Not likely.

Linderman knew that he had to go west soon. There were discrepancies between LaGrange's listing of employees and their pay compared to the roster that Linderman maintained in Washington. In addition, decisions needed with the construction of the new mint in San Francisco were by themselves reason enough. In particular, the method of refining needed to be resolved. It was around this time that John Cochran's 12 charges preferred against Hugh LaGrange hit Linderman's desk. Unlike Harmstead, the former melter and refiner was not going to go quietly. He had been replaced at the mint by John Eckfeldt, further angering him. In his accusations, Cochran detailed numerous instances of LaGrange's malfeasance in office, starting with fraudulent subscriptions from the employees for political campaigns. There were the unreported sales of surplus equipment and supplies. There were the phantom employees. There was the copper that the mint purchased from Pinney. And there were the extensive frauds surrounding the purchase of coal and other supplies.[22]

Linderman's response was to postpone his visit and order James Pollock to San Francisco to investigate the validity of these accusations. Linderman authorized him to take a clerk to transcribe testimony.[23] It would be called the Pollock Commission. Behind Linderman's back in the community, it would be known as the Whitewash Commission.[24]

LaGrange was tied up in knots, and the source of his anxiety was George Pinney. Over dinner one evening at LaGrange's home, he and Pinney had tense moments. LaGrange wanted surplus zinc returned or the proceeds paid over to the mint. Pinney wanted the zinc carried as a loan. Then he offered to pay for the zinc. LaGrange refused, saying Pollock would believe that LaGrange had pilfered the money and was now putting it back in a mea culpa. After more harsh words, Pinney agreed to replace the zinc while depositing with the superintendent the money from the sale until the zinc was delivered.[25]

Whitewash or not, LaGrange was spooked over the possibilities, besides the dealings of Pinney, that Pollock might uncover. He now called upon those vendors to whom he sold surplus or excess supplies at discount prices to pay up.[26] Pinney in turn had his own concerns about the investigation. The chief clerk at the Navy Pay Office had died, and Pinney would assume his position in the winter of 1873-74, opening up even more possibilities for personal gain.[27] Pinney was not about to mess up that opportunity. When LaGrange, after squeezing his favored vendors, still came up short, Pinney loaned him $1,000. He even magnanimously told the superintendent he could have $10,000 if he needed it to stymie the inquiry.[28]

LaGrange need not have worried; Linderman was in a tight spot. His nomination for director would come before the Senate for confirmation in early December. He absolutely could not let this investigation get out of hand. When finally he arrived in San Francisco, he huddled with LaGrange, counseling the superintendent in concealing his questionable and illicit dealings with Pinney from Pollock's investigation.[29,30]

The inquiry was conducted in secret. None of the witnesses, mostly mint employees, was required to testify under oath. John Cochran, acting as a quasi-prosecutor, was denied the assistance of an attorney to press his questioning. Worse, Pollock claimed that he lacked authority to subpoena witnesses. Under this scenario, Pinney had a field day. He freely testified that he never knew copper to be purchased that was not delivered or purchased in excess of the market price.[31]

In mid-January 1874 Linderman, now formally confirmed as director of the mint, received Pollock's report. In a short note to LaGrange, he told the superintendent that no public use of the report would be made and that LaGrange should consider the matter closed.[32]

For Jos Harmstead, his suspension was like a door being slammed shut on his life. He and his wife held some rental property and started a small shop to sell preserved flowers. While Harmstead was proud of his wife's initiative, it was hardly a fulfilling occupation for him. He found himself visiting the construction site of the new mint almost daily. Harmstead had offered his consulting services, at no cost to the government, almost prior to groundbreaking, but his offer had been spurned.

Instead, John Eckfeldt was given the position of assistant supervisor of construction once Cochran had displaced him as melter and refiner. Now Eckfeldt's two government positions, plus his outside wire-works business, stretched him thin. As a result, Harmstead, during Eckfeldt's absences from the construction site, answered questions from the workmen and offered helpful suggestions. Unlike Cochran, Harmstead remained loyal to the Mint Service in spite of his mistreatment.

From the workers, Harmstead learned of Linderman's presence in San Francisco during the investigation and that he would be inspecting the construction site. Here, Harmstead grabbed what time he could with the man. Linderman responded politely to the former coiner's desire to return to any position at the mint and promised that he would look into the matter.

Jos Harmstead waited until February 1874 when, having heard nothing, he wrote to Linderman. It was a pleading letter. Harmstead was a man of very limited means; he had passed the whole of his manhood in the Mint Service, with no surplus means set aside, he must keep doing what he knew best as long as he had the strength to do it. Linderman made the effort, writing to the supervising architect, A. B. Mullett: "Can you not give Harmstead something to do at your works in San Francisco? I find it impossible to do anything for him at this mint. He is a good man and should be cared for." However, Mullet was unwilling to help and dumped the preparation of a rejection letter to Harmstead on an assistant.[33]

In later years Billy Ralston's reputation as a civic leader and a man of unlimited generosity would assume superhuman proportions. Stories would abound of his giving large sums of money to down and out people on the street. Yet what he did without a second thought, crushing Jos Harmstead who dared to stand up for what was right and honest, was simply despicable.

Chapter 16

HUMPTY DUMPTY SAT ON A WALL

When James Fair walked into the offices of *The Territorial Enterprise* in Virginia City in late October 1874, Dan DeQuille did not know quite what to expect. DeQuille was the most astute mining reporter on the Comstock and a former colleague of Mark Twain. The two had both worked for the newspaper and roomed together. It was said that DeQuille possessed the better writing skills of the two men.

Fair called out loudly, "Those city papers have been abusing us long enough. I won't stand for it! Where's Dan? I want him to go down to the mine. I'll show him what we are doing."

The mine was Consolidated Virginia, its operations overseen by Jim Fair. Whatever his motive, he invited DeQuille "to go in and climb around" the mine's workings. Fair promised to leave the reporter alone and let him make up his own mind. DeQuille spent half a day below, taking ore samples from a 200-foot mine-face.[1]

What came out of that visit shook the status quo of Virginia City and, ultimately, San Francisco. DeQuille reported that the Consolidated Virginia and neighboring California mines were in bonanza, not just in the quantity of ore but the quality as well, the likes of which had never been seen in the Comstock Lode. He conservatively estimated the ore body had the potential to churn out profits of $36 million per year for ten years.[2]

Fair and his partners would ever after be known as the "Silver Kings."

The first public acknowledgement that the Consolidated Virginia Mine might be something special had come the previous year. The *Carson Daily Appeal* reported that the mine's prospects were never more flattering, that there remained only 85 feet to connect the exploratory drift driven from the neighboring Gould and Curry mine to the main shaft. (Using a neighboring mine to develop a new one was common in the Comstock Lode.) However, the going was slow. The end of the drift was intensely hot and water was expected to be a problem as the main shaft was bored lower.

Still, the *Gold Hill Daily News* speculated that it would not be many months before the Consolidated Virginia would take its place on the list of dividend-paying mines.[3] The few comments from Jim Fair were misleadingly less than enthusiastic regarding the assay of the ore.[4]

Fair and his mining partner John Mackay, together with their financiers, James Flood and William O'Brien, had used Consolidated Virginia to acquire a controlling position in the adjacent inactive California Mine property through a recapitalization. They then declared a stock dividend of 7/12 of a share payable for each share of Consolidated Virginia.[5] They also formed an umbrella holding company, Pacific Mill and Mining.[6] It was clear something big was on the horizon.

Indeed, Consolidated Virginia began paying dividends in May 1874. The *Gold Hill Daily News* speculated that there were plenty more dividends in sight as the mine showed continued improvement in its lower levels. The great ore body had a fair chance to develop into equal importance with the bonanzas of Belcher and Crown Point. The paper speculated that this bonanza even gave assurances of the continuation of ore deposits in the Comstock Lode to illimitable depths.

In short, this was an excellent mine though no better than others; but, more importantly, the great silver ledge that comprised the Comstock Lode appeared to be never-ending.[7]

For over a decade everything Ralston touched had turned to gold. Now he started rolling snake eyes. The end of the bonanza at Belcher was within sight. He had just been forced to borrow $2 million from William Sharon to complete his grand dream in San Francisco, the Palace Hotel.[8]

Yet from all outward appearances, one would never have guessed that Ralston was on the verge of a crash. The lavish parties continued at his country home. When not there, Ralston was attending the California Theatre in San Francisco where Edwin Booth was performing Shakespeare. Here he became enamored with the beautiful English actress Adelaide Neilson, deluging her hotel room with flowers and bestowing on her an expensive diamond necklace.[9] The man seemed to know no bounds.

The first venture to come up snake eyes was the new trade dollar. Mint Director Henry Linderman was overly optimistic about its success. He told Hugh LaGrange at the San Francisco Mint to give priority to depositors presenting refined silver bullion to the mint for conversion to trade dollars. He authorized overtime so that the minting of gold coins that had priority would not interrupt the flow of trade dollars into commercial channels.[10] When Philadelphia fell short of its quota of trade dollars, Linderman authorized LaGrange to pick up the slack. He even told LaGrange to build in inventory to ensure demand was met. Linderman was quite certain that trade dollars would be the favored form for export of silver.[11]

Billy Ralston harbored no such illusions as Linderman about the trade dollar. On the front lines of gaining acceptance for this coin in the Orient, Ralston worked diligently with Jack Robertson, Oriental Bank's representative in Yokohama, Japan. Robertson admonished Ralston straight up not to send these coins to Japan; the country was converting to the gold standard.[12] For starters Robertson was looking for official proclamations from Hong Kong and Saigon declaring the coins legal tender. However it would take the trade dollar five to 10 years to fully penetrate the oriental markets.[13] Robertson suggested trying a "tip" on some of the Cantonese mandarins.

By September Ralston was at his wit's end. Robertson's man in China had told him that "tips" would not do. When the trade dollar did not gain immediate acceptance in Hong Kong, Ralston in frustration told Robertson to "sink John Bull." Robertson chided Ralston that neither man could afford to do that, the English were entrenched. For the trade dollar to gain acceptance there, they needed a proclamation declaring legal tender status and then everything in the East would be all right."[14]

Things weren't all right. The Oriental Bank representative in Hong Kong was thrown from a horse and died. The British bureaucracy in the colony continued to drag its feet.[15] A notice from the colonial government was not forthcoming, and there were concerns that the British government might strike their own trade dollar in competition. Meanwhile, the north of China remained closed to the trade dollar. Ralston pleaded with Robertson to "crack his whip," to no avail.[16] Ralston had to back away from this market; he had not the time to nurture its development.[17]

Twice before the Comstock Lode had come to Ralston's rescue. Now he needed another silver strike to keep going, and the Ophir Mine—next door to the Consolidated Virginia and California—would certainly share in this bonanza. He must acquire with his bank friends a controlling position before the Ophir shareholders' meeting in December 1874. William Sharon was all in, purchasing shares for his personal account. Even Ogden Mills joined in the game. However, there was one obstacle: E. J. "Lucky" Baldwin, a real estate investor and speculator, had acquired Ophir shares in payment for a debt for a pittance in the very early days, held them, and was now the controlling shareholder. He would have to be bought out by Ralston.

There was another fly in this ointment—Sharon. In the spring of 1874, he announced that he was running on Nevada's Republican ticket to replace Bill Stewart in the Senate. Sharon caught Stewart at a weak moment. The senator had relied on the Bank of California and the Southern Pacific Railroad to provide the muscle behind his candidacy.[18] Now Sharon had just removed the Bank of California, and the railroad was so unpopular in Nevada as to be a political liability.

Stewart had another problem as well. He had just completed a home for his wife, Annie, known as the Castle on DuPont Circle in Washington. In addition, her spendthrift habits and trips to Europe had further drained his bank account.[19] Bill Stewart had no money. He now had no choice but to put his home up for rent in Washington and return to his law practice in San Francisco to restore his fortune.

In this senatorial contest, really centered on the four populous counties around Carson City and Virginia City, Sharon was determined to win. The newspapers had hurt him in his unsuccessful Senate contest with former mine superintendent John P. Jones, one paper likening Sharon to a hyena.[20] Now he owned the *Gold Hill Daily News* and *The Territorial Enterprise* in Virginia City. He had another ace up his sleeve. Into the ear of every Republican candidate for the state legislature, he whispered in confidence to buy Ophir stock. A bonanza was certain and those on the ground floor would make a killing.[21] With this scheme, Sharon was actually making Ralston pay more for his shares.

In September, Ralston sought the help of James Keene, the leading broker on the San Francisco Stock and Exchange Board, to corral the necessary Ophir shares for control. He was considered one of the shrewdest operators on the Board. Keene asked and received carte blanche from Ralston to do whatever it took. It mattered not to Ralston that Keene bought in his personal account and then sold to Ralston at a higher price.[22] In the first week of October, the stock sat at $46 and climbing on rumors and speculation.[23]

Then DeQuille's article on the Consolidated Virginia Mine came out and the mining stocks on the San Francisco Stock and Exchange Board went into a frenzied bull run. The *San Francisco Chronicle* described men and women of every class and level of society pouring in their orders to purchase the bonanza stocks. They saw a pot of gold at the end of the rainbow, there for the taking. Consolidated Virginia, California, and Ophir were the primary beneficiaries but active buying pushed all the mining shares higher. Whether Fair meant to or not, he had hit Billy Ralston where it hurt the most, his pocketbook.

William Sharon was not a shoo-in for senator this time around in spite of his money. Adolph Sutro actively opposed Sharon. Sutro was the man driving the tunnel, in the face of Ralston's intense opposition, to access the Lode from underneath, draining the water and providing a better way to move the raw ore. To combat Sharon, Sutro started his own paper in Virginia City.[24] He called Sharon a monopolist and "an occasional lodger" in Nevada. Sharon had moved his primary residence to San Francisco two years previously.[25]

With the election seemingly in doubt, Sharon took an action that hurt Ralston even more. He needed to get money into the pockets of the Republican state legislators to ensure their unwavering support. His newspapers in Virginia City began publishing observations highly favorable to the prospects of the Ophir Mine. Upward the stock price moved.

Early November saw Ophir shares rocket past $90. Ralston and his group, still lacking control, had no choice but to open negotiations with "Lucky" Baldwin for the shares he personally held. Ralston paid Baldwin $2.64 million including a $125,000 premium over market. Billy Ralston now had controlling interest of the Ophir mine.[26] The great silver strike would bail Ralston out of his cash worries at the Bank of California. However, he failed to focus on the fact that Ophir's market capitalization had reached an unbelievable level.

In December Senator Jones and Alvinza Hayward had a falling out at Crown Point.[27] Ralston and Sharon stepped in and purchased Hayward's stock for a rumored $1.6 million.[28] Ralston had just doubled down in an over-heated market.

On January 12, 1875, William Sharon was elected by the Nevada legislature to the Senate seat he so coveted.[29]

George Pinney had a foolproof scheme to take other people's money to play the stock market in San Francisco. Now that he was the chief clerk in the paymaster's department at the Mare Island Navy Yard, there were no checks on his activities and no accountability. The paymaster, Rufus Spalding, naively trusted him implicitly. Pinney put his brother-in-law, Joe Crawford, in as his assistant and was off to the races.

In the paymaster's Department of the Navy, it was customary for vendors furnishing supplies or performing work to receive certificates from the paymaster stating that their billings had been examined and found correct. A genuine certificate was a guarantee of payment. The vendor could then take this certificate to a moneylender as collateral security for a loan, bridging the gap until the warrant authorizing payment arrived from Washington, D.C.[30] The ever-trusting Spalding would sign blank certificates for Pinney without question.[31]

Pinney's angle involved issuing certificates for two or three times the amount requested by the vendor. He would then have available funds until the warrants arrived. In cases where the amounts had been inflated, the certificates would be rolled over rather than cashed out.[32] The vendors might or might not be aware of Pinney's actions but held no liability regardless. To make the system work, Pinney needed a bank that did not ask the hard questions.

Charles Felton made the necessary introductions.[33] E.W. Burr, president of the San Francisco Savings and Loan Society, signed on, charging Pinney a usurious one percent per month on the outstanding balance.[34] In addition, Pinney had to pay Burr a 5 percent commission on the side.[35] Also in on the deal was W.H. Culver of the Masonic Bank.[36] There would be others, but Burr and Culver were the two major players.

Pinney had one more problem to address: Rufus Spalding's appointed term expired in mid-1874. Pinney turned to Senator Aaron Sargent for help. By now the yard was commonly known as "Sargent's Naval Yard."[37] Employment would jump by 1,000 or so men before an election. The naval commander of the yard had had the audacity to tell Sargent he was running the yard, not Sargent. Sargent had him removed. Sargent made it clear to those aspiring to replace Spalding that they must retain Pinney. After all, he was a good man and gave a good speech. There were no takers, and Spalding was appointed to a second term.[38,39]

With the reappointment accomplished, Sargent used his influence to gain a third clerk for the office under the unusual arrangement that Pinney's salary would be used to pay the man. Thus Pinney was freed up for campaign activity as well as his own stock speculations. However, it wasn't all roses between the two men. In January 1874, Sargent took the extraordinary step of rebuking Pinney in writing when his shakedown of vendors became too blatant.[40,41]

Pinney speculated in other ventures but his big score was in Ophir stock.[42] Thus, he was able to buy one of the costliest homes in Oakland. Ample grounds beautifully ornamented with shrubbery and complemented by serpentine walks, green lawns, and flowerbeds surrounded the home.[43] Still constantly looking over his shoulder, he put the home in his wife's name.[44] Even in these good times, though, Flora would recall that the beatings in varying degrees of severity occurred almost daily.

Hugh LaGrange was in the difficult position of trying to please two masters, the Republican ring in California and Henry Linderman in Washington. The politically driven merry-go-round of new hires continued at the San Francisco Mint with Linderman taking exception as they were reported in January and July 1874.[45] The following October Linderman went so far as to put a temporary hold on LaGrange's appointments.[46]

Linderman was also watchful over the flow of raw bullion from the San Francisco Mint to the San Francisco Assaying and Refining Works and the return of fine bars. He asked for a statement detailing the transfers and returns.[47] Linderman also wanted to know why the mint paid 8 cents per ounce for all raw bullion deliveries to the refining works but only collected 6 cents on lower quality deposits from the dealers and brokers.[48]

The bullion fund continued to be a bone of contention between the two men. LaGrange wanted to increase the silver bullion fund to coin more trade dollars in advance of the summer peak demand for the Chinese export market while maintaining maximum production of gold coins. Linderman insisted that payments come out of the gold bullion fund instead.[49]

It was clear that trade dollar demand was straining the capacity of the San Francisco Mint in advance of moving to the new facility. As early as March 1874 Linderman was telling LaGrange that he wanted work to press ahead for the new mint with no excuses,[50] at least on the coin production side. Refining was a different story. Linderman knew that the sulfuric acid method of parting raw bullion was more efficient and yielded gold with a higher fineness than the nitric acid method.[51] Yet he procrastinated making this decision. Linderman had a report in hand from R.E. Rogers, professor of chemistry at the University of Pennsylvania, recommending the sulfuric acid method. Still he delayed, waiting to reveal the projected startup date of July 1875 in his request for appropriations for the coming year.[52]

Sensing that plans to place the new mint into operation might not be well formulated, the mint director in mid-June sent Martin Davis from the Bureau of the Mint to confer with LaGrange and John Eckfeldt as to its readiness. The mint director also sent his brother, Albert, to serve as clerk to Davis. In reality, Albert received per-diem pay, boarded at a nice hotel, and enjoyed fine dining while adding nothing much to the equation.[53]

Melter and refiner Eckfeldt, responsible for fitting up the new mint's machinery and fixtures,[54] now felt the resulting stress. This position had provided a salary prior to his being reappointed melter and refiner. Prohibited from drawing two salaries, Eckfeldt now was performing this function for no compensation. He wrote Linderman in July, in reaction to Davis's inspection trip, that the detail of pushing to finish the fitting as soon as possible was terrible.[55]

In spite of Eckfeldt's worries, final work at the new mint proceeded well. So it came as a shock when LaGrange telegraphed Linderman on October 8, 1874, that John Eckfeldt had committed suicide that morning. Linderman, accompanied by Arthur Orr, partner in the firm providing much of the coining equipment for the new mint, immediately headed for San Francisco to assess the work remaining to fit up the machinery.[56]

What came as a bigger shock was the size of the estate left by Eckfeldt. In addition to the wire works known as Eckfeldt & Graves, he left securities valued at $78,588 and cash of $24,703 and a total estate of $141,600.[57] Linderman requested a settlement of Eckfeldt's accounts as melter and refiner.[58,59] Had Linderman only known that there was more; the gold buried below Eckfeldt's house.

With Eckfeldt gone, Jos Harmstead began almost daily visits to the new mint. LaGrange had assumed Eckfeldt's responsibilities for the fit-up, meaning day-to-day decisions were left up to the contractor. Thus, Harmstead was given permission to come on site and observe the equipment move close up and provide comments and suggestions.[60] However, there were limits as to what Harmstead could accomplish. A subsequent investigation would reveal "gross incompetency" in the erection of the machinery. The layout of the steam plant was such that enormous amounts of steam were flushed down the city sewer.[61]

Coining operations at the San Francisco Mint began rather inauspiciously in December 1874.[62]

Chapter 17

Humpty Dumpty Had a Great Fall

The Bank of California failed at 2:30 p.m. on August 26, 1875. The next day, Billy Ralston's body was fished out of the San Francisco Bay. He was 49. Some would say that it took two years for the Panic of 1873 to reach the Pacific Coast and that was what brought down Ralston. Others would say that his unrelenting drive to do the next great deal, to stay on top of the heap, caught up with him.

For over a decade the Bank of California had thrived as both a retail bank and an investment bank. Ralston's success had been based on a profit model that siphoned funds from the low-risk, low-return retail side into the high-risk, high-return investment side. The body blow to this profit model came on May 19, 1875, the date of incorporation of the Nevada Bank of San Francisco by the Silver Kings with a capitalization of $5 million in gold.[1] The rumor got back to Ralston that the Silver Kings, with their $5 million and another million and a half in coin from Donohoe, Kelly & Company, were going to break the Bank of California.

The year 1875 had opened with Billy Ralston seemingly at the peak of his game. Ophir stock shares at the beginning of January were $205. A week later they hit $325. The speculation on Ophir stock carried the other mining shares upward as well. The market had not been this frothy since the boom just before the bust in May 1873.

Share prices broke downward for no apparent reason the following weekend with Ophir leading the decline.[2] In retrospect, it was easy to point the finger at Bill Sharon as the stock had hit his target sell price on January 3. It was said that he even shorted the stock on the way down.

A month later, sanity had returned to the market. The *Gold Hill Daily News* observed that "the millionaires of Christmas are as poor as the turkey that Job forgot to fatten for the festival!" Ophir was now selling at $70 per share.[3] Ralston had ridden out the boom-bust cycle of these mining stocks before. What was important was the expected sharing through his Ophir holdings of the bonanza of the Consolidated Virginia and California mines.

All through February, March, and April there appeared optimistic reports that it was only a matter of time until Ophir was in bonanza. At times the stock bumped upward reaching above $100 per share. On May 6, 1875, the bloom came off the lily when the *Gold Hill Daily News* asked what was the matter with Ophir. The assessment of those in the know was that there was no substantial bonanza extension into Ophir from its neighboring mines. The anticipated giant ore body had, in actuality, pancaked out at depths of 1,500–1,600 feet.[4] Ophir was in essence a dry hole. Billy Ralston had rolled snake eyes again, this time in a really big way.

Seemingly unfazed, Ralston looked closer to home for his now badly needed next bonanza. San Francisco's sole supplier of water was the Spring Valley Water Company. Its principal water source was a series of reservoirs in the rugged peninsular mountains south of the city. With a virtual monopoly, Spring Valley Water was very profitable, paying out on average 60 percent of revenues as dividends.

Ralston saw opportunity when Spring Valley opened contentious negotiations with the city. While the company wanted to maintain its franchise, it was obligated in that agreement to supply water for public purposes free, something it no longer wished to do. The city responded that given the profitability of the company, they would not renegotiate. This dispute underscored what everyone knew. The growth rate of San Francisco would soon outstrip the company's ability to supply the needed water. Instead of allowing Spring Valley to meet this need, the city's Board of Supervisors decided to buy the company and do their own expansion.

Before the city was ready to move, Ralston, in combination with Charles Felton, bought the watershed identified as the best new source to meet Spring Valley's expected growth. The two men also moved on the company's stock. They had no cash. They offered more than market for the stock and paid for it with certificates bearing a 9 percent interest rate. In this way they accumulated a majority of the shares outstanding. Then in May 1875 Ralston and Felton sold the watershed to Spring Valley for $1,012,000 compared to their original cost of about $100,000. They then offered the water company to the city for $15.5 million a 50 percent premium over market.

The *San Francisco Bulletin* and *San Francisco Call* were up in arms over this deal. Feeling the political pressure, the Board of Supervisors rejected Ralston's offer. An election of the supervisors was to be held in September, and Ralston mounted a campaign to elect men favorable to the deal. The two newspapers responded in kind, questioning Ralston's business ventures through the Bank of California. Daily front-page blasts over Ralston's dealings, particularly on the Comstock, began to take their toll. Mining shares, even Consolidated Virginia and California, began to break downward. However, Ophir, once again, led the slide. Ralston was in a bind.

Matters improved in early August. The vitriol spread by the *Bulletin* and *Call* had begun to backfire. Stocks had strengthened somewhat from their lows of July. Then in mid-August the New York newspapers picked up the Associated Press reports out of San Francisco predicting bank problems in California. Funds were already tight due to high coin demand from California's agricultural region for the coming harvest season. On August 23, Ralston turned to the Oriental Bank to tide him over the cash squeeze. He blamed his problems on two of the Silver Kings, Flood and O'Brien, locking up all the available coin as they readied the opening of Nevada Bank. By now the New York reports had reached London, and Ralston was refused. In turn, Ralston telegraphed the Sub-Treasury in New York for the transfer of $1 million. For the first time in his experience, he was refused. The wolves were circling his door.

The dawning of 1875 found Henry Linderman wrestling with the issue of the refinery for the new San Francisco Mint. Leaning toward the sulfuric method of refining, he instructed Hugh LaGrange to contact John Hewston, superintendent at the San Francisco Assaying and Refining Works, to ascertain the terms upon which he would *oversee* construction of the refinery. He also ordered LaGrange to prepare a new estimate of the cost.[5]

At this point LaGrange threw Linderman a curve ball. The coiner had just caused a mechanical failure of the big, new Ajax coin press. It was total and inexcusable incompetence and it put Linderman in a difficult position.[6] The production of double eagles and trade dollars would be directly impacted until a replacement part could be manufactured and shipped.

February found Linderman pushing LaGrange to close out the construction accounts for the new mint. He was hoping there would be some unexpended funds available to supplement the refinery appropriation. LaGrange was slow in response, irritating Linderman. By the end of the month, Linderman had no choice but to ask treasury Secretary Bristow for an additional appropriation for the refinery.[7]

Finally on March 9, 1875, Linderman was ready to move. He informed Bristow that he would use Professor Rogers from the University of Pennsylvania to plan and superintend construction of a sulfuric acid refinery at San Francisco.[8] John Hewston had asked for $10,000 in gold to provide these services while Rogers was willing to take $500 per month and expenses in greenbacks.[9] Linderman was trading Hewston's practical hands-on experience in exchange for Rogers's theoretical knowledge of chemistry and the apparent cost savings. Unsaid, Hewston's fee would have come out of the refinery appropriation while Rogers's services could be covered within salaries at the mint.

Then, without explanation, in the middle of initiating construction of the refinery, Linderman ordered the assayer in charge of the Denver Mint, Professor Jacob Schirmer, to go to San Francisco unannounced to take charge of the cashier's vault to count and verify that the coin on hand tied to the books of account and that the ordinary fund was in order.[10]

While Schirmer found no obvious discrepancies at San Francisco, his observations resulted in a blistering letter from Linderman to LaGrange. The chief clerk, Bernard Lande, was often not on the job, tending instead to his private business. The bookkeeper did not keep regular hours on the grounds that the salary set by law was insufficient to attract a competent individual. Linderman wanted the man's pay increased or a replacement found.[11] Schirmer must have found the accounting records in such deplorable condition that he could not reconcile the books to the cash on hand.

By now Linderman had determined that there was $10,000 in unused funds from the construction of the mint that could be moved over to the refinery.[12] Still the mint director was in a bind over funding. The first hint of what was in store came when Linderman asked LaGrange if he had disposed of his porcelain pots used when the mint was refining with nitric acid.[13] LaGrange had not, a stroke of luck. Professor Rogers had a solution using nitric acid. He and Linderman set up a trial run at Philadelphia, being so confident of success that they invited Secretary Bristow to view the results.[14] Linderman deemed the trial a success though they had refined a mere 100 ounces, hardly a rigorous test. Linderman proudly proclaimed this nitric acid process was superior in all aspects to the sulfuric acid method, required less space and time, and was very economical.[15] However key to this decision was Rogers' estimate that many thousands could be saved in the initial outlay for the refinery.[16]

Linderman now sent Rogers west to serve as superintendent of construction accompanied by Albert Linderman, his wayward brother, who would serve as foreman.[17] Linderman even went so far as to boast that when this process was in place at the beginning of July, the San Francisco Mint would have capacity nearly great enough to refine all the bullion coming out of the Comstock. In particular, Linderman wanted to be in a position to part all the doré silver, recovering the small amounts of gold from that unique bullion. Otherwise, it would go to the export market where foreign refineries possessed the means to capture that gold.[18]

With the refinery issue settled, Hugh LaGrange reentered the picture. This time it was an entry in his accounts of mint activity for April. It read: "unsettled exchange of unparted bullion $103,634.11." It raised alarm bells in Linderman's mind, and he immediately asked for an explanation.[19] LaGrange's answer was that the San Francisco Assaying and Refining Works had one month's inventory of raw bullion waiting to be refined.

Linderman accompanied by his wife left for the Pacific Coast on June 18, 1875, wanting to be present for the annual settlement.[20] He was coming into a soured situation. LaGrange had been angered by the not-so-subtle lack of faith the director had shown by having Schirmer inspect the cash in the vault. Linderman had also sent a man from the Mint Bureau in Washington to serve as LaGrange's chief clerk. LaGrange had taken umbrage over this action, refusing to accept him.

Upon arrival, Linderman discovered $11,000 in bills held over for payment after the June 30 fiscal year-end closing. Linderman sent his brother to rifle the chief clerk's desk to ascertain the exact details of the held invoices.[21] That move was discovered the following day and tempers flared. Then Linderman called for layoffs among the adjustors. LaGrange discouraged him on that count, as a political hornet's nest would be stirred up.

Matters finally cooled when the annual settlement of accounts came off without problems. Linderman buried the sword saying that time would heal the wounds.[22] The two men then traveled together to Virginia City to tour the Comstock Lode.

A reporter from the New York Tribune had been on the ground in Virginia City for some two weeks when Linderman arrived and arranged a tour of the Consolidated Virginia Mine for him. Accompanying the director and LaGrange were Rogers and James Crawford, superintendent at the Carson City Mint.

Linderman shared with the reporter that he had contracted for substantial amounts of silver bullion from the Consolidated Virginia and that the mine had easily delivered. He told the reporter that there was $10 to $15 million of ore in plain sight at the mine face. Professor Rogers claimed the ore seemed practically inexhaustible. LaGrange agreed.

The reporter wrote about his descent into the mine. In some places the drifts hit temperatures of 130 degrees. LaGrange was overcome and had to return to the surface. To handle the heat, the miners worked in teams, trading out places every few minutes. As the reporter explored each cross-cut, he was constantly in ore—above, below, in front, to the right, and to the left. He described Henry Linderman as half-crazy with excitement. The mint director had never seen so much money in his life and did not expect to do so again; he thought it was time to resume specie payments. Under the headline "The Big Bonanza," this story was page-one news on the East Coast the next day.[23] While not enough to stanch mining shares on the San Francisco Stock and Exchange Board that day, its impact would be felt in the coming months. Linderman would instruct Rogers, with virtually no mining experience, to make a report of bullion reserves for the Comstock Lode that the director would incorporate into his annual report that fall.[24]

Linderman had planned to continue east after his inspection tour but now he suddenly returned to San Francisco in an absolute panic.

Billy Ralston knew he was on thin ice yet, could he bluff his way out of his financial mess?

On August 25, a clerk from Flood and O'Brien presented Ralston with a sealed note. The clerk had no idea of the contents. Ralston, looking at the contents, told the clerk to tell Flood that he would send him back to selling rum over the Auction lunch counter. That was the name of the saloon operated by Flood and O'Brien before their Comstock ventures. A few minutes later the clerk returned with a message from Flood. Flood said that in a short time he would be able to sell rum over the counter of the Bank of California. Ralston's bluff had been called.

In fifteen minutes the two men met in Flood's private office. Ralston could not honor the $300,000 check that the clerk had originally delivered drawn on Flood's Bank of California account in favor of his Nevada Bank. The two men agreed to three checks instead, to be presented over the following three days. The first check drawn by Donohoe, Kelly & Company cleared on the 26th. Later that day, D. O. Mills, the former president of the Bank of California, came to Flood asking for help or the bank would go under. Flood refused. For Eugene Kelly, whose company would become the New York agent for Nevada Bank, the revenge had been a long time coming.[25]

The fatal blow came from the San Francisco stock market. Weakness at the start of the week turned until a wholesale rout on Thursday, August 26. At 11 o'clock, Bill Sharon dumped a huge block of his remaining holding in Ophir shares. Then as the selling commenced, it became apparent that Sharon had sold his holdings in Consolidated Virginia and California as well. Tremendous amounts of gold coin would be needed to settle transactions and meet margin calls. Flood and O'Brien were largely protected, incurring only paper losses. Like a cat thrown out of a window, Sharon landed on his feet with his fortune intact. However, Ralston's bank was in real trouble.

That same day, the Board of Supervisors caved to Ralston's pressure and voted to buy Spring Valley Water Company, only to have the mayor veto their action. Clearly, with time, a negotiated sale could take place, given the supervisors now supported the purchase. However, it was too late.

Ralston was finished. By 2 o'clock the lines at the Bank of California had formed with people milling in the street outside. The bank run was on. Pressure had been building all that morning with withdrawals actually beginning to seriously escalate at 1 o'clock. The bank failed at 2:30, just half an hour before closing.[26]

That night Ralston conveyed all his personal property including his homes in a deed of trust to Bill Sharon for the benefit of his creditors. He trusted Sharon to do what was right. The next morning, Ralston revealed to his board that he owed $9.5 million against assets of $4.5 million. He asked that the board allow him to stay on at the bank in order to straighten out this mess. The directors, including Sharon, expressed shock. On a motion from Sharon, Ralston was removed as president.

Shortly after Ralston left the office, Sharon came out of the boardroom and called for the envelope marked: Contract of William Sharon to be delivered to W. C. Ralston only. Slitting open the envelope, he took out the paper within and replaced the envelope. Later when questioned, he claimed "there was nothing in it." Sharon had shared on the upside with Ralston; he was not sharing on the downside.

That afternoon, perspiring heavily, Ralston headed toward North Beach to the Neptune Bath House. He left his clothing in charge of the attendant, something he had never done before. Ralston entered the water and proceeded to swim into the tidal currents. Ralston had always been an expert swimmer and often used swimming to relieve stress. This time witnesses saw Ralston's body contort. Once rescued, efforts to revive him failed.[27] There exists a story that Mackay, one of the Silver Kings, asked: "Could not they revive him? Could not they save him?" To which the little man (inferring Sharon, who was short in stature) conversing with him said: "My God, for a while I thought they would!"[28]

Linderman arrived back to a San Francisco racked with financial chaos. He was worried about an investment made by his wife with Ralston and needed to discuss it with the Nevada Bank.[29] Concurrently, there were rumors that Ralston had taken bullion without regard to ownership from the San Francisco Assaying and Refining Works to the mint to exchange for gold coins that had been used in the failed attempt to stave off the run at the Bank of California.

Now, Linderman learned what it really meant to have an unsettled bullion balance with the refining works. LaGrange had ordered a midnight withdrawal of raw bullion from the firm without regard to proper ownership. He then suspended full payment for gold bars brought to the mint, withholding 10 to 15 percent pending assay, for four or five days. This allowed him, working his men overtime, to refine in his new facilities the bullion taken from the private refinery. By the end of August, LaGrange was able to present a balance sheet that showed the mint's books perfectly balanced. Linderman coldly told him never to take that action again.

Meanwhile, Linderman had three separate interviews with Senator Aaron Sargent pushing him to name LaGrange's replacement. Sargent at first delayed but then consented. Word promptly leaked back to LaGrange, and he submitted his resignation to Sargent.[30] On that same day, Linderman, never divulging his meetings with Sargent, asked LaGrange to submit an undated resignation that he would hold on file in case the politicians came after the superintendent that winter. Linderman would, of course, seek to secure a diplomatic mission for LaGrange that would be favorable to his health should he have to use the resignation. However, San Francisco business leaders interjected, seeking to retain LaGrange.[31] Sargent wobbled.[32] It then took a direct letter by LaGrange to Secretary Bristow asking to retain his appointment or at least hold it for a little more time to enable him to pay interest on stock purchases made under Linderman's advice. LaGrange had survived.[33]

The San Francisco Assaying and Refining Works, now twice looted, declared bankruptcy. The bullion that disappeared belonged to the Silver Kings and others. Yet Nevada Bank kept quiet over the removals. On October 5, 1875, Flood, O'Brien, and Fair, among others, were named directors of the newly incorporated Pacific Refinery and Bullion Exchange that assumed the assets of the failed refinery formerly controlled by Ralston.[34]

No notice was taken when George Pinney failed. At the beginning of 1875, he was a made man, chief clerk to the Navy paymaster, even serving for a time as head of the Alameda County Republican Central Committee. When the San Francisco Stock and Exchange Board decided to expand the number of brokerage seats, Pinney paid $25,000 for a seat. He was in tall company with the likes of Ralston, Sharon, Flood, O'Brien, Felton, and Senator John P. Jones also purchasing seats.[35]

This all came to a crushing end when the Bank of California folded. Pinney's bankers called their advances on the Navy Pay Certificates. Pinney had no liquid assets to satisfy the calls. He asked his wife to transfer title to their home to him. When she refused, he gave her a beating that she would long remember.[36] He had no alternative but to go to Bill Carr, the Bay Area Republican political boss.

Subsequent testimony of events between the two men was muddied at best as nothing was ever straightforward with Pinney. He produced a copy of an agreement that purported to transfer to Carr an interest in a quicksilver mine, shares of an Oregon coal company, and other assets. In exchange, Carr agreed to cover Pinney's advances from the Navy Pay Certificates at three banks totaling $488,500. In addition, the agreement called for Carr to pay Pinney $100,000 in gold within one year in settlement for assets of Pinney's held by Carr. Even using Pinney's numbers, the math did not work.[37]

Carr had a completely different version. Basically, he inferred that Pinney's assets were close to worthless and that the agreement with Pinney never existed. Only a fool would sign such a document. One fact was clear: On the day the two men met, Carr wanted Pinney out of town, as far away as possible, and he was willing to pay $12,500 toward that end.

Pinney fled the country for Valparaiso, Chile, on September 1, 1875, with a girlfriend to keep him company.

As the dust settled and the creditors tabulated the assets of the Bank of California, Henry Linderman appeared on the books owing $60,000. In another report, Linderman appeared on the books of the Bank of California as a creditor, even though he was not a depositor.[38] What in the world was that and how did he get on both sides of the ledger, so to speak?

Part 4
John Sherman

Chapter 18
RESUMPTION

In later years John Sherman would remember exactly where in September 1873 he learned of the failure of Jay Cooke & Company that started the Panic of '73. It was Buffalo, New York, and he was part of a Senate committee examining public improvements, especially water transportation at the mouth of the Mississippi River and the Great Lakes along the Canadian border. Each of the senators knew in an instant that their committee duties were at an end. There would be no funds available for public works.

Sherman watched helplessly as the panic spread like wildfire, affecting industries far and wide inside of a month. Banks were compelled to call in their loans, withhold their circulating notes and generally contract their business in order to shore up their balance sheets to withstand the downturn. Like wise Treasury had precious little cash on hand. With revenues from tariffs in rapid decline, the federal government cut back on expenditures, compounding the disaster.[1]

President Grant in his message to Congress on December 3, 1873, called for an elastic circulating medium just sufficient to transact the nation's business. He wanted a currency that could expand to meet increased demand for harvesting crops in the nation's interior. He also wanted increased capital available to reflect the nation's post-Civil War population growth. That currency was gold coin.[2] His message was purposely vague. It would be up to John Sherman as chairman of the Senate Committee on Finance to sort out what was politically doable.

Senator John Sherman, deservedly or not, was commonly called the Ohio Icicle.

On the day Grant's speech was read to both Houses of Congress, Senator Justin Morrill of Vermont, often the voice of Sherman, called for resumption of specie payments by Treasury and a substantial reduction in the reserve required for each national bank to issue its currency.[3] Opposition flared, and Morrill's bill died in committee in April 1874.[4]

Then President Grant vetoed a bipartisan bill that would have increased the ceiling on national bank notes, providing some stimulus to the economy. Westerners threatened a breach with the Republican Party. Kentucky Congressman James Burnie Beck summed the situation up nicely for the Democrats: "The President is mistaken if he thinks the mouth of the Mississippi can be dammed with straw. That [veto message] gives us Democrats the president next time."[5] No veto override was possible in the Senate, and the first session of the Forty-Third Congress ended June 23, 1874.

Meanwhile the country, with the exception of the Pacific Coast, was sinking deeper and deeper into a serious depression. It should have come as no surprise to Republicans when they were soundly defeated in the midterm elections that fall. For the first time since the Civil War, the Democrats would hold the majority in the House of Representatives when the new Congress convened in December 1875. In the interim, John Sherman had one last chance to gain resumption and unsnarl the currency issue. The second session of the current Congress would convene December 7 and adjourn at its expiration, March 3, 1875.

At year-end 1874, total outstanding United States Notes (greenbacks) were $382 million, Fractional Notes convertible into legal tenders, $44 million, and national bank notes, $356 million for a total of $780 million. Each paper dollar was worth a fraction less than 89 cents in gold coin. Right or wrong, Sherman counted himself part of that body of Northeast financiers that believed the excess speculation that led to the Panic of 1873 could only be remedied by a return to sound, honest money—specie payments.[6]

Sherman wasted no time. Meeting in Republican conference, he moved that a committee of 11 senators be created to formulate a resumption bill. With him as chair, the committee included William Boyd Allison, George Boutwell, Roscoe Conkling, George Edmunds, Thomas Ferry, Frederick Frelinghuysen, Timothy Howe, John Logan, Oliver Morton, and Aaron Sargent. Boutwell and Conkling represented the Northeast gold interests, Logan and Morton, the Midwest soft money advocates, and

Allison and Sargent, the pragmatic centrists.[7] Of utmost importance, these men were the leaders of the Republican Party in the Senate; their support for resumption of specie payments by the government was critical.

At the first meeting, Sherman asked each member to state how far he would go in the direction of specie payments. With all opinions thus put on the table, Sherman felt almost stymied. The differences were so great that an agreement seemed impossible. Yet all knew that failure to agree meant a major disruption for the Republicans.

The unanimous result was S.1044, a bill for specie payment resumption that Sherman brought out of his Committee on Finance on December 21, 1874, and moved the next morning that the Senate take under consideration. Sherman was his typical brusque self, stating that he did not think a long discussion necessary; the subject of resumption had already been thoroughly discussed in the Senate. It was a short bill, only three pages long, and he meant to see it passed that day

The opposing senators knew that if Sherman's motion passed, the bill would also pass. There were objections to moving so quickly; senators wanted time to consider the bill and gain feedback from the financial institutions of the country. Thus, there was a strong sentiment to table the bill over the Christmas recess. Sherman wasn't having any of it, pressing the presiding officer to call the vote. Time would only serve to chip away at the delicate consensus within his special committee. His motion to consider easily carried.[8] Now debate would begin on the bill, S.1044.

Sherman began by describing the bill in his typical oversimplified and abbreviated fashion. The first section of the bill provided for the redemption of 10-, 25- and 50-cent Fractional Notes, the exchange of the hated shinplasters for subsidiary silver coins through the Treasury Department. He pointed out without explanation that this action could be taken without any loss of revenue. He shied away from explaining that seigniorage, the government's coinage profits, would benefit from the declining price of silver bullion on the London market, thus more than offset the minting costs.

The second section removed the inducement to export gold bullion to Great Britain, a country with long established laws that allowed gold coinage at the Royal Mint free of charge. Sherman never mentioned specifically the removal of the one-fifth of one percent charge for coining gold bullion. The senator kept to himself his true feelings that the removal of the coinage fee was an unjust concession to the gold miners.[9]

Sherman, in addressing the third section of the bill stated, in an offhand manner, that it contained only two or three affirmative proposals. Any national bank would be empowered to increase its currency to any extent within the limits of the existing banking law. In this way the currency could be increased in case business in the community demanded it. Coupled with that provision, the secretary of the Treasury would retire United States Notes amounting to 80 percent of the additional currency issued by the national banks until the outstanding United States Notes were reduced to $300 million.

The final provision called for the redemption of United States Notes beginning January 1, 1879, at the will of the holder for gold or silver. In essence the holder of a greenback could present it at will and receive its face value in gold or silver. However, Sherman omitted telling the senators that the bill authorized the secretary of the

Treasury to use any surpluses as well as the proceeds from bonds issued at not less than par in coin to carry out this provision.[10] Sherman did not want the distracting debate over the national debt.

John Sherman was adamant that the bill not contain any clauses addressing the reissue of greenbacks redeemed. The reason was simple: The 11-man committee could not agree on the issue. Sherman was under the strictures of the committee not to comment either way in his presentation of the bill. Furthermore, he must maintain the integrity of the bill—meaning no amendments—or risk defections from the special committee. That would spell doom for S.1044.

Criticism of S.1044 was immediate, led by the Democratic senator from Ohio, Allen Thurmond. He had done his homework effectively arguing against the bill. Summing up, Thurman called S.1044 a study in ambiguity by keeping the people in the dark as to whether it meant inflation or not.

This sort of discussion was exactly what Sherman did not want. However, he had the votes. Once it was completely obvious that no modifications would be allowed, the question was called and the bill passed.

The House passed S.1044 on January 7 without debate, but not without a hiccup. Eugene Kelly through his proxy, George Edelman, got up a paper attacking contract refining with the intention of gaining an adverse amendment in this bill.[11] Linderman got involved, stopping the effort cold, and President Grant signed the bill into law on January 14, 1875.[12]

Sherman had crafted legislation that offered concessions to the opposing political views on the economy. The Western silver producers gained from the redemption of fractional currency. The charge at the mint to coin standard gold bullion, in place since 1853, was gone, removing the export incentive. National banks had the ability to respond to local currency needs. The secretary of the Treasury had the ability to inflate the currency and the authority to issue bonds to finance the return to specie payments. There was something for all parties affected in this bill.

This legislative victory was Senator John Sherman at his best.

Chapter 19

NO REDEMPTION FOR THE DOUBLE DIME

John P. Jones was in his second month of his first session as a senator when Mint Director Henry Linderman named him to the prestigious 1874 Assay Commission.[1] Charged with meeting annually to verify the accuracy of the weight and fineness of American coinage, that appointment, both an honor and a responsibility, was highly unusual for a freshman senator. Clearly Linderman was currying favor here. But he also saw something more.

Jones was not going to hold to the Senate custom that new senators were seen and not heard for the first year. He chose as his first endeavor, the correction of something that had aggravated him in Virginia City. He had been shorted so many times using a quarter for a ten-cent purchase only to have the merchant give him a dime in return.[2] While it really was no imposition on Jones, it placed a real burden on the laborers who worked the Comstock mines.

The heart of the problem was twofold. First, the quarter was an inefficient denomination in a decimal monetary system. The root of its origin was the Spanish dollar, upon which Alexander Hamilton had based the monetary system. The Spanish dollar was divided into eight reales, or bits, each worth 12-1/2 cents that had been legal tender in the United States until 1857. Thus the quarter was worth two bits. The problem was the dime, which quickly became known as the short bit.

The second piece of the puzzle was that no minor coins circulated in the West. Only the Philadelphia Mint was authorized to strike pennies and nickels. The

The Philadelphia Mint struck Assay Commission Medals to recognize the annual meeting of the commission to verify the accuracy of U. S. coinage. This example is from 1874, the year Jones participated.

Treasury Department was not going to pay the freight to move minor coins any great distance so what pennies and nickels circulated in the West came in the pockets of travelers. Thus, when the half dime was eliminated in 1873, the dime became the smallest monetary unit in the Western states.

Jones introduced his bill, S.468 authorizing a twenty-cent piece or "double dime," on February 10, 1874. It was routinely referred to the Committee on Finance.[3] A freshman senator could introduce a bill as well as any veteran senator but the odds against it going anywhere were overwhelming. However, Jones's action coincided with the convening of the Assay Commission in Philadelphia, implying that his bill had Linderman's approval.

On April 20, 1874, Linderman ordered James Pollock, Philadelphia Mint superintendent, to prepare pattern designs for the new coin. He acknowledged that the size difference between the double dime and a quarter would be quite small. Therefore, it would be necessary to give the new coin distinctive devices and employ a plain, rather than reeded, edge to make it easily distinguishable from the quarter. Linderman preferred the trade dollar obverse that had been prepared by artist-engraver Joseph Bailly paired with engraver William Barber's eagle from the adopted reverse of the trade dollar. Linderman proposed one of the mottos be applied in sunken letters around the edge of the coin. He also wanted to try for increased concavity on this coin, much as had been achieved with the new German twenty-mark coin.[4]

Linderman's instructions for the pattern designs left the engraver absolutely no leeway for creativity. The mint director had not been happy with Barber's engraving for the trade dollar. The coiner at Philadelphia, Loudon Snowden, complained that some of the cuts for the design on the die were so deep that he could not bring them up, even on the proof pieces.[5] However there was more that aggravated Linderman. Barber's son, Charley, was employed as an assistant engraver. When the mint upgraded in 1869 to the Hill engraving machine, "Barber and son" took possession of the old machine for use in their outside business.[6] Linderman had wanted the machine returned to the mint to be salvaged.[7]

Dutifully, Barber executed the one pattern design requested and a second variation, employing the denomination surrounded by an open wreath on the reverse, forwarding them to Linderman in August. Linderman called them excellent but made no decision, choosing to wait instead for passage of Jones's bill.[8]

Pattern strikes of the proposed designs to be considered for the new twenty-cent piece.

The Senate passed S.468 on the last day of the first session of the 43rd Congress.[9] It went over to the House and languished throughout the second session. Again on the last day of this session, the House passed the bill authorizing the twenty-cent piece without amendment or debate,[10] strongly indicating that Linderman was active throughout the process.

A week after the bill became law Linderman pulled the trigger on the design selection. The obverse would bear the same Seated Liberty as the other subsidiary silver coins. The reverse would employ the eagle from the trade dollar. On March 31, Pollock sent the director impressions from the new die. Yet there was still doubt about the design in Philadelphia resulting in two more rounds of pattern pieces based upon designs used on existing United States silver coins. Also at issue was whether the piece should be expressed as "20 Cents" or "1/5 of a Dollar."[11]

In addition to these retread designs, William Barber created a head of Liberty for the obverse and a shield with the numeral 20 incused for the reverse.[12] Pollock clearly liked this last design, calling it peculiar, meaning unique, and very beautiful. Indeed, while Linderman acknowledged the beauty of the design, he did not feel he had the latitude within the law to omit the eagle from the coin's reverse.[13]

Linderman stuck with his original design selection. The obverse was the same as that for the quarter. The difference in the eagle on the reverse was not readily distinguishable from that of the quarter. The only real difference was the smooth, plain edge.

The final design for the twenty-cent piece was flawed because it was not distinct enough compared to that of a quarter.

The first double dimes were struck at the Philadelphia Mint on May 19, 1875, with little fanfare.[14] Such was not the case on the Pacific Coast, where Senator Jones was present at the Carson City Mint when the first two pieces were struck on the afternoon of June 1. Jones, now known as the father of the twenty-cent piece, was presented with the first strike. The *Carson Daily Appeal* declared the coin more needed than any other.[15] The *Gold Hill Daily News* called it a "diminutive quarter."[16] But would these two coins circulate side by side. Mintages for 1875 were equal to or greater than the those of the quarter at both San Francisco and Carson City. However, mintages of this coin fell off a cliff the next year.

Meanwhile the Resumption Act of 1875 had hit a snag—the redemption of the hated shinplasters. There simply were not enough subsidiary silver coins in the government coffers to make the exchanges to retire the Fractional Notes. With the convening of the 44th Congress in its first session in December 1875, it was clear that corrective action would have to be taken.

Henry Linderman inserted himself into the drafting process in the House, proposing the quarter be omitted in favor of the twenty-cent piece. Seeing a nascent demand for the demonetized standard silver dollar, he proposed a slightly heavier coin with a legal tender cap of $20 in any one payment except customs duties and interest on the public debt. It also removed the legal tender status of the trade dollar, the intrinsic value of which had now fallen to 94.5 cents in gold, effectively restricting its use to the bullion-based oriental markets.[17]

Once redemption was complete, Linderman wanted the subsidiary silver coins to be issued only in exchange for gold thus preventing overproduction and maintaining their purchasing power. If this legislation were enacted, he said, it would make the American monetary system perfect.[18] Once introduced in the House and Senate, this bill went nowhere.

When an alternative bill authorizing redemption of the shinplasters passed the House, Sherman struck out the clauses dealing with the standard silver dollar and the trade dollar to gain passage. It wasn't that he was against the standard silver dollar, he just wanted its coinage limited and the silver bullion necessary to be purchased by the government to gain the seigniorage, the excess of face value over the value of the silver plus the cost of coinage. In this version both the double dime and the quarter survived.

Sherman's version became law on April 17, 1876. Next a resolution was introduced in the House for the issue of the necessary subsidiary coinage. Linderman desperately wanted the resolution amended to remove the legal tender status of the trade dollar that had now fallen in value at the end of May to 89.95 cents in gold.[19] Brokers were capturing this growing spread between bullion and face value (more than nine cents per coin after deducting the coinage charge) by placing these coins into domestic circulation.

In the end, after much wrangling, this resolution passed, providing for the mintage of $50 million in subsidiary silver coins and removing the legal tender status of the trade dollar.[20]

For the next two years, every mint would be employed to the maximum in the production of subsidiary silver coins. When it came to redeeming 25-cent notes, the quarter had the upper hand; no minor coins, meaning the nickel, had been authorized. In the press to get the coins minted and the fractional paper redeemed, the twenty-cent piece simply got shoved aside. Its mintage fell off a cliff in 1876. For all the wrong reasons, it became the little coin that couldn't. A bill was introduced to repeal authorization of the ill-fated double dime in July 1876 and finally passed in May 1878.[21]

Chapter 20
DOGFIGHT

The San Francisco Mint was never very far from Henry Linderman's mind now. In its new facilities, it should have been the crown jewel of the American Mint Service. It wasn't; in fact, it was far from it.

Once Linderman returned to Washington from San Francisco in September 1875, he began to realize that he had a real problem with the new mint's refinery. The additional porcelain pots required to fully implement Professor Rogers's nitric acid–based refining method were simply nowhere to be found. With no appropriation for operating expenses for the refinery, he was forced to allow Hugh LaGrange to cover refining expenses by drawing unused funds from the mint's refinery construction account and from appropriations to the contingency fund. This workaround would at least allow refining doré silver. Now that resumption of specie payments was set to begin in 1879, it was imperative that as much gold as possible be coined rather than sent abroad as bullion.

Initially Linderman had nowhere to turn in this refining dilemma with the San Francisco Assaying and Refining Works bankrupt and its assets idled. On September 29, 1875, he set forth his thoughts on the subject to two of the Silver Kings—James Flood and William O'Brien. Linderman spelled out the difficulties with the refinery at the San Francisco Mint and shared his thinking that sulfuric acid refining was better done in a building specifically constructed for that purpose and not at the mint. He closed by coyly asking as to the present ownership of Ralston's refinery.[1]

Linderman's letter gained him one piece of intelligence: He now knew that certain of the Silver Kings controlled Ralston's refinery, newly renamed Pacific Refinery and Bullion Exchange Company. He forthrightly told Flood and O'Brien that without additional appropriations, he would have to restrict refining to only doré silver, about 200,000 ounces per month. In Linderman's opinion, it would be convenient if they restarted the idled private refinery as soon as possible.[2]

Having received a proposal in response, Linderman signaled on November 2, 1875, that he was ready to make a contract with Pacific Refinery.[3] However this time, Linderman ordered LaGrange to exchange unparted bullion at the mint only for gold coins, fine bars, and trade dollars. There were to be no unsettled balances as had occurred with Ralston.

Once the contract was in hand, Linderman ordered LaGrange to apply no more operating expenses for the refinery against its construction account.[4]

It only took two months from the commencement of this refining contract for LaGrange to ignore the stipulation that raw bullion transfers be offset by refined bullion or coin from the Pacific Refinery. March 6, 1876, found Linderman writing in frustration asking LaGrange to explain the entry in the San Francisco Mint accounts: "advanced Pacific Refinery $50,000."[5]

Even before the issue of the refinery, Henry Linderman was concerned over the coal supply for the San Francisco Mint. In the first months of 1875 labor unrest had spread through the anthracite coal districts of eastern Pennsylvania. Anthracite was the coal used at the mints and San Francisco, burning 940 tons annually of the coal, was at the extreme end of the distribution chain. Any shortages would be quickly felt.[6]

Faced with the need to replace the Fractional Notes with subsidiary silver coinage, Linderman could not afford to see production at this mint impaired for want of coal. He was not without experience regarding the Pennsylvania coalfields. His father-in-law, George Davis, had been a pioneer coal operator in the Wyoming and Carbon anthracite coal districts. His brother, G. B. Linderman, had production in the neighboring Luzerne district.

By April the coalfield work stoppages had spread and were approaching general strike proportions. The miners wanted a 10 percent pay hike, ill received by the mine owners in the midst of a depression. Violence was imminent with the National Guard being called out from Philadelphia to protect the mine sites.[7] By May 1, coal shortages were occurring up and down the Eastern seaboard threatening the Philadelphia Mint.[8]

In spite of this difficult environment, Linderman still attempted to acquire anthracite coal for San Francisco though the vendor quote stopped him cold.[9] By the beginning of June, the strike lost its steam, but it would be a period of time before market prices returned to normal.

Linderman waited through the summer before moving once more. On October 4, he asked his brother for a quote on 500 tons. A week later he presented the transaction to LaGrange as a done deal. He had negotiated a price delivered around the Cape not to exceed $19 currency per long ton (2,240 pounds.) By comparison, LaGrange had paid $27 per ton in currency for equivalent anthracite coal.[10] Linderman directed that 100 tons go to the Carson City Mint. Also, the mint director stated that this coal had long been in satisfactory use at the Philadelphia Mint.[11] Linderman had his brother send the invoice for the coal directly to his office.[12]

The coal arrived in San Francisco in March 1876 with LaGrange not knowing that it came from Linderman's brother. While there was a problem with excessive fines from abrasion caused by the long ocean voyage, its combustion characteristics were admirable. However, LaGrange had a problem with the price. It delivered to the mint at $24.09 per ton, not $19 as promised. On a gold basis, the coal cost $21.69 per ton while its equivalent could be had in San Francisco for about $14.50 per ton and had been steady at that price for six months.[13] In response, Linderman considered the price comparison faulty—there was no adjustment for long tons or the superior heat content of his coal.[14]

Nevertheless, Linderman backed off; his attempt to have his brother supply all three operating mints with coal, a piece of very bad judgment, was dropped.

Linderman's relationship with Hugh LaGrange took a turn for the worse when Frank Cicott was promoted to assistant coiner in March 1875.[15] Cicott was Republican political boss Bill Carr's man and a significant inroad for the Republican ring into the coiner's department.

Of course, Frank Cicott had absolutely no prior knowledge of minting machinery, or machinery of any kind for that matter. He had learned bookkeeping at a business college, then taken employment at the Pacific Box Company. His uncle was a business associate of Carr, and Cicott gained a mint appointment through these two men on December 16, 1874. Subsequent to joining the mint, he was accused of embezzling $100 at the box company; however, the firm had closed its doors, and nothing could be proved.[16]

With Billy Ralston dead, his man Jefferson Babcox, the coiner at the San Francisco Mint, was exposed, and Cicott was the tool the ring used to remove him. Babcox's account books all balanced. There could be no theft of bullion, as daily transfers to the coining department were strictly monitored. However, the coiner was required daily to deliver finished coin in even thousands to the treasurer. This was a loophole as a substantial sum would accrue through the remnants of this rounding in the coiner's vault until the month end close. Funds could be "borrowed" in the interim if they reappeared at month end. It was here that Babcox's problem arose as Cicott also had access to the coiner's vault.[17]

On December 22, 1875, Horace Beach, the cashier, asked Cicott to exchange ten-dollar gold pieces (eagles) for twenty-dollar gold pieces (double eagles). Babcox being out, Cicott opened the coiner's vault to find there were no eagles to make the exchange. Later that day, Babcox appeared, and Cicott informed him that there was a deficiency in his eagle account. At first Babcox feigned ignorance but then admitted that he had invested the money in stocks. He would liquidate those stocks and make restitution that night, asking Cicott to say nothing of the incident. The next morning Babcox left the building and did not return until afternoon, failing to replace the money. Cicott then went to LaGrange who was at his home in Oakland. The following morning, Christmas Eve, LaGrange had Babcox open his vault in his presence, revealing a shortage of $12,355.

Faced with suspension, Babcox chose to resign. On December 29 surreptitiously supplied funds covered the loss.[18] No one wanted to cross Charles Felton who was on Babcox's bond.[19] Given there was no loss to the government, LaGrange immediately left for Washington to lay the case for Babcox before Treasury Secretary Benjamin Bristow. However, Linderman stopped him, saying that Bristow was a straight arrow and would take LaGrange's head off over the affair.[20] The director was right in that regard. Benjamin Helm Bristow, a unionist Kentuckian, had not hesitated to take on the Ku Klux Klan in his previous position as solicitor general. And this was in spite of significant Confederate sentiments in his extended family. LaGrange backed off, and Cicott gained the coiner's office on January 15, 1876.[21]

Secretary Bristow, upon learning of the defalcation, referred the case to United States District Attorney Walter Van Dyke. LaGrange had to testify before the grand jury, but as no money was lost to the federal government, the case went no further.[22]

In the aftermath, Babcox's key men, including the foreman of the adjusting room, either resigned or were suspended. As replacements, Cicott brought in the ring's political hacks, allowing the coining operations to continue on autopilot.[23] In fact, it got so bad that LaGrange was forced to bring Babcox back on a per diem basis for 12 days in March 1876 to oversee the green hands and return some semblance of order to the coining operations.

The *San Francisco Chronicle* broke the story of the defalcation on March 23, 1876. An evasive and embarrassed LaGrange failed to tamp down the furor. When the reporters attempted to follow up with Babcox, he was nowhere to be found in the city. In fact he was in Nevada, far from their prying questions, superintending the construction of a quartz mill in which Carr was rumored to be an investor.[24,25]

Meanwhile, at the annual meeting of the Assay Commission in February 1876, Henry Linderman noticed some poorly struck dimes from the Carson City Mint. He expressed surprise, as he had not seen this problem on his trip west the previous summer.[26] Linderman now had an uneasy feeling about both his western mints.

The director ordered Fred Eckfeldt from his office to go west on an inspection trip. Eckeldt's father currently served as the assayer at the Philadelphia Mint, and John Eckfeldt had been his cousin.[27] The Mint Service was in his blood, and Linderman trusted the young man implicitly. His instructions were to examine the method of receiving supplies and attendance of officers, clerks, and men at San Francisco and to look in detail into coining operations at Carson City. Linderman termed the defective dimes there indicative of a lack of skill or gross carelessness on the part of their operative officers. In addition, Eckfeldt was to suggest that Superintendent Crawford hire Jos Harmstead as a general foreman of machinery.[28]

A little more than two weeks later, Linderman changed Eckfeldt's marching orders in regard to San Francisco. The execution of the silver coinage at that mint was unacceptable and die usage was inordinately high. Eckfeldt was to review the qualifications of the coiner and his key employees and ensure that the coins were well struck.[29] He was to make changes if any of these men lacked the necessary skills to turn out well-executed coins.[30]

The problem of poorly struck dimes went down differently at Carson City. The dies had been improperly hardened. Hardening required tempering with heat. Too little heat had made the dies soft, causing weak strikes, particularly with the smaller dime dies. Also, two basic follow-up steps had been omitted: the acid washing of the tempered dies and a final polishing.[31] Linderman suggested that Crawford hire Harmstead and sealed that deal by telling the superintendent he would hold him responsible for the issue of any more defective coins.[32] Harmstead reported for duty April 8, 1876, although his wife remained in San Francisco. There was an immediate improvement in the problem at Carson City.[33]

Amidst dealing with the Carson City dimes, Linderman learned that the big Morgan & Orr Ajax coin press in San Francisco had been damaged again. The press had been working gold coinage, striking $1 million worth in nine hours. Allowing for work stoppages, the press had been run at 90 rpm when it should not have exceeded 75 rpm.

Linderman met with Arthur Orr, the primary Morgan & Orr partner who had accompanied him to San Francisco at John Eckfeldt's death, to review the situation. Orr did not mince his words. The way the Ajax press had been run was bad, displaying a gross ignorance in operating such machinery. He cared not for any excuses. All that was required in running a coin press was brains.[34]

Fred Eckfeldt's report on San Francisco hit Linderman's desk on April 4, 1876. The poorly struck dimes extended back to Babcox with Cicott subsequently failing to raise a red flag. The cutting punches had become worn from frequent use, resulting in planchets (sometimes called coin blanks) being cut larger than standard practice dictated. To reduce them to size, heavy milling of the edges was required, raising a rim around the edge of the planchet. The result in most cases was a weakly struck dime and cracking and chipping of the working die. Compounding the problem was a complete lack of skill in the die hardening process.

A week later, poorly struck dimes from San Francisco arrived at the treasurer's office in Washington for use in the currency redemption. Linderman could no longer contain the problem within the bureau and took LaGrange to task.

> If these matters shall not be fully and effectively corrected without delay, such reorganization as may be necessary to that end will have to be made at the close of the fiscal year.[35]

Linderman learned on that same day he wrote his fiery reprimand to LaGrange that the superintendent was back to his old habits of not fully disclosing hires and removals. It was like throwing gasoline on the fire. Linderman promptly halted hires at San Francisco for the remainder of the fiscal year.[36] Five days later he went a giant step further, rejecting two appointments in the melter and refiner's department.[37] And a week after that, more hires were disapproved.[38]

On April 19, Linderman gigged LaGrange again. That morning the treasurer had shown the mint director defective quarters from San Francisco. He sent the superintendent a well-struck dime from Carson City "due chiefly to the employment of a competent expert at general foreman of the coining department."[39] Linderman wanted LaGrange to consider hiring someone from the Philadelphia Mint to straighten out the mess.[40]

LaGrange, in response, placed the blame for the defective coinage on Jefferson Babcox. Linderman tartly rebutted that it did not exonerate Cicott, at the time assistant coiner, or the pressroom foreman.[41]

Now Linderman brought the heavy guns to bear, detaching Martin Davis indefinitely from the Bureau of the Mint in Washington to San Francisco with an intermediate stop at Carson City. The choice was a good one. Davis had served in the 90th Pennsylvania Volunteer Infantry Regiment during the war. He had seen fighting in all the major battles from a raw recruit in the cornfield at Antietam to a survivor at the surrender at Appomattox.[42] Hugh LaGrange would not intimidate him.

Davis's first report back elicited another letter from Linderman to LaGrange on May 15, 1876, questioning whether the superintendent had been diligent in his duties, including general inspections of the coins struck. There also was the question of careless setting of the coin dies. Again, Linderman stated that if not corrected, he would send experienced men from Philadelphia to do the job.[43]

The next day Linderman sent a formal letter to Secretary Bristow, setting forth the problems encountered at the western mints and the actions taken. He relayed that both superintendents had been censured, and any continuation of the problem would result in a change in officers. However, Linderman was now confident that measures had been taken to ensure proper execution of the coinage. He had impressed upon the superintendents the need to employ only the most skilled workers. Linderman also gave the excuse that with the failure of the Bank of California, there had been heavy demand for the coinage of gold and trade dollars that continued for some months afterward.[44] It all sounded so logical and designed to put Bristow's concerns at ease.

In fact, Bristow's focus was elsewhere, being prominently mentioned as a reform candidate for the Republican presidential nomination at their convention convening on June 14. On June 8, rumors floated in Washington that Grant wanted a change at Treasury after the convention adjourned.[45] This rumor proved true; Bristow resigned on June 20, 1876. His successor, Lot Morrill, came over from the Senate to serve as a placeholder for the remaining months of the Grant Administration. Under Morrill, Linderman could do as he pleased, either clean house or cover up the mess.

At a time when LaGrange should have been hunkered down, he stuck his neck out. He complained about having to inspect his inventory of dimes before sending them east to Treasury. In LaGrange's view, after ninety days of circulation the public would not be able to tell the difference anyway. Linderman failed to budge.[46]

LaGrange further antagonized Linderman by sending a letter showing the workings of the San Francisco Mint over the past eight years in a very positive light with a copy to Senator Sargent. An irritated Linderman pointed out that LaGrange had gone over the head of the secretary of the Treasury with this action.[47] Yet by doing so, LaGrange had reminded Linderman that he must deal with Senator Sargent if he were to seek LaGrange's removal.

At this point, Director Linderman had had enough of his San Francisco superintendent. He must have felt like the little Dutch boy trying to plug the leaks in the dike and making no progress. He sent his trusted associated, Professor Rogers, to San Francisco along with Edward Leech from the bureau and A. W. Downing, coining room foreman at the Philadelphia Mint to make a thorough review of the operations at San Francisco and Carson City. Davis would also be pulled from his other duties to help cover Carson City. They were to conduct their investigation during the annual shutdown in July. Downing would examine the coining operations, Rogers, the refinery, and Leech, the records of the superintendent and operative officers.

The ink was hardly dry on Linderman's instructions to Rogers before he was forced to amend them. Stephen D. Mills, a special agent for the Treasury Department, had been in San Francisco,[48] apparently to investigate irregularities at the Customs House. Either he stumbled onto issues at the mint, or former melter and refiner John Cochran, stirred up by the Babcox defalcation, renewed his allegations. Nevertheless, charges had been made to Mills that there were individuals on the mint payroll that performed no duties as well as complaints about the superintendent.[49]

With an outsider potentially meddling in the affairs of the San Francisco Mint, Linderman needed to get in front of this issue or risk losing control of the narrative. He requested through a Treasury Department solicitor that Mills be instructed to meet with Rogers to provide names and furnish any proofs behind the allegations. Linderman did mention to Rogers that a naval officer from Mare Island was one potential witness. That could only have been Navy paymaster Spalding. Rogers was empowered to take testimony under oath and allow cross-examination by the accused. Linderman's only caveat was that any hearings must be conducted without publicity.[50]

As the time of Rogers's departure approached, Linderman again added to the scope of his examination. He now knew that the dime problem at San Francisco was much larger than anticipated with $1 million of potentially poorly struck dimes on hand. Rogers must make the call if these were to be melted.[51] In addition, Davis had told Linderman that light trade dollars had knowingly left the mint indicating a problem in the adjusting department.[52]

Linderman did not wait for the results of Rogers's examination, informing LaGrange that if the adjusting problem were not fixed, he would be compelled to suspend coinage at San Francisco.[53] At this point a communication hit Linderman's desk that the cylinder in the large steam engine at San Francisco was cracked, necessitating a major repair.[54] Venting, he wrote Rogers that the frequent removals at San Francisco were one of the primary causes for the silver coinage problems.[55]

Once again, Linderman expanded Rogers's scope of investigation to include the chief adjustor and the foreman of the drawbench, both with critical roles in keeping the coin weights within their legal tolerances. In addition, he threw in the chief engineer in charge of the mint's power train. The director wanted to know the actual experience of these men at hiring and to be provided with a copy of their certificates of qualification if such existed.[56] In this case, the chief engineer was H. F. Fisher who had in previous times been Senator Sargent's barber.[57]

June 29 was another rough day for Linderman. Rogers told him the entire $1 million in dimes should be condemned. Without the slightest hesitation, Linderman ordered LaGrange to melt them on June 30.[58] Next, the director ordered Davis to investigate purchases in San Francisco to ensure that supplies were being purchased at market prices and being delivered in full.[59] Then he shut down the employment merry-go-round, disapproving all pending nominations by LaGrange.[60]

At this point, the Mills accusations proved to be a tempest in a teapot. The special agent sent a letter to Rogers making less than definitive charges and providing evidence of a vague nature before leaving town. Linderman was unwilling to press these charges, believing that Rogers's examination of the operations would fully uncover any irregularities.[61]

Linderman's relations with LaGrange improved with the satisfactory results of the annual settlement during the shutdown.[62] It did not last. LaGrange appeared to make wholesale changes in the adjustor's workforce. Digging into the situation, Linderman learned from LaGrange that all these ladies had been working as substitutes in the positions of the women they were now to replace. It was clear that inexperienced ladies had been employed in the adjusting room in an underhanded manner to avoid the need for Linderman's approval.[63]

With the annual shutdown over, Rogers returned and gave Linderman a verbal report. If Linderman had expected Rogers to place the noose around LaGrange's neck, his friend let him down. Rogers reported that the San Francisco Mint was now turning out beautiful coins. However, the verdict was still out on the coiner, Cicott. Linderman told LaGrange that he would await Rogers's written report before deciding to remove the coiner. Yet it was a gentler Linderman that explained to LaGrange that his objective was to encourage and strengthen the superintendent in every effort that the man might take to meet the problems.[64]

Linderman transmitted the first of Rogers's written recommendations on August 19, 1876. LaGrange was to cut his payroll by 15 percent through terminations and wage reductions. Linderman also mandated that wages in the melting, refining, and parting of bullion must be covered by the charges to the depositors for refining their bullion.[65]

Next Linderman called for the assistant coiner under Cicott to resign and Martin Davis to be appointed in his place.[66] The problem here was that Linderman neglected to clear this with Davis in advance.[67] Davis wanted no part of the toxic environment in the coiner's department. The preceding May the transfer clerk had taken exception to Cicott's bookkeeping. The clerk called Cicott a fool and an imbecile and the coiner responded by punching the clerk in the nose. In the ensuing scuffle, the clerk grabbed Cicott from behind by the neck and clawed his face removing skin and whiskers. Both men took time off, and LaGrange transferred the clerk.[68] Ultimately an unrepentant LaGrange appointed M. J. Cady, George Gorham's nephew, to be assistant coiner.[69] Prior to coming to the mint in 1870, Cady had been a plumber.[70]

On August 21, 1876, Henry Linderman conveyed the Rogers report to LaGrange. Linderman had sent a technician, albeit highly skilled, and had received a technician's report. Linderman's action beyond wage reductions through new and tightened regulations was window dressing, plain and simple. His response was significant for what it did not do: Linderman did not remove the coiner.[71]

So it was business as usual at the San Francisco Mint with Linderman constantly playing catch up to offset the transgressions of the Republican ring through the overly pliant LaGrange. If Henry Linderman had been truly honest with himself, he would have realized that the San Francisco Mint had been in a state of decline since the suspension of Jos Harmstead in 1873.

After the fact, Linderman would admit that between the dimes and the appointments at San Francisco and the hassling with Congress over appropriations he was all done in. He and LaGrange had stood toe to toe in August 1876, and Linderman had blinked. It would come back to bite him.

Chapter 21
TURNING POINT

At the beginning of 1876, John Sherman assessed his chances of gaining the Republican nomination for president at the June National Convention to be held in Cincinnati. The Resumption Act of 1875 had given the Republican Party a safe harbor of sound monetary policy after President Grant had vetoed a modest increase in circulating national bank notes. However, Sherman's shoving the resumption bill to enactment had come at great personal cost. Hard-money advocates called the law a political trick, an evasion of public duty, and totally inadequate. The soft-money men just simply opposed the act and were determined to repeal it at any cost. Sherman had alienated everybody. His political salvation now lay with the successful resumption of specie payments called for in the law on January 1, 1879.

Out of the running, Sherman's decision on the presidency seemed simple enough. He was very much against a third term for Ulysses Grant. At the same time, he could not support the front-runner, fellow senator James G. Blaine of Maine. Without hesitation, on January 21, 1876, Sherman endorsed Rutherford Hayes for president. Hayes was a long shot, a dark horse, a political unknown outside of his home state of Ohio, where he was about to be inaugurated for a third term as governor. Sherman knew Hayes well. They had canvassed Ohio together the preceding summer.

Yet Sherman's endorsing letter was hardly glowing in praise. Hayes had been a good soldier during the Civil War, performing his full duty but not greatly distinguished. As a member of the House of Representatives, he was not a leading debater or manager of party tactics but held true to his convictions. As governor he had shown good executive abilities and maintained a good reputation with both Republicans and Democrats. For Sherman, the deciding point was Hayes's position on currency. He was thoroughly sound on the issue, yet not committed to any particular measure so as to be able to cooperate with any plan that might promise success. Sherman believed the currency question would play a major role in the election.[1]

Sherman had good reason to be concerned with control of the House passing to the Democrats in the 44th Congress. In a positive move, the Democrats named Michael Kerr, a gold man, their elected speaker. He proceeded to pack the Ways and Means and Banking and Currency committees with like-minded Democrats.[2] Bills that called for the repeal or sidetracking of resumption would be buried in these two committees. Still, it would push John Sherman as he had never been pushed before to hold the line on resumption.

As Sherman feared, trouble had not been long in coming. When Treasury purchased 8.25 million ounces of silver to provide sufficient coin to redeem the Fractional Notes, Secretary Bristow hoarded $10 million afraid the coins would not stabilize in price when valued in greenbacks and would disappear from circulation. The result was that Treasury continued to print and issue new Fractional Notes, necessitating the call for a supplemental appropriation from Congress. Samuel Randall, chair of the Committee on Appropriations, introduced the necessary bill to fund the budgetary deficiency in the Printing and Engraving Bureau and for the issue of silver coin in place of the shinplasters on March 2, 1876.

However, the committee had instructed Randall to allow amendments from the floor, resulting in a legislative free for all.[3] A 412.8-grain standard silver dollar with a legal tender of $20 for any one payment made its appearance.[4] In addition the trade dollar lost its legal tender status. The sentiment in the debate had been to increase the use of silver through the standard dollar with a higher legal tender status. Gold Democrats had abstained, allowing hard-money Republicans to carry the day against the soft-money Democrats. Sherman observed as debate progressed that a substantial portion of the Democrats in the House would vote against any measure that aided implementation of the Resumption Act.[5]

When Sherman got his hands on this bill in the Committee on Finance, he struck out the section dealing with the silver dollar and trade dollar. On April 10 in a speech before the Senate in support of the slimmed down bill, Sherman stated he believed the price decline in silver was temporary. He argued that if the subsidiary silver coinage was capped at the number of Fractional Notes to be redeemed, there was room for a silver dollar but with limits to coinage. Overall, this additional silver coinage would counteract any contraction of the currency.[6]

The debate was now on. Lewis Bogy, speaking for the soft-money Democrats in the Senate, wanted a complete re-monetization of silver and called the Coinage Act of 1873 a blunder. Regardless, the bill became law on April 17 and provided the issue of subsidiary silver coins of standard value in the redemption of an equal number of Fractional Notes whenever presented.[7]

Sherman still had a problem: the legal tender status of the trade dollar. Bristow and Linderman were pleading with him to fix the situation. Sherman recognized that to leave legal tender in place for the trade dollar both deprived the government of the seigniorage that would accrue from a standard silver dollar and placed no legal caps upon trade dollar coinage. If he did nothing, he left in place a back door for an inflationary unlimited domestic silver coinage through the trade dollar.

Sherman's efforts in April had only brought frustration. In floor debate, Senator John P. Jones asserted that the bi-metallic standard, silver and gold, would help immeasurably in returning to specie payments while ending the depression, now nearly three full years in duration. He argued that silver had been removed as a monetary standard within the Coinage Act of 1873 in the interest of creditors, both domestic and foreign, who could then be assured of receiving gold only for bond-principal repayments. That act was a grave wrong committed unwittingly yet certainly in the favor of a few capitalists in England and Germany that held U. S. government bonds.[8] This rhetoric was not what Sherman wanted; it would make bimetallism a political football in the upcoming presidential election.

Next had come a joint resolution introduced in the House on May 1 to expedite the issue of silver coin and the retirement of Fractional Notes. The resolution was referred to the House Committee on Banking and Currency where it sat. Frustrated, Sherman attempted to force the situation before the convening of the Republican National Convention by resurrecting in the Senate legislation that provided for a silver dollar with limited legal tender status to $20.[9] This effort died, but it broke the logjam in the House.

The Committee on Banking and Currency reported the expediting resolution favorably. However, the devil was in the details. This resolution called for an additional $10 million of subsidiary silver coins to be issued in exchange for an equal number of greenbacks that would be destroyed. A second resolution that called for $20 million of subsidiary silver coinage, without any greenback redemption clause, was also placed on the floor for consideration. Democrat Richard Bland who would become silver's main cheerleader made a futile attempt to amend this resolution to remonetize the standard silver dollar. With most hard-money Democrats again abstaining, the Republican minority was able to pass both measures.[10]

Here matters had sat until the two major parties held their national conventions to nominate their candidates for president. In actuality, there was a third, the Independent Party, more commonly known as the Greenbackers, but no one took them seriously. Meeting in Indianapolis, they had a single issue, inflating the currency, and their nominee Peter Cooper, founder of the Cooper Institute in New York, was too old at 85 for the active campaign required to bring the party national recognition. Their platform, after initially rejecting a position on coinage, called for making the old silver dollar legal tender. It carried and would roil American politics for the remainder of the 19th century and beyond

The Republicans kicked off their sixth national convention on June 14.[11] The party's platform played a distant second fiddle to the anticipated battle for the presidential nomination. It would take 377 delegate votes for nomination, and the handicappers were having a field day. James G. Blaine was still the favorite with Roscoe Conkling from New York trying to chip away Blaine's support in the early balloting. Oliver Morton from Indiana and Bristow followed. Bristow seemed the wildcard in this affair. No one was seriously considering Rutherford Hayes whose support was limited to his home state of Ohio.[12]

With no special efforts having been made for Hayes, delegates filled the auditorium well in advance of the 10 o'clock June 16 start of voting with Bristow men growing more confident as the time neared. The first ballot showed Blaine strong but not strong enough with 285 votes. Morton and Bristow followed, with Conkling a disappointing fourth. Hayes stood at a paltry 61 votes, barely more than a "favorite son." The second vote was delayed when Senator Donald Cameron, chair of the Pennsylvania delegation, attempted to suppress Blaine votes through the unit-voting rule. Still, Blaine picked up a few delegates, but otherwise there was no real shift of support. The deadlock continued, ballot after ballot.

On the seventh ballot, Bristow withdrew, throwing his support to Hayes. In addition, Cameron threw his votes that were not going to Blaine over to Hayes. The momentum swung with the anti-Blaine vote going to Hayes, giving him the nomination.[13] On June 19, 1876, a grateful Hayes penned a very personal note to Senator Sherman.

"I trust you will never regret the important action you took in the inauguration and carrying out of the movement which resulted in my nomination. I write these few words to assure you that I appreciate, and am gratified for, what you did." [14]

The Democrats met in St. Louis for the first national convention to be held west of the Mississippi River on June 27. New York Governor Samuel Tilden was the front-runner, easily gaining the nomination on the second ballot. Their platform, among other issues, called for hard money and repeal of the Resumption Act. In other words, Tilden was running on payment in coin, but was it gold or silver? The Democrats were not specific. However, they definitely were going to make Sherman and the Resumption Act an issue in the coming presidential election.

In the middle of this political theater, Sherman was still faced with the dire need to demonetize the trade dollar. The hardline Republicans in the Senate would not support legislation passed in the House that also remonetized the standard silver dollar. By default, Sherman chose the June 10 House resolution that called for $10 million of additional subsidiary silver coins and amended it on June 21 to remove legal tender status for the trade dollar. It passed that day, but the House refused to concur, amending the Senate version on June 28 to fully remonetize the silver dollar.

By this point Sherman had become thoroughly frustrated, expressing weariness with the manner in which, like some ill-timed jack-in-the-box, the monetary standard question kept intruding into the discussion of subsidiary coinage measures. Sherman had wished that he needed to say nothing additional about this resolution, for he was as tired of it as he was of any legislative measure in his life.[15] The resolution now went to a conference committee. In its final form the resolution called for the $10 million in additional subsidiary silver to be exchanged for a like number of greenbacks that would be held in the Treasury. It also capped subsidiary silver coinage authorized at $50 million in aggregate. Last, but not least, the trade dollar was demonetized. No longer was there a back door to the free coinage of silver through these coins. No longer could brokers pass these coins, acquired at their lower intrinsic value, into the domestic market at their legal tender value.

This conference report had passed the House on July 13 but not without debate. By now there was a shortage of both Fractional Notes and subsidiary silver in the country, bringing pressure on the House to act. Had there been knowledge that Linderman had ordered the melting of 10 million defective dimes at San Francisco two weeks before, all hell would have broken loose. Had the mint director's action been in support of Sherman and the hard-money men?

Two silver Republicans, Joe Cannon and Horatio Burchard, both of Illinois, came around to support the conference report, carrying the resolution to the finish line in the House.[16] The resolution passed the Senate on July 22.[17]

In a final act for this session of the Forty-Fourth Congress, in August the House and Senate authorized a monetary commission to study the subject of re-monetization of silver. On the commission were both John P. Jones and Richard Bland. All but two of the members were favorable to restoration of the silver dollar at full legal tender.[18] This cake was baked before it was ever placed in the oven.

When Congress adjourned on August 15, Sherman hit the campaign trail for Hayes like he had never done before. He spoke nearly every weekday in one of the five or six states that he traveled to, right up to the election. Everyone believed the race too close to call. When the dust settled, Tilden won the popular vote. The Democrats still held the House and the Republicans, the Senate.

Yet, there remained the possibility that Hayes could win. The vote was disputed in South Carolina, Florida, and Louisiana with Hayes needing every one of these states' electoral votes to win by one vote in the Electoral College. In February 1877, a compromise was struck. Hayes received the electoral votes needed, and in return, he agreed to remove the military from the former Confederacy that would bring an end to reconstruction.

Now president-elect, Hayes wanted Sherman for his secretary of the treasury, bluntly telling the senator that he was "by all odds the best fitted for it of any man in the nation." There was no refusing the man. In addition, Hayes requested that Sherman secure William Evarts to be secretary of state.[19] When Hayes came to Washington a few days early for his swearing in and inauguration, he was Sherman's houseguest. It was obvious that Sherman was going to play a much larger role than just running the Treasury Department in this administration.

John Sherman now found himself in an extremely powerful position to make resumption a success on January 1, 1879. Meanwhile, Hayes had announced that he would be a one-term president. For Sherman, 1880 was shaping up to be his year. And it was not lost on him that Senator Cameron had played a pivotal roll in Hayes's nomination. The one wildcard in this affair was re-monetization of the silver dollar.

Chapter 22

Art Breaches the American Consciousness

John Sherman no doubt found the grand opening of the Centennial Exposition in Philadelphia on May 10, 1876, a welcome respite from the tedious financial debates and presidential politics swirling around him in Congress. A special excursion train had left Washington at 3 o'clock the afternoon before, bound for the opening festivities, carrying dignitaries and their families from Congress. Even his brother, General of the Army William Tecumseh Sherman, had hitched a ride.[1]

Philadelphia was decked out like a Fourth of July celebration. Houses throughout the city displayed flags, and many added banners celebrating all the nations participating. Even the mint decorated for the event, spending $200 to decorate the Chestnut Street side of the building. They were afraid that lack of decoration would be quickly noticed and severely criticized.[2]

Whether the mint was adequately decorated was the least of Mint Director Henry Linderman's concerns. With the redemption of Fractional Notes, subsidiary silver coinage was once again in circulation. Complaints about their designs were not far behind, first in the *Galaxy* magazine and then picked up and given fuller exposure by the *New York Times*.

Without a doubt, the articles declared, American silver coins were the ugliest among the coins of civilized nations. They were mean in aspect, weak, commonplace, and without character. They had the look of poorly designed and executed medals. The superiority of earlier American coins was due chiefly to their comparative boldness and simplicity of design. In a direct suggestion as to replacement designs, the article called for Washington and Franklin to be considered as emblematic of Liberty.[3]

Thus, for Henry Linderman, the Centennial Exposition crystallized in his mind a growing concern that his engraving staff was inadequate to the task. When the opportunity presented itself, would his engravers have the necessary artistic skills to deliver?

For one thing, the engraving staff seemed an independent, willful lot. The mint director continued to refer to engraver William and assistant engraver Charles Barber as "Messrs Barber and Son" as if they were a commercial enterprise. The father-son team still had the old reducing machine that had been replaced at the mint in 1869. Linderman could not get an answer from the Philadelphia superintendent, James

This half dollar with its companion quarter featured the design, first issued into general circulation in 1840, that was so complained of in the Eastern press.

Pollock, as to the ownership of this machine. In January 1876 he had flat told Pollock that if the machine belonged to the mint, it should be returned and kept there.

Assistant engraver George Soley took matters a step further. When the Philadelphia Mint retired its nearly forty-year-old steam coin press, Soley purchased it for his small engraving shop. To complement this press, Soley had constructed a duplicate to the mint's new Hill Engraving Machine, a clear patent infringement. Linderman told Pollock to get Soley and the engraving machine under his direct control.[4]

The Centennial Exposition had proven a bonanza of outside work for the Mint's engravers. The decision had been made early on that there would be no changes in the circulating coin designs to celebrate the event. It would be better to strike medals for the exposition with more appropriate emblems, devices, and inscriptions. Thus, the engravers received commissions to design the medals and prepare the dies, acceptable as long as it was not done during regular working hours.[5]

The medals that were forthcoming from his engraving staff for the centennial did little to inspire confidence in Linderman. The official medal of the exposition and, therefore, the most important was designed by William Barber. It showed a belligerent Liberty rising from a recumbent position with sword in hand, wholly inappropriate for the nation's circulating coinage. The other centennial designs by assistant engravers William Key and George Soley were a plethora of centennial buildings, Liberty Bells, a seated Liberty, and George Washington. There was nothing of note here except the image of George Washington. Finally, there was a "Nevada dollar" struck from Comstock Lode silver and engraved by William Barber. This design, both obverse and reverse, was a mess. Barber even failed to center the sun on the reverse within its gloriosa. Interestingly, Charley Barber took no credit for any designs for the event.

The official medal of the1876 Centennial International Exposition (HK-20) was designed by William Barber. The design struck a belligerent pose reflecting the mood of the nation following the veiled interference of Great Britain and France during the Civil War.

With no congressionally sanctioned commemorative coin program for the nation's centennial celebration, the assistant engravers produced a series of designs on dollar-sized planchets later to be known as so-called dollars. The examples shown here are HK-23 and HK-55.

This so-called dollar (HK-19) was designed by William Barber using silver bullion from the Comstock Lode.

Nevertheless, Linderman had asked Philadelphia Mint Superintendent Pollock on May 1 to have William Barber prepare sketches for a new dollar coin. He wanted on the obverse a head of Liberty bearing an inscription of Liberty somewhere within the device. For the reverse, he wanted an olive wreath or branches of olives surrounding the denomination, spelled out. He was striving for a European look to this design.[6]

Workmanlike designs came back a week later with a head of Liberty distinctly like every other one William Barber had prepared over the prior few years. In addition, he prepared a seated Liberty very close in likeness to the trade dollar.[7] He had plowed no new ground. Still Linderman gave the go-ahead to prepare dies and strike pattern pieces.

Anticipating legislation reauthorizing the standard-weight silver dollar, Henry Linderman instructed William Barber to begin preparing pattern designs (J-1462/J-1467) in 1876.

On May 23, 1876, Linderman further advanced his thinking in regard to the design with Pollock. He wanted a classic head of Liberty. The single motto, "In God We Trust" was adequate, wanting "E Pluribus Unum" dropped. He wanted coin denominations to replace the eagle on the reverse, believing the obverse and reverse design more likely to strike up in this pairing. This said, the mint director closed with a real zinger. Citing the phrases from the *Galaxy* and *New York Times* articles,

Linderman told Pollock, "It would be well to consider any improvement in respect to engraving within our reach."[8] Henry Linderman was going outside the mint for designs.

Just days later, Linderman reached out to a variety of outside candidates: Hermann Faber, a Philadelphia artist well known for his etchings; Henry Mitchell of Boston, who had prepared an official medal for the Battle of Lexington Centennial in 1875; and the Wyon brothers of Great Britain. (Linderman had coordinated the setup of their medals display at the Centennial Exposition.) Here he turned to his friend, W.C. Fremantle, deputy master of Great Britain's Royal Mint, to transmit his proposal to the Wyons.[9]

Mitchell was prompt in answering Linderman's request, submitting several sketches. Linderman particularly liked the head of Liberty shown on Mitchell's rendering for the quarter and wanted a similar design for the proposed new dollar coin. He also threw Mitchell a bone; he had provided the engraver's name as the best artist in the country to the Centennial commissioner in charge of preparing the award medal for exhibitors. Linderman even threw out a suggestion for the design.[10] Mitchell took the commission.

On June 11, Linderman moved to get Secretary Bristow up to speed. He told the secretary in broad terms that he was contemplating improving the appearance of American coins as well as facilitating the impressions of the designs to be brought up more readily in striking. To expedite matters, Linderman had drafted a short bill containing the necessary changes in provisions that he wanted referred to the Senate Committee on Finance, in other words to John Sherman. However, Linderman's bill was not a quick fix. He included the sticky issue of removing legal tender status for the trade dollar. The three-dollar gold piece would be discontinued. And his design proposals for the silver coins dropped the eagle on the reverse. While Linderman supported retention of the motto "In God We Trust" where space permitted, he was silent on "E Pluribus Unum," which meant he wanted it dropped.[11] Linderman's political timing for once was terrible, given that Bristow, feeling the political fallout from his failed presidential bid, would resign on June 20.

Linderman was still sorting out his options for obtaining new coin designs a day later with a second letter to Freemantle. Could the deputy mint master find a first-class die sinker who would be willing to take the position of assistant engraver at Philadelphia. He would need to be able to produce finished hubs and, if he understood modeling and bronzing, he would be even more valuable. Linderman could pay $8 per day.[12]

July turned into August, and it was apparent that Linderman was not going to get a short bill dealing with designs out of Sherman's Committee on Finance. Meanwhile William Barber had prepared copper impressions for his dollar design that Pollock forwarded to Linderman. The director called the head of Liberty equal to if not superior to anything prepared at the mint.[13]

Coincidentally, at the same time Henry Linderman was praising Barber's work, he received a letter from Fremantle recommending George Morgan as an assistant engraver. The man had a solid background in the technical metallurgical skills and had exhibited at the Royal Academy of Arts. Though clearly overqualified, Morgan faced limited opportunities for advancement in England.[14] Just as importantly, Morgan

In 1875 a medal was issued to celebrate the 100th anniversary of the battle of Lexington at the beginning of the American Revolution. This so-called dollar (HK-16) was designed by Henry Mitchell, a Boston engraver better known for his work with the Bureau of Printing and Engraving.

Henry Linderman smoothed the way for Henry Mitchell to gain the commission to design the award medal given to exhibitors at the 1876 Centennial International Exposition.

had queried Linderman directly about submitting designs and executing dies for the Centennial award medal.[15]

Linderman now penned a letter to James Pollock at Philadelphia. He enclosed Freemantle's recommendation of Morgan and a small package of specimens of the man's engraving.[16] Backpedaling on employment terms, Linderman told Pollock he would hire Morgan on a temporary basis, leaving the question of permanent employment until they had tested his qualifications with the preparation of new designs for the silver coins.

Linderman believed this arrangement would relieve Pollock from all the embarrassment in respect to the personal pride of the engraver and his assistants, notably son Charley.

Almost as an afterthought, Linderman told Pollock he was free to inform William Barber if he so desired.[17]

Linderman received a sign-off from Pollock on August 16. He would offer Morgan an engagement with the Philadelphia Mint for six months. In a postscript, Linderman told Pollock that he would not object to the change that the superintendent suggested in the matter of "young Barber."[18] That change, not revealed, was obviously designed to placate any concerns that Charley might have relative to Morgan.

Linderman waited through most of September but heard nothing from either Freemantle or Morgan concerning the job offer. Finally on September 29, 1876, Linderman, anxious to move forward with designs, authorized Pollock to have William Barber prepare dies using the Liberty Head design forwarded to the director in August for the dime, quarter, and half dollar.[19]

Three days later Linderman had George Morgan's acceptance in hand. Linderman told Pollock to have Morgan travel directly to Washington when he landed in Philadelphia so that the director might confer with him. He explained that Morgan would be acting under instructions from the mint bureau in Washington, communicated through Pollock. Then in a statement intended for William Barber's eyes, Linderman laid down the ground rules for Morgan's relationship with the engravers.

"It is not intended that the lawful functions of the engraver shall be interfered with nor infringed upon but it is necessary in order to accomplish the result which we have in view that Morgan should have the fullest opportunity for the display of his professional skill and that he should not be subjected to any restriction."[20]

Ominously, Linderman, upon completion of this letter to Pollock, sent him a telegram: "Take no action for the present on the pattern dies for silver coins."[21] If there was any doubt in the minds of the Barbers, father and son, where Linderman was headed, this action removed it.

Linderman, 18 months later, let slip his feelings about Charley Barber when he suggested to Pollock that the man should go to the San Francisco Mint; he had a brighter future in the Mint Service there.

This image of George Morgan is from his early years at the Philadelphia Mint.

It would have completely shocked Henry Linderman that the future of American coinage designs, while having its roots at the Centennial Exposition, rested not with him but with a young totally inexperienced sculptor. The exposition's smallest building, Memorial Hall, housed displays of sculpture, painting, engraving and lithography, photography, and ceramic decorations and mosaics.[22] Americans were shocked yet captivated by the nudity of the Italian and French sculptures, reflecting classical Greek and Roman themes.[23] The major American art houses, Tiffany and Gorham, were well represented. Thomas Moran even provided a recent painting of Yellowstone.[24]

However, not to be overlooked among the exhibitors, a talented young artist was looking to make his mark in American art circles. His name was Augustus Saint-Gaudens. In short order, Saint-Gaudens would burst forth rising to the pinnacle of the American art world. Though his monumental works would be judged as exceptional, it was his last work for which he would be most recognized by posterity—his American gold coin designs. But, at this moment, that he even exhibited at the Centennial Exposition was no small feat in itself.

Augustus Saint-Gaudens wasn't even one year old when his French shoemaker father, Bernard, and Irish mother, Mary, emigrated from Ireland in 1848, ultimately settling in New York City. His father's shop featured "French Ladies Boots and Shoes" at a time when the wealthy of New York were crazy for anything French. Customers included Horace Greeley and some of the Astors and Belmonts. Consequently, the Saint-Gaudens family lived comfortably enough in the lower middle class of the city.[25]

Even as a young boy, Gus showed an unusual artistic ability. He drew sketches at recess and painted on the fence behind his house, using his saliva instead of water to mix his paints and getting sick to his stomach in the process. When the Saint-Gaudens family followed their clientele uptown, setting up a shoe shop at 268 Fourth (Park) Avenue. Gus happily flourished at a new school and started sketching the cobblers at work in his father's shop. In another show of his innate ability, he had a keen eye for arranging the shoe display in the store window.[26]

Saint-Gaudens's scholastic career came to an abrupt end after one year at his new school when Bernard apprenticed him out to a French cameo cutter. Then in September 1862, he enrolled his son at Cooper Union in a night school art class. This school offered free education in the mechanical arts and sciences with an emphasis on practical education for working class men and women.[27] That Gus was 14, two years below the minimum enrollment age, was not a problem once he demonstrated his innate drawing ability. So every night for six days a week, Gus received instruction for an hour but stayed often for another three hours honing his skills.[28]

In 1864 the cameo cutter that employed Saint-Gaudens fired the young man for not cleaning up his work area after his lunch. Gus found new employment with Jules LeBrethon, a shell-cameo cutter. His employer possessed an unused stone cameo cutter. The easy-going LeBrethon agreed to teach Saint-Gaudens the basics of carving and gave him extra time to practice. This fundamental experience in small-scale, low relief work would pay dividends to the young man in years to come.[29]

At age 19 Saint-Gaudens reached a crossroads; could he advance in his chosen profession or would he remain in the working class. While others had turned to the western frontier, California and Nevada, for their future, Gus looked to the artistic culture to be found in Europe.

The plan was for Saint-Gaudens to see the Paris Exposition of 1867, gain admission to the Ecole des Beaux-Arts for nine months to learn sculpture, and return home. The problem was he had no idea what he was getting into. To gain admittance to the Ecole des Beaux-Arts, he must make application through the American minister to France. That took nine months alone. Gus cut cameos to feed himself, moving to smaller and smaller apartments as his money dwindled to nothing. Literally with only the shirt on his back, he began his career.[30]

Saint-Gaudens's circumstances were looking up in 1870. He had scored accommodations with another American artist with better means to support himself, Truman Bartlett.[31] This happy arrangement ended with the start of the Franco-Prussian War that forced Saint-Gaudens to flee Paris for Rome. Here he took a giant step forward, setting up a small studio that drew in wealthy Americans, many customers of his father's shoe shop. From one such customer, former governor and senator Edwin Morgan, Gus obtained a major commission that gave him much needed visibility in New York. His career was taking hold.

Saint-Gaudens had originally planned a monumental work for the Centennial Exposition. However, the cold reality was that he could not afford such an extravagance. In the end, he settled on an already completed bust of the soon-to-be secretary of state, William Evarts, a canny marketing move. The young sculptor had met Evarts in Rome where the two discussed the possibility of a portrait bust. Saint-Gaudens had returned briefly to the states in 1874 to complete the Evarts commission. What resulted, modeled from life, was a classically influenced head, looking to the right with undraped shoulders undercut on a plain square pedestal. Although an early work, it would survive the test of time as Saint-Gaudens's style matured. Gus won no prizes at the Centennial Exposition with this work, but it acted like a magnet, drawing in others of the Eastern establishment wishing the same for themselves.[32]

Chapter 23

A Gathering of Scoundrels

When George Pinney defaulted and fled the country, a door was slammed shut in hopes he could never return. Navy Paymaster Spalding for whom he had worked as chief clerk at the Mare Island Navy Yard, reported him absent without leave and, therefore, a deserter. In December 1875, two charges of forgery were brought against him by a grand jury.[1] In addition, more details of his dealings in the Navy Pay Office became known at Spalding's court martial in May 1876. A contractor had testified that Pinney issued a pay certificate for work completed in the amount of $2,460. Then after Spalding approved it, Pinney had altered the amount to $32,460.[2] In total, pay certificates over Pinney's hand were issued for more than $1 million, covering $120,600 of work completed.[3] Pinney's reputation was now thoroughly destroyed.

Nor had Pinney considered actions that his wife might take. He had fled the country with another woman. Flora was stunned, essentially left with no means of support, the abandoned wife. The tragic death of their seven-year-old son in January 1876 jolted her back to reality.[4] On May 1, 1876, she filed for divorce on the grounds of adultery, naming names and providing witnesses. The divorce, along with custody of their surviving daughter, was granted by decree.[5]

Flora was represented by the attorney for Republican political boss Billy Carr. Pinney did not miss the connection, accusing Flora of venturing too near the precipice and then covering her tracks with the divorce.[6] In fact, the alleged affair with Carr was such common knowledge that the *San Francisco Chronicle* would subsequently feel free to write that the attentions of a certain prominent citizen of Oakland toward her were well known.[7]

That his wife would betray him in this matter was something that Pinney could not bear. He went on about it in letters to San Francisco Mint Superintendent Hugh LaGrange. She was his property, and he would return to reclaim her. The facilitators in Pinney's return were the two men who had the most to gain: E.W. Burr and W.H. Culver, the bankers who had been burned the worst by the Navy Pay Certificate scheme. Pinney agreed to help the bankers recover his assets left in Carr's care in exchange for their promise to clear the way for his return and not prosecute him for fraud.[8] No surprise, it was suddenly found that Spalding had granted Pinney, prior to his fleeing the country, an indefinite leave, invalidating the desertion charge.[9]

William "Billy" Carr served as the Republican political boss of Oakland, California. He would later "retire" to the Central Valley to develop large agricultural holdings he acquired under questionable circumstances in federal land sales.

Vague rumors circulated in San Francisco at the end of April 1877 that Pinney was back.[10] This was confirmed on May 5 when Pinney walked into the district attorney's office and surrendered to face the two outstanding forgery charges against him.[11]

It was only natural that Pinney turned to the *San Francisco Chronicle*, consistently critical of the San Francisco Mint, to strike the first blow in what would become a bruising battle. It came in the form of a special dispatch from Washington, D.C., printed by the *Chronicle* on May 7, creating such a stir in the city that a second edition was exhausted almost immediately.[12] The most damning allegations centered upon Hugh LaGrange's purchase of a memorandum book from Flora Pinney that detailed George Pinney's illegal transactions at the mint on behalf of the superintendent. The *San Francisco Bulletin* called for an investigation of LaGrange and his removal if Pinney's accusations were sustained. Purchase of the memorandum book was proof enough that wrongdoing existed.

The *Bulletin* tracked down Senator Aaron Sargent at a local hotel. He was in complete surprise when confronted with the allegations contained in the Pinney "special dispatch" concerning the ring's activities, threatening libel proceedings against the *Chronicle*. Carr was quoted as boasting that he would own the *Chronicle* before he was done. LaGrange refused comment except to deny purchasing the memorandum book from Flora Pinney.[13]

President Hayes summoned Mint Director Linderman and Treasury Secretary Sherman to the Executive Mansion on June 5. In office just two months, he was in no mood to start his administration with a scandal. He wanted a commission to get to the bottom of the mess in San Francisco. Linderman left for the West Coast to constitute that commission on June 17, facing the unenviable job of putting out the fire without getting burned.[14]

The Republican political ring struck back with a vengeance. Through a quirk in the laws, individuals had the right to prosecute cases in the Municipal Criminal Court in San Francisco. Billy Carr filed 15 charges against Pinney on May 31, and bail was set at $75,000.[15] The next day charges totaled 79 against Pinney.[16] Carr's attorney was none other than former senator Bill Stewart, back in San Francisco to restore his finances. Stewart would spare no effort to damage Pinney's integrity as well as question the motives of the two bankers.[17] However, the ring was not finished. They searched over the entire state to find a venue suitable to pursue libel charges against the *San Francisco Chronicle*, finally settling on Placerville, 200 miles from San Francisco.[18]

Linderman was charged with appointing two additional members to the Treasury Commission before taking testimony. With Sherman's approval[19] F.F. Low, an intimate friend of Charles Felton, was to serve as chair of the commission. Low was a former governor, congressman, collector of the Port of San Francisco, and minister

As chair of the Treasury Commission, F.F. Low presided over hearings that sometimes degenerated into a free-for–all.

Henry Dodge, as the third member of the Treasury Commission, rarely spoke out during the hearings. Subsequently, Director of the Mint Henry Linderman secured his appointment as superintendent of the San Francisco Mint to succeed Hugh LaGrange.

to China.[20] He was currently serving as president of Anglo-California Bank, controlled by the Selig Brothers of New York City. Unspoken was the fact that Linderman had purchased substantial quantities of silver from Low's bank for the subsidiary coinage. Henry Dodge rounded out the commission. By profession a commission merchant, he was a member of the Republican State Central Committee and formerly twice a member of both the Board of Supervisors and the state senate. Linderman bragged to Sherman that when the commission finished its work, all questions would be quelled.[21]

With the commission constituted, Linderman's first action was to reconcile the bullion and coin on hand at the mint to the books. That done with no discrepancies found, the first public meeting of the commission was held in the Palace Hotel in San Francisco on Monday, July 2. Linderman was totally unprepared for the donnybrook that ensued.

Low started by stating the commission would oversee a thorough examination of the mint's books. He stated further there would be no whitewash and every facility would be offered to those who had charges to make. Civilities ended at that point.

George Parkinson, one of Jos Harmstead's foremen, immediately gained the floor to ask how it could be proven that a person drew pay while performing no work if the payroll books could not be examined. Low hedged. LaGrange waded in, spicing his language with profanities, saying that Parkinson wanted a job at the mint. Former California Attorney General Frank Pixley, who would assume the role of self-styled prosecutor in the hearings, immediately jumped up to complain about LaGrange's intemperate language. Low then brought the meeting back to order.

LaGrange made an opening statement in which he refuted all charges. Then shifting gears, he attacked Pixley, questioning his role in the hearings. Pixley replied that he was appearing as a friend of the president. LaGrange made an insulting retort setting off a hot exchange between the two. LaGrange then called Pixley the counsel of the *Chronicle*. Pixley asked just what that meant, adding that he would not be bulldozed. He had been out of politics for eight years, and there was no dirty business about him. LaGrange became extremely angry and declared that no one, including Pixley, was going to bulldoze him.

At this point a reporter observed that it looked like the situation would come to blows. Low tamped down emotions by recessing the hearing for dinner.[22] After these fireworks, Linderman immediately found that he had pressing business at the Carson City Mint and left town.[23]

The commission reconvened the hearing on July 14. In the interim, they had completed their examination of the mint's books to their satisfaction.[24] Low opened the meeting by establishing the powers of the commission. Persons making written charges would be allowed to examine and cross-examine witnesses. However, no attorney would act as prosecutor.[25]

Pixley gained the floor now to ask if the person making the charges would be allowed to examine the books of the mint at the expense of that person. Low refused. Pixley complained that if such were the case, the prosecution would be virtually paralyzed at the outset. Low cut off the discussion, stating that the commission was now prepared to hear charges.[26]

Frank Pixley assumed the role of prosecutor during the Treasury Commission hearings in San Francisco.

On the following day George Pinney made his first appearance, accusing LaGrange of selling material belonging to the mint and pocketing the proceeds and paying suppliers for material that was never delivered. Pinney submitted these accusations in writing and presented a true copy of a memorandum book detailing some of the questionable transactions. Next mint employees testified, stretching over two days. The tediousness of this testimony was only broken when Pixley would reveal each man's ties to either Carr or Sargent. The *Chronicle* sarcastically called it the "harmonious accord of the testimony of the brigade."[27]

On Saturday, July 21, Pinney began his much-anticipated testimony by calling his wife, Flora, to the chair. She described finding the memorandum book of mint transactions and a note for moneys owed by LaGrange to Pinney in late December 1875. Flora went to LaGrange and over the next several weeks the negotiations through her brother, Joe Crawford, continued. She finally settled for $600, a note for $650, and the voiding of LaGrange's two notes against Pinney in exchange for the memorandum book that promptly disappeared. However, she kept a copy.

Next Crawford was called to the stand. He had made the copy of the memorandum book. Learning of this fact, LaGrange told Crawford that if he did not reveal the existence of the book, he would give him a salary. On the other hand, if Crawford said anything about the book, LaGrange would kick him down at the first opportunity. He could shoot and smile at the same time. Unemployed, Crawford needed the money. However, Carr vetoed the deal.

Pinney was sworn in next and questioned by Edward Marshall, representing LaGrange. Quoting from the copy of the memorandum book in cipher that had been retained by Flora, Pinney described various transactions involving kickbacks and unusually large commissions he conducted for LaGrange while at the mint.

Pinney was at pains to point out that his commissions always came from moneys he had paid over to LaGrange. Marshall interrupted; asking how many lies from that book would have to be corrected? Pinney smiled and said Marshall would have to ask his client how many lies he was going to respond with in his testimony and that would give him his answer. There were more allegations involving coal, borax, and zinc. The details of the coal transactions were difficult to sort out. The coal dealer, George Hoag, had conveniently died, and the books of his company were missing, allowing everybody to tailor their testimony to suit.

At this point Low asked if at the time he made the book, Pinney had intentions of holding it over LaGrange's head. Pinney emphatically denied it. Was the book made for extorting money? No. Since returning, had Pinney offered to destroy the book? No. Did Pinney either inform LaGrange directly or through a third party that for a sum of money he would not appear before the commission? No. Low was openly dubious of this answer. With this exchange, the excitement surrounding Pinney's testimony petered out.

In the evening session, Pixley called John Cochran, the former melter and refiner, to the stand. His testimony largely rehashed his complaints from charges filed at his dismissal. LaGrange attacked Cochran, questioning his motives but accomplishing little. For his part Cochran attempted unsuccessfully to introduce into the hearing the rumors surrounding the deceased John Eckfeldt's involvement in the massive gold losses that had been blamed on Augustin Haraszthy when he was a mint officer.

Throughout this Saturday session, the *Chronicle* observed a portly man listening intently to the proceedings: William Carr.[28]

On Monday evening, July 23, LaGrange brought Bill Stewart with him. Stewart's presence meant the ring was still in LaGrange's corner. Stewart characterized the commission proceedings as a mockery of justice. Pixley responded that it was impossible for his side to compel the production of vouchers and papers that would show the most corrupt mint administration ever. Here was bunkum for bunkum. The audience broke into applause.

Pinney was summoned back to testify and counterattacked requesting correspondence from LaGrange to then Mint Director James Pollock. He also wanted vouchers that would back up his memorandum book. Finally, he wanted all records of money LaGrange reimbursed to the government as a result of Pollock's 1873 investigation. The commissioners promised to consider his requests.

Bill Stewart now commenced to aggressively attack Pinney, starting with the coal transactions with Hoag. Pinney and Hoag had fallen out over the payment of a commission resulting in a lawsuit. Stewart forced Pinney to admit that he had perjured himself in that lawsuit. Then Stewart went after Pinney's testimony to Pollock about copper purchases. Did Pinney or did he not give testimony as to the correctness of copper purchases in the Pollock investigation? Pinney agreed that he might have said it; it was true in one way but not in another.

After more aggressive questioning by Stewart, Pinney offered to make a voluntary statement to the commission under oath. Pinney stated that he had received overtures from LaGrange to not appear before the commission. LaGrange asked what Pinney wanted. Was it money? No. LaGrange wanted Pinney to stop his attack on him.[29] Pinney replied that Billy Carr must call off his hounds. Then he might refuse to appear.

It was nearing midnight as Stewart finished; he had dealt real body blows to Pinney's creditability.

On the evening of July 24, the hearing opened with Pinney sparring with Low over correspondence from the Pollock investigation. Low stated that the papers requested would not be produced. Pinney called them essential. And so it went with more arguing between Pinney and Low over access to the mint's records. Within this exchange Pixley announced that without the mint records it was impossible for him to continue, and he scaled back his participation accordingly.

The following evening was an abbreviated session. LaGrange complained that certain persons representing themselves to be agents of the commission were pressuring merchants who did business with the mint to allow them to examine their books seeking evidence against LaGrange. Low stated that the commission had no such agents. George Parkinson volunteered that the charges were in reference to his activity. He denied having represented himself as an agent of the commission but admitted that he had attempted to convey that impression. Low called his conduct reprehensible.

Pinney then addressed the commission at length complaining of the manner in which he had been treated and again asking that the books of the mint containing the transactions in question and associated vouchers be brought before the commission. Low replied that he had no power to order the books from the mint, and even if he did, he would not do it, given the present excitement in the city over this hearing. The commission was in session a total of fifty minutes.[30]

Testimony on the evening of July 27 dragged past midnight. Felton was called to the stand to testify as to the integrity of the bullion fund. He stated that he had sole control of the fund. Low asked if Felton had ever loaned money belonging to the mint or given it upon any collateral at any time to the Bank of California. Felton answered that he had never loaned from the vaults of the mint any money to any person living or dead or to any corporation for any purpose whatsoever. This all neatly avoided raw bullion advances to the San Francisco Assaying and Refining Company and that portion of the bullion fund held by the assistant U.S. treasurer in San Francisco.

At the hearing on Monday, July 30, Jos Harmstead was called to the stand. Harmstead presented in a matter-of-fact manner the terminations of experienced men in his department by LaGrange. He also addressed the issue of too many female adjustors. Pixley asked him about the consumption of anthracite coal. Harmstead estimated that coal usage was about one half of what the records had indicated as purchased.[31] Furthermore the price paid was $6 to $10 per ton over market.

The infighting resumed the next evening between Pinney and LaGrange. Later in the night George Parkinson was called. His testimony supported the statements by Harmstead. He gave several examples of phantom employees that were friends of Carr and Gorham. Finally, after much indirect abuse from the prosecution, Billy Carr took the stand. By his count he had only two men at the mint. To Parkinson's question, Carr admitted to recommending Cicott for coiner.[32]

At this stage in the proceedings, Linderman had failed to keep the hearings low-key and noncontroversial thanks to Pixley and Parkinson. It was obvious that, by intent, there was no accountability in the purchasing process. Pricing was rich for the vendors and deliveries on bulk material such as coal had virtually no oversight. And now the whole city knew what Linderman had known all along about employment at the mint; it was rotten to the core. Yet Linderman had approved all hiring and dismissals, and Treasury had reviewed all invoices. No monetary damages had been established. If the hearings were adjourned now, LaGrange would retain his position. Linderman now found himself in a real box.

And then the situation worsened. On July 31 the *Chronicle* received an unsigned postcard asking for a meeting at a jewelry store. The city editor went to the location and met with David Levy, the proprietor. Levy claimed knowledge of unfinished coin outside the mint. After a missed follow-up, Levy appeared in the *Chronicle* editorial offices on August 2 and stated that he was in possession of the mint material and made arrangements to turn it over to a reporter while revealing the full story, as he knew it.

Sometime previously, a Mrs. Black came into the jewelry store with some gold clippings and a few silver blanks and snips, clearly from the mint, worth maybe $25 to apply against her account. Levy thought nothing more of it until the Treasury Commission hearings.

After the missed follow-up, Levy had gone to LaGrange in his office. He found the superintendent lying on a lounge. When Levy explained that he had blanks and clippings, LaGrange immediately became interested and wanted to know if anyone else knew of the situation, particularly the *Chronicle* people. LaGrange demanded to know the name of the person from whom Levy obtained the gold and silver. LaGrange also asked to see the material, and Levy initially agreed. However, the merchant had a change of heart, putting off LaGrange. LaGrange, in turn, assumed a friendly manner toward Levy saying if the man had come forward earlier, he would have been in a position to reward him handsomely. With a patronizing hand on his shoulder, LaGrange suggested Levy meet with Low.

Levy agreed and quickly found Low wanted what LaGrange wanted, namely to see the gold and silver and to learn the name of the person originally in possession of the pieces. Levy balked, in part, saying he would show Low the gold and silver but not divulge the name until appearing at the commission. Low said he would come to the jewelry store at 5 p.m. to see the material. From Low's office Levy came directly to the *Chronicle*. He believed that Low and LaGrange were intent upon destroying the evidence. A reporter went with Levy to his home and retrieved the coin blanks and clippings and subsequently turned them over to a deputy U. S. marshal.

Promptly at five o'clock, Low came to the store with Linderman in tow, and LaGrange appeared almost immediately behind them. The meeting was very brief. Low and Linderman demanded Levy turn over the gold and silver and divulge the name of the person giving him the scrap metal. Levy refused. The three men left Levy and walked to a nearby corner where an animated conversation took place. LaGrange separated but then came back and more words were exchanged. Then LaGrange went his way.

At 6:15 p.m. LaGrange appeared before the assistant United States attorney and swore out a complaint against Levy, charging him with wrongfully conspiring to commit offense against the United States, involving certain pieces of gold metal belonging to the United States. Levy was arrested an hour and a half later and released on a bond of $2,000.

Later in the evening of August 2, a *Chronicle* reporter went to the home of Mr. and Mrs. Black. Both were in bed. Mr. Black was unaware of his wife's actions and refused to awaken her. Then Mr. Black came to the *Chronicle* at 12:30 p.m. on August

3 with a different story. The wife of Samuel Keith, a weigher at the mint who had just testified positively about practices within that institution before the commission, gave the silver and gold blanks and clippings to his wife. That story was unimpeachable as Samuel Keith's wife was now dead.[33]

The commission reconvened on August 3 and not a word of the errant gold and silver reported that day by the *Chronicle* was mentioned. Midway on August 5, making no further progress, the prosecution rested its case against LaGrange.

The superintendent opened his defense with testimony from his wife and sister, using them to introduce statements that, out of proper decorum, would not be questioned by the prosecution. Then LaGrange launched into his own statement.

The most revealing material came in the contents of the full correspondence provided by LaGrange that the two men conducted after Pinney fled the country. At that time, LaGrange wrote that he believed Pinney a man who intended to do not only right but to do generously by all men. Pinney had overreached only to be deserted by cowardly partners and false friends. They urged Flora to obtain the divorce. Pinney had never committed a forgery nor did he owe the government one dollar. He piously said that he had been willing to sacrifice almost everything to provide a comfortable home for his wife. Besides, he did not get drunk anymore and had quit whoring around in a great measure. LaGrange told Pinney that he had employed Flora's mother at the mint to help out the family. Finally in February 1877 LaGrange told Pinney that the only way he could return would be to strike a compromise beforehand with the bankers holding the worthless navy pay certificates.

In closing, LaGrange stated that had he known of Pinney's grave crimes before coming to San Francisco, he would never have hired him. There were indeed frauds in the mint vouchers that he had discovered in the past month from that time period. The signatures were forged. Here were new accusations; but what had prompted this attempt at preempting the introduction of evidence? It would only be that Martin Davis, posted to the San Francisco Mint by Linderman, had made the discoveries after a thorough examination of the mint's records.

Now came the *mea culpa*. LaGrange held himself legally but not morally bound by the acts of Pinney as a result of carelessness or over confidence on his part. He offered to immediately replace any material found sold but not accounted for by Pinney.[34] LaGrange was offering to pay and make the whole affair go away. That had worked in the past, specifically the Pollock investigation. It was dead on arrival here.

Finally, on the night of August 6, the focus shifted to the Levy affair. Samuel Keith from the mint was questioned, sticking to his story that he had found the pieces in September 1874 and that his wife had subsequently given some or all of them to Mrs. Black. A detective followed, producing the gold and silver. Mrs. Black had told him that she kept the lot of clippings for three years, and six weeks previously had given them to Levy in exchange for a credit on her account of $2.25. The detective judged the pieces were worth about $12 by weight. At this point the commission adjourned to allow LaGrange to leave town for two or three days.[35]

LaGrange had to go to Placerville for the libel trial against the *Chronicle*. Much to the delight of the de Young brothers, owners of the newspaper, the proceedings had degenerated into the Republican Ring defending its actions. The *Chronicle* noted that LaGrange came to the trial one day quite late, well after testimony had commenced. He spent an inordinate amount of time combing his considerable mustache, his only remnant of military greatness. The reporter speculated that he did this to display his large emerald ring. The paper sarcastically noted that surely this ring was purchased from his salary at the mint.[36]

The commission did not reconvene until August 22 with Low informing the commission that Pinney had telegraphed from Placerville that he wanted to cross-examine LaGrange that night. Pinney was not now in the room. Low asked Pixley if he had any questions for LaGrange. He did not.

Low pressed LaGrange on Pinney's involvement in the borax, copper and zinc transactions. Then Low asked incredulously why LaGrange did not know of Pinney's poor character after the Hoag coal transactions came to light in the court case involving Pinney. LaGrange answered that he felt Hoag was lying. Continuing, Low could not understand why LaGrange had not called his loans to Pinney when the man became prosperous.

Clearly, in the commission's recess the mood of the commissioners had turned ominous; the questions posed were pointed and negative in implication. By that point, Martin Davis had had time to ferret out and brief the commissioners fully on the questionable dealings enumerated in the testimony.[37] They were clearly dealing with a pack of scoundrels and uncooperative vendors who did not want to kill the goose that laid such a lucrative golden egg at their doorstep. LaGrange's attorney, Edward Marshall sensed the change in tone and attempted to have LaGrange's examination stopped. He said the man loved to talk and that it was impossible for him to keep talking this way and not incriminate himself.

LaGrange got it together for a few moments until Pinney came into the hearing room. Pinney complained that he had not been told that the cross-examination of LaGrange was going to take place on this night. LaGrange for his part refused to answer any question of Pinney. The two men shouted at each other until Low rapped for order. Marshall told the commissioners that they could see what questioning from Pinney would cause. Pinney had more words for Marshall. Marshall, upon hearing Pinney's vitriol once more, said that that ended the matter, and he wished the investigation closed. The commissioners in unison rejected Marshall.

After a short, whispered conversation, the commission ruled that LaGrange should submit to Pinney's cross-examination. Marshall consulted with LaGrange and agreed, but the two parties must agree to be placed at opposite ends of the conference table. The commission agreed and ruled that it would take place the next evening in order to allow Pinney time to read the night's testimony.[38]

Meanwhile, the libel trial in Placerville came to a conclusion on August 24 after eighteen days with a hung jury. The *Chronicle* had not expected an acquittal. But in reality, a hung jury was just as good as the Republican Ring could not stand the adverse publicity of a retrial. The *Chronicle* noted, tongue in cheek, that there were miracles in politics as well as religion.[39]

Delayed a day, the commission hearing reconvened the evening of August 24. The early cross-examination dealt with whether LaGrange had received kickbacks for the sale of "condemned" materials. Pinney accused from the memorandum book and LaGrange denied. The questioning took a serious tone when Pinney produced a letter in LaGrange's hand asking that moneys from the sale of the condemned materials be applied against the mint's contingent fund rather than refunded to Treasury, written after the fact. Pinney danced around Marshall's question as to whether he ever stole letters out of LaGrange's letter book. Marshall asked why he had kept the letter so long. Pinney stated that it was a good thing to have in the house. People sometimes made mistakes under oath. It was a good thing to have handy. There was laughter in the room.

Finally, Pinney's questions hit upon a very sensitive subject--advances in gold coin to the San Francisco Assaying and Refining Works before equivalent refined bullion was deposited at the mint. LaGrange denied making any advances during the time Pinney was there. However, he did subsequently make advances to the refiner. LaGrange denied saying that if those men with whom he had accommodated with the advances did not stand in on the Pollock investigation that he would drag them all down. That was explosive; so explosive that none of the commissioners asked any follow-up questions.[40]

Pixley had no such qualms, asking if, at the time of the suspension of the Bank of California, LaGrange advanced on gold bars from $1 to $3 million dollars to various persons. LaGrange said that one evening, either before the suspension or on the night of the suspension, that he did receive a dray load of bullion after office hours. He had kept the mint open to receive the gold bullion, being requested to do so by the depositors. LaGrange would not identify the depositors. LaGrange could not state if the coin exchanged for the bullion had been to assist the banks. He could not remember the amount, but part of it came from the San Francisco Assaying and Refining Works. LaGrange had been to the refining company earlier that day to see about the delivery. The man in charge, Louis Garnett, had told him they wanted to make a large deposit later that day. LaGrange was certain that the works had not received coin from him before they delivered the refined bullion. However, if Garnett were to testify otherwise, LaGrange would have to accept that as fact because he regarded Garnett's word highly.

After more testimony with accusations flying, the commission adjourned to meet at the call of the chairman, this being the last of its regularly scheduled public sessions.

In an attempt to offset the damaging testimony in the final days of the hearing, Edward Marshall gave a spirited defense in a closing argument in LaGrange's behalf on August 31. The sewers reeking with the filth of this investigation were at last closed. All the lies had been told and had crystallized into perjuries. He assailed Pinney, denying him the possession of any cardinal virtue or even the shadow of one. The man had no soul. The administration of LaGrange at the mint had been the best in the history of San Francisco. Marshall expected a verdict of "not proven" from the commission.[41] In all, Marshall spoke for two and a half hours. He outlasted the opposition as no one wished to make a rebuttal.[42]

Linderman wrote Sherman that the hearing was now complete; however, the commission would hold off making a report for a period of time.[43] Yet the story was not quite done. A week later, the assistant United States attorney had finally fixed a date for the hearing of charges against Levy; however, Samuel Keith could not be found, having evidently left the city. The *Chronicle* noted that Mrs. Black had not been called before the commission to testify on the defalcation. The paper asserted that Keith's story was further in doubt as the clippings were more recent that he had claimed. The *Chronicle* questioned why Keith had not been arrested on the spot. Then the newspaper dropped the bombshell. It was well known in the neighborhood that Mrs. Black and Mrs. Keith were not on the best of terms before Mrs. Keith's death. On the other hand, Mrs. Black was very intimate with Mr. Keith.[44] Five days later the *Chronicle* reported that Keith was in Mexico, and the whereabouts of Mrs. Black was unknown.[45] They had arrested the wrong man, or maybe it was the right man in order to suppress the story.

Near the end of October, the *Chronicle*, having heard nothing, raised the issue of LaGrange's fate. The report given by the commission to Secretary Sherman on October 15, while whitewashing a daub, still presented charges strong enough to remove LaGrange.[46] The *Chronicle* was hearing rumors that LaGrange and the ring were getting up excuses for LaGrange and rounding up supporters to oppose his removal. Could it be that the ring was afraid that LaGrange, if sacrificed, might "peach" on them? LaGrange knew the inner workings of the ring and his testimony would obliterate their power base. Some who professed to know the true inwardness of the man believed Linderman to be open to attack. LaGrange's crime constituted a felony, and he should have been indicted by the United States grand jury.[47]

On November 24, 1877, the *Chronicle* broke the story that Hugh LaGrange would be allowed to resign, effective January 1, 1878. The newspaper did not want a replacement acceptable to Sargent or Linderman. They need not have worried about Sargent; he was finished politically. The newspaper wanted the president to appoint a man acceptable to California reform Senator Newton Booth.[48] That was not to be, the political plum went to the Treasury Commission's own Henry Dodge with his ill-defined relationship to the ring; he was Linderman's man.[49]

Pinney never served time and would go on to pursue a career as a stockbroker, ultimately on Wall Street, specializing in mining stocks.[50] Nor did Pinney ever make good on the fraudulent Navy Pay Certificates. Poor Flora Pinney just disappeared into the pages of history. Meanwhile, Billy Carr retired a gentleman farmer. All this time he had been amassing public lands at a steep discount in California's Central Valley.

Chapter 24

Dollar of Our Daddies

From his perspective of the secretary's position in the Treasury Building, John Sherman could look back at the Second Session of the Forty-Fourth Congress that opened on December 4, 1876, with some degree of relief; both he and the Republican Party had survived. While the newspaper headlines dealt with the deadlocked presidential election, Sherman had had his hands full in the Senate controlling the silver movement while, to a lesser extent, deflecting attempts to repeal resumption of specie payments. His efforts had been restricted by the need to avoid generating any controversy as the Republican party moved to secure Rutherford Hayes's election.

But Sherman was up against Missouri Representative Richard Bland, an uncompromising advocate for silver. Barely a week into the session, "Silver Dick" introduced legislation for a 412-1/2-grain standard silver dollar with unlimited legal tender, except where payment of gold coin was required by law. After two hours of debate in the House, the bill passed by an overwhelming majority.[1] The westerners viewed the bill as a market for the immense amount of silver coming from the Comstock Lode.

In the Senate, Sherman, again chair of the Committee on Finance, had dragged his feet.[2] He must maneuver to limit the legal tender of the silver dollar and restrict its coinage to preserve the gold standard while not generating controversy that would derail Rutherford Hayes's election.

On January 16, 1877, Sherman reported Bland's bill out of committee without recommendation. He would postpone action until the Silver Commission (established

Richard Bland entered the House of Representatives in 1873. He immediately became an uncompromising advocate for silver. Ultimately campaigning for the Democratic presidential nomination in 1896, he would lose to William Jennings Bryan on the fifth ballot.

at the end of the 1st Session of the 44th Congress) issued its report, for which the Senate had just granted an extension. At such time he would offer a substitute.[3] Sherman had just given qualified support for a legal tender silver dollar without fully staking out his position.

On February 4 Sherman tipped his hand. His substitute bill called for a standard silver dollar issued for the redemption of United States Notes on demand of the holder. This limited the issue of the proposed dollar. The bill also directed that the silver dollars were legal tender for all debts of the government except interest and principal of bonds expressly payable in gold.[4] Sherman had delayed for three more weeks; he had four more to go to the adjournment of this Congress.

A significant number of senators wanted the Silver Commission report in hand before considering action.[5] That report missed its new deadline, being delayed another week, leaving no time to debate the silver bills in the Senate before the Forty-Fourth Congress expired. Sherman had won this skirmish, but the battle was still to be fought.

The majority report of the Silver Commission was signed by John Percival Jones and Lewis Bogy from the Senate and Richard Bland and William Groesbeck from the House. In their view, the cause for the recent decline in the value of silver relative to gold was due mainly to Germany's demonetization of the metal, combined with the other European countries' switch to the gold standard. These actions in turn led to falling commodity and real estate prices, diminishing public revenues, and declining wages—all leading to multiple bankruptcies.

Led by Jones, the majority had just adroitly framed the political issue that would drive American politics for the rest of the 19th century. If only the United States would go to a bimetallic standard, "returning the dollar of our daddies," silver prices would advance to a par at the old ratio with gold. The deleterious effects of the Panic of 1873 would be reversed, and prosperity would reign across the country.[6]

Senator George Boutwell presented the minority report. He deemed it not expedient to authorize a silver dollar until a convention of the major commercial nations could agree upon a fixed relative value between the two metals. If done unilaterally by the United States, gold, having the superior value, would rapidly fall out of circulation and the demonetized and discarded silver of every nation would flow to the United Stated, causing the value of silver to steadily decline.[7]

With the battle lines drawn, Secretary of the Treasury John Sherman now had until October when the Forty-Fifth Congress convened to sort out his position.

Mint Director Henry Linderman's primary problem over this time period was of a simpler nature—effectively employ George Morgan within the engraving department at the Philadelphia Mint. Also should a standard silver dollar be authorized, Linderman would need a design in place to commence striking these coins immediately.

The first difficulty arose when Superintendent James Pollock could find no room for Morgan in the engraver's department or anywhere else, for that matter, at the Philadelphia Mint. Linderman had been forced to ask Morgan, freshly arrived from England, to conduct his work in his boarding house room. Consequently, Linderman felt it necessary to instruct both Pollock and engraver William Barber to afford Morgan every proper facility that he might require.[8]

Settling into his boarding house, Morgan visited the Philadelphia Academy of Fine Arts for the purpose of brightening his ideas and studying American art. He quickly made the acquaintance of the well-known artist and volunteer instructor at the academy, Thomas Eakins. The two became warm friends, and Morgan would use Eakins's home some two blocks from his boarding house as a makeshift studio.[9]

Once the Englishman was in place, Linderman created a competitive environment involving Morgan, William Barber, and in a new wrinkle, former assistant engraver Anthony Paquet. They were to submit new designs for the subsidiary silver coins—starting with the half dollar, using a head of Liberty and a heraldic eagle. By the end of October, Morgan already had one mold ready for the reducing machine. That indicated that he had arrived with design concepts in hand.

With the advent of 1877, Linderman pushed each artist to make experimental dies and provide him with wax impressions of their proposed designs. It was clear that Morgan was the frontrunner. Linderman waxed eloquent in his praise of the obverse paired with multiple reverse designs.[10] Liberty from a hub cut for the mint by Morgan was unlike any that had come before on United States coins. Linderman sought artistic critique of the work and asked Morgan to consider refinements to Liberty's chin and cap. The reverse design, an eagle with upraised wings surrounded by two laurel branches, Linderman thought good and had no suggestions.[11]

Up to this point, Morgan had kept his designs out of the mint. Linderman now foreclosed that option by asking that working dies for a half dollar using Morgan's design variations be prepared. However, Linderman tipped his hand stating that he was in no particular hurry for completion.[12] He was really looking for designs scalable to the size of a silver dollar.

Linderman did suffer one setback. The previous December, he had lost Philadelphia coiner Loudon Snowden, the most experienced in the organization, having been with the mint nearly 20 years.[13] Snowden left to take an appointment as postmaster of Philadelphia. His replacement, assistant coiner O.C. Bosbyshell, would prove competent enough, as time would quickly tell.

On February 20 Linderman was back communicating with George Morgan over his designs. Morgan had placed a distinctive inside ring of pearling within the inscriptions that defined the area for the head of Liberty. Linderman wanted to see the models without that ring. He also had seen some European coins with the prominent figure of a lion upon a coat of arms. He would like to try for a reverse using an eagle like that of the 20-cent piece placed upon a shield. Finally, he wanted modifications of Liberty's hair on the obverse.[14]

William Barber got wind of this request and commenced working on reverses of his own, employing an eagle upon a shield. A miffed Linderman told Pollock to have Barber in the future submit drawings to his office for consideration before progressing further with his designs.[15] Barber complained in response, requiring another note from Linderman to Pollock in which he admitted that it was quite proper for the engraver to have an opportunity to display his skill in the preparation of a die that had the figure of an eagle on the shield. The engraver was welcome to submit one or more drawings of new devices for Linderman's review. Then he added a postscript: Barber's work on new designs must not interfere in the least with the regular work of the engraver's office. One of the reasons for employing Morgan was so the engraver would not be required to perform work that would interfere with his regular duties.[16] William Barber had just lowered the chance that one of his designs would be chosen.

At the end of March, Anthony Paquet submitted his design for the proposed half dollar. Linderman praised it but made no effort to critique the design. The obverse head of Liberty was quite different and appealing. The reverse eagle, however, plowed no new ground. Perhaps Paquet hurt his chances when he asked Linderman to reimburse him for the preparation of the design's dies. He had had George Soley do it on his machine rather than take it to William or Charley Barber. Linderman refused to consider the payment.[17]

Under the guise of a competition for a new design for the half dollar, Henry Linderman actually was anticipating passage of silver dollar legislation. Linderman charged Barber, Morgan, and former assistant engraver Anthony Paquet with preparing designs for consideration: From Barber, J-1501 and 1502, and J-1524–1539; from Morgan, J-1503–1523; and from Paquet, J-1540 and 1541 (selected examples shown).

Barber (J-1526 and J-1538)

Morgan (J-1510 and J-1512)

Paquet (J-1540)

George Morgan now had the inside track in this design competition, wherever it led.

John Sherman had been secretary of the Treasury for less than a month when he quizzed Linderman on the manner in which the Bureau of the Mint acquired its silver bullion. Purchases of silver bullion for the subsidiary silver coinage were a major outlay for the public treasury. Linderman's rule was to purchase silver below the London rate and in no case to pay above it. Linderman would fix the acceptable price, and the superintendents of the mints and New York Assay Office would execute the purchases. If supplies still came up short, Linderman's office would make special purchases subject to the approval of the secretary of the Treasury.

There had been a deviation from this practice when the Nevada Bank of California negotiated an exclusive supply contract with payment made in 5 percent bonds priced at the gold equivalent for currency at New York or in gold coins at the preference of the secretary and concurrence of the seller. This agreement fell apart in August 1876 when silver prices in San Francisco, driven by the seasonal demand from the Far East, greatly exceeded the London market. Thereafter, Linderman bought on a non-exclusive basis from the Nevada Bank.

Linderman also frankly told Sherman that large purchases by the mint had moved the markets from time to time. The Far East demand coupled with the American needs for subsidiary silver had drained the silver supplies in Europe and the United States. Since November 1876, Linderman had been able to make no large purchase of silver without overpaying.[18]

As the summer of 1877 waned, debate over the form a re-monetization of the silver dollar heated up. Stanley Matthews, the man who took Sherman's seat in the Senate, spoke in Cleveland to Ohio Republicans advocating for a limited issuance of standard silver dollars[19] And, James Burnie Beck, now a senator, speaking at a mass meeting in Mason County, Kentucky, pledged that Southern Democrats were for the unconditional repeal of the Resumption Act of 1875 that Radical Republicans had fastened upon the country in the interest of foreign and domestic bondholders. Beck promised to restore the old standard silver dollar as a unit of value equal to gold. The dollar was demonetized in 1873 by fraud, falsehood, and suppression of the truth by the Radical Republicans and their foreign allies.[20] Beck had very adroitly given silver a place in Southern politics.

Answering on August 17, 1877, before a hometown crowd in Mansfield, Ohio, Sherman defended the Hayes Administration's monetary policy. He noted that the Treasury secretary was authorized under the Resumption Act of 1875 to issue bonds as well as use surplus revenues to accomplish redemption of greenbacks in gold. The balance of trade was in favor of the United States, meaning gold was flowing into the country. European demand for American agricultural products was surging. Sherman also tipped his hand that he was counting on a re-monetized, restricted-issue standard silver dollar to help secure resumption. On the other hand, Democrats were looking to an unlimited issue of re-monetized silver dollars as a step to inflating the monetary base.

Sherman had not been specific enough in his speech, and uncertainty over monetary policy began to take hold in October. Silverites knew that President Hayes favored resumption and would veto any bill repealing it. However, they believed he would not veto re-monetization. Reacting to this environment, a gold syndicate, led by financier August Belmont, charged with marketing the government bonds needed to generate the funds necessary for resumption, began to fear that re-monetization would grant legal tender status to silver dollars for the payment of the public debt. The syndicate pressed Sherman for a firm statement from the president on this issue. The Treasury secretary sidestepped, assuring them amendments in the Senate would stop any threat to the public credit by guaranteeing repayment of government bonds in gold alone. Sherman was counting on maintaining a close relationship with the Committee on Finance to carry this issue.

The Forty-Fifth Congress was called into special session on October 15, 1877, to address military appropriations. On that same day, Director Linderman recommended suspension of the receipt of deposits for coinage into trade dollars at the New York Assay Office and the Philadelphia Mint. Unspoken, he had fears that brokers would leak them into domestic circulation at face value, a substantial premium over their bullion value. There was a general shortage on the East Coast of one- and two-dollar notes with banks paying a premium for them to serve their customers. This problem would act as an accelerant for the domestic circulation of trade dollars. However, Linderman did not want the suspension to apply to either the San Francisco or Carson City mints. Sherman promptly approved the move.

On October 18 word had reached San Francisco of this action, and banker F.F. Low telegrammed in cipher to Linderman requesting confirmation. Linderman did not answer that day. Instead, the following day he asked Sherman to extend the suspension to San Francisco and Carson City. The San Francisco Mint now had on hand sufficient trade dollars to meet any demand in the immediate future on the West Coast. Sherman again concurred. In turn, Linderman sent the order to LaGrange at San Francisco by telegram that same day. However, Linderman went a step further that same day, notifying F.F. Low, fellow member of the former Treasury Commission, of the order.

LaGrange was the first to alert Linderman that the mint director had boxed himself into a corner. In a telegram LaGrange stated he could get no doré silver for his refinery because the depositors wanted trade dollars in return. Low put it more forcefully; if Linderman failed to coin trade dollars, his order would give Nevada Bank control of all the bullion business, including the doré silver. That telegram, in cipher, got Linderman's attention. He telegraphed back the following day that there were nearly two million trade dollars accumulated in San Francisco, proving there was little demand for export.

In a long letter, Low responded that this accumulation included 1,250,000 trade dollars in the bullion fund, and with the mint now closed for trade dollar deposits, those coins might just as well be on the moon. Low went on to complain that nearly all the trade dollars outside of the mint were in the control of Nevada Bank, and their management, in light of Linderman's suspension, had raised the price of trade dollars by two cents. Low, no friend of the Nevada Bank, even told Linderman that the San Francisco Mint was at that point almost idle. On November 5, Linderman yielded, asking Sherman to approve an order rescinding the suspension for the San Francisco and Carson City mints.[21]

On that same November 5, "Silver Dick" Bland again introduced his silver dollar bill in the House. It called for complete and unlimited re-monetization of the standard silver dollar, knowing full well that the Senate would make restricting amendments, necessitating compromise. There were 94 representatives absent in the House that day, tending to elections at home. While the vote in favor was overwhelming, when allowance was given for paired voting, a practice permitting members to vote in absence, the true majority was almost exactly two-thirds.[22]

Two days later, Belmont's gold syndicate also charged with refinancing outstanding Civil War debt at a lower interest rate told Sherman that the broad legal tender provision in the Bland bill would cause problems. Hayes considered the paying of public debt with silver coin a violation of the public faith. He supported silver dollars when treated as a subsidiary silver coin with limitations on legal tender. Had he gone public with his stance, the ensuing chaos in the market for the bonds would have been avoided.

Another two days after Sherman had been warned, the price of these refunding bonds fell below par in spite of the syndicate's repurchasing efforts to stabilize the situation. Sales were halted first in New York and then in Europe. Sherman would take no action, saying that the issue was still before Congress and therefore unresolved.[23]

The syndicate's point was that if silver was worth 92 cents in gold, the four percent bonds used for refinancing the public debt, selling at par based upon repayment in gold, would drop immediately from $100 to $92 if repayment in silver were permitted. Existing bondholders would dump their holdings onto the market, further damaging the public credit. Likewise, the price of imports would increase an equal amount to compensate for the prospect of being paid in the lower-valued silver.[24]

William Boyd Allison, viewed as a moderate on the issue of silver, was the successor to Sherman as chair of the Committee on Finance. His committee marked up the Bland Bill on November 20 and reported it to the full Senate the next day. In a blow to President Hayes and Sherman, the committee refused to limit the proposed silver dollar's legal tender status. However, it struck out the free coinage clause that allowed the bullion owner to have his silver coined at the mint for no cost.

In a concession to Sherman, Senator Allison insisted that these silver dollars be limited through a clause that authorized the secretary of the Treasury to purchase no less than $2 million per month of bullion or more than $4 million for their coinage. Without this limitation, Allison feared he would lose the moderate support necessary to hold a two-thirds majority. Both Allison and Senator Jones believed that, even with this restriction, the price of silver would increase to a point that a silver dollar would be equal in value to a gold dollar.[25]

William Allison came to the Senate in 1872. Serving as chair of the Committee on Finance in 1878, he put forth a compromise that satisfied neither the silver nor the gold interests but assured the re-monetization and mintage of the standard silver dollar.

Allison also announced his intention to offer an amendment calling for the president to invite the governments of the Latin Monetary Union as well as other European nations to a monetary conference for the adoption of a common ratio between gold and silver for the purpose of establishing an international bimetallic standard. Such a conference would be assured of success once the silver dollar had obtained parity with a gold dollar.

There was a problem with the bill. It instructed that the silver dollars would be issued in exchange for greenbacks and no other way. These United States Notes that would be redeemable in gold starting January 1, 1879, had a value greater than silver, meaning that no one in their right mind would exchange them for silver dollars. The only way these coins would leave Treasury was to be paid out on public debt obligations. However, these coins would then be scooped up and come right back to Treasury in the form of customs duties. In other words, the coins would not circulate.[26]

Syndicate sales of bonds slowed once again. Still, Allison held to his belief that Senate passage of a bill that exempted explicitly repayment of government debt in silver would be impossible. On November 23, another blow against sound money came from the House when it passed a bill repealing resumption by a vote of 138 to 120. Not veto proof by any means, but it put another crack into Sherman's armor.[27]

President Hayes now felt compelled to respond. He used as his medium his annual presidential message sent to Congress at the beginning of its regular session on December 3, 1877. His basic premise was that the working masses should be compensated in money that was of a fixed and unchangeable value. This permanent quality of money could only be gained by resumption of specie payments. In addition, Hayes was adamant that the outstanding bonds must be paid in gold. Hayes did grant that if a stable ratio of value could be maintained between silver and gold, the coinage of silver dollars would afford material assistance to the resumption of specie payments.[28] Everyone inferred from this message that Hayes would veto re-monetization of the standard silver dollar.

In the Treasury Report that followed the president's message, Sherman was unequivocal that under existing law the payment of principal and interest on government bonds in coin of less value than authorized by law at time of issue would not be tolerated. He meant to pay in gold coins.[29]

Sherman made a last personal appeal to Senator Allison in a letter of December 10. He wanted Allison to amend the bill such that it would not arrest the refunding of the public debt at the lower interest rate or prevent the sale of the 4 percent bonds so necessary for specie resumption. If not, the United States would not be able to sell bonds.[30]

As it became clear that no vote in the Senate on re-monetization would occur until after the holidays, petitions against the silver bill poured into Washington from the financial centers of New York, Boston and Philadelphia. In the far West, public enthusiasm for re-monetization of the silver dollar transformed John P. Jones into a political hero, earning him the political sobriquet: "Daddy of our dollars."

Ominously in early January, a meeting was called of the New York City Clearing-House, where balances from daily financial transactions were settled amongst its members. It was attended by the presidents of the largest and strongest banks, trust companies, and insurance companies in the city. In addition, representatives from the clearing-houses in Boston, Philadelphia, and Baltimore sent observers. It was decided to urge through the various financial institutions that the merchants, traders, and manufacturers place themselves upon a gold basis. Silver could be made by Congress a legal tender, but it could not be forced upon a community that refused to accept it.[31]

Debate on the silver dollar legislation commenced in earnest in the Senate on January 29. Various propositions began to take shape, the strongest being to increase the weight of the standard silver dollar to the point of equivalency, 434 grains, with the gold dollar. Those against the bill hoped that senators advocating an increase in weight would vote against a 412-1/2-grain silver dollar if they could not get their amendment passed.[32]

In early February California Senator Booth added a new consideration calling for the ability to deposit silver dollars at Treasury in exchange for silver certificates. These certificates would be receivable for customs, taxes, and all public dues. Booth wanted to address the cumbersomeness of the silver dollar in commerce.[33]

As the debate grew more spirited, the *New York Times* observed that there were two classes in the Senate clamoring for restoration of the silver dollar. One led by James Birney Beck insisted it would make money cheaper, and the other led by Senator Allen Thurman of Ohio insisted that it would equalize the value of the gold and silver dollars. Both could not be right, but both could be wrong.[34] However, it was now obvious that the most important aspect of the coming Senate vote would be whether the bill gained a two-thirds majority approval, making it veto proof.

A last-minute amendment to the bill authorizing silver dollars allowed depositors at the Mint to accept certificates in exchange for their bullion that would be used as currency. They would become known as Silver Certificates.

When the Senate convened on February 15. An exasperated Allison asked senators to finish debate on the silver bill and not adjourn until a vote was taken.[35] Allison got his way. On that Friday, the Senate rejected the free coinage clause of the House bill. A proposed international conference was accepted. At one point, it appeared that the vote would be at hand by four that afternoon. Yet, the *New York Times* went to press that night with no vote.[36]

The bill finally passed at 5 o'clock on the morning of February 16. The majority of the time had been taken rejecting amendments that increased the weight of the silver dollar or limited its legal tender. At 2:30 that morning, an amendment was passed that permitted the holders of silver bullion to deposit it at the mints in exchange for certificates to be used as currency. It eliminated the delay for coining and offered a convenient alternative to the heavy silver dollar in daily commerce. Its acceptance was in doubt when Senator Newton Booth stepped in with an amendment that the dollars first be coined and deposited at Treasury before being exchanged for certificates. This was the last serious and successful amendment to the bill.

The late-night debate had been an embarrassment to the decorum of the Senate. The *New York Times* noted that, as happened in night sessions, senators showed the effects of too much whisky and champagne. The scenes that early Saturday morning were considered extremely disgraceful. One account had seven senators deeply drunk before the early morning vote. Regardless, the margin gained was veto proof.[37]

The Silverites in the House acquiesced to the amended Senate version of their bill, in their consideration mutilated, reasoning that they could not, otherwise, get a needed two-thirds vote in the Senate to override the expected veto.[38] For Sherman the handwriting was on the wall; he ordered suspension on February 22 for a second and final time of coinage of the trade dollar that would be confusing in domestic commerce. As expected, President Hayes vetoed the bill, and it was promptly and perfunctorily overridden on February 28, 1878. This law would be known as the Bland Allison Act.

Linderman was prepared, announcing that the new silver dollars would be available at the Philadelphia Mint March 13.[39] The only hitch was that the mint and Treasury Department would only accept gold coins in exchange for the new coins.

After Linderman had returned from the San Francisco Treasury Commission investigation and settled into his office, he dropped all pretenses as to the purpose of the silver coin designs he had commissioned, ordering Barber and Morgan to prepare without delay dies for a silver dollar. He was specific with Morgan as to which design he wanted. With Barber, he wanted a reverse die with a representation of an eagle that he would pair with whichever head of Liberty the engraver preferred from his earlier work.[40] Senator Jones was even in this mix, wanting a six-piece set of the proposed designs for the new standard silver dollar.[41]

In November, Linderman was pressed on the capacity of the mints to strike silver dollars. New Orleans could add additional coinage when properly fitted up. Another mint, newly erected at Omaha or someplace in the Northwest would likewise augment coinage.[42] Before the dust settled from this legislation, Linderman would also have to provide an estimate to place the Denver Mint in service to strike gold and silver. Here he had to admit that the existing building was not capable of supporting a minting operation; the only savings accruing would be the cost of the land.[43]

On December 8, 1877, Linderman gave Secretary Sherman specimen dollar coins of Barber and Morgan. Sherman, in turn, took them to the president. The secretary stated that they went off like hot cakes.[44] Linderman then asked Superintendent Pollock for additional pattern coins to distribute, including those that Jones had requested. Afterwards Linderman expanded the distribution to include officers of the Philadelphia Mint but instructing that the coins only be struck in gold and silver as using other metals had led to complaints from coin collectors.[45]

While no official designation of the design to be used for the new dollar coin had been made, by February 1878 it was obvious in the engraving department that it would be Morgan's work. Linderman pushed Superintendent Pollock to have trial specimens to provide the Assay Commission when they met in the middle of the month.[46] While in Philadelphia for that meeting, Linderman asked Morgan for some slight changes to the reverse. He told Pollock to press Morgan on the changes on February 21, revealing to the superintendent that this was the design he intended to use for the dollar coin. It was Sherman's intent to issue these coins as soon after the bill became law as possible.

Linderman also shared with Pollock the basis for his choice. The designs of both Morgan and Barber exhibited high skill as well as artistic taste with little difference, if any, in their merits. Linderman based his selection on the design with the lowest relief requiring the lightest striking pressure to bring up the devices and inscriptions.[47]

The formal recommendation of Morgan's design from Linderman to Secretary Sherman was issued February 28, the date that President Hayes's veto was overridden. Transmitting a specimen, the mint director provided a full description.

> The obverse of the coin bears a free cut head of Liberty crowned with a Phrygian cap decorated with wheat and cotton, the staples of the country. On the reverse surrounded by an olive wreath is an eagle with outspread wings bearing in his talons a branch of olive and bundle of arrows, emblems of peace and war. This specimen has been selected not only for quality of design but also for the exceptionally low relief of devices, ensuring protection from abrasion and enabling them to be brought up in striking by a minimum pressure.[48]

President Hayes and Secretary Sherman approved the choice and requested the first and second pieces struck respectively.[49]

There was one more chapter to this story. Linderman wanted changes to the reverse of the dollar coin, specifically reducing the tail feathers of the eagle from eight to seven. Morgan completed the new hub for this modification on March 25. But the working dies would not be ready until April 2. However, Morgan offered to "enter this hub" into 50 dies made from the old hub and have them ready in a couple days.[50] In the press to get silver dollars into circulation, the decision to re-hub was made. A screw press was used to impress the positive image from the new seven tail-feather hubs into the existing negative image of eight tail feathers on the working dies. These "double-impressed" working dies were then placed into production, creating the 7 over 8 Tail Feathers silver dollar. Linderman's penchant to tinker would exhibit itself again, resulting in two more slight variations of the seven-tail feather variety as the year progressed.

At 52, Henry Linderman was in full stride now as director of the Mint. When his term expired the following December, there was no question in anybody's mind that he would seek and receive another five-year appointment.

The new standard silver dollar would become known as the Morgan dollar for its designer.

Chapter 25
Linderman's Demise

If Henry Linderman had left San Francisco at the conclusion of the Treasury Commission hearing feeling he had successfully avoided a potential political black eye and that all would be well, he was sadly mistaken. For starters his report hardly condemned Hugh LaGrange, holding him responsible for $4,245 of goods purchased but not delivered to the mint and another $2,430 missing from the sales of old material.[1] Linderman, while taking the necessary action to remove LaGrange, had erred in applying too much whitewash to the wrongdoings in the commission's final report. For those in the know, this report grossly understated the illicit activities at the San Francisco Mint.

Infuriated, the editors of the *Chronicle* began to dig, picking apart Linderman's most recent annual report issued on November 13 that year. In that document, Linderman stated that he had purchased 26.6 million ounces of silver over the eighteen previous months at an average rate below the London market. The newspaper pointed out that these numbers were slanted; seven-eighths of the most recent purchases were above the London market rate. They believed that no one man in government should have the power at his sole discretion to purchase $30 million of silver in trades with banks of his choosing instead of in the open market. The *Chronicle* went further, insinuating a cozy relationship existed between Linderman and the Nevada Bank and Frederick Low at the Anglo-California Bank. The paper accused Linderman of communicating with Low in cipher, conveying valuable information in advance of public knowledge.[2] Someone was feeding inside information to the newspaper.

The *Chronicle* continued to do its their homework over that winter of 1877-78. Charges were made and forwarded to an investigative committee of Congress. However, the newspaper held back on making anything public until leaks appeared in Washington. On March 6, 1878, just in time to tarnish the new silver dollars, the charges were published in systematic and comprehensive form.

The *Chronicle* claimed that Henry Linderman spearheaded an effort to head off a *bona fide* investigation of every arm of the federal government in San Francisco, run as a political machine with certain spoils men making large illicit gains. The peculiar commission that Linderman constituted had no authority of law, no power to subpoena papers or testimony. Taking care to publish each session, every witness was placed in the unenviable position of an informer, some even being browbeaten by the commissioners. Still testimony had revealed a major theft of copper; yet that was suppressed from the commission's final report. LaGrange was allowed to resign when he should have been prosecuted. The new superintendent had ties to the Republican ring and no house cleaning of the political appointees at the San Francisco Mint had taken place.

A specific charge that would subsequently prove to be distorted stated that Linderman advanced information through coded telegraph messages to F.F. Low at Anglo-California Bank in October 1877 revealing the pending suspension of the coinage of trade dollars. When that order became public knowledge in San Francisco thirty-six hours later, the price of trade dollars, in the face of strong commercial demand, advanced 4 percent. Subsequently an employee of Western Union was discharged for sharing these dispatches with the newspaper.[3]

Three days later, the *Chronicle* made another allegation. Linderman was the head of a "Mint Ring" and was at the bottom of the demonetization of the silver dollar in 1873, one of the most flagrant jobs ever afflicted upon the people of the United States. It was well known that he was in personal speculations with Billy Ralston and that the Bank of California recognized his claim as a creditor for $25,000 at its failure, even though he was not on the books as a depositor. The paper implied that the silver questions currently plaguing the country were the unintended consequences of this trick that the mint ring played on the people.[4]

As if on cue, the *Cincinnati Commercial* swung the next blow on March 25. Their topic was the bullion fund and the cozy dealings of the mint with the San Francisco Assaying and Refining Works. The article charged that as much as $1 million of the bullion fund was removed from time to time and that Linderman was fully knowledgeable of this fact. The newspaper then spelled out in terms any reader could understand how Ralston gained unsecured loans with Charles Felton's aid and advances of refined bullion by the San Francisco Assaying and Refining Works to the Bank of California. The paper questioned why Linderman did not look into the allegations that Ralston was using the bullion fund at the time of the removal of Cochran and Harmstead. It then speculated whether Linderman's personal intimacy with Ralston and the generous hospitality extended to him at Ralston's country mansion had anything to do with it.

Next the *Cincinnati Commercial* related the story of LaGrange's removal of bullion from the refining works at the time of Ralston's demise. The paper, however, printed key details that LaGrange had failed to provide in his testimony before the Treasury Commission and that did not come to light in subsequent questioning by the commissioners. The removal of a million dollars of bullion occurred at midnight on the night of the Bank of California's failure. It was rumored in San Francisco that LaGrange had acted upon receipt of a telegram from Linderman instructing the superintendent to save the government from loss from the failure.

The day following the removal of bullion from the San Francisco Assaying and Refining Works, it became known that the main portion of the bullion taken was not owned by Ralston but primarily by the Nevada Bank of James Flood and William O'Brien. No public complaint was ever made or even threatened. Instead the assets of the refinery came under control of the Nevada Bank. Whether this action made Flood and O'Brien whole, no one would ever say.

There was more; Ralston was acting as stockbroker for the director of the mint. Among the assets of the Bank of California at its failure was the indebtedness of Linderman for $60,000 by reason of either the bank or Ralston having carried stock purchased on margin for Linderman's account. When mining share prices declined, Ralston carried Linderman rather than make a call for the cash necessary to cover the loss in value.

After Ralston's financial collapse, the Nevada Bank assumed Linderman's indebtedness to the Bank of California. What was of more importance to the Silver Kings was Linderman's inspection of the Consolidated Virginia and California Mines just prior to the Bank of California's failure. Mining share prices had plummeted from already low levels in the ensuing financial disarray. The report issued by Professor Rogers under Linderman's influence was published in October and vastly overstated the reserves of the two mines, influencing the value of their shares as well as the value of the whole Comstock Lode.

Linderman's favors were not yet done. The Nevada Bank attempted to "bull" the English silver market in 1877 by purchasing one million ounces of the metal. They were hoping to firm up the market price and then unload a large inventory built up at their two mines. Just the opposite happened; the price of silver dropped precipitously, leaving the bank more exposed than ever. Linderman agreed to come to the bank's aid, purchasing one million ounces at a previously agreed price some 2.5 cents above the then current market quote. What made the situation reek was that at the time of the purchase, the San Francisco Mint posted a notice that silver was not needed in the immediate future and no bids for purchase would be taken.[5]

Leave it to the *Chronicle* to dig even deeper into the stock transactions that seemed to be at the root of the questionable actions of Linderman after the bank failure. The story went all the way back to the fall of 1869 when Linderman and John Jay Knox came to San Francisco on their investigative tour. Vague rumors were making the rounds of Ralston's surreptitious removal of gold coins from the sub-treasury that previous July. Instead of looking into the matter, Linderman had urged Secretary Boutwell to authorize gold transfers from the East Coast to the West Coast by telegraph through the sub-treasuries. Ralston had been so appreciative of this help that he bought on-margin a block of Crown Point and Belcher mining stocks for $3,500 in Mrs. Linderman's name. More importantly, should the transaction ever be questioned, Linderman was in the clear. The Victorian standards of the times dictated that a wife would never be questioned concerning the dealings of her husband.

Linderman subsequently badgered Ralston over and over concerning Mrs. Linderman's stock holdings. Ralston caught Belcher stock on a rise and sold, clearing a profit on the Linderman holding of $25,000, a tremendous return on the initial investment. In the summer of 1875, Linderman telegraphed Hugh LaGrange to draw Mrs. Linderman's profits from Ralston. It was at this meeting with LaGrange that Ralston called Linderman an old hog.

Ralston had had a problem. He had reinvested the money as part of a transaction to purchase 1,000 shares of Consolidated Virginia and California on margin in an effort to demonstrate to Flood and O'Brien that he had faith in their mines. Mrs. Linderman's share of the purchase was 300 shares. Then the downward break in mining share prices occurred. The value of Mrs. Linderman's shares dropped out of sight and faced a margin call of $60,000. It then fell to LaGrange to deliver the bad news to Linderman that his profit was not only lost but he was deeply in debt.

With the failure of the Bank of California, Flood and O'Brien picked up this indebtedness and promptly wrote it off. Not withstanding this break, Linderman did not let up on Bill Sharon, serving as executor of the Ralston estate. He became intolerably annoying to Sharon, insisting that he be given the profits from the sale of the Belcher stock. Finally on the day following the announcement that operations of the reorganized Bank of California would resume, Linderman sent a letter to Sharon congratulating him on his herculean efforts to re-establish the bank. Could not his wife's claim be settled now? Opening the dispatch, Sharon showed it to a person present and asked, "How is that for taste?" The *Chronicle* snidely observed that it was the taste of a hog! Linderman got his wife's $25,000.[6]

Unbelievably, there was more of a personal nature. The *Chronicle*, complained that when A.B. Linderman accompanied his brother to the West Coast, he always drew an exorbitant salary and performed work easily done by others on site in San Francisco. When Henry Linderman's son came to San Francisco to serve as clerk to the Treasury Commission, someone else did the work while the young man stayed at the Palace Hotel drinking and playing billiards.

Waiting a couple days to allow readers to digest the latest accusations, the *Chronicle* next revealed the coal purchase from Garret Linderman at prices supposedly above market. The report that LaGrange made to Linderman on the trial of this coal at the mint was printed in the paper.[7] Also, there was the contribution of the four operative officers at San Francisco of $1,000 for poor Mrs. Linderman's welfare.[8]

The final blow came as a result of the actions of A.B. Linderman while supervising the construction of the nitric acid refinery in San Francisco. He overstepped his authority as the project neared completion by letting of a two-year contract to provide the acid for the new refinery. The total value of the contract was estimated to be $100,000. A.B. Lindermen awarded the contract to the low bidder and sent a telegram in LaGrange's name to his brother seeking approval of the action. Linderman sent his concurrence directly to LaGrange who now became aware that all was not right in the process. A short time before the first delivery, LaGrange learned that A.B. Linderman had received a note payable to him for $1,000 from the supplier. LaGrange told the contractor that he would decline to receive any acid deliveries unless A.B. Linderman returned the note. The contractor insisted the note was a forgery. At this point, Henry Linderman arrived in town and when presented with the note by LaGrange, wrote cancelled on it and put it in his pocket. Still another $14,000 in notes were given to A.B. Linderman extending over the life of the contract. They were subsequently offered for sale at a discount to Flood and O'Brien. Flood declined to purchase the notes. Meanwhile the notes became public knowledge, putting both Linderman brothers in hot water. A.B. Linderman was packed off on the next train east. Henry then met with Flood and threw the notes into the fire.[9]

In fact, the articles in the *San Francisco Chronicle* did get their desired response in Washington. George Parkinson traveled east as an expert in the matter, meeting with Senator Newton Booth and Representative John Glover in mid-May 1878. He even gained an audience from President Hayes. Parkinson presented seven charges broadly structured around the revelations printed in the *Chronicle* the preceding two months.[10,11] John Love, attorney general for California when Booth was governor, had assisted in drawing up the charges.[12] Parkinson was clearly Booth's man and Booth wanted control of the San Francisco Mint. The other expert in this affair was George Edelman, the former deputy treasurer in the New York Assay Office. It had been Edelman who worked on behalf of Eugene Kelly in attempting to block the legislation that facilitated the exclusive refining contract between the San Francisco Mint and the San Francisco Assaying and Refining Works. However, the most damaging of the allegations and substantiating information could only have come from one man who was not going to be present to testify—Hugh LaGrange!

Representative John Glover conducted numerous investigations into expenditures in the Treasury Department, most of which came to naught or implicated members of his own party. He flubbed the one real case he uncovered against Mint Director Henry Linderman.

The questionable link in this affair was Representative John Glover, chair of the House Committee on Expenditures in the Treasury Department. He had first been elected as a Democrat to the Forty-Third Congress, beginning March 4, 1873. His performance had been so lackluster that it took 227 ballots before he gained the Democratic nomination in his state political convention for the Forty-Fourth Congress.[13] Now in his third term, he had latched onto this committee, designed to harass John Sherman, as a pathway to a more prominent role in the House of Representatives.

Even the *New York Times* had taken note of Glover. In April 1878 they reported gleefully upon his activity. The man was now on the highway to success as an investigator of crooked dealings and corrupt practices. His net had been cast many places but hauled up empty. Or rather his net tended to bring up Democrats and not Republicans.[14] Then in June 1878 he claimed that he had discovered $19 million missing from Treasury from the time of Secretary Hugh McCulloch in the 1860s. This accusation was quickly claimed as totally absurd by the United States treasurer as an amount so large as to be impossible to hide.[15] Glover was a loose cannon with no one taking him seriously.

After the fact, the *New York Times* reported that Glover's investigative technique was unorthodox at best. Glover often examined witnesses alone. Other times it was an "expert" that officiated at the examination. Few knew the accusations brought against them. However, the *Times* complimented Glover for raising the committee from a non-entity to a fourth-class power.[16]

Linderman could see the inquisition that was coming and reached out to Glover in mid-April asking that the Congressman afford the mint director the opportunity to be heard. The first inquiry on the April 27 concerned the suspension of trade dollar coinage in October 1877 in San Francisco. The use of cipher in F.F. Low's communications with Linderman seemed to indicate that the banker was receiving advance knowledge of the order. Linderman maintained it was Low who initiated the use of cipher and that Linderman had communicated the stoppage to others that same day.[17]

Linderman also stonewalled Glover when he could. Glover asked for the amount paid for the services of the commissioners and clerks during the Treasury Commission hearings in San Francisco. Linderman replied that he had no record of these payments. They were paid from an appropriation made by Congress for that purpose and administered by the secretary of the Treasury.[18]

Matters began to grow testy in May. Glover asked for backup paperwork and telegrams regarding doré silver purchases in certain months of 1875. George Edelman, acting on Glover's behalf, asked for certain correspondence of Louis Garnett of the San Francisco Assaying and Refining Works which Linderman provided. On May 11 Linderman reminded Glover that at the last meeting of his committee, the congressman had directed the stenographer to allow Linderman to examine all statements and testimony given by Edelman and others. As Linderman did not know how to locate the stenographer, he would call on the committee's room in hopes of being able to see that testimony. At that same time, he would help to unscramble any cipher needed.[19] That was a not-so-subtle quid pro quo.

Now the pressure began to ratchet up on Linderman. Instead of answering questions, he was going to have to testify before Glover's committee. To better prepare his testimony, Linderman called for Martin Davis, now assigned to the Philadelphia Mint to come to Washington for three or four days of official business.[20]

The Senate seemingly joined the fray on May 10, asking in a resolution for all correspondence regarding the suspension of trade dollar coinage in October 1877. The originator of this resolution was Aaron Sargent. Linderman provided the requested papers showing his responses were never in cipher and justified his actions as needed to prevent trade dollars from entering domestic circulation. The timeline of the correspondence was such that F.F. Low could not have gained any advantage unless LaGrange delayed in making the order public.[21] Sargent had seemingly lobbed a softball at Linderman, allowing him to hit it out of the ballpark. However he had an ulterior motive. It also exonerated both the Anglo-California Bank and the Nevada Bank. The last thing these banks wanted was for the committee to come to San Francisco on a fact-finding mission. The *Chronicle* would still maintain there had been profits made on trade dollars from inside information but the evidence was far from conclusive.[22]

Next Linderman had to deal with the accusation by Edelman that his examination of the New York Assay Office had been obstructed by its superintendent, Thomas Acton.[23] There were also claims of favoritism shown to certain of the depositors at the assay office. Linderman wanted Acton and Davis to testify and he wanted an opportunity to question Edelman. Linderman claimed that Edelman had made false statements and he trusted that the privilege of cross-examining the man would not be denied.[24]

It was not to be. Linderman was forced to submit Martin Davis's written and notarized statement.[25] Even worse, Glover's requests for more correspondence kept coming. Linderman apparently learned of the testimony of George Parkinson from an article in the *Chronicle*. May 30 found him requesting a copy of Parkinson's testimony and offering to send a clerk to perform the work so as not to inconvenience Glover.[26] On June 3 Linderman submitted his final answers to Edelman's statements.[27]

With testimony complete, Linderman on June 8 filed an addendum. This addition addressed the committee's question concerning Linderman's ownership of mining stocks. Linderman had replied in the negative. Now he was admitting that it had slipped his mind but a warm personal friend, Alvinza Hayward, had voluntarily purchased and held for a time for Linderman some shares of a mining stock. No profit resulted and Hayward had not been a seller of silver bullion to the mint.[28]

Linderman's last appearance before the committee was June 14, 1878.[29] With the adjournment of this session of the Forty-Fifth Congress pressing, Glover rushed his committee report, submitting it to Secretary Sherman and President Hayes. Sherman abruptly concluded that no action would be taken until an inquiry could be made that was fair to Linderman, giving the mint director a full opportunity to defend himself.[30]

With Sherman failing to take immediate action, more sinister forces came into play. An unauthorized article purporting to come from Glover appeared on June 17 in *Philadelphia Press* and *National Republican* newspapers. The source was George Wedell, formerly of the New York Assay Office and currently an expert for Glover's committee.[31] One statement that had not previously been aired in the *Chronicle* involved the payment well over market for a purchase of silver bullion.[32] Linderman went to Glover to complain about the leak and persuaded the congressman to issue of letter on June 24 stating that the article publicized was unauthorized. The points contained in the article were never developed before the committee.

Edelman, when confronted with the article, felt compelled to send a letter to the *Philadelphia Times* and *New York World*, setting the record straight. In fact, Glover had authorized Edelman's letter that summarized the key charges against Linderman that were based upon in the various findings published in *Chronicle*.[33]

Linderman, upon seeing the Edelman letter, made public the letter from Glover over the unauthorized allegations. Confusion reigned over whether or not the Glover letter referred to the Edelman letter. Thus Linderman effectively blunted Edelman's charges. By the time Glover wrote a letter to the *Philadelphia Times* setting the record straight on July 8, first impressions had been set and the damage was done.[34] Linderman, sensing matters shifting to his favor, pressed Sherman to move forward with an inquiry.[35]

As this investigation was playing out, Linderman also had to address the need for added capacity to fulfill the silver dollar mintage requirements of the Bland Allison Act. New Orleans was the front runner simply because the facility was in place with only equipment upgrades and replacements necessary. This mint had the added advantage of easy access to Mexican silver. The two big bonanza mines of the Comstock had peaked and were now starting to deplete with no deeper finds expected, raising questions about the ability of domestic production to solely meet the mint's needs.[36]

No sooner had the moneys been appropriated than a yellow fever epidemic in New Orleans caused the death of the melter and refiner. The coiner then moved over to take the melter and refiner's position. Linderman was forced to stop preparations for ninety days.[37] During the interim, the superintendent, Michael Hahn became embroiled in local politics and ended up on the wrong side of President Hayes. Hayes removed him in December and in an unfathomable move, appointed the ancient politician Henry Foote, Bill Stewart's father-in-law, to the position. This left Linderman free to send Martin Davis to be the new coiner; he needed someone with actual coining knowledge.[38]

Finally, in an ultimate irony, Linderman told Sherman on July 11 that there was no more room at the Philadelphia Mint to store silver dollars. The coin was not circulating in the East.[39]

The investigation and subsequent trying of Linderman's case in the newspapers left the mint director a used up man. He had held the job for almost five years and his detail-oriented management style, delegating little to his subordinates, had taken a toll on his health. He took an extended leave of absence on August 2 that was planned for five weeks but extended an extra five days. October found him out again.

By December it was common knowledge that Linderman was in ill health; he had been absent from Washington for a month or more. With his term of office expiring December 7, 1878, there was open speculation about his reappointment that had been up in the air since the Glover hearings. With Congress coming back into session, Hayes would have to make a move.

Sherman gave the first indication. On December 6 the secretary rejected a request by Glover to be permitted to examine Linderman's papers on a fishing expedition. Sherman would however furnish the originals or copies of any specific documents Glover desired. Glover's own party had not re-nominated him for another term; he was now a lame duck and Sherman easily brushed him off.[40]

Still President Hayes did not send Henry Linderman's name to the Senate for confirmation. Glover would later reveal that he had an understanding with the president that Linderman would not be nominated until the investigation had been completed.[41] The *San Francisco Chronicle* speculated that Linderman would get that nomination. However there were two other names in the running: Loudon Snowden, the current postmaster at Philadelphia and James Pollock, although the former director's support was not considered strong.[42]

After Christmas, Henry Linderman made an appearance in the office working partial days until the end of the month. He had celebrated his fifty-fourth birthday the day after Christmas.

Henry Linderman passed away at his home in Washington on January 27, 1879. His family bitterly stated that Glover's investigation had aggravated his sickness and hastened his death. John Sherman seconded the family's emotions; being quoted as saying that Glover's committee had hounded Linderman into his grave on false charges

In this image of Henry Linderman, the Mint director shows the toll his detail-oriented management style at the Bureau of the Mint had taken upon his health. He had just turned fifty-four at his death.

For John Glover, the one big fish ensnared in his net had just escaped. Glover accused Linderman of deliberately stalling the investigation in order to prevent the issuing of a report before that session of Congress adjourned in June. Glover ungraciously claimed that Linderman, when he saw that the investigation was going to drag into the December session of Congress, took to his bed ill. After his death, the Republican on the committee objected to releasing a report on a dead man and asked that the evidence be printed without the concluding report. In response Glover placed in the *Congressional Record* some negative remarks against Linderman.[43]

Henry Linderman should have been considered the father of the modern Bureau of the Mint. Yet his place in history would be tarnished by his greed.

Chapter 26
Grasping the Golden Ring

John Sherman was never known for his outgoing personality; he exuded no magnetism. Behind his back he was known as the "Ohio Icicle." Yet as the "Season" in Washington, D. C. kicked off on New Years Day 1878, his home was the center of attention. It was totally out of character and yet there was an obvious reason.

The object of this attention was his niece, 20-year-old Elizabeth Sherman. Lizzie had been invited to spend the Season with her uncle's family. This young girl immediately attracted all the eligible young men in town. One would never at this point have guessed that her future would involve an intimate friendship with the noted historian Henry Adams. That Lizzie would be an advocate within the Sherman family for Augustus Saint-Gaudens. So much so that the family would see her personality in Saint-Gaudens' Angel of Victory in the Sherman Monument—the inspiration for his standing Liberty design for the twenty-dollar gold piece.

For Lizzie's mother the attention of the young men was the point; she was anxious to obtain a good match for her youngest daughter. Lizzie's father, Charles, the retired judge for the United States District Court of Northern Ohio, was in failing health and the family's finances were precarious.

This was Lizzie's second Season in Washington, so she knew the ropes. She had the social connections through the Sherman family name. She also had the beauty and charm without the vanity that made her all the more attractive to her male suitors. The receptions were dazzling, and John Sherman made sure that the family attended

Donald Cameron

all of them, including at the Executive Mansion. She even met Madame Modjeska, in town to play Camille in the Dumas play about a Parisian prostitute. The strait-laced John felt the play too much, so Uncle "Cump," the grizzled old general, William Tecumseh Sherman, agreed to escort Lizzie. Besides, she was his favorite niece. It was a time of freedom and gaiety for Lizzie. She had just allowed her family to push her into rejecting a suitor back in her hometown of Cleveland. And yet, there were rumors that this young beauty was not available; Uncle John had arranged a match.

Gradually the name of Donald Cameron began to be mentioned in Lizzie's letters to her mother in Cleveland. Cameron had succeeded to his father Simon's Senate chair the preceding March. As such, he was heir to his father's Pennsylvania political machine. He was a 44-year-old widower with six children, ages 7 through 20. To those in Washington, it seemed an odd alliance. The two families had not been close with Cump running afoul of Simon Cameron early in the Civil War when Cameron, as secretary of war, questioned the general's mental stability. However, all the doubters had to do was look at the map. Pairing the Keystone State with Ohio created a formidable political power in the center of the United States. Nor was it lost on John Sherman that Donald Cameron had produced the shove that propelled Hayes to the Republican presidential nomination in 1876. Still there were risks. Cameron in a conversation discussing the upcoming 1880 presidential election had been quoted that it was not a personal matter with him. He was sincerely patriotic, but he was for the man who could win.

Lizzie made it only to the end of January before agreeing to marry Cameron. However, her terms were not the most encouraging for the proposed union. She insisted that the engagement remain a secret until she decided to make it public. She intended to have a gay time over the course of the Season, and she would flirt as much as she wished. She kept the senator at arm's length during this period, seeing him only once or twice a week. Love was nowhere to be seen in this arrangement. One gossip writer had the nerve to call the pair the "Beauty and the Beast."

When the engagement was announced, Lizzie's mother was, of course, satisfied. Her father and Cump said nothing. None of Cameron's children was pleased, particularly the eldest daughter who would be bumped from serving as the senator's hostess for Washington events. John Sherman's wife suggested the wedding be held in

Washington. Lizzie declined; perhaps she understood that her wedding would become a sideshow in a veritable political circus if held in the nation's capital. It would be in Cleveland, but the date now became an issue.

On the evening of Saturday, March 9, 1878, the betrothed couple was met by Lizzie's brother and sister at a suburban rail station outside of Cleveland. General Sherman was part of the party that disembarked the train. It was to be a low-key but formal visit to the home of the intended bride. Nevertheless, the press gained advance notice and described the party as quite fatigued by the journey with Lizzie being lame, scarcely able to walk and supported by the senator and her brother from the railcar to the carriage. Lizzie had sprained her ankle. Cameron returned to Washington the following Monday while Lizzie stayed on in Cleveland.[1]

Lizzie was using her sprained ankle as an excuse to postpone the wedding until the following fall. Cameron balked; he wanted the marriage that spring. It was Cump who drew the short straw to convince Lizzie that a May wedding was in the offing. May 9 was to be the appointed date.

John Sherman had more on his mind than the wedding of his niece that winter and spring of 1878. Thomas Ewing's bill for the outright repeal of resumption had passed the House and was in the hands of the Committee on Finance in the Senate at the start of 1878 and promised real trouble. Ewing, a fellow Ohioan, was the son of the former secretary of the Treasury and related by marriage to Sherman. Nevertheless, he was a staunch foe.

The combination of this repeal bill and the pending silver dollar re-monetization had brought sales of the 4 percent bonds needed for resumption to a standstill. To date, Sherman had in the treasury $25 million in proceeds from these bonds and a revenue surplus over prior expenditures of $30 million. These funds were not enough to ensure resumption. However, the prospects were still positive. The export of bullion had been stopped while exports of domestic products had greatly increased, adding strength to the budding economic recovery. Perhaps most important, agriculture prices were firming.[2] On January 14, 1878, Sherman terminated the agreement with August Belmont's syndicate that included the Selig Brothers charged with placing the bonds to fund the resumption in hopes of gaining better pricing in light of the strengthening economy.

Sherman's actions were further complicated by a move in Congress to force repayment in U.S. Notes of the 5-20 six-percent bonds issued during the Civil War being called in the concurrent refunding. To head off this movement in Congress, Sherman, after the passage of the Bland-Allison Act, gave testimony to the committees with oversight in both Houses. The more important of the two was the House Committee on Currency and Banking where Sherman could expect a real grilling. The committee chair, A. H. Buckner of Missouri was not disposed to interfere with the experiment of resumption. However, Buckner had his doubts. On the third day of testimony, Buckner believed Sherman had faith in the success of resumption. However, he observed that if Sherman failed, he would be the "deadest man politically" that ever lived.[3]

In the Senate, Sherman had a different kind of problem. Thomas Ferry was president pro tempore and on the Committee on Finance. The bill repealing resumption had sat in committee during the entire session. Indications were that the bill would be reported out favorably by a majority of one, including Ferry. Sherman had had frequent conversations with Ferry on the subject. While a veto certainly would be forthcoming from Hayes, passage of the repeal bill would greatly weaken Sherman's hand in negotiating the sale of the needed bonds.

With maybe an inkling of what Ferry would do, Sherman had to move forward with the financiers now that Congress had received his testimony. The secretary traveled to New York, meeting first with the Belmont Syndicate that included the Selig brothers. Initial negotiations hung up when the syndicate told Sherman they would have to wire their principal backer, Rothschild, in London in order to move forward. Sherman contacted the New York bankers the following day for an alternative offer. On the third day the bankers withdrew from consideration. After some tense back and forth, Sherman found himself waiting while the syndicate again sought permission from Rothschild to do the deal. That approval came on the fourth day. Now Sherman could borrow the necessary funds to implement resumption of specie payment on January 1, 1879.

Sherman was hailed in the Eastern newspapers when the deal was announced. In the West where the financial issues were less well understood, the press was either indifferent or opposed. More importantly, the logjam broke in the Senate's Committee on Finance on the House bill repealing resumption. The bill that was reported on April 17 gutted the House version.[4]

The wedding approached all too soon for Lizzie. On the appointed day, she threatened not to go through with it, but the Sherman women gave her no choice. Lizzie had evidently been so vocal in her reluctance that the *New York Times* felt justified in printing the rumor that she was opposed to the marriage.

The wedding was one of the most brilliant and costly affairs that Cleveland had witnessed. Senator Cameron had wanted a private ceremony, but the Sherman clan, having lost in the attempt to hold the celebration in Washington, would have nothing but a big event in Cleveland. Saint Paul's Episcopal Cathedral, where the event was held, was covered in the interior with flowers, so many that additional blooms and greenery had to be brought in from New York. Inside the cathedral, crowded 1,000 invited guests. The mob of onlookers outside the cathedral was so large as to virtually block traffic on the surrounding streets. Donald Cameron's gifts to the bride included a double-strand oriental pearl necklace and a pearl and diamond pendant. The total value of the gifts was estimated in the newspapers to be $100,000. In addition, there was a prenuptial agreement giving her the income from $160,000 of securities.

The ceremony began at 8 p.m. Afterwards, the marriage party greeted selected guests at the home of Lizzie's sister and brother-in-law, a prominent Wall Street financier. At 9:30 the couple retired and appeared half an hour later dressed in traveling clothes to depart for the senator's private rail car attached to the 10:30 train to New York.[5]

Many years later, Lizzie would confide to a friend that on her wedding night, spent on the train in the palace car Ohio, her first encounter with sex was a virtual rape.[6]

With resumption of specie payments now likely, the opposition sharpened their knives to come at Sherman personally. If they could not stop resumption on a straight-up effort, a scandal would do just as well. First came an article in the *National Republican*, a mouthpiece for the Radical Republicans, accusing Sherman of carving out for himself a share of the commissions to be paid on the bond issue. The article observed that Sherman came to the Senate a poor and perhaps honest man. Yet now he paid taxes on a computed property value of more than half a million dollars, all made during his senatorial term on a salary of $6,000 per annum.[7]

Yet the investigation with the least creditability, surprisingly, had the most potential to stop resumption cold. The Glover investigation contained the alleged sweetheart trade dollar dealings between the Anglo-California Bank and the U.S. Mint. It was only a matter of time until Seligman ownership of the bank came into the public focus, placing the syndicate's bond issue in jeopardy. Thus, when Aaron Sargent introduced his resolution in the Senate in May calling for the correspondence between Low and Linderman, it was to diffuse the issue, not aggravate it. When the *National Republican* picked up on the Glover investigation in June 1878, the newspaper totally missed this connection. In addition the House did not vote to publish Glover's report on alleged excesses at the mint before adjourning on June 20. Sherman was home free to make resumption happen.

There were still plenty of naysayers over the summer. Representative Ewing advanced the idea that successful resumption would require gold coin enough to cover redemption of all the greenbacks and national bank notes plus all the deposits in the banking system. The *New York Times* simply called that a false theory.[8] Sherman certainly disagreed with Ewing; by the start of July, he had $121 million in his resumption fund. That amount approximated 40 percent of the greenbacks outstanding, the same target that the Bank of England maintained for its specie reserve. The secretary expected legal tender notes to reach parity with gold by October 1.[9] If Congressional opponents made another run at repeal at the start of the next session of the Forty-Fifth Congress, he would start resumption early.[10]

In fact, Sherman felt confident enough of his position that the United States treasurer authorized banks to begin paying out silver dollars in general commerce for personal checks and small denomination greenbacks and national bank notes in addition to gold coin.[11] Sherman really had no choice as the mints, by law, were coining silver dollars well in excess of demand, and Treasury was running out of vault space. Adding to his dilemma, the international monetary conference called per the Bland-Allison Act was a complete failure. There was not even a vote taken on the American proposition to fix a ratio between gold and silver for monetary purposes.[12] Silver prices had fallen since passage of the act, and a silver dollar in the fall of 1878 was worth only 83 cents in gold. Sherman could only hope that Congress further limited their coinage or altered the law to increase the silver content of the coin.[13]

John Sherman had a bigger and more immediate issue concerning silver dollars and resumption, the payment of principal and interest on U.S. bonds. Allied with that concern were the actual mechanics of resumption. Sherman met with a committee from the member banks of the New York Clearing-House Association in early November. He told the bankers that they should not consider silver a bugbear. There was but $5 million of silver dollars in circulation. If more would be called for, he would have it under lock and key in the treasury vaults where it was capable of doing no more harm than if it were in the mines.[14]

These talks led to a proposal by the New York City banks on November 12 that Sherman accepted the following day.[15] These banks, within their power, would strive to keep the value of government and bank paper at par with gold but would distinctly recognize and, as far as they could, enforce the intrinsic difference between silver money and gold or paper convertible into gold. They would settle all balances between banks at the Clearing-House either in gold coin or legal tender notes. They would receive silver dollars upon deposit only under special contract to repay the same in kind and they would allow no payments of balances at the Clearing-House in silver dollars or Silver Certificates except in small numbers.[16] That action effectively dealt with payment of principal and interest on the bonds too. They would be in gold.

The Boston Clearing-House followed suit two weeks later.[17] Philadelphia concurred the next week with one exception: That clearing-house declined to treat silver dollars as special deposits payable in kind.[18]

In December with Congress back in session, the silver proponents threw in the towel; resumption should have a fair trial.[19] As a first indicator, the First National Bank in New York began paying out gold coin at par after Christmas.[20] In preparation, Sherman ensured that $100 million in gold coin was in New York at the end of December. Resumption would start there and spread to the other large cities in February.[21] On January 2, 1879, there was no run on the New York banks for gold coin. Nor would there be. Resumption was an accomplished fact.[22]

What John Sherman had accomplished for the United States with resumption of specie payments was every bit as significant as his brother's military exploits in the Civil War. Now with alliances seemingly set and resumption an accomplished fact, Sherman could concentrate on the prize at hand—the presidency.

Chapter 27

CHANGING OF THE GUARD

Sherman had his hands full finding a director to take the deceased Linderman's position. It would leak into the newspapers that President Hayes had had no intention of reappointing Henry Linderman. In December, the president offered the position to Loudon Snowden, a man whose prior experience as the Philadelphia coiner made him imminently qualified. Snowden refused as a friend of Linderman and knowing the man was seriously ill. After Linderman's death, Hayes again offered the position to Snowden, but the man again refused, this time stating a reluctance to relocate to Washington.[1] Unsaid was the fact that Snowden was financially entrenched in Philadelphia.

Philadelphia Mint Superintendent James Pollock offered advice: With Snowden's rejection, he suggested Robert Preston from the Bureau of the Mint. Preston had the prerequisite knowledge and with the financial policy of the government now being substantially set, there would be little occasion for experiments in the coinage.[2] Then Pollock abruptly resigned to take a Hayes appointment to the position of naval officer at the Philadelphia Customs House. Upon leaving the mint, Pollock received from the officers and employees a gold watch and chain, standard fare. However, they also gave him two easy chairs, a wrapper and pair of slippers, and a life-size crayon portrait of himself.[3] It was a mixed message.

This time when the president reached out to Loudon Snowden to quit the Post Office it was to replace Pollock instead. He accepted. The Snowden and Pollock

A. Loudon Snowden twice refused the position of director of the mint. As an alternative, he was offered and accepted the position of superintendent of the Philadelphia Mint. Snowden would operate this mint virtually independent of Washington.

Horatio Burchard was an Illinois Congressman until ousted by silver men. John Sherman then placed him in charge of the Mint. Over his term in office, he generally deferred to Robert Preston and Loudon Snowden in the day-to-day operational issues of the Bureau of the Mint while retaining firm control of any political matters.

nominations were referred to the Senate on February 9, 1879. This action had all the earmarks of Sherman wanting Snowden and willing to force Pollock out to make it happen. However, there was a twist to this story: Senator Cameron had not blessed Pollock's move to the Customs House. Therefore, the Senate failed to act upon that nomination. Pollock, his son, and nephews, employed together at the mint, were now out of their jobs while Snowden soldiered on.[4] Pollock would eventually gain confirmation as naval officer and serve until 1883.

Meanwhile back in Washington, Hayes turned to Illinois Congressman Horatio Burchard to be director of the mint on February 14, 1879. A long-standing member of the House Committee on Coinage, Weights and Measures, Burchard, regularly voting with the Eastern establishment but accomplishing little in the way of legislation, had not been renominated and would be unemployed at the end of the Congressional session on March 3. The Republicans in his district wanted someone more Western in attitude.[5] That was political speak for a staunch silver supporter. Burchard certainly knew the politics of the mint. His key support in conference for the subsidiary silver legislation of 1876 certainly helped him with Sherman. However, running a manufacturing operation was entirely another thing. In the interim, Robert Preston would fill the void at the bureau as acting director.[6]

It was the chair of the House Committee on Coinage, Weights and Measures, Alexander Stephens, who in February pushed Preston and Sherman where they did not want to go. John Kasson, formerly the chair of Stephens' committee, was now serving as minister to the Austro-Hungarian Empire and once again advocating an international coinage. He wanted a coin equivalent in value primarily to those of the Latin Monetary Union. The whole unit closest in value was four dollars.

Stephens sought outside help that resulted in a four-dollar gold piece, termed a Stella, that would tie to a metric double eagle. Stephens, in turn, asked Sherman to have trial samples struck. The reverse would include a five-pointed star and replaced the motto "In God We Trust" with "Deo est Gloria."

Sherman rightly saw this coin as going nowhere, dumping it on Preston to address. Preston argued he was not authorized to strike such a coin and no funds were budgeted for such purposes. Stephens instantly saw through that bureaucratic explanation. Trial or pattern pieces were duly authorized.[7]

Charley Barber designed an obverse Liberty with flowing hair, drawing heavily on a design prepared by his father the preceding year for the five-dollar gold piece. George Morgan designed a Liberty with coiled hair. There was little artistic difference between the two heads with the exception that Barber's might have been a bit more masculine looking. Word got out, and the mint was covered with Congressional requests for this novel coin, creating a small but significant mintage and a numismatic rarity.[8]

Flowing Hair (J-1635)

Coiled Hair (J-1638)

In 1879 and 1880 the Mint issued a four-dollar gold piece known as a Stella in a last attempt to devise an international coinage. The obverse featured competing designs by Charles Barber (Flowing Hair) and George Morgan (Coiled Hair). The obverse inscription reads *6G*.3*S*.7*C*7*G*R*A*M*S*. G stands for gold, S for silver, and C for copper.

As a companion piece to the four-dollar gold piece, the Mint also struck in 1879 a metric twenty-dollar gold piece (J-1643) that consisted of 30 grams of gold, 1.5 grams of silver, and 3.5 grams of copper.

Without Linderman at the helm, other pattern pieces came out of the Mint in 1879, featuring a scaled-down version of Morgan's adopted silver dollar obverse for the subsidiary silver coins. In addition, Morgan and both Barbers prepared new versions of Liberty for the larger silver coins. Morgan's "School Girl" image was superior to any design produced up to that point at the Mint.

George Morgan designed this "School Girl" pattern silver dollar (J-1608) in 1879 that is far superior to the design adopted the previous year.

Charles Barber appeared to be the dark horse to succeed his father as engraver. However, over brandy and cigars in Washington, Loudon Snowden prevailed with Burchard to give the job to Charley.

William Barber took ill while vacationing at the beach in New Jersey and died August 31, 1879, at the age of 72.[9] He had entered the Mint Service in September 1865 as an assistant engraver before succeeding to his position as engraver upon the death of his predecessor. Burchard sat on this, not making a move to appoint a new engraver until December 3, 1879, when Snowden pressed him for a decision. They agreed that Snowden would come to Washington the following Saturday evening and bring samples of the work for each of the applicants to be considered.[10] Belatedly on that Saturday, an embarrassed Burchard wrote Secretary Sherman that Barber had died three months previously, apologetically saying he thought that fact had already been reported.[11]

In reality the open engraver's position was of considerable interest. Anthony Paquet recruited a very able advocate in Judge Kelley. Kelley called Paquet the most capable man in the United States for this position. He was an artistic genius without the eccentricities that so often accompanied that gift. Kelley believed that Paquet would both reduce the expenses of the engraving department while improving its work.[12] This was a strong recommendation as Kelley and Burchard had served on the Committee on Ways and Means in the House together.

George Morgan, now ensconced in the mint as space had become available with William Barber's death, was not without his cheerleader. Deputy Mint Master Charles Fremantle wrote Burchard that Morgan would make a superior engraver. His artistic merits were recognized by many of England's leading artists.[13]

There were no outside recommendations for Charley Barber, making him seemingly the dark horse for the position. However, he had a most able presenter in Loudon Snowden. Snowden was a strong supporter of a system of advancement at the Philadelphia Mint that had become the uniform rule—that of promoting the son to the father's position. He believed that over the years it had added much to the efficiency of the organization.[14]

The two men met that Saturday night and literally over cigars and brandy, Snowden set forth his recommendation. That Burchard had reservations became obvious when on the following Wednesday, he asked Snowden to make his recommendation for engraver in writing to be presented to Sherman.[15] Charles Barber would become the sixth engraver at the United States Mint on January 20, 1880.

Chapter 28
We Want Garfield!

Now that resumption was in place and Rutherford Hayes a one-term president, John Sherman's time had come. But there were cracks in Sherman's foundation of support. Two Democratic silver men, Allen Thurman in the Senate and Thomas Ewing in the House, hailed from Sherman's home state. Appealing to the financially ignorant, the cries of "Crime of '73" and "Dollar of our Daddies" would present obstacles to be used by his opponents.

The first move Sherman made in his run for president was to turn away an overture by Ohio Republicans to draft him in May 1879 as their candidate for governor. Sherman believed that his resigning from the cabinet to accept that nomination would be viewed as a desertion of the public trust in favor of his personal ambitions, thus hurting his chances for the presidency.[1] Yet, he could not totally avoid getting drawn into Ohio politics. Charles Foster and Alphonso Taft went into a dogfight over the Republican gubernatorial nomination, and it took Sherman's coming to Ohio to settle the issue in favor of Foster.[2]

In a letter written concurrently, Sherman stated that he believed the true issues of the 1880 election would be national supremacy in national matters, honest money, and an honest dollar. Sherman's definition of honest money was that a dollar in paper should be worth a dollar in gold or silver anywhere in the country and that paper money under any circumstance should be exchangeable anywhere in the country for silver or gold.[3]

By September 1879, a good crop harvest in the United States combined with strong demand in Europe produced good times with the country awash in gold coin. Charles Foster easily defeated Thomas Ewing for the governorship of Ohio, and the Republicans gained control of both houses of the Ohio legislature, dooming Thurman's drive for a second term in the Senate. The Ohio Republicans would give that plum to Congressman James Garfield. Sherman's two Democratic antagonists were now on the sidelines.

In December 1879, Sherman had cause to regret staying in the Hayes cabinet. The president in his annual message to Congress called for the suspension of silver dollar coinage and the retirement of United States Notes. Sherman was against both actions. In his report to Congress, he attempted to squeeze through the eye of the needle, urging the importance of adjusting the coinage ratio between gold and silver by treaties with commercial nations. Short of this event, Sherman wanted tighter limits on the coinage of silver dollars to the extent that the Treasury could easily maintain the gold standard while keeping gold dollars and silver dollars at par with each other.[4]

Going into the New Year, Sherman opened a campaign office in downtown Washington to generate expanded political correspondence. Grant definitely would be a candidate under the premise that a four-year hiatus between terms removed the stigma of a third term. The other strong candidate was James G. Blaine. Sherman believed that in a knockdown, drag-out battle between Blaine and Grant, he was a viable alternative should neither man prevail at the convention.[5]

Recognizing that he must have a firm, dependable base that would stay with him if an initial deadlock occurred in the balloting, Sherman announced that he would not be a candidate unless Ohio Republicans gave him substantial support. Prior to the state Republican convention in May 1880, James Garfield sought a meeting with Sherman to offer his backing.[6] Even with Garfield in the Sherman camp, there was strong sentiment for Blaine. The state convention finally passed a resolution instructing the delegates-at-large to vote for Sherman and requesting the district delegates to do likewise. Sherman was now forced to go to the national convention knowing a minority in his state's delegation would ignore instructions, supporting Blaine.

The 1880 Republican Convention convened in Chicago on June 2. The location was the Interstate Industrial Exposition Building that had risen like a phoenix, gleaming steel and glass, 1,000 feet long and 75 feet high, from the ashes of the Great Chicago Fire of 1871. However, there was nothing glorious about the party that met within its massive confines. The Republicans were split into two warring factions, although neither wanted anything to do with silver. The Stalwarts, formerly radical Republicans, were in opposition to President Hayes's efforts to reconcile with the former Confederacy. They also opposed civil service reform and were determined to keep the spoils system alive at all costs. Aligned against the Stalwarts were a group of moderately liberal Republicans that the Stalwarts derisively called the Half-Breeds, meaning Republicans in name only. Led by Blaine and Sherman, the Half-Breeds backed Hayes's Southern policy, or as Sherman so deftly put it, national unity on national issues. They also favored civil service reform. Sherman liked Blaine; the two men were friends. Blaine said it best for Sherman that the Treasury secretary was as eminently fit for president as any man in America.[7]

James Garfield arrived at the convention having agreed to place John Sherman's name in nomination. While a skilled speaker, he had reason to regret this commitment to Sherman. He had procrastinated in drafting his speech. The words were slow in coming and the distractions, never ending. Hotel space was tight, forcing him to share his room with a stranger. Furthermore, Garfield was well aware that Sherman, by picking him to make the nomination, ensured that the Ohio delegates would not defect to him.[8]

Sherman's concern was real, and Garfield hated the position in which he found himself. The day before Garfield's arrival in Chicago, the *Cincinnati Commercial*, the recognized organ of John Sherman, admitted in an editorial that the senator's cause was hopeless and advised the Ohio delegation to move to Blaine. The paper noted that Senator Garfield was again being talked of prominently as a presidential candidate and that the Sherman people were terribly disgusted with such a proposition.[9]

The nominating process began the evening of Saturday, June 5. Blaine was the first to be nominated. Seconding that nomination was Frank Pixley.[10] That somehow seemed like poetic justice after Linderman's Treasury Commission in San Francisco steamrolled him. Garfield followed New York Senator Conkling's nomination of Grant. Conkling, given the grand stage, had filled his speech with theatrics making Garfield's job all the more difficult.

As Garfield prepped his audience to get their attention he asked, "And now gentlemen of the Convention, what do we want?" From within the audience came an answer that mortified Garfield. "We want Garfield!" It took a visible effort for Garfield to regain his composure and get to the meat of his speech.[11] However, Garfield performed well.

The applause from supporters that followed Sherman's nomination made up in noise for what they lacked in numbers.

Afterwards, the chair of the convention stood firm that no balloting would take place after midnight and that the convention would rest on the Sabbath. That meant all day Sunday the backroom politics would go full tilt. It also meant that Garfield was approached on the possibility of his name being placed in nomination. He flat refused, declaring his vote for John Sherman.

To gain the nomination a candidate had to garner 379 votes. On that first ballot, Sherman was a distant third with 93. He lost nine in his own state to Blaine. He had some strength in the African American delegates of the South, although Grant had a decided edge in this group. In Pennsylvania Donald Cameron, a solid Stalwart, did nothing for Sherman. He gained but three votes out of 58 that state cast. California, a state solid for gold where Sherman could have been competitive, cast its twelve votes for Blaine. Here was payback for the perceived whitewashing by the Treasury Commission. In spite of these setbacks, Sherman was still alive. Grant fell well short of the needed votes, recording only 304 with Blaine trailing at 284.

On the second and third ballot the deadlock continued. And so it went, back and forth.

On the 32nd ballot, support for Blaine began to crack. Sherman made a run on the 33rd ballot but stalled out with no help from Cameron, recording only 110 votes.[12]

As the deadlock continued, Sherman and Blaine held a conference in Washington. Their floor managers had assured both men that it was impossible for either to win the nomination. To defeat Grant, they must settle upon some man who could secure the anti-third term vote. The managers suggested Garfield. Blaine had no preference between Garfield and Sherman, but his supporters still opposed Sherman. Facing the need for an alternative, the two men agreed to concentrate their support upon Garfield.[13]

On the 34th ballot a switch took place in the Wisconsin delegation. Garfield garnered all but two of their votes. Garfield attempted to protest, but the chair refused to recognize him. On the 36th ballot more gains came for Garfield until it came time for Maine, Blaine's home state, to cast its ballots. They went to Garfield; it was over.

The story of how New York native Chet Arthur gained the vice-presidential nomination came out some thirty years later. Garfield's supporters in the Ohio delegation settled upon Arthur as an unobjectionable sop to the Stalwart wing of the party. Garfield could not win the presidency without New York, and he could not win New York without the support of the Stalwarts. These men approached Arthur directly, which irritated Conkling, the political boss of the state. Conkling told Arthur to "drop it as you would a red-hot shoe from the forge." Arthur refused, calling the office a greater honor than he could have dreamed of.[14] Sherman simply called it a "ridiculous burlesque."[15]

John Sherman did not take his defeat gracefully. In June, he ordered the dismissal of William Hayne, a former enslaved person, as inspector of customs at Charleston, South Carolina. Hayne had been a South Carolina delegate to the convention, voting for Grant on every ballot.[16]

Sherman's anger went much deeper; he believed he had been sold out. In a blistering letter to Charles Foster, he accused the governor of harboring a desire to see Blaine nominated and only half-heartedly supporting Sherman. Sherman believed that Foster had turned away feelers from other delegations seeking to support Sherman. He cited an example where Foster had sidestepped Blaine people in Pennsylvania looking to shift their support.[17] Without giving his source, it could only have come from Senator Cameron.

Sherman also burned his bridges with Garfield. He criticized Garfield's acceptance letter to the nomination. He felt it yielded too much on the issue of civil service. He also brought up the silver question that was proving more vexing by the day. Congress must come together to either arrest the coinage of silver dollars or increase the silver content of the coin to achieve par with a gold dollar.[18]

The fall campaign was virtually devoid of any national issues. In the end it turned on getting out the vote. Garfield won by less than 10,000. In the nation's first presidential race since the end of Reconstruction, the South went solidly Democratic. The Electoral College was not nearly so close. There were two battleground states that turned the electoral votes and, therefore, the election to Garfield—New York and Indiana. New York was no surprise. However, Indiana raised eyebrows, and rumors abounded after the election given that the Democratic vice-presidential candidate hailed from that state.[19]

Sherman was hardly out of a job. He decided to stand for Garfield's vacant Senate seat. When Garfield took office on March 4, 1881, John Sherman moved from the Treasury building and up Pennsylvania Avenue to resume his position of power on Capitol Hill.

With the potential alliance between Sherman and Cameron dead, where would Elizabeth Sherman Cameron turn, stuck in a marriage that she did not want?

Part 5
Rising Giants

Chapter 29
TRIUMPH AND TRAGEDY

If Augustus Saint-Gaudens were being totally honest with himself, he would have admitted that the Farragut commission had been a very close thing. After getting the commission only by the skin of his teeth, there had been several points in the evolution of this monumental work where failure had been more likely than success. As Gus was fond of saying, the whole process had been a tug.

Admiral David Farragut, the Civil War hero of Mobile Bay, died in August 1870. An association was organized in New York City on December 9 to commission a monument in his honor. This would be one of the first of the great commissions honoring the Civil War leaders of the Union. Subscriptions were not to exceed $100, and funds were to be sought from all classes.[1] However this was a politically connected memorial association. The president, John Dix, would serve as governor of New York from 1873 to 1875. Two months later at a second meeting, additional members were elected to the association, including Edwin Morgan, just finishing his term in the Senate. They also formed an executive committee, but it excluded the president and the treasurer, leaving a real question of just who was running the show.[2] Not surprisingly, matters at this point languished.

Saint-Gaudens returned from Rome at the end of April 1875.[3] Gus had an agenda. He was ready to marry Augusta "Gussie" Homer, whom he had fallen in love with in Rome, as soon as he could establish himself with some substantial commissions. Specifically, he had two projects in mind—the proposed memorial to Admiral Farragut

A young Augusta Homer, with her own connections to the art world, would soon marry Augustus Saint-Gaudens.

and a mausoleum for Morgan who had given him his first major commission while in Rome, the *Hiawatha*. For the Farragut project, he had come back from Italy prepared, having brought with him a sketch of Farragut's head.[4] Saint-Gaudens knew that the Farragut could make his reputation.

September 1875 found Saint-Gaudens actively lobbying to get the Farragut Memorial Association to award the commission. He also very coolly assessed his chances of getting the commission, if it were let immediately, as good. He viewed John Quincy Adams Ward, a well-established and competent American sculptor, as his major competitor.

Not surprisingly, the association that had largely sat dormant since its establishment, failed to respond to Saint-Gaudens's overtures. They were short funds, having just $11,000 cash in hand but with the expectation more. In frustration Gus penned a letter to Morgan asking that the man inform the association that Gus was willing to do the Farragut for $15,000 and build enough flexibility into the completion schedule to allow sufficient time to raise the additional funds.[5]

Morgan, in essence, told the sculptor to back off. Gus now had no choice but to finish his model and try to get as many members of the executive committee and subscribers as possible to come and look.[6]

Winter of 1876 turned to spring with no movement on the executive committee's part and Saint-Gaudens still struggling to identify the decision makers. June found Saint-Gaudens in the dumps. Gus was afraid that he would have no good matrimonial news for Gussie when she arrived back in the states from Italy at the end of the month.

Worried to the point of distraction, Saint-Gaudens wrote a letter to his perceived competitor, Ward. He was about to make a proposal on the Farragut commission, and his chances would be a great deal better if he could refer the committee to Ward for an opinion of his past work. Saint-Gaudens knew it was a delicate request. Yet, Ward acquiesced. Saint-Gaudens could refer to Ward in any manner he chose.[7]

Matters finally turned favorable when the executive committee met on December 12 and unanimously elected Morgan a member. The executive committee was to meet and finally make a decision the following week, and Morgan would be attending.[8] What Gus did not know was that Morgan's involvement would essentially neutralize James Montgomery, the association's secretary who was lobbying for a relative to get the commission. The man had twice asked for Morgan's help to secure a consulship for him.[9] Morgan had had no luck with the Grant administration, but with Hayes, there was a glimmer of light. Therefore, Montgomery was not going to antagonize Morgan.

What happened next is all second-hand. Gus wrote in his memoirs Morgan told him that, to his great surprise, the work had been awarded to Saint-Gaudens. However, it was only by the skin of his teeth as five of the executive committee had voted for giving the commission to a sculptor of high distinction even though the reality of this vote meant that they would have to return to the subscribers for more funds.[10] Saint-Gaudens's son, Homer, in finishing and amplifying these memoirs, was a little more enlightening. When the initial vote was taken, it was six to five in favor of J. Q. A. Ward. Ward declined, and used his influence to direct the work to Saint-Gaudens.[11] In Adeline Adams's biography of John Quincy Adams Ward, she quoted the sculptor as saying: "Give the young man a chance."[12] It was a magnanimous gesture. However, there was most certainly a contributing factor. With ample work, Ward simply had no available time to take on the added burden of the Farragut.

Lost in all of this detail is the fact that Morgan's vote the second time around, while never disclosed, had to be the tiebreaker for Gus. The politically astute Morgan had delivered for Saint-Gaudens. Not unexpectedly, within a month Montgomery was again asking Morgan's help in securing a good consulship.[13]

Even with the selection made, the executive committee dawdled. It would take a visit to Saint-Gaudens's studio to look at the sculptor's latest version of his proposal, his third model, to get matters moving. From the contract that was signed on May 23, 1877, it was obvious that Saint-Gaudens had cut his fee to the bone to get the commission. He was to receive $9,000 for his work.[14] However with a $2,000 advance per the contract, he could now get married and return to Paris to execute the commission.

The Farragut was not the only work going to Paris. He had several smaller projects that must be addressed before he could start on the Farragut. In addition, the Morgan Mausoleum project that had lain dormant for some 18 months was back on the front burner. Morgan was ready to commit. So the newlyweds settled into Paris with one large commission in hand and another in the offing. Gus rented a large studio through December where he could begin work. It was the young couple's plan to leave Paris in December for Rome where work in earnest must begin on the Farragut.[15] Gussie handled the household expenses, working closely with her father who invested their funds and oversaw letters of credit for them.[16]

The move to Rome accomplished nothing. In a hint as to the design concept, Saint-Gaudens decided that he must have Admiral Farragut's sword from the family in America later in the process.[17] Early April 1878 Rome had lost its allure and the couple was back in Paris looking for another studio.

Rome was not alone in losing its allure. In a letter from Gussie to her parents, Gus added a cartoon that noted his wife's increasing waistline. In another cartoon, he referred to her as "fatty." Throughout his life, Saint-Gaudens would use crudely drawn cartoons to express what he could not or would not say. Gussie admitted to her mother to being disturbed by his actions. Then she noted, tongue in cheek, that French courts did not recognize divorce so she must grin and bear it.[18]

Activity did not commence at the new studio until May 17.[19] Even then a week later, Gussie was writing her mother that work at the studio went on but slowly. Gus needed carpentry work done, and he could not find competent help for love or money.[20] It had now been 12 months since the Farragut agreement was signed. In this first year, the sculptor had devoted one month of sustained activity to this project.

Distractions seemingly aside, Saint-Gaudens was finally seriously into the Farragut.

In the middle of this frenzied activity a letter arrived from Stanford White. He and Charles McKim, promising young architects and good friends of Saint-Gaudens, were coming to Europe for an extended stay with Gus. Once they arrived at Saint-Gaudens's studio, they began to pester him to take a walking tour to the south of France. Gus refused. Members of the Farragut association, with wives in tow, were coming to look at his two-foot model.

McKim related afterwards that the viewing did not go well, putting Saint-Gaudens in a quandary. Gus asked some of his fellow artists over to critique the work. They were not kind. In disgust, Gus removed the head and toppled the plaster sketch to the ground.[21] He left for the two-week walking tour at the beginning of August. When Gus returned, Gussie wrote home, speaking vaguely, yet revealingly, of the trip.

"Aug returned Tuesday night having had a most successful trip. He feels that he has learned a great deal from travelling with his architect friends."[22]

Meanwhile, word of the visit had gotten back to Morgan in New York where he expressed concern to Gus's father.[23] Clearly the Farragut was at a crisis point. Just who from the association came to Paris in the first place? Saint-Gaudens was silent on that point. It wasn't Morgan. Dix was terminally ill. It had to include James Montgomery, by now consul general to Switzerland. Gus would obliquely make note a year later to being reluctant to approach Montgomery, having had a "diplomatic row" with the man.[24] Regardless, the association representatives had to be dismayed to find 15 months into this project only a two-foot rough model.

Gus must now fix his Farragut. Twenty years later, in a conversation with one of his best assistants,[25] Saint-Gaudens gave insight as to how his thinking changed during his time in the south of France. He had initially patterned his work after François Rude's Marshall Ney. His resulting model of Farragut imparted great action with a drawn sword and wide-open mouth.

Having distanced himself from the studio and, no doubt, talked at length to White and McKim, Saint-Gaudens realized that this approach was wrong. His model reflected action near at hand rather than a gesture that could grasp the field of battle. With this observation, Gus sheathed the sword and had Farragut lean into the wind with a piercing stare, surveying his command.[26]

Gus had just set his own ground rules. Forget the contract details and deadlines. Writing to Morgan, his most sympathetic supporter, he delivered the bad news softly. He was hard at work on the statue and would have it done within a few months of the time named in the contract. He believed a few months sooner or later in the completion of the work was not of so much importance as that the work should be good, and that nothing should stand in the way of its being so.[27]

Throughout the fall of 1878, Saint-Gaudens made steady progress. He shut himself up in his studio and allowed no one to see the work. By February 1879, Gus

Stanford White, close friend of Augustus Saint-Gaudens.

began to feel better about the Farragut. At this point Gus and Stanny White were deep into design of a suitable pedestal. Gus wanted to avoid a disagreeable contrast that would arise from pairing the bronze with granite. It was White who suggested blue stone. It was as durable as granite, gave a good finish, and was more harmonious with the bronze statue.

Stanford White was a guiding light in the architectural firm of McKim, Mead and White. He was a close friend of Augustus Saint-Gaudens, providing many of the bases for the sculptor's monumental works. However, he had a dark side; he and Saint-Gaudens were noted for late night carousing New York.

As the months of June and early July 1879 progressed, Gussie began again to see progress on the Farragut. He and his brother Louis, now working at the studio while studying at the Ecole des Beaux-Arts, had been putting in 12-hour days. They had begun to finish the body of the Farragut, and the head was nearly done.[28]

This optimism was unwarranted. Saint-Gaudens suddenly regressed to working on the life-sized nude, expecting to put the clothes on shortly.

Meanwhile, White, finally returned to New York, moved quickly to address the need for funding of the pedestal that ultimately required a meeting with Morgan. White and Morgan were not on the best of terms. When White finally broached the subject of the pedestal with him, Morgan exploded. He did not like the proposed bas-reliefs of "Loyalty" and "Courage" that would be incorporated and thought Saint-Gaudens was wrong in attempting anything beyond the contract. The executive committee would not guarantee a cent. Saint-Gaudens had a contract, and he should stick to it. As to the idea of asking for more money, the executive committee wouldn't pay a cent, nor would they go begging to the subscribers. Afterwards a subdued White was told not to mind Morgan. Morgan's doctors had told him that he could not live more than two or three years and that put him constantly in a morbid and depressed state.[29]

Back in Paris, Gussie in December began to fret. She wrote her parents that the days were so short that Gus seemed to get nothing done. In a hint to the real problem, she noted that the legs are always the principal trouble in a statue.[30]

Saint-Gaudens could not dawdle; his studio lease expired February 1, 1880, as the building was scheduled for demolition.[31] Into this turmoil his other good friend, the noted publisher Richard Watson Gilder arrived with his family. By mid-January Gussie observed that Gus seemed to be in agony over finishing the Farragut. He was very nervous and would take more time on it if he could.[32] Gilder, years later, quite proudly recalled standing for the legs from time to time.[33] Gus was going to hang up on the legs until the very end.

February 1880 found Gus still hard at work; he had gotten an extension of a week before the building would be torn down. On the sixth, he set up sheets behind his work in clay for the photographer who would commence the picture taking for the Farragut association the next day.[34] Two days later on Sunday, he opened the studio for a few people to see the "finished" work.

At this point it became apparent to all that Saint-Gaudens had an overriding reason to push completion of the Farragut. Gussie was pregnant and would be in her sixth month in June.[35] She wanted to be with her parents when the baby was born. For once procrastination was out of the question; Gus had no choice but to come home. He booked his return passage for June 19.[36] The Farragut must also be finished and cast by that date.

At the beginning of April, Saint-Gaudens felt confident enough of his work to have a second plaster cast made to exhibit at the upcoming Paris Salon. Gus wanted to see how his work compared with that of others at the salon.[37] Instead he received a lesson in the ways of French exhibitions. The Farragut, modeled for an immense space with light surrounding it, was placed under a side gallery with light coming from only one direction and the head poorly illuminated. All Gus could accomplish was to get the pedestal elevated to five feet.[38] . Ultimately the work would receive an honorable mention, leaving Saint-Gaudens to speculate on what might have been had he been given a more favorable placement.[39]

On June 5 trouble once again developed. The lower half of the statue was cast that day and due to an oversight on the part of the founder, it was a failure and the mold destroyed. The founder finally committed to a second casting date of July 9. That would place Gussie at the end of her sixth month, which was acceptable. So July 10 was the new departure date.[40]

Once back in New York Saint-Gaudens faced the task of finishing the pedestal within the funding limits imposed by the Farragut Memorial Association and gaining approval from the Parks Commission for a suitable location for his monumental work. White would have to forego his architect's commission for his work on the pedestal. Also, an exception from city regulations on the size and material used for the pedestal had to be granted.[41]

Meanwhile Gussie was encouraged by her mother to plan for extended convalescence.[42] After son Homer's birth on September 28, Gussie remained bedfast for a month. However, she did not start to move about freely until mid-December, another 45 days.[43] Perhaps in reaction, Gus spoke freely of the fine attributes of the New York models compared to those of Paris.[44] Then, to compound the situation, Gussie's father died after a very short illness on Christmas day, 1880. Gussie had to then take over the family's financial affairs placing her in conflict with Gus, who refused to be concerned with such matters.

The *Farragut* was dedicated May 25, 1881. The ceremonies were set to commence at three that afternoon. The crowd began to gather at noon, and fully 10,000 people were on hand for the ceremony in the limited seating and from windows and rooftops. Dignitaries, both military and civilian, participated. Politicians abounded, but the

Saint-Gaudens's figure through the use of the binoculars, advancement of the right foot and the wind whipped jacket gives a feel to the viewer of being at Farragut's side during the Battle of Mobile Bay

Richard Watson Gilder was the influential publisher first of *Scribner's Monthly* and then of *The Century Magazine.* He served as a mentor to Augustus Saint-Gaudens over much of the sculptor's professional career and enjoyed the ear of Presidents Cleveland and Roosevelt.

sculptor was unseen. The papers, while unstinting in their praise of this work, made no mention of his presence.[45] Sculptors were often overlooked in these ceremonies.[46] At about this same time, Watson Gilder gently took Saint-Gaudens aside and explained to him that gentlemen from the press could be his best friends if he would let them and that genius without publicity would simply not be recognized.[47]

As if to emphasize the advice he had given to Saint-Gaudens, Gilder ran an article in *Scribner's Monthly* on the *Farragut*, giving the sculptor national exposure. The article praised Saint-Gaudens for holding true to the essential spirit of the Greek taste but with an influence of Florentine Renaissance in his work.[48] It even went so far as to suggest that there were opportunities to employ this decorative style on American coinage.[49] It was Gilder's opening shot in what would prove to be a very long battle to improve the designs for United States coinage.

James Garfield would have done well to heed John Sherman's cautionary notes about the excesses caused by the American political patronage system. Even before his inauguration, Garfield had had to deal with Roscoe Conkling and the Stalwart wing of the Republican Party. Beyond the standard patronage, Conkling wanted the right to name the next secretary of the Treasury. He obviously wanted a gold man but also his man in the position. He brazenly told President-Elect Garfield that his administration could not be more successful than Conkling wished it to be.

Roscoe Conkling was the egotistical and vain senator from New York and boss of the state's Republican Party.

If Garfield had any suspicions about Conkling, they were removed the day of his inauguration. The day before, Senator William Boyd Allison had agreed to take the position of secretary of the Treasury only to renege that morning. Garfield blamed Allison's desertion on Conkling. Nor did Garfield have an ally in Chester Arthur who was Conkling's houseguest before the inauguration. The adversarial situation was hardened when Garfield offered Senator James G. Blaine, Conkling's mortal political enemy, the key position of secretary of State. In making this offer, the president exacted a promise from Blaine that he would not run for president again; Garfield wanted no divided loyalties in his administration.[50]

Once in office, Garfield faced difficulties well beyond Conkling; office seekers were lined up out the front gate of the White House and onto Pennsylvania Avenue. There were neither hours enough in each day nor jobs enough in the federal government to satisfy this every fourth-year gathering of vultures. Included in this witches' brew, Garfield had to deal with an evenly split Senate that customarily remained in session only briefly after the Inauguration to confirm presidential appointments.

Democrats had gained control of the Senate for the first time since the Civil War in the preceding Congress, giving them, among other things, the right to name the secretary of the Senate. Thus, George Gorham had found himself out of a job in 1879. He then landed the editorship of the *National Republican*, now the voice of the Stalwarts.

When the Senate convened on March 4, there were 37 Democrats and a like number of Republicans plus two independents. One independent announced he would caucus with the Democrats. When the vote came on March 14 to organize the Senate, every senator waited with bated breath for Virginia's William Mahone, from a breakaway faction of state Democrats, to vote. When the time came, he cast it with the Republicans. It turned out that George Gorham had brokered a deal with Mahone in an attempt to get his old job back. With Vice-President Arthur's tie-breaking vote, Republicans would control the chamber.

The Republican advantage quickly evaporated due to illness and absences for home state obligations. The Democrats in turn failed to answer quorum calls, tying the Senate up in knots and keeping Garfield's appointments in limbo.

Among the hoard of office seekers was Charles Guiteau, a lawyer by training but totally unqualified to hold any position of importance in the government. His object was an appointment as minister to Austria or maybe France. His claim was an acquaintance with Vice President Chester Arthur who, in the face of repeated approaches, had finally relented to let the man give a very short speech in support of Garfield's election in New York City. The speech was enough to give Guiteau the confidence to appear at the Executive Mansion day after day, seeking President Garfield's favor.[51]

The opening round of the struggle for supremacy between Garfield and Conkling began quietly enough. Garfield on March 22 routinely submitted five nominations of Conkling men to the Senate for approval. However, the next day he submitted William Robertson to be collector of customs at New York City. Robertson was president pro tem of the New York State Senate and had served in Congress with Garfield. It was said that Robertson led the last-minute bolt for Garfield of the New York delegation at the Republican Convention in outright defiance of Conkling.

By appearances the president had consulted with Conkling and possibly Thomas Platt, the other New York senator and an ally of Conkling, over the earlier nominations. Now he was balancing that action by naming a man from the Blaine wing of the party to the collector's post. However, to the two New York senators, this action was a complete surprise and totally unsatisfactory.[52] When it came to patronage, there simply was no difference between the Stalwarts and the Half Breeds. They were different wings on the same vulture. There would be a fight over confirmation.

Conkling threatened a contest over senatorial privilege in the nominating process. He insisted the nomination of Robertson should be rejected in the interest of the Republican Party of New York and gave notice that he would use every effort to accomplish that result. If necessary, he would carry the fight onto the open floor of the Senate. Garfield simply withdrew the nominations he had made of the five Conkling men. Many wanted to reject Robertson to avoid an embarrassing intraparty fight. A compromise was offered up that Robertson's nomination be postponed to the regular session the following December in hopes that Senator Platt and the president could reach a satisfactory settlement of the issue in the interim. Ominously, some senators considered Conkling's action as offensive. Others simply wanted this stumbling block removed so they could get on with the other confirmations, adjourn, and go home.[53]

On May 12 the workings of a possible compromise surfaced.[54] Then on May 14 cracks in support of Conkling began to appear. All ideas of a withdrawal of Robertson's nomination had been abandoned. The next day there was even an olive branch thrown out by Garfield's people. If the opposition were not too bitter, the names of most of the New York Conkling nominees would be resubmitted.[55]

On May 16 at the convening of the Senate, Roscoe Conkling announced his resignation. Most senators were in conversation, reviewing papers for the start of the day, and did not hear the reading of the resignation by the Senate clerk. The clerk was forced to read the brief letter of resignation a second time. That done, the clerk then read the resignation of Thomas Platt, who had been in the Senate only since March 4. Nearly every senator was alienated by these actions. Worse for the

Republicans, they would have to share power in the Senate. In the ensuing compromise George Gorham was out, his political comeback thwarted. The once all-powerful California Republican ring had just taken a serious hit to their power base.

The *New York Times* speculated that neither Conkling nor Platt intended to permanently retire from the Senate. Platt had just visited Albany, and it was suspected he had prepared the legislative allies there for their return to the Senate. It was expected that the legislature would fill the vacancies on May 24, the first date under the law that they could do so.

Conkling went straight to Albany, supremely confident that he and Platt would be returned. His supporters were boldly declaring that nothing could prevent the reelection of the two men. Yet the state Republicans refused to go into caucus until both factions, Stalwarts and Half Breeds, were in joint convention.[56]

Conkling forced the Republican leadership to call the caucus on May 30. It blew up in his face when the caucus failed to secure a quorum.[57] Yet Conkling's huge ego would not permit him to acknowledge failure. All through June the Republicans remained deadlocked with no one able to secure a majority of votes in caucus.

On July 1, Platt surprised everybody by withdrawing, leaving Conkling to soldier on in certain defeat.[58] Reflecting the fact that Platt had allowed Conkling to draw him into this foolish gambit, political pundits now called him "Me Too Platt." Yet given the tragic events that would overtake the country in the next 24 hours, he probably saved his career with this withdrawal. Still, it would take Thomas Platt a political lifetime to regain what he had just thrown away.

On the morning of July 2, Garfield was scheduled to leave Washington to join his wife in Massachusetts before continuing to his 25-year reunion at Williams College. The worry over his wife's recent illness, coupled with the stress of dealing with Conkling, made the president look forward to this journey. He traveled by carriage to the Baltimore and Potomac Station with Secretary Blaine at a leisurely pace as the two men discussed political affairs. The president's itinerary had been published in advance.

The mentally deranged Charles Guiteau, against Garfield's nomination of Robertson and believing the president to be a danger to the Republican Party, was waiting in ambush. He shot the president in the back in a wound that should not have been fatal. However, the medical treatment Garfield received *was* fatal, leaving him to die in agony on September 19, 1881. The American public was aghast, clearly comprehending that the political spoils system was totally out of control.

Chapter 30
The Pendleton Act

With Chester Arthur now at the helm, all appeared business as usual for the Stalwart Republicans. The spoils system was alive and unchecked. And President Arthur refused to acknowledge the storm clouds gathering from Garfield's assassination.

As usual the mints were in the thick of it. San Francisco Mint Superintendent Henry Dodge had struggled to restore stability to that operation after LaGrange's exit. He had come into almost immediate conflict with Congressman Horace Page, the surviving member of the Republican Ring.

Both Secretary Sherman and President Hayes had quickly become aware of the quagmire Dodge faced. The superintendent forwarded to Sherman a letter from a woman wishing her daughter to be employed at the Mint as an adjuster. The angry mother stated that there were some adjusters at the Mint that were "unworthy the holy name of woman." An embarrassed Dodge offered her daughter an appointment at the earliest vacancy.[1]

Dodge made his move on Congressman Page in April 1880. The issue centered upon the removal of three employees, one being Page's son. Page in turn stirred up a hornet's nest accusing Dodge of dismissing skilled Republican Mint employees of long standing, men owing their appointment to Page. He also raised a new issue concerning refining charges for low-grade silver bullion, claiming favoritism to certain depositors.

Page's action had forced Mint Director Horatio Burchard to circle the wagons. With doré silver from the Comstock Lode in decline, San Francisco's refinery was in the process of converting to the sulfuric acid method of parting.[2] Now Burchard suspended the project.

To understand the extent of the problem, Burchard had ordered Dodge to provide a full and detailed explanation of all dismissals during his tenure. Dodge's response in a lengthy telegram clearly demonstrated the influence of Page over past hiring practices at the San Francisco Mint.[3] Next he had traveled to San Francisco to reinforce Dodge's dismissal of some eight or ten employees.

Page, not to be deflected, had written President Hayes, questioning the removals of two men and the advantageous transfer of another, conveniently omitting from the complaint his son's termination. The addition of the employee transferred was a direct shot at Burchard. The individual in question was Burchard's brother-in-law.

Dodge had taken the high road in a report to Burchard refuting these charges. However, he did point out that one man was incompetent, having poured molten silver on his shoe. As to Burchard's brother-in-law, the man's loyalty and character had never been questioned while employed at the Mint.[4] Burchard had taken this letter and added his own in the formal response to Secretary Sherman. The director wasted no time in mentioning Page's son was one of the men terminated. He also endorsed Dodge's effort to satisfy party demands while maintaining an efficient operation.[5] Here the matter rested and should have stopped.

Page bided his time. Once the Garfield administration was in place, he brought his charges, retooled, and this time the mud stuck to the wall. His opening shot on April 27, 1881, requested that the secretary of the Treasury provide the amount of silver bullion delivered by the San Francisco superintendent to the melter and refiner in fiscal year 1880. Burchard stonewalled Page with a long and technical response.

Page proceeded anyway, making his charges against Dodge to the president on May 21. His major allegation surrounded the receiving of low-grade silver bullion from the Anglo California Bank without the proper deduction for refining expense. In addition, Page claimed equivalent low-grade bullion from other suppliers was rejected.[6]

Dodge went immediately to Washington to confer with Burchard.[7] But, it was too late for damage control. In June, Burchard delivered the bad news to Dodge. There would be a special commission appointed to inquire into Page's charges, and the books of the Mint would be made available to the examiners as well as specific entries provided to Congressman Page.[8]

The special commission convened on July 23, 1881, at a very familiar venue, the Palace Hotel. The collegial ties of the five commissioners to President Garfield and John Sherman were plain as day. The verdict was preordained.

The hearings opened with counsel for Page submitting ten additional charges that represented an expansion of the charge that Dodge had failed to make the proper deductions upon base bullion, that being silver bullion at or below 600 fine. The coiner, Frank Cicott, had provided input on this expansion. Perhaps it was poetic justice that his support of Page cost him his job. He had been removed effective July 1.

Pivotal to Page's charge concerning the low-grade bullion was that Dodge had used it as a vehicle to benefit the Anglo California Bank and its president, F.F. Low, in recognition of Low's support of Dodge for the superintendent's appointment. Yet Page could produce no witness to testify to any favoritism toward the bank. All the bullion dealers testified that they were always treated fairly by Dodge. None of these people were going to bite the hand that fed them.

Testimony from Low was likewise effective in undercutting Page's charges. Low, at the time of LaGrange's removal, did not know that Dodge was an applicant for the job. Low did reveal that Dodge had traveled to Washington about the position at Director Henry Linderman's request. The banker did not talk to Dodge about the situation until after the man's return. Only when Linderman requested, did Low write a recommendation for Dodge. In fact, Low had suggested Charles Felton as LaGrange's replacement. Low further testified that no low-grade bullion was ever received at the Mint by specific order of Dodge.[9]

The commission found that Dodge followed the laws honestly, had operated the Mint in an efficient manner, and had maintained a corruption-free administration. Friends of Page most likely "miscommunicated" to Page in their desire to support him politically. Had they not done so, these charges probably would not have been made.[10] Page would lose his bid for reelection from a solidly Republican district in 1882.

With coiner Frank Cicott gone, the last of the LaGrange influence left the San Francisco Mint. Jos Harmstead, sensing his opportunity, asked Senator John P. Jones to write a letter of recommendation to the secretary of the Treasury for his transfer back to San Francisco. Dodge duly initiated the necessary request and Harmstead returned on December 5, 1881.[11] On Harmstead's first day on the job, Dodge talked with him. He knew of Harmstead's troubles under LaGrange but that his record since had been exemplary. He also pointed out to Harmstead that he had been a member of that commission that had found LaGrange responsible for his subordinates' actions in 1877.[12] It was as close to an apology as Harmstead would ever get.

No sooner were issues simmered down in San Francisco than the cauldron began to boil at the New Orleans Mint. Martin Davis had moved over from coiner to the superintendent's office in June 1880, at the death of Henry Foote. Davis had needed Maximillian Bonzano's recommendation to seal the promotion. Bonzano had been the melter and refiner at the Mint before the Civil War. He returned to New Orleans with the federal occupation of 1862 and became the assayer-in-charge when the Mint was reconstituted as an assay office in 1876. Bonzano, again the melter and refiner knew the local Republican players well, making him the power to be reckoned with at the Mint.

The conflict started innocently enough in July 1881. The new coiner, J.W. Helffrich, moved to dismiss certain employees without obtaining Davis's approval. Davis went to Burchard to reinforce the fact that only he had the power of removal at the Mint.[13] When Davis asked for specific reasons from the coiner for the removals, Helffrich had none. Davis reinstated the men, causing the coiner to promptly resign.[14,15] The fight to fill this vacancy would bring Davis into full conflict with Bonzano.

Davis placed the assistant coiner, Benjamin Butler, in charge. By October, there were five applicants for the position. Butler had the support of Senator Benjamin Harrison of Indiana.[16] He had competition; Frederick Jones, an employee in the melter and refiner's department, had Bonzano's support as well as that of James Albrecht, the assayer.[17] He also had the support of Louisiana Republicans, including Senator William Pitt Kellogg and Representative Chester Darrall. Against this support, Davis could only delay the selection and risked making powerful enemies.

Concurrently Davis kept receiving corrections to reports filed with the bureau from his mint. His bullion reports were late. Reports would be returned for minor errors. Some of the comments on sloppy reporting came under Burchard's signature; some, in his absence, came under Preston's signature. However, the wording, the focus on detailed mistakes and necessary corrections, could only have come from Robert Preston. Preston even chided Davis to pay more attention to the preparation of the accounting statements from his mint.[18] It was apparent that Horatio Burchard had ceded the day-to-day affairs of the Bureau of the Mint to Robert Preston.

November dragged into December with no action to fill the coiner's position. Davis pressed the issue with a personal note to Burchard on January 13, 1882.[19] It was a futile effort with Jones gaining the appointment at the end of that month. Davis had no choice but to get Butler out of the coining department, requesting Burchard's approval to appoint the man to the cashier's position.[20]

Trouble of an entirely different nature was quick to follow. Davis notified Burchard on February 4 that, according to a newspaper article, a discharged employee would be filing an affidavit stating that Davis, during his tenure as coiner, had culled out some 1,500 trade dollars for melting to destroy their identity, a violation of the law. There were other matters as well contained in the article, and Davis demanded an investigation. Burchard responded that if formal charges were received, he would promptly initiate a thorough examination.[21]

The fog of politics began to envelop the New Orleans Mint in March. Davis telegraphed Burchard that the new coiner had made a recommendation for his assistant. Burchard then turned to Senator Kellogg for approval as well as the transfer of Butler to the position of cashier.[22] Butler passed the vetting, and, in fact, Burchard complimented his statement of accounts as acting coiner.[23] The appointment of an assistant coiner was another matter as Burchard, a week later, was again urging that an experienced man be chosen for the position.[24]

Martin Davis found himself in a box with no way out at the beginning of April. The chairman of the finance committee of the Louisiana Republican State Central Committee had requested Davis provide a complete listing of officers and employees at the Mint with rank and pay to serve as a basis of future assessments for voluntary contributions. Davis shared this request with Burchard. The Mint director in turn conferred with Treasury Secretary Charles Folger and both were of the opinion that it clearly violated the law.[25] By declining the request, Davis stayed within the law but alienated the local Republican establishment. It wasn't long until formal charges against Davis surfaced in Washington.

In addition, Davis had to put up with Bonzano snitching to Robert Preston over any perceived wrongdoing. The parting charge in gold assay reports was in excess of that authorized by regulations.[26] Persons appointed to positions at the Mint had allegedly not reported for duty. Preston wanted a listing of leaves of absence granted.[27]

Worse, it was Preston who broke the news to Secretary Folger that Burchard was in New Orleans investigating charges against Davis.[28] Congressman Darrall had presented seven formal charges to Burchard in mid-April. Leading the charges, Davis, while coiner, delivered to the melter and refiner, Bonzano, clippings of a large number of trade dollars that were ultimately coined into standard silver dollars. Another charge raised a serious hint of scandal. Davis throughout his term as superintendent had "corrupted or attempted to corrupt in a manner grossly scandalous" the female adjustors in the coiner's department. However, the most damaging charge was that Davis forged and used the names of B.F. Flanders, the customs collector for New Orleans, Bonzano and Albrecht in the decisive telegram to the director endorsing Davis for the superintendent's appointment.

Burchard arrived in New Orleans on April 22 and over the next six days took statements and testimony. As a letter from Bonzano to Congressman Darrall had been submitted with the charges to Burchard, he started his investigation by asking the melter and refiner to produce any evidence in his possession substantiating the charges. The only item that Bonzano could produce was a letter detailing the trade dollar transactions.[29]

Davis testified that he had received some 230 trade dollars from the bookkeeper of the Mint. He sought the permission of then Superintendent Foote to receive the coins. He defaced them and turned them over to Bonzano for melting. By rendering them into standard silver dollars, the government gained 7-1/2 grains on each coin. Davis had taken this action openly and had no economic interest in the trade dollars.

In the instance of the telegram, it seemed that Davis went to the Customs House to obtain Flanders's signature. Finding him out and in a haste to get the telegram to Washington, Davis went directly to the telegraph office rather than returning to the Mint, a considerable distance away, and prepared and forwarded the dispatch containing the recommendation, omitting only Flanders's name. Upon returning to the Mint, he wrote both Bonzano and Albrecht of his action and neither objected. Burchard disliked that Davis had cut this corner but refused to sustain the charge of forgery. However, the telegram had been instrumental in securing the appointment for Davis. The Mint director had previously been reluctant to support Davis for superintendent "for reasons that had been communicated" to Burchard and had advised Secretary Sherman to put the appointment on hold until a personal interview could be held. Those negative comments most likely had come from Robert Preston.

In regard to the female adjusters, Burchard found no improper action of Davis as superintendent. On the last day of oral testimony an affidavit from a woman stating she had applied for a position at the Mint and that Davis had offered to use his influence in return for "conditions dishonorable and insulting." Davis denied the charge, and with no supporting testimony, Burchard declined to submit the evidence.

Burchard had hardly left New Orleans before racially charged political accusations hit the press. The account was accurate in that it stated all that was material to the charges had been disproved or mitigated so as to show no criminal intent. The newspaper went further, alleging that the war on Davis had grown out of his refusal to "Africanize" his workforce at the demand of local Republican politicians. He refused to remove experienced men who were Democrats appointed by his predecessors to make room for "illiterate and incompetent negroes." In addition, Senator Kellogg and Congressman Darrall were in a fight for control of patronage for the Third Congressional District, and Darrall had taken offense, claiming Davis was giving preference to Kellogg's friends.[30]

Senator Kellogg was quick to smell blood, submitting his choice for the superintendent's position on June 1. The whole situation left Secretary Folger sitting on the fence. As June drew to a close, Folger pressed Burchard to make some kind of recommendation. Burchard noted that the heart of the charges concerned actions prior to Davis's appointment as superintendent and, as such, did not afford cause for removal. However, Davis's reputation and standing had been diminished. Therefore, Burchard believed the Mint Service would be promoted by requesting his resignation. If he refused, Davis should be removed.[31] Burchard had let Bonzano and Preston color his judgment.

Still there was no action as strong support for Davis had developed. In fact, the superintendent took a leave of absence to fight his case.[32] However, the bad news broke in the *New York Times* on August 5, 1882, that Dr. Andrew W. Smyth would be replacing Davis at the beginning of September.

As August drew to a close, the male employees of the New Orleans Mint gathered to present Davis with a gold-headed cane. The female employees gave him a pair of monogrammed cuff links. His wife was present for the ceremony and complimented. Every employee contributed to the gifts.[33] In addition, the handover of the various accounts to the new superintendent showed no deficiencies on the part of Martin Davis.[34]

Thus, Martin Davis left the Mint Service. He would never have the opportunity to rise to the position of director of the Mint; Robert Preston had seen to that. However, in recognition of his Civil War service and perhaps that the case against him was weak, Davis was appointed secretary to the Internal Revenue Commission.[35]

It wasn't six months until Bonzano was complaining about Superintendent Smyth to Robert Preston.[36] Congressman Darrall reinforced this action with a direct contact to Burchard that resulted in a trip to Washington for Davis's successor.[37] The political meddling subsided when Louisiana Democrats swept Kellogg and Darrall, reconstruction Republicans, out of office in the 1882 elections. Burchard finally removed Bonzano in November 1883.[38]

While the turmoil in New Orleans was playing out, President Arthur began to place Stalwart Republicans in positions throughout his administration. The president kicked Thomas Acton, the longstanding superintendent of the New York Assay Office, upstairs to be assistant treasurer for the New York Sub-Treasury. Then he put his close personal friend, Pierce Van Wyck, into the superintendent's position. Van Wyck promptly placed his son in the key position of chief clerk at the assay office.[39] It was all orchestrated and coordinated as Edwin Morgan went on Acton's performance bond for the assistant treasurer's position.[40]

Meanwhile in California, Jos Harmstead ushered in the New Year 1882 quietly at home, reunited with his wife. As the year progressed, Harmstead began to hear rumors that President Arthur intended to make changes in the federal offices in San Francisco. When Harmstead returned to work after the annual settlement of accounts, the outside watchman told him a new superintendent and coiner were in place. As the 68-year-old Harmstead progressed to the coining department, he learned that others within his group were being discharged. It was a relief for him to learn that he was not one of them. The new coiner took the time to tell Harmstead he had heard many good things about him, and he was looking forward to working with him.[41] What Harmstead did not realize was that he was the glue that held the coining department together.

The new superintendent was Edward Burton, a close friend of Chester Arthur, having worked for him at the New York Customs House.[42] Charles Gorham, George's brother, was the new coiner. Aaron Sargent was on Charles Gorham's performance bond.[43] The San Francisco Mint was backsliding.

Throughout this period, Loudon Snowden and the Philadelphia Mint appeared lily white. As a Civil War officer, although on the home front, he was acceptable to the Stalwarts. However, there were problems at Philadelphia. Snowden and O.C. Bosbyshell presided over a flood of restrikes, experimental pieces, die mulings, and off-metal strikes that flowed through the back door of the Mint, somehow ending up, for a price, in the hands of numismatists. Snowden, after leaving office, would be accused of profiteering from the purchase of machinery and supplies for the Mint. In addition, he kept irregular hours at the institution, devoting more of his time to his position as president of the Fire Association, a well-known large fire insurance company.[44]

What a fine mess this all was. Yet the Mint was no worse than other federal bureaus and departments when it came to patronage politics. The problem lay in its unique position within the federal government as both a manufacturing operation and a financial instrument.

The concept of federal civil service reform was well ensconced in the public consciousness when Charles Guiteau assassinated President Garfield. In fact, significant legislation establishing needed reforms was on the drawing board of the Senate in the closing moments of the Forty-Sixth Congress, before Garfield's inauguration. George Pendleton, a Democratic senator from Ohio, introduced such a reform bill on February 10, 1881.[45] It being late in the session, this bill was going nowhere; it was meant to stake out a political position.

Pendleton had been a staunch advocate of repaying the national debt with greenbacks, an anathema to John Sherman. Yet there was more to Pendleton than that single issue. He had been George McClellan's running mate in the 1864 contest against Abraham Lincoln. He had suffered the long dominance of Republicans in his home state, losing to Rutherford Hayes in the 1875 gubernatorial contest. So it was no surprise, in spite of his seeming lack of legislative experience, when Democrats voted him to be the chair of their Senate caucus for the Forty-Seventh Congress.

Senator George Pendleton was the author of the act that established the Civil Service Commission.

When the Senate and House convened in their opening legislative session in December 1881, Senator Pendleton lost no time reintroducing his bill. He argued that his merit-based system would result in the appointment of men who were honest, capable, and faithful, those proven to be the best.

The concept embodied in Pendleton's bill was the development of a set of classifications within which federal government jobs across the spectrum would fall. These jobs were to be filled from those graded highest on competitive examinations. Promotion would be on the basis of merit and competition. The bill established a commission whose members were to be appointed by the president to promulgate and enforce the necessary regulations necessary.[46]

Pendleton built some limiting factors into his bill. The classification system would initially only apply to federal employees in Washington, post offices employing fifty or more people, and the customs houses at the major ports of entry. Existing employees would be grandfathered into the system. Pendleton's bill was tabled, and there it stayed until the tsunami touched off by the mid-term elections.

Republicans completely misread the mood of the electorate, thinking the recent strong economy would be enough to keep them in power. They were wrong! When the dust settled after the mid-term elections, Democrats held nearly a two to one majority in the House of Representatives. Somehow the Republicans held their narrow majority in the Senate. The defeat at the state level was just as bad. In New York, Democrat Grover Cleveland captured the governorship by a huge majority. And in Pennsylvania, Donald Cameron, the successor to Roscoe Conkling as the supreme Stalwart spoils man, took a near fatal blow to his organization. Thomas Platt called the debacle the worst thing to happen to the Republican Party since its founding.

Republican leaders saw the defeat as a backlash against the spoils system. If the Republican Party was to have a fighting chance in the presidential election of 1884, civil service reform had to happen to diffuse the issue before the new Democrat-dominated Congress convened on March 4, 1883. Republicans now breathed new life into Pendleton's bill.[47]

Democrats were ambivalent toward Pendleton's measure, believing that they would be the winners in 1884 by prolonging this issue. Pendleton countered this line of thinking, reminding his colleagues they would retain the support of the electorate only so far as they responded promptly, honestly, and earnestly to the issue of civil service reform.[48]

Put on a fast track, Pendleton's bill was signed into law on January 16, 1883. As originally constructed, the bill covered only a fraction of the federal government's total employment. Exempted from the act were all presidential appointments subject to Senate confirmation. However, the law empowered the president to expand the reform by adding employees into the system. This provision was also a loophole; it allowed Arthur and his successors to lock in their political supporters in any expansion of coverage.[49] Its initial limited application did not include the mints, only the headquarters staff.

The act set up a three-man commission to oversee civil-service reform. The tools were there to bring the spoils system into check. Now it only required a commissioner willing to get his hands dirty to make it all work.

Chapter 31

Stirrings of Controversy and Conflict

Loudon Snowden had long been an advocate of a uniform design across the minor coinage. He reasoned that the different designs then employed were confusing. With Horatio Burchard taking a hands-off attitude, Snowden took the lead. The Philadelphia superintendent had an ally in this endeavor—Joseph Wharton, long a supporter of a nickel-based alloy for the minor coinage. Wharton had continued to be the primary supplier of nickel to the Mint. However, once the low-denomination shinplasters had been retired, demand for the copper-nickel three-cent and five-cent pieces plummeted, leaving Wharton with very little market.

As 1881 played out, Snowden charged Charles Barber with executing a design suitable for these two coins plus the one-cent piece. The resulting minor coinage would be distinguishable by proportionate changes in diameter and weight. Snowden wanted a head of Liberty for the obverse and a wreath of cotton, rice, tobacco, and wheat surrounding the Roman numeral of the denomination for the reverse. Barber's Liberty reflected a classic Greco-Roman style to which he added a coronet with cotton bolls and wheat ears attached. This obverse had a certain sameness when compared with the image of Liberty on Morgan's dollar. On the reverse, Barber employed several different wreaths on his pattern pieces, one of cotton and wheat and another of cotton and corn. Here the project sat until the end of the year.

J-1665

J-1668

J-1671

Loudon Snowden initiated the first assignment in 1881 for Charley Barber to provide a uniform design for a set of minor copper-nickel coins.

On November 12, 1881, the Treasury Department, facing an increase in demand for five-cent pieces, ordered Burchard to begin striking these coins in significant quantities.[1] While nothing could be done in the short term, Snowden used this renewed demand to push for new designs. He reasoned the design of the existing nickel, using an ornamental shield representing the Union, did not conform to the coinage law, requiring a device emblematic of liberty. On this basis, Snowden believed that the director of the Mint had the authority to authorize a change without going to Congress. He also had a problem with the diameter of the piece. With a required weight of five grams, the resulting planchet was too thick for its diameter, causing difficulties bringing up the design devices due to the hardness of the copper-nickel composition. Die life was also shortened as a result of the increased striking pressure utilized. Because weight and composition changes would be required on the one- and three-cent pieces that would necessitate legislative approval, Snowden reasoned that they could wait upon the completion of the work on the nickel.[2]

On December 22, 1881, Burchard asked Snowden for six or seven of the new pattern five-cent pieces.[3] Barber had two variations at this point. Both presented

Liberty on the obverse with the inscription "United States of America" on the perimeter. The reverse featured the Roman numeral V surrounded by a wreath of wheat and cotton. A second version contained the motto "In God We Trust" in small lettering in an arc above the opening in the wreath.[4] As if on cue, two days later Joseph Wharton was awarded a supply contract with the Philadelphia Mint as the lowest and best bid for 20,000 pounds of pure nickel.[5]

Little additional effort was put forth over most of 1882. Barber turned out a third version of the reverse, substituting "E Pluribus Unum" for "In God We Trust." A problem for the new design was the requirement from the Coinage Act of 1873 that United States of America appear on the reverse of the nation's coinage. Snowden pressed ahead regardless, requesting authority to adopt the new design on December 20. When Burchard presented the request to Charles Folger, the Treasury secretary balked. Folger admitted that there was much force to Snowden's arguments for placing "United States of America" on the obverse. However, if any design change were to receive his sanction, he believed the new coin ought to conform to the requirements of the law. Burchard gave Snowden and Barber no choice but to rearrange the inscriptions.[6]

Charles Barber quickly rolled out the fix: Thirteen stars now surrounded Liberty on the obverse. The wreath was shrunken on the reverse to accommodate "United States of America." "E Pluribus Unum" shifted to the bottom edge of the coin in a smaller font to fit the available space. The diameter for the new coin was set at 21 millimeters, an increase of 0.5 millimeters from the earlier nickel. Burchard sent approval, countersigned by Folger, on January 8, 1883.[7]

The comments in the press came swiftly. The new coin was nearly as bad as the Seated Liberty of the subsidiary silver coins. The only argument in its favor was that when carefully gilded, it could be palmed off upon a newly arrived immigrant as a five-dollar gold piece.[8]

Burchard had argued the reverse should include the inscription "Cents." Folger had overridden Burchard.[9] In addition, the coin's diameter was now almost exactly the same as the half eagle or five-dollar gold piece. As the newspapers had related, con artists immediately found they could use a quarter eagle gold coin to gold plate the new nickel and pass it into commerce as a half eagle. By the first of March, Barber had moved "E Pluribus Unum" to the open top of the wreath to make room for "Cents" at the base of the reverse.[10] The result was horribly crowded. This design change had been more a fiasco than an improvement.

George Morgan was active at this time as well, focusing on a uniform design to replace the Seated Liberty on the subsidiary silver coins. His Shield Earring pattern design, named for the unique earrings that adorned Liberty, was exceptional. The eagle on the reverse was a variation of the eagle he had employed for his Schoolgirl Liberty design of 1879. This latest version, beautiful as it was, went nowhere. Morgan instead found monetary reward designing quasi-commemorative coins in bronze and silver for the various American Revolution centennial events. His pieces, named "so-called dollars" because of their comparable size to a silver dollar, included the Battle of Yorktown and, perhaps his best, the British evacuation of New York. However, his work had no real audience with mintage measured in the hundreds of coins.

Charley Barber's design was adopted for the five-cent piece in 1883. However, on the reverse the inscription omitted "Cents," assuming the "V" would be sufficient. Conmen immediately began gold-plating the coin and passing it off as a newly designed five-dollar gold piece. Consequently, the inscriptions were rearranged on the reverse to make room for "Cents."

In 1882, the last year of prolific creation of pattern pieces, George Morgan designed the "Shield Earring" silver dollar (J-1700), a piece equivalent in beauty to his pattern silver dollar of 1879.

George Morgan's so-called dollar (HK-125a) celebrating the centennial of the evacuation of New York City by the British. Struck in high relief, it artfully employs the coats of arms of the Washington family and the city, and it is judged to be one of his best works.

Perhaps Richard Watson Gilder was not the first to recognize that technological advances in the reducing lathe in Europe opened to sculptors and artists a world that had been the exclusive domain of Mint engravers—the designing for coins and medals. However, he certainly would have been exposed to the latest developments from the European-trained American artists attending his Friday night salons at his home in New York City.

Gilder was in a unique position to be a catalyst for design change. The periodical he edited had been revamped and renamed *The Century Magazine*. Its name came from the Century Association, whose club was located next door to Gilder's home. Almost overnight, it had become the premier illustrated monthly magazine for Americans. Now, Gilder launched a personal effort to improve American coin designs.

As an opening act, he sent Augustus Saint-Gaudens and Alexander Drake, the art editor for *The Century*, to the office of Mint Director Horatio Burchard in Washington. Saint-Gaudens and Drake had been classmates at Cooper Union. They found Burchard initially to be open-minded. The two men launched into a discussion of the aesthetic effect of fine coins upon the taste of the people. They displayed some beautiful Greek and Roman coins. Finally, to clinch their point, Gus pulled from his pocket a particularly rare Greek gold piece of exquisite design. Burchard was not moved, pulling from his pocket Morgan's silver dollar and saying, "Now we think this is a very beautiful coin." Both men knew that they would get no farther with this man.[11]

The second act occurred on the floor of the Senate on December 5, 1883. Justin Morrill was now chairman of the powerful Committee on Finance.[12] Morrill's first shot was directed against opposition to high-relief coinage designs. Upon the larger coins, having the central portions slightly concave and the figures in bas-relief and further protected by a gradually raised outer border would minimize the loss of value from abrasion. This action had the additional benefit of providing added depth for greater boldness in the figures. It would also make it difficult for counterfeiters to split the coins and substitute base metals for the inner part extracted.

Next, Morrill got to the real point of his diatribe on coin designs. The eagle representation on the ten- and twenty-dollar gold pieces best represented a flattened skin of some wild bird of prey packed away in the vaults of the Smithsonian. Whoever looked at these birds might well croak and utter Poe's doleful raven slang of "Nevermore." America's eagles exhibited too little of truth and grace of form. As to the silver coinage, the country was able to command the best and highest art resources yet appeared to be content with the poorest.

A follow-up point was a bombshell. Morrill stated that in accordance with the Coinage Act of 1873, the Mint did not have any discretion in regard to existing designs. They could not be changed unless authorized by Congress. The engraver could not show any skill except when new coins were authorized. Nor could his ambition be greatly stimulated by his rather limited compensation.

In conclusion, Morrill called for change. Our coins should by their size and character be easily distinguishable by sight or touch, and there should be no nickel or silver coins that could be gilded and passed off as gold coins. Morrill went further, declaring there was too much alloy in the silver coins, causing them to become dull as the dullest lead after a short period in circulation. Our standard fineness should be raised to that of British sterling silver, 925 fine. Finally, Morrill stated that the design and artistic execution of our coins should not be inferior, as they presently were, to any foreign examples.[13]

Morrill's speech had an unintended chilling effect upon the Mint's engravers. All efforts to design pattern pieces, prototypes to replace the tired Seated Liberty on the subsidiary silver, stopped.

It would have been a mistake for anyone to believe that the controversy surrounding the standard silver dollar would dissipate with the passage of the Bland-Allison Act that reinstituted its coinage in 1878. Barely four years later, John Sherman, freed from the restraints that came with being secretary of the Treasury and at least temporarily removed from presidential politics, expressed his opposition to its continued coinage. The silver dollar was only kept at par because, of the 100 million minted, the government held 65 million in vaults. The Silver Certificates issued alongside these coins had been freely exchanged for gold by the government. Had these certificates been redeemable only in silver, they would have declined to the bullion value of a standard silver dollar.[14]

A House report aired on June 6, 1882, framed the issues once again from a gold perspective. If coinage of the silver dollar and the issuance of Silver Certificates went on without an increase in the silver content of the dollar coin or an agreement on an international coinage ratio between the leading commercial nations to secure equivalency to gold, depreciation in the value of United States currency would commence and gold withdrawn for export. The problem was that no one could predict with any creditability exactly where that tipping point would be reached.

In an outgrowth of this report, a bill was introduced in the House that would limit the coinage of silver dollars to their circulating requirements and suspend the issue of Silver Certificates. Those in favor of passage argued the real results of the coinage of the "dollar of our fathers" was to compel the government to expend more than $100 million in buying and coining silver when the people wanted only one-third of them.[15]

The silver forces promptly retaliated. The decision of the New York Clearing-House to maintain a de facto gold standard, particularly in regard to United States bonds, had long irked them. Now they responded with legislation that would force clearing-houses to accept both gold and silver without bias. Ultimately the debate brought forth a compromise that provided no national banking association could be a member of any clearinghouse in which Silver Certificates were not received in clearing-house settlements.[16]

Once the banking reform legislation was in place, the New York Clearing-House agreement in favor of gold was effectively abrogated. However, this abrogation was in name only as a tacit understanding was substituted that neither the U.S. assistant treasurer for the New York Sub-Treasury nor any other clearing-house member should offer silver or Silver Certificates in payment of balances. This nullification was done with the full knowledge of the secretary of the Treasury.[17]

Putting the political debate aside, there was a more immediate practical problem. Treasury was running out of secure places to store the unwanted silver dollars. Vaults had been constructed at the New York, San Francisco, and Philadelphia Sub-Treasuries in 1878, at the San Francisco Mint, Baltimore Sub-Treasury, and Philadelphia Mint in 1880, and at both the sub-treasury and mint in San Francisco in 1882. At the end of 1882 those vaults were practically full. The tightest storage situation was in San Francisco where no space was available and surplus silver dollars were being transported to the East.

Treasury Secretary Folger was forced on January 23, 1883, to send a letter to the speaker of the House pleading for relief. Unless the law mandating the coinage of silver dollars were repealed, a supplemental appropriation must be enacted to provide the storage of 27 million more silver dollars, less those absorbed through demand into commerce. Pessimistically, Folger pointed out that only about one-and-a-half million silver dollars had been absorbed into circulation in the most recent twelve-month period.[18] Neither side wanted the fight over repeal; it was much easier to just appropriate the money for more vaults.

President Chester Arthur inflamed the silver forces in his annual message to Congress in December 1883 by asking for the recall of trade dollars.[19] These coins had not been struck for commercial purposes since 1878. That the trade dollar contained more silver than the standard silver dollar but commanded a lower value was an embarrassment. This anomaly needed to be addressed. There were two issues standing in the way. Would the silver bullion from the recall reduce the amount of required monthly purchases of silver during the melt period?[20] And what amount would be paid out for the recalled coins?

Discussion of valuation centered on the fact these coins had had their legal tender status removed without a grace period.[21] The government had a moral obligation to redeem the coins at their original legal tender value. In the back of every legislator's mind was the knowledge that now brokers or banks held most of the trade dollars.[22] The only consensus on the issue was that trade dollars counter-stamped, chopped by Chinese merchants, would not be accepted for recall. Hours of debate would drag this issue out until 1887. Only when the silver interests gained the concession that the bullion from the recalled trade dollars would not count toward the monthly silver purchases, would the trade dollar's fate be sealed.

The silver debate hit a new low when Richard Bland took to the House floor complaining that silver could not reach par with gold at a 16-to-1 ratio unless it had the same privileges of unlimited free coinage at the mints. When asked why he advocated the coining of silver when no one wanted it, he retorted that everybody wanted it in the West. Bland blamed the government for the large accumulation of silver dollars in storage. According to him, Treasury was deliberately not paying them out. The opposition branded his call for free silver as suicidal.[23]

The debates and jousting in Congress over silver seemed at times incoherent, disjointed, and lacking focus. However, one point was clear; silver was again emerging as a national issue. Arguing points would be sharpened, and opinions hardened going forward.

Chapter 32
In Death's Shadow

The double funeral was held on Saturday morning, February 16, 1884, in the fashionable Fifth Avenue Presbyterian Church. The pews were crowded with friends and members of the extended family. Before the altar were two rosewood coffins, covered with wreaths of roses, lilies, and green vines. At the door to the church stood two hearses, side by side. The services were simple but unusually touching. After the choir opened with a hymn, the Reverend John Hall preached a brief sermon upon the work and influence of Christian lives. The man was painfully affected, and every reference of a personal nature brought forth responses in tears and sobs from the many mourners. When the benedictions had been pronounced, and while the people still stood with lowered heads, the coffins were borne out through the congregation and out the church doors on their final journey to Greenwood Cemetery.[1]

They had died on Valentine's Day, the mother from typhoid fever and the wife in childbirth from complications due to Bright's disease, a type of kidney disease.[2] The blow to young Theodore Roosevelt was crushing. His worst nightmare had become his reality.

After his father had died unexpectedly, Roosevelt returned to Harvard determined to move forward. He had put his childhood sweetheart, Edith Carow, aside that following summer. Arriving on campus in September 1878, he was offered membership in the prestigious and exclusive Porcellian Club. In October he met Alice Hathaway Lee, daughter of a Boston banker, and quickly determined to win her hand. They became officially engaged on February 14, 1880. Courtship, however, did not interfere with his studies; Theodore Roosevelt graduated Phi Beta Kappa from Harvard on June 30, 1880. He married Alice Lee on his 22nd birthday, October 27, 1880.

The newlyweds started their domestic life at 6 West 57th Street; they were living in the Roosevelt family home with Theodore's mother. However, the couple had dreams and plans, purchasing a hilltop property at Oyster Bay on Long Island only a few weeks after the wedding. Roosevelt enrolled in Columbia Law School. He also moved forward his to-be-critically-acclaimed work, *The Naval War of 1812*. Yet, it was the third activity that raised eyebrows when he became a regular at the 21st District Republican Headquarters. Here he had to put aside his upper-class credentials, including membership in Mrs. Astor's elite social listing, to mix with the mostly Irish political class.

There was a specific reason that Theodore Roosevelt was going to get actively involved with politics. An event just prior to his father's death had been seared into his being.

The triggering of the sordid affair had been the determination of President Rutherford Hayes and Treasury Secretary John Sherman to clean up the New York Customs House, through which two-thirds of all customs receipts flowed. A Treasury Commission had been constituted to investigate and make recommendations. This commission had broken their investigation into four separate reports.

The first report had found appointments were based upon political influence without regard to an individual's ability. In addition, the Customs House was so grossly over-staffed that the commission recommended an across-the-board force reduction of 20 percent. However, no fault was found with the collector of customs, Chester Arthur. Arthur's sin was keeping very lax hours and looking the other way. Unsaid, the New York Customs House was under the complete control of Senator Roscoe Conkling. He would fight to retain that power.

Three more reports, each painting a picture of a totally dysfunctional, politically driven operation, were issued. President Hayes, after reading the last of these reports, made the decision to clean house and start over. It fell to Sherman to handle the removal of Arthur.

Sherman had soft-pedaled it. He met personally with Arthur, and in the process Secretary of State William Evarts offered the consulship at Paris as a consolation prize. Much to everyone's disappointment, Arthur declined this plum appointment. He would simply sit on the sidelines and let Hayes and Sherman duke it out with Conkling.[3]

In the first week of October 1877, Hayes made his move. A *New York Times* reporter questioned Secretary Evarts as to the replacements. Evarts would neither confirm nor deny that Theodore Roosevelt, Sr. would be nominated by Hayes to serve as collector.[4]

Theodore Roosevelt, Sr. had just turned 46. He had recently retired from the family plate-glass business to devote himself full time to charity work. His service to the community was exemplary, his reputation, unblemished. The *Times* gave Roosevelt its full support, describing him as a gentleman of the very highest character with executive abilities of no common order.[5]

On October 16, the nominations of Roosevelt and two subordinate officers were officially announced and sent to the Senate, in special session, for confirmation.[6] The Committee on Commerce, chaired by Conkling would review these nominations.[7] Fellow senators knew the outcome; Conkling saw to it that the three men were rejected. Chet Arthur continued as collector of the port in spite of the president.

Hayes had not accepted this defeat. With commencement of the regular session of Congress in December, the president submitted all three nominations again for confirmation. In the wee hours of the morning of December 2, Conkling reported the nominations out of his committee with an adverse recommendation.[8] Again, the nominations went to the floor of the full Senate. Again, the nomination of Theodore Roosevelt, Sr., was rejected.

Two days later the senior Roosevelt had collapsed with a diagnosis of acute peritonitis. He seemed to rally as Christmas approached, with the burden of this nomination and subsequent rejection receding into the background. He had much to rally for with the return that Christmas of his son, young Theodore, from his first-year studies at Harvard.[9]

Young Theodore Roosevelt would return to Harvard with no comprehension of the seriousness of his father's illness. Recovery was not to be, the son who idolized the father never saw him alive again. Theodore Roosevelt, Sr., had died on February 9, 1878. The stain of the political rejection, followed so swiftly by the father's death, left its mark upon the son. Theodore Roosevelt would embrace a political career with a clear-eyed perspective, bringing to bear the principles of honesty and fair dealing imbued in him by his father.

In the fall of 1881, Roosevelt immersed himself in the Republican nomination for state assemblyman from the 21st District. The incumbent was a Stalwart Republican machine politician. Roosevelt, against returning this man to Albany, stood on firm ground. Others in the district believed that Garfield's assassination combined with Conkling's theatrics put machine politicians in a bad odor. Roosevelt became their man, easily gaining the Republican nomination on October 28, 1881. Afterwards, Roosevelt announced that he would be strongly Republican on state matters but independent on local and municipal affairs. The 21st District that included the Roosevelt residence was staunchly Republican. After an eight-day campaign, the young man, barely 23, was swept into office.[10]

Whether Theodore Roosevelt realized it or not, his career as a professional politician commenced on January 3, 1882, at the opening session of the New York State Assembly. To the veteran legislators, there was but one question upon his arrival at the capitol: "Who's the Dude?" His stylish formal dress coupled with his upper-crust accent made him an easy mark for the crusty hardcore politicians at Albany. The "Dude" quickly attracted a small group of like-minded reformers. However, they were greatly in the minority; the majority, drawing from both parties, was there for the power and personal gain.

The activities of the Assembly were so openly corrupt that for Roosevelt to find a suitable target was like shooting ducks in a rain barrel. His opportunity came midway in the session. He had heard rumors that Judge T. R. Westbrook was in the pocket of the edgy New York City financier, Jay Gould. By sheer force of perseverance, Roosevelt gained the necessary two-thirds vote of the Assembly to launch an investigation. The Judiciary Committee, charged with carrying out the investigation, wrapped up its report with only days left in the session. Rumors leaked out the day before their report was to be made public, that the committee would recommend impeachment. However, money flowed in the intervening hours, and the recommendation came down against impeachment.[11]

Pictured here in about 1882, the dapper Theodore Roosevelt cut quite a figure among the rough-hewn politicians of Albany.

Roosevelt was furious. Yet in fighting from the moral high ground, he had, over the course of the session, gained the favorable attention of the newspapers. *Harper's Weekly* praised him for his public service. A testimonial dinner was held June 13 at Delmonico's in his honor.[12] The point was made at the dinner that, impeachment or no impeachment, at least one duck in the rain barrel had gotten its wings clipped. There were even rumors that Roosevelt might be considered for party leadership in the next session.

Roosevelt spent the summer of 1882 at leisure on Long Island. The fall election brought him back to reality. Though he breezed to reelection; everywhere else followed the national trend, a Democratic deluge.[13] Regardless of the dismal outlook for his party, Roosevelt became the minority leader. He wasted no time in introducing a civil service reform bill that drew the attention of the new governor, Grover Cleveland. Roosevelt had wanted to meet Cleveland, having formed a favorable impression of the Democrat. However, Cleveland beat him to the punch. He summoned Roosevelt to his executive office to discuss ways to get the reform bill out of committee, where it was hopelessly stalled, and onto the floor for a vote. The two men talked for an hour, and it was Cleveland that sized up Roosevelt as an ally for good government.

The hugely overweight, cautious governor and the energetic "Dude" from New York City made an odd couple. However, Cleveland took his erstwhile ally in careful doses. He was quoted saying, "There is a great sense in a lot that he (Roosevelt) says but there is such a cocksuredness about him that he stirs up doubt in me all the time."[14] Nevertheless, when a Roosevelt ally successfully got the civil service reform bill to the assembly floor, Cleveland gave it his full support at great personal political cost. The bill came out of the Assembly and passed the state Senate on the last day of the session. This new law put Grover Cleveland on the national stage.

Roosevelt's return to New York City was marked with pressing family matters. Alice was pregnant. Nevertheless, September 1883 found Roosevelt bound for Dakota Territory to an area around Medora to hunt bison. The daily hunts were arduous, made worse by inclement weather. Capping it off, game was scarce. On the positive side, evenings were filled with conversation around a fire. Here Roosevelt confided to his hunting companions that he was seriously thinking of investing in the cattle business. As the bison hunt extended futilely for days, Roosevelt focused more and more on the issue at hand—to invest or not to invest.

Finally, Roosevelt struck a deal to invest in a herd of cattle to be managed by local cattlemen, Sylvane Ferris and Bill Merrifield. He wrote a check on the spot for $14,000 as an initial down payment. Asked if he wanted a receipt, he declined. Roosevelt was taking a large risk; there were limits to the money he had inherited from his father, and he was already committed to building the home on Long Island. However, the enchantment of the Badlands had fully captured Theodore Roosevelt's imagination. Here the vast countryside with its endless unspoiled vistas gave him a sense of freedom that he could not experience in the East.[15]

The fall election of 1883 had been good for New York State Republicans; they regained control of the Assembly. Roosevelt as the sitting minority leader believed his chances excellent to win the speaker's position when the new Assembly convened in January. However, Warner Miller—Thomas Platt's replacement in the Senate, and a Half Breed—had promised the position to another individual. Votes changed, and Miller's man prevailed. Defeat never suited Roosevelt particularly well, and he threw himself into the legislative fray, promising through reform legislation to break the power of the political machines in New York City. However, weekends were for family now that Alice was entering her final weeks of pregnancy.

And then the unthinkable happened. On February 14, 1884, Theodore Roosevelt drew a large "X" in his diary and wrote: "The light has gone out of my life."[16]

The day after the funeral, Alice Lee Roosevelt was christened. It seemed off-handed, but the grieving husband and father placed the care of this little baby girl in the hands of his spinster sister, Anna, or "Bamie" as she was more familiarly known among family and friends. Only in those days immediately following Alice's death did he utter his late wife's name. His little girl became Baby Lee. Yet, he knew he must go on.

He returned to Albany on February 18 to push his New York City reform legislation. The family moved quickly to sell 6 West 57th Street. Roosevelt did sign the contract to commence construction of Leeholm on Long Island but espoused no plans to move in upon its projected completion. Roosevelt basically left everything in New York City up in the air for Bamie to sort out.

Politics resumed front seat for Theodore Roosevelt with the convening of the New York State Republican Convention on April 23, 1884. At stake was the election of delegates to the national convention including four delegate-at-large seats. Over a long night of protracted negotiations, Roosevelt led the at-large voting. Coming in a distant fifth was his rival, Senator Warner Miller. Flush from this victory, Roosevelt got in the humiliated Miller's face. Here was payback for the underhanded dealings over the speakership and he meant for Miller to know it. Roosevelt's grief in the emotional stress of the moment had poured forth in pure vengeful anger.[17]

Roosevelt had one last chore to accomplish in Albany, the enactment of his suite of bills for the reform of New York City government. The assemblyman was confident that Governor Cleveland would sign his legislation into law. He was wrong. Cleveland simply told Roosevelt that he could not sign the bills as presently drawn. Instead of looking for common ground such as a bill with technical fixes to cure the legislation, Roosevelt just stood in front of Cleveland and blustered. The legislative session was near its end, and the vetoes killed Roosevelt's reform effort. Intentionally or unintentionally, it also healed the rift between Grover Cleveland and Tammany Hall, the Democratic political machine in New York City, over the governor's support for civil service reform.

With the convention less than a month away, Theodore Roosevelt received a letter from Henry Cabot Lodge, a Republican state party leader from Massachusetts. Lodge, too, was a delegate-at-large from his home state and supported well-regarded Senator George Edmunds of Vermont. The letter was favorably received as Roosevelt was on the verge of writing Lodge for the same reason. Lodge was eight years senior to Roosevelt, but the two men had much in common, both being Harvard graduates and Porcellians. Roosevelt promptly invited Lodge to come to New York on May 16 and be his houseguest. As they were in the process of breaking up the house on West 57th Street, Theodore apologized that it might seem like camping out. Lodge accepted.[18]

If Roosevelt and Lodge were seeking to promote the candidacy of Senator Edmunds, Richard Watson Gilder was the man to see. *The Century*'s associate editor, Robert Underwood Johnson, described the meeting. Roosevelt was full of humorous anecdotes from the New York State Assembly. The stories proved so good that Gilder suggested that he pull them together for an article for *The Century*. Theodore easily won over Gilder and Johnson by his humor and democratic fervor. Johnson noted how attractive Roosevelt's spirit was when one met him face to face.[19]

The Republican National Convention convened the first week in June 1884 in Chicago. Roosevelt and Lodge had an

Henry Cabot Lodge early on formed a close friendship with Theodore Roosevelt. He was Roosevelt's political confidante, helping to craft a course planned to put Roosevelt in the White House in 1904.

almost immediate problem. Senator Edmunds had made it clearly known before the convention that he did not want the Republican presidential nomination.[20] On the other hand, John Sherman did want the nomination. Sherman had made several canvassing trips around the United States prior to the convention but was clearly reduced to the status of a favorite son in spite of strong support from the financial community in New York City.[21]

The problem for all the candidates was that James G. Blaine had name recognition among party regulars. Blaine wrapped up the nomination on the fourth ballot. Sherman picked up votes late but without a deadlock between Blaine and Arthur, he was not a factor.[22]

The departing senators and representatives exhibited little enthusiasm for the ticket of Blaine and Senator John Logan. In fact, they could hardly conceal their disappointment; but there was no move by the Stalwarts to bolt the party. The independent Republicans, however, including Roosevelt and Lodge, were a question mark.

The balloting over, Theodore Roosevelt headed west to heal his soul. From his point of view, the only thing good to come out of the convention was his friendship with Cabot Lodge. Indeed, Lodge would be both a friend and valuable ally over the rest of Theodore's life.

Just the thought of the Badlands, as the miles began to slip by, helped his mind settle down. While changing trains at St. Paul, a reporter accosted him, demanding to know if he would accept Blaine's nomination or bolt. At any earlier moment, the answer might have been colorfully newsworthy. Instead, Roosevelt said he would not bolt; he had nothing against Blaine personally.[23] He would burn no bridges with the Republican Party.

Other reform-minded Republicans, sick of machine politics and its associated corruption, felt differently. With the nomination of Grover Cleveland, they bolted and were derisively called "Mugwumps." Watson Gilder, one of the frustrated defectors, wrote to Roosevelt on June 10.

> The paper has conflicting accounts as to your intentions with regard to the Blaine & Logan outrage. Personally, I have too small an acquaintance with you to venture to advise or exhort—but as one who has had unbounded admiration for and faith in your career will you let me make an earnest and (illegible) hope that today's news (in the *Tribune*) is untrue and that the enormous body of genuine though independent Republicans in the state of New York will not have to lament a lost leader in this crisis.

In 1898 Gilder penciled at the bottom of this letter that Roosevelt told him that this was the only remonstrance that made him feel badly.[24]

With the dedication of the *Farragut*, the career of Augustus Saint-Gaudens reached heights never dreamed of by the sculptor. Even before the formal dedication, he declined to enter any competitions for commissions, insisting instead to negotiate directly with the prospective client or walk away from the work. In this manner, in

February 1881, he initiated discussions to provide a large bas-relief plaque honoring the 54th Massachusetts Volunteer Infantry Regiment, the second African-American unit organized to fight in the Civil War.[25] This unit took heavy casualties, losing its colonel, Robert Gould Shaw, in front of Fort Wagner outside of Charleston in 1863. Plans called for a commemorative plaque to be mounted on the wall in front of the state capitol on Beacon Street in Boston. While not really a monumental work, it nevertheless had symbolic importance and would become known as the *Shaw Memorial*.

In spite of this adulation, Gus had a problem: the Morgan Tomb project was far from completed. As contracted, Stanford White was to design and oversee construction of the mausoleum to be erected at the Cedar Hill Cemetery in Hartford, Connecticut. Saint-Gaudens was to provide the statuary to adorn the mausoleum. Even while Saint-Gaudens was in Paris at work on the *Farragut*, Morgan had had suspicions that the sculptor was not focusing on his commission. He had asked Stanford White for photographs of the models, forcing White to say they were too rough for any pictures to be taken.[26]

The plan, as the *Farragut* neared completion, was for Saint-Gaudens to acquire a very large marble block from which a grouping of four angels would be carved in place. The work would then be placed atop the completed mausoleum. Finally progressing, the sculptor sent White photographs to critique of his concept, now reduced from four angels to three.

At this point, White did Saint-Gaudens a disservice. He wrote that, while the angels in the photographs were "busting," the ensemble looked like a musical party. Morgan and his wife were "blue-nosed" Presbyterians and might think of death as a gloomy performance instead of a resurrection.[27] Presented with a quandary and unwilling to consult his client, Saint-Gaudens set the angels aside.

In March 1880 Saint-Gaudens, with his days in Paris drawing to a close, finally communicated with Morgan. He was ready to commit for the block of marble.[28] He had been sick, and the angels were not as far along as he wished.[29] Unsaid was that this project was hardly even in an initial stage.

Morgan answered that he was "very anxious that his tomb should be completed as soon as possible." The remains of his son and daughter-in-law were deposited in an unsecure receiving vault in Hartford. Morgan wanted to know when Saint-Gaudens would complete the models. Saint-Gaudens answered that he was still working on the angels and would show Morgan a carver's model upon his return to New York at the beginning of July.[30] In May, he told Morgan that the angels were almost up in half-sized models that he intended the carvers to use.[31]

Saint-Gaudens held true to his word upon returning to New York. By October two marble blocks, rather than one large one that had proved too expensive, had arrived. Also Morgan had paid an installment of the commission, meaning that some small models of the angels must have been completed.[32] However, the fly in the ointment this time was the mausoleum; it would not be ready to accommodate the marble blocks until July 1881 at the earliest.[33]

The two marble blocks were shipped from New York and up the Connecticut River to Hartford in June 1881. Morgan immediately pressed Saint-Gaudens to start on cutting the figures in place.[34] Gus promised that he would begin on the first angel figure as soon as the blocks were positioned on top of the mausoleum. On the surface it was a reassuring answer, but much was again unsaid. Morgan had yet to see the model that most likely was not nearly finalized.[35]

Morgan refocused upon Saint-Gaudens in November. The marble blocks were now in place. Had Saint-Gaudens made provisions to protect the workmen during the cold weather? Morgan had been told that the work did not look well in its present condition; he was anxious to have it completed both for Saint-Gaudens's account and his. In this he sidestepped his concerns over his failing health.[36] Gus seemingly was on top of the situation, telling Morgan that his carver had just made the necessary arrangements for a shelter at the mausoleum and that he was doing all he could to have the work finished by next May or June as promised.[37]

In spite of these exchanges, Gus made no progress on the Morgan angels. Seemingly distracted, Morgan did not badger Saint-Gaudens again until May 1882. At that point, Gus confessed that no progress had been made over the previous winter on the carving; he was still modeling the figures. The old man now worried that the wooden frame structure around the two marble blocks that formed the shaft might look bad and should be taken down.

Saint-Gaudens responded that he would either pull down the shed or make it look presentable. That was not the action that Morgan wanted. Putting politeness aside, he told Saint-Gaudens that he was mortified beyond expression at the long delays.[38] Sadly, this outburst accomplished the opposite of its intent. Gus, as he had before in the face of strong emotions from Morgan, only ceased all communications with him.

The next exchange between the two men came four months later. Morgan sent Saint-Gaudens a note on Thursday, September 14, asking that he call on him at his home. Gus was out when the note was delivered and did not return to his studio until late that Friday. He called Saturday and learned that Morgan was no longer in town. He shared with Morgan in a follow-up note that he was at work on the angel group and that rapid progress was being made.[39] However, he was about to leave town for a week or ten days. And so, Saint-Gaudens ducked the old man.

Davida Clark became Saint-Gaudens's mistress and mother to his child. The sculptor would support this second family throughout his lifetime.

Only in November 1882 when Saint-Gaudens believed that he was back in Morgan's good graces did he reopen correspondence. Saint-Gaudens had found that he was constantly interrupted at his studio. To give his undivided attention to the Morgan group, Gus had started working at another studio that no one knew about. He was now absolutely undisturbed and making rapid progress. He felt that Morgan would have no further reason to complain of delay on his part. He closed by sincerely thanking Morgan for his patience.[40]

What was really going on here? Gus had found a model for the central figure of the angel holding a scroll. From the fact that this same figure appears in later works, it is clear that the model for this angel was Davida Clark.[41] Gus had fallen in love, and this new studio was his hideaway.

Saint-Gaudens was to father another son with Davida and support this second family until his death.

As if on cue, although not having seen Gus's newest letter because the sculptor had not yet mailed it, Morgan showed up at the "official" studio. Upon learning of the visit, Gus penned a second note. If Morgan wished to see his group of angels, Gus asked that he name a day, just not that particular day, as Gus did not wish Morgan or anyone else to see them just now.[42] It was a strange note that only served to raise more questions than it could ever answer. The models that he had been working on since at least the spring of 1880 were not yet ready to be seen. How many compositions had Gus worked through only to start over again? It also was the last correspondence between the two men.

Morgan's health was rapidly slipping. Suffering from severe chest pains, Morgan died on February 14, 1883.[43] Thus, the man was interred in his mausoleum without having left any evidence of ever having seen the models of the angel group for his tomb.

With Morgan gone, the pressure of the deadline slipped. In mid-August 1883 Gus finished models for two of the angels and forwarded them to Albert Entress, the local stonecutter he had selected to do the work.

With the project finally started, Saint-Gaudens then took two months off to tour the West with Stanford White. Upon his return, he went to Hartford to discover that Entress had not commenced the work. In defense of Entress, the third angel, the central figure with the scroll that Gus had been working on at the undisclosed location, remained unfinished.[44] In addition, archival photographs of the models lend credence to the assumption that Gus had held to his original intent of supplying models at half scale, encumbering the pointing process necessary for transferring the work into the marble.[45]

Matters came to a head at the end of January 1884; Gus needed $1,000 from the Morgan Estate to meet the expenses of the marble cutters. He now admitted to the executor that the model for the angel with the scroll was still not done. He was having trouble getting this last angel right. A photo of this single figure he also enclosed to give a sense of how the scroll would be held.[46]

The Fourth of July, 1884, found Saint-Gaudens writing to the estate again for money. This time it was $1,500. He also sent a new photograph of the third model-the central figure. Gus had finally turned this work over to the carvers.

July that year found Gus, as usual, alone in New York as Gussie had gone to Boston and would depart shortly for Halifax. There were problems financially. Gussie had taken a duplicate checkbook with her, and Saint-Gaudens was having trouble keeping track of the combined checks written. Not surprisingly, he was overdrawn at the bank.[47]

On August 20 Saint-Gaudens was alone at the studio; he found it lonely.[48] That afternoon it became uncomfortably hot, and Gus knocked off work at 6 p.m. Thunderstorms during the night cooled the city down. There seemed to be no issues with the Morgan angel grouping. Had the need arisen, he could easily have run over to Hartford in a day trip. The train service was frequent. There even was an express leaving Hartford as late as 10:35 p.m. for New York City nightly.[49]

Then it happened. Friday morning, August 22, Gus's quiet summer came to an abrupt end with the arrival of a telegram.[50] The shed around the Morgan tomb had caught fire the previous night, destroying the nearly finished work of the angel group. Saint-Gaudens hurried to catch the 11 a.m. train to Hartford.[51] What Saint-Gaudens saw that afternoon was a crumbling, worthless column that had once been the shaft that towered twenty-five feet above the mausoleum. The charred debris of the protective structure surrounded it. The granite roof of the mausoleum had been damaged by falling pieces of the shaft, but there had been no apparent damage to the interior. The fire had been discovered about 11 p.m. by the family of Robert Scrivener, custodian of the cemetery, who lived in a cottage at the entrance gate.

There was much speculation as to the cause of the fire. The officers of the Cedar Hill Cemetery Association were quick to initiate an investigation. The facts of the event were that the shed had been closed and locked as usual that Thursday night at 5:30 p.m. Entress stated that no fire had been on the premise that day. The source of the fire was a mystery. There was no difficulty between the men, no ill feeling toward Entress or the cemetery management and employees.

Saint-Gaudens presented several proposals to restore the original design. Morgan's widow did not share her husband's love of art. Furthermore, she harbored great bitterness over the affair, believing strongly that Saint-Gaudens should have long since completed his work.[52] The family would repair the roof of the mausoleum and walk away from the whole affair.

There is another version of the fire that has lingered in the shadows. Some months after the tragic event, Truman Bartlett, now an art critic in Boston, was asked to come to Hartford to critique a statute of Nathan Hale being sculpted by Enoch Woods Smith. It was Bartlett who had allowed Saint-Gaudens to move into one of his two studios when the artist was down and out in Paris. Over the subsequent years, Bartlett developed an intense dislike and jealousy for Saint-Gaudens that seemed to escalate as Saint-Gaudens's career prospered while his own languished.

While in Hartford, Bartlett learned that Albert Entress wanted to see him. Of course, knowing of the fire, Bartlett took the time to meet the marble cutter. At that meeting Entress complained of having trouble with Saint-Gaudens. A day or two before the fire, Entress went to Morgan's agent in Hartford to say he could do nothing more with the work and that it was in such a condition that he did not want to have anything more to do with it. The agent then wired Saint-Gaudens and received a reply that he would come at once by train, arriving early in the afternoon preceding the fire. Saint-Gaudens did not appear that afternoon but did appear according to the story very early on the morning after the fire. Saint-Gaudens supposedly gave no explanation for the delay. Entress now harbored a suspicion that Saint-Gaudens set the fire.[53]

There are holes in this story. Bartlett had been urged to interview Morgan's agent to corroborate the story but, inexcusably, failed to do so. Saint-Gaudens was writing to his wife at 11:30 on the morning of the fire, and he was in his studio to receive the telegram from Entress the next morning telling of the fire. These alibis seemingly contradict Bartlett's statement as to Saint-Gaudens's whereabouts. However, the train schedules were such that Saint-Gaudens could have traveled to Hartford the afternoon of the fire and return by early morning to New York.

The story now lay dormant until Saint-Gaudens's death. At this point, Albert Entress gave an interview with the *Hartford Daily Courant.* Quoting from that article, there was little doubt as to the origin of the fire. "There was no question the fire was set by incendiaries or vandals. In the morning cloths saturated with kerosene were found on the ground." The stone carver also related that he was a heavy loser in the fire, being badly crippled financially.[54]

The final chapter in this story occurred in 1913 when the Saint-Gaudens autobiography, completed posthumously by his son, Homer, was published. The Hartford newspaper did another story on the fire, sending a reporter to interview Robert Scrivener, the cemetery custodian, who was still living. His memory of the fire was sharp.

> I had gone to bed and woke out of my first sleep to see a blaze in the sky. At the same time I heard neighbors talking of the fire, and dressing, I ran out to see if I could help. It was the tomb that was burning. When I ran up no one was there, and the fire was burning fiercely. I succeeded in dragging away one side of the shed, by the stairs, so that the plaster models from which the workmen were carving the marble were saved, slightly scarred but still useable.

Scrivener then went on to talk about the next day.

> When Saint-Gaudens came I was very reserved, and refused to ride out to the tomb in his carriage. The thing that he seemed greatly interested in was his plaster models and he seemed much relieved when I told him that they had been saved.

After the fire, the broken and chipped marble statues lay around for some time. Ultimately some of them were used for foundations, and one piece still remained in Scrivener's lawn. Naturally the reporter asked Scrivener whom he thought started the fire. He said there was no doubting its incendiary origin. He ventured to the reporter that the officers of the cemetery association had a very definite idea as to the origin of the fire but would not divulge it.[55]

Saint-Gaudens would never be accused openly of starting the fire. On the other hand, Saint-Gaudens was guilty of gross abuse of his client. Edwin Morgan was responsible more than any other individual in seeing that Saint-Gaudens received the *Farragut* commission. The true root of this tragedy that caused so much angst for Morgan's family over the failed commission was undeniably the procrastination of Augustus Saint-Gaudens.

Chapter 33
CHANGE BUT NO CHANGE

In the general election of 1884, the Democrats pounded Blaine's connection with the Crédit Mobilier scandal. The Republicans countered with the ditty, "Ma, Ma, where's my Pa," alluding to the child Cleveland fathered out of wedlock. Cleveland addressed the extenuating circumstances surrounding the child in a straightforward manner, allowing him to run on his record of civil service reform.

Grover Cleveland's running mate was Thomas Hendricks from Indiana. The election was close. The Democrats carried the Solid South, and the Republicans carried everywhere else except Indiana and the Middle Atlantic states. However, the key to the contest was New York. Whoever took New York carried the Electoral College. For two days the vote was so close neither candidate could claim victory. In the final count, Cleveland carried New York by a razor-thin 1,149 votes. The independent Republicans, Mugwumps, had played a major role in the victory. Gilder and Cleveland would become close friends. Having regained the White House after an absence of 28 years, the Democrats took the Republican ditty and turned it on its ear by adding a second verse: "Gone to the White House, ha ha ha!"

Horatio Burchard breathed a sigh of relief when the Senate adjourned its special session for approval of presidential appointments on April 2, 1885. His five-year term as director of the Mint had expired in early 1884; at which point, President Arthur reappointed him. Now no move had been made to oust him while the Senate was in session, leaving him to believe he would remain in place through Cleveland's four years in office.

That was not the case with the mints or even the backwaters of the bureau, the several small regional assay offices. Local and state Democrats, having been out of power for so long, were determined to reap the spoils of victory. The new secretary of the Treasury was Daniel Manning, and having just been chair of the New York Democratic Party, he was Cleveland's eyes and ears to the politics of this administration. One look at the man said that he was more at home at a Tammany Hall conclave than at a cabinet meeting. Thus, he would not stand in the way of this political housecleaning. The mints were no exception. Only Andrew Mason at the all-important New York Assay Office survived.

Yet the messiest situation proved to be the Helena Assay Office. Its assayer-in-charge, Russell Harrison, was the son of Senator Benjamin Harrison. An 1877 graduate of Lafayette College, young Harrison had taken courses in mining and engineering, thus paving the way for his appointment to the Helena Assay Office in January 1879. He brought with him a friend from Indiana, L.A. Walker, to serve as one of his clerks.[1] Once settled into his position, Harrison branched out into the cattle business. He formed the Montana Land and Cattle Company and brought in outside investors to fund the business. Again, Walker served as clerk for Harrison's cattle operations.

In 1884 everything was going Harrison's way. Mining activity was on the rise, lifting the importance of the assay office. At the beginning of the year, he married May Saunders, a Washington debutante and daughter of former Nebraska Senator Alvin Saunders.[2] As a proper abode for his new wife, he built what was considered the finest example of Queen Anne architecture in Helena. That showplace home was in keeping with his position as a director of the Montana National Bank of Helena. In August, Harrison was elected secretary of the Stock-Growers Association of Montana.[3] Thus, Harrison sat atop the twin pillars of power in Montana Territory—mining and cattle. Still there was speculation in April 1885 that Harrison might be removed.

While all roses to an outsider, on the inside there were problems. With the increase in deposits, the quality of the clerical work was slipping, raising the ire of Robert Preston at the Bureau of the Mint. Also, Harrison's expenditures against his contingent appropriation were deemed excessive. However, management of the bullion fund was the major concern.

Standard operating procedure at an assay office was to pay the depositor for bullion presented. If coin on hand at the assay office was insufficient, the depositor received a draft payable by the assistant treasurer at the New York Sub-Treasury. From time to time, the assayer would routinely request advances to be placed in his bullion fund to cover these drafts. On April 1, 1885, Harrison routinely requested by telegram an advance of $50,000. On April 2, Harrison was advised by mail that due to the large amount of cash in his custody, no further moneys would be placed to his credit in New York until the cash in his vault had been paid out. Meanwhile, Harrison, expecting a routine approval, had issued some $30,000 in drafts that the assistant treasurer in New York refused to honor.[4] It was a major embarrassment for Harrison, but the Bureau of the Mint was not without fault.

This matter of the bullion fund was hardly resolved when Treasury Secretary Manning handed Mint Director Burchard formal charges made against Harrison by John P. Donaldson.[5] Donaldson was a sometime miner and fight promoter. His major claim to fame was having gone eleven rounds with John L. Sullivan before being dispatched.[6] It was an odd source for the complaint. Nevertheless, Burchard pursued it. He detailed his brother-in-law, W. P. Lawver, employed at the bureau, to take testimony for the investigation. It seemed unusual that he did not turn the investigation over to Edward Leech, the comptroller of bullion. Delays occurred, and Lawver did not reach Helena until the last week of May.

In the meantime, a different problem with the bullion popped up. Bars of bullion sent from Helena to the New York Assay Office for separating gold and silver contained less gold by weight than silver. Departmental policy prohibited the assay offices from purchasing bullion that contained less than 50 percent gold by fineness. Thus, these bars would be treated as silver, and all silver purchases must be handled through the secretary of the Treasury. Treasury did not want even the slightest taint that silver could be presented for purchase at will at a mint facility. Procedure dictated that these bars should have been returned to the depositor rather than purchased. There had been previous times when the gold content of a bar or two had fallen below the 50 percent threshold. However, this time it covered 17,228 ounces of silver combined with less than 2,000 ounces of gold in sixteen bars. Angry at this blatant ignoring of settled procedures, Burchard took this to Manning as it represented a breach of the secretary's authority.[7] Behind this dispute was the implication that Harrison had shown favoritism to one of the large mining interests.

Harrison did not back down. He recalled during his interview with Burchard in Washington after he had accepted the position in Helena that Burchard told him he would be permitted to make purchases of bullion when the value of the gold exceeded that of the silver. Burchard countered that he remembered telling Harrison that he could not accept bullion where the weight of the gold was less than the weight of the silver.[8] This was a slick move on Harrison's part; he had just put the dispute into a gray area for which there could be no resolution.

One of Lawver's first acts when finally on the ground in Helena was to offer protection to any employee against removal should they wish to testify.[9] Seemingly out of nowhere, H.B. Wilkins Jr. came forward. Although a clerk in the assay office, this man was a surprise. He had been a groomsman in Harrison's wedding the preceding year. At that time, he had been private secretary to the territorial governor. He had since resigned and accepted a clerkship in the assay office.

The two men met in a saloon, and Wilkins afterwards boasted that he had "fired fourteen cocktails into Lawver and fixed him all right." Whether Lawver remembered any details of the conversation the next morning, June 1, made little difference as Harrison fired Wilkins on the spot.[10] Burchard promptly ordered Wilkins reinstated.[11] Harrison ignored Burchard and refused to let Wilkins return to his desk.[12] Then Harrison argued that Burchard did not have the authority to countermand his removal of Wilkins. Failing on that point, he used the argument that he removed Wilkins to protect the man who provided the clerk's bond.[13] Burchard saw that as a ruse and refused to reverse his disapproval.[14] It was still not over. Burchard was next forced to go to Secretary Manning, who, in turn, bucked it over to the solicitor of the Treasury, Alexander McCue, for a decision.[15]

In this heated atmosphere, Lawver began his investigation. Of course, the accuser, Donaldson, was out of town, and Burchard instructed that the proceedings go forth without him. The proceedings were not open to the public. Not even the formal charges leaked into the newspapers. Street gossip had Harrison using public money for private purposes.[16] The charges certainly addressed excessive absences of Harrison from his office. The testimony covered both Harrison's public and private affairs over the five years he had been assayer-in-charge.[17]

On June 12 Burchard telegraphed Lawver wanting to know how much longer the investigation would take. He wanted Lawver to meet him at his home in Freeport, Illinois. He closed by saying that all was well.[18] With Congress adjourned, Burchard was ready for his annual summer vacation at home. The situation suddenly changed with Burchard telling Lawver four days later to come directly to Washington if testimony was closed.[19]

Things were not all well. Secretary of the Treasury Manning had requested Burchard's resignation on June 10. Burchard protested. There had been no malfeasance or misconduct on his part. Manning's stated reason was that the position of director of the mint was intimately associated with the administration, and the secretary wanted the privilege of selecting his own man. Burchard countered that the Coinage Act of 1873 set the term of office at five years precisely to avoid turnover with each change of administration. Therefore, Burchard saw no reason why an exception should be made and that he should be allowed to continue in office for his full term.[20] That line of reasoning fell flat on its face with Manning.

Now a lame duck, Burchard basically told Lawver to tie a string around his testimony and dump it on Manning's desk. Lawver provided no summary of findings. Burchard made no recommendations when he formally conveyed the report to Manning on June 27.[21] Manning, in turn, conveyed the report to Alexander McCue, placing the solicitor on the spot to provide cover for whatever decision was to be made. McCue made his findings on July 3, 1885. He had examined the charges made by Donaldson and found the evidence against Russell Harrison to be neither clear nor satisfactory. McCue suggested that no further action be taken.[22] Manning sat on this report.

Burchard's replacement, James P. Kimball, walked into the director's office on July 1 with an interim appointment. Given the potential for Senator Benjamin Harrison, actively involved in his son's case, to cause embarrassment during the confirmation hearings when the Senate reconvened the following December, Manning and the new director were in a delicate spot.

Kimball was not a politician. He was a competent mining engineer and had played a major role in developing iron mines in Bedford County, Pennsylvania, just prior to taking on the job of director of the mint. He would prove to be a very capable mint director, but it was late in the game regarding the Harrison investigation.

Kimball's first act in the affair was to deny John Donaldson's request that he be reimbursed for travel expenses for his return to Helena to give testimony.[23] Next came a telegram from Russell Harrison, raising the issue of Wilkins's removal.[24] That was still pending. However, Kimball was more supportive of Harrison's assertion that removal of the clerk was on grounds having nothing to do with immunity for testifying.

President Cleveland's director of the Mint, James Kimball, pushed for efficiencies in coin production and disrupted some of the cozy business relationships that had existed for several generations at the Philadelphia Mint.

Shortly after this telegram, Kimball relayed to Harrison the personal wish of Secretary Manning that a certain individual be employed at the Helena Assay Office. Harrison tartly responded that he would hire this individual if the department would rule in his favor against Wilkins.[25] Faced with a political deal that was sure to blow up in his face, Kimball pressed McCue for a ruling on Wilkins. McCue found in favor of Harrison, and Wilkins was removed effective June 1, 1885.

The investigation mercifully reached its end for Russell Harrison on August 20. That was the day Kimball conveyed to him a letter written on July 31 by the acting secretary of the Treasury that concurred with the solicitor's opinion that no further action be taken in the case.[26] Manning had washed his hands entirely of the affair and would not even sign his name to the document exonerating Harrison. On September 4, Robert Preston informed Harrison that it had been decided to accept the transfer of the substandard bullion to the New York Assay Office, but Harrison was to make no more such purchases.[27] Harrison resigned September 30, 1885.[28]

James Kimball belatedly received his Senate confirmation on May 14, 1886.[29] Nothing more was heard on the investigation until Wilkins filed a suit in the U. S. Court of Claims in Washington in December 1886 for wages from June to September 1885.[30] Just as quickly as this suit appeared, it was made to disappear.

Once Kimball settled in, he concentrated on cost reductions in ways not experienced before at the various operations. He questioned the long-standing cozy relationship between the Philadelphia Mint and Arthur Orr. In addition, he terminated assay work done for outside parties at the mints and assay offices.[31]

In November Kimball did the unthinkable. The coining operations at the Carson City Mint had been temporarily suspended in June and then extended indefinitely by Secretary Manning in July.[32] Raw bullion deposits then trailed off because payment was in draft form rather than coin, and a charge for transporting the bullion to San Francisco for refining was instituted. Now Kimball recommended suspension of bullion receiving, meaning the complete closure of the Carson City Mint. Kimball retained the superintendent and a watchman and terminated the remaining workforce.[33]

In 1886–87, Kimball was able to make improvements in the steam plant at Philadelphia. He wanted more; the machinery and appliances at Philadelphia had been introduced a half century before and were far behind foreign mints and private operations domestically. Kimball strongly believed, at the very least, a third floor should be added at Philadelphia or adjacent ground purchased to support an expansion. However he considered construction of an entirely new facility to offer the best alternative.[34]

The director of the Mint, in this same timeframe, clamped the lid down on the thriving side business of restrikes. No coins would be struck after the year of their date or in any other metal or alloy. Trial pieces, struck for mint purposes only, could not be issued, circulated, or sold. The revised statutes prohibited such pieces, and Kimball would enforce the regulations.[35] To prove he meant what he said, he had previously stopped the auction of Henry Linderman's coin collection by his widow that had been scheduled for June 28, 1887. More than a dozen lots from the original catalog were removed before the auction was allowed to take place.[36]

There was a notable exception to side activity at the Philadelphia Mint. The engravers still had free rein to take on whatever additional design work came their way. George Morgan executed a beautiful high-relief so-called dollar celebrating the centennial of the Constitution. Charles Barber even joined with an excellent piece recognizing the gift of the *Statue of Liberty* by France and its designer, Auguste Bartholdi.

George Morgan's design for the centennial of the Constitution (GW-1009) was an excellent example of his artistic skills.

In 1886 Charles Barber began his participation in the genre of so-called dollars with a design celebrating the erection of the *Statue of Liberty.*

Kimball in his annual report for the fiscal year 1888 could not resist taking one good shot at the Mint Service as it was then constituted. European mints were favored with permanent organizations, skilled supervision and skilled labor. The mints in the United States were subject to quadrennial changes in the entire personnel, incompatible with the business methods of a high-class manufacturing establishment. He also stated that only two mints were necessary to serve the country's needs.[37]

Jos Harmstead had survived that first force reduction at San Francisco. That was the least of his worries as his wife had suffered a debilitating stroke in February 1885. That fall, his wife suffered a second catastrophic stroke. Harmstead took a leave of absence to be with her during her last days.

As 1886 played out, Jos Harmstead realized that he was struggling to perform even some of his basic tasks. His hands were stiff, and he needed to sit down frequently. His co-workers teased him, calling him an old codger. That was not the case with coiner Charles Gorham. He found nothing funny about the teasing; he would often come and lend a hand if Harmstead had a problem.

On August 12, 1886, Superintendent Israel Lawton called Harmstead to his office. Lawton had troubles finding the words, but Harmstead knew at age 72 that his time had come. A fine dinner was held later that month with Harmstead receiving a gold watch and fob for all his years of dedication to the service. Harmstead would pass three years later.[38]

With Kimball in charge of the mint, Watson Gilder was ready to mount a full assault on the federal government to gain new coin designs. The March 1887 issue of *The Century* let fly a full salvo at the existing designs. Of all civilized nations, America and the United States mint mothered the most barbarous products.[39] Gilder even penned:

> It rests simply with the Treasury Department to consign to oblivion when it will our gawky fowls and disjointed goddesses ... The Administration which is the first to adopt this reform will win for itself high and deserved honor.[40]

Suggesting that there had been a coordinated effort, Kimball wrote Gilder that he was about to invite designs for all six of the non-gold circulating coins. He asked Gilder to provide him with a list of New York artists whom he might send a circular letter announcing a competition. Particularly, he wanted Saint-Gaudens's address.[41]

Kimball had done his homework. Four days previously he had drafted a circular to outside artists calling upon them to submit proposed new designs, and Secretary of the Treasury Charles Fairchild (Manning having resigned due to poor health) had approved the draft three days later.[42] Each competing artist would be required to submit a plaster model no more than 2-1/2 inches in diameter for both the obverse and reverse of the coin being considered for change. The models should be free of all lettering, date, and denomination. These were elements that the engravers' reducing machine was not capable of addressing and were still hand-punched. The design should be low relief to minimize excessive abrasion occurring in high relief works. The designs must be submitted on or before June 1, 1887. The winning design would receive an award of $500. However, in a departure from standard artistic practices, the mint reserved the right to combine the obverse and reverse designs from different artists.[43]

Matters were still on track when Kimball wrote Tiffany & Company on April 9 to see if any of their artists wanted to be considered, enclosing a circular in the process.[44] Where was Robert Preston in this process? He knew better; either he stood by and let Kimball walk into trouble, or he warned the director and was ignored. Either way the results were the same. Senator Justin Morrill put a stop to the process, citing the Coinage Act of 1873. Kimball had no such authority to initiate design changes for existing coins.[45]

Kimball immediately went on the defensive. He was admittedly acting on an ambiguous interpretation of Section 3510 of the Revised United States Statutes that had its foundation in the Coinage Act of 1873. The new silver dollar design had been brought forth under this law in 1878, and the new nickel design in 1883. If Morrill was right, these design changes had been illegal. He had no choice but to call in Treasury for a ruling.[46]

It was a chastised Kimball who wrote Morrill on April 15. Kimball was suspending the circular until further notice. Morrill was right; an act of Congress would be required to change designs.

Neither Kimball nor Gilder would give up. Kimball addressed the issue head-on in his annual report for fiscal year 1887. Under the revised statutes, Kimball was without mandate to change U. S. coinage designs. A mechanism was needed that would allow design changes administratively. Kimball believed that a public competition would not be successful. Instead, he was proposing that leading artists in their fields be engaged to provide new designs. A jury appointed by the secretary of the Treasury would then judge their work. However, he cautioned that the high relief of the ancient coins was not practical to meet modern cost-efficient, high-volume minting requirements. Kimball also acknowledged that valid issues concerning changing the designs existed. Too frequent changes would result in confusion as the public associated designs with the respective coin values.[47]

In 1888 editorials supporting legislative action to change the designs appeared in the *New York Times*, *Evening Post*, *Sun*, and *Boston Globe*. These had been drawn from a pamphlet prepared by Kimball and forwarded to Gilder for distribution. In total, supporting articles appeared in fourteen papers in New York, Boston, Washington, and St. Louis as well as two magazines in April, May, and June of 1888.[48] One editorial went so far as to point out that America had at least one artist capable of providing acceptable new designs. The writer was Mariana Van Rensselaer, a well-respected art critic and good friend of Augustus Saint-Gaudens.[49]

Kimball proceeded to draft a legislative amendment, and Morrill introduced it in the Senate.[50] Richard Bland introduced a companion bill in the House. Changes for existing coins were to be no more frequent than every twenty-five years. Also, in a backhanded acknowledgement that the current designs on the dollar and nickel had been implemented without proper authority, those two coin designs were exempted from the initial twenty-five year requirement.[51]

Progress was nil with the legislation bottled up in committee in 1888 and the 1889 rump session of the Fiftieth Congress.[52] The problem was in the House, again controlled by the Democrats. Speaker John G. Carlisle was single-mindedly pursuing administration policy to reform and lower tariffs on imported goods.[53] In such a politically charged atmosphere, legislation to provide changes in coin designs did not stand a chance.

Sherman had been right in cautioning President-elect Garfield that the silver question had not been settled with the Bland Allison Act of 1878. Silver was now a major political issue.

As President Cleveland's term was set to begin, John Sherman once again was forced to address the issue. The original silver dollar legislation sought to restore the former 16 to 1 ratio between silver and gold. That had not happened, and the weight of a standard silver dollar would now have to be increased from 412-1/2 to 480 grains to have an intrinsic value equal to a gold dollar. He also pointed out that the silver dollar would not circulate.

Still Sherman was pragmatic. It was foolish to propose any alternative to the present situation. The political positions on both sides of the question were so hardened that the Bland Allison Act could not be changed. Until popular sentiment in the country demanded it, or some great danger threatened to drain the country of its gold, no remedy would move forward.[54] Given that the wealth of the nation, valued in gold, was held by less than one percent of the population, this silver issue was going to fester.[55]

Grover Cleveland in his first annual presidential message to Congress on December 5, 1885, made it clear that he was a gold man. He ascribed totally to the position of Senator Sherman. International conferences to set a common ratio across countries for silver and gold had failed. He wanted the striking of standard silver dollars suspended.[56]

There was another factor now entering into the silver equation. The United States was producing one half of the silver and one third of the gold mined annually in the world. However, at least 25 percent of American gold was a by-product of silver mining. On the other hand, Great Britain was a gold standard country as well as the largest holder of American bonds. England supplied India with silver, where $1 billion of that metal were in circulation. Above all other nations, Great Britain was invested in making silver cheap. For every ounce of American silver that England bought, she made more than 25 cents profit coining it into rupees for India. Paying for Indian imports in rupees then forced down the price of competing American goods denominated in gold.[57] In particular, the majority of Indian exports to Great Britain were wheat and cotton. Imports of wheat from India to London had grown from 94,000 bushels in 1873 to 45.5 million in 1885. Brokers would pay for the crops in silver rupees and then sell the excess over domestic needs into the European market for gold at rates still profitable but undercutting the American competition. Thus, the

John Percival Jones picked himself up by the bootstraps rising from a mine foreman in the Comstock Lode to a leading United States senator and leader of the silver movement.

William Morris Stewart had become a fixture in the Senate by the time this image was taken. Once a friend of Abraham Lincoln, he held a position of respect in the Senate.

American farmers in the Midwest and South saw gold as an international tool that depressed the prices received for their crops.[58]

When, on March 4, 1887, the Fiftieth Congress convened, new members were called forward to take the oath of office. Among them in the Senate was William Morris Stewart. The Nevada silver barons had found a seat in the Senate not to their liking and had retired from office. Riding the coattails of the silver movement and funded by his former San Francisco client, the Southern Pacific Railway, Stewart was back. Silver had gained an effective, if not always logical, proponent on the national stage.

Cleveland, attempting to preempt the silver issue's growing strength, turned to the resolution passed at the end of the Forty-Eighth Congress that called for international negotiations to secure free coinage of silver. He charged Edward Atkinson, the Boston industrialist, to visit the financial centers of England, France, and Germany to ascertain the feasibility of establishing a ratio of value between gold and silver necessary for the free coinage of both metals.

Atkinson had gained national prominence by his advocacy for the increased use of silver in the developing nations in both hemispheres. Given the imperialistic nature of many of the European countries, it was felt that Atkinson's approach to silver might lead to a sustainable ratio for the two metals. Cleveland instructed Atkinson to use every effort to achieve this goal.

Atkinson made his report on October 1, 1887. In his interviews with European officials, he attempted to make it understood that the United States was faced with a contraction of its currency should the standard silver dollar lose its legal tender status. That action in turn would induce a heavy draft for gold coin upon the reserves in Europe to fill the gap. Atkinson asked what steps could be taken in Europe to restore free coinage of silver at full legal tender status at an agreed ratio to gold so that suitable measures might be taken by the United States government and Congress.

Upon his return to the United States, Atkinson reported that there was a dread in Europe of an "avalanche of silver" from the United States that was causing an unwillingness to even consider bimetallism. There was also fear of the consequences should a sudden change take place in this country's monetary policy that would lead to a termination of silver coinage and also an attempt to dispose of a considerable portion of the existing stock of standard silver dollars in storage. Atkinson found the Europeans had little or no understanding of silver certificates that had passed into circulation and maintained their value at par with gold due to interchangeability.

In conclusion, Atkinson observed that he met resistance at every turn. He held out no hope in his report of any present action to restore free silver or full legal-tender silver. Atkinson concluded that the standard silver dollar at a ratio of 16 to 1 must be suspended or no proposition for a bimetallic treaty for the full legal tender of silver coin would be entertained by European nations.[59]

Atkinson's report quelled not one bit the conflict surrounding silver coinage.

Chapter 34
The Sherman Clan

The stylishly dressed, strikingly beautiful young woman stepped up to the door and brashly knocked. There were strict rules, and this was just not done in the staid Washington society of the 1880s. Not only that, it was the home of Clover and Henry Adams. Clover was notorious for speaking her mind, generous with her friends, but deadly when she did not care to be bothered. The two women had met at a January 1881 reception hosted by Clara and John Hay to which both the Cameron's and the Adams's had been invited. At that first meeting, Lizzie had asked if she could come to tea at Clover's home without waiting for the necessary invitation. Now Elizabeth Sherman Cameron showed herself above Washington's strict social protocol. Given Lizzie's brazen action, Clover had every right to snub her. However, when the door opened, Lizzie entered into an unshakeable friendship with Henry and Clover Adams.[1]

The Adams's had moved to Washington to escape Boston in 1877. They were both very much at home in the highly charged political atmosphere of the capital city. Henry, grandson and great grandson of presidents, was a former Harvard professor and historian by training. Here he would author under pen names fictional books tightly based upon characters and events swirling around him. Clover was a highly skilled photographer, maintaining her own darkroom in their basement.

Adams was close to John La Farge and, through him, maintained contact with Augustus Saint-Gaudens. He had watched the sculptor in his one painting endeavor, working for La Farge on the Trinity Church in Boston. When visiting New York,

Clover and Henry would often dine with La Farge and Saint-Gaudens.[2]

Clover Adams offered Lizzie art and culture as an alternative to the boredom she was experiencing with her middle-aged husband. Lizzie had no desire to be sequestered like a wallflower in drab Pennsylvania towns while Don Cameron inhabited smoke-filled hotel rooms, dishing out senatorial plums to his political chums in order to stay in power. Cameron had no affinity for his legislative function; no acts of Congress would ever bear his name. It was the power of the position that he craved.

Sensitive to Lizzie's impossible situation, Clover took her under her wing, helping the young woman become one of the most sought-after hostesses in Washington. Dinners were often enlivened at her house with "Uncle Cump" Sherman in attendance. When a dinner conversation dragged, his favorite niece could always lure him into rehashing his march to the sea.

Elizabeth Sherman Cameron at first was dismayed when shown a photograph of this painting by Anders Zorn. Done in 1900, the painting conveyed an element of realism that Lizzie found uncomfortable. Yet there is a noticeable resemblance to Saint-Gaudens' *Head of Victory* from the *Sherman Monument*. Lizzie's dissatisfaction apparently eased when presented with the portrait itself. It would adorn her Paris apartment and be found hanging in her home when she died in 1944.

Lizzie reveled in this Washington scene. When not hosting or attending a dinner party, she was going to the opera or the theater. Her husband was a no-show at these affairs; his trips to the opera had ended with the wedding. He often pleaded illness to avoid attending.

Lizzie and Senator Cameron made the grand tour of Europe in 1883. The young woman was captivated by London, which included presentation to Queen Victoria. In her absence, Henry Adams and John Hay bought two adjoining lots at 16th and H Streets where they would build connecting houses. Henry drew upon inherited wealth. John, the one-time private secretary to Abraham Lincoln, had married well.

Tragically, Clover's family had a history of depression and suicide. Her husband stood by helpless as Clover started to descend this dark alley in 1884. Her father died in April 1885, and the madness seemed to accelerate. Swallowing a mixture of cyanide and other chemicals from her darkroom, Clover committed suicide on December 6, 1885. Henry Adams was left adrift, consumed in grief. His home was ready for occupancy at the end of that year, but Adams instead joined John La Farge on a six-month journey to Japan. Meanwhile in the summer of 1886, Lizzie and Don moved into the Ogle-Tayloe House on Lafayette Square across from the new abode of Henry Adams.

Adams came back from Japan in October 1886 not healed but with a concept for a suitable memorial at Clover's gravesite in Rock Creek Cemetery. Traveling to New York, Adams, reuniting with La Farge, met Augustus Saint-Gaudens in his studio on West 36th Street. They were afraid that Saint-Gaudens, now hopelessly overloaded with commissions, would refuse the project. Adams described what he wanted in general terms, a figure in the vein of a Buddhist goddess symbolizing the acceptance, intellectually, of the inevitable. Intrigued, Gus tried several poses before he hit upon one to which Adams could relate. He then called his assistant over and put him in the pose. Next, he picked up a blanket and draped it over the assistant's head. The burlap-like material fell in heavy folds, enhancing the dramatic elements of the pose. Henry Adams considered the pose settled. Here the project would sit for the next two years with Gus demolishing at least three models before he settled on his interpretation.[3]

Henry Adams was an astute observer of the Washington scene in the Gilded Age. His was the most exclusive salon in Washington, D.C. The great tragedy of his life was that he could not express his feelings for Elizabeth Cameron. They were like two ships passing in the night.

Adams emerged slowly from his grief, gradually settling in to host an elite salon for elegant noonday breakfasts. His guests were admitted, not invited. There were the regulars that included La Farge and Hay. Also in the group were the newly arrived young British diplomat Cecil Spring-Rice and Cabot Lodge. Adams included his female acquaintances that he termed his nieces. Above them all, not to be compared or role-cast, was Lizzie Cameron. She was best friend, confidante, and could have been much more.

Within this group, Saint-Gaudens was always welcomed. He was put off and inarticulate, believing his wit and education inadequate. Yet Adams was drawn to the sculptor with his energy and ability to create with his hands. Put simply, Saint-Gaudens was the accomplished doer, and Adams was the consummate observer.

At some point, either at his studio, always open to visitors, or at Henry's salon, Saint-Gaudens met Elizabeth Sherman Cameron. He was enamored with her poise and beauty. On her part, Lizzie openly offered her friendship and sparkling personality.[4] Lizzie was that way with men; she would flirt and she would tease, she would kiss and cajole. However, she simply would not please. Still, she could do no wrong in the sculptor's eyes. That she was General Sherman's favorite niece only added to the allure.

In August 1890, La Farge and Adams left for another extended journey, this time to the South Seas. Adams, understandably, began to worry from a distance about the lack of progress on Clover's memorial. He asked Lizzie to keep an eye on work at the gravesite. Finally in March 1891, Lizzie reported that the bronze figure had at last been positioned.

Lizzie bravely reported in her frequent letters to Henry that his brother, Charles Francis Adams, said the work looked like a mendicant in a horse blanket. However, John Hay weighed in, writing to Henry that the work was indescribably noble and imposing. Upon returning to see the work for himself, Adams grasped its greatness.[5] From this point forward, Saint-Gaudens was a friend of great merit in the eyes of Henry Adams. And Adams was always constant to his friends.

Some chose to entitle this Saint-Gaudens work at the grave of Clover Adams in Rock Creek Cemetery in Washington, D.C., *Grief*. Saint-Gaudens, however, was reluctant to give it any title.

The presidential bug had once again bitten John Sherman. Blaine had no desire to run again, retreating to Europe for an extended tour well in advance of the Republican convention. Surely there would not be another "Garfield Miracle." John Sherman's turn, well earned, appeared to be at hand.

The campaign kicked off for Sherman with the Ohio Republican state convention of April 18 and 19, 1888. The convention unanimously went for Sherman, giving him 46 delegates. The at large delegates included Governor Joseph Foraker, former Governor Charles Foster, and Representative William McKinley.[6] Mark Hanna, the Cleveland industrialist, wealthy from coal and iron, would be the convention manager for Sherman. It was a familiar role for Hanna, having served Sherman in the same position in 1884. If Sherman could hold at bay the ambitions of Foraker and McKinley, it was a formidable lineup.

Going into the Republican convention in Chicago, Sherman not only held Ohio, but also a good portion of Pennsylvania and the largely African-American delegates from the South. William McKinley would be chairman of the resolutions committee, charged with drafting a party platform suitable to Sherman.

McKinley's platform espoused the Republican position on tariff policy limiting cuts to those imported goods not produced at home. The monetary plank backed the use of both gold and silver as money and accused Cleveland of working to demonetize silver. McKinley's committee was straddling the currency issue.

In the nominating process, Sherman's name, as the most important, was held to the back of the pack. Benjamin Harrison's nomination stirred some interest as Indiana was considered a swing state. Thomas Platt's New York delegation nominated

Chauncey Depew. He was a placeholder. Platt was holding his delegates until it came time to vote them in a block that yielded the most benefit to him and his state's Republicans.

Voting commenced on Friday evening, June 22. On the first ballot, Sherman led the field with 229 votes, both disappointing and far short of the number needed for nomination. Harrison, a regional candidate at 94 votes, was not a factor. Sherman gained slightly on the second ballot but lost steam on the third round. It appeared the strategy of those really in favor of Blaine was to put the convention into a hopeless deadlock and then turn to Blaine to save the party from chaos.[7]

Voting resumed on Saturday. By the fifth ballot, Sherman stood at 224 votes to Benjamin Harrison's 212. At this point the convention adjourned leaving a fertile field for the party bosses to wheel and deal.

In the recess there was a growing feeling that Sherman could not win. Foraker defected to Blaine. At the same time, a movement budded for McKinley as a rising name in the party. Platt and the other party bosses were prepared to support the congressman. However, McKinley refused to be drafted, staying firmly in Sherman's camp. Hanna wired Sherman stating that only a McKinley candidacy could prevent a stampede to Blaine. Sherman wired back to let his name stand, that he preferred defeat to retreat.

On Sunday morning, Andrew Carnegie, hosting Blaine at his Scottish castle, wired that Blaine was not a candidate and favored Harrison. That Sunday afternoon Platt met with a key Harrison advisor and believed afterward that he would be secretary of the Treasury under Harrison with control of Treasury patronage.[8]

On the first ballot on Monday, New York swung to Harrison. Still, it would take two more ballots to nominate Benjamin Harrison.[9] Sherman would never name Platt as the man behind his downfall. Instead he claimed that one delegate controlled the whole New York delegation and that a corrupt bargain made that Sunday, transferred the great body of that state's vote to Benjamin Harrison.[10]

Mark Hanna had several takeaways from this convention. William McKinley had comported himself with dignity and honesty; Joseph Foraker had not. McKinley had delivered the goods for Sherman as chairman of the resolutions committee and had held firm for Sherman throughout the balloting. Depending upon whether Harrison was successful in the general election, McKinley showed promise for either 1892 or 1896. Hanna also saw the Southern delegates, lacking strong, controlling state organizations, as low-hanging fruit, easy to harvest with a minimum of effort. Finally, he learned that the nomination needed to be won on the first ballot. Otherwise, the political bosses took over and unsavory deals were needed to carry the nomination.

Augustus Saint-Gaudens had always admired William Tecumseh Sherman. "The general had remained in my eye as the typical American soldier ever since I had formed that idea of him during the Civil War."[11]

When Sherman removed himself from the Washington scene and set up residence in New York City in the fall of 1886, it was only natural that Gus would want very badly to have the general sit for him. He wasn't alone; any New York artist worth his salt wanted a shot at the general. Stanford White approached the general's daughter, Rachel, on Saint-Gaudens's behalf.[12] However, she wasn't the best go-between, being considered within the family as a spendthrift.[13] In typical fashion, the crusty old general would have none of it. He simply refused to be pestered by any more "damned sculptors."[14]

It was not in Saint-Gaudens's shy personality to approach the general directly. So, the rest of 1886 and most of 1887 passed without action. Then Saint-Gaudens teamed with Stanford White for one last try. Sherman, since moving to New York, had been lionized by its high society.[15] Naturally White, although pessimistic of success, had an angle that was worth a try. The architect was in the process of renovating the Villard house that had been purchased by Whitelaw Reid.

Reid, originally from rural Ohio, was an accomplished newspaperman. Using his wife's money, he had just acquired the *New York Tribune*, where he had been the long-time managing editor.[16] He and the general had become close in New York in spite of Reid having crossed swords with Sherman as a war correspondent.[17] White thought an approach through Reid was worth a try. The editor was agreeable, going again to Rachel and reaching the same dead end. Then when the general paid Reid a visit in his home, the newspaper editor tackled him in person. In Reid's words, "He swore a little, but finally consented to give Saint-Gaudens the sittings."[18]

Gus was ecstatic over his success, emotionally proclaiming that his *Sherman* would be a labor of love. That meant no money would change hands. He optimistically promised the general that he would complete his work with two sittings a week over one month. Sherman, perhaps well aware of the sculptor's reputation for interminable delays, meant to hold him at his word. Starting on January 3, 1888, every Tuesday and Saturday promptly at 2 p.m. the general appeared at Saint-Gaudens's studio for a two-hour sitting.[19] Sherman proved to be a good sitter, with one exception. He appeared uneasy when Gus would walk to one side or the other to study his profile. His eyes would alertly follow the sculptor. If Gus moved too far, his head turned too.[20] As progress was made, Gus grew optimistic over the results, saying, "I have not spoiled it yet thank God, in fact I'm sure it's better."[21]

January stretched into February with each session taking the full two hours. The general's patience was wearing thin. At one point Gus stepped over the line. He could not get General Sherman to button his coat and look his high rank. In exasperation, he turned to Sherman and said, "Look here, General! Where you see portraits of Bismarck, Von Moltke, and other great generals, their coats are always buttoned up tight to the throat, and they look their rank. Do just for a short time, button yours up and set your tie straight so I can get it as it should be!" Gus had gone too far. Sherman fixed the sculptor with a hard stare and finally said, "Saint-Gaudens, I don't give a tinker's damn how men choose to wear their coats, but I want you to know that the General of the Armies of the United States of America will wear his coat any damn way he pleases." Well afterward, Gus told of sweat breaking out all over his head. He was in jeopardy of "not getting the man," so necessary to the greatness of the piece.[22] Yet it was Gus's mistake and not Sherman's. If Gus had gotten the general to do as he asked, a masterpiece would never have been achieved.

Finally on March 6, after eighteen sittings, the portrait bust was completed.[23] But, not without Sherman threatening to stop the sittings.[24] He even insisted upon a "confidential presentation" when the work was done.[25] Though one month had stretched into nine weeks, Gus was timely, the first in his career, in this work. In the process, he had become even more attached to the general. Gus had had the rare benefit of seeing the real man without the trappings of fame.

The bust faced forward with the head slightly turned to the proper left.[26] It was as if Cump Sherman might be watching as Saint-Gaudens walked around him to get a better look at his profile. However, the masterstroke was simply that the general's coat was unbuttoned at the throat and his string tie askew to one side of his careless turned-over collar.[27]

Saint-Gaudens's bust of William Tecumseh Sherman captured the forceful character of the Civil War general.

As his work drew to a close, Gus knew he wanted more. He had tried midway into the sittings to get the general to sit upon a horse. Sherman point blank refused, saying he had gotten through doing that twenty years previously.[28] This time Saint-Gaudens did enlist Lizzie. He wanted General Sherman on a horse so that he would have an excellent likeness from which to do an equestrian statue sometime in the future. Still Sherman refused, saying that no general ever did or would sit for an equestrian statue. More softly, he told Lizzie that he could not help but smile at her picture of him sitting upon Saint-Gaudens's hobby horse for an indefinite time for a statue that the sculptor would erect some fifty years hence. Saint-Gaudens had enough with the bust to complete a plaster cast that could be enlarged to life size after he was gone.[29]

Chapter 35
A Rooseveltian Return

Benjamin Harrison faced Grover Cleveland in the fall general election of 1888. As the incumbent, Cleveland had gained the Democratic nomination by acclamation. The Republicans had chosen Harrison's running mate with an eye to the Electoral College, picking Levi Morton, a former congressman from New York. The Democrats chose Senator Allen Thurmond for Cleveland's vice-presidential candidate. It was a bad choice; Thurmond was too old for a vigorous campaign and in the end could not even carry his home state of Ohio.

The campaign turned on the issue of tariffs. President Cleveland wanted dramatic reductions, arguing that high tariffs were unfair to consumers. Harrison wanted high tariffs to protect American industries and their associated factory jobs. It did not help Cleveland that he opposed expanded Civil War pensions and supported the gold standard.

Harrison's campaign manager was Senator Matthew Quay from Pennsylvania. He was also chairman of the Republican National Committee. Quay's rise had been meteoric, having been a lowly state treasurer just over a year before. In fact, Don Cameron's one-time lieutenant had outmaneuvered him and was now head of the Republican machine in Pennsylvania. Don's displacement had come that quickly, and Simon Cameron, at age 89, no longer had the political stamina to save his son.

Not unjustly, Quay was considered one of the ablest political bosses the country had ever produced. He enjoyed politics and was quick to assess the opposition's weak points. He understood that this presidential election would be no different than the last two-close and turning on the vote of New York. He was also convinced that Tammany Hall had turned the 1884 election against Republicans on vote manipulation in New York City. Well before the election, Quay sent his operatives into New York City under the guise of preparing a citywide directory. Instead, they quietly compiled a comprehensive list of eligible voters. Two weeks before the election, Quay announced that any fraud attempted on Election Day in New York City would be detected and the guilty parties would go to prison. Quay's action effectively suppressed Democratic votes in the city.

Harrison carried New York by a slim margin of slightly more than one percent. He also carried Indiana. Further cementing Quay's hold on the Republican Party Harrison's winning margin in Pennsylvania of 79,000 votes was the largest of any state. Still, Cleveland won the popular vote, but the victory in New York gave Harrison the Electoral College and the presidency. Harrison proclaimed, "Providence has given us this victory." Quay, upon hearing this responded, "Providence hadn't a damn thing to do with it."[1]

Thomas Platt did not receive the appointment as secretary of the Treasury. However, Platt was not to be denied his patronage. He was given the collector of the port and the postmaster positions for New York City. That patronage alone would be enough, along with the ancillary appointments, to shove aside Warner Miller and cement his position as the Republican boss of New York.

It was the postmaster appointment that blew up in President Harrison's face. Henry Pearson had been the postmaster in New York City since his appointment by Garfield and then, reappointment by Cleveland. He had come up through the ranks, starting at the bottom in 1860 at age 18 and was known for running an efficient operation.[2] Even so, the public was inured to turnover of political appointments. It was his replacement that stuck in the craw of Progressive Republicans.[3]

Cornelius Van Cott was a machine politician who gained his first experience as a volunteer fireman in New York City. In his only exposure to the post office, he once held a contract for a brief period to repair government mailbags. Theodore Roosevelt called him Platt's henchman. To him it was a horrible contrast to Pearson, an awful black eye to the Republican Party, simply a criminal blunder. Roosevelt observed to Henry Cabot Lodge that Platt seemed to have a ring in the President's nose in regard to New York.[4]

Yet the outcry did not seem initially to be widely heard in the public forum. New York City was agog with preparations for the celebration of the 100th anniversary of the inauguration of George Washington. This was the capstone for a series of national centennial events that had kicked off with the Centennial Exposition in 1876. New Yorkers actually considered this celebration the centennial of American government.

Platt would have emerged unscathed had not Pearson sickened and died at age 47 on April 20, even before he could handover his office to Van Cott.[5] His death thus propelled the issue of his political removal into public focus. With the president due in New York in nine days to lead the city's celebration of the inauguration centennial, something had to be done and quickly. Their solution was Theodore Roosevelt.

Yes, Theodore Roosevelt was back. In some ways he had never left New York's political arena. Winter months, when there was little or no work to be accomplished on his ranch, found him a semi-permanent boarder at the home of his sister, Bamie, 422 Madison Avenue. There were other short durations when he returned as well. The fact was that he never really disengaged from the New York State Republican Party, faithfully attending their conventions.

The rigors of operating a cattle ranch had hardened and matured Theodore Roosevelt as nothing else could. The emotional wounds of his double loss of 1884 were healed but not forgotten. However, there was one void in his life that must be addressed before he could fully resume his political career.

Oral history has it that one day in October 1885 Theodore returned to the Madison Avenue home and, upon opening the door, met the 24-year-old Edith Carow coming down the stairs. It must have been an awkward moment for these two former childhood sweethearts. As teenagers, they had socialized together until a falling out that summer before he met Alice in Boston. All Edith would ever say about the breakup was that Theodore had not been nice. Since the funeral, Theodore had avoided Edith in spite of her being his sister Corrine's best friend and a regular visitor to Bamie's home. In the summer of 1884 Theodore had even told Bamie to warn him if a certain old family friend came to call so that he could arrange to be away.[6]

Theodore Roosevelt had attempted to avoid Edith Kermit Carow after his wife's tragic death. When he did chance upon his old childhood chum and sweetheart, pictured here in 1885, the courtship was whirlwind.

Edith and Theodore were secretly engaged within a month. They did not even confide the engagement to Bamie. To announce it publicly would not do; under the constraints of Victorian society not enough time had elapsed for a proper grieving period.[7] January and February 1886 Theodore's closest friends saw him often with Edith but suspected nothing. It seemed they looked as brother and sister. In March, Theodore headed west. In spite of both extreme caution and absence from the city, rumors of the engagement leaked out in the August 29 society column of the *New York Times*. It was an embarrassed Roosevelt who wrote Bamie to confirm the gossip as true.

Late summer 1886 had brought forebodings to Roosevelt about his Badlands investment. That summer had been hot and dry; yet more cattle were moved onto the range. Three years before, Roosevelt had found the area to have plentiful grasslands capable of supporting additional stock, but now the reverse was true. He had lost $10 a head on his fall sales that year. By now Roosevelt had $85,000, roughly half of his inheritance, invested.

As Roosevelt had prepared to return east, always the naturalist, he noticed that the migratory birds were leaving early. There were rumors in the community that snowy owls had been seen in Montana, a rare event.[8]

Roosevelt arrived in New York as battle lines were being drawn up for the mayor's election. It would be a three-way race between the traditional Republicans, Democrats, and the Labor Party. The Republicans were looking for a youthful leader to take advantage of the squabble they expected between the Democrats and Labor over the left-wing vote. Party leaders wanted Roosevelt. He was in a box; Edith was expecting a December wedding in London followed by a three-month honeymoon on the Continent. However, a refusal of the nomination was not an option.

On Roosevelt's birthday, October 27, 1886, Republicans convened their county convention at Cooper Union. Wall Street lawyer, Elihu Root, chairman of the Republican County Committee, called the meeting to order and introduced Thomas Acton, former superintendent of the New York Assay Office and assistant treasurer, to chair the meeting. Acton rallied the crowd, saying here is the "Cowboy of Dakota. Make the Cowboy of Dakota the next mayor!"[9]

The campaign over the last days of October and first days of November was fought on a high plain, addressing the issues of capital versus labor, municipal reform, and social justice, extremely remarkable for the times. Even Watson Gilder climbed down from his Mugwump pedestal and spoke for Roosevelt. But Roosevelt was soundly defeated on Election Day when the Republican machine threw its support to the Democrats to block the labor candidate. The only good news that evening was that Cabot Lodge had won a Congressional seat.[10]

On November 6, 1886, Theodore Roosevelt, Corinne and her husband, Bamie, and little Alice set sail on the *Etruria* for England to rendezvous with Edith.[11] On board, they encountered Cecil Spring-Rice returning to Great Britain to prepare for his first posting in the British diplomatic service to the Washington Legation. Theodore and "Springy" hit it off so well that Spring-Rice would serve as best man for the wedding.[12]

On a very foggy Thursday, December 2, 1886, Theodore and Edith were married at St. George's Church on Hanover Square in London.[13] The fog permeated the church, giving the nave an eerie feel when viewed from the back of the sanctuary. Spring-Rice had even convinced Roosevelt to wear bright orange gloves.[14]

Edith suddenly found herself transitioning from close friend of Theodore's two sisters to wife of their brother. For the unmarried Bamie, idolizing Theodore and raising little Alice, soon to be returned to Edith and Theodore, that transition was particularly difficult. In addition, the couple had issues to sort out. Living in the West was not a realistic option. The house at Oyster Bay, now named Sagamore Hill, posed a dilemma. Roosevelt could not afford both a town house in New York City and the home at Oyster Bay. There was also the overriding issue for him of whether to resume his political career or turn to writing.[15]

The young couple made a dynamic duo, their strengths complementing each other. Edith had a good sense of art and literature. Theodore observed that she was both cultured and scholarly. She knew instinctively what was right and appropriate.[16] Roosevelt would learn that any time he went against Edith's advice, he paid for it.[17] Spur of the moment decisions could get him into trouble. Edith, on the other hand, exhibited a judgment that was well weighed, free from impulse.[18] Over the years, built upon the rock-solid foundation of their marriage, they would become a formidable team.

The newly married Roosevelt's journeyed from London to Italy. All was not bliss, however, as Theodore realized that his finances had deteriorated. He *must* live well within his income and begin paying off his debt, no matter what the cost, even to shutting up or renting out their home.[19]

In the beauty of Renaissance Florence, the couple went for a long winter's walk in the solitude of the Boboli Gardens and reached a decision. Theodore did not have the heart to sell Sagamore Hill. That meant that he would move his residency out of New York City. After his thrashing in the New York City mayor's race, Roosevelt had no political future. He must take what literary commissions he could glean and put the farm operations at Sagamore Hill on a paying basis.[20]

Near the end of their honeymoon, the newlyweds experienced an unusual snowfall in Venice. The Piazzo San Marco was covered in a pristine blanket of pure white snow. The domes of the Basilica de San Marco shimmered in their snowy caps, contrasting against the brilliant gold mosaics that graced the exterior of the cathedral.[21]

Meanwhile half a world away it was also snowing, but there was no beauty here, only a hellish death for any man or beast caught in its grip. The first of the terrible snowstorms rumbled through the northern tier of states in mid-January.[22] Sadly, it was only the harbinger for the blizzard that struck the Bad Lands on January 31. The mercury in St. Paul, Minnesota, sank below zero and stayed there, ranging from 20 to 35 degrees below zero for two days.[23] Driven by the wind, snowdrifts were reaching heights of eight feet. At Bismarck, Dakota Territory, a train coming from the east pulled by four engines failed to arrive, stalled in a massive snowdrift. Numerous settlers isolated on the prairie were just simply lost.[24] By February 4, wood fence posts were disappearing and outhouses dismantled for firewood.[25]

Now the cattlemen were in trouble. Made crazy by the intense cold, the cattle moved constantly, burning up their reserves of fat. When the wind whipped up the snowdrifts, their forage became locked in a frozen vault. Unable to replenish their energy, the cattle died. The situation was compounded by the fact that most of the vast herds were owned by easterners who returned home for the winter, taking their cash with them and leaving their foremen in charge of the herds. Thus, in the dead of winter there was no coin, or very little circulating, that could be used to buy forage.[26]

Unfortunately, Mother Nature was not done with the cattle ranges. Another massive blizzard rolled through in mid-February.[27] It was followed at the end of the month by yet another storm.[28] When the thaws came, the ground was littered with carcasses. Cattle that survived were walking dead. A stockman with a loss of only 50 percent of his herd could consider himself extremely lucky.

Roosevelt returned to the United States in March and hurried west at the first possible moment. He called it a perfect smashup all through the cattle country of the Northwest. The losses were crippling. He admitted in a letter to Cabot Lodge that for the first time he was utterly unable to enjoy his visit to his ranch.[29]

It would be another year before Roosevelt could cut his losses in his cattle operations. In September 1888, he told Bamie he had "made pretty good sales of his cattle."[30] That was like polishing a rotten apple. He was liquidating into a bear market, driven down by all the investors exiting the cattle business. He was more truthful to Cecil Spring-Rice, telling him that the ranch almost "burst" him.

Organizing for New York City's celebration of the Centennial of the Inauguration of George Washington started in 1887. The event enjoyed widespread support among the leading citizens of the metropolis. Theodore Roosevelt was quick to participate, being named to the executive committee on January 11, 1888. He also served on the General Committee and the Committee on States. It was this last committee that gave Roosevelt national exposure through its responsibility for handling arrangements for attending out-of-state dignitaries. However, the Art and Exhibition Committee carried the heaviest load. From this committee came the Washington Arch, conceived by Stanford White. It was also within this committee with Watson Gilder as its secretary that the decision evolved to strike a medal recognizing the event.

The concept of a celebratory medal started innocently enough. At a committee meeting on November 30, 1888, a suggestion was made that its stationery be marked with an appropriate device. Alexander Drake and William Coffin, manager of the committee and art critic for the *Sun*, were drafted to secure a design. From this start, the idea expanded to include a commemorative medal that would double as the device on the stationary. When Gilder was added to the subcommittee, Saint-Gaudens became the clear choice to do the work.[31]

Saint-Gaudens begged off; he simply had no time to do justice to the effort. Gilder persisted, and Gus relented with one condition. He would design the medal and supervise its modeling, to be done by his former assistant, Philip Martiny.[32] Saint-Gaudens rightly believed that the design was nine-tenths of the effort. With Martiny doing the modeling, he avoided the dreaded deadline. Saint-Gaudens would take no compensation for this effort.

Work initially progressed well with Saint-Gaudens beginning his research into the basic design. Gilder offered to put *The Century*'s dictionary department at his disposal for this work.[33] The bust of Washington would come from a previous effort by Martiny.[34] Even so, there was little time to complete the work. The intent was that the official committee badges be miniatures of the medal.[35]

As the work hit full stride, Gilder wrote Director of the Mint James Kimball on February 13, 1889, to raise the possibility of having the Mint strike the badges.[36] Kimball answered that he could strike medals of a national character, and he believed that this badge qualified. The work could be done out of pocket. However, in regard to the mechanical and artistic execution, Kimball was concerned that the work undertaken would not satisfy Saint-Gaudens. He recommended using a private establishment to give Saint-Gaudens more control. Then he went further:

> I may also remark that the personal equation of such work in this case might be against the very best results as the personal disposition of the engravers at the Mint does not seem to be in favor of doing justice to designs prepared outside.[37]

This statement was amazingly blunt, a fire bell in the night. It was perhaps too negative in that one engraver, George Morgan, was participating in the inaugural celebration.

Gilder promptly made the decision to have Tiffany & Company prepare the badges. In a tip-off to Gilder's thinking, these badges were exactly the size of a twenty-dollar gold piece. Ultimately seven of the official badges would be struck in gold.[38] Thus Gilder was showing what could be accomplished in small scale suitable for coinage. Gilder expanded upon this point, hoping that the medal in an indirect way would have an ultimate effect upon the nation's coinage.[39]

While not generally recognized, George Morgan produced a well-designed so-called dollar (GW-1126) in celebration of the Inauguration Centennial.

As the March deadline approached, problems began to develop. Gus was caught up in what seemed a never-ending process of changes through trial and error. There were also issues with the arrangement of the inscriptions. To Gus the inscriptions were an integral part of the composition.

Tiffany & Company began to pressure Martiny and Saint-Gaudens about the badges. The deadline came and Saint-Gaudens made more changes. William Coffin came to Martiny's studio to find the artist "mad all through." Martiny said he was "done out." Coffin then went to Gus for a long talk. The long and short of it was that while work would continue on the medal, Martiny would make casts of his most recent wax. They would be released for preparation of the badges the next day.[40]

Ultimately Gorham cast the medal in Renaissance style. The design showed a number of characteristics that would carry over into Saint-Gaudens's future work on the coinage. On the reverse, a magnificent eagle with wings spread bore a shield with the motto "E Pluribus Unum" inscribed upon it. Held in the eagle's talons were an olive branch and arrows. To one side was the New Amsterdam coat of arms. Around the perimeter were thirty-eight stars for the states of the Union.

The central device of the obverse was a profile high relief half bust of Washington in continental costume, a change from the norms of the time that generally followed the unadorned Houdon work. Breaking the symmetry to the right of Washington's bust was the fasces. The Latin phrase "Pater Patriae" (Father of his Country) appeared but was not overbearing.[41] The centennial dates were in Roman numerals. Most imaginative was the way Saint-Gaudens broke the inscriptions with the design motifs on the obverse and managed an unwieldy inscription on the reverse. He knew the little details made the difference. The resulting medal was not merely a good one but a great one. Two thousand medals would be cast and sold for $2 apiece.

As the day of celebration approached, Theodore Roosevelt's mind returned to politics. Roosevelt had made a campaign swing through the Northwest for Benjamin Harrison the preceding fall, even taking Edith along.[42] Russell Harrison was now living in New York City. Like Roosevelt, his cattle investments had turned into a disaster. Unlike Roosevelt, he simply pulled up stakes, leaving a bunch of sore investors back in Helena. February 1889 found Theodore with an attorney friend taking Russell Harrison to lunch at the Down Town Club. His friend suggested they get Harrison drunk to learn about the new cabinet appointments.[43]

In March, Lodge wrote that he had approached secretary of State James Blaine about the possibility of Roosevelt being appointed assistant secretary of State. Blaine had diplomatically declined.[44] Blaine would subsequently write that his real problem with Roosevelt was that he lacked repose and patient endurance required for an assistant secretary. There was danger that Roosevelt might be too quick in execution. Matters were constantly occurring that would require the most thoughtful concentration and the most stubborn inaction.[45]

Here matters stood when the removal of Henry Pearson coupled with his sudden death on April 20 turned into a nasty problem for the Harrison Administration. With the president at the center of attention in the coming celebration, the mess needed to be cleaned up quickly. Suddenly Roosevelt had appeal to the Harrison people. The offer of civil service commissioner was most likely made at a dinner hosted by Chauncey Depew at his home on April 26. Attending were D. O. Mills, surviving quite nicely after the demise of Billy Ralston, General Sherman, Warner Miller, Whitelaw Reid, Theodore Roosevelt, and Russell Harrison. Harrison was most likely the messenger bearing the offer.[46]

Lodge arrived April 27 as Roosevelt's guest for the festivities. He was aware of the offered appointment and advised Theodore not to take it. The job paid but a pittance of $3,500 per year. The commission was fraught with bureaucratic entanglements and deliberately underfunded by Congress. Besides, Roosevelt would be forced to take positions that were bound to make him unpopular in Washington. Roosevelt heard his friend out and then accepted the appointment. Authoring books had proven to be a meager existence.

The great celebration kicked off at the ugly hour of 1 a.m. on the morning of April 29 in Washington. The assembled presidential party that included Russell Harrison and his wife entrained for a nine-hour journey aboard eight Pullman Palace cars and one private car supplied by the Pennsylvania Railroad for the president and his family. The destination was Elizabethport, New Jersey, the point where Washington, after seven days by coach, boarded a barge to cross over to New York.[47]

This final version of the 1889 Inauguration Centennial medal came from the estate of Richard Watson Gilder, accounting for its near perfect patina and cast. There is what appears to be a casting flaw on the fasces. However, it is roughly in the shape of an oak leaf added for this piece at the last minute. It was not extraordinary in Roman times to nail an oak leaf to the fasces as a symbol of strength and justice.

President Harrison's formal welcoming to the city occurred within the Equitable Building, recently expanded and touted for its nine stories complete with elevators and electric lighting. President Harrison entered from Broadway where a detachment of the Fifth Artillery and members of the New York Commandery of the Loyal Legion were drawn up in two lines leading to the great staircases.

Next, the presidential party took the elevators to the Lawyers Club where 2,000 gentlemen, including, Theodore Roosevelt, paid their respects. At three o'clock the reception ended, and the president, in a select company of guests, marched within the building to the private banquet hall of the newly opened Café Savarin. Theodore Roosevelt made the cut while Russell Harrison did not. Roosevelt was being put on prominent display.[48]

The celebration wound up on the evening of April 30 with the Centennial Ball, billed as the largest in American history, held at the Metropolitan Opera House. Both Roosevelt and Gilder had prime seats on the floor close to the presidential table. Lodge was in the last row of tables that ran along the circumference of the hall. Grouped at the table next to Lodge's were the artists that included Saint-Gaudens, who stood out with his red hair.[49] It would seem very probable that Gilder would have introduced the sculptor to Roosevelt in passing, particularly given his proximity to Lodge.

Roosevelt's appointment was picked up in the press on May 8, 1889. Harrison had two slots on the commission to fill and the other one, by law, went to a Democrat, in this case, ex-Governor Hugh Thompson of South Carolina. Thompson had originally been nominated by President Cleveland and then held in limbo by the Republicans in the Senate. Now Harrison was taking pains to appear supportive of the commission by reversing his party's opposition to Thompson. The *New York Times* observed that Roosevelt had the party prestige to uphold Harrison in support of civil service reform and even perhaps to hold him to such support. However, there was a note of caution as New York Republican politicians scornfully disapproved of Roosevelt's criticism of the removal of Postmaster Pearson. The test of wills between Theodore Roosevelt and Thomas Platt, the easy boss, had begun. In what proved to be, in the best of times, an uneasy alliance, Platt would need Roosevelt as cover for the exercise of his political power while Roosevelt would learn that he simply could not avoid Platt if he were to be successful in the exercise of his elected power.

Theodore Roosevelt arrived in Washington on May 13, 1889. He would temporarily board with Cabot and Nannie Lodge as Edith was pregnant with their second child. He soon met Hugh Thompson and formed a bond of friendship, driven by common beliefs that would extend beyond his time as a commissioner. And just like that, with Thompson at his side, Roosevelt took control of the three-man commission.

Toward the end of September 1889, James Kimball turned in his resignation as director of the mint, effective October 25. He had tried to bring mint standards up to the best practices of the day. However, with the superintendents and operative officers appointed by the president under the influence of political patronage, he had lacked the whip necessary for implementation of the needed changes.

Horatio Burchard now reappeared on center stage seeking his old job back. He had formidable support; both Illinois senators and most of its Congressional delegation endorsed his nomination.[50] Even so, he had not a chance. In the Harrison Administration, it was now apparent that office seekers must go through Russell Harrison to ensure receiving their desired appointment. Not surprisingly, the press had picked up on this fact and cynically dubbed the young man "Prince Russell."

Russell Harrison had some outstanding debts left over from his time as assayer-in-charge at the Helena Assay Office. One repayment went to his personal friend and former clerk, L. A. Walker. It was rumored that Walker had helped smooth over issues in Helena during the assay office investigation.[51] However, the real surprise came when President Harrison nominated Edward O. Leech to be director of the Mint.

When Burchard initiated the Helena Assay Office investigation, he had heard rumors that Leech had some connection to the Montana Land and Cattle Company operated by young Harrison. As a result, Leech had been pulled from the investigation in favor of Burchard's brother-in-law. With Burchard's removal, Leech inserted himself back into the process, serving as an advisor to the solicitor for Treasury, Alexander McCue, who had no technical knowledge about the mints or assay offices. The newspaper reports strongly implied that Leech orchestrated the cover-up and received the director's position as his reward.[52]

Edward Leech gained the support of President Harrison's son, Russell, for the position of director of the Mint. He would be plagued by an independent-minded Philadelphia Mint.

As thorough as the press was in their reporting, they missed one element of the purported cover-up entirely. McCue had been appointed to the plum position of assistant treasurer for New York Sub-Treasury in March 1889. Perhaps they gave that story a pass as McCue died of a stroke on April 2, 1889.

Thus, before he could ever take the reins of the Mint Service, Edward Leech, was damaged goods. Leech had one other problem. Oliver Bosbyshell had come out of "retirement," having lost his coiner's position in the Cleveland Administration, to become superintendent of the Philadelphia Mint after Matt Quay and Don Cameron together visited the White House on October 17, 1889.[53] He would operate this mint on a standalone basis, paying little heed to Leech's authority.

Chapter 36
PANDORA'S BOX

Perhaps the first sign that the Harrison Administration was going to be favorable to silver was the appropriation to reopen the Carson City Mint.[1] Senators John P. Jones and Bill Stewart of Nevada had pressed on this issue.[2] However, President Harrison's first annual message to the Fifty-First Congress in December 1889, made the message strong and clear.

In his report, Harrison noted that in the fiscal year that ended on June 30, 1889, government receipts had substantially exceeded expenditures and were expected to continue in this vein. To President Harrison, this situation justified a reduction in taxation. He also pointed out that there had been a net reduction in National Bank Notes circulating of $114 million, driven by the retirement of bonds necessary to secure the issue of these notes. This shrinkage offset the expansion of Silver Certificates issued under the Bland-Allison Act of 1878. Harrison observed that when that act was passed, silver stood at $1.20 per ounce. It was now $0.706 per ounce, causing fear that a further reduction would result in a depreciation of Silver Certificates.

The president wanted a revision in tariff rates such that reasonable protection of home industries was maintained. He left it his Treasury secretary, William Windom, to present the administration's plan for silver. He wanted the mandatory coinage provision in Bland-Allison repealed. In its place Treasury would purchase an increased amount of silver bullion each month and pay for it with a new paper currency.[3] Harrison had just opened Pandora's Box or was it simply a can of worms.

The administration's strategy was to advance the tariff and silver legislation at the same time as a package. They reasoned the Western men would support a tariff they did not like in exchange for increased silver purchases. The Easterners, on the other hand, would support the new tariff legislation while rationalizing their fears over the silver legislation.

Republicans controlled both Houses of the Fifty-First Congress. Thomas Reed of Maine was the new speaker. The untimely death of Senator James Burnie Beck from a sudden heart attack in the Baltimore and Potomac Railroad Station on May 3, 1890, cost the Democrats his leadership.[4] Beck had been an effective voice in advocating his party's position on both tariffs and silver.

Senator Justin Morrill introduced Treasury's silver bill on January 28, 1890. It called for the purchase of $4.5 million of silver bullion monthly, provided the current market price for 371.25 grains of silver (the amount of pure silver in a standard silver dollar) did not exceed $1. This purchase amount was so large that it was essentially a backdoor way to free silver—unlimited coinage of silver. To pay for these purchases, the bill authorized the issuance of Treasury Notes, later to be called Coin Notes. In addition, the mint was obligated to coin two million ounces of silver monthly from these purchases until July 1, 1891. Thereafter, only sufficient silver dollars to support redemption of the Treasury Notes need be coined.[5]

The House passed their legislation first. It contained a different concept concerning redemption of Treasury Notes. It gave the secretary of the Treasury the option of redeeming these notes with silver bullion at market rates.[6] Known as bullion redemption, it gave the secretary a safety valve if gold reserves ran too low. The silver men accused the administration of using the power of patronage to gain adoption of this provision in the Committee on Coinage, Weights and Measures.[7]

When this bill reached the Senate, it was accepted by unanimous consent as a substitute for the Senate bill. Now the focal point of the silver men shifted to the detested bullion redemption clause. It placed a check on silver coinage and was all the more hateful to silver supporters because it appeared to have the full support of President Harrison.

With deliberations commencing in the Senate, John Sherman, on June 5, argued that this legislation needed to reflect what that chamber desired to accomplish. The majority of senators desired to provide an increase in the money supply to meet the needs of the rapidly expanding American population and to replace the retiring national bank currency. It was also the desire to increase the value of silver both domestically and internationally in hopes that the metal would advance to its ratio with gold mandated in the Bland Allison Act.[8]

The silver lobby had been active from the beginning of this Congress; they had been anticipating the Harrison Administration's moves in favor of silver. The point man for their efforts was Francis Newlands, the outside manager of the National Silver Committee. He had the ear of President Harrison as well as holding the president's opinions in confidence.

Newlands was not a westerner by birth, studying law at Georgetown College. He then moved to San Francisco to begin his law practice. Here he hit pay dirt of a different sort; he married Bill Sharon's daughter. He was at Sharon's side as the man laid dying in 1885, dictating how his estate should be handled. Now as the sole trustee,

Newlands had more than a passing interest in the silver issue.

Reflecting a level of expertise not previously seen on the silver issue, petitions, protests, and requests poured in upon the Senate and House, all similar. They resembled the printed forms distributed by agents of the silver men who had been traveling the countryside to preach the gospel to the plain folk. These lobbyists, at Newlands's direction, put into practice the belief that the most effective way to influence a congressman was to light a bonfire in his home district.

Newlands knew every twist and turn the silver bill had taken to get to this point. He made the call as to when a proposition ought to be accepted or rejected. As the bill reached the Senate, Newlands served as a sort of moderator between the two sides. When the anti-silver men made a case that too much silver would drive gold out of the country, Newlands argued statistics to refute their position. Still the silver men were becoming anxious that they would lose on key issues within the bill. It was at this point that Newlands went to President Harrison.

Francis Newlands developed his political skills under the tutelage of Nevada senator William Sharon. His skills as a lobbyist for silver were instrumental in the passage of the Sherman Silver Act of 1890. He would become John Percival Jones's replacement in the Senate.

Harrison frankly told Newlands that he was a friend of silver; he wanted to maintain its value, not depress it. However, he feared the potential flooding of the domestic market with foreign silver. He wanted gradual steps toward free coinage of silver and to be sure of every step made. Harrison also was in favor of bullion redemption in the House bill. Newlands told the president that bullion redemption was the one point silver men could not concede. The Treasury Notes created by the bill must only be redeemable in coin, not in silver bullion. Silver in bullion form was strictly a commodity and that would defeat the principles inherent in the bill. Harrison told Newlands that he wanted a compromise. Excluding free coinage of silver, his mind was tentative about all other provisions of the bill.

Newlands came back to Harrison in a letter saying that the bimetallists would agree to a bill calling for the purchase of 4,500,000 ounces of silver per month and elimination of the bullion redemption provision. Then Jones and Stewart went into a conference with House leadership and Newlands. Immediately afterwards, the two senators met with the president. It was reported afterwards that Harrison stood his ground; there must be a compromise. He believed bullion redemption would fix the value of the existing Silver Certificates and maintain them at parity with gold until the nations of the world took up free coinage. However, the president was willing to concede bullion redemption in exchange for a bill calling for monthly silver purchases of $4,500,000. The two senators were accepting of this position although they believed the price of silver was going to steadily increase, thereby diminishing the volume of monthly purchases. Jones and Stewart knew they could not override a veto.

Afterwards, Newlands followed up with Harrison. The president was determined to have a party measure. He did not want a bill passed that had a majority of Democratic votes. Newlands left this meeting still hoping that purchase by weight could be attained in the final language of the legislation.[9]

On June 17, Senator Preston Plumb, a Republican from Kansas, offered an amendment to the silver bill providing for the free coinage of any acceptable silver bullion presented to the mint. The amendment, with a majority of Democrats passed. Among supporting Republicans was Donald Cameron, now irrevocably cast as a silver man.[10] Jones and Stewart recognized they risked a veto, but were willing to try for free coinage of silver if it could be had.[11]

Matters reached another critical point on June 25. Speeches were made for and against free silver in both the House and the Senate. It was a hot summer day in Washington, but it got a lot hotter in the Senate. Sherman called the current version not a practical bill but only an uneasy and fatherless ghost of no account. Then Stewart vehemently began harping on the "Crime of 1873." At issue was the elimination of the standard silver dollar in the Coinage Act of 1873. Stewart claimed he and other senators did not know they were voting to demonetize the silver dollar because the implementing amendment was never read in the Senate. Sherman had the records from that debate brought to the floor. The two senators then pitched into each other, and each made the record prove what he wanted.[12]

It was quieter in the House. The Republican leadership held their coalition and the House refused to concur with the Senate on its amendments to the silver bill.[13] The differences would have to be hammered out in conference. Among the conferees were Sherman and Jones from the Senate and Richard Bland from the House.

Newlands now began to apply pressure to gain the best bill for silver possible out of the conference. He gave a speech in Salt Lake City to the effect that Western and Southern silver men were willing to sacrifice the tariff bill over the silver bill. Immediately afterwards, the National Silver Committee sent telegrams to Western state and local Republican committees asking that they request their senators hold up the tariff bill until the silver bill was passed.[14]

Matters finally came to a head in the Senate on July 7. The Committee on Finance attempted to have the tariff bill taken up for passage but was defeated by the silver men. Three hours later, the conference report on the silver bill was presented.[15] Once the silver senators had a day to look over the compromise bill, they saw John Sherman's fine hand all over it. They got their purchase by weight and Treasury Notes that were, like the silver dollar, legal tender for all debts, public and private. As expected, bullion redemption was gone but so was free coinage of silver. However, there was too much discretion in the bill. There was a loophole that allowed the secretary of the Treasury to purchase less than the monthly requirement if the full amount was not offered. There was also a statement that bothered them to the effect that "it being the established policy of the United States to maintain the two metals at the legal parity with each other upon the present legal ratio, or such ratio as may be provided by law." This looked to Democrats as a plain notice to the secretary of the Treasury to continue paying out gold and doing the public business on a gold basis. In fact, Windom would do just that.

Silver Republicans did not see these issues as something to worry over. They expected another effort for out-and-out free coinage of silver in a year or two. In the end, even Bill Stewart, the most outspoken proponent of silver, agreed that the final bill should receive the vote of every friend of silver.[16]

The *New York Times* had a slightly different take on the silver bill. Its real danger was in the accumulation of silver in the Treasury. If that continued indefinitely, a time would come when to obtain the gold needed to keep the Silver Certificates and Treasury Notes at par with gold, the credit of the government would be severely strained. But that was a long way ahead and the silver purchases could be paused or turned back by law if needed.[17]

The bill was agreed to on July 14, 1890. Senator Sherman was perplexed that the law would commonly be known as the Sherman Silver Purchase Act. He took no part in framing the legislation until it reached conference. The law's chief benefit was that it stopped the coinage after one year of silver dollars that no one wanted. However, as silver prices continued to decline in the face of new discoveries in the West, Sherman saw the error of his thinking and began to advocate for repeal of the law.[18] In fact, naming this law after Sherman was more like pinning the tail on the donkey.

With the reconvening of Congress in December 1891, the silver men again began pushing for free coinage of silver. However, on the first day of the session, Representative Alexander Dockery, a Missouri Democrat, introduced a resolution calling for an investigation into an alleged silver pool. It was claimed that certain well-known senators and representatives bought silver on the margin while the silver bill was being debated in anticipation of a price increase.[19] Apparently Seligman & Company and other New York bankers knew something about these transactions. The resolution was promptly referred to the Committee on Rules and put to sleep.

When the press raised a stink about bottling up Dockery's resolution, the full House took it out of the hands of the committee. There seemed to be fertile ground for an investigation. During the prior session, Representative Abner Taylor, a member of the Committee on Coinage, Weights and Measures, had introduced a bill that required Treasury to purchase 12 million ounces of silver from an undisclosed entity.[20]

Speaker Thomas Reed, with his hand forced, appointed an investigative committee of his friends. It quickly came out that Francis Newlands was involved in the speculation. However, he was under no ethical restrictions in this regard. At this point, Senator Vest of Missouri asked to be heard. On the day appointed for his testimony, he was not called. When the committee did meet again, it was just after the Republican caucus in Pennsylvania had voted to support Donald Cameron for a third term in the Senate. Vest was now called and testified that Cameron told him he had bought and sold silver. Cameron, in defense, saw nothing wrong; it was no different than speculating in corn or wheat. His actions were not influenced by his position in the Senate, and it had been done after the bill, in its amended form, passed the Senate.[21]

Cameron took the witness stand on January 26. He revealed that he put up $8,000 on his silver purchase and netted a profit of $1,100 on the sale. He knew nothing about an alleged silver pool. He knew no other senator or representative who bought silver. No member of Congress asked him to exert his influence in favor of the silver bill.[22] It was the end of the line; the investigation died there.

Senator Cameron made a handsome return on his $8,000 investment. However, it fell into the old Kentucky adage that pigs get fat while hogs get slaughtered. The behind-the-scenes political deal appeared to be that Cameron would be given time to secure his senatorial nomination in the Pennsylvania Republican caucus before being outed for his silver transaction. Unsaid, if silver did not prevail during Cameron's third term, it would be his last. Quay would be waiting at the exit doors of the Senate with a one-way train ticket for Donald back to the Cameron family farm, Lochiel, in rural Pennsylvania.

The House investigative committee never called Representative Taylor to question him about details behind his bill directing the specific purchase of undisclosed silver bullion. The connection with Seligman Brothers was never pursued. Both argued that silver speculation during the debate was probably more widespread. After all, Newlands, who interfaced with everybody in Washington, had admitted to speculating. However, no one in power wanted this investigation to go beyond Senator Cameron.

Where were the Harrisons, father and son, in this affair? Their ties to Montana silver interests through the Helena Assay Office left that an open and valid question. The single connection was Representative Tom Carter from Montana. Carter was a good friend of Russell Harrison, and the *New York Times* mentioned him in the same breath with Richard Bland as being one of the most effective proponents of silver in the House.[23] In addition, Carter had a seat on the Committee on Coinage, Weights and Measures. Carter lost his bid for reelection in the fall of 1890, making him a lame duck in this last session of the Fifty-First Congress. Yet President Harrison appointed Representative Carter to the annual Assay Commission for 1891 with no apparent political motive.[24]

There were fissures appearing in Lizzie Cameron's world. She had given birth to a daughter in 1886, but that had not helped the marriage. Simon Cameron, being an incorrigible lady's man, had always been enamored of Lizzie, serving as her advocate in the family. With his death in 1889, the grown children from Cameron's first marriage sharpened their knives, and there was no one to hold them at bay. Worst of all was the obvious decline in Donald Cameron's political power.

One bright spot had been the friendship with Theodore Roosevelt and then his wife Edith, when she joined her husband after the birth of their second son. Roosevelt had made a name for himself as a leader of the reform movement through his role on the Civil Service Commission. Roosevelt's close friendship with Cabot Lodge guaranteed entrée to Adams's salon. Adams was fascinated by Theodore's vitality, so opposite of his retiring personality. Yet Edith, in her own right, thrived in these surroundings and would develop a lifelong friendship with Henry.

With the death of Clover Adams, Lizzie's relationship with Henry had grown into very deep mutual feelings. With the end of the 1890 social season, Adams and La Farge had departed for the South Seas. Lizzie in June departed for Massachusetts with her daughter. Roosevelt upon her departure wrote, "You cast a gloom over us by your dreadful threat that as you had been good this winter you intended to be bad next winter. On behalf of the family I protest."

Thanksgiving and Christmas at Lochiel with Donald were an onerous chore for Lizzie. Then a real emotional blow took her to a new depth of sadness. Uncle Cump, her surrogate father for so long, died on February 14, 1891. He was only 70 years old.

The great general's passing saddened all of New York City and the nation. Charles Beaman, the long-time friend of Augustus Saint-Gaudens, stepped in to arrange for the taking of the death mask. Saint-Gaudens would arrive at the family home the night of February 16, accompanied by friend and fellow sculptor, Daniel Chester French. Upon arriving, Saint-Gaudens broke down, leaving French to take the death mask.[25,26]

The citizens of New York wasted no time in forming a committee to erect a proper memorial to the general who had chosen their city as his final home. At once Saint-Gaudens wanted this commission. However, there were thoughts of having either a limited or an open competition. A competition would not do for Gus; he would decline.

Coincidentally this was the same time that Saint-Gaudens was coordinating with Lizzie to place the Adams memorial at the gravesite in Rock Creek Cemetery. She thought the bronze "inexpressibly noble and beautiful."[27] And so it was that Lizzie found herself advocating for Saint-Gaudens to gain this commission.

On April 9, the committee met and announced their decision. They had considered both a limited and open competition. They dismissed an open competition because of the possibility of having someone other than an American create the work. Then they rejected a limited or invited competition as well. Saint-Gaudens was to receive the prize. They believed the circumstances were exceptional. Saint-Gaudens had recently completed a bust of the general, much to everyone's satisfaction. He had been the choice of the family to make the death mask. Most important, members of the family were very desirous that he be selected to design the statue.[28] Gus was to provide both an equestrian bronze of Sherman and a figure of "Victory."[29] And so the long journey to the gold coin designs had begun.

In the fall of 1891, Henry Adams, returning from his extended sojourn in the South Seas, met Lizzie in Paris. They could not resolve their relationship. She proved unwilling to face the social stigma of divorce. Henry could not make himself risk losing their special friendship in order to gain a more significant relationship. They were like two ships passing in the night, and the opportunity tragically for them was lost forever.

Chapter 37
Barber's Masterpiece

For Richard Watson Gilder victory was at hand. For almost a decade he had worked to replace the tired and dated designs on American coins. With a sense of self-satisfaction, he believed a glorious renaissance in American art upon the nation's coinage was at hand. The roadblock was gone; American artists would see that his dream was achieved.

With the silver bill out of the way, Congress could focus on two pieces of legislation that set the Mint's long-term operational mandates. The first empowered the secretary of Treasury to change coin designs administratively every 25 or more years. The second streamlined American coinage by eliminating the three-cent nickel minor coin and the one- and three-dollar gold pieces. These coins had either outlived their usefulness or were never popular with the public.[1]

The bill authorizing design changes passed the House on February 24, 1890. One sentiment expressed in the House was that the motto "In God We Trust," though not mandated, ought to be retained. [2] As the Senate wrapped up debate on the silver bill in June and prepared to take up this bill, Mint Director Edward Leech grew so excited about the prospects for passage that he could not contain himself.

Leech proudly announced that he would advertise for new designs. There would be a contest open to all—amateurs and professionals—with rewards to the winners of not less than $500. Leech proclaimed there would be a new design for the silver dollar, exempted from the 25-year rule, bluntly stating that he did not believe that the

Philadelphia schoolmarm's head on the dollar signified Liberty. He wanted something different, perhaps an image of George Washington. On the reverse, he wanted an eagle that was of heroic design, not one that looked like a turkey buzzard.

Leech should have left well enough alone, but instead proceeded to critique the other current designs. He wanted all three of the subsidiary silver coins—the dime, quarter, and half dollar—to have the same design. He thought the existing eagle on the back of the Seated Liberty design that had been around since 1809 a very creditable sort of bird. Confusing the obverse Seated Liberty design with that of the trade dollar, he opined that he wanted to do away with the young female sitting on a bale of cotton. He also wanted the stars on the circumference of these coins to correspond to the number of states currently in the Union.

Then he turned to the penny. "The Indian must be wiped out, it is a well-executed head, artistically speaking; but the law says the design on the face of a penny must typify Liberty." He did not see how an Indian typified Liberty, unless it is "Liberty very badly abused, with an overdose of bad whisky thrown in." Tossing a compliment to engraver Barber, Leech thought the nickel was a pretty fair-looking coin. The gold coin designs would not be changed; they were admirable as they were. He considered the double eagle gold piece the best design of all the United States coins. When questioned about "In God We Trust," Leech was not prepared to say the motto would be removed.[3]

Public Law 51-286, giving Treasury the authority to make design changes, was enacted on September 26, 1890. Almost as an afterthought, on October 3 Gilder received a note of thanks from Treasury for his work on behalf of the legislation.[4]

With authority in place, Leech asked Charles Barber for input should designs be sought from outside artists. Barber responded that models should be in low relief from four to eight inches in diameter and include all inscriptions required by law. Barber was adamant that it was essential to judging any design to consider how the inscriptions and date were placed within the design's field.[5]

Then suddenly someone above Leech in Treasury applied brakes to the project. The director, giving the reason of time needed to complete his annual report, announced the postponement of the design competition until late spring 1891.[6]

Leech knew that he must rely heavily upon the New York artists in order to ensure a successful competition. Bypassing Charles Barber, he wired Andrew Mason, in charge of the New York Assay Office, on April 2, 1891, for a list of the prominent artists to be considered. In response, Mason sent his chief clerk to interview the artists. First on his list was Augustus Saint-Gaudens.

Saint-Gaudens was honored but stated that he would not be willing to enter such a competition although he certainly would be proud to provide designs if invited. Gus did make several recommendations, suggesting that the competition be limited to qualified artists. If possible, they should be compensated. Saint-Gaudens even volunteered names of sculptors he thought might participate.

John Quincy Adams Ward was also interviewed that day. He agreed with Saint-Gaudens that a great deal of time and effort would be involved for the participants. He certainly did not want to see the commission go "to incompetent hands." He too provided names but felt Saint-Gaudens and Olin Warner the two most qualified.[7] On

April 3, Mason sent Leech ten names: that included Saint-Gaudens and all the most prominent artists in the city.[8]

Leech also sought additional input from Charles Barber. The engraver wanted the diameter specifications for each coin to be set forth as part of the process; a design might be suitable at one size and not at another. Barber did not believe that advertising in newspapers for designs would produce satisfactory results. Furthermore, he pointed out that compensation for any time expended in submitting the designs should be considered. Barber also provided potential names that included Saint-Gaudens.[9]

Leech wasted no time, setting the process in motion on April 4, 1891. Each artist on Andrew Mason's list received a copy of a circular letter of invitation that called for two separate design submittals: One for the obverse and reverse of the dollar and one for the obverses for the half dollar, quarter, and dime to be submitted for judging no later than June 1. The models must be in low relief, suitable for coinage, and bear all the legally required inscriptions. The payment for each accepted model was $500.[10] Leech was, at this point, content with the reverse of the Seated Liberty design and wished only modifications at most to the eagle and shield. Leech followed with a press release setting forth this action and also stating that the motto, "In God We Trust," would be retained.[11]

Leech had ignored Charles Barber on two critical points. While not adequately publicized and unknown to the New York artists, Leech sent some two thousand circulars throughout the country.[12] This action precluded Leech from considering compensation beyond that to the winning designers.

The circular was greeted with consternation by the artists in New York. Finally on May 20, Saint-Gaudens and seven others met to draft, sign, and publish a response to the circular. The artists wanted the designs to be judged by a competent jury of individuals of standing in the profession, to be chosen by vote of the competitors. They wanted three months to prepare sketches and six months for the preparation of completed models. Compensation was to be given for each completed sketch and an additional sum for any models submitted. They wanted $1,000 for the winning designs. Finally, they wanted the obverse and reverse of any coin to be designed by the same artist, and they wanted the existing reverse of the dime, quarter, and half dollar abandoned.[13]

It was reported in the New York papers that all of the artists, including Saint-Gaudens, signed the letter. Gus, however, had second thoughts. The letter implied that he would compete if the terms were modified. He would not; he was withdrawing.[14]

Leech could not understand why the artists had waited to respond until only ten days before the close of the contest. If he extended the deadline, he would be showing obvious favoritism to a select group of artists. As to the financial terms, no moneys had been appropriated for such payments. Here Leech was assuming that the New York artists were aware that he had issued a broad invitation. He did assure the artists on one point: A competent jury would be selected to judge the entries.[15]

On the margin of Saint-Gaudens's letter withdrawing his name from the competition are written in Leech's hand the names of Saint-Gaudens, Ward, and Gilder. This may have been Leech's first take at a jury to judge the designs. It would have been an excellent choice, had he stayed the course.

Leech regrettably changed his mind with only Saint-Gaudens surviving to make the final cut. Added were Charles Barber and Henry Mitchell.[16] Mitchell was a noted engraver of stamps and seals from Boston. He had one major numismatic effort to his credit: The official medal for the Philadelphia Centennial Exposition in 1876.[17]

This final selection was tainted. Both Charles Barber and Henry Mitchell had a vested interest in the outcome. If the competition were a failure, both saw themselves capable of providing new designs.[18] It is a shame that Gilder fell out of consideration. He had no agenda except the betterment of the nation's coin designs.

The three-man jury convened on June 3. The submittals were disappointing, with Gus rejecting all out of hand.[19] He even confided to Leech that he had studied the situation and only four individuals were capable of doing such design work. Three lived in France, and he was the fourth.[20] Maybe Gus did have a personal agenda after all, but only after it was apparent the competition was a failure.

When Leech, in turn, tried to constructively suggest to Charles Barber that he retain someone to assist him should this work now be done at the Mint, Barber bristled. He knew that Saint-Gaudens preferred a design from the ancient Greeks featuring high relief. A general circulation design done in this same manner was absolutely out of the question. In addition, high-relief coins would not stack for bank counting purposes and would be easy prey for counterfeiters. Barber rebutted that he knew of no one who could even assist him in preparing acceptable designs.[21]

The 1890 Joseph Francis Medal was modeled by Louis Saint-Gaudens and engraved at the Philadelphia Mint by Charles Barber. The Mint's Hill reducing machine required substantial touching-up by Barber to produce a finished die. In addition, Barber was instructed to rework the lifeboat on the reverse that had been inaccurately depicted in the model. This was the first professional contact between the two men, and most likely Augustus Saint-Gaudens took offense because of these modifications.

Leech had now put himself in a corner. His only option was to have the design work done in house. On June 11, Leech instructed Barber to prepare sketches for the half dollar, quarter, and dime. He was content to leave the Morgan dollar, with its expected drastically reduced coinage requirements starting that July, in place for the time being. He was looking for one obverse design based upon the head of Liberty as depicted on the French five-franc piece. The design need not be an exact copy. For the reverse, Leech was holding to the present eagle on the half dollar and quarter. If changed, he would want the shield either on the eagle's breast or in its talons.[22]

At the end of June, Saint-Gaudens had his say in *Harper's Weekly*. A limited competition might be better than depending upon one artist although the designs should be in the hands of an artist capable of doing the work well. And the only means of getting such an individual is through the offer of a proper reward. Every possible concession should be made and no effort spared to reduce to a minimum the sacrificing of the artistic side to the mechanical and technical requirements of coining. However, none of the technical requirements can be disregarded. On both sides some concessions will be necessary. In the present effort to secure models of artistic beauty for our coinage the government is deserving of praise rather than blame.[23]

In response, Leech defended his decision to use Charles Barber on July 20 in a brief report in the *Boston Transcript*.[24] He believed the recent competition was a wretched failure. The result was not flattering to the artistic development of the country. He doubted whether such a competition would ever be tried again.[25]

In what was now degenerating into a war of words, Richard Watson Gilder, responded in the *New York Tribune*. Gilder recognized that the design solicitation had been a failure. However, he questioned giving the Mint—in effect a manufacturing facility—artistic control of the new designs. In his opinion, the Mint director should have continued the process within the artistic community until an acceptable solution was reached.[26]

Oliver Bosbyshell served as superintendent of the Philadelphia Mint during the Harrison Administration and enjoyed the support of both Pennsylvania senators. He had previously been the coiner under Loudon Snowden.

It should have ended there but it did not. On August 9 Leech's answer reached New York. The engraver at Philadelphia had prepared some new designs that he had shown to both Leech and Henry Mitchell. However, Leech was still not entirely satisfied and expected that the changes would take some weeks more. The letter then took a defensive tone. "Artistic designs for coins, that would meet the ideas of an art critic like yourself, and artists generally, are not always adapted for practical coinage." If he could get improved designs by staying within the Mint Service, he saw no good reason to look beyond it.[27]

Leech's statement that he was reserving final judgment on Barber's new designs for the subsidiary silver coinage set the stage for a test of wills. The design first proposed by Barber for the half dollar ignored Leech's directions for the obverse. Its principal device was a standing female figure representing Columbia. In one hand was a liberty pole topped with the liberty cap, a theme identical to the Seated Liberty coins. In the background behind Columbia was an eagle with wings upraised, standing on a rock.[28] The reverse was no better. It consisted of the heraldic eagle from the Great Seal of the United States, downsized and surrounded by sunrays and an oversized wreath of oak leaves. The proportions were wrong, and the elements impossibly crowded. Why have eagles on both the obverse and reverse of the design?

Leech was not satisfied with the obverse and asked Barber to prepare a design in accordance with his original suggestion. Barber complied with a head of Liberty drawn most likely from a composite of images emanating from France.[29] Barber left the reverse unchanged but was beginning to have second thoughts about the inclusion of a wreath.[30]

Leech, after showing this latest design to the secretary of the Treasury, proceeded to critique the image of Liberty and ask for the reverse with and without the wreath and to strike pattern pieces.[31] Charles Barber bristled. The engraver stated that he was perfectly willing to make any changes in design, provided the suggested change was, in his opinion, a good one. Barber was sorry to say but as an artist, he begged to differ with the director.[32] Superintendent Bosbyshell took this letter and attached one of his own in support of Charles Barber.[33]

An irritated Leech wasted no time in responding. He was having none of it.

Leech did not care how many dies were prepared. If a modification, however slight, improved the design in his opinion, that change would be made. It was his objective to get as nearly perfect a work as possible. Any criticism given in the proper spirit and aimed to beautify American coinage should be cheerfully received and fairly considered.[34]

If Leech were expecting to find an apology in the text of Barber's response, there was none. What he got was more a tedious recitation about the olive leaves, scroll, and star points. The overall tone of the response remained argumentative.[35] Charles Barber then prepared three more versions of the reverse, each incorporating clouds above the eagle.

It did not end here. The clouds now became an issue. In the first week of November, two more variations were submitted.[36] Leech gathered these patterns and forwarded them to President Benjamin Harrison. On November 6, 1891, the president and his cabinet reviewed Barber's work and chose the pattern without the clouds. On November 7, Leech ordered the adoption of this design, and the saga was over.[37] Barber then adapted the design to the smaller quarter. Leech's preference for the existing reverse of the dime carried the day. Only the obverse of the dime was changed to incorporate the new head of Liberty.

J-1766

J-1762

J-1764

J-1765

Charles Barber produced four pattern pieces in 1891 for the redesign of the subsidiary silver coins. His first effort (Judd-1766) exhibited an eagle on both the obverse and reverse of the coin. In addition, the reverse was so overcrowded as to eliminate the negative space needed to highlight the central element of the design. The three subsequent patterns (J-1762, J-1764, and J-1765) substituted a head of Liberty for the obverse. However, the reverses still suffered from overcrowding.

The newly adopted design in 1892 for the subsidiary silver coins would come to be known as the Barber coinage. However, Edward Leech played a major role in cleaning up the reverse design elements for the quarter and half dollar to give the needed negative space.

"The mountain had labored and brought forth a mouse," declared *Harper's Weekly* when provided a photograph of the model for the new half dollar that November. Kenyon Cox was disdainfully quoted.

> Every time the government has anything to do in art matters it shows its utter incapacity to deal with such things. It [Barber's design] is beneath criticism. I think it disgraceful that this great country should have such a coin as this.

Another artist declared that the image of Liberty was evidently the work of an amateur who had mastered very few of the rudiments of modeling. He then went to the extreme saying that the head of Liberty appeared unintelligent and that the face suggested that of a disreputable woman just recovering from a prolonged debauch!

A "learned" numismatist commented only upon the promise of anonymity to protect his business relationship with the Mint. He called it inferior to the several pattern designs developed in the 1870s at the Mint but not adopted.[38] What he was questioning in a veiled manner was the passing over of George Morgan's lovely School Girl design of 1879 as well as the assistant engraver's exclusion from the entire design process.

The most-lively criticism in the article was that of Saint-Gaudens. His attitude had significantly deteriorated since his last *Harper's* interview in July. Gus injudiciously ranted:

> There are a hundred men who could have done a very much better job than this. This is inept; this looks like it had been designed by a young lady of sixteen, a miss who had taken only a few lessons in modeling. It is beneath criticism. . . I cannot see that it is any improvement in any regard upon the old coins.[39]

Saint-Gaudens's emotions were too intense in the *Harper's Weekly* interview. Beneath his unwillingness to enter a competition, Saint-Gaudens must have harbored a desire to have his design on a circulating American coin.

Part 6

An Affair for the Ages

Chapter 38

The Greatest Show on Earth

Augustus Saint-Gaudens remarked early in the planning that the World's Columbian Exposition had brought together "the greatest meeting of artists since the 15th century."[1] That was a bit bombastic, but he certainly was correct that the nation had never previously experienced anything approaching this concentration of artistic talent. Even so Saint-Gaudens declined to provide a monumental work for the Fair. However, he gladly accepted a paid oversight role, as all wanted his unfailing critical eye. It was a heady time for him, working with the other architects and artists, but with no real responsibility and no deadlines to meet.

The stated purpose of this national celebration was to recognize the 400th anniversary of Columbus's discovery of the Western Hemisphere. The World's Columbian Exposition would be both a fair and an exposition, the likes of which the nation had never before attempted. The concept had first been proposed in 1887 as an intellectual and scientific exposition under the control of the federal government and located in Washington, D.C. As the idea gained ground, the emphasis shifted to an industrial exposition with New York, Chicago, and St. Louis vying to be the host. The field then narrowed to Chicago and New York. Civic feelings were strong with so much scorn poured New York's way in the Chicago press that their counterparts in New York dubbed Chicago the "Windy City."[2] When Congress tardily enacted the necessary legislation in April 1890, the fair was delayed a year. Chicago had carried the day, but the legislation only appropriated $1,500,000 for the expenses of the federal government's participation. Much work needed to be done in just the three short years to the Exposition's opening date. Complicating matters, there were two competing management structures with overlapping authority.

The leading citizens of Chicago formed the World's Columbian Exposition Company to finance and build the Exposition. Through a stock subscription and bonds issued by the City of Chicago, they successfully raised $11 million to fund the effort.[3] To expedite construction and hold down costs, building exteriors were to be constructed of staff, a mixture of plaster of Paris and hemp. The enabling legislation likewise set up a World's Columbian Commission that had responsibility for approving the plans and construction activities of the Exposition Company as well as oversight of the exhibits.[4] This commission was composed of two appointed members from each state, one Republican and one Democrat, plus at-large members. It was a political body. Committees under both organizations sprang up overnight like mushrooms, causing wholesale confusion. As construction expenditures skyrocketed, infighting between the two groups developed.

Much of the credit for meeting the May 1893 opening day deadline would go to Daniel Burnham, who mid-way through the project became the construction czar. Concurrent with this appointment, the Columbian Commission under George Davis became subordinate to the Exposition Company. Burnham was a member and prime mover of the Board of Architects for the Exposition Company that included most of the leading architectural firms in America. He was the ideal man for the job. He had a favorite saying: "Make no little plans; they have no magic to stir men's blood."[5] Under Burnham's leadership, the buildings and more importantly, the Fair itself, would embody the Beaux-Arts tenants of scale, harmony, and ensemble.

For those in charge of paying for this Fair, it was not so heady of a time. By May 1892 it was apparent that the Exposition Company was in need of additional funds; construction budgets for the Fair had been inadequate. A supplemental appropriation of five million dollars would be needed from Congress. The Exposition Company encountered support in the Senate but stiff resistance from the fiscally strict Democrats in the House. An outright appropriation proved impossible, necessitating a compromise. Five million dollars worth of souvenir half dollars would be authorized instead.

Never before had the United States struck a legal tender coin designed for a specific occasion. Bullion was to be provided from obsolete and underweight silver coins removed from circulation. For the government, the only cash cost of this action would be for melting and re-coining.

Even with this workaround, there was continued resistance in the House. That body was in a foul temper. They had received a formal report in May accusing the Columbian Commission of paying exorbitant salaries.[6] On the day of adjournment, August 5, 1892, a compromise was reached. The authorization was cut back to 2-1/2 million dollars.[7]

Fair officials easily saw the way to recoup their lost appropriation by selling these souvenir half dollars for one dollar. They reasoned that ten to fifteen million fair goers would want one. Hence, a premium could be supported. Cooler heads, notably the Chicago financier, Lyman Gage, doubted the magnitude of the markup. A few thousand might be sold at that price but the remainder would be left in the hands of the Exposition Company.[8]

For the Exposition Company, time was of the essence. There was a desire to have some coins dated 1892. The more pressing concern was to have coins available as soon as possible to help fund construction that was now starved for cash. Word from the Mint was that preparation of the designs and dies would take at least five months.[9] Using in part the promise of future sales from the coins as security, the Exposition Company proceeded to float their own bonds. Public acceptance of these coins was going to be critical in the coming months.

Well in advance of the passage of the necessary legislation, a test of wills had developed over the basic design theme for this souvenir coin. A key player was James Ellsworth, a noted numismatist and member of the board of directors of the Exposition Company. He was the owner of the Lorenzo Lotto period portrait thought too be Christopher Columbus. He wanted his portrait to be the basis for the likeness of Columbus on the half dollar. Taking the initiative, at Frank Millet's recommendation as head of exposition design, Ellsworth had contacted the noted sculptor, Olin Warner, for the design work. Word also came from Assistant Secretary of the Treasury William Edmond Curtis that the Executive Committee of the Exposition Company should get the design process under control.[10] Daniel Burnham also took a lead, going to several eminent artists who recommended Philip Martiny as capable of giving a good design.[11] Meanwhile Mint Director Leech was willing to leave it largely up to the Exposition people.

Ellsworth moved. Assistant Secretary Curtis was urging action, fearing the Mint would involve a number of artists in a competition, jeopardizing the chances that the Lotto portrait would be the basis for the coin design.[12] Ellsworth gained the endorsement of the Columbian Commission's Committee on Design for his portrait. It wasn't enough.

On August 6, 1892, with ink on the enabling legislation hardly dry, Treasury announced that the designs for the souvenir half dollar had been selected and would bear a likeness of Columbus from a bust based upon the Lotto portrait on the obverse and the Administration Building of the Exposition on the reverse.[13] That press release was entirely premature.

On August 15, Charles Barber volunteered his preliminary design.[14] Robert Preston, acting in Leech's absence, forwarded Barber's sketches to the Commission's Director General Davis for his review. The obverse showed Columbus in profile, based on the Lotto portrait, while the reverse depicted an image of the western hemisphere with a caravel in the background.[15] Perfunctorily, Preston asked Davis to provide suggestions that he might think proper. However, he closed by saying that Davis would be afforded an opportunity to consult with the Mint before the designs were finalized.[16]

Davis balked.[17] He provided Barber's crude Mint sketches to Ellsworth who in turn showed them to artists working at the Exposition. This group drafted a protest calling the design proposal absolutely inartistic, unsuited to purpose and unworthy of the country and the occasion. Among the signers were Daniel Chester French, Philip Martiny, and Olin Warner.[18] Even worse, the press said Barber's Columbus looked like a namby-pamby, smooth-faced, longhaired professor instead of the ruler of the sea.[19]

James Ellsworth lost his temper and promptly withdrew permission to use the Lotto for the souvenir coin's obverse design.[20] It seemed as if chaos was rapidly approaching.

Now Olin Warner, at Frank Millet's suggestion, tried his hand at a design. The obverse was not based upon the Lotto portrait. The reverse featured a caravel symbolic of the *Santa Maria* above two globes representing the hemispheres. Fourteen and 92 flanked the two globes.[21] This did not suit.

The whole affair then landed in the lap of the Finance Committee of the Columbian Exposition Company, of which Ellsworth, now having regained his temper, was a member. Faced with no consensus in the Finance Committee,[22] its chairman, Ferdinand W. Peck, forwarded only Warner's sketch for the reverse of the coin to Leech. This package landed on Leech's desk early in September. A September 3 story with a Washington dateline claimed a radical change had been made in the souvenir coin's designs. The Lotto likeness would be replaced with a profile from a medal struck in Spain. For a reverse, a representation of the "Western Continent" would be used.[23] This story was at odds with the Finance Committee with respect to the reverse.

Leech went to Philadelphia on the fifth and sixth to confer with his people before replying on the ninth.[24] He mentioned that Barber was going to move forward with a model of the head of Columbus. Corrections could be made to the head when the Spanish medal was received. Leech then stated that the officers of the Mint did not think the proposed reverse would show well as a coin. Barber was proposing an alternative that consisted only of the western hemisphere nestled in a half wreath of oak leaves.[25]

Meanwhile, Olin Warner had moved on, starting work on the directory badge for the dedication ceremonies scheduled for October. His depiction of Columbus was more nearly in line with the Lotto portrait. The bust of Columbus, done in high relief, extended to the lower rim of the badge, adding a sense of animation to the design.[26] This work was finished early in September and was immediately seen as a possible alternative to Warner's proposed obverse for the souvenir half dollar.[27,28]

Perceiving an impasse, George Davis determined that a face-to-face meeting with the Mint would be necessary. At that meeting on September 17 at Leech's office in Washington, Charles Barber was present.[29] It was a clash of wills. Davis wanted to use Warner's reverse design in conformance with the Finance Committee's wishes. Barber pushed for a design that would show the coin well in low relief. Davis lacked the technical expertise to argue the issue of relief. No decision was reached. On September 21, Leech authorized Barber to travel to Chicago to consult further with Davis.[30]

The meeting took place between Barber and the Finance Committee on September 23.[31] In the only indication of the committee's position, the news release the next day noted there would be a slight alteration removing the cap from the Lotto head.[32] It was a roundabout way of saying that Warner's second (Lotto) version of Columbus

The badge for the World's Columbian Exposition, designed by Olin Warner, was the basis for the obverse of the 1892 Columbian commemorative half dollar.

from the badge would be used. In a September 28 letter to Davis, Leech signed off, finding the selections fitting and the designs handsome.[33]

Barber, his pique showing, wrote Ellsworth on September 29, petulantly asking that a letter be provided authorizing the use of the Lotto head and the caravel and globes for the coin.[34] He made no reference to the fact that these were Olin Warner's designs. On the next day, there appeared in the *New York Times* quotes from the engraver objecting to Warner's designs for the souvenir half dollar. Artistically there were too many objects in the reverse field. When the model was reduced to the size of the coin, the results would be unsatisfactory. The relief of the coin was also too high. The finished coins would not stack, and the coin presses would not be able to strike off the pieces rapidly. The designer had forgotten that this piece was to be a coin for circulation and not a medal.[35] On the surface, it appeared to be gross insubordination. That Barber got away with it indicated that he had solid support within the Mint bureaucracy.

In translating Warner's badge into an effective coin design, Barber was faced with two difficulties. First, Warner's final obverse design did not have the proper inscriptions.[36] Barber was faced with either coming up with a unique approach to incorporate inscriptions or making a major modification to provide necessary negative space. Second, the details of the head and face were strongly emphasized, in a pronounced, but tolerable high relief and slightly off center. Metal flow problems could arise during the striking, resulting in an uneven rim.

Barber also had an issue with the reverse. Warner's model of the ship lacked details. Barber immediately asked Ellsworth for a photograph of the caravel at the Exposition in order to fine-tune this design element.[37] He feared that people would look at the caravel and then compare the reverse of the coin to the ship. If the likeness were not perfect, his work would be subjected to criticism. Ellsworth sent photos but they also were lacking in sufficient detail. Barber had a solution: He turned the reverse over to George Morgan.

On November 11, Barber wrote Ellsworth. He had just supplied him with impressions of the coins. He told Ellsworth that he was providing the Philadelphia superintendent with his plaster model. The work was rough because he preferred to do his final touches in the steel die. While others relied upon a better model and allowed the reducing lathe to make the necessary cuts in the master die, he had clung to the old ways. He might have added that this skill was necessary because the Mint's reducing lathe was not capable of making exact, extremely detailed cuts. Barber expected to have working dies ready in a week, and striking of the souvenir coins could begin immediately.[38]

Minting of the souvenir coins commenced on Saturday, November 19. Ellsworth was present.[39] A million of the half dollars were planned for November and December.[40] At Barber's suggestion and then Superintendent Bosbyshell's, 100 were to be struck on highly polished planchets using specially selected dies to yield a mirror-like Proof finish.[41]

It was a major undertaking for the Mint. The first coins arrived in Chicago on December 19 to great fanfare. Fifty thousand coins came in five stout oaken kegs, five bags of 2,000 coins each per keg. Each keg weighed 400 pounds.[42], [43] It was front-page news in the *Chicago Daily Tribune*. Every detail from the opening of the wooden kegs to the distribution of the coins was described. The first coin struck had already been auctioned for $10,000 to the Remington Company, a typewriter manufacturer.[44]

Buried in the last of the article were several critical assessments. Opinions were somewhat negative although good points were noted. Almost to a person, the interviewees wished for higher relief. Details of the image of Columbus had been lost in the need to both reduce the relief and shrink the image to make room for the inscriptions on the circumference of the coin. Ominously, one individual called the design weak and predicted that sales of the coin would be poor. Nevertheless the enthusiasm of the common people at the event was infectious.[45] A premium of 25 to 50 cents over the dollar asking price quickly developed.[46]

Ellsworth clipped this article and sent it to both Barber and Warner. Immediately, Barber, thin-skinned when it came to criticism directed at him, poured out his invective against the critical comments. In a five-page letter, Barber replied to Ellsworth on December 22, addressing each and every negative point. Much of his rebuttal was

The 1892 Columbian half dollar was issued to help finance the Fair's construction. It was the first legal tender commemorative coin authorized and issued by the United States government. Within the total mintage were 100 Proof coins originally intended for distribution to railroad executives but later diverted to Fair dignitaries.

a justification for low relief. Barber ended by suggesting that the newspapers of Chicago should restrict their publishing of "opinions of people who display a deplorable amount of ignorance and likewise seem inclined to say, 'Stinking Fish.'" The papers would be much better off trying to promote sales in support of the Exposition.[47] The Christmas spirit eluded Charles Barber that year.

Warner's response to Ellsworth, without understanding the reasons behind Barber's alterations, was one of resignation. He told Ellsworth, "I have not seen the souvenir coin yet, but I'll wager it doesn't look like the model."[48] Warner's initials were conspicuously absent from the souvenir half dollars.

On a more serious note, sales of the Columbian half dollar slumped. By February 1893, the newness of the souvenir coins had worn off and the problem was serious enough to affect Exposition Company finances. To generate quick cash, some two million of the half dollars were turned over to Chicago area banks to be held as part of their legal reserve requirements. The banks in turn advanced face value for the coins to the Exposition Company. It was a desperate but successful move to generate enough cash to keep going until the Fair opened and revenues began to flow in May.[49]

In March to add insult to injury, Congress, seeing the sluggish coin sales, unfairly expropriated 1,141,760 of the souvenir half dollars to pay the estimated costs of the Columbian Commission for judging and making awards to the exhibitors at the Fair.[50]

Chapter 39
A BREACH OF FAITH

Confound the Shaw Memorial Committee! Now Augustus Saint-Gaudens was in a pickle and he must find a way to get out.

This mess went all the way back to February 1881, when Saint-Gaudens initiated discussions to provide a large bas-relief plaque honoring the African-American Fifty-Fourth Massachusetts Volunteer Infantry Regiment and its colonel, Robert Gould Shaw. He had finally signed a contract in 1884 with a completion date of 1886. By his own admission the sculptor in the intervening years had spent more time thinking about the work that actually working on its completion.

Matters had come to a head in a December 1891 meeting with the committee. As Saint-Gaudens had progressed on the *Shaw*, so many more possibilities for composition had presented themselves, each in turn needing to be worked out.[1] It now was too large to go upon the State House wall requiring Gus to seek a new location across the street on the edge of Boston Common. Site preparation would be required. There was not money enough in the Shaw Memorial Fund, thus requiring an appropriation from the city. There was another problem. John Murray Forbes, the New England industrialist and strong personality on the committee, disliked the allegorical angel that capped the bas-relief, calling it Cassandra-like and hoping that Gus's "better angel" would encourage the sculptor to improve it or leave it out.[2] Forbes had an emotional tie to the project. His wife was a good friend of the mother of the late

Colonel Shaw who was killed during his regiment's assault of the Confederate Fort Wagner in South Carolina.

There was also an underlying irritant at that meeting for the Shaw Memorial Committee. Saint-Gaudens had just taken the *Sherman* commission with a contractual completion date of May 1, 1894. The committee was tired of being permanently at the back of the queue. Like a cat with nine lives, Saint-Gaudens had somehow survived this meeting but his relationship with the committee was strained.

On December 24, 1891, with the city approval and funding in hand for the change in location, Edward Atkinson, charged by the committee as the liaison with Saint-Gaudens, had called the sculptor to account for all of his procrastinations and delays. If Saint-Gaudens needed additional money to finish this work, the Committee would make such advances. They would much rather take this course than have Saint-Gaudens take on additional commissions of a potboiler nature to support his studio. Then Atkinson had thrown his spear. He believed that Saint-Gaudens was under an obligation to devote himself exclusively to this work. He likened it to a moral obligation of a businessman to not waive the terms of a contract for any reason, artistic or otherwise, except by consent of both parties.[3]

The problem that Saint-Gaudens now faced involved the award medal for exhibitors at the World's Columbian Exposition. The legislation authorizing the souvenir half dollar also appropriated $60,000 for the design, engraving of the dies, and striking of medals to award outstanding exhibits under the supervision of the secretary of the Treasury.[4,5] Almost immediately, Secretary Charles Foster sought the advice of the Columbian Commission Awards Committee[6] for input as to appropriate designs and devices.

The committee formed the Awards Subcommittee led by John Boyd Thacher. As both a manufacturer and former mayor of Albany, NY, he was comfortable in both corporate boardrooms and the smoke-filled back rooms of American politics. In fact, as chairman of the executive committee within the Awards Committee, he held the power.[7] Holding responsibility for the appointment of exhibition judges as well as oversight of the exhibit awards, his influence really extended far beyond the confines of the committee.

Thacher wasted no time, contacting the Treasury Department on August 22, 1892, to set the process in motion. Foster, in turn, laid the groundwork for the process in a communication to George Davis, the director general of the World's Columbian Commission. Foster was reserving for the Mint the right to engage an artist. If the Awards Subcommittee desired, a competition could be conducted. He suggested considering Saint-Gaudens, Will Low, Henry Mitchell, and possibly the Mint's own Charles Barber.[8]

Three weeks later, Director Leech prompted Thacher to make a decision. While the medal would be in high relief, the extensive inscriptions would prevent any elaborate artistry. Time was critical. The design and the engraving work would be under Leech's control; however, the Mint lacked the capacity to strike the required medals, necessitating a contractor. Leech promised that if an outside designer were considered, he would seek to secure the best talent available.[9] In early October, Charles Barber "consulted" with Thacher in order to instruct the Awards Subcommittee of the Mint's ability "in procuring a fine design."[10]

John Boyd Thacher as chair of the Awards Subcommittee of the World's Columbian Exposition thought he could bull through the opposition of the Shaw Committee to have Augustus Saint-Gaudens prepare the award medal for exhibitors at the Fair. His manipulation ultimately led to Saint-Gaudens taking the commission under questionable circumstances that were made even worse in the ensuing imbroglio with Secretary of the Treasury Carlisle over the medal's portrayal of a nude youth.

John Boyd Thacher had other ideas. There was no time. He had to sacrifice a competition in return for the assurance that a competent designer would make what he hoped would be timeless art. On October 5 at a meeting in Washington, Thacher and his subcommittee determined to invite Saint-Gaudens to prepare the medal. The design was to be submitted in the form of a plaster model no more than three times the diameter of the proposed medal. That diameter had not yet been set, but it would be either three or four inches. The dies would be engraved at Philadelphia for the use of a private contractor to strike the medals.[11]

There was one hitch; Gus turned them down. He forthrightly explained that he needed to obtain permission from the Shaw Memorial Committee before taking on any new commissions.[12]

Leech then suggested that Thacher consider J. Q. A. Ward. However, Thacher would not budge. He had some reason to be optimistic. Over the summer, Saint-Gaudens had progressed on the *Shaw Memorial*, and the Shaw Committee had become optimistic that completion was imminent.[13]

Wasting no time, Thacher wrote to John Murray Forbes. That was a mistake. Forbes was opposed but left it to Edward Atkinson to deal with outside matters.[14] As October drew to a close with no reply from Forbes, Thacher began to look for leverage. He learned that one of the committee members, M. P. Kennard, was the assistant treasurer for the Boston Sub-Treasury. He immediately induced Secretary Foster to apply pressure for Saint-Gaudens's temporary release.[15] [16] There was even a letter from the sister of Colonel Shaw to the committee supporting Thacher's request.[17] Thacher described himself to Edward Leech as firing hot shot into the Boston camp.[18]

By now the Shaw Monument Committee had begun to react. On November 5, John Foord, secretary of the Awards Subcommittee met with Atkinson, telling him that if Gus did not take the medal commission, the alternative was obnoxious. It would take Saint-Gaudens about three weeks to complete the commission if he were to be released. Foord's approach was straightforward and favorably received by Atkinson.

Atkinson immediately followed up on November 9 with a query to Saint-Gaudens as to the sculptor's wishes. If the sculptor could give a certain specific time frame there might be a chance that the committee would relent.[19] Saint-Gaudens was direct and to the point in his reply.

> In the matter of the medal I am much troubled. I only wish to do it to keep it out of the hands of the man at the mint who I am positively assured by Mr. Thacher and Mr. Ford *[sic]* will certainly do it if I don't. If I thought that it were at all possible that one of two or three other artists could obtain the work, I should certainly refuse to have anything to do with the matter. As that is not the case I should be glad to do it but it will take three months as it is a very serious matter.[20]

Thacher made one last effort, appealing to Forbes's patriotism. The enterprise was of both national and international importance and should not be looked at in the same vein as a private commission. Thacher also brought to bear the appeals of several distinguished individuals, including Vice President Levi Morton, for Saint-Gaudens's release.[21]

Thacher's actions were for naught. These men on the Shaw Committee were not about to be moved by such rhetoric. In fact, Forbes, when he first learned of the proposal in October, had referred to Thacher and his committee as crazy folks.[22] The differing estimates of the time required for completion of the medal only served to raise a red flag. Atkinson wrote Saint-Gaudens that three months was unacceptable. It would effectively delay completion of the Shaw by a year.[23] Citing the incapacity of artists to measure their own time, the Shaw Committee unanimously rejected the Awards Subcommittee's request on November 18, 1892.

This action seemed to close the door finally and completely on the Awards Subcommittee. Then suddenly Thacher appeared to prevail. On November 30, he told Gus that Treasury was treating his original rejection as withdrawn. The medal was his to design. Optimistically, Thacher hoped that the sculptor would have the work well in hand by the first of the coming year.[24] Saint-Gaudens's acceptance, reported in the newspapers on December 4, 1892, was greeted with much satisfaction.[25] Thacher boasted that if Saint-Gaudens's work turned out well, the world would see that America could do quite as well as any other country if not distinctively better.[26]

Had anything happened to change the Shaw Committee's position? Thacher would not explain to the Awards Subcommittee on paper what he had done. However, he would explain in detail personally.[27]

The Shaw Committee had a very good idea of what had happened. They first received word in mid-December that Saint-Gaudens was going to do the medal on the sly, in the evenings. Yet the sculptor had contended in the past that he needed to think solely and continuously upon one design. If that were truly the case, he was being dishonest to the Shaw Committee to distract his mind by taking on the medal commission.[28]

Edward Atkinson went to New York. Saint-Gaudens confessed that Thacher had told him that either he must do the medal or it would surely go to Charles Barber. To avoid an artistic catastrophe, Gus was going to do the medal on weekends and at night. His work on the Shaw would take place during the day when he could judge the effect of light upon his composition.[29] The committee viewed Saint-Gaudens's actions as a breach of contract in spirit if not in fact.[30] Thacher had used Gus's distaste for Barber's skills as an artist to strong-arm him when similar efforts with the Shaw Committee had failed.

Reflecting federal funding of the awards medal, the commission of $5,000 would be given by the secretary of the Treasury. There was to be no contract and, therefore, no technical violation of the moral obligation to the *Shaw* people. It was a handshake deal between Augustus Saint-Gaudens and John Boyd Thacher.

Gus intimated to Thacher that he had the ambition to make this medal the chief work of his career.

Chapter 40
The Sum of All Evils

The big bust-up could be fixed to an exact date. Unlike the Panic of 1873 where the American economy was collateral damage to the crack-up in Europe, this mess was made in the U.S.A. It would be called the Panic of 1893. Undeservedly, John Sherman's reputation would suffer irreparable damage. Yet there had been warning signs of the coming catastrophe.

Following the recession of 1884–85 that caused a temporary outflow of gold, Treasury receipts began once more to build but their sources shifted dramatically. The growing American economy produced a constantly decreasing surplus of merchandise exports over imports that turned negative in 1888. Offsetting this drain, the British and European financial markets developed an insatiable appetite for American securities to fund that domestic expansion. In fact, the eagerness of English financiers to invest in American companies, particularly railroads, made Great Britain our largest creditor.[1] As a result the net importation of gold persisted in what could be called a "false positive."

Correspondingly, the large increase in our imports added greatly through tariffs to the receipts of the government. That and other factors, including western land sales to homesteaders, led to the rapid accumulation of an unprecedented surplus at Treasury. The logical remedy, advocated by the first Cleveland Administration, would have been to reduce tariffs. However, the Republican-controlled Senate stalemated this move. By default these funds were then used to retire government bonds that otherwise would have been available to meet the holding requirements of the national banks necessary to issue their currency. That resulted in an unwanted currency contraction.[2]

When Benjamin Harrison defeated Grover Cleveland in the Electoral College in the Presidential contest of 1888, he preceded to implement the two key planks of his presidential platform, selective tariff adjustments (The McKinley Act increased tariffs on discretionary items and reduced tariffs on necessities) and increased silver purchases. If surpluses remained, Harrison in his first message to Congress called for additional appropriations for domestic programs. This was something every legislator could get behind, and they became known as the Billion Dollar Congress. Leading the entitlement expenditures were two large pension increases for Civil War veterans. It was a tax-and-spend policy.[3]

During this period of prosperity, suspension of gold payments was not even an issue. However, the need to keep silver in circulation was a constant problem. Only with such artificial measures as the substitution, starting in 1886, of one- and two-dollar Silver Certificates for small denomination United States Notes, or greenbacks, could Treasury maintain any semblance of silver circulation. However, as the small denomination greenbacks were withdrawn from circulation, they were replaced with larger denomination certificates. Too large to be of use in everyday commerce, these large-denomination greenbacks quickly passed out of the hands of the general public to the banks, meaning they would be presented to Treasury for redemption in gold very quickly should the need arise.

In addition, the added Silver Certificates in circulation were legal tender for customs receipts. Thus, when used for such they displaced the normal inflow of gold to the Treasury. Indirectly, it had the same effect as redeeming these Silver Certificates for gold.[4]

The Sherman Silver Purchase Act of 1890 did not really repeal the Act of 1878 that re-monetized the silver dollar. It replaced the coining of a specific amount of silver dollars with the purchase of an even larger amount of silver bullion. In total, Treasury's purchases of silver bullion were now doubled to about $50 million annually. It was also the stated policy of the United States to maintain silver and gold at a legal parity with each other. In order to achieve this requirement, Treasury redeemed in gold the new Treasury Notes issued to pay for silver bullion purchases. Thus, the Sherman Act further facilitated the withdrawal of gold from the Treasury.[5]

British expansion during the 1886–90 period mirrored that of the United States. However, theirs had an element of speculation into risky securities. In response, the Bank of England raised its discount rate at the beginning of 1890, quelling much of the excess. However, at mid-year, certain of these speculative investments turned sour. Thus, the British, facing a financial breakdown, were forced to liquidate their American holdings, in the main, railroad stocks. The situation reached a nadir on November 15, 1890, with the collapse of a British banking house.[6]

When these American securities were liquidated in Great Britain, it meant they came back into the United States market in exchange for a settlement in gold. Suddenly in late summer 1890, gold on a net basis began to flow out of the country. This came at a time when agricultural activity in the South and West was beginning its annual harvest-driven demand for funds. Trouble for the New York banks, and therefore the American financial markets, was not long in coming. Twice during this period, reserves at these banks fell below the 25 percent minimum settled balances in gold. Now in a work-around, they issued clearing-house certificates in place of gold. The banking associations in Boston and Philadelphia soon followed suit.

Meanwhile, the financial health of American industries, including the railroads, remained strong over this period. Year-over-year earnings showed improvement, and profit margins widened. They proved a firewall that prevented the financial difficulties of the major banks from spreading into the interior of the country. Yet the harvest for 1890 had been lower than previous years and demand from England and Europe down, resulting in reduced gold inflow. This reduction was further aggravated by increased imports, driven by the desire to avoid certain tariff increases under the McKinley Act scheduled to take effect in July 1891. As a result, gold continued to flow out of the country over the first half of 1891.[7]

Democrats regained control of the House of Representatives in the Fifty-Second Congress that convened in March 1891. Yet they did not counter President Harrison's effort to spend the surplus. Not only was the surplus wiped out, the Treasury was threatened with a deficit. Added to this swing in fortunes was the termination of the required coinage of silver dollars on July 1, 1891, and thus the issuance of Silver Certificates. In their place, the increased purchase of silver bullion brought on the new Treasury Notes redeemable in gold. These new notes added up to a massive expansion of the currency in circulation that was not justified and could not be absorbed by the economy.[8]

The situation was touch-and-go by late summer 1891, and then prices in the international grain market firmed in response to a depressed harvest in Europe and in Russia, a complete failure. Into this market flowed a bumper crop of wheat and cotton from America. Augmenting this swing in financial fortunes, the British returned as purchasers of American securities. Exports of gold ceased in July and quickly reversed for the remainder of the year as the trade balance swung in favor of America. With the prospect of sound finances restored, the country appeared ready to enter a period of unsurpassed prosperity.[9]

In November 1891, with the harvest complete, idle currency began moving from the western and southern banks to the Eastern money centers, particularly New York. The Eastern bankers were quick to understand that this buildup of excess currency would get worse when the issue of Treasury Notes was considered. It was easy to project that this mass of currency would quickly exceed the banks' required gold reserves. Almost immediately, gold used in clearing-house settlements diminished. After May 1892 settlements were almost exclusively in greenbacks and Treasury Notes.

The next step taken by the banks to reduce their legal tender note holdings was to work them off by applying them against customs dues. Consequently, gold paid to the government from tariffs fell to 25 percent and less. Secretary of the Treasury Charles Foster, confronted by this situation, reacted by stopping government disbursements in gold through the New York Sub-Treasury to the New York Clearing-House. However, that move only slowed the steady decline in the gold holdings of Treasury. In effect, both the government and the banks were hoarding gold.[10]

The continued agitation of the silver question in Congress, with the fear that Senator Bill Stewart's free silver coinage legislation would be passed, merely added fuel to the fire. Just days before the June 1892 Republican National Convention in Minneapolis, John Sherman took the Senate floor for two days in a successful effort to stop the momentum in favor of Stewart's bill. In doing so, he clarified the Republican monetary position in advance of the presidential nominations.

Sherman doubted whether under the law requiring the annual purchase of 54 million ounces of silver bullion that gold and silver could be permanently maintained at the same value as money at the existing ratio of 16 to 1. Sherman would repeal or materially change the Sherman Silver Purchase Act of 1890. He would also change the legal ratio of silver to gold given the steady price decline for silver in spite of increased purchases by Treasury.[11] Sherman would follow up his efforts against free silver with a bill to repeal the Sherman Silver Purchase Act but would not push it in the face of the upcoming presidential election.[12]

Alarmed by the strength of the free silver movement, British and other foreign investors lost confidence in the American government's finances and again began liquidating their American securities holdings. In spite of a significant excess of exports over imports, the securities liquidations were so large that no gold flowed back into the United States in 1892. Starting in July 1892 checks payable in legal tender notes were issued in exchange for bills of exchange from London and other European financial centers. The foreign bankers were then faced with only two ways to convert their American currency. They could present them to Treasury for redemption in gold. Treasury had no choice, as the alternative would result in the legal tender notes being discounted against gold. The second manner of conversion was for the foreign bankers who needed gold for export to present the legal tenders to Treasury. In particular, the greenback, with its large denomination bills, was the vehicle for this redemption.[13]

In these troubled waters, the presidential election of 1892 took on an added importance. This contest would be a rematch of the 1888 election. Both Harrison and Cleveland won the nomination of their respective parties on the first ballot. However, there was dissatisfaction within Republican ranks. New York's Thomas Platt was behind a dump Harrison campaign, hoping to resurrect Blaine. Sherman declined to be considered; he wanted no part of a bitter battle should he enter the contest. He was lukewarm to Harrison and really wanted new blood, being William McKinley.[14] Mark Hanna, too, wanted McKinley to run. McKinley was now governor of Ohio after having been gerrymandered out of his safe House seat in the redistricting of 1890. However, he was ambivalent and pessimistic about his chances in the general election and threw his weight to Harrison. It seemed the convention settled upon Harrison by default.

The presidential campaign centered on the McKinley Tariff of 1890. In addition, Cleveland was firmly for the gold standard while the Republicans sat on the fence supporting bimetallism. Complicating matters, the newly founded Populist Party had strong support from the silver states and the farmers. Cleveland carried a plurality of the popular vote and won his home state for an easy victory in the Electoral College. It was a strong indicator for maintenance of the gold standard. However, his inauguration on March 4, 1893, was a long way off from the viewpoint of the international financial markets.

Just prior to the presidential election, the Harrison Administration called for an international monetary conference to be held in Brussels in November 1892. Harrison appointed Senators William Boyd Allison and John P. Jones as delegates. He also added Congressman James McCreary, a Democrat from Kentucky with little practical financial background. From the academic world, he chose Dr. James Anderson, president of Brown University. From Chase Bank in New York came Henry Cannon, a former comptroller of the currency.[15] Mint Director Leech accompanied the delegation as the representative of the executive branch.

The delegates met with Secretary Foster in Washington on November 10, 1892. Harrison, now a lame duck, seemed to back away from any direct involvement. Afterwards the press could learn nothing of their instructions.

Upon arrival, the delegation was met by skeptical Europeans. Silver Certificates, kept at par solely by our government's pledge to redeem them in gold, were a point of concern. The Europeans openly speculated that a time would come when this pledge could not be kept. Thus, the Americans were calling together all the countries of the world to ask them to adopt some means of averting a domestic disaster. Yet the solution was to stop the purchase and coining of silver and that must be done in Washington.[16]

Into this vacuum of ideas, the American banker, Henry Cannon, did all he could to promote various proposals. However, he held the basic belief that it would be necessary for the United States to rescind the Silver Purchase Act and wait for Europe to reach an agreement in regard to silver.[17] The Americans put forth several attempts to reach some consensus on the silver issue. However they were not willing to suggest a ratio of value necessary to arrive at a bimetallic system. There was nothing new in the proposals and they fell upon deaf ears.[18]

The last session of the Fifty-Second Congress convened on December 5, 1892. Sherman again did not press his bill to repeal the monthly mandatory silver purchases, though strongly urged to do so in the Eastern newspapers. He still faced a majority of senators led by Bill Stewart who were for free silver. He feared the worst—pressing his bill would lead to passage of free coinage of silver. Should that happen, Sherman expected that the lame duck Harrison would either sign it or allow it to become law without his signature.[19]

By January 1893, Treasury's reserve of gold had fallen to $108 million, barely above the $100 million mandated by law as necessary to maintain the gold standard. By hook and by crook, this gold reserve held at this level into February as the Harrison Administration reached to the end of its life.[20] Still Sherman could see the handwriting on the wall. Treasury would soon break the minimum and be forced to borrow to replenish its gold stocks. He tried in the closing days of the Congress to gain permission for Treasury to borrow medium term at lower rates for this purpose. It went nowhere; the silver faction simply did not care if the United States defaulted on its gold obligations.[21]

Cleveland's choice for secretary of the Treasury was John G. Carlisle. His qualification was defending the gold standard for Cleveland while Carlisle was speaker of the House. In early February 1893 Carlisle came to New York to meet with Cleveland. They talked so long that Carlisle missed his train back to Washington. On the list of discussion items was repeal of the Sherman Silver Purchase Act. Trouble was brewing, and Cleveland and Carlisle knew it.[22]

As a career politician from Kentucky, Secretary of the Treasurer John G. Carlisle quickly found himself in troubled waters dealing with the American economy.

Upon entering the office, Carlisle was faced with a gold balance in the government's vaults of $101 million. While he should have been concerned with keeping open communications with Wall Street, Carlisle instead haughtily cancelled a dinner in New York City arranged to introduce him to the bankers shortly after Cleveland's inauguration.[23] Clearly, he was hoping to work through this crisis without their help.

A key barometer for the banks watching the government's gold holdings decline was the issuance of Gold Certificates for gold deposited in the Treasury, authorized as long as gold reserves remained above $100 million. On April 15, 1893, Carlisle suspended their issuance. Then several days later the markets grew feverish on the rumor that Carlisle intended to abandon the policy of redeeming Treasury Notes in gold. That action would mean the formal abandonment of the gold standard.

To counteract this rumor, on April 20 Carlisle issued a statement that he would redeem Treasury Notes in gold as long as he had "gold lawfully available for that purpose." This statement alleviated none of the fear; in fact, it reinforced the rumors that Carlisle was in league with the silver interests. The *New York Times* would report circumstantial evidence that Carlisle did plan to pay out silver for Treasury Notes if gold holdings fell below the required $100 million.[24]

On April 22, Cleveland effectively countermanded Carlisle by issuing a statement: The "President and his Cabinet are absolutely harmonious in the determination to exercise every power conferred upon them to maintain the public credit, to keep the public faith, and to preserve parity between gold and silver and between all financial obligations of the Government." This added statement could not undo the damage of Carlisle's pronouncement two days earlier as the gold reserve fell below $100 million that day. Furthermore, it aggravated the silver Democrats who complained that Carlisle lacked a backbone. The Panic of 1893 was now in full swing.

A rush of investors to liquidate their holdings now enveloped the financial markets. Worsening matters, several small brokerage houses were unable to protect themselves from the massive selloff of securities and were forced to suspend payments. Depositors quickly concluded that the banks were not going to be in a position to quickly convert their balances into gold. This feeling was particularly strong in the interior of the country.

Under the provisions of the National Banking Act, national banks were required to maintain a reserve of 15 percent of their deposits. Only two-fifths of this reserve had to be held in their respective vaults. The other three-fifths could be kept on deposit at reserve banks in designated cities. With light demand for currency except in harvest season, the bulk of their reserves came to be held by certain Eastern reserve agents, particularly the New York banks. By late May and June, a run on the banks in the West started as hoarding of money now spread to individuals. In response, a steady withdrawal of funds from New York developed to stem the bank runs in the country's interior.

The inevitable result of this general hoarding was shrinkage of the money supply in the East. Loans were difficult to obtain and by the early part of August, a premium developed for gold, silver, and currency of any kind. In response, banks extended the float time on check-clearing activity. In addition, clearing-house certificates reappeared. In this tight environment, failures in the private sector reached pandemic proportions. National banks went into liquidation. A number of the major rail systems went into bankruptcy.[25]

Internationally, silver markets went into a downward spiral. On June 26, the British government, without warning, closed the Indian mints to silver. India would stay on a silver standard, but the unlimited silver coinage of prior years was at an end.[26] The British were in damage-control mode but with a nefarious motive. They believed the closing of the Indian mints with its concurrent negative impact on silver prices would make it more likely that the United States would abandon its silver purchase program.[27] That would in turn help ensure that American financial obligations, specifically those held by English banking firms, would continue to be met with gold payments.

On June 30, 1893, President Cleveland, with his back to the wall, called a special session of Congress to convene on August 7. He had agonized for days over the decision. In justifying his action, Cleveland stated that the current economic conditions were largely the result of financial policy that the executive branch of government found embodied in unwise laws that must be executed until repealed by Congress.[28] Former President Harrison was interviewed in New York after the call. He claimed there were other causes besides the Sherman law, but he did not care to discuss them. However, he was in favor of its repeal.[29]

Sound money Democrats ignored the cries of the silver men and joined with Republicans in the House to repeal the Sherman Silver Purchase Act on August 29.[30] Repeal of the Sherman act in the Senate was going to be a close thing with Bill Stewart promising a filibuster.[31] Obstructive debates over free silver dragged for six weeks.[32] However, in the end, the repeal forces managed a vote and carried the day on October 30. The Sherman Silver Purchase Act was no more. However, it was done with a majority of Republican votes and only a minority of Democratic votes. Grover Cleveland had split his party, yielding future advantage to its silver faction. With repeal official, confidence in the financial integrity of the country was restored. However, recovery of the economy was altogether another matter.

John Sherman's reputation would forever suffer from having his name attached to the Silver Purchase Act. During the 1892 Republican Convention, Sherman was quoted as likening himself to an old rebel down South. His brother was gone, and he sensed his time was drawing to a close. He just wanted to be left alone.

Chapter 41
PRIDE AND PREJUDICE

By the time the World's Columbian Exposition opened in May 1893, the financial panic was the undeniable dark mass of clouds threatening on the horizon. Yet hard times seemed not to dampen the enthusiasm for the Fair.

Called the "White City," it mattered not a whit that the Fair itself had little to do with Columbus. When the World's Columbian Exposition closed the following October, some twenty-seven million visitors had admired its many exhibits. Given that the population of the young country in the 1890 census was just under sixty-three million, the great Fair was an unqualified success.

The Exposition boasted some 65,000 exhibits housed in the various buildings on the grounds.[1] There was the commonplace such as a 22,000-pound block of Canadian cheese. It had required a collaboration of 10,000 cows giving 27,000 gallons of milk to produce. At the other end of that spectrum was the interior of the Schlitz Brewery pavilion in the shape of two immense beer casks.[2]

Yet there was more to this Fair than catchy gimmicks; it was a showcase for American technology. The Page Belting Company displayed the largest conveyor belt in the world, 200 feet long, 8-1/2 feet wide and weighing 5,176 pounds.[3,4] There was an entire hall of electricity, exposing fair-goers to the uses of an energy source just becoming available at affordable prices to middle class Americans. As if to make that point, there was an 82-foot-tall tower within the hall strung with 18,000 lamps.[5] In

The massive, steam-powered Ferris wheel was invented for the Exposition. A round trip in one of its sixty-person cars lasted twenty minutes.

the U.S. Government building, the Mint mounted a display of a virtual operating facility—although no legal tender coins were struck, only the official souvenir medal.[6]

The Fair also offered an amusement section, known as the Midway Plaisance. Entertainment of this sort had never before made an appearance at a world exposition. Included was George Washington Gale Ferris's magnificent giant wheel, with gondolas taking riders up 25 stories. This never-before-seen structure was Chicago's answer to Gustave Eiffel's tower at the Paris Exposition of 1889. There was simply no answer for "Little Egypt" and her belly dancing at the Streets of Cairo exhibit.

The World's Columbian Exposition was a precursor for the American mass culture that would grow to dominate the world of the Twentieth Century. Put simply, with this Fair, America announced its arrival on the world stage.

Theodore Roosevelt, with family and his sister, Bamie, in tow, arrived on May 11. Bamie was a representative of New York State on the Fair's Board of Lady

Managers. They stayed eleven days, enthralled with the exhibits and the Midway. Edith looked forward to the art exhibits and sculpture. Theodore, on the other hand, had taken a personal interest in the location of the hunting camp exhibit of Boone and Crocket, an organization he had been instrumental in founding.

Yet not all was roses with the Roosevelt family at the Fair. Bamie was frustrated that her role with the Board of Lady Managers had been hampered because of "imperfect tools and hindering associates."[7] And now she and the family had ringside seats at a drama that had unfolded matching the Board of Lady Managers against the Bureau of the Mint. It would be the Roosevelts' first experience with that institution and it would not be a positive one.

Bertha Palmer, chairperson of the Lady Managers, was a headstrong lady not to be trifled with. Her husband was Potter Palmer, the famous Chicago hotelier. Watching the struggle of the Columbian half dollar authorization in Congress in the summer of 1892, the Board of Lady Managers had decided to postpone their effort for a souvenir coin of their own to its next session.[8] Congress dallied, finally authorizing a souvenir quarter dollar on March 3, 1893, its last day in session, as a form of funding a $10,000 appropriation. Total mintage of this second commemorative coin was to be limited to 40,000 pieces.

Bertha Palmer was determined that the commemorative quarter for the Board of Lady Managers would avoid the troubles encountered in the design of the Columbian half dollar.

Palmer was annoyed that the devices and designs for the coin were to be prescribed by the director of the Mint with the approval of the secretary of the Treasury. She had not been impressed by the Mint's souvenir half dollar and wished the ladies "to have credit of being the authors of the first really beautiful and artistic coin that has ever been issued by the government of the United States."[9] She also sought a woman to design the coin, consistent with the Board of Lady Managers' desire to showcase the abilities and progress of women.

Ultimately the burden of recommending an artist fell upon Augustus Saint-Gaudens. He endorsed a former student, the twenty-three-year-old Caroline "Carrie" Peddle. Though inexperienced, she was well trained, gutsy and ready to take on the challenge of this commission.

Mint Director Edward Leech, now facing his eminent political removal as a

Harrison appointee, contacted Palmer on March 14. He asked if any work had started on the designs. He was quite willing to conform to the wishes of the ladies. He even offered to send Charles Barber to Chicago.[10] However, there was more at work here behind the scenes. He had received letters from Barber and Philadelphia Superintendent Bosbyshell prompting him to take the initiative. His proposal to send the engraver to Chicago to meet with the ladies was at Barber's instigation.[11] Barber was making a concerted effort to keep this design process under his control.

Palmer was just as diplomatic in her reply. The Board of Lady Managers had decided what should be placed on the coin. They wished to commemorate the part played by Queen Isabella in the discovery of America and the action of Congress in creating the Board of Lady Managers. She would be glad to have the Mint director come to Chicago to consult once the Board of Lady Managers had finalized their suggestions. She closed with a masterstroke. Would the Bureau of the Mint wish to submit a design embodying the ideas that she had indicated for competition?[12] Like Barber, Bertha Palmer had every intention of controlling the process.

Next Palmer set her sights on the new Cleveland Administration and, in particular, Secretary of the Treasury John Carlisle. She chose Chicago Congressman Alan Durborow, a former Carlisle colleague and chair of the House Committee on the Fair, to carry her message to the secretary. His charge was to broach the subject of a female designer and secure acceptance. He also carried a copy of a letter that she had sent to Carlisle setting forth her design proposal.[13] Given that Bertha Palmer had already settled on Caroline Peddle as the designer, Durborow had no choice but to be successful.

In her charge to Peddle, Palmer was most explicit about the design motifs. The one side should have a figure of Isabella and the other, in addition to the prescribed requirements, an inscription "Commemorative Coin Issued for the Board of Lady Managers of the World's Columbian Exposition by Act of Congress, 1492 – 1892." Peddle would be free to arrange and choose the lettering style for the inscription in such a manner as to "permit a most artistic appearance."[14] However, Palmer had failed to instruct Carrie Peddle that she should submit her sketches to the Board of Lady Managers for approval.

Carlisle and Leech had no real choice but to give in to Bertha Palmer. The secretary wrote her that the director of the Mint was willing to allow the modeling of the commemorative quarter by a woman and that the head of Isabella should appear on it.[15] The proposed design for the reverse was another issue altogether. Carlisle felt that the inscription was reminiscent of a tradesman's advertising token.[16] A different design would have to be formulated.

Leech now had to keep peace with his Philadelphia staff. On March 27 he sent a short note to Bosbyshell. It was probable that the Board of Lady Managers would have some sculptor model the obverse of the souvenir coin. However, Charles Barber should start work on some alternative designs for the reverse.[17]

The next day, Palmer informed Leech that Peddle would be preparing the obverse and reverse models for the proposed souvenir coin. The Mint director politely agreed; however, there would be constraints. Specific instructions would be provided for the preparation of Carrie Peddle's work product. He confirmed that a head of Isabella would be an acceptable subject. He would have Barber prepare a suitable design for the reverse to be submitted to Bertha Palmer. Of course, no real progress could be made until the designs approved by the Board of Lady Managers had been prepared and submitted for review at the Mint.[18]

Leech in a separate letter placed Peddle in an awkward position stating that he and Secretary Carlisle must approve her models. There would be no objection to using the head of Isabella for the obverse and that part of the work could begin at once.[19] The most onerous letter for Leech was the one to Bosbyshell explaining that Barber might not be doing the reverse after all.[20]

Events now unfolded rapidly. On April 3, Peddle forwarded a design of the original inscription for the reverse that had been provided by Mrs. Palmer to Leech. She felt it was cumbersome and required the entire reverse of the coin. She asked Leech's help in shortening it. She had questions about the style of lettering and if she could include "Isabella" on the obverse.[21]

On that same day, Peddle also opened a line of communication directly to Bosbyshell. He had just provided her with the instructions for model preparation that Leech had promised.[22] She was proposing using a *figure* of the queen rather than a head in profile. Bertha Palmer had spoken of a figure of Isabella to Peddle. A rough sketch was included of the seated queen based upon one of the engravings provided by Palmer. Peddle believed the design more pleasing than a head unless it reduced poorly. She closed by asking that they telegraph their response.[23]

While Peddle was complying with Leech's instructions in good faith, that trust was not returned. On that same April 3, Leech informed Bosbyshell that Barber should continue work on the reverse. It was not his intent to allow Miss Peddle to *design* the reverse. That would be done at the Mint.[24]

On April 4, Bosbyshell and Barber dismissed Peddle's obverse sketch out of hand in a letter to Leech. They felt the foreshortening of the legs of the seated figure would produce an unacceptable appearance after any reasonable amount of wear from circulation. Bosbyshell and Barber continued to be obsessed with the belief that these commemorative half dollars and quarters would enter general commerce. In their opinion, a profiled head would be more appropriate.[25]

Meanwhile that same day, Leech wrote Peddle that the reverse inscription was unacceptable. Carlisle would write Mrs. Palmer to that effect and changes would have to be made. Leech went on to say that he had asked Barber to prepare the reverse. Once completed, he would send it to Mrs. Palmer for her review.[26]

Adding to Carrie Peddle's confusion and frustration, Bertha Palmer both wired and wrote to her on April 6. She wanted to know what progress had been made on the coin. The design for the reverse had been changed. Possibly Peddle had not received an earlier letter setting forth this decision. (There was no record of it in Palmer's letterbook.) Palmer now wanted Peddle to use one of the drawings from the Women's Building as the central theme on the reverse.[27]

On April 7, Peddle wrote to Leech. She was unhappy. She had been complying with Mrs. Palmer's instructions with her previous design for the reverse. She could not consent to having her work muled. She had been commissioned to prepare models for both sides of the quarter. She now threatened to quit work on the obverse model.

Then a letter from Bosbyshell pushed Peddle over the edge. In the superintendent's opinion, a crowned head on an American coin would be inappropriate. Also

Charles Barber would be modeling the reverse.[28] With that communication, Caroline Peddle had had enough. On April 8, questioning the role of the engraver in dictating the designs for the coin, she resigned her commission.[29] Her frustration had lasted eleven days.

Bertha Palmer was beside herself with anger that spilled out in a letter to Saint-Gaudens. She considered it a "direct discourtesy" that Caroline Peddle had communicated directly with Treasury officials, thereby frustrating the plans of the Board of Lady Managers and more particularly, herself, for the souvenir quarter. She wanted Saint-Gaudens to know that the whole matter had been arranged with great effort and that the ladies would have been able to take care of themselves as well as Miss Peddle. Gus was a bit chagrined in his reply. He was very deferential to Bertha Palmer but he did not duck the issue. When Carrie Peddle told him that the reverse of the quarter was to be modeled by the incompetent designer at the Mint, he agreed with her that it would be dignified to refuse the commission.

On April 24, Leech sent two models of the head of Isabella to Mrs. Palmer for her choice. One represented a frontal view of a mature queen and the other, a profile of a young queen. Both bore crowns. For the reverse, Secretary Carlisle relented to the inscription, "Board of Lady Managers" on a design "emblematic of women's work" prepared by George Morgan.[30] Bertha Palmer had at least carried the issue most dear to her heart. The ladies would be represented on the coin. At their board meeting of May 5, the women chose the young head and their ordeal was over.[31] So it was too for Edward Leech. He left Mint employment in mid-May to become cashier of the National Union Bank in New York City.[32]

The quarter for the Board of Lady Managers was far from the artistic design the women had hoped for.

Winding up this affair, the Mint began striking these "showy quarters," to use Charles Barber's words, on June 13.[33] The first one hundred of these coins plus the 400th, the 1,492nd and the 1,892nd were struck in Proof.[34]

Chapter 42

SEEKING TO BEST THE MINT

Saint-Gaudens was in a panic. In mid-April 1893, driven by the onset of the financial collapse and Carrie Peddle's bad experience with the Mint, the sculptor began questioning John Boyd Thacher, first as to the validity of the award medal agreement under which he was working, and second as to just exactly what work product he was to provide the Mint. Overriding these issues, Gus was concerned about the money. Because of the *Shaw* obligation, the financial panic caught him in a period of tight cash flows. In an undated note to his friend Richard Watson Gilder that year he described himself as being "bust absolutely" but hopeful of some large payments in the offing.[1] Even his wife was forced to ask her mother for a loan to tide the sculptor over.[2]

Thacher set up a meeting in Washington at the end of April 1893 for Saint-Gaudens with Carlisle and Leech. He also wanted to know when the award medal would be done. It was imperative that one side be done now. Thacher told Gus that he thought Leech to be in sympathy and would help in the matter.[3]

On his way to the meeting, Saint-Gaudens stopped at the Philadelphia Mint. He met with Charles Barber to review the Mint's methods of reducing models and preparing dies for medals. Gus revealed that the model was complete. However, it was between three and four feet in diameter, far larger than the capability of Barber's reducing lathe - no more than three times the diameter of the actual medal. Gus acknowledged that he knew of no reducing machine in America that could bring this model down to the size of the award medal. Coyly, Saint-Gaudens admitted thinking of shipping his oversized model to France. He went further, suggesting that it might be well to have the dies cut there too.[4]

Both sides now knew the issues for the meeting as Gus came to Washington. The decision-maker in the meeting was the acting secretary, Charles Hamlin, sitting in for Carlisle. He assured Saint-Gaudens that he would be paid the $5,000 in conformance with the understanding with the Awards Subcommittee. Saint-Gaudens forthrightly stated that he had sent his plaster models to Paris for reduction as well as to have the dies cut. The government then conceded the obvious. Gus could do whatever he wished in order to have the final model comply with the size restrictions. The reduction work could proceed in Paris, but the dies would have to be cut in Philadelphia.[5] One last appeal, after the meeting, by Saint-Gaudens to Hamlin went nowhere. The liability of adverse criticism was too great if the dies were cut outside of the country. The reductions, once completed in Paris, must be delivered to the Mint as soon as practicable.[6]

His temper flaring, Saint-Gaudens in a June 2 letter to Thacher drew a red line in the sand:

> Now, as what I wish seems to be an impossibility in making of the dies, I cannot be held responsible for them and if any liberties are taken with my work at the Mint such as have been taken with others I shall certainly publish it.[7]

Exasperated by the delay and not fully comprehending Gus's concern, Thacher wrote to Secretary Carlisle, expressing ignorance of the vehemence of Saint-Gaudens's stance. He offered as an explanation that the Lord made artists differently from other men. Thacher hoped that Carlisle would placate Saint-Gaudens and have the dies cut in Kamchatka if that were the artist's desire. Thacher even threw out for consideration a compromise of having an outside party cut the dies under the direction of the Mint.[8]

Carlisle would not budge; the dies must be cut at Philadelphia. The secretary did give every assurance that the award medal dies would be a faithful reproduction of Saint-Gaudens's design and that not the slightest deviation from the model would be made. Carlisle was confident that the work would be executed to the sculptor's entire satisfaction.[9] Here matters sat over the summer while Saint-Gaudens waited on the models to be returned from France.

On September 27, 1893, Robert Preston was nominated by President Cleveland to be Mint director.[10] There was immediate speculation that the silver forces in the Senate would act against Preston's confirmation. Their public opposition revolved around Preston dragging his feet over the summer on silver purchases, acquiring less bullion than was specified under the Sherman Silver Purchase Act. He had acted under the provision in the act that allowed the secretary of the Treasury to purchase only that silver offered at market rates. Those in favor of the nomination argued that Preston had acted under the direction of Carlisle and should not be held accountable.[11] That said, the Senate in executive session failed to take up consideration of Preston, leaving the man hanging by a thread.[12] Once the special session to repeal the Silver Purchase Act had ended, Carlisle acted, gaining for Preston an interim appointment on November 6, 1893.[13]

Having spent nearly his entire career in the Bureau of the Mint, Robert Preston achieved his much-sought-after position of director in 1893.

In October, Saint-Gaudens delivered the models for the award medal to Thacher's subcommittee. Still seeking to cut Barber out of the process, Saint-Gaudens had gained the agreement of both Gorham and Tiffany & Company to engrave the dies and strike the medals within the Congressional appropriation.[14]

The Awards Subcommittee asked on October 19 that Preston come to Chicago for consultation. Preston declined, claiming to be unable to travel due to legislative matters and the preparation of his annual report.[15] Simply put, given his precarious position, he could not leave town while the Senate was debating repeal of the Silver Purchase Act. However, he sent a clear message to the committee by reiterating that as soon as Saint-Gaudens delivered the models to Philadelphia, Charles Barber would begin preparation of the dies.[16] The subcommittee did not buckle under to this unyielding response. Potential bidders to strike the medal would be asked to provide the engraving work as part of a package bid.

Wishing to avoid a damaging public dispute, acting director Preston wrote Superintendent Bosbyshell on October 25, asking that he instruct Barber to cut the dies following the models precisely with all possible dispatch. He reminded the superintendent that Saint-Gaudens had wanted the dies cut in France. Preston wanted to give Saint-Gaudens no cause for complaint with the engraving department.[17]

With the Fair now closed, on November 4, Preston wrote Saint-Gaudens asking for a brief description of the designs. He was receiving numerous requests for this information from the press. He had declined to give out any description in accordance with Saint-Gaudens's previous request that the designs not be made public.[18]

Preston got more than he asked. Saint-Gaudens sent the eight-inch models to Washington.[19] He also followed up with a description of the medal for public release, provided Thacher approved. In his words, on the obverse Columbus was represented stepping ashore in the New World with a gesture of thanks to God. The reverse depicted the Spirit of America as represented by a young man in full vigor of life.[20]

That description was not the one that appeared in the Washington papers on November 7. That storyline had the obverse being a bust of Columbus and the reverse, a chubby faced boy, typical of youth and energy. The diameter of the medal was now supposedly set at three and one-half inches.[21] Preston sent the models to Philadelphia that same day, standing firm that Barber should proceed with engraving the dies.[22]

On November 8, Bosbyshell responded, asking that work on the dies be put on hold. John Woodside, a Philadelphia businessman and the Awards Subcommittee's liaison to the Mint, had called on Bosbyshell. Woodside reiterated the subcommittee's wish that the engraving be included in the bid package for these medals. He argued that by combining these two processes, there would be no finding fault with the dies by the party receiving the contract to prepare the medals. Furthermore, both Tiffany and Gorham desired to submit bids on this basis. Bosbyshell, not wishing to unduly antagonize a politically connected World's Fair Commissioner, now acknowledged the validity of Woodside's argument.[23] Just as likely, Barber, with the models in hand, knew that his reducing machine could not accurately duplicate deep cuts needed for the high relief design. He would have to make hand adjustments in the dies, opening himself to Saint-Gaudens's ire.

With Bosbyshell wavering, Preston was left with no alternative but to acquiesce to Saint-Gaudens's desire that no die cutting be done at the Philadelphia Mint. Preston wanted the sculptor to supply him with a list of firms that could contractually carry out the combined work.[24] To Woodside, Preston was more specific; he was placing the matter of the medal entirely under the Awards Subcommittee's control. The Mint would not seek proposals by public invitation; they would simply send a circular letter to firms known to be capable of meeting the Mint's production standards. He did request that the Scovill Manufacturing Company, which had a complete metalworking plant capable of doing coining work, be included on the list of bidders.[25] Seemingly, Gus had carried the day.

However, Preston had second thoughts about turning over complete control of production of the award medal to the subcommittee and on November 22 authorized Bosbyshell to accompany Woodside on a visit to the manufacturing facilities of Tiffany & Company, Gorham, and Scovill.[26] Bosbyshell and Woodside visited Tiffany's plant in Newark, New Jersey, with Saint-Gaudens on Monday, November 27. When queried, the Tiffany people were strongly in favor of having the dies made in the United States. Without Gus, the two men continued on to Gorham in Providence, Rhode Island. Here they learned that Gorham would prefer the dies to be made at the Mint, although they had a reducing lathe capable of doing the work. Gorham also preferred a three-inch diameter for the medal even though they had not seen the design. The trip ended in Waterbury, Connecticut, at Scovill.

On November 29, the men returned to Tiffany & Company headquarters in New York City. Saint-Gaudens was again present, having received in the interim three cast bronzes from Paris. The medals, in the diameters of two, three and four inches, astonished Bosbyshell with their beauty. He concluded that any of the three firms was capable of executing the contract, whether the medals be struck or cast. He even recommended that if the costs could be contained, a four-inch cast medal should be executed.[27]

The design, in medallic form, submitted by Saint-Gaudens for the World's Columbian Exposition Award Medal.

December 1893 found Woodside asking Preston why there was a delay issuing the circular letter. The Mint director relayed that Secretary Carlisle had determined the specifications unsatisfactory given the unresolved size and the ambiguity over whether the medal would be struck or cast. Preston wanted Woodside to provide fuller specifications, which he promptly did.[28]

Still the process dragged. Now, Gus queried Preston as to the status of the bids. Curiosity was intensifying over the designs. What Gus did not reveal to Preston was that even if the process was ready to move forward, he might not be. He had carefully examined the four-inch cast piece and determined that Columbus' left leg must be modified.[29] It appeared to just dangle in the medal. However, it was a detail that could easily be addressed once the contract was let. Preston waited four days before answering him that only Gorham had submitted a bid to that point.[30] It was a very brief letter answering Gus's specific question and nothing more.

What Preston did not explain to Saint-Gaudens was that no additional bids had been received because the circular had not been issued. The Mint director was forthcoming as to just why on January 6, 1894, in a letter to C.P. Goss, head of Scovill. Goss had wanted to meet with Preston to discuss Scovill's bid. Preston related to Goss that he had delayed on the circular while he investigated the possibility of striking the medals in aluminum. New technology had greatly reduced the cost of production for this metal. A great number of badges and medals had been struck in aluminum for the Fair and were well received.[31] He had just learned that the delays would be great and that there was considerable opposition. Preston closed by saying that he would issue the circular calling for bids the following week.[32]

Meanwhile, the newspapers, sensing widespread public interest, were now more accurately reporting the obverse to be a representation of Columbus stepping ashore from a boat. Surrounding him were three companions, one holding a banner of Spain aloft. On the reverse Saint-Gaudens had supposedly replaced the typical female figure with that of a vigorous upright American male.[33]

All looked in place for Saint-Gaudens to have maneuvered around Charles Barber and his World's Columbian Exposition award medal to be issued to great acclaim.

Chapter 43

And All Hell Broke Loose

As the year 1894 opened, Treasury Secretary Carlisle would have rolled his eyes if he had known that the Award Medal for the World's Columbian Exposition was going to blow up into a major issue. Frankly, at this point it was the least of his worries.

Repeal of the Sherman Silver Purchase Act did not stop the gold drain. Worse, with the deteriorating economic conditions, tariff collections necessary to fund the government were dropping like a rock. With the notable exception of patronage jobs, Carlisle had clamped down on expenses. Silver dollar coinage was suspended, and force reductions put in place for the Mints at Philadelphia, New Orleans, and San Francisco. The Carson City Mint was closed entirely.[1] Preston's idea of striking the award medal in the more expensive aluminum was a loser before it ever hit the starting gate. However, Carlisle could only do so much economizing; he was saddled with bloated entitlements in the form of Civil War pensions that were untouchable.

Now Carlisle faced a political dilemma: He must maintain the $100 million gold reserve in the Treasury while addressing the expected budget deficit. The Treasury secretary met on January 10, 1894, behind closed doors with the Senate Committee on Finance to deliver the bad news. A deficit of $50 to $60 million was expected by the June 30 fiscal year end that would effectively cut that gold reserve by more than half.[2] Carlisle's only authority to borrow came from the Resumption Act of January 14, 1875, and that was a stretch.

Based on feedback from the Committee on Finance, Carlisle plowed ahead, issuing a circular calling for bids on 50 million dollars' worth of new issue bonds. The reaction in the London market was immediate and positive with prices on American securities strengthening.[3] Carlisle was going to use his authority to borrow to maintain the minimum gold balance and also provide cover for silver men in his party by saying the proceeds would be used to cover the deficit.

Opposition in the House was immediate. Silver Democrats introduced a resolution on January 15 that stated Carlisle had no authority under existing law to issue and sell bonds except to provide for the resumption of specie payments.[4] The silver Democrats were willing to split the party wide open and allow financial chaos if it brought down the gold standard.

Carlisle appeared to wobble in the face of the House challenge. He admitted that he did not believe he had perfectly explicit authority to use bonds to pay the current expenses of the government. However, he would use what means he had.[5] With the validity of Carlisle's authority in question even by the man himself, the bankers in New York sent a message that the "Blue Grass Secretary of the Treasury," referring to Carlisle's rural northern Kentucky roots, needed to come to New York to allay fears.[6]

Carlisle, faced with a summons, came to the bankers on January 29. Whether it was a bluff or not, the Treasury secretary told the bankers that he had full authority to issue the bonds and that neither Congress nor the courts would raise any obstacles or interfere with his plan. The proceeds of the loan would be available for the general purposes of the government. However, what the bankers heard from this statement was that the gold standard would be maintained and thereby the bonds would be repaid in gold, not depreciating silver. The only skepticism from the bankers was whether the amount borrowed would be enough.

On the next day, Assistant Treasury Secretary William Edmond Curtis brought Carlisle the good news. His reception by the bankers had been favorable; the bond issue would be a success.[7] In fact it would be oversubscribed, bringing in $54 million.[8] It wasn't enough.

As Treasury prepared for the first bond issue, all hell broke loose for Augustus Saint-Gaudens on January 12, 1894. A crude likeness of his award medal design

This crude, inaccurate facsimile of Saint-Gaudens's design created a firestorm when it became public.

appeared in the newspapers. The obverse was the least accurate. Christopher Columbus stood in a meaningless pose without banner or sword. The men in the background were supposedly representative of five different types of nations, all in contemporary clothing including derby hats. The reverse was much more accurate. The nude male that represented America was faithfully rendered although with a slight paunch. All in all, it was an inept attempt to reproduce Saint-Gaudens's work. Nevertheless, a sudden firestorm over the issue of male frontal nudity enveloped the sculptor. His wife, Augusta, in a letter to her brother Tom, gave some idea of what was happening:

> The house has been besieged with reporters as well as the studio. One man came at 2 a.m. and was almost kicked out of the house by the irate sculptor, only as his feet were bare he thought it would hurt him more than the man's feelings.[9]

There was even precedence for the use of a nude male. The exhibition judges appointed by John Boyd Thacher had been so biased that the French had withdrawn all their exhibits from consideration. Instead, they commissioned the noted French medalist, Oscar Roty, to prepare a separate award medal just for them. Its obverse featured a nude winged male in frontal view. However, it was not so boldly obvious as Saint-Gaudens's design.

The award medal prepared by the French for their exhibitors at the World's Columbian Exposition.

Where was the leak? It wasn't Preston in Washington; he did not have possession of the models. Part of the answer comes from a newspaper interview with the executive officers of Page Belting Company, a New Hampshire manufacturer. They related that George F. Page, the company president, visited the Philadelphia Mint on Saturday, December 8, and was shown the models of the medal by "officers of the Mint." Page apparently did have a letter of introduction from Senator William Chandler of New Hampshire that he had presented to Robert Preston the previous summer. Preston in turn had given him permission to make the visit.[10]

Seeing the models was not the primary purpose of Page's visit; he was seeking business from the Mint.[11] He examined the models and later made a drawing from memory for use on advertising circulars.[12] The medal had real commercial value. He was entitled to the two medals his company had been awarded at the Fair and the business advantages that they would bring. [13] This circular then found its way into the newspapers.

Circumstantial evidence would point to Charles Barber as the source of the leak, given that he had physical possession of the models. However, Barber, as the engraver, would have had no real reason to have any contact with George Page. Up to this point, Barber still had a working relationship with Saint-Gaudens. He basically had no motive.

Philadelphia Superintendent Oliver Bosbyshell was another story altogether. A long letter from Bosbyshell to James Ellsworth, chairman of the Committee on Liberal Arts, under the pretext of setting up the Mint exhibit at the World's Columbian Exposition on March 13, 1893, laid the foundation for the motive. Bosbyshell asked that Ellsworth put in a good word for him politically. He was in jeopardy and afraid that Cleveland and Carlisle would remove him.[14]

Coincidental to Preston's interim appointment as director, Bosbyshell again wrote Ellsworth on November 3. He was still "doing business at the stand." However, "some little stir" was being made just that week. Any assistance that Ellsworth could give to help him retain his position would be felt with greater force.[15] Clearly something about the appointment of Preston had Bosbyshell on edge.

When George Page showed up at the Philadelphia Mint and asked to see the models of the award medal, Bosbyshell was not going to refuse the request. While he had been instructed to allow no photographs, a simple viewing would seem harmless.[16] Seeking to curry favor, Bosbyshell had motive; he was the unwitting culprit. Ironically for Bosbyshell, Secretary Carlisle asked for his resignation on December 14.[17]

Trouble was immediate in coming. An embarrassed George Davis, representing the World's Columbian Commission, declared it an outrageous thing to be distributed among the exhibitors. It represented neither art nor science nor industry and appeared to be indecent.[18] Of course the press jumped all over this quote.

Then having calmed down, Davis wrote to James Ellsworth on the December 15 that he was only reacting to the caricature in the *Tribune*. However, he was afraid that if the medal were anything like the caricature, the general public would not regard it as up to Saint-Gaudens's standard. On the other hand, the general exhibitor would not care much about the depiction of Columbus or the "statue of a man."[19]

Saint-Gaudens lashed out in anger. He called the actions of Page Belting Company's representative disgusting, dishonorable, and dishonest. That was the expunged version printed in the *New York Tribune*. Gus actually called the Page Belting representative an "idiot" and a "New Hampshire ass."[20] At his instruction, a letter claiming damages and criminal activity was sent to Page Belting.[21] However, his attorney, Charles Beaman, explained that while the case was a good one in New York, Gus would have a hard time proving damages to a jury of New Hampshire farmers.[22]

Early on, William F. Vilas, chairman of the Senate Committee on the Quadro-Centennial with oversight for the Fair, voiced his objection to the design and asked that the models be brought to Washington for his committee's inspection on January

18.[23] When the models arrived, there was more in the box. Peter Krider of the medal firm in Philadelphia had provided seventeen proposed designs for the award medal. He was offering them free of charge should the government decide to reject Saint-Gaudens's work.[24]

The lack of a formal approval procedure for the award medal design now hurt Saint-Gaudens's case. Confusion reigned. Assistant Secretary Curtis, speaking for the Treasury Department, supposed that the Awards Subcommittee accepted the design, and in his opinion that was where the responsibility rested. The *Chicago Tribune* reported on January 13 "it is understood that Mr. Thacher has approved the design. In acceptance with his manner of doing business, he has not consulted the wishes of the Exposition officials, whose superiority he declines to recognize."[25] The handshake agreement had come back to haunt Saint-Gaudens.

Treasury Secretary Carlisle conveyed the Committee on the Quadro Centennial's objection to the award medal to Saint-Gaudens on January 23. Carlisle noted that the design was unobjectionable as a work of art. However, it was not suited to the general distribution that would result from the awarding of more than 20,000 of the medals. He closed by asking that Saint-Gaudens submit a design that covered the figure's genitals.[26]

By not being firmer in his diplomatic letter to Saint-Gaudens, Carlisle had done the sculptor a disservice. Four days before he wrote Saint-Gaudens, Carlisle had had a conversation with Vilas.[27] Here, Carlisle was much more forthcoming. He was in agreement with the committee that the present design must be changed. Either a new design must be prepared or the existing one remodeled so that no "exhibition of vulgarity in art" appeared.[28] He was just as blunt in his correspondence to Thacher, again stating that he was directing that the design be changed.[29] Carlisle's reputation was such that there would be no appeal; the decision was final. When queried by the press for a public response to Carlisle's request, Gus would not comment other than to say he was "tired of the whole thing."[30]

Tired or not, Saint-Gaudens fought back. In a letter to Carlisle, he conveyed a three-inch model, the size set for the medal, in hopes that upon seeing the design in smaller scale the Treasury secretary and the Senate committee would reverse themselves. However, should the committee still wish a change, he preferred to submit a design rather than have someone else do it. In closing, he reserved the right at some time to publish the correspondence between the two of them.[31]

Carlisle duly forwarded the model with the objectionable reverse to actual scale to the committee on January 27, seeking their conclusions in writing.[32] George Page was in Washington that day, indicating that the committee made the effort to determine the circumstances of the unauthorized leak of the medal's design.[33] Gus felt confident that once the committee had a chance to review his work in proper scale, he would be vindicated. Saint-Gaudens probably believed that he had an advocate in one of the members of the committee, Don Cameron. What he did not know was that Carlisle and Cameron were whisky-drinking, poker-playing buddies of long standing.[34] There seemed but one voice from the committee, that of condemnation.[35]

On January 29, 1894, newspapers quoted Carlisle as saying that he had taken the position that since Treasury had paid Saint-Gaudens the $5,000 commission, his work was the property of the United States government to do with as it saw fit. Carlisle was reserving the right to have the design altered if he so chose, either by Saint-Gaudens or by someone else if the artist was unwilling.[36] The Committee on the Quadro-Centennial wasted no time. Upon a second review, committee members rejected the reverse of Saint-Gaudens's medal on February 1.[37]

Why was Carlisle taking the time away from the pending bond issue, critical to the nation's financial health, at the end of January to address this distraction? Carlisle was vaguely involved in a scandal involving his protégé, W.C.P. Breckinridge, known behind his back as "old Billy Breck," the sitting congressman from Lexington, Kentucky. A young woman, Madeline Pollard, was suing Breckinridge for breach of promise. It seemed that Breckinridge had had a long-standing affair with the woman and promised marriage when his wife died, only to renege when the opportunity arose. At this time depositions were being taken, and the trial promised national press coverage. Breckinridge knew that the woman had approached Carlisle in the summer of 1893 through a letter seeking the secretary's attentions. Carlisle had gossiped about the approach. If true, it would put an end to the lawsuit. Carlisle refused to come forward. There was scandal here. If he allowed the nude male that graced the award medal design to stand, it would only add fuel to a fire that he needed to ensure did not flare up and consume his political ambitions that were aimed at the presidency.[38]

In the press, Gus reassured Mint Director Preston that he would replace the offending reverse design if the Senate committee's objections continued. Preston relayed this information to Philadelphia and that he was willing to give Saint-Gaudens a reasonable length of time to do so. He also instructed Charles Barber to begin preparing the dies for the obverse of the medal.[39] Preston, confirmed as Mint director by the Senate on January 12, had regained the initiative.

Carlisle took his time communicating the official rejection of the reverse design to Saint-Gaudens. It came in a letter dated February 21 that enclosed a copy of the Senate committee resolution stating that the reverse ought to be changed.[40] He requested, in accordance with his earlier communication to Saint-Gaudens, that the sculptor should submit a new design as soon as possible. However, there would be no additional expense to the government.[41]

On March 15, at Richard Watson Gilder's urging, Saint-Gaudens relented.[42] He submitted three modified reverse designs. In two, he strategically placed a ribbon over the offending anatomy. It was so suggestive as to not really help matters much. In the third version, he replaced the ribbon with a fig leaf. Following a suggestion from Gilder,[43] he asked Carlisle to submit these alternatives and his original model to a committee composed of the heads of the principal art societies or men of recognized standing in these matters such as Ellsworth in Chicago.[44]

Carlisle had no intention of following Saint-Gaudens's recommendation. He submitted the revisions to the Quadro-Centennial Committee.[45] They then carefully pointed out that no formal meeting of the committee had taken place. Their opinions were only of an advisory nature. Ultimately, authority rested with the secretary of the Treasury to accept or reject the work of Saint-Gaudens.[46]

At this point, Carlisle fired a shot at Saint-Gaudens in the press, saying that if the sculptor did not provide another design, he would ask Charles Barber to supply an acceptable reverse. Years later, the engraver confessed reluctance to undertaking this assignment, which he considered a no-win situation for himself.[47]

Saint-Gaudens heard nothing for three weeks. Finally on April 26, 1894, Preston notified Gus that Carlisle had formally rejected his alternate reverse designs. Carlisle desired that Saint-Gaudens prepare a new design as soon as possible. However, the obverse design was acceptable. Preston wanted to assure Saint-Gaudens that the reproduction of his design by the Mint would be exact in every "practical" way.[48] That was a significant retreat from the former assurance of a faithful reproduction without the slightest deviation.

At this very moment, the Shaw Committee reentered the picture to further bedevil Saint-Gaudens. The preceding November when the medal work seemed at a conclusion, Gus had traveled to Boston to quietly sit down with John Murray Forbes to resolve the bitter feelings. Forbes cynically felt that Saint-Gaudens had asked for the interview with him because the sculptor knew he was a soft touch compared to others on the committee. Forbes humored Saint-Gaudens, avoiding anything that would stir him up emotionally. Peace was made between the two men temporarily.[49]

As the medal controversy reached full stride in February 1894, Atkinson told Saint-Gaudens that if he did not put aside all causes that seemed to crowd his time to finish the *Shaw*, he would be making the mistake of a lifetime.[50] Days later, Atkinson followed up asking specifically if the medal stink was distracting Saint-Gaudens.[51] However, satisfactory progress made the committee feel at the end of March that Saint-Gaudens was at last approaching completion of his modeling work.[52]

Meanwhile Gilder prodded Gus to take action on the award medal. He told Saint-Gaudens to put the controversy behind him and make an acceptable reverse design. Gus emphatically responded that he was going to do an alternative. In fact, he had communicated on May 18 in a letter begrudging the review process to Preston that he was commencing another model for the reverse.[53] Saint-Gaudens still wanted his next design submitted to a jury of "persons of standing" in the profession.[54] The nude would be entirely gone. Only a standing eagle surrounded by a wreath would remain. Of all the reverse versions, this rendition was Saint-Gaudens's best by far. Preston, in a fit of optimism, told the press that the medal would be ready to strike six weeks after Saint-Gaudens had completed his latest design. Everything was in readiness for the obverse, and there was a chance medals could be struck by July 1.[55]

In June 1894 Augustus Saint-Gaudens finally yielded to Secretary of the Treasury Carlisle and provided an acceptable alternative reverse. He also billed the secretary $1,000 for the extra work involved in preparing the new reverse.

Gilder's pressure, however, was not the real cause of Gus's capitulation. Saint-Gaudens's ego had gotten the better of him. In spite of Columbus's dangling leg, the sculptor had allowed Paul Bion, an old friend from his student days in France, to submit on his behalf the award medal designs to the Paris Salon for 1894. Approval from Paris would provide him with ammunition to resist changing the reverse. Bion attended the preview on April 29 to see how Gus's work was positioned. He was embarrassed for his American friend. The medal had been grouped with the work of some amateurs and "skyed"—that is, placed high up, toward the ceiling (or sky), while the works considered the best in an exhibition were placed at eye level. Having one's entry skyed was an artist's worst fear.[56] The French had just told Saint-Gaudens this medal was at best average. It was a stinging rebuke.

With his eagle reverse model received by Preston by June 23, Saint-Gaudens included a bill for $1,000.[57] No doubt he had incurred legitimate additional expenses to comply with Carlisle's directives. Also, his difficulties with the Shaw Committee were still pinching his cash flow. He revealed to Stanford White that he was short of cash.[58] "Every blooming cent that I have has all poured out and I don't see how I am going to fix it," he lamented.[59]

This supplemental billing was a big-time blunder. Carlisle no longer had to consider the merits of his art. He only had to point to the audacity of Saint-Gaudens to include a bill for his services.

Preston presented the model to Carlisle on June 25.[60] Suddenly on June 27, Gus received a rejection at the same time as the Mint announced that a reverse by Charles Barber had been adopted. True to form, the rejection letter specifically pointed out that Saint-Gaudens's work was to be done at no additional expense. The Awards Subcommittee had been completely cut out of the process. Saint-Gaudens had given Carlisle the opening, and the Treasury secretary had taken it.

The press reacted, proclaiming that Saint-Gaudens had been wronged by having his work combined with that of a vastly inferior designer. The government's dealings with Saint-Gaudens over the award medal design had been disgraceful. However, this last action was of a coolness that took one's breath away.

Gilder now came strongly to Saint-Gaudens's defense. He turned to Assistant Treasury Secretary Curtis, a former New York attorney. On July 3, Gilder wrote Curtis that he had been instrumental in convincing Saint-Gaudens to put aside important work to furnish the last reverse for the award medal. Now to have it replaced by one from a "vastly inferior hand making a hodgepodge of what

The final World's Columbian Exposition Award Medal included the reverse replacement ordered by Secretary Carlisle and executed by Charles Barber. Saint-Gaudens would never forgive this muling of his obverse with Barber's reverse.

promised to be a memorable piece of medal work" was an extraordinary proceeding. He felt the Treasury Department would be criticized for all time for this act by those both inside and outside the country who had knowledge of art. Gilder wanted to know if there were any unstated reasons for the rejection of Saint-Gaudens's third effort at a reverse design. He closed by offering his help.[61]

When Gilder received Curtis's reply, he burned it. There is no record of its contents. But by July the environment in Washington was one of fear. The Panic of 1893 was now a deep depression with jobs being cut and wages reduced as companies fought to stem the bleeding from lost revenues.

The real trouble had started when workers struck at the Pullman Palace Car factory in Chicago on May 11, 1894. Then the American Railway Union ordered its membership to stop working trains that included Pullman cars. That boycott quickly spread to freight traffic. Passenger traffic snarled, particularly around Chicago.[62] By July 1 the work stoppage was being called the greatest strike in history.[63] It got worse; riots broke out in Chicago on July 6 with thousands of freight cars put to the torch. It took local police and state militia, backed up by regular army troops, to quell the lawlessness.[64] With the military camped on the lakefront, order was effectively restored on July 11, and the spread of the strike to other cities stopped.[65]

In spite of the national trauma from events in Chicago, the usually judicious Gilder turned around and wrote a much stronger second letter to Curtis. Gilder was forced to defend Gus's action of sending a bill with his third reverse design for $1,000. Gilder held nothing back in this second letter. The offending nude was entirely gone. Saint-Gaudens had carefully prepared this last design, and it was astounding that it should be thrown aside for another seemingly made in competition to Saint-Gaudens's work. What really moved Gilder was that this country would do so gauche and inexcusable a thing as to cast aside the work of its most noted sculptor and patch on something from a man of no artistic reputation. If possible, Carlisle should be "saved from making so glaring an error as this." Gilder even went so far as to tell Curtis he could show his letter to Carlisle if it would do any good.[66] It wouldn't. Carlisle was not going to budge.

It took Saint-Gaudens two drafts to come up with a letter that would be printable in his promised public protest of his treatment. He offered to waive the additional charge of $1,000. He noted that rejection of the eagle reverse could only have been on the basis that it was not acceptable as a work of art. In actuality the rejection added the gratuitous insult that Saint-Gaudens was incapable of making a proper reverse for his own medal.

While there was no formal answer, Saint-Gaudens's protest had been heard. In an interview with the *New York Sun*, Robert Preston gave the Mint's reply. In it he revealed that the medal controversy had gone all the way to Grover Cleveland—no doubt thanks to Watson Gilder's personal friendship with the President.

> He sent in a model with appropriate lettering covering all of the face accept a little space at the top on which a very impertinent-looking eagle strutted on a wreath of laurel; and a panel below in which the name of the prize winner was to appear. The whole thing looks as if Mr. St. Gaudens had run it off in an idle hour. With this new effort came a modest bill for $1,000 which was promptly returned unpaid.

> And, by the way, it is not generally known that the president himself passed on Mr. St. Gaudens's first design. His criticism was not at all on the nudity of the figure. He remarked that the left leg of the young man looked as if it had been broken and set badly.[67]

Robert Preston had just made this sordid affair personal for Augustus Saint-Gaudens.

In November gold reserves were again below the required minimum. Carlisle on November 10 vehemently denied that there would be a second bond issue. The secretary even went so far as to state that the bond issue was being urged by a lot of selfish bankers and brokers in New York. This action put the secretary in an embarrassing position when President Cleveland announced on November 13 that the government would return to the bond market for another $50 million.[68] Twice now Cleveland had overcalled his secretary of the Treasury. Rumors flew that Carlisle should resign. Political wags, however, pointed out that the man had spent his whole life in politics and had nowhere to go. In regard to his presidential ambitions, Carlisle had just neutered himself.[69]

On February 4, 1895 J.P. Morgan, the uncrowned king of Wall Street, accompanied by Bob Bacon, a classmate of Theodore Roosevelt's at Harvard, checked into the Arlington Hotel in Washington; speculation was rampant that a deal was to be made.[70] In January Treasury's gold holdings had hit a low of $45 million; it was apparent to all that the November bond issue had been only a stopgap measure.[71] On February 8, Cleveland sent a message to Congress that he would issue $65 million of 30-year bonds payable in coin under the authority of the 1875 Resumption Act. Also, in a real twist of tails, Cleveland stated that Morgan's syndicate had consented to a clause that would allow the issuance of bonds specifically payable in gold at a lower interest rate, should Congress approve.[72]

A resolution favoring the issuance of bonds payable in gold was voted upon in the House on February 14. The gold Democrats needed the support of Republicans to gain approval. However, Tom Reed, leader of the opposition Republicans and with his own presidential aspirations, straddled the fence, giving only tepid support for the resolution. The silver Democrats on the other hand were over the top in their rabid opposition. William Jennings Bryan from Nebraska said he would prefer death to seeing this infamous bargain approved. His fellow representatives, however, met this declaration with laughter and shouts of derision that so unsettled Bryan that the rest of his speech fizzled. Still, the resolution died, and the bonds would be issued at a higher interest rate.[73]

While the silver men were obstinate, Cleveland was winning this battle over gold. Overlooked in the debates that winter was the fact that half the proceeds of the February bond sale came from overseas. The flow of foreign investment funds had reversed. While Cleveland would need one more bond issue to hold the line on gold, the nadir of the depression had been reached, and the road to recovery, though bumpy, was in place.[74]

Chapter 44

A Tale of Two Men

For Augustus Saint-Gaudens the evening of May 20, 1895, began innocently enough. He was a guest at a celebration of a tenth wedding anniversary held at a photographer's studio. That the wife was away touring Europe caused the sculptor not the slightest hesitation; in fact, it promised a good time.

Maybe a meal of sixteen courses was a bit excessive. Champagne was the wine of choice for the evening and maybe an alleged consumption of 144 bottles was a bit much. However, it was the seventeenth course that put the affair over the edge. As the men were lighting their cigars, there came a knock at the studio door. Six waiters entered carrying an enormous pie in the shape of a sphere. The headwaiter cut the crust with a silver knife. As if by magic, the pie parted, and a great bevy of canaries flew into the room. But there was more. Out popped 16-year-old Susie Johnson in filmy black gauze with the likeness of a black bird upon her head. That she wore nothing else was apparent to each of the guests. As she made her appearance, all in the party broke out with "Sing a Song of Sixpence."[1]

It had been a good month for Gus; he had gotten his revenge against Charles Barber. On May 6, in a setting worlds apart but still in New York City, the Joint Committee on the Improvement of United States Coinage, an ad hoc group formed from the American Numismatic and Archeological Society and the National Sculpture Society, opened an exhibition to showcase the results of their call the previous year for new designs for the silver dollar. This was a blue-ribbon effort with widespread

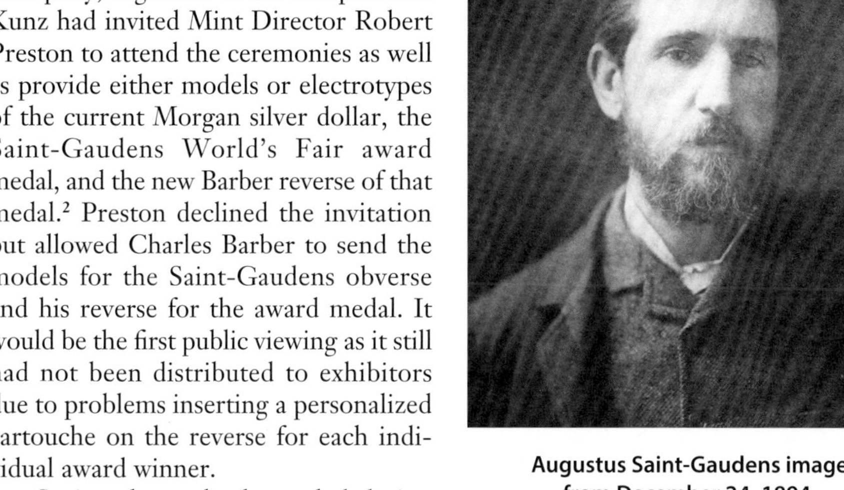

Augustus Saint-Gaudens image from December 24, 1894.

support. After the opening ceremony, there would be a dinner that night at the home of George Kunz of Tiffany & Company, organizer of the competition. Kunz had invited Mint Director Robert Preston to attend the ceremonies as well as provide either models or electrotypes of the current Morgan silver dollar, the Saint-Gaudens World's Fair award medal, and the new Barber reverse of that medal.[2] Preston declined the invitation but allowed Charles Barber to send the models for the Saint-Gaudens obverse and his reverse for the award medal. It would be the first public viewing as it still had not been distributed to exhibitors due to problems inserting a personalized cartouche on the reverse for each individual award winner.

Seeing that only the muled design would be displayed, Saint-Gaudens took matters into his own hands. He made available his rejected reverse design that dropped the nude theme. When interviewed at the exhibition by the *New York Tribune*, Saint-Gaudens stated he was very much disgusted by his experience with the government. Then in a payback for the blistering over the affair that Robert Preston had administered him in the *New York Sun* the previous year, Saint-Gaudens told the *Tribune* he could understand why some people objected to his first design with a nude figure although no person "of judgment in matters of art had any criticism on that account." He then draped the nude, but it met with rejection as well. Finally he prepared "a simple and typical" model. They rejected that one too. Perhaps, he concluded, "they thought that whatever was plain and simple was not artistic."[3]

Saint-Gaudens was serving on the jury of awards with Daniel Chester French and Olin Warner. Some twenty-five obverse and reverse designs for the silver dollar were exhibited. It had been intended that the winning designs be made available to the United States government at the conclusion of the exhibit. However, the jury went to pains to point out that their awards, dictated by the terms of the competition, in no way amounted to an endorsement of the winning designs. In other words, the competition was a bust. With no remuneration given for models submitted, none of the prominent New York artists had participated.[4]

Charles Barber took the opportunity to visit the exhibit on May 13. The manner in which the electrotypes of the award medal were displayed deeply angered him. The problem's source stemmed from the Mint's treating the side with the awardees' names, being Barber's design, as the obverse while everyone else considered Saint-Gaudens's rendering of Columbus as the obverse. Upon receiving the display case, the Barber and Saint-Gaudens electrotypes had been reversed by unknown hands, returning them to their proper order. The result was that the Saint-Gaudens obverse was now displayed more prominently. Also, in the course of making this change, the electrotypes had been mishandled in the remounting process.

In Barber's opinion, there had been "but one desire of those into whose hands the exhibit fell, namely to disgrace it."[5] In his letter of complaint to George Kunz, Barber never mentioned Saint-Gaudens or the fact that Saint-Gaudens's third reverse was on display. From this point forward, Charles Barber would harbor personal bitterness toward Saint-Gaudens for this public humiliation.

Truth be told Saint-Gaudens had better things to be doing that spring; the *Shaw* was still not completed. At the end of 1893 when Saint-Gaudens had met with John Murray Forbes, the man had been so worked up over the lack of real progress that he had proposed, only somewhat tongue in cheek, the committee consider a new monument to Shaw by Daniel Chester French. He valued Saint-Gaudens's work very highly but confessed to deep shame for having the *Shaw* linger at a snail's pace without a protest that would have either given the committee a monument or left it free to seek another sculptor.[6]

Now Forbes had resigned himself that molasses caught more flies than vinegar, but his silence brought little progress.[7] In April 1895, Edward Atkinson asked for an update. Gus optimistically answered that the allegorical angel for which Forbes never had a good word was in place and required only a few final touches. The rest of the relief was complete. He expected to put up the completed work in Boston in October.[8] Then in July, Saint-Gaudens told Atkinson that he had just finished the angel. He was going away for a week, and the work would be ready upon his return. He would then look at it one more time before having it cast in plaster.

There was anticipation that Saint-Gaudens would request a draw against his contract. This advance would allow him to go abroad for the summer and rest while the statue was being cast in bronze.[9] These positive status reports seemed to lull the Shaw Committee to sleep. They should have known when progress did not develop that Gus, upon his return after a week's break, had embarked upon yet another round of changes on the angel.[10] Upon seeing the enlarged flying figure, Gus had become convinced that it should be smaller.[11]

Saint-Gaudens missed his self-imposed October 1895 deadline. The Shaw people sat on the sidelines with little they could do beyond keeping a tight hold on their purse strings.

On that same May 20, 1895, Theodore Roosevelt was at a dinner of an entirely different nature from that of Augustus Saint-Gaudens. This dinner was a one-on-one with Reverend Charles Parkhurst and the two men were discussing how to clean up the New York City Police Department. It was appropriate as Roosevelt was the President of the New York City Police Board. Parkhurst had been at the forefront of a move to document corruption in the police department. Illicit trade in liquor, gambling, and prostitution were thriving in the city, greased by bribes from precinct captains down to patrolmen on the beat. Parkhurst had begun his campaign in February 1892, and by 1895 it had grown into a society promoting honest government and bent upon ridding the police department of all corruption.[12] Parkhurst's efforts had played no small part in Republican Mayor William Strong's victory the previous fall. Their conversation that night centered on the removal of two of the most corrupt precinct captains and the chief.

For Theodore Roosevelt this position was a consolation prize. He knew the timing was right for a Republican victory in the mayor's race. However, he had sat out the race in deference to his wife's wishes. Edith Roosevelt was concerned about the family's finances should he lose. Theodore had yet to totally liquidate his cattle investment in North Dakota.[13] Still he needed to get out of his Civil Service commissioner's job in Washington. When the offer of the position on the police board came, he accepted.

On that day of the opening of the silver dollar design exhibition, Mayor Strong swore in Theodore Roosevelt as a commissioner on the New York City Police Board. The board members would be bipartisan and were of a like mind for reform. Key decisions would require a unanimous vote where one board member could deadlock the commission. Yet at this point, that was far from the minds of the four commissioners. At their first meeting shortly after being sworn in, Roosevelt was elected president of the commission.[14] He gained no real power from this position with one exception—he handled all speaking engagements and interviews for the commissioners.[15] Theodore Roosevelt was refreshed and ready for this job.

The Civil Service position had proven to be onerous, as Cabot Lodge had warned. In spite of civil service reform, the post office had remained very fertile ground for political spoils. It was only a matter of time before Roosevelt had run afoul of the Postmaster General, John Wanamaker. It stemmed from corruption in the Baltimore Post Office. Roosevelt reported on the situation and recommended 25 federal officials be dismissed. Neither Wanamaker nor President Harrison was disposed to act upon Roosevelt's recommendation; in fact, Roosevelt had become a thorn in the side of the Republican Administration. Wanamaker had gone so far as to conduct his own investigation into Roosevelt's charges of wrongdoing. The matter had finally come to a head when the Democrat-controlled House Committee on Civil Service opened an investigation on April 19, 1892. The conflict had taken on a personal tone and boiled over into the public arena. Ultimately, the House committee found in Roosevelt's favor, giving Wanamaker a complete black eye in a Presidential election year.[16]

When Grover Cleveland returned to the White House victorious in March 1893, Roosevelt had expected to be removed. However, Cleveland had had other ideas, asking Roosevelt to hold over for a couple years. Expecting a better relationship than he had with Harrison and troubled by the Panic of 1893, Roosevelt accepted.

That trouble would have developed anyway first came in the form of an innocuous little piece in the newspapers in September 1893. In regard to the supervision within the Treasury Department, no action would be taken without the personal consideration of the secretary of the Treasury.[17] No reasons were given for the sweeping dismissals of the Republican clerks. In their place came Democrats, mostly southern.[18] It was obvious even to the most detached observer that Secretary Carlisle was intending to build up a personal power base in the Treasury Department.

By that October, Roosevelt had had his eyes specifically fixed on Treasury. It was much worse managed than it had been under Harrison. Logan Carlisle was a curse and he acted with the full approval of his father.[19] No surprise then when Roosevelt to his sister, Bamie, described John Carlisle as smooth, rather cowardly, able and vindictive.[20] It was not a pretty picture.

By March 1894, Roosevelt was in open conflict with Carlisle, comparing him to Wanamaker. A frustrated Roosevelt dressed down Carlisle in a report to the Senate for which Carlisle was very angered. Theodore's retort was that he expected Carlisle would try to have him removed and he did not care a rap.[21]

Carlisle's move was much more underhanded. One of his clerks, hailing from Georgia, published an article in the *Washington Post* attacking the commissioners and Roosevelt individually based upon previously disproved charges. Roosevelt called the action lacking in nerve, spiteful and as silly as it was contemptible.[22]

Roosevelt had also been disgusted that the "head devil," Logan Carlisle, paid attention to the color line in making dismissals and to reducing and promoting for sectional and political reasons. The commissioner had read in *Harper's Weekly* that Secretary Carlisle possessed the best traits of trained English legislators who made a learned profession of their calling. Whoever wrote that article; Roosevelt wanted to feel their head![23]

At the end of that June, Theodore again let his hair down to Bamie. Not even Wanamaker was a meaner, smaller cur than Carlisle; he was dishonest, untruthful and cowardly.[24] It was in this vein that Roosevelt had led the Civil Service Commission to advocate for a sweeping expansion of the civil service, placing all the Treasury units not already covered under its regulation. It would bring in all the operating mints and assay offices. Cleveland had tabled the recommendation, afraid of its impact on the looming mid-term elections.[25] It was time for Roosevelt to go.

After Roosevelt's resignation Cleveland had begun to see merit in his position. In May 1895 he had announced a new policy at the mints. Officers of the mints should be selected by the president on the advice of the secretary of the Treasury. These appointments should not be made factors in the distribution of patronage among state and local political party functionaries in the future.[26]

Theodore Roosevelt kicked off his tenure on the Police Board with a bang. At the end of May 1895 the Irish-born police chief, Thomas Byrnes, and one of his captains resigned. On June 7, Roosevelt began the first of his midnight rambles. Accompanying him was Jacob Riis, a police reporter and future muckraking journalist. Roosevelt would become the scourge of sleeping cops on the night shift. Woe unto the beat cop he found belly to a bar enjoying a late-night beer. Once busted by Roosevelt, the offending policeman would be summoned to the next meeting of the commissioners where no mercy would be shown. With Riis documenting the jaunts, it made great press for Roosevelt, and it struck fear into the rank and file of the police force. But it also exposed Roosevelt to a poverty-stricken side of the city that he had never before experienced first-hand in such detail.[27]

Theodore Roosevelt had an uncanny ability to digest and retain information. He is shown here at work at his desk as a New York City police commissioner; the trash basket is full and the floor littered with discarded minutiae absorbed, a necessity for him to function effectively.

Roosevelt still faced a much bigger problem. Saloons had violated the Sunday closing laws since the Civil War, and prostitution catered to all levels of society.[28] In fact, the saloons were at the heart of much of the prostitution as well as illegal gambling in the city. On Sunday, June 23, 1895, two thousand policemen surrounded a significant portion of the saloons in New York. On that hot summer day, New York's working population, in search of a cold beer on their day off, got a rude awakening. Even the side doors, the ladies' or family entrance, to the bars were locked. Meanwhile Roosevelt spent the day with his family at Sagamore Hill.

Organized opposition dug in immediately. At the forefront were the German immigrants who enjoyed family outings to biergartens on Sunday. Representatives of the German-American Reform Union quickly confronted the mayor in a stormy public meeting. Roosevelt wrote to his sister, Bamie, that he had now run up against an ugly snag. While the Sunday closing law was altogether too strict, he had no honorable alternative but to enforce it, despite the furious rage of the saloon owners and many good people for which he was sorry.[29] What he did not say was that the exclusive clubs and hotels were exempt from the closing law.

In this imbroglio, Roosevelt had the support of temperance groups, women's rights organizations, and the churches. Arrayed against him, however, were Tammany Hall and workingmen, and they voted.[30] On election night in November it was apparent that the Democrats, siding for local option, had scored a landslide victory in New York City, sweeping the judgeships, electing ten of twelve state senators and thirty of thirty-five assemblymen from the city. New York City voters had soundly repudiated Roosevelt's Sunday closings.[31]

One police effort, cleaning up the rampant prostitution of the city, still seemed to have strong support. Yet the police managed to create a post-election public relations nightmare for Roosevelt. They arrested a young woman after dark for talking to a stranger. Her defense was that she was seeking directions. She went to the workhouse for three days. Next the police chief ordered an upscale brothel be raided. Again, a young woman was arrested on the premises in spite of no obvious connection to the illegitimate activity. The press had a field day. On December 11, Roosevelt was greeted to a front-page cartoon in the *New York World* of the Statue of Liberty under arrest for being an unaccompanied female out at night.[32] Not one New York City newspaper was supporting Roosevelt; Whitelaw Reid had gone so far at the *New York Tribune* to ban all but negative or unavoidable mention of Roosevelt.[33]

On Sunday, October 13, 1895, on the first page of the second section of the *World* was the unthinkable that left little to the imagination: An artist's ribald rendering of the May 20 anniversary celebration. Discretion was the rule of the day for such things. Now, it was public knowledge and Saint-Gaudens's distinctive profile as sketched among the guests could simply not be missed. In a time when the immigrants in the city were lucky to earn a dollar a day, this dinner cost $3,500, according to the *World.*

In the "Pie Girl" dinner sketch, Augustus Saint-Gaudens is at the far right. Also present were his architect friends, McKim and White, and Morgan's lieutenant, Bob Bacon.

Though never mentioned in correspondence, there could be no doubt that the Shaw Committee saw the sketch.

Chapter 45

A Cross of Gold

William McKinley, now the former governor of Ohio, was reluctant to endorse gold. He had staked his presidential campaign on the maintenance of a strong tariff. In spite of high tariffs being blamed by Democrats as a cause of the Panic of 1893, they were now viewed as the means for the economy's revival. McKinley had urged in campaign speeches that American labor would prosper with the tariff-afforded protection for domestic industry. Tariff protection would create jobs, raise farm prices, and restart the nation's mines, smelters, and factories. McKinley avoided speaking on the currency, calling it a dead issue.[1]

The two senators from Nevada did not consider currency a dead issue. John P. Jones accused McKinley of being neither flesh, fish, nor fowl on currency but rather a straddler, pure and simple. Bill Stewart was even more direct. He demanded in a curt letter to know if McKinley was for the gold standard or a restoration of the bimetallic standard that existed before the Coinage Act of 1873. McKinley did not answer Stewart. Instead, just before the convention, his supporters issued a circular that quoted from his speeches in Congress. McKinley stood opposed to the unlimited coinage of silver under existing conditions. He believed whatever dollars the nation must have must be good dollars, worth 100 cents, whether it was gold, silver, or paper.[2]

Looking from a distance on June 10, Theodore Roosevelt told Lodge that it was evident that McKinley had the nomination sewn up. However, he did hope that the party platform would have a most vigorous gold plank and be against unlimited silver coinage (free silver) at any ratio. The Democrats would go for free silver, and if the Republicans assumed a timid or halting position, they would get whipped and disaster awaited the country.[3]

For just this one time, Roosevelt and the New York Republican boss, Thomas Platt, were in agreement. Platt called a meeting in his private hotel rooms for the evening of June 14 of the leading gold proponents at the convention; none were McKinley supporters. In attendance among others were Henry Cabot Lodge and Pennsylvania Senator Matthew Quay. Platt wanted these men to stand by him in his demand for a gold plank, no matter what. Lodge was willing to cooperate, declaring that the very life of the party depended upon an unquestioning expression for gold. Quay took the same ground, thinking it would force McKinley to stop his straddle. After an hour and a half, they settled on a draft statement for adoption by the convention's committee on resolutions.

> We favor the maintenance of the existing gold standard and are opposed to the free coinage of silver except by international agreement for bi-metallism with the leading commercial nations of the world.

Immediately after the meeting, Lodge and Quay went to Mark Hanna, McKinley's campaign manager, to inform him of the move. The reaction was vexation; Hanna wanted to avoid a bolt of silver Republicans from the convention.[4] The next day Hanna coolly told the Platt people to run the proposed plank past the New York representative of the McKinley campaign.[5] That was capitulation; no New York Republican was strong enough to oppose Platt on this issue. An exultant Lodge easily carried the day for a strong gold plank in the resolutions committee and was reaffirmed when the convention soundly rejected a silver substitute. Afterwards, twenty-three delegates did leave the convention.[6]

Roosevelt quickly got on the bandwagon, declaring McKinley upright and honorable with considerable ability but not necessarily a strong man in a crisis.[7] The *New York Times* observed post-convention that it was not McKinley, whose nomination was almost preordained, that people talked about. Instead, it was the gold plank. Republicans and Democrats alike were surprised that the convention mustered up enough courage to take this unequivocal stand.[8] Thomas Platt knew better; after all he was a serious coin collector. He knew the difficult history of money in the United States. Platt would always consider this action his one shining moment.[9]

William McKinley spent his whole political career championing protective tariffs. Yet when he gained the Republican presidential nomination in 1896, he quickly found that he could not straddle the fence when it came to the silver movement.

In fact, Mark Hanna was sore at Platt for forcing McKinley's hand on gold. Afterwards, Roosevelt would encourage Platt to make the first move toward reconciliation, believing Hanna would be receptive. In was simple economics: Hanna needed Eastern money to help fund the campaign.[10]

The Democrats, a majority of their convention delegates pro-silver, wanted nothing to do with Grover Cleveland. Cleveland had tried at the beginning of the year to defuse the situation. Treasury Secretary Carlisle ordered that silver dollars be struck in quantity again at the mints. The reason given was that the appropriation for subsidiary silver coinage had been consumed while moneys remained available to strike silver dollars. Rather than furlough mint workers without pay, they were put to minting standard silver dollars again.[11] No minds were changed.

The New York Democrats wanted a platform that called for an international agreement setting the ratio between gold and silver, fearing a unilateral move on the issue would flood the country with silver, debasing the nation's currency. Richard Bland counter-argued that free coinage of silver would instead drive the price up to the point that it supported a ratio of 16 to 1. The problem with Bland, however, was his health. He had not actively campaigned in the run-up to their convention. The way was open for a silver dark horse.[12]

Now President Cleveland could see the waning influence of gold Democrats upon his political party. Salvaging what he could, Cleveland turned to Roosevelt's position as advocated in the 1894 Civil Service Commission annual report calling for an expansion of the classification system. With one stroke of the pen in his presidential directive of May 6, 1896, he nearly doubled the size of the classified positions falling within civil service authority, adding 30,000.[13,14] He thus locked into position his Democratic supporters and limited the inroads that could be made if either the silver Democrats or the Republicans gained the presidency. Included were all the mints and assay offices.[15] Finally, the Mint Service was freed of the patronage system that had proved so detrimental to its efficiency and productivity for the past half century.

Grover Cleveland would now acknowledge the obvious and prepare to leave the presidency. He had labored diligently to fix the disastrous financial policies of the Harrison administration. Yet, in the end, Cleveland would still take the blame.

The Democrats convened their convention in Chicago on July 7, 1896. Republican Senators Teller and Jones attended under the silver banner with Teller even seeking the Democratic presidential nomination. The fireworks came July 9 with the presentation of the party's platform. If the gold Democrats hoped for a reasoned document, they were disappointed; the silver Democrats needed only a majority in the committee, and they were unwilling to compromise. It was a populist document through and through, advocating for free coinage of silver, an income tax, a reconstruction of the Supreme Court, and repudiation of the obligation to repay the public debt with gold. Voices of reason rose up in protest. Senators David Hill of New York

William Jennings Bryan swept his way to the Democratic presidential nomination in 1896 with his "cross of gold" speech. He captured the spirit of the silver movement and thus became the antithesis to Theodore Roosevelt. Bryan's expected candidacy in 1908 was at the core of Roosevelt's desire to redesign the gold coins.

and William Vilas of Wisconsin made the point that this radical document would cost the party the election. It fell to ex-Congressman William Jennings Bryan to rally the delegates in favor of the platform with its silver plank that he had drafted several weeks previously.

Bryan had come a long way since that moment in Congress when his fellow representatives derided his overly emotional call against gold. He had criss-crossed the country since his leaving Congress in 1895, after a failed run for the Senate, giving speeches in support of silver and honing his oratorical skills. He was ready.[16]

He pronounced this a battle between the holders of idle capital and the struggling masses that produced the wealth and paid the taxes. Republicans legislated to make the well-to-do prosperous with that prosperity leaking down to those below. Democrats legislated to make the masses prosperous, and their prosperity would work its way up and through every class that rested upon it. Restore bimetallism and then let England have bimetallism because the United States had it. Next Bryan got to the heart of his emotional speech, coming out with his crown of thorns comparison. He closed with "you shall not crucify mankind on a cross of gold." He then dropped to his knees and extended his hands to symbolize a crucifixion before walking off the stage in silence.[17] It was pure theatre and the convention went nuts.[18] Wisconsin, overwhelmingly for gold, declined to participate further in the nominating process but nobody cared.

On the following morning, balloting for the presidential nomination commenced. The Bland forces were relying on support from the South and the simple fact that Bland had carried the torch for free silver so long and so well. When the votes of the first ballot were tabulated, it showed Bland's core support well short of the two-thirds needed for nomination. On the fifth ballot, the convention stampeded for Bryan, the "Boy Orator of the Platte," the youngest man, at thirty-six, to be nominated by a major political party for president.[19]

Theodore Roosevelt called the Chicago Democratic convention a witches' Sabbath. Lodge had long maintained that the hardest fight the Democrats could give the Republicans in the presidential campaign was the free silver issue. Roosevelt felt the Democrats had chosen wisely if one disregarded the question of the morality of their position.[20]

Chapter 46
A Glorious Retreat

On Friday, July 31, 1896, Theodore Roosevelt left the city for a long weekend at Oyster Bay, an increasing occurrence as the police commissioner job wore him down that summer. However, this was no ordinary weekend; his houseguests were Maria and Bellamy Storer who had maintained a ten-year close friendship with William McKinley. Theodore seemed like a younger brother to Maria, and Bellamy was godfather to Edith and Theodore's son, Archie. Yet when Maria recalled this meeting in a magazine article in 1912, their relationship had completely fractured so that some of her observations of that weekend must be tempered.

Theodore took Maria rowing on Oyster Bay. She had always found him entertaining. He seemed like a boy who would never grow up, and one never knew what he would say next. Theodore had the oars, and his rowing was spasmodic as he started talking about his future in a depressed way. He had done all he could on the police board, and he could not stay there any longer; too many wanted him out. Yet, he had no idea what he would do. He called himself a melancholy spectacle to his children, writing books that would not sell. He had no future.

About this time the wake of a passing steamboat nearly capsized them, causing Maria to suggest they continue this conversation on dry land. Back at the house, Theodore bared his soul. There was one thing that he would do but he had no chance of getting it—assistant secretary of the Navy. He knew that McKinley did not like him. Maria also knew that to be true but stayed silent. Instead, she volunteered that both she and her husband would advocate Roosevelt for the position.[1]

After the Storers left Sagamore Hill, the grind at the police board continued. William Jennings Bryan came to town and fell flat. In Roosevelt's words, "He fell with a bang here." There might have been more to it. The police department was charged with keeping order at the location of Bryan's speech. Somehow a significant number of gatecrashers gained admittance to the auditorium, while legitimate ticket holders ended up on the outside, looking in.[2]

After an extremely contentious police board meeting on August 20, Roosevelt headed West to his ranch the next day to lick his wounds and rejuvenate. September and October were going to determine Roosevelt's future.

After a brief sojourn at his ranch, Theodore Roosevelt returned to New York City ready to throw himself into the presidential contest between Bryan and McKinley. Roosevelt polished his stock campaign speech at a Sound Money luncheon in New York City where he used outsized props of gold and silver coins. Not surprisingly, this election was going to be fought with coins. The Bryan people were issuing satirical dollars struck in white metal, called "Bryan Money." In this talk, Roosevelt, in a play for the intrinsic value of gold, even accused Bryan's free silver supporters of violating the Commandment "Thou Shall Not Steal." He was taking no prisoners, and the audience ate it up. At this point, Cabot Lodge told Roosevelt that he had convinced New York State Republicans to allow Roosevelt to accompany him on a campaign swing through the state for McKinley. The only catch was that Roosevelt had to make peace with the Republican bosses. This he did, striking a deal that he would stay out of New York City, only campaigning upstate.[3]

McKinley's traditional front-porch campaign dictated that Republicans send out a phalanx of speakers to counter Bryan's campaign. On the strength of Roosevelt's New York performance, he gained a plum assignment of trailing Bryan, rebutting the "Boy Orator of the Platte" at huge rallies in Chicago and Detroit and points in between.[4] Michigan, in Roosevelt's opinion, was very much in play.[5]

Oblivious to the political turmoil playing out before him and pinched by the depression, Saint-Gaudens in May 1896 was forced to alert the Shaw Committee that a "construction difficulty" would prevent the *Shaw* from being put in the hands of the molder for a few weeks. The delay had nothing to do with the artistic portion of the work. However, the holdup was inconveniencing him financially, and he needed a bridge payment from the committee of $500 or $1,000.[6]

Edward Atkinson visited Saint-Gaudens's studio ten days later. The work was ready except for the allegorical angel. The figure was itself complete and was being molded in plaster. Unsaid was that what work had been done on the *Shaw* over the winter consisted of tinkering with the angel in an attempt to get it right by trial and error. Still, Atkinson agreed that Saint-Gaudens's work was essentially done. On that basis, the committee acceded to Saint-Gaudens's request for the bridge payment.[7]

The situation blew up in June. Saint-Gaudens decided to again reconstruct the angel. Colonel Shaw's mother and the committee were upset that they were not being given any say in this matter.[8] After fifteen years with Saint-Gaudens, Atkinson was exhausted and felt he was at fault for not somehow forcing the *Shaw* to completion. He bluntly told the sculptor that they were at a parting of the ways. Upon Saint-Gaudens's assurance, he had authorized the bridge payment. Atkinson told Saint-Gaudens that if the work were not complete by the following May, he would resign as treasurer of the committee and consider his performance as incompetent.[9]

Again, Saint-Gaudens promised that the *Shaw* would be complete by May 1897. Saint-Gaudens knew that the one member of the committee he absolutely could not afford to alienate was Atkinson. However, John Murray Forbes was a different matter. In a letter to Atkinson, he referred to Saint-Gaudens as "your Saint" and talked of the "cussed angel." Saint-Gaudens was demanding pay for clay when he should have long previously provided the bronze. Forbes closed by saying, "Brass is your Saint's proper metal, and I should like to see a horse collar fastened around his neck."[10]

This time, Saint-Gaudens delivered. The committee came together at his studio at 11 a.m. on September 3, 1896, to view the essentially completed work.[11] Not trusting Saint-Gaudens's solvency, the committee paid the foundry directly for casting the bronze. There would still be tinkering on the angel to the very end, but the crisis of a failed commission had narrowly been averted.

The *Chicago Tribune* billed Theodore Roosevelt as police commissioner of New York City and nimrod of the West. He was an Eastern intellectual who could explain the complexities of the gold standard in terms a cowboy could understand. The mass meeting at the Chicago Coliseum, attended by 13,000, had the aspects of a religious revival with the audience enthusiastically swaying to the singing of national songs. Robert Lincoln escorted Roosevelt through the crowd to the speaker's platform. Roosevelt spoke for two hours using props.[12]

Roosevelt continued addressing crowds at Michigan City, Indiana, and listening to Bryan at Jackson, Michigan, before speaking himself in that city. However, he saved his best for Detroit at a meeting of sound money men at the Majestic Building. Silver men were scattered through the audience, but there were no interruptions. Roosevelt was simply too quick on his feet. When a dog started barking loudly, Theodore agilely exclaimed, "Another vote for Bryan."

Laughter aside, Roosevelt was dead serious in the message he delivered. Congress had the power to coin money and regulate its value. Congress had the power to try to make money pass at the ratio of 16 to 1. It could, if it so chose, establish a ratio of 1 to 1. There was no provision in the constitution that forbade Congress from doing foolish things. If Congress chose not only to be foolish but dishonest, it could repudiate the national debt, allowing repayment in silver. Congress had the right to make a fool of itself. What Republicans were fighting for in this campaign was that the United States should not make a fool of itself.

Roosevelt rolled on. At the beginning of the campaign, Bryan was fighting for a 53-cent dollar. However, silver had fallen, and he was now fighting for a 50-cent dollar. Silver would continue to fall in value. No matter what the politicians did, they could not make people in this world take something for what its value was not.

Roosevelt was highlighting in simple terms that silver prices had gone into decline with the repeal of the Sherman Silver Purchase Act and Great Britain's closing of the Indian mints to silver coinage.[13]

Now Roosevelt turned to the roots of the debate. The crime of 1873 was done stealthily and that stealth took the queer form of 158 pages of the Congressional Record in speeches and debate. The bill was printed stealthily thirteen times. It was passed on the grounds that it gave the nation a gold dollar and that workingmen needed a gold dollar. Roosevelt quoted from the debate: "The question never will be settled until you determine the same question again, whether the laboring man is entitled to have a gold dollar if he earns it and whether you are going to cheat him with something else." That quote came from Bill Stewart.

Roosevelt then held up two silver Mexican dollars. Each was a little larger than a French five-franc piece that he also held up. Each of the Mexican coins had an intrinsic value of slightly more than the five-franc piece. Yet Roosevelt purchased the two Mexican coins for one dollar and the five-franc piece also for one dollar. Why was that the case? The Mexican dollars represented free and unlimited coinage of silver. The French piece had gold back of it.

On it went. In closing to prolonged applause, Roosevelt asked that his audience vote against free coinage and riot, vote against repudiation of debts. He asked that they do it not merely because it was in their self-interest but to do it as Americans. In this crisis of the nation's fate, he asked them to be loyal to America and to leave us "so that we may hold our heads up high when **we say we are citizens of the republic ever brightened by the rays of the morning.**"[14] Roosevelt told Lodge that the audience in Detroit went mad with enthusiasm.[15]

The final blow to Bryan was the rise in wheat prices in October. Actually, they had been strengthening for some time. Bryan had argued that wheat and silver moved in tandem. Free silver was needed to firm up silver prices and in turn help the farmer. However, just the opposite had happened. The crop in India had failed, wheat production in Australia was not enough to meet domestic demand, and Russian production was lower than expected.[16] However, what many observers overlooked was the crop failure in India eliminated the British practice of price undercutting of American agricultural products into Europe. With a reviving economy, McKinley won convincingly.

Roosevelt now had a dilemma, whether to go to Canton and lobby directly with McKinley for a job in his administration, or let others do the heavy lifting for him. Before Thanksgiving, the Storers visited McKinley and made a plea for Roosevelt to be the next assistant secretary of the Navy. Maria Storer related that McKinley's response was that he wanted peace. While he did not know Roosevelt well, he had been told that the man was always getting into spats with everybody. McKinley was afraid that Roosevelt was too pugnacious. Mrs. Storer urged McKinley to give him a chance and he might prove peaceful.[17] Everyplace that Roosevelt had served, he had been placed in order that he might fight. McKinley chewed on that for a moment or two and then said he would think it over.

Henry Cabot Lodge went to Canton next. After a wide-ranging discussion of policy, McKinley initiated the discussion on Roosevelt. The president-elect respected Roosevelt's abilities. He did have one question. Would Roosevelt arrive in

Washington with preconceived plans that he would want to drive through immediately? Later in the conversation Lodge came straight out and asked as a personal favor that McKinley consider Roosevelt. After lunch, McKinley volunteered to Lodge that he knew the one thing close to Lodge's heart and that he should say no more about it.[18]

Lodge was not done on the subject, phoning Boss Platt on December 7. Platt was reluctant; he did not want Roosevelt making war on him from the Navy Department. Lodge was taken aback, asking how that could be. The answer was the Brooklyn Navy Yard. Platt wished very much that Roosevelt would come see him.[19] Clearly any issues with the Brooklyn Navy Yard were going to be worked out when the two men met. Both wanted to get Roosevelt out of New York.

December greeted Roosevelt with a botched vice raid and more brawls within the police commission over promotions. This all came at a time when Roosevelt needed to keep his head down and his name out of the press, give no more speeches, so as not to spoil his best chance for extracting himself out of a clearly difficult position.

Meanwhile the communications line from the McKinley camp went dark. Lodge worked those people as best he could, pulling in his friend, John Hay, to put in a good word for Roosevelt. When former Massachusetts Governor John Long was named the incoming secretary of the Navy, Lodge wasted no time getting his approval of Roosevelt. Even Thomas Platt, now returning to the Senate, kept quiet. After the

Zorn quickly finished this etching of Gus and Hettie and then left to catch a ship back to Sweden. Records indicated some fifty copies of the etching were produced but the actual number is nearer fifteen.

inauguration, Vice President Hobart asked how he could help.[20] Still there was no movement.

In March the door cracked open a bit. Platt's lieutenants were urging him to support Roosevelt.[21] Lodge heard the rumor that Platt would welcome having Roosevelt out of New York if Platt could influence the mayor's choice for a replacement police commissioner.[22] It was clear Platt was dragging his feet, angling for whatever political concessions he could extract in exchange for his endorsement of Roosevelt.

Then the door seemingly closed. On April 1 McKinley offered the position of assistant secretary of War to Roosevelt's fellow police commissioner, Fred Grant, son of the former president. That would fill the administration's quota of New Yorkers. Then the door opened once again when Grant refused the position. On April 6, McKinley sent Roosevelt's name to the Senate for confirmation as assistant secretary of the Navy.[23]

With the *Shaw* now behind him, Saint-Gaudens turned to the long overdue *Sherman*. The sculptor had found an Italian peasant model approximating Sherman's build and holding his head in much the same manner as the general.[24] Also, Phimister Procter had previously modeled Sherman's horse. On February 14, 1897, Gus had a go with the figure for the Angel of Victory. He was not backing off a composition that paired

In spite of the angel that Saint-Gaudens struggled to perfect, his *Shaw Memorial* is one of the greatest bas-reliefs of all time.

an allegorical angel with the rough-hewn general in spite of his troubles over that concept with the *Shaw*. The model was Harriette "Hettie" Eugenia Anderson. Hettie was an African American woman of light complexion from Columbia, South Carolina.[25] The sculptor had first learned of her through Stanford White some two years previously.[26] In Gus's opinion, she had the figure of a goddess.[27]

The Swedish painter, Anders Zorn, spent that February day with Gus. They had known each other since the days of the World's Columbian Exposition. The man was a genius with his etchings, mastering contrasts between light and dark. As Gus worked, so did Zorn. It took Zorn about an hour, etching directly on the copper, to produce the scene of Gus seated with fatigue on his face while Hettie rested in the background, having just completed a modeling session.[28,29]

On Decoration Day 1897, the saga of the *Shaw* came to an end. The work was dedicated in Boston to great acclaim. The grizzled old African American survivors of the 54th Massachusetts Volunteer Infantry Regiment marched, many bent and crippled, one last time past this fitting memorial.[30] The genius of Saint-Gaudens was apparent in this wonderful relief.

In spite of the acclaim, there were criticisms of Saint-Gaudens from Europe to the effect that his works would not show well on the continent. The sculptor had no choice but to go to France, exhibit a monumental work at the Paris Salon and subject his creative ability to French critics. In November 1897, he and his family arrived in Paris.[31] The figure of Sherman, the horse, and the angel went with him.

When reporters told Police Commissioner Andrew Parker, Roosevelt's main protagonist on the police board, of Roosevelt's appointment as assistant secretary of the Navy, the man laughed for a very long while and then said: "What a glorious retreat."[32] The same could appropriately be said of Augustus Saint-Gaudens.

Part 7
Victory in Hand

Chapter 47
LAYING THE FOUNDATION

The election results were barely finalized, making William McKinley the 25th president of the United States when Matt Quay moved. On November 7, 1896, a Quay lieutenant gave a statement to the press that it was time for a Philadelphian to succeed Donald Cameron in the Senate. With that said, the man scampered down to Florida to spend three weeks as Quay's guest.[1] Donald Cameron's political career was finished.

By this stage, Don Cameron was prone to drinking sprees. The alcohol consumption left him moody and irascible. Lizzie was torn by the harsh reality that she must either endure her bad marriage or risk the social stigma of separation. Her husband, out of office and constantly underfoot, quickly put her in the condition of a "nervous breakdown." She took to her bed for several weeks and then was confined to limited physical activity. Worse, her husband let the house on Lafayette Square to the incoming vice president, Garret Hobart.

Lizzie was homeless but not helpless. In spite of her prostrated condition, she managed a trans-Atlantic crossing to meet Henry Adams in London. Henry then helped her to find suitable accommodations in Paris. From here in early winter she returned to New York where her health fully recovered. She wrote Adams after the New Year that she feared nothing, even winter at Cameron's farm.[2] Yet in truth, she had just successfully navigated a trial separation from her husband.

Without the deadweight of political patronage, Frank Leach took over the San Francisco Mint and turned it into an efficient, first-class operation. Over his ten years as head of that Mint, he rose to become the most respected superintendent in the Mint Service.

The telegram came out of the blue, like a bolt of lightning, on the evening of March 7, 1897. It was from the California Congressional delegation stating that he was their choice to be superintendent of the San Francisco Mint. It closed by presumptuously offering congratulations. Several minutes later a second telegram from on old friend, Congressman Samuel Hillborn, was even more forceful: "You will be tendered the superintendency of the mint. I earnestly entreat you to accept the position."[3] Frank Leach did not know what to do. He had not sought the position, had not even entertained it. Yet the minting procedures were not entirely alien to him; he had served on the 1891 Assay Commission in Philadelphia.[4]

Frank Leach, after thirty years in the publishing business, was at the top of his profession. In 1886, with a partner, he had purchased a small tri-weekly Oakland paper that was essentially an advertising sheet and turned it into a powerhouse daily, the *Enquirer*. In pulling off this move, Leach took an unsecured loan for $2,000. When it was paid, Leach learned that Aaron Sargent had provided the funds for the loan.[5] Had Leach not retired the note, he would have been under Sargent's thumb for political influence. That was how it was done in Oakland, and Leach had dodged a bullet.

Over time, Leach grew quite active in the community. In 1895 he turned his paper over on Washington's Birthday to the Women's Christian Temperance Union. The women had free rein over the paper's content that day, and the proceeds from its circulation and advertisements went to benefit their organization.[6]

As publisher, Leach made the *Enquirer* into a voice for good government. His support was critical in local politics. Then in 1894 he supported Hillborn's candidacy for the House of Representatives over that of the Republican machine.[7]

Thus by 1897 the endorsement of Leach and the *Enquirer* seemed tantamount to election. Frank Leach was very uncomfortable with that perception; it resembled too much a political machine. His support for one faction of the Republican Party against an opposing faction was bound at some time to result in open conflict, hurting all participants.[8]

There was one more factor at work in Frank Leach's mind. He was past the point of living hand to mouth financially. In addition, his wife had an inheritance. When her father, Abraham Powell, died in 1895, his Puget Sound Lumber Company was one of the largest lumber operations on the Pacific Coast.

Leach took a day before sending his reply to Hillborn. "If the president offers me the position, I shall take it."[9] It happened quickly because Treasury Secretary Gage wanted his own man in place when the money, including an immense amount of gold, was counted at the close of operations for the fiscal year at the Mint. Leach was nominated on June 8, 1897, and confirmed three days later.[10]

All Frank Leach had to do was read the San Francisco newspapers to see what he was walking into. When President Cleveland placed the Mints under civil service regulations, John Daggett, the Democrat-appointed superintendent, was first at sea over his loss of patronage. He quickly saw wiggle room; temporary positions were exempt, and he could still make terminations for cause.[11] The *San Francisco Call* sarcastically observed that Daggett was going to oil up his guillotine to create more vacancies that he could use to his advantage.[12]

With the nomination in place, Frank Leach made an announcement; He would not consider any application for appointment to the Mint. Every office was under civil service rules, and even the current superintendent's secretary had every right to expect to be retained. Anyone that expected an appointment had better pass the civil service examination and then get in line.[13] In one simple statement, Frank Leach had gained the confidence of every employee at the San Francisco Mint.

Reflecting on Leach's leadership in his first six months, the newspaper headlines at yearend 1897 proclaimed that the San Francisco Mint was setting new records for coinage. Gold from Alaska and imports from Australia were flooding into San Francisco in volumes undreamed of just a couple years previously.[14] For one brief shining moment, Leach had the operation assuming its rightful place as the lead Mint of the United States. Frank Leach was going to be a very different kind of superintendent.

As quick as Treasury Secretary Gage was to fill the superintendent's slot at San Francisco, he dragged his feet appointing a new director of the Mint, leaving Robert Preston in place. It wasn't until January 25, 1898, that George Roberts was nominated for the position.[15] Preston resigned and resumed his old position of examiner in the bureau.

The director's slot was now filled, but it had come about in a very odd manner. George Roberts was an Iowan and publisher of the *Fort Dodge Messenger*. As the politics of silver had heated up, Roberts found himself squarely behind the gold standard and sound currency.

Roberts's visibility rose substantially when he penned a persuasive rebuttal to the simplistic pamphlets issued by the silver movement. Roberts's work came to the attention of Lyman Gage, at that point president of the First National Bank of Chicago.

Gage, upon assuming the office of Treasury secretary, took with him Frank Vanderlip, one of the leading financial editors of Chicago. Both Vanderlip and Gage were very leery of the fire that Bryan had ignited over silver. Vanderlip advocated with Gage to hire George Roberts. Gage balked, "We haven't the money to employ such a person."

"Make him director of the mint," suggested Vanderlip, "and let him spend part of his time helping out in this campaign of education."[16] In later years Vanderlip would say that he always regarded George Roberts as the most lucid writer in the country on the subject of business economics.[17]

George Roberts was a kindly man with a wry sense of humor. He assumed his office on February 14, 1898. On the next Sunday, he went to church and wrote home afterwards that he had arrived just in time to help with the capital campaign to retire their debt.[18] He also was just in time to oversee the implementation of the most aggressive transformation ever undertaken by the Mint Service.

George Roberts became director of the Mint when Secretary of the Treasury Lyman Gage needed a place for this accomplished economics author. Roberts would preside over an unprecedented expansion of the Mint Service. However, when it came to coin design changes, Roberts's management style consisted of consensus building.

The struggle to replace the Mint at Philadelphia opened up all the arguments that had swirled around the authorization of its existing building. Move the Mint to Washington. No, move it to New York, the center of the nation's finances. When funding finally was authorized, the appropriations did not occur. The nation was locked in the depression of 1893 and discretionary government expenditures were on hold. Treasury Secretary Carlisle did not move to purchase land until the end of 1895.[19]

Philadelphia finally moved forward with the building completed at the beginning of 1900. The carving of the granite stone for the exterior had taken almost a year.[20] It would take another year to acquire and erect the equipment for the Mint. The Mint was placed in service on June 13, 1901, at a total cost of more than $2 million.[21] It was proclaimed to be the finest and best equipped in the world. Refining would be converted to the more efficient electrolytic method the following year.[22] Engraving was the one department where little change was put in place. The reducing lathe was not upgraded. However, medal presses were added to expand the medal-striking capability of the Mint. Otherwise, it was business as usual for engraver Charles Barber.

Fortunes also turned favorable for the Denver Mint in 1895. The production of gold in Colorado and the surrounding states had doubled in the preceding three years.[23] The move to upgrade the Denver facility quickly progressed from seeking to authorize coinage to the erection of a modern mint in place of the dilapidated assay office.[24]

The third mint structure in Philadelphia was placed in service in 1901. Billed as the finest mint operation in the world, it would leave the engraving department largely unchanged, including the Hill reducing machine, acquired in September 1867.

As with Philadelphia, this mint would be on a pay-as-you-go basis. Plans dragged. Construction startup was expected by mid-1897. Yet bids were not opened until January 1898. The building went under roof in the fall of 1900.[25] When George Roberts stated in May 1901 that work on the machinery would be commenced and carried on without delay, the Colorado newspapers interpreted that to mean sometime in the next five or six years.[26] There was real concern that Treasury would let the building sit idle.[27] In fact Treasury did just that; trial strikes on the coin presses did not occur until 1905 with circulating coinage issued in 1906.

There were also changes on the Pacific Coast. Gold was pouring in from the Klondike and the beaches of Nome. Congress acted with unusual quickness in 1898 to establish an assay office at Seattle; otherwise, the gold would flow into Canada at Vancouver.[28] In San Francisco an upgrade at the Mint was approved in 1902. Leach would convert from coal and wood to gas from the city gasworks for annealing purposes and electrify his minting equipment, eliminating the need for steam power. And like Philadelphia, electrolytic separation would be installed for refining.[29]

Throughout this process, the New Orleans Mint was the odd man out. Director Roberts repeatedly called for the Mint to be closed in his annual reports. He wanted its machinery transferred to the new Denver Mint, explaining the foot dragging there. Appropriations would repeatedly be omitted for its operation only to be reinserted by the Louisiana Congressional delegation with the promise of just one more year of operation. New Orleans kept alive on silver dollars and foreign coinage contracts, including Mexican dollars.[30] Money for operations would run out and the Mint close on June 30, 1909.

Overriding any issues at the Bureau of the Mint, the McKinley administration faced two major monetary issues. As of June 1, 1898, there remained in Treasury an uncoined silver bullion hangover from the Sherman Silver Purchase Act of 1890 of 97,507,425 ounces. Secretary Gage thus seized upon the potential seigniorage from coining this bullion as one piece in the puzzle to finance the Spanish American War that was now in full swing. To do that, he had to devise a way to monetize this seigniorage that basically amounted, after deducting the cost of the bullion used and the direct expense of mintage, to about 40 cents per dollar coined. He gained Congressional authorization to coin one million ounces of silver dollars monthly until July 1, 1901, for the redemption of Treasury Notes. After that date, as many silver dollars would be issued as necessary for the further redemption of the 102 million dollars' worth of outstanding Treasury Notes.[31]

In the midterm elections of 1898, Republicans had predictably sagged in numbers in the House of Representatives in spite of the resounding victory of the United States over Spain. However, they still held a solid majority, even after allowing for the defection of any silver men in their numbers. In the Senate, Republicans actually increased their numbers, commanding an overwhelming majority. Thus, Republicans were in a position to dominate the Fifty-Sixth Congress. First on their agenda on December 11, 1899, was HR.1, a bill to define and fix the standard of value such as to maintain parity of all forms of money issued or coined by the United States and for other purposes. In other words, it would place the United States unequivocally on the gold standard.[32] The timing was no accident. World gold production would double from 7.6 million fine troy ounces in 1893 to 14.8 million fine troy ounces in 1900.[33] The gains were coming from the gold strikes in the Yukon and Alaska, Australia, and South Africa.[34]

Lyman Gage, William McKinley's secretary of the Treasury, led the drive to place the United States firmly on the gold standard in 1900.

HR.1 was too simple and in some cases did not go far enough. Ultimately the Financial Act of 1900 was passed and signed into law on March 14. It defined the unit of value for the dollar to be 25.8 grains of 900 fine gold. Furthermore, it was the duty of the secretary of the Treasury to maintain all forms of money issued or coined at parity with this standard.

The act placed $150 million in gold coin and bullion into a redemption fund that was separate from the general fund. This fund was to be used for the redemption of United States Notes and Treasury Notes when exchanged for gold within the general fund. However, redeemed notes could not be used to meet deficiencies in current revenues. That clause was intended to break an endless chain of redemptions. If the redemption fund fell below $100 million, the secretary of the Treasury was empowered to restore the fund. He was specifically empowered to issue bonds if necessary for this purpose.

Gold Certificates would continue to be issued for deposits of gold coin for the convenience of commerce, as had been done since the end of the Civil War. Never before a major vehicle of value, they would assume a more important role due to the increased gold inflows. However, that authority would still be suspended should the gold redemption fund fall below $100 million. Likewise, the secretary had the option to suspend the issue of Gold Certificates whenever the Silver Certificates and United States Notes in the general fund exceeded $40 million, a protective measure to sustain the redemption fund.

For the bonds outstanding specifying repayment in coin, the act authorized the secretary of the Treasury to issue 2 percent gold bonds in a refunding exchange. Thus, the ambiguity that so plagued bondholders in times when the gold redemption fund was in jeopardy would be removed.

The act reaffirmed that the bullion from the Sherman Silver Purchase Act of 1890 was to be coined into silver dollars coupled with the issuance of Silver Certificates to provide for the retirement of Treasury Notes. It also allowed this bullion to be diverted to subsidiary silver coinage. Ultimately, the silver bullion surplus would be exhausted in 1904 and the striking of silver dollars discontinued.

Finally, the act authorized national banks to issue circulation notes up to 100 percent of their required holdings of Treasury bonds. Initial capital to organize a national bank was dropped from $50,000 to $25,000, and startups would be allowed in towns with as little population as 3,000.[35]

This legislation made real progress with one exception. Demand for money in the heartland was still seasonal, peaking during harvest. In the interim periods, the money moved to the financial centers in the East, primarily New York City, fueling risky speculation in the stock markets. As long as Congress was not ready to cede monetary control to a central bank, there were going to be times when excess speculation, either domestic or international, would bring about a serious economic downturn.

On March 4, 1897, John Sherman resigned from the Senate to become secretary of State under President McKinley. Mark Hanna succeeded Sherman into the Senate, much to the pleasure of William McKinley. Declining health and a failing memory forced Sherman to resign from the cabinet on April 25, 1898. John Sherman passed away October 22, 1900. As strong as his leadership in the Senate had been, his career should have been so much more.

Chapter 48
BARBER'S REVENGE

Charles Barber had been stung by the treatment of the muled Columbian Exposition award medal in its New York exhibit. He believed Saint-Gaudens to have been behind it, either directly or indirectly. He would bide his time, but he would have a last word in this feud with the sculptor.

With the upcoming United States participation in the French Exposition Universelle of 1900, a grassroots movement was initiated to erect a statue of Lafayette in Paris. In January 1899, the Lafayette Memorial Commission went to Congress to ask for supplemental funding in the form of 100,000 souvenir half dollars to be sold for one dollar apiece. At that point, it was contemplated that the design would incorporate a miniature of the proposed Lafayette statue on one side and a symbol significant to the event with an appropriate inscription on the other side.[1]

Congress instead saw these commemorative coins as an opportunity to unload some of the excess silver bullion. They would appropriate $25,000 for 50,000 ounces of silver bullion. On its last day of its last session, the Fifty-Fifth Congress authorized the issue of 50,000 circulating silver dollars to be struck and sold to the public for two dollars apiece.[2]

On April 5, 1899, George Roberts met in Washington with Robert Thompson, the secretary of the Lafayette Memorial Commission. Roberts was in favor of a design using the heads of Washington and Lafayette in jugate on one side and the monument on the other. However, the commission had other ideas. Roberts suggested that

Thompson meet with Barber to refine possibilities for the design. However, one point was clear: The design for the Lafayette Dollar would not originate from an outside artist.

The head of the commission, Ferdinand Peck, wanted Lafayette's Prayer as part of the coin's inscriptions. Barber resisted it in his meeting with Thompson. A prayer of this length would eliminate all possibilities for beauty and originality on the side of the coin on which it was to be employed. Thompson countered by asking if the size of the dollar coin could be increased. Barber rebutted that the reduced thickness of the coin would leave less metal available to be moved. It would be impossible to obtain a suitable impression from the dies using one strike of the coin presses. The Mint was already pushed to the limit striking the dollar coin used for general circulation. This problem would especially be true if Roberts, as Barber expected, picked the jugate heads as one of the design motifs. This style required a greater relief for an effective appearance.[3]

Peck was unyielding; he wanted the prayer. Charles Barber rightly rebelled. This proposal had no artistic merit.[4]

Barber proceeded to prepare sketches for the coin that Roberts forwarded for the Lafayette Commission's review on April 22, 1899. On the obverse were the jugate heads of Washington and Lafayette and on the reverse, a representation of the statue. Roberts went on to set forth the Mint's objections to including a prayer using Barber's arguments and added that the coin would be of interest in Paris where good art was recognized.[5]

At first Peck gave in, accepting the designs proposed by Roberts and Barber. Then he reopened the issue. Peck now wanted to include at least a part of Lafayette's Prayer. He enclosed a sketch showing how it might be done with separate representations of the faces of Washington and Lafayette.[6]

Barber was harshly critical of Peck's representations of the two men—mere masks.[7] That earned the engraver a trip to New York City to meet with the Lafayette Memorial Commission. Paul Wayland Bartlett, sculptor for the memorial, and member of an advisory group would be at the meeting. Roberts assured Barber that the artists with whom Peck was conferring would surely side with the engraver.[8]

Indeed, Barber returned from the meeting feeling vindicated that the Mint would hear no more of the prayer. Peck now understood that space on the coin for decoration was really limited, given the desire to have the monument displayed. In consequence, the commission now was asking that the monument be represented without the pedestal. As soon as Barber had a photograph from Bartlett of his model, he would make more sketches.

While Barber was indeed in concurrence with the commission, he came away from the meeting with a serious concern. There was real potential for delay well into 1900 if the depiction of the monument on the coin's reverse was to be accurate. Bartlett's work still must be submitted to a committee for approval.[9]

After some additional correspondence, the project sat idle. On July 6, Barber wrote to Roberts stating he would begin die preparation as soon as he was provided a rendering of the equestrian statue.[10] For the next three months Barber took no initiative.

Dialogue reopened in October. Thompson had seen a newspaper interview with George Roberts in which the director supposed that the Lafayette dollar would not be issued until the coming year. The secretary of the Lafayette Memorial Commission reacted instantly, having understood that the coin would be into their hands for distribution in time for holiday sales.[11] Roberts in reply was forced to admit that he had disengaged himself from the project. He had learned of changes underway on the monument and had deduced that the coin would be delayed as well, given Barber's desire that the statue be accurately represented on the reverse. He had to admit that he had not conferred recently with Barber and that Thompson might be better informed than he as to where Barber stood with the engraving.[12] The nicety of an exact final replica of the Lafayette statue on the coin was going to be foregone.

On November 23, the first "specimen" coin was forwarded to Roberts from Philadelphia.[13] The director duly sent it on to Ferdinand Peck.[14] A very pleased Peck replied three days later. He had shown the coin to Frank Millet. Millet had charge of the decoration of the U. S. government's pavilion at the Exposition Universelle and was on the selection jury of the fine arts jury for the overall exposition as well.[15] Millet pronounced the coin artistic and better in every way than the regular dollar coin.[16] The Treasury Department, in releasing this statement to the press, was praising Charles Barber at the expense of his assistant, George Morgan.[17]

Conceived to help fund a statue of Lafayette in Paris, this commemorative silver dollar, bearing a date of 1900, was designed by Charles Barber—his best work as engraver.

The commission requested a small ceremony with the press in attendance to celebrate the first strike.[18] Roberts set the event in Philadelphia for December 14, the 100th anniversary of the death of George Washington.[19] Fifty thousand of these dollar coins were minted that day. However, the event was all a show. The first striking, a proof, had been sent to the Mint director the day before.[20] Ultimately, President McKinley would convey that coin to the Republic of France.[21,22]

Overall, this issue was a modest commercial success with sales amounting to 36,000 coins. Most of the remaining 14,000 of the authorized issue ultimately were melted.[23] Subsequent critics would point out flaws in Barber's work. To ensure that the design struck up well, Barber washed out much of the obverse relief, giving the busts a linear appearance. Barber was also scored for the lack of originality of the obverse composition. The final result was all too close to the medal by Peter Krider struck for the centennial of the battle of Yorktown in 1881.

Yet the critics of Barber's work overlooked one small detail on the reverse design. On the plinth, clearly spelled out was the last name of the sculptor, Bartlett. Coming from the engraver who had given no credit to Olin Warner for the Columbian half dollar, this sudden desire to share credit was out of character. Paul Bartlett was the son of Truman Bartlett, the man who had made a profession of questioning the abilities of Saint-Gaudens and had actively spread the malicious rumor that Saint-Gaudens had started the fire that consumed the Morgan Tomb. Barber had gotten in a subtle and effective shot at Saint-Gaudens.

Chapter 49
In the Bright Sunlight of Morning

The weather smiled on Saint-Gaudens for his homecoming. Fresh southerly winds pushed white clouds across the blue skies, and temperatures hovered near 80 degrees.[1] However, as he sailed into New York harbor on July 23, 1900, it was nothing like what he would have envisioned it.[2] He could not enjoy the *Statue of Liberty* or bask in the fact that he was a shining example of all that it symbolized. During the voyage he had suffered from mental and physical exhaustion. His wife, Gussie, alerted by an advance telegram, met him at the gangplank.[3]

The country was in the midst of a presidential campaign. McKinley was seeking reelection. However, Saint-Gaudens had not the slightest interest. In 48 hours his wife had Gus checked into Massachusetts General Hospital. The operation to remove the cancerous tumor in his lower intestines was performed on July 28. Almost miraculously, Saint-Gaudens escaped infection and survived the surgery.[4] However, the cancer discovery had come late. As part of the surgery, a colostomy was performed.[5] The attending doctors expected another operation would be necessary in five to seven years.[6]

Most of August was spent recuperating at the hospital.[7] Saint-Gaudens wrote Stanford White that he was as full of holes as porous plaster.[8] When sufficiently recovered, he journeyed to his summer home at Cornish, New Hampshire. October passed well enough, but November found Gus back in another Boston area hospital, St. Margaret's, for a second surgery. Gussie tersely said that it was not a success.[9] An attempt had been made to reconnect the colon and eliminate the need for the colostomy.[10]

It was not supposed to have turned out this way.

In what must have seemed like an eon ago to the sculptor, Saint-Gaudens had arrived in Paris in the fall of 1897 and endured the agony of finding suitable space for a studio. The task was made more complicated because of the space requirement for the equestrian *Sherman*. He also had other projects, even bringing along a plaster cast of the *Shaw* to tinker with, regardless of the fact that it had been cast and dedicated. However, the *Sherman* came first. The Sherman Committee had been upset with the lack of progress; the contractual completion date had long since come and gone.[11] To placate them Gus had brought Phimister Proctor to model Sherman's horse while he struggled with the *Shaw*.

Saint-Gaudens found four connected studios on the Left Bank and proceeded to combine them into one large space with a separate inner sanctum.[12] To help in the studio, Gus initially had only one assistant.[13] Subsequently he brought Henry Hering to Paris. Hering had studied under his guidance for four years at the Art Students League in New York.[14] Gus's brother, Louis, came and went.[15] In 1899, Gus added James Earle Fraser. The young man had won the prize in the 1898 Paris Salon for best work by an American. He was currently studying at the Ecole des Beaux-Arts. More importantly, Fraser had won the American Art Association's Wanamaker Prize for which Gus had been a juror.[16,17] His winning exhibit had been a model of his western Native American themed *End of the Trail*. Fraser recalled later that Gus liked his Indian.[18]

Even with this help, conditions in the studio could be chaotic. An accident happened to the cast of one of the horse's hind legs on the *Sherman;* Gus was not concerned. He had a duplicate cast of the horse in Cornish. He sent a man back to retrieve the duplicate leg and oversee its packing. Returning three weeks later, the man had the wrong hind leg. Later it would make a great story, but at the time it put grey hairs on his red head.[19]

When Saint-Gaudens was enthusiastically at work on the *Sherman*, days came and went rapidly.[20] His goal was to exhibit the completed *Sherman* in the 1900 Exposition Universelle in Paris. He wrote Gussie on February 26, 1898, that the model, including the Angel of Victory, was entirely finished.[21] Of course, Gus was not allowing for the endless refinements that he must work through.

The "finished" Angel of Victory soon suffered under his critical eye and underwent modifications. The head of Victory no longer resembled the bust he had made of Hettie Anderson. Gus was also struggling with drapery for the angel. He always considered arranging flowing draperies a complicated task. He used muslin calicoes that had a little starch in them.[22] It was a matter of personal taste. He took four weeks before settling on a final arrangement.[23]

As 1898 drew to a close, Gus was well along with the *Sherman*, writing confidently to Stanford White that the model was done. He was planning some travel as his assistants translated the model into plaster.[24] Then the same hind leg on the full-sized model of the horse plagued him again. It seemed that the leg had a tendency to sag. Each time, his assistants would patch the resulting cracks without his knowledge. Over time, the leg had thus lengthened by three inches.[25] His eye had finally caught the problem.

The general's cloak became the next point of frustration. He described his trials with the cloak to his son, Homer.

> I've just remodeled the cloak over for the 10,000th time and today it seems beautiful. Tomorrow it will probably appear hellish and so things go.[26]

With the help of a manikin, he was finally able to satisfy himself with a much simpler arrangement for the offending cloak.[27]

Gus's plan was to exhibit the *Sherman* first at the 1899 Paris Salon. He intended to show Sherman on horseback in full size, accompanied by a small model including the Angel of Victory. This Salon would give him his first indication of how well he was progressing and perhaps how the Paris critics would receive his work. If all went well, he would then exhibit the completed *Sherman* at the Exposition Universelle in 1900.

If possible, Gus's personal life was even more chaotic than his studio life during this period. Gussie did not particularly like Paris the second time around. In the summer of 1898 she left for the spas. The following summer and fall she returned to Cornish in a visit prolonged by the death of her mother. Meanwhile at some point in 1899, Gus brought his mistress, Davida, and their son over. In a letter of exasperation to his brother that fall, Gus said that Gussie didn't like Paris and was coming back on November 1. Davida didn't like it either and wanted to leave. He called it a funny world.[28]

Depression now plagued the sculptor. Henry Adams told of a time in Paris when Saint-Gaudens showed up at his doorstep to pour out his woes. In Adams's words, the sculptor was suffering from an oppression of life and dread of death. In typical Adams fashion, Henry flippantly replied that he never felt any other way and actually rather liked it.[29]

Counterbalancing the depression and perhaps as a result of it, there were periods of relaxation when Gus left the studio behind. His friendship and affection for Elizabeth Cameron, now separated from her husband and living in Paris, seemed to grow.[30] They exchanged mildly flirtatious notes concerning social engagements. Gus dined with her to celebrate the Fourth of July in 1899.[31] There were also motoring expeditions with Adams through the French countryside.[32]

The opening of the Salon for 1899 was scheduled for May 1. As April waned, the studio became a bedlam. Saint-Gaudens had eleven molders working night and day on the *Sherman.* Sometimes Gus would laugh, sometimes cry, and sometimes both during the process.[33] For what might have been a first in his life, he met the deadline.

Now, as the *Sherman* stood in the place of honor in the center of the garden at the Champ-de-Mars, Gus for the first time could feel cocky.[34] Still he would come to the garden with his assistants for additional work from first light until the Salon opened at ten in the morning.[35] Henry Adams in his strolls stopped almost every day to admire the colossal work.[36]

When Gussie returned to Paris that fall, she found, to her surprise, her husband still poking around on the Angel of Victory that she had expected to be long since completed.[37] As the exhibition on the Champ-de-Mars ended, the angel had acquired a free forward-swinging gait and her features were youthful, soft, and sweet.[38] Now in the late fall Gus had changed the model again. Gussie called it very stunning.[39] Saint-Gaudens had pulled it all together. The angel grasped a palm leaf in her left hand. Her right hand was raised with authority, as if she were clearing away a path for horse and rider.[40] Her stride was bold and confident. Her head was crowned with laurel. The face had matured. She had a clear-eyed gaze, firm but rounded chin and straight nose.[41]

Was it Elizabeth Sherman Cameron? In Saint-Gaudens's autobiography, Homer Saint-Gaudens said of his father that in his ideal sculpture, little or no resemblance could be traced to a model. Saint-Gaudens was always quick to reject the least taint of what he called "personality" in such instances.[42] In general, that statement is true. Gus would tinker with his work until the likeness to the model was washed out and an idealized portrait emerged. However, there were exceptions. Characteristics of Davida Clark are clearly visible in his *Diana* and the *Amor Caritas*.

Arline Tehan, in her book *Henry Adams in Love*, made a strong case. Citing Sherman family legend and studio gossip,[43] Tehan noted the similarity of the facial features of Lizzie to those of the angel. She also stated that Gus sent the Anders Zorn etching to Lizzie.[44] The innuendo is there.

Saint-Gaudens himself gave another clue. Some five years after his return to America when he was in New York, Lizzie sent him a ticket to *Parsifal*. He responded that he had wanted to see this Wagnerian favorite but had lacked the executive ability to make it happen. "Now like a good angel you send me one."[45]

Tehan cited another example. In her final years, Lizzie lived with her son-in-law in England. A young Cambridge graduate student from America came to visit her. His father, an architect, had been a close confidant of Lizzie in a friendship dating to 1903. The young man drove up to the old Georgian mansion that Lizzie called home. He "suddenly caught sight of her standing on the steps, her head thrown back, her arms outstretched and held slightly backward, looking for all the world like the Angel of Victory."[46] That young man was Burke Wilkinson, future biographer of Augustus Saint-Gaudens.

There is one last piece of secondary evidence that comes directly from the Sherman family. In October 1902, Rachel Sherman (now Mrs. Paul Thorndike) wrote Saint-Gaudens after having seen the finished *Sherman* for the first time. She was deeply moved and wrote a long letter to the sculptor revealing her innermost emotions. Nothing of consequence appeared until the closing when Rachel, knowing of Gus's penchant for unending changes added, "Please do not change the Victory. I shall never forget her face that morning (of the viewing)." Rachel had instantly recognized the resemblance.[47] So it was for those who knew her that Elizabeth Sherman Cameron, intended or not, became the "Angel of Victory."

With the success of the Paris Salon behind him, the desired recognition came Gus's way. At the end of 1899 he was elected a member of the Institut de France. To cap that, Saint-Gaudens was awarded the cross of the Legion of Honor, in which he was made an *officier*. The ultimate compliment occurred when the French government purchased the original bronze of his *Amor Caritas* for display at the Luxembourg.[48] In gratitude he presented the Louvre with casts in three diameters of his World's Columbian Exhibition Award Medal.[49] Gus was very much in demand but also making his point about the snub of his medal in 1894.

The Exposition Universelle of 1900 opened on April 14. The French hosted these expositions on eleven-year cycles. The *Sherman Monument* was ready. Saint-Gaudens was again very cocky about the work, particularly with its Angel of Victory.[50] It received "special placement" among the sculptures in the Grand Palais. However, Gus was not happy with the overall presentation. He wrote that "such a collection of sculpture, rammed together ignominiously, has never been seen nor ever can occur again."[51]

The *Sherman* appears in the center of this image of the exhibition hall for sculpture in Paris.

Still the *Sherman* achieved high recognition, receiving a Grand Prix and a gold medal. There was a final recognition of his work that involved no medal, no honor. Saint-Gaudens also exhibited the "touched up" *Shaw* plaster at the Exposition Universelle. Auguste Rodin, in one of his extravagant gestures, doffed his hat before it and stood bareheaded in tribute.[52]

Gussie left Paris in June sharing in the glow of her husband's triumph but frustrated over his health. He seemed all used up.[53]

With the pressure of preparing for the exhibition at an end, Saint-Gaudens resolved to consult the doctors about the illness and the exhaustion that seemed to be his constant companions. He worried that he might have a heart condition.[54] The diagnosis of intestinal cancer, far worse, left Gus in complete shock and denial. As bad as the diagnosis was, the prognosis was worse. Antibiotics did not exist, and the probability for deadly infection from the surgery was extremely high. He was being struck down at the moment of his greatest triumph.

The young Fraser recounted Saint-Gaudens's dreadful reaction to this tragic twist.

> I was working in the studio early one morning when he suddenly burst through the street door and went directly from our studio into his own. In a few minutes I heard the outside door in his studio slam. It was all so unusual that I was rather startled, but thought possibly he might have been in a hurry and got on with my work.
>
> In about an hour and a half he came in again and said, "Fraser, come into my studio, I must tell you something." I went in and I noticed that his look was unusual and very excited, and he said. "I have just had the most extraordinary experience. You know I have never been ill in my life—as a matter of fact, I never thought of death, but it now appears that I am seriously ill and must go home for an operation. I am greatly worried and have been sleepless for many nights. Suddenly this morning, I decided that I would end it all, and when I came here I had definitely made up my mind to jump into the Seine. As I left here I practically ran down the Rue de Rennes toward the Seine. As I looked up at the buildings they all seemed to have written across the top a huge word in black letters—Death, Death, Death. This on all the buildings. You can readily understand my mental state. I ran—I was in so much of a hurry! I reached the river and went up on the bridge and as I looked over the water, I saw the Louvre in the bright morning sunlight, it seemed wonderfully beautiful, and suddenly everything was sufficient to me, the Louvre was wonderful—more remarkable than I had ever seen it before. Whether the running and hurrying had changed my mental attitude, I can't say—possibly it might have been the beauty of the Louvre's architecture or the sparkling water of the Seine—whatever it was, the weight and blackness suddenly lifted from my mind and I was happy and found myself whistling", and he still seemed excited and happy and I felt that he had passed a dreadful crisis and was safe for the time. [55]

Whatever the cause, the depression lifted as a veil and Gus lost all desire to do away with himself.[56] Yet Saint-Gaudens did nothing. He did not schedule the operation. He did not book passage back home. He was in this condition of mental paralysis when Stanford White discovered him, took matters in hand and booked passage for Saint-Gaudens back to the United States.[57]

Just how good was the *Sherman Monument?* Yes, it had received a Grand Prix and a gold medal at the Exposition Universelle. However, the Exposition had generated 42,790 awards in total. Included were 2,827 Grand Prix and 8,166 gold medals.[58] The *Sherman* awards were just two among many. The final judges would be his countrymen.

Chapter 50
To Buffalo and Beyond

Saint-Gaudens, successfully mending after his ordeal of two surgeries, enjoyed that first winter of 1900–01 in Cornish but wasn't prepared for the spring thaw. Early spring snow melts led to flooding with the mud season reigning supreme.[1] Wanting nothing to do with this kind of dismal weather, Gus fled to Henry Adams's home. In fact, for Saint-Gaudens, spring with Henry Adams in Washington would become an annual ritual.[2] He found the comings and goings of the salon regulars entertaining. Henry was as acidic as ever; his drawing room was open to all and yet closed to but a few of his truly close associates. He had endured the inauguration of McKinley who had easily overcome William Jennings Bryan for a second term, again losing only the "Solid South" and the silver states. At the end of the Washington social season, Adams would leave to join Lizzie Cameron in Paris.

Yet there was a decided difference to the salons now. Theodore and Edith Roosevelt were back in town. As McKinley's running mate, Roosevelt had carried the heavy burden of the campaign, giving speeches against Bryan and silver throughout the country.

Saint-Gaudens had more on his mind that spring than the mud of Cornish. His *Sherman* had no home. Charles McKim was providing the pedestal and had fronted for

Shown here in the small Kentucky town of Mt. Sterling, just one stop among many, Theodore Roosevelt served as the point man in McKinley's campaign for reelection in 1900.

the sculptor during his time in Paris in finding a suitable location in New York City for its erection. McKim's original intention had been to locate the memorial at the south end of the mall in Central Park. Such a plan, if executed, would have presented the *Sherman* most favorably. However, it also would irreparably alter the original design and concept for this portion of the park.[3]

At the end of March 1900, the city's Parks Commission had decided that all statuary, existing as well as proposed, must harmonize with the scenery of the parks. There was already too much statuary in the parks, and it had been placed without regard to the best interests of art and landscape gardening. The adopted regulations were sweeping; no statue would be erected in any New York park where scenery was predominant. Statues could be placed as adjuncts of buildings, bridges, or viaducts to heighten and beautify the effect of the scenery. Only statues of great artistic beauty and of great national or universal interest could be placed in small parks or at the intersection of two or more avenues.[4]

Concurrently, McKim's planned location leaked into the public domain. On April 10, the *New York Times* ran an inflammatory editorial. Without naming Saint-Gaudens or McKim specifically, the editorial called them artistic vandals. The proposed placement of the equestrian statue would destroy the effect of the mall for no better reason than that it was the most conspicuous site that could be found for the monument. It was the most serious disfigurement of the park ever proposed.[5]

Other alternatives met with a host of different objections so that for the time being, the *Sherman* was homeless. Saint-Gaudens's illness then put this issue into an extended holding pattern.

In March 1901, William Coffin, who helped to bring the Washington Inauguration Centennial medal to closure, began writing Saint-Gaudens in Cornish. He had seen Gus in Paris and gotten a commitment from the sculptor to exhibit a plaster of his *Shaw Memorial* and some lesser works at the upcoming Pan-American Exposition. This exposition was the first major American effort since Chicago and hopes were riding high for its success. As director of the Exposition's Fine Arts Division, Coffin was determined to have the *Sherman Monument.* He was adamant, pestering Gus with letters almost daily in April. Gus was reluctant. The plaster cast of the *Sherman* had arrived damaged and there were the never-ending modifications to be made. Coffin was persistent, offering to pay all the costs of mounting. Gus relented. He sent Henry Hering to oversee the installation and patch the damage.[6]

The opening of the Pan-American Exposition was set for May 20. Saint-Gaudens came to New York City well in advance. This being the first American exhibition of his equestrian group, Gus was anxious about its reception in America. He had already been to the exposition fairgrounds to inspect the erected work. Coffin had been true to his word. The *Sherman* had a prime location in front of the Fine Arts Building, facing south. Coffin had even removed a fountain that was in the way. Although the *Sherman* faced the Fine Arts Building, Gus was content with the nearby Delaware Park Lake as a backdrop. His only objection was the pedestal; it did not suit. As a result, Coffin had the offending surfaces hacked out and a new pedestal created.[7] Saint-Gaudens was being grandly treated in Buffalo.

Vice President Theodore Roosevelt had the honor of officially opening the exposition. The man had come a long way very quickly since exiting the New York City police commissioner's job in 1897. With the advent of war with Spain, Roosevelt had resigned as assistant secretary of the Navy to raise a volunteer cavalry regiment composed of adventurers and cowboys, nicknamed the Rough Riders. He had assumed second in command of the regiment and ultimately commanded it in an assault at Kettle Hill outside Santiago de Cuba that made him a national hero. Of course, it helped that Roosevelt made good press for the war correspondents, thus ensuring his exploits captivated the American public.

After all the dust had settled, Mark Twain likened Roosevelt's public recognition to a political Klondike.[8] Upon Theodore's return from Cuba, the New York Republicans nominated him for governor. Thomas Platt had found himself needing a squeaky-clean candidate or face loss of the governor's mansion to the Democrats. Two years later, Platt had had all Governor Roosevelt's reform he could stomach. The second spot on the McKinley ticket was available after the untimely death of Vice President Garret Hobart. Platt had been persistent in pushing for Roosevelt's selection for the post at the convention. Roosevelt had been publicly reluctant. Mark Hanna had had grave misgivings exclaiming: "Don't any of you realize there is only one life between this madman and the presidency?" Cabot Lodge counseled Roosevelt to accept in preparation for a run for the presidency in 1904. In the end, Roosevelt accepted the nomination.

On the appointed day in Buffalo, Vice-President Theodore Roosevelt arose to do his duty in the opening ceremonies. He used the occasion to renew the principles of the Monroe Doctrine.[9] He based his speech in part on six or seven quotes from among those that Richard Watson Gilder had been asked to provide for the

Thomas Platt reigned as boss of New York State Republicans but he could not rule over Theodore Roosevelt.

exposition.[10] The exposition people had used the quotes to adorn the buildings of the Fair. As Roosevelt spoke, he made eye contact with Gilder who was seated with Edith Roosevelt. He would come over toward Gilder and hurl one of the inscriptions directly at him. Everyone praised the inscriptions that left Gilder saying that he had never had so much taffy.[11]

Saint-Gaudens was there only to take a brief walk around the *Sherman* to see again how it appeared in the light. He was satisfied with the figure but still was not happy with the horse that he thought looked as if it were trotting into a barn.[12] After the speeches, there were tours and special activities arranged for Roosevelt's party. Edith was particularly taken by the *Sherman*.[13] Likewise, the press hailed the *Sherman*'s arresting beauty.[14]

It was an interesting time for the otherwise bored vice-president. On the way back home, Theodore, Alice, and Edith stopped at Genesco to visit friends and go horseback riding. Edith then wanted to spend some time in Albany. The afternoon of May 28 found Roosevelt traveling alone back to Oyster Bay.

Hermon MacNeil designed the exposition's award medal. Black Diamond served as the model for the reverse. James Earle Fraser would later use this same animal for his nickel design.

G.T. Brewster designed the official souvenir medal (HK-287) for the exposition. Its obverse depicts a Native American on a soaring eagle.

On the train he happened upon Saint-Gaudens, traveling with Finley Peter Dunne. Now the loquacious Theodore and the shy Gus with Finley Peter Dunne thrown in for leavening took lunch together.[15] All three were master storytellers. Theodore tended to overuse the first-person singular in his tales, but they did not lack in color. Dunne was a nationally syndicated political satirist, renowned for his "Dooley" stories patterned after an old-time Irish saloonkeeper in South Side Chicago. Dunne, at the end of 1899, had parodied Roosevelt's book *The Rough Riders* in a tongue-in-cheek review saying the book should have been titled "Alone in Cuba." Gus was no slouch himself. He was noted for his vivid descriptions and scene setting. He was also a good listener. Only Roosevelt recorded the chance meeting, and it was scant in detail. He wrote his son that it was great fun talking with the two men and that he liked them both.[16]

Roosevelt wasted no time in cementing the bond. He wrote Saint-Gaudens on May 31 to invite the sculptor and his wife to come to Sagamore Hill as houseguests. But there was more.

> Probably you never will realize what a real comfort and source of pride you have been to me. I am very proud of America and very jealous of American achievement. It has been to me a source of real regret and concern to see how our writers have passed away and left no one to take up their plumes and as no amount of mere material achievement seems to me worth while, if taken purely by itself—I mean mere increase in wealth and industrial facilities—it is always a relief to think that there is one American in the prime of his powers who is leaving us the *Lincoln*, the *Farragut*, the *Sherman*, the monument to Shaw, and so much else that represents a real addition to the national sum of permanent achievement.[17]

Roosevelt not only admired Saint-Gaudens's works, he had just critically identified the sculptor's very best public monuments.

Back at Cornish, Gus erected a third plaster of the *Sherman* in the shed. He had brought James Earle Fraser to help him work through the never-ending improvements. He modified the tail of the horse and added tiny angles and stiff marks of age to the animal that he felt increased its "nervous snap."[18] Sherman's cloak and the mane of the horse received more work. To the everlasting discomfort of white Southerners, he added pine boughs to the base of the statue to symbolize Georgia.[19]

The plaster cast of the *Sherman Monument* and staff at Cornish after the exposition. James Earle Fraser is second from the left, and Saint-Gaudens third from the left.

As the summer waned, the various juries of award for the Pan-American Exposition announced their recommendations. The three-man Jury of Awards for the Fine Arts Division that included Daniel Chester French and Phimister Proctor singled out Saint-Gaudens for the extraordinary and altogether exceptional merit of his work. The jury unanimously recommended the sculptor for the award of a special diploma and Medal of Honor, above and apart from all other awards and created solely for his work. Certainly an honor, but it carried a taint of home cooking, given that French and Proctor were friends. On August 2, 1901, the Superior Jury adopted this recommendation.[20] James Earle Fraser would receive the commission to create this special award medal.

Theodore Roosevelt spent the summer at Oyster Bay with his family. It had not been this peaceful for him since before the Spanish American War. He took two trips west to Colorado and Minnesota. Little note was made that President McKinley would be touring the Pan-American Exposition during the waning days of summer. Theodore was in Vermont, a guest of the Vermont Fish and Game League on September 6 when he learned the president had been shot by a young anarchist, Leon Czolgosz. Roosevelt rushed to McKinley's side. The president had a serious abdominal wound. However, McKinley was so recovered that all thought it appropriate on September

James Earle Fraser designed the special Medal of Honor awarded to Augustus Saint-Gaudens at the Pan-American Exposition. However, Fraser did not complete his work until after the death of Saint-Gaudens.

10 that Roosevelt leave, projecting an air of confidence to the situation. Theodore gathered Edith and two of their children for a climbing expedition in the Adirondacks. On September 14, it happened. McKinley had taken a turn for the worse on the day before, and Roosevelt was summoned back to Buffalo. First by buckboard and then by a waiting train that hurried through the night, Roosevelt arrived too late. Theodore Roosevelt became the 26th president of the United States. He was going to be a catalyst for change and the United States would never be the same.

Theodore Roosevelt arrives at John Milburn's house to take the oath of office. He has yet to change into formal dress for the ceremony.

As Theodore and Edith moved into the Executive Mansion, they were presiding over a city that in the post Civil War period had experienced unbounded growth, straying far from L'Enfant's original plans. A paramount issue was the integrity of the Mall being threatened by a Pennsylvania Railroad proposal to expand its station, at Sixth Street, NW.[21] In addition Colonel Theodore Bingham of the Army Corp of Engineers and head of the Office of Public Buildings and Grounds was proposing to expand and substantially alter the Executive Mansion.

That whole affair had started the preceding year as efforts got underway to celebrate the centennial of the establishment of the nation's capital at Washington. A centerpiece of the celebration called for the restoration of the Mall. A measure had been introduced in the Senate in May 1900 calling for a board of experts in architecture, landscape architecture, and sculpture to address the Mall, the Executive Mansion, and other issues. It died in the House. Joe Cannon, the dictatorial chairman of the House Committee on Appropriations, strongly believed any activity even remotely associated with the fine arts would degenerate into a raid on the federal treasury. [22]

In a second effort, Senator James McMillan, chairman of the Committee on the District of Columbia introduced a resolution calling for a master development plan that again failed in the House. Not to be denied, in a backroom maneuver, McMillan gained approval for his committee to report to the full Senate plans for the development and improvement of the entire parks system of the District of Columbia. Thus, the Senate Park Commission was born on March 19, 1901. [23]

McMillan wanted Daniel Burnham with his reputation from the World's Columbian Exposition, to head the committee. McKim was quickly added followed by Frederic Law Olmstead, Jr. son of the designer for New York City's Central Park. It wasn't long afterwards that McKim gained approval to bring Augustus Saint-Gaudens on board as the fourth member.

In the summer of 1901, Charles McKim in particular began to devote full time to the Senate Park Commission report. The game plan was to finish by the end of the year, but there were problems to be addressed. The Victorian building housing the Smithsonian Institution on the south side of the Mall was at odds with the Beaux Arts classicism to be incorporated into the master plan. Acknowledging the fact that razing the

Charles Follen McKim was a true friend to Augustus Saint-Gaudens. McKim also relied heavily upon the sculptor's unfailing critical eye.

building was unlikely, the committee settled on the solution of using a screen of trees to mask the building's facades.[24]

A thornier question was the location of a memorial to Abraham Lincoln. Gradually through the adroit hand of Elihu Root with John Hay in the background, the Senate Park Commission came around to the position that the spot at the west end of the Mall nearest the Potomac should be reserved for Abraham Lincoln.[25]

Yet Burnham scored the biggest coup. A. J. Cassatt, president of the Pennsylvania Railroad, had previously retained him to design the railway station that would open onto the Mall. Being the artist Mary Cassatt's brother, the man was sympathetic to Burnham's cause. Still he would not yield a position of value without receiving something in return. If the Senate would appropriate $1,500,000 to assist in tunneling under the Capitol Building, he would relocate the planned station to the north of the Mall.[26] Learning of the proposal, Senator McMillan pushed the necessary appropriation forward.[27]

On the morning of January 15, 1902, McKim formally unveiled the plan to the Senate Committee on the District of Columbia. It was clear to all that the inspiration for this plan was the White City of the World's Columbian Exposition of 1893. The reception was positive. At noon, the report was submitted to the full Senate. That afternoon Congress, the cabinet, and President and Mrs. Roosevelt attended a follow-up special presentation in the Corcoran Gallery.[28] This president was going to take an active role in the process, compared to the passive McKinley.

John Hay, with an obvious concern for the man he had once served as secretary, went straight to the proposed location of the Lincoln memorial. He understood the significance of its axis with the Capitol and the Washington Monument and liked it.[29] In Hay's opinion, nothing should be near the Immortals.[30] This location did that for Lincoln.

The presentation was a success. However, the question of whether the Washington politicians would follow the plan remained unanswered.

Chapter 51
The Art of Governance

For Edith Roosevelt in that first winter in the Executive Mansion, there was a more immediate and pressing matter than the plan for future development of Washington. Her new home was ill-prepared to handle a young family with six children. The second floor of the mansion provided both the office for the president and his living quarters. Edith made do as best she could with the cramped quarters. She appropriated the library as her personal space. It had a private door into Theodore's office. In this manner the two could consult between Theodore's meetings.[1] Frequently the president had to appropriate the library for a conference or a waiting room for special visitors. Edith would afterwards say, tongue in cheek, the windows had to be opened "to let out all the politicians!"[2] Accommodating overnight visitors added another layer of complexity. The first of a steady stream was Watson Gilder.[3] With only one room normally available for guests, Edith found herself in the awkward position of needing to know beforehand if a husband and wife shared the same bedroom. To top it all off, there were only two bathrooms on the second floor.[4]

With the opening of the 1902 social season, Edith served notice that she would be a different first lady. She had a personal agenda before it became the accepted norm for first ladies. She would use the traditional first lady's weekly reception to promote the fine arts in the form of musicales. She did it after discussing its appropriateness with Theodore.[5] She started simply with light chamber music in the Green Room.

Adding his own touch, the president was on hand to give autographed copies of *The Rough Riders* to departing guests.

As the season wound down, Edith stepped out in what would become her standard in the years to come. She invited the renowned pianist, Ignace Paderewski, to perform on the evening of April 3.[6] Her guest list for the evening reflected the importance of the occasion. She invited among others, Augustus Saint-Gaudens and his wife. The guests were received in the Green Room and then moved to the East Room that had been converted into a music hall. Gus and Gussie had front row seats.[7] The performance began at ten. A magnificent grand piano with a solid gold-leaf cover had been wheeled between the double east doors. Afterwards a light dinner was served where Theodore and Edith mingled freely with the guests.[8] It was a brilliant evening for all.[9]

Edith Kermit Roosevelt, pictured here in 1900, retained her youthful beauty that belied the inner strength that she brought to bear as Theodore Roosevelt's wife in the White House. Written upon this photograph in Theodore's hand is the notation "Mistress of Sagamore Hill."

Edith's next effort started innocently enough. Congress had appropriated some $16,000 for the routine upkeep of the Executive Mansion, now more familiarly known as the White House. She was in a quandary as to how best to spend the money. Instinctively, she wanted to do right by the structure so she turned to Charles Follen McKim.

Yet McKim was not prepared for what he saw on his walk-through of April 15, 1902. He told Edith that the appropriation would not even pay for a proper cleaning of the mansion, much less repairs. After he left the White House, he went to see Charles Moore, who served as liaison to the Senate Park Commission. The two men had become fast friends, and as McKim unburdened himself, Senator McMillan came from the Senate floor. There was a brief conversation. How much would it take, Moore wanted to know. McKim pulled a number out of the air, for starters at least $100,000. There would need to be some accommodation for added office space that would cost another $10,000 to $15,000. With that McKim left for New York City, feeling depressed, and McMillan returned to the Senate.

When McKim arrived in New York there was a telegram awaiting him. McMillan had pressed the Senate Committee on Appropriations to add $150,000 for repairs to the White House and another $15,000 for an office space.[10] McKim was ecstatic, telling Moore it was a miracle. The only hesitancy was over the temporary office quarters to be added to the White House. McKim felt that a permanent separate building should be constructed as soon as possible. Daniel Burnham had warned him earlier that anything temporary in Washington would soon become permanent.[11]

Roosevelt was in New York the following weekend and invited McKim to meet that Saturday. The president was aroused and understood that the renovation would be radical. Roosevelt summoned McKim to his lunch table on the following Monday, April 21, in Washington. He would make the White House available to him for a thorough inspection on the following day.[12] When McKim arrived for lunch, Edith made herself available both days.[13] Theodore and Edith wanted the White House returned to an eighteenth-century purity. Any expansion must be along the lines conceived by Thomas Jefferson, employing a colonnaded terrace.[14]

Charles Moore accompanied McKim on his Tuesday inspection. Both men were appalled at what they saw. Sanitary conditions were unspeakable. The place was infested with rats that provided the Roosevelt boys no end of entertainment. Of a more critical nature were severe structural problems and defective wiring. There were even signs still of the fire of 1814.[15] The architect repaired to New York, knowing that he had his work cut out for him. The president had given him a deadline of four months. To make it happen, everything must fall into place.[16]

Edith immediately sought to follow up with Moore. It was a chilly day for May when she received him in the handsome second floor oval library. A customary fire was burning in the fireplace. Moore shared his easy chair with young Archie Roosevelt and a collie. The informality of the setting belied the importance of the meeting. Edith was beginning to grasp the radical nature of the proposed changes. However, it was clear to Moore, as it had been to McKim, that Edith would manage the renovations.

On May 10, 1902, McKim got his marching orders from Theodore Roosevelt. The renovation must be complete before Congress reconvened in December; Roosevelt wanted no Congressional oversight. There was just one problem; someone had to go see Joe Cannon before the first hammer could be lifted. That someone was Charles Moore. He called it "confronting the lion."[17] Moore found the chairman in his domain in the rooms of the House Committee on Appropriations. Cannon's initial response was less than enthusiastic, expressing frustration that McMillan had stolen the show with the Senate Park Commission. Nevertheless, the ice was soon broken. Cannon didn't care how much the renovation cost to put the White House in proper shape. His only concern was that money requests not come dribbling in, year after year. Put the entire appropriation together immediately, and Cannon would see that it got through the House.[18]

McKim got the phone call. His estimate had to be ready the next day with enough cushion to avoid going back to the well. The final document had pencil marks through line items as cushions were added. At the bottom of the page in pencil the total was $369,050, a number well beyond everybody's expectation.[19] Moore went first to the White House where he found the president about to be shaved. As Theodore was being lathered up, he told Moore to fire away. Moore told him the amount, and he about jumped out of the barber's chair. Resignation then settled in. However, Roosevelt volunteered Moore for the assignment of telling Cannon of the higher amount. Several days later, Cannon's consent was relayed to Moore.[20]

On the evening of Saturday, June 14, McKim met with Roosevelt for the final review. The temporary executive offices in the form of the west portico with colonnade would take the place of the greenhouses. This addition in combination with the reconstruction of the east portico and colonnade would relieve the main building of a number of office requirements. Old prints and plans for the White House's original design had been discovered in the Library of Congress. The work envisioned would put the building into the condition first planned but never carried out.[21] The only remaining problem was that construction of the east portico would require seven to eight months. However, it would not interfere with Roosevelt's deadline for use of the other portions of the White House.[22]

The appropriations bill was signed into law on June 20, and demolition began immediately.[23] Trouble was not far behind. The source was not unexpected: Colonel Theodore Bingham. Colonel Bingham had traveled to New York City at the beginning of June to talk with Thomas Hastings, an architect of substantial standing. His purpose was to convince Hastings that his designs for the wings to the White House were superior to McKim's. Hastings very strongly told him not to interfere. After the interview ended, Hastings promptly warned McKim. McKim was shocked.

Armed with the knowledge that Bingham was not a friend, McKim then sought clarification on procedures to pay contractors. He knew that all payments had to be made through the Office of Public Buildings and Grounds. McKim wanted Bingham to have nothing to do with the work or have any authority to question amounts certified for payment.[24]

At the heart of everything, McKim was fretting about the deadlines that Roosevelt had imposed. He would wait thirty days to see how the project was going. If delays looked imminent, McKim would enlist Edith's help.[25] Colonel Bingham had a different solution for project delays. He proposed a $200 per day forfeiture for McKim's architectural firm, McKim, Mead, and White for each and every day work was delayed beyond the agreed deadlines.[26]

Then as work progressed, the issue of forfeitures and prompt payment of the contractors returned to the forefront. In addition, Bingham was proposing to apply purchases of items for the White House, not included in the appropriation, against the project. McKim could take no more and asked for a meeting with George Cortelyou, the president's personal secretary. That meeting was called for July 14 at Oyster Bay. William Mead accompanied McKim. When they arrived, they found Elihu Root as well as Theodore and Edith. Root as secretary of war was Bingham's boss. As they sat on the porch, the president sent for Cortelyou and dictated a letter. Each and every issue was firmly addressed.

Attention then shifted to interior decorating. Again Edith was very deferential in her communications with McKim, saying, "The president and I have consulted." As part of the interior changes, she brought back the George Watts painting *Love and Life*, which had been banished from the White House for its nudity. For this first lady, nudity in art did not equate to crudity in art.[27]

Meanwhile, articles began to appear in the Washington papers critical of the renovation. McKim suspected Bingham was the source.[28] A positive article would counter the negative stories coming out of Washington. McKim turned to familiar ground, Richard Watson Gilder and *The Century*. However, Edith requested the galleys before the article was printed. She would leave nothing to chance.[29]

The White House renovation was the end of Bingham. In March 1903, he was transferred to Fort Riley in Kansas.[30] The colonel did not exit gracefully.[31] His departure was the subject of much speculation in the Washington papers. One political cartoon showed Belle Hagner, Edith's personal secretary, dragging Bingham by the ears from the White House grounds. In a subsequent unpublished autobiography, Hagner strongly denied any role in Bingham's departure.[32] However, by implicating her, the newspapers were subtly pointing a finger at the first lady.

Meanwhile the *Sherman* site remained unresolved. It was the kind of conflict that Gus detested. If there had been any doubt in Saint-Gaudens's mind about his work, the Pan-American Exposition had removed it.

As 1902 dawned, McKim decided to make a major push to get the statue located in the Central Park mall despite the previous objections.[33] It was rejected.

The person behind the rejection was Samuel Parsons. He was the widely respected landscape architect for the Parks Department. Having served in a variety of positions overseeing Central Park, Parsons was the last surviving link within the department to the original designers of the park, Frederic Law Olmsted and Calvert Vaux. The man was a skilled defender of Central Park, believing in the preservation of its natural beauty.[34] His standard procedure was to speak first to the commissioners. If unsuccessful, he would then turn to anyone who would listen, including the editorial writers for the *Times* and the *Tribune*.[35]

In March, with a new administration in place, McKim again attempted to gain resolution of the location problem. Again, there was no favorable response to the Central Park location.

A public hearing was called. After discussion of locating the *Sherman* at the site of the Grant Tomb, opposed by the Grant family, matters appeared at an impasse. Then old Samuel D. Babcock stood up. He said that it had been so long since he had first chaired the Sherman Monument Committee that he could not remember all the various proceedings. However, he did remember that every proposed location had been refused by the Parks Department. In his opinion it was up to the Parks Department to find an acceptable spot.[36] It was a masterful move that boxed in the Parks Department. Parsons would have to compromise his principles and offer up a spot suitable for the *Sherman*.

It was not what Gus had wanted to hear, and he had left that meeting in disgust.[37] Now, the only decent site left was the plaza at 59th and Fifth Avenue. McKim called it the tulip bed site. The decision was made.

Now Saint-Gaudens lobbied for changes to the chosen location. The circle needed extending as the statue was best viewed from 65 feet away.[38] One would have to step into the street to admire the *Sherman* from the proper distance. The sculptor requested that the grass plots be eliminated and "some redisposition" of the trees surrounding the circle made.[39]

The issue of the modifications to the 59th Street site continued to swirl around. Finally on May 26, under the new strictures, the proposed location, with an attached approval from Parsons, was presented to the Art Commission for consideration. There was also a memorandum from Saint-Gaudens and McKim, Mead, and White agreeing to no major alterations to the site at 59th Street. It was a rare capitulation for Augustus Saint-Gaudens and Charles Follen McKim.[40] Sherman and the Angel were no longer homeless.

Saint-Gaudens had always been very particular that his works have the right patina. Now he made an unusual decision, opting to gild the *Sherman* entirely.[41] In his typical fashion, he said only that he was sick of seeing statues that looked like stove pipes.[42] Perhaps his real concern was that a bronze *Sherman* would not stand out sufficiently against the background streetscape at the 59th Street site.

Still matters dragged. The pedestal with its inscriptions must be resolved. The end of 1902 found McKim pleading with Saint-Gaudens to make decisions. Those days were not a good time for Gus. Son Homer's fiancé noted in January that Saint-Gaudens was in need of a doctor day and night.[43]

Finally in March 1903, all was in readiness with one exception. Gus could not abide the elm trees blocking the view. First, tearing a page from Parsons's book, an editorial appeared in the *New York Evening Post.* It acknowledged the special uniqueness of trees but argued that an exception should be made for the *Sherman* at the 59th Street site. The rebuttal was quick in coming, strongly expressing Parsons's views. "We must not forget that the parks are not made for statue but that the placing of statue with the parks is an incidental feature."[44] The trees would stay.

The dedication for the *Sherman* was set for Decoration Day, May 30, 1903. Gaetan Ardisson was in charge of the erection process. Nominally a molder in the studio, he was Saint-Gaudens's long-time lieutenant in the whole sculpture process from sketch to bronze.[45] Still, Gus would not let go of the tree issue. They were big elms, each some twenty inches in diameter.[46] Ardisson had been able to cut some of the offending tree branches from the erection scaffolding. Then the Parks Department began to have second thoughts and sent a work crew to trim more of the concealing limbs. Ardisson bribed the men with whiskey and even more limbs came down.[47] Then two of the elms were removed. The reason given: The trees would obstruct the view from the reviewers' stand.[48]

The day of the dedication finally arrived. The lowering skies and the constant threat of rain did not dampen the celebration. The festivities started at nine sharp with regular army soldiers followed by the New York National Guard stepping smartly off from the Washington Arch in Washington Square. These men were sixteen abreast, forming a solid phalanx from curb to curb. The pace was brisk; the soldiers had 54 blocks to march in an hour and a half to reach the *Sherman Monument* at the entrance to Central Park.

At 42nd and Fifth, the veterans fell in behind the column.[49] First came the Loyal Legion made up of former officers of the Union Army. Then came the men from the various posts of the Grand Army of the Republic. While some marched well, these men mostly came at a slow pace, their ranks thinned by the ravages of time. Proudly they bore their tattered, war-torn battle flags. Slouched hats were doffed as the veterans marched the course.

At 10:20 with the parade column nearing the reviewing stand, the guns of the First Battery boomed, the sound magnified by the low hanging clouds. William Tecumseh Sherman Thackara, the seventeen-year-old grandson of the general, pulled a cord that allowed a veil of bunting that had been covering the monumental work to come down. Well, most of it came down. A swirl of wind caught part of the material on the spur of the general's boot and would not budge. As the column of soldiers closed on the reviewing stand, at the side of the statue, a city employee scrambled to bring a ladder to rectify the dignity of the situation. Meanwhile The Old Guard Band struck up "Marching Through Georgia" and then, as if to make amends, followed with "Dixie."

Finally freed of the bunting, the horse and rider of the *Sherman Monument* appeared. They seemed imbued with a spirit of restless advance, following the path where Victory pointed the way.[50] Many in the crowd were familiar with the work in plaster, having either seen it in person or in pictures from the exhibition in Buffalo. However, they were not prepared for the stunning effect of the gilding.[51] They also had not seen the elegant pedestal with its encircling bench for seating. At its top, the pedestal became the rock over which the horse briskly trotted.

The crowd gathered, some with umbrellas to fend off the rain, in anticipation of the dedication ceremonies that were about to begin.

As the young soldiers and grizzled old veterans passed by in review after the unveiling, Alice Roosevelt, all grown up and a celebrity in her own right, escorted by Mr. and Mrs. Whitelaw Reid, cheered enthusiastically from a front row seat. It took an hour and a half for the column to pass. Showers broke out intermittently and necessitated umbrellas at one point; yet the crowd's spirits remained undampened.[52] Gus and Gussie viewed the festivities from an inconspicuous spot. As was his habit, he had briefly inspected the statue the previous day.[53]

Rain or not, it was a grand day for speeches. Root was in from Washington for the keynote address. In the preliminaries, Parks Commissioner Willcox who had been so disdainful of the *Sherman Monument* pledged to "at all times guard this statue with affectionate care."[54]

With the speeches over, the politicians and generals adjourned to the nearby Metropolitan Club for a luncheon hosted by the Sherman Monument Committee. Gus was present but most of the men attending were at best acquaintances of the sculptor. At least McKim was there to keep him company.[55] Among the politicians was none other than John G. Carlisle.[56] Gus had never really recognized Carlisle as his true adversary in the award medal controversy from the World's Columbian Exposition.

For Saint-Gaudens, it was a grand day of achievement and recognition. He was an acknowledged leader of the American art establishment and friend of the president and first lady. On the other hand, why would Carlisle have come to this occasion? He had never recognized the travesty of his decision to mule Barber's work with that of Saint-Gaudens on the award medal. For John Carlisle, it was one last fleeting moment of recognition for what he had once been and of the power he had once wielded. His New York law practice, while taking on some high-profile cases, had never been monetarily rewarding. The self-styled defender of the workingman could never quite make himself into a corporate lawyer. Now, he was without his two sons who had died in early adulthood. His subsequent life had been a vivid contrast compared to the continuing success of Augustus Saint-Gaudens.

That evening, Whitelaw Reid gave a dinner party for the Sherman family and Mr. and Mrs. Saint-Gaudens. Reid felt it fitting that the affair ended where the relationship between William Tecumseh Sherman and Augustus Saint-Gaudens had all begun, at his home.[57]

On the Fourth of July, 1903, Daniel Chester French sent his compliments to Saint-Gaudens.

> I told you the other day that I had something to say to you about the *Sherman* but I missed the opportunity and I have been trying for the last hour or so to write you what I feel. The result sounds so cheap and commonplace that I fear I must be content to express my approval with my congratulations and let it go at that.
>
> Yet I do want you to know how really and rarely great—I feel—I *know* the statue to be—great as few works of sculpture, ancient or modern are. Not only have you scored a great success, but the note you have struck is so entirely fresh that the statue stands in a class by itself. To say that it is better than this or next in rank to that is as idle as to compare a rose with an orange. It is one of the wonders of the world. Let that suffice![58]

It was the highest compliment a fellow sculptor could pay. French had just told Saint-Gaudens that he was not capable of such a work as Gus had created. Saint-Gaudens had successfully married the allegory to the reality with the *Sherman*, something he had struggled over with the *Shaw*.

That following August, Saint-Gaudens received a letter from the president.

> Now to my mind your *Sherman* is the greatest statue of a commander in existence. But I can say with all sincerity that I know of no man, of course of no one living, who could have done it. To take grim, homely, old Sherman, the type and ideal of a democratic general, and put with him an allegorical figure such as you did, could result in but one of two ways—a ludicrous failure, or striking the very highest note of the sculptor's art. Thrice over for the good fortune of our countrymen, it was given to you to strike this highest note. [59]

Saint-Gaudens wrote back humbled.

> I don't know how to thank you for your more than kind words about the *Sherman* and my other work. And when I realize that you have taken the time to say this to me, amid the multitude of other things on your mind, it is a fact that touches me deeply and your letter will be set aside and treasured for those who come after me.[60]

Now Saint-Gaudens truly had received the recognition of his countrymen that his work so richly deserved.

Chapter 52
In His Own Right

As a student of history, Theodore Roosevelt would have known that no vice president succeeding unelected into the presidency of the United States had ever achieved election to that office in his own right.

The Cleveland Wing regained control of the Democratic Party in 1904 and at the Democratic convention nominated Judge Alton Parker of New York for president. Parker had been on the bench for eighteen years and was at that point chief justice of the New York Court of Appeals. William Jennings Bryan had fought a rear-guard action at the opening of the convention that resulted in no currency plank in the Democratic platform. However, Parker came out late in the convention solidly on the side of the gold standard. Silver Democrats left the proceedings uninspired to work for Parker.

Theodore Roosevelt was apprehensive of the Parker candidacy. While he chafed at the bit, as the campaign progressed, he observed presidential traditions and stayed out of the fray. On the other hand, George Cortelyou as his campaign manager took heavy heat as the supposed "bag man." Innuendos abounded that Cortelyou was trading favors for cash. Roosevelt, covering himself, felt the need to remind Cortelyou that he had instructed him that no favors were to be granted whatsoever. Cortelyou bristled back that he was conducting the campaign on as high a plane as Roosevelt had conducted the presidency.[1]

J. Pierpont Morgan was at the height of his power on Wall Street as Theodore Roosevelt assumed the reins of power. His moniker, Jupiter, was well earned. Since his intervention to turn the tide at the crucial point in the Panic of 1893, the financier had met with success after success. Yet Theodore Roosevelt was no shrinking violet in the face of such power. The overarching question was how would these two men interact?

In 1901 Morgan had financed the merger of Carnegie Steel, Federal Steel, and National Steel to form the first billion-dollar corporation—U.S. Steel. Elbert Gary of Federal Steel would run the combined operation.

In a controversial move that same year, Morgan, in partnership with James J. Hill, merged the Northern Pacific Railway, Great Northern Railway, and the Chicago Burlington and Quincy Railroad into an entity named Northern Securities. Second in size only to U.S. Steel, the combined entity held a virtual monopoly on freight movements across the northern tier of the Great Plains.

Yet there was more to Morgan. He believed the business of America should be honestly and decently managed by a few of the best people who just happened to be friends and associates of his. He liked the order and efficiency that the combination of entities into large business units produced. He disapproved of the speculative gangs who plunged in and out of the market, heedless of the properties they were toying with. When Morgan put his resources behind a company, he expected to stay with it. It was how a gentleman behaved. Morgan's integrity was as solid as a rock.

Two of the leading players in Morgan's circle were George Baker, president of First National Bank, and James Stillman, president of National City Bank, both in New York City. Baker was the closer of the two. Stillman and Morgan did not always see eye to eye. Though competitors for securities underwritings, the three men mutually respected one another and worked together when the circumstances dictated.[2]

Theodore Roosevelt had a different take on corporations. "They are indispensable instruments of our modern civilization, but I believe that they should be so supervised and so regulated that they shall act for the interest of the community as a whole." In another instance, Roosevelt expanded upon what limits should be imposed. "One great problem that we have before us is to preserve the rights of property, and these can only be preserved if we remember that they are less in jeopardy from the socialist and the anarchist than from the predatory man of wealth. We must pursue the policy of asserting the right of the nation, as far as it has the power, to supervise and control the business use of wealth, especially in the corporate form."[3]

Yet there were exceptions to Roosevelt's concerns about corporations. Much later he would state that while the existing antitrust laws forbid all combinations, they should discriminate between those that do good and those that are evil. The antitrust laws should not prohibit those combinations that benefit the public.[4]

While Pierpont Morgan and Theodore Roosevelt had spheres of belief concerning corporations that were mostly at odds with each other, there was common ground where these spheres overlapped. Within this overlap, trust could be developed; outside of it, there would be conflict.

Believing that Northern Securities Trust was not in the best interest of the people of the United States, Theodore Roosevelt instructed his attorney general, Philander Knox, to develop a case to reverse the merger of the three railroads on antitrust grounds. Without advance notice and even keeping key members of his cabinet in the dark, Roosevelt gave the authorization and Knox filed suit on February 19, 1902.

To Morgan, Northern Securities represented the culmination of decades of work consolidating railroads, putting them on a stronger financial footing and eliminating harmful competition brought about by over-building. Morgan was furious over the means by which the suit had been brought. He believed Roosevelt should have given him advance notice and an opportunity to address objections. The two men had had their differences over the years, but Morgan had always considered Roosevelt a gentleman. Morgan had contributed $10,000 to Roosevelt's gubernatorial campaign in 1898.[5] In 1901 after his election as vice president, Roosevelt had hosted a dinner in Morgan's honor.

More confrontation for Theodore Roosevelt was just around the corner. In May 1902 John Mitchell took 150,000 United Mine Workers in the Pennsylvania anthracite coalfields out on strike. As president of the miners' union, it was a calculated risk on Mitchell's part. In February, Mark Hanna had instigated a meeting between Mitchell and Morgan. Morgan exercised ultimate control over the mines and railroads in the anthracite fields, but his power was not absolute. Mitchell would say of the meeting that Morgan told him that he would do what was right when the opportunity came for action. If the railroad presidents who controlled the mines were wrong, Morgan would not sustain them. If the miners were wrong, he would not help them.[6]

As the first cold spells of fall began to descend upon the Atlantic and New England states where this fuel provided heat for homes, Roosevelt felt compelled to act. The president summoned the mine owners and John Mitchell to Washington for a meeting on October 3, 1902. The owners had to this point refused to enter any discussions until the miners returned to work. After the public announcement of this meeting, Morgan told a reporter that Roosevelt had his full approval.[7]

At the meeting, the president implored that mining resume. Mitchell, for his part, was willing to meet with the owners to discuss a settlement. If an agreement could not be reached, he was willing to submit the issues to an arbitration panel. On the other hand, the mine owners obtusely demanded that Roosevelt order federal troops to restore order. There was no middle ground between the two sides. After the meeting, Roosevelt dejectedly told Senator Hanna that he had tried and failed.[8]

The day after the failed conference, Morgan announced that he would buy 50,000 tons of coal in Wales and ship it to New York where it would be distributed free of charge. For Morgan the strike had become a public embarrassment, and public resentment could spill over directly upon him and his interests. On October 9, Morgan summoned George Baer, lead negotiator for the mine owners, to his offices in New York. That same day Secretary of War Elihu Root wrote Morgan to ask his help in arranging arbitration. Root went further, gaining Roosevelt's permission to approach Morgan as a private citizen. Aboard Morgan's yacht, the two men hammered out the framework of a solution to the impasse. There would be no arbitration. Instead, all issues between the owners and the miners would be submitted to a fair tribunal, appointed by Roosevelt for resolution. After the meeting, Morgan placed a long phone call to Baer. The owners still objected in important ways, particularly to the makeup of the tribunal.

Progress again stalled and Morgan sent Bob Bacon and George Perkins, his other trusted lieutenant, to Washington in a desperate move to find a solution. Even Morgan could not make the mine owners budge. Both Bacon and Perkins were scared that if talks failed, the country would slip into anarchy. In the end, the controversy was not over the makeup of the tribunal but the respective expertise assigned to each position. In the early morning hours of October 16, a resolution was reached. Roosevelt simply switched titles, and the labor representative became an imminent sociologist. The miners ratified the resulting agreement and began returning to work on October 21. Afterwards Roosevelt wrote a personal note to Morgan thanking him for the service he rendered to the American people. He did not see how the strike could have been settled without Morgan's intervention.[9]

Even with Roosevelt's attempted rapprochement after the miners' strike, Morgan remained against the president. In 1903 Morgan would join other businessmen to implore Mark Hanna to challenge Roosevelt for the nomination in 1904. Hampered by failing health, Hanna was happy to settle for a second term in the Senate instead.[10]

Still, there was common ground. When Roosevelt signed the act that established the Department of Commerce and Labor that would bring both business and labor under government oversight on February 14, 1903, he used two pens. One went to George Cortelyou, the department's first secretary, and the other went to George Perkins of J. P. Morgan & Co.[11]

Morgan lost the Northern Securities suit before the Supreme Court on March 14, 1904, by a five-to-four vote. Yet in May of that year, Morgan played a central role in financing the American purchase of the French rights for the building of a canal in Panama.[12]

In spite of this often-frosty relationship, George Cortelyou in the 1904 election did not hesitate to solicit Morgan for help. It was fertile ground as Mark Hanna had died on February 15, 1904. In October 1904, Morgan first contributed $100,000 and then another $50,000. Perhaps the *New York Sun* expressed Pierpont Morgan's sentiments best in its endorsement of Roosevelt— "Theodore! With all thy faults."[13]

Years later a Congressional committee would grill Morgan over his contributions to Roosevelt's 1904 campaign. Morgan testified, "I want it distinctly understood that J.P. Morgan & Company never made a single subscription to any election with any promise or expectation of anything or return in any way, shape, or manner, and we never made it without we deemed it advantageous for the government and the people." Put simply, all Morgan wanted was a square deal. It was here that the two spheres of belief overlapped, and each trusted the other.[14]

On November 8, 1904, Theodore Roosevelt traveled by private rail car to Oyster Bay to cast his vote. He arrived back in Washington at 6:16 p.m., quickly exiting his car coupled to the rear of the regular Pennsylvania Railroad evening service to the capital. He walked briskly half the length of the train, cordially acknowledging the greetings of other passengers and bystanders. He then took a side door to his waiting carriage for the ride back to the White House and his family.

The president did not have long to wait in suspense. By 7 p.m., he knew he had carried New York by a plurality so large as to be really astounding. More bulletins followed from other states as the polls closed. Soon after dinner, Roosevelt, joined by John Hay and other family and friends, waited for the late returns. Tension quickly changed to exuberance. At 9 p.m., Judge Parker sent a telegram to Roosevelt offering his congratulations. Theodore Roosevelt had won the presidency in his own right by a historic landslide.

Once the congratulatory telegrams had been received from his supporters, Roosevelt left his small gathering and went to the executive offices to receive the congratulations of the reporters. It was here, in a moment of euphoria over the victory and in the presence of the Washington newspapermen, that he made a pledge that caught everyone by surprise. Summoning his personal secretary, William Loeb, he commenced dictating while the newspapermen listened in rapt attention.

> I am deeply sensible of the honor done me by the American people in thus expressing their confidence in what I have done and have tried to do. I appreciate to the full the solemn responsibility this confidence imposes upon me, and I shall do all that in my power lies not to forfeit it. On the fourth of March next I shall have served three and a half years, and this three and a half years constitutes my first term. The wise custom which limits the president to two terms regards the substance and not the form. Under no circumstance will I be a candidate for or accept another nomination.[15]

Roosevelt's announcement was received favorably in the conservative *New York Sun*. The newspaper's editors recognized that a second term, what Roosevelt would have considered a third term, was a distinct possibility given his popularity with the American people. Yet to his everlasting honor, in his hour of triumph, he had deliberately renounced this not unreasonable theory.[16] It might have been honorable, but it was certainly premature. A cynic would have taken the *Sun*'s praise as a sigh of relief that, although four years away, there was light at the end of the tunnel. Edith Roosevelt, standing nearby as he dictated his proclamation, was seen to flinch. She would later say that had she had any inkling of what Theodore was going to do, she would have done everything to stop it.[17]

Theodore Roosevelt had just conferred upon his presidency an impotent "lame duck" status. To overcome his handicap, he would have to keep Republicans at bay by designating an heir apparent to carry forward his policies. No president since Andrew Jackson had been able to pull off this feat. To prepare the way, Roosevelt, while at the height of his power, had to also attack the key issues of the Democrats. Given his stunning victory over Parker and the gold wing of the Democratic Party, Roosevelt could fully expect the resurgence of William Jennings Bryan. The president would have to address gold versus silver. Given Edith and Theodore's support of the fine arts, it would not be unreasonable to assume that art would have a role to play in this effort.

Chapter 53

A Medal as Millard Fillmore and More

Seated three places to the left of William Eames, the president of the American Institute of Architects, Augustus Saint-Gaudens surveyed the dignitaries assembled for this annual dinner of the association. He had been looking forward to this event with great anticipation, even if he did have to "utter ten of his classic words."[1] It was a Wednesday night, January 11, 1905, in Washington, D.C. The place was the Arlington Hotel, tops in the city, enjoying a prime location at an angle to Lafayette Square.[2] St. John's Episcopal Church was across the street, and the White House was a just a short walk through Lafayette Park. They were gathered in The Dining Hall. The high table at which Gus enjoyed a prominent position stretched to three sides of the hall to accommodate the seventy-five dignitaries.[3]

Although part of the annual meeting of the AIA, the dinner had taken on a much deeper meaning. First and foremost, it was an occasion to further cement the work of the Senate Park Commission. This evening would help official Washington to refocus on the commission's crucial recommendations concerning the Mall. Also, among other points, the meeting was a quiet affirmation of the successful renovation of the White House that stood for all to see.

For Charles Follen McKim, this night was the fulfillment of long years of hard work, furthering the arts in America. He had devoted seven months to the arrangements, and getting the dignitaries to commit had been like herding cats. Everyone called it "McKim's Dinner."[4] Seated directly on Gus's right at the head table was

Secretary of State John Hay. McKim had had Gus write to Hay, urging his attendance.[5] To the other side of William Eames sat Elihu Root, recently resigned as secretary of War. Among others in attendance were Pierpont Morgan, a strong supporter of the arts, James Ellsworth, active in the commemorative half dollar for the World's Columbian Exposition, and Whitelaw Reid, the newly minted American representative to the Court of St. James.

McKim had thoroughly planned the event, only scheduling the dinner the preceding October after clearing the date with President Roosevelt's calendar. It was to no avail. On January 3, just eight days before the dinner, he learned that certain prominent members of government, including Joe Cannon, would be unable to attend due to a conflicting dinner at the White House scheduled by the president.[6] Envisioning the entire event falling apart because of the scheduling conflict, McKim had written to William Loeb, pleading in the name of Republican justice that those summoned to the conflicting dinner at the White House be allowed to attend. With the topics at hand for the dinner, there were certainly enough reasons for Roosevelt to adjust his schedule sufficiently to deliver a speech to the group assembled. In closing, McKim stated that a box was being improvised for a few ladies, a first for the staid Arlington Hotel. Roosevelt's two sisters, Corrine and Bamie, were planning to attend.[7] Then McKim applied the *coup de grâce.* He was proposing to place the box at the disposal of the first lady and had written as much to her.[8] The dinner was now back on track.

When First Lady Edith Roosevelt entered the dining room with her party and made her way to her special box, a quartet of male voices sang "Hail to the Fairest." The president of the AIA then gave one of the many toasts of the evening:

> To the gracious lady whose presence is inspiration,
> because her thought is ever on the things that are true.[9]

The toast alluded directly to a quote from Keats:

> Beauty is truth, truth beauty—That is all
> Ye know on earth and all ye need to know.

As the meal was completed, the time for speeches began. In the middle of these proceedings, the president and his party arrived, and Roosevelt made his way to the podium. In his speech, he went on record supporting the Senate Park Commission.[10] That act was fulfillment enough to call "McKim's Dinner" a success.

The speeches dragged on until past midnight. When it was over, McKim sat for two hours talking to Root and the others of the night's events. At 1:30 Gus rolled out, returning to Henry Adams's home where he was staying. The following day, Edith Roosevelt was joining the Adams salon for breakfast, and afterwards there would be a reception and dinner at the White House.

January 12, 1905, was the date of the Annual Diplomatic Reception, the highlight of the Washington social season. The diplomats appeared in full court dress. Their wives and daughters were attired in gowns carefully selected and ordered from abroad for the occasion.

The reception was scheduled to begin at 8:45 that evening. The south portico would be made available as a second entrance for the diplomatic corps, cabinet, Supreme Court justices, and special guests that included Saint-Gaudens.[11] At the stroke of nine, the president and his cabinet entered the Blue Room. The ladies of the cabinet took their respective positions to the right of the first lady. Edith, quite naturally, was the center of attention; fluent in French, the diplomatic language, she was at ease in her setting. The newspapers the next day would say that her gown of soft yellow silk exemplified a return to the last century's fashions. The skirt was trimmed with streamers of dark brown and black velvet ribbon, to which were tied clusters of large flowers. Around her waist, white lace was festooned becomingly. All the ladies carried bouquets to eliminate shaking hands in the reception line. Only Roosevelt shook hands. All told, between 2,200 and 2,300 guests were presented to the president. Afterwards, they were free to mingle. Ice water was the beverage of choice; in fact, it was the only beverage offered. The public reception ended promptly at 10:45.[12]

Now the first lady felt distinguished to be having supper with Henry James, John La Farge, and Augustus Saint-Gaudens who were among the 100 select guests invited to stay for the affair.[13] Saint-Gaudens found himself seated at the president's table. With him were Elihu Root and Whitelaw Reid, friends he was comfortable being around. Also at the table was Secretary of the Treasury Leslie Shaw; his presence was for an altogether different purpose.[14] At that moment, Gus was feeling cocky.[15] It was a very high honor but no accident as Edith always prepared the seating chart for Theodore's approval.[16]

Secretary of the Treasury Leslie Shaw would preside over much of the effort toward the redesign of the gold coins. His role was nebulous given that President Roosevelt dealt directly with Augustus Saint-Gaudens on the commission.

An old friend was also among those attending. Elizabeth Sherman Cameron was seated at Edith's table. Lizzie Cameron was using the Diplomatic Reception as a suitable debut for her daughter, Martha. She had pressed Henry Adams into service to ask Edith for the invitation.[17] Still estranged from her husband after eight years, this was the best that she could manage as a coming out for her daughter. So far had Lizzie fallen socially in Washington that the papers the next day would barely take note of her presence.

As Saint-Gaudens sat down to supper, Theodore Roosevelt had a specific project in mind for the sculptor. Perhaps it was only coincidence that Watson

Gilder had come to Washington seeking a few words with Roosevelt in early December.[18] They had had lunch together on December 9.[19] Regardless, on December 27, 1904, Theodore had written to Secretary Shaw.

> I think our coinage is artistically of atrocious hideousness. Would it be possible, without asking permission of Congress to employ a man like Saint-Gaudens to give us a coinage that would have some beauty?[20]

This note prompted a cursory examination that brought to light the 1890 amendment to the revised statutes allowing changes in any coin design in service at least twenty-five years. Theodore had what he needed. He could act through the secretary of the Treasury to change the designs immediately on the eligible coins—the cent and the four gold coins.[21]

Both Roosevelt and Saint-Gaudens admired the high-relief coins of ancient Greece. Why could not the United States produce a coin as beautiful as the Greeks? If Gus would design a modern version, Theodore would have the Mint produce it. [22] Theodore made light, saying: "You know, Saint-Gaudens, this is my pet crime."[23] Roosevelt particularly disliked the existing gold coins. He thought the eagle on the reverse looked like a grilled squab, and he didn't like grilled squabs. There was never enough there for a full-grown man to eat![24] Gus was initially taken aback. He had long wanted to see the designs on United States coins improved but felt any effort in this regard would be futile.

This image shows Augustus Saint-Gaudens in 1905 at age 57. His battle with cancer has clearly taken its toll, as shown in his face.

In fact, there was give-and-take in the conversation. Gus had come to the reception with an agenda of his own. He and his brother, Louis, were in the initial stages of undertaking a commission, at the request of John Hay, to prepare a medal honoring Benjamin Franklin in 1906. Adding to the significance of the occasion, one medal would be specially struck in gold for presentation to the French government. Inquiries to the Philadelphia Mint had raised a roadblock regarding the time required to prepare the dies and strike the medal. The environment had not changed at the Mint. Gus was straightforward in describing the problem and blamed engraver Charles Barber. In a letter to his brother Louis after the dinner, he described the ensuing conversation:

> Barber is an S.O.A.B. but I had a talk with the president who ordered Secretary Shaw in my presence to cut Barber's head off if he didn't do our bidding.[25]

These were heady words coming from the mouth of the president. Still Gus must weigh the president's desires that he undertake the coin design commission with his other obligations. His health was a question mark. He knew from experience that working with the Mint would be impossible. Individuals close to him had begged him to take no more commissions.[26] The sculptor was noncommittal, describing this time with Roosevelt as intense.[27]

Roosevelt's challenge to Saint-Gaudens that night was more than to collaborate on a "pet crime." The president believed a nation's coinage should convey a message to all who touched it. It would add to the beauty of living and therefore to the joy of life.[28] But there was more to it than that; the message that Roosevelt wanted to convey was that gold, not silver, was key to the prosperity of Americans. His solution was to increase Americans' familiarity with its coinage by stimulating interest through the new designs. This approach might seem simplistic, but there were grounds for Roosevelt's reasoning. Ever since the great gold discovery of 1848, this yellow metal in the form of coins had driven the California economy. With gold coins in abundance, the silver movement never took hold within that state.

Following up on January 13, Director of the Mint George Roberts wrote to Saint-Gaudens. No designs had been prepared, and there was nothing definite in mind. The Treasury Department was not even ready to give a commission, but the counsel of artists such as Saint-Gaudens was desired. If Saint-Gaudens happened to be in town, the director would be pleased to have an interview with him.[29] Saint-Gaudens's reply was polite but equally noncommittal. He would give the subject some thought and would be happy to meet with Roberts on his next visit in March.[30]

Secretary Shaw was to blame for this exchange of letters. Roberts had been unsure whether Shaw wished to consult with artists other than Saint-Gaudens. Clearly, Shaw had not conveyed to Roberts the unique circumstances of Saint-Gaudens's participation. In actuality, the Mint director was in full agreement with the president concerning the coin designs, thinking them artistically poor.[31]

Throughout early January, preparation of the official inaugural medal had continued with little notice, driven by the March 4 inauguration. It was a repeat design from the presidential medal quickly prepared upon Roosevelt's 1901 ascension to office, with only the date being changed. The Inaugural Committee had not been happy with a recycled image of the president but had not sought other alternatives.[32] The Mint had let the project slide during November and December, thereby preempting the Inaugural Committee's ability to change the design. Also, in spite of Barber's recent upgrading of the Mint's medal department, Philadelphia lacked the necessary equipment to strike the required 3,000 medals so the work had been contracted to Joseph K. Davison's Sons of Philadelphia.[33] This medal seemed to be lurching towards the March 4 deadline as much from benign neglect as anything.

The official inauguration medal for Theodore Roosevelt in 1905 was executed by Charles Barber and George Morgan.

Two days after the Diplomatic Reception, a letter arrived at the White House as if shot from a cannon. It was addressed to Edith. Frank Millet, who had become close to the first lady, was addressing her in hopes of affecting a change. He had been stirred by a story on official medals issued by the Mint in the Sunday magazine section of the *New York Herald.* It was not that the official Roosevelt inaugural medal was declared ordinary; it was that it compared so poorly with the others highlighted in the article.[34]

> The [inaugural] medal … has no nobility about it; it does not satisfy any of the cannons [sic] of the medalists and it is commonplace (even worse) it is a libel. … Cannot you bring it about that the president shall have a medal which will at least hold its own? Why can't he have a medal as Millard Fillmore, for example?

Millet had said enough. Edith's mind was made up. Now it was up to Theodore to implement the change. He moved quickly, requesting that an outside artist be employed by the Mint to provide a design for another inaugural medal. What he learned was both discouraging and consistent with what Millet had said. The director of the Mint readily admitted in a letter to Secretary Shaw that the Mint's medal work was not up to the standards of the French or some of the other foreign Mints. Efforts had been made over the previous three years to correct this deficiency through equipment upgrades. However, there were no funds to employ outside artists. If Roosevelt wanted a different inaugural medal, it would have to come through unofficial channels.[35]

Saint-Gaudens was due back in Washington for a meeting with the president and the secretary of the Treasury on the evening of January 16. Gus had raised enough issues about dealing with the Mint to necessitate this follow-up discussion. In this meeting, the president was determined that Saint-Gaudens provide at least one design for the gold coin series and made it clear to Shaw that Saint-Gaudens should have total artistic control of his design and its execution. He wanted no interference from the Mint.

Then Roosevelt raised a totally new issue; he wanted an unofficial inaugural medal. Saint-Gaudens hedged. There was so little time and so many hurdles. Roosevelt was adamant. He would give Saint-Gaudens, or whomever Saint-Gaudens and Millet chose, an absolutely free hand. In following up after their meeting with a letter to Shaw, Roosevelt asked that his desires and concerns be communicated to the director of the Mint. To ensure that the president's concerns were heard, he freely lifted sections from Millet's letter to Edith in his communication with Shaw.[36]

As Saint-Gaudens returned again to New York, his head must have been spinning from the onslaught of Theodore and by proxy, Edith. While on the train, he sketched out a basic design for the inaugural medal.[37] In Philadelphia he stopped for consultation. In the sculptor's discussions with the president, he had asked Roosevelt to provide him with his favorite motto for inclusion in the inscriptions on the medal. Roosevelt had preferred "A Square Deal for Every Man" from his recent campaign.[38] Gus needed help rendering this motto in Latin.[39]

On the January 17, Theodore was again pushing Gus to accept the commission to provide new designs for the gold coins and the one-cent piece.[40] Concurrently, Roosevelt also queried General John Wilson, chairman of the Citizens' Inaugural Committee to determine if funding for a second medal could come from that source. In justification of this additional expense, Roosevelt observed that it was out of the question for an ordinary government employee, meaning Barber, to design a medal that would add to the stock of artistic achievement of the nation.[41] Wilson had no choice but to find the funds to make this second inaugural medal happen.

Two days later, Wilson wrote Saint-Gaudens formally asking that he undertake the special inaugural medal.[42] Wilson followed this letter with a telegram on the next day alerting Saint-Gaudens to the request.

Had Gus waited for the formal engagement letter to arrive, he might have hesitated about moving forward. It was everything that he abhorred. Funds would limit his artistic license. The diameter was entirely too small for his liking. The deadline was absolutely impossible for him to meet. But Gus did not wait. Like Wilson, he was reluctant to say no to his president. Upon receiving Wilson's telegram, he immediately replied directly to Roosevelt.

> If the inauguration medal is to be ready by March the first, there is not a moment to lose. I cannot do it but I have arranged with the man best fit to execute it in the country. He has a most artistic nature, extremely diffident but would do an admirable thing. He is also supple and takes suggestions intelligently....

> He is so interested that he begged me to fix any price. I named $250. That is a low sum for such work.

Saint-Gaudens would personally see to the medal's design. The sculptor he wanted to use was Adolph Weinman, his former assistant from 1895 and 1896. There was more; Gus supposed that the dies would be cut at the Mint. If not, Tiffany & Company and Gorham could do the work. Then he scribbled a quote from Tiffany for making the dies and striking the medals.[43] Gus was pushing to see how far the president would go in supporting him. He also told Roosevelt that he would communicate in a couple of days on the coin project. On that note, Roosevelt would gradually learn the artist's definition of a couple days.

Obviously Saint-Gaudens had given the medal advance thought. On the obverse would be Roosevelt's portrait. He intended keeping inscriptions in the simplest form to aid the dignity of the arrangement.[44] On January 23 Gus had his answer. The president had shown his letter to General Wilson. Wilson was requesting that Weinman come to Washington to meet the president. Saint-Gaudens and Weinman would do the unofficial inaugural medal. What Saint-Gaudens did not know was that Roosevelt had written a personal note to Wilson asking that Saint-Gaudens be given absolutely what he wanted in this matter.[45] Wilson was going to have little say in the matter of this inaugural medal.

On February 19, Saint-Gaudens in a letter to Wilson proposed a three-inch diameter medal, much larger than the "official" medals of recent inaugurations. Unsaid was that with the larger diameter, Saint-Gaudens would have the medals cast, always his preference. It would add to the costs, but he felt it worthwhile. He suggested as a cost savings compromise that the silver medals might be made at a 2-1/2-inch diameter, however regrettable that would be. To sugar coat this bitter pill, Gus held out hope, having now seen Weinman's model, that the gold medal could still be ready in time for the inauguration.[46]

Gus had great trepidation as to whether this proposal was going to fly. The following day, Weinman called on Henri Weil of Deitsch Brothers in New York City. Weil, a Frenchman trained in Paris, was working the firm's Janvier reducing machine, the latest technological innovation from France and the first of its kind to be imported to America. Weinman was seeking from Weil a bid in addition to the one from Tiffany & Company.

Next Saint-Gaudens sent Weinman to Washington to meet first with William Loeb and then with John Wilson. The sculptor pointed out that a three-inch diameter doubled the cost. Wilson was simply amazed. At first he would not even entertain another appropriation from his inaugural committee. President Roosevelt was unmoved by Wilson's objections.

Saint-Gaudens carried the day. At the February 23 meeting, Wilson's committee accepted his recommendation for a diameter of three inches. There would be two gold medals and 120 bronze medals cast. As a compromise, the silver medals were dropped from consideration. Now Gus could begin his "fine tuning" of the design.

Theodore Roosevelt was closer to onlookers than to dignitaries when giving his March 4, 1905, Inaugural Address. With brows furrowed, he read his brief address from a few sheets of notepaper. His key point, that much had been given to Americans and much would be expected from them, had its basis in the New Testament of the Bible.

March 4, 1905, dawned as a bright and windy but cold day in Washington, D. C. His speech was uncharacteristically brief—less than ten minutes. Its shortness served to emphasize his two main points. "Much has been given to us and much will rightfully be expected from us."[47] "Upon the success of our experiment much depends, not only as regards our own welfare, but as regards the welfare of mankind." These two phrases succinctly captured his vision for this, his second term. However, the highlight of the day was not the president's inauguration speech but the three and a half-hour parade that followed, including a full phalanx of Rough Riders.

Once the inaugural festivities were behind him, John Wilson focused anew on the medal, optimistically querying Tiffany & Company as to when it would be ready.

The answer was jarring. They had no models from which to commence the casting, and they had had no word from Weinman. Tiffany immediately alerted Gus to the potential trouble.[48] Gus promised Tiffany that the models would be complete in ten days or a fortnight.[49]

For the reductions, Weinman wanted to use Weil at least for the portrait side because of the absolute accuracy of the Janvier machine and the neatness of its execution. Weil could also increase or reduce the relief at will, although Weinman was happy with the relief as modeled.[50]

On Friday, March 10, the models were finished and shipped. Roosevelt's bust was in the Renaissance fashion. The pince-nez, being inconsistent with that style, was gone. Roosevelt personally disliked having the glasses in any sculptured likeness anyway. For the reverse, Gus approved the design of a standing eagle without a shield.

Edith Roosevelt, posing in her inaugural gown, still retained her youthful appearance but added was the poise and confidence of a very accomplished first lady.

It fell to Weinman to take the completed models to Washington to gain the president's approval. Years later Weinman related, "Teddy Roosevelt came in about 80 miles an hour, said 'Bully, bully' and dashed out."[51]

Still there was more back and forth as Saint-Gaudens changed the size of the lettering on the obverse. Weil now was reducing both sides.[52] His paraffin reductions reached Tiffany & Company on April 10. When Saint-Gaudens saw the first gold casting of the medal, he was not happy with Tiffany's work and rejected it. There then developed a back and forth between Tiffany & Company and Saint-Gaudens over the quality of their workmanship.

Finally at the end of the first week in June, Tiffany & Company delivered two more gold casts to Weinman. The patina of the second was that of an old gold coin that he found pleasing.[53] Weinman thought the quality of the casts good. Gus would not accept his word and wanted the medals sent to Cornish.[54] With this last review, Gus signed off.

Saint-Gaudens was never fully pleased with the gold casting. As the process came to an end, he sent the president a bronze medal instead for his review on July 6.[55] Roosevelt wrote back in glowing terms to Saint-Gaudens, saying he felt that they had suddenly imported a little of fifth or fourth century BCE Greece into America.[56] Roosevelt would tell Cabot Lodge that he particularly liked the eagle on the reverse and the Latin rendering of his campaign slogan— "*Aquum Cuique.*"

At the instigation of First Lady Edith Roosevelt, Augustus Saint-Gaudens designed an unofficial medal that was then modeled by Adolph Weinman. This particular medal was given by Theodore Roosevelt to his son Archie. Its flawless cast and beautiful patina argue that it was the medal that Saint-Gaudens forwarded to Roosevelt and that lay before Edith Roosevelt as she wrote her note of high praise and thanks to the sculptor in July 1905.

For some reason, Theodore was ambivalent about his likeness on the medal; Edith, however, was unstinting in her praise.

> Your medal lies before me as I write and I must say how very fine I think it and how happy I am in its possession. To me it is wonderfully good and I am indeed grateful that you were able to undertake the work—to me such an important one.

Written across this letter in the sculptor's hand when he read it was the notation: "Must I reply?"[57] Gus was flustered by the emotions in the first lady's note.

Saint-Gaudens now had no concerns about Roosevelt's ability to deliver on his promises. The president indeed wielded a big stick. With the conveyance of the bronze medal on July 6, Gus told Theodore that he was ready to take steps about the coinage designs. Accordingly, he would write directly to the secretary of the Treasury.[58]

Chapter 54

An Unwanted Interference

On July 10, 1905, Saint-Gaudens began an exchange of letters to define his commission with Mint Director George Roberts. Key within this correspondence was Saint-Gaudens's proposal to have the dies for his designs cut outside of the Mint. His reasoning being that the existing reducing lathe at the Mint required retouching the dies by hand; a "modern" one would obviate the need, reducing the models and cutting the dies entirely, including the lettering. He absolutely did not want Charles Barber retouching his work.[1]

On July 29, the Treasury secretary set forth the terms of the agreement. Two designs would be provided, one for the four gold coins and a second one for the one-cent piece. The fee would be $5,000, well below the sculptor's going rate. Saint-Gaudens had admitted that he had this project so much at heart that he would take what was offered by the government. Shaw had taken him at his word and went on to quote the statutes regarding design requirements and inscriptions. He noted that the eagle should be omitted from the reverse of the one-cent piece.[2] In a separate letter, Roberts pointed out that the sculptor was to provide only models, no dies. Also, the rim on his models would have to be higher than the design devices to facilitate stacking of the coins.[3]

In actuality George Roberts was a step ahead of Saint-Gaudens. He had sent Charles Barber to Europe in June to study modern minting practices. In his report to Roberts, Barber noted several pertinent issues. One involved the European method of milling coin blanks. The American practice called for basining the dies instead to add convexity that eliminated the need for milling. It was a technical subject but left unresolved how much additional relief could be imparted to a coin design using the American method. Barber also noted that the Janvier reducing lathe was in use at the mints in France, Italy, London, and Vienna. This machine could raise or lower relief or add a camber or basin to the background for coin models. Barber was investigating this issue because the Mint had a contract in place to replace their existing Hill reducing machine. He suggested, should the effort underway not prove satisfactory, consideration be given to purchasing a Janvier machine.[4]

Meanwhile at Cornish, nothing happened. The root of the problem went back to the fall of 1904. The American Philosophical Society had gained enactment of legislation authorizing the issuance of a medal commemorating the 200th anniversary of Benjamin Franklin's birth on January 17, 1906.[5] The celebration was to be sponsored by the State Department. Secretary Hay naturally asked Gus to serve on the committee charged with overseeing the medal's preparation. Harrison Morris, managing director of the Pennsylvania Academy of Fine Arts, was the chairman. The other committee members were American Philosophical Society President Edgar Smith and Charles McKim. The design was already dictated, the head of Franklin would be on one side and on the other the Muse of History would record Franklin's accomplishments with dedicatory wreaths for diplomacy, science, and philosophy. It looked to be an easy commission.

The project did not get off to a smooth start. Morris called for a meeting of the committee at the end of September 1904.[6] At the last minute Gus had to cancel because of illness.[7] The meeting was rescheduled to October 21.[8] Thus Gus was in New York for, among other things, this meeting on the Franklin Medal when his studio in Cornish burned to the ground. It was an ill omen, and much time would be required for its reconstruction.

At the meeting, Louis Saint-Gaudens was given the commission under Gus's oversight. Through the years, Gus had tried to take care of Louis by throwing commissions his way. Gus felt that Louis was truly more of an artist than he. The problem was that while Louis could create, he could also be indolent and disliked the work of modeling. He was absolutely incapable of the final effort to get the work into marble or bronze. He also lacked the necessary people skills: directing the workmen, conciliating the clients, and making the contracts.[9] A deadline of January 1, 1906, was set for distribution of the medal.

On Inauguration Day 1905, Morris, at Gus's suggestion,[10] queried the State Department whether the Franklin Committee must use the Mint to prepare the die for the medal.[11] The answer: There was nothing specific in the act that required the medal be struck at the Mint.[12] However, the money to pay for this outside work must come out of the appropriation, money that would otherwise be paid to Louis Saint-Gaudens as his commission.

At the end of June, Gus again entered the process to recommend Deitsch Brothers for the die preparation.[13] The Janvier quote from Paris was lower, and their work would be superior, but the time involved for delivery was unacceptable, given the project's deadline. Morris accepted Gus's recommendation and on July 3, 1905, received State Department permission to proceed.[14] Henri Weil, with his Janvier lathe would again be working with Saint-Gaudens.

The plaster cast of the Franklin Medal as first prepared by Louis Saint-Gaudens.

During July 1905, work on the Franklin Medal seemed to take both a step forward and a step backward. Louis finished the plaster reduction of the obverse and began work on a wax model of the reverse.[15] This obverse model then sat in Gus's studio for ten days while he experimented with variations in the inscriptions. In Louis's words, Gus had taken an interest, and it rested with him to say when the work was good enough to be called done.[16]

Was Louis expressing frustration or resignation? The answer was not forthcoming. A copy of the plaster obverse and photographs were promised to Morris but did not materialize.[17] In the meantime, Saint-Gaudens wrote Morris that his constant inquiries to Louis were upsetting his brother and interfering with the quality of his work. Future correspondence should be addressed to Gus.[18]

In August, Gus told Morris that a new composition for the head of Franklin had occurred to Louis and him. Fresh off the success with the Roosevelt Inaugural Medal, the two brothers were giving Franklin a Greek look. It would take a fortnight to complete. So, at the end of August, Morris still had not seen a model.[19]

Saint-Gaudens's including his brother in the text of the design change was a cover. Louis Saint-Gaudens had left Cornish abruptly.[20] Gus had taken on the artistic direction of the project in addition to the production end.

Now came the tedious work with Deitsch Brothers in preparation for cutting the dies. Henri Weil told Gus that they could cut the dies with one reduction if the models were from 15 to 18 inches in diameter and assuming that the medal itself would be either 4 or 4-1/2 inches in diameter. If the models were larger, a double reduction would be required. In either case Weil would like to have bronze castings made from which to cut the die directly.[21] Whether they would cut a die or a hub, from which a die would be made, Weil could not say until he had seen the models. Therefore, Gus would have to send the plaster casts in both positive and negative to accommodate.[22]

Meanwhile Morris was waiting for the photograph that had not come. Gus, still tweaking the obverse model, was not ready to let it go. Morris was beginning to get nervous; he knew that Louis had wanted to finish the design and modeling work by the end of September.[23] Weil was anxious as well and ready to start.[24] Gus finally released the obverse model on October 11. Yet, there was a change in the inscriptions even before it reached Weil.[25]

Still with no images in hand, Morris traveled to New York to see the obverse at Deitsch Brothers. There was the issue of approval by the committee members, a mere formality in this case. The design was also subject to the approval of the secretary of State and that was no mere formality. With John Hay's untimely death, Elihu Root had taken his place.[26]

At this point, Weil had made decisions in his approach to cutting the die for the obverse. Gus was trying to achieve the look of a cast medal even though the law specified a struck medal. As a result, the sculptor wanted a medal thickness of only one-eighth inch, requiring the additional step of cutting a hub. Intermediate bronze castings would also be necessary since the models were large enough to require a double reduction.[27]

Saint-Gaudens insisted not only upon inspecting the castings but also the paraffin reductions before allowing Weil to cut the die.[28] With the added work, Deitsch Brothers now raised the issue of additional pay.[29] Gus, admitting to acting as an intermediary for Louis, felt the overall charges too high. However, he would acquiesce for the time being.[30]

While the work on the Franklin Medal was distracting, it should not have been time consuming; Saint-Gaudens had assistants to execute the various changes. Though he believed his cancer was still in remission, there was no denying that his health was declining. He was suffering from night sweats, fever, and loss of appetite. He had progressed from codeine to morphine for his pain.[31] X-ray treatment was also being continued.[32] In addition, his bowels required constant attention. He was on a specialized diet of sweets and coffee. Occasionally he was able to have his beloved ice cream.[33] Golf in October and November was continuous, sometimes eighteen holes on the little course he had constructed at Cornish.[34] He was falling back upon vigorous exercise as a way to combat his pain.

Suddenly, the coin design project caught up with Saint-Gaudens. On November 6 Theodore Roosevelt wrote asking for an update. He had been looking at some gold coins of Alexander the Great and was struck by their high relief. Would it not work to have coins with high rims that would meet bank-stacking needs for ease of counting and still maintain high relief in the design?[35] Gus took five days to reply, agreeing with the president that a coin as Roosevelt had described was feasible.

Saint-Gaudens took the opportunity in his reply to also set forth his concept of the design for the gold coins. On the one side would be a standing eagle much like the one on the reverse of Roosevelt's inaugural medal. On the other side, he would place a figure of Liberty, possibly winged, striding energetically forward as if on a mountaintop holding aloft in one hand a shield bearing the Stars and Stripes with the word Liberty across the field. In the other hand, there would be perhaps a flaming torch. Liberty's drapery would be flowing as if in a breeze. Gus wanted to make it a living thing, typical of progress. This image embodied Roosevelt's view of America first expressed in his campaign speech in Michigan during the 1896 presidential election and expanded upon in his recent inaugural speech.

Saint-Gaudens recalled their conversation of the morning after the Diplomatic Reception dinner. Clearly the men had talked of the president's vision of an America rising that day as expressed in the sculptor's preliminary concept. Gus also noted that Theodore had spoken of a head of an Indian. That would be a superb thing to do but would it be emblematic enough of Liberty as required by law?[36] Here Saint-Gaudens was attempting to deflect the president; none of his preliminary sketches at this point included a Native American.

Theodore Roosevelt responded immediately, promising to press forward with the Mint people for high relief with a raised rim to placate the bankers and businessmen. He was hoping for a relief between that of the ancient Greeks and the low relief of the circulating coinage. He proposed that Saint-Gaudens have a design struck off in a tentative fashion, meaning preparing a model in high relief to determine if such a coin would be feasible. The president was content with the sculptor's concept of Liberty as beautiful, but could it be possible to give the image an Indian feather headdress?[37]

On November 22 Gus conceded the headdress issue to the president. Now he wanted Roosevelt's help dealing with Secretary Shaw on the mottos required for the gold coin design. He wanted to add either "Justice" or "Law" to "Liberty" and to know if "In God We Trust" was required. The end result was that a tack on to "Liberty" faded away; but it was clear that the law did not require the motto "In God We Trust." It could be dropped.

Mercifully there were no more letters from Roosevelt until late December, allowing Saint-Gaudens to put every effort into meeting the January 1, 1906, deadline on the Franklin Medal.

This likeness with a laurel wreath first used for the 1906 Franklin Medal was a radical departure from the image of Benjamin Franklin with which most Americans were familiar. When the commission was completed, the State Department asked that all artist proofs of this first version be destroyed. The gouge in Franklin's check was Tiffany's act of compliance. No other such pieces have appeared in the marketplace. Saint-Gaudens did receive permission to strike several uniface medals with the first or laurel wreath head.

Meanwhile, back in November, Morris had written Saint-Gaudens after seeing the obverse at Deitsch Brothers. He called it "chastely beautiful and correct in every way to celebrate the large but simple character of the man." Morris also now knew that the Mint would not be striking the medal and was pleased. He described the Philadelphia Mint as "incivility in a lump." However, Morris again raised the point that Root must approve the design. Gus's rebuttal was to the effect that there was no time to spare. Submitting the models to Root was virtually a matter of form.[38]

Time now was becoming a major concern. Morris again traveled to New York to catch up on the status of the reverse, finding it to his liking but not as much as the obverse. Again, the man pressed Saint-Gaudens to send models of both sides of the medal to Root.[39] Ignoring this request, Gus asked Morris when the medal should be completed. He received the same answer as before, January 1, 1906.

On December 19, Gus, in New York, gave the contract to strike the medals to George Kunz at Tiffany & Company. All was on track to meet the deadline. Gus now addressed the need to get design approvals. However, he dumped it on Morris, saying he would send the man plaster casts to show to "whoever is to see and approve of it."[40]

Meanwhile Gus returned to Cornish two days later feeling the work near completion.[41]

He was dead wrong as he found out on Christmas Day 1905. His son, Homer, had talked to Morris on December 22 about doing an article on the Franklin Medal. Morris told him that he could not allow publicity until the medal's release in April due to strictures placed upon it by the American Philosophical Society.[42] Homer related this conversation to his father on Christmas Day, and Gus instantly knew that January 1 had never been the actual deadline.

Now Gus was distressed and wrote Morris emotionally. He had taken on the finish of this medal at both a loss of time and money. More importantly, he had allowed things on the reverse to go uncorrected. He would wire Kunz to stop everything so he could get a better reverse.[43] At least that was what the final version of the letter said. In a scribbled draft Gus said something much different: He had let other projects slip or go unattended. [44] At the top of that list was the gold coins design.

On January 2, Saint-Gaudens received the Deitsch Brothers bill of $545 for their work preparing the first set of dies. Gus was at a loss to understand how it could be that much.[45] Deitsch in turn was at a loss to understand Gus's frustration with their bill. Their workload had increased well beyond the scope of the original quote.[46]

Gus sat on the Deitsch Brothers letter of explanation for several days. Finally on January 9, he sent a check, but he made it clear he was not happy with the situation.[47] Here work on the Franklin Medal paused.

Theodore Roosevelt was back in the mix, writing just before Christmas to see how his coin project was progressing. At least Saint-Gaudens had decided upon his design. For the reverse he intended using a standing Roman eagle. He had always admired a flying eagle but had ruled it out. The reason was that on the obverse he was going to employ the figure of Liberty with outstretched wings, straight from his Angel of Victory. If he matched his obverse with the extended wings of a flying eagle, there would be, simply put, too many feathers.[48]

With his reprieve on the Franklin Medal, Saint-Gaudens moved his focus to implementing the obverse and reverse design for the gold coins. On January 2, he asked Adolph Weinman to persuade Hettie Anderson to come to Cornish for a couple or three days.[49] The studio fire had destroyed his original plaster model using her for the Angel of Victory. Weinman forwarded this letter to Miss Anderson, and Gus recalled in his earliest draft of his autobiography that upon her arrival, she was just as splendid as when he had first set eyes upon her. [50]

On that same January 2, Saint-Gaudens wrote Secretary Shaw. Here he enlightened Shaw concerning his correspondence with Roosevelt. The two men had concluded that a trial between the extreme high relief of the Greek coins and the very low relief of the modern coins might show that a higher relief than currently prevailed would be permissible. In his closing sentence Saint-Gaudens acknowledged that any design would require a rim as high as the highest point of relief on the coin to facilitate stacking for counting purposes.[51]

Harriette Eugenia Anderson was an African American of light complexion from Columbia, South Carolina. In Saint-Gaudens's opinion, she had the figure of a goddess.

That letter sent Shaw running to Roosevelt's office. Roosevelt reminded the secretary that this project was his "pet baby." Roosevelt told Saint-Gaudens that Shaw was very nice about it. The president paraphrased Shaw's response. There were always a certain number of gold coins that had to be stored up in vaults, and that there was no earthly objection to having those coins as artistic as the Greeks could desire. Theodore observed to Gus that he thought this project would increase mortality seriously among the employees of the Mint. However, they would perish in a good cause![52]

With Roosevelt's letter in hand, on January 7, Saint-Gaudens again wrote Weinman asking for the loan of an Indian headdress.[53] Weinman located the headdress and threw in some photographs of eagles for good measure.[54] Two days later, Saint-Gaudens responded to Roosevelt, stating he would proceed along these lines to obtain high relief. Both the obverse and reverse models were well in hand. Whatever resulted would certainly be better than the inanities presently on the coinage. However, Saint-Gaudens was much more realistic as to the reaction at the Mint. There was "one gentleman there, however, who, when he sees what is coming, may have the 'nervous prostitution' as termed by a native here, but killed, no. He has been in that institution since the foundation of the government and will be found standing in its ruins."[55]

Saint-Gaudens was absolutely right about the reaction at the Mint. George Roberts wrote Shaw on January 13, protesting any design in high relief. However, recognizing the reality of the situation, he set forth two criteria that a high-relief gold coin design must meet. It must require only one blow of the coin press to permit cost-effective minting. It also must not lose weight and, therefore, value through excessive wear and abrasion on its highest points from circulation. Shaw relayed these requirements to the sculptor. The Treasury secretary and the director of the Mint, both, also wanted Saint-Gaudens to visit the Philadelphia Mint to carefully inspect its coining operations.

Suddenly in mid-January all progress on the commission stopped. Gus's health was in serious jeopardy. The doctors were recommending six meals a day to relieve him of his discomforts and to help him regain his strength.[56] Pain wracked Saint-Gaudens's body on the bad days. He needed medication to sleep at night. His increasing bowel irregularity was a symptom that a blockage was growing in his intestines. On January 15, Gus admitted in the daily log he had been keeping of his pain and medication to experiencing great depression and crying.[57] He wrote to his doctor that day in despair.[58]

The *Head of Victory,* also known as Nike Erene, or Victory Peace, has its origin in the Angel of Victory from the *Sherman.* It was a way for Saint-Gaudens to make additional income from his monumental works beyond the commission.

In spite of this rough spell, at the end of the month Saint-Gaudens decided to make a trip to Washington. However, no interim stop was made in Philadelphia to visit the Mint. Upon arrival, Saint-Gaudens visited Henry Adams and attended the Congressional Reception at the White House.[59] Yet he could not deny the pain. The trip to Washington sapped his strength. On the return journey to Cornish, he stopped first in New York City where he was so sick he could not eat.[60]

Still, Gus took this time for a little personal touch. Since well before January, Edith Roosevelt had been immersed in planning for the White House wedding of Alice to Congressman Nicholas Longworth. The Saint-Gaudenses now sent as a wedding present, a bronze of his *Head of Victory*.[61] Knowing Edith's preference for the *Sherman Monument*, from which the *Head of Victory* was derived with modifications to give a more youthful appearance, he was not surprised when Edith wrote promptly to say they were overcome by the gift.[62]

Upon arriving at Cornish, Saint-Gaudens focused once again on the Franklin Medal. The sculptor now was ready to send the obverse to Root for approval, relating to Harrison Morris that there had been a "misunderstanding" at Cornish over the matter that had now been corrected.[63] Still Saint-Gaudens delayed. He was waiting for the cast of the reverse to be completed, having rejected Tiffany's first attempt in which the inscriptions appeared crowded.[64]

A surviving model fragment of the offending Franklin image points to the probability that it was cut out of the center of the working model and Louis's first profile dropped into its place.

Then real trouble started. Elihu Root rejected the obverse of the medal. He didn't really reject it in the manner that John Carlisle had done in 1894. He was much more circumspect. He approved the design but doubted the laurel wreath upon Franklin's head, believing it a mistake and out of character. He had shown it to Roosevelt and the French ambassador, and they were in agreement.[65]

Morris was in a tizzy. He disagreed with Root; but he would leave Saint-Gaudens to mount any charge against the secretary. He assumed that Root's interference would disconcert Gus.[66] It was worse than that; Gus was now seriously sick and bedridden.[67]

Calmly Saint-Gaudens wrote to Morris that if Root and the others preferred Franklin without the wreath, it was useless to try to persuade them otherwise. He had had his assistant Henry Hering talk with Kunz and Deitsch. Kunz's advice had been particularly valuable.[68] The consensus was that a new obverse die could still be done without unduly delaying the completion of the medal.[69]

On March 7, Gus could take it no longer. He left with Gussie for the Corey Hill Hospital in Brookline, Massachusetts.[70] On March 13, he was put under ether, and an operation was performed on his artificial opening. While he was sedated, the doctors took the opportunity to examine his intestines. The prognosis was not good. Of the two doctors performing the surgery, one said the cancer would not return for five or six years. The other said it would return much sooner. Both men concurred that when the cancer returned, it would be inoperable. Gussie agonized, finally telling Gus that the doctors found no recurrence of the tumor but nothing more.[71]

After the surgery, Gus even wanted to hold Gussie's hand, which she found touching.[72] Recovery from the operation was slow. Gus did not attempt to return to Cornish until March 28.[73] In his later correspondence, he called it an "ugly time."[74]

Morris resumed his correspondence with Gus on April 4. While Morris preferred the figure with the wreath, he had accepted the change. Kunz believed the medal in its final form the handsomest produced in America. The presentation medal was struck in Alaskan gold, giving it a greenish tint.[75] The bronze medals would be done in this tint, too.

Once again Root stepped into the process. He did not like the green tint of the Alaskan gold. He wanted a new presentation medal using 18-karat gold. The bronze medals likewise should reflect a natural "brown" tint.[76] This time Gus had no objections.

Tiffany & Company now took on the Department of State. The end result was that the green tint would remain on the bronze medals but be reduced to about one-third in intensity. Also, the dies must be broken up and all copies, except those called for by statute, destroyed.[77]

Finished bronze medals reached Gus on April 20. He was not feeling well that day, and the medals were the last straw. The compromise green patina disappointed him keenly. Kunz had had trouble maintaining its consistency across the medals.[78] Yet he knew he must not be too tough on George Kunz; the man had moved mountains to get this medal completed on time.[79]

The 1906 Franklin Medal exhibited a green patina that did not suit Saint-Gaudens. However, he kept his objection to himself as those involved with the medal had moved mountains during his recent illness to have the medal completed on time.

Regardless of the patina problems, the official presentation occurred on April 20, 1906, in Philadelphia. It went off without a hitch with Secretary of State Elihu Root saying nice things.[80] But the focus of all in attendance, including the newspapers, was elsewhere. The event was pushed to page four of the *Philadelphia Inquirer*. The celebration seemed a non-event, as the world learned the horrific details of the catastrophe that had struck San Francisco two days before.

Chapter 55
Trial by Fire

By 1906, Frank Leach had become the longest serving superintendent in the history of the San Francisco Mint. With that extended tenure came experience. When engraver Barber made his report of European minting practices to George Roberts in the summer of 1905, the Mint director forwarded it to Leach for comment. Leach responded that Barber's discussion of milling of coin blanks in Europe needed to have taken the issue further. Leach implied that European reliefs were too low. What he could not say though was how much relief could be achieved at the American mints. At some point too much relief would cause excess wear on the most convex portions of the die.[1]

It was clear that Frank Leach had the full confidence of George Roberts and was effectively the lead superintendent within the Bureau of the Mint. Still the journey had not been without its bumps along the way. The worst of these had been the defalcation of his chief clerk, Walter Dimmick. Yet Frank Leach was about to be tested as no other superintendent in the Mint Service ever had or perhaps ever will.

When Frank Leach went to bed on the night of Tuesday, April 17, 1906, it was doubtful that he had any thoughts beyond the contemplation that tomorrow would be a beautiful spring day in the Bay area. The weather that day had been gray and sullen with fog lingering over San Francisco. Tomorrow would be a pleasant change; the forecast was calling for warm and balmy weather.

Oakland, where Leach lived, was not spared the fury of the earthquake that struck along the San Andreas Fault, reaching San Francisco at 5:13 a.m. on April 18, 1906. Leach awoke to the creaking and cracking noise of his house; the walls and ceiling of his bedroom were twisting. The house was in his words "dancing a lively jig," jumping the better part of a foot at each undulation of the earth underneath. There was the crash of falling glass and porcelain from the bric-a-brac collected over a lifetime. Bricks from the chimney thudded upon the roof. It seemed the shaking would never stop with each succeeding tremor feeling more violent. Leach was terrified. Seeing debris falling past his window, he decided staying in bed was as safe as anything he could do. Yet as horrifying as the shaking seemed, Oakland was some distance from the fault line. Though Leach could not have known it, San Francisco sat between two fault lines with the city center only eight miles from the San Andreas Fault.[2] The San Francisco Mint was at ground zero. The force of the earthquake would actually move the building two feet but leave it structurally intact.[3]

Finally the earthquake's violence subsided. In a room filled with dust, Leach hurriedly dressed and then went outside to assess the destruction. Buildings all around were damaged, but the extent of that damage did not, at first glance, seem particularly bad. The water and gas mains were still functional. However, Leach was taking no chances; the family fixed breakfast on a camp stove in the backyard. After breakfast, he decided to walk toward downtown Oakland, as much in curiosity as anything else.

As Leach walked, he saw nothing that even hinted at the disastrous nature of the quake. Then he got to a vantage point where he could look across the Bay to San Francisco. Up to this point, Leach could be described as being a somewhat detached curious spectator. He would admit later that not until he saw San Francisco had one thought of the Mint's condition crept into his mind. What he now saw horrified him: A massive cloud of black smoke hung over the city. Not only had San Francisco been hit by the quake, the city was on fire.

Leach propelled himself toward the trains that would carry him to the ferry slip. Then, if he was lucky, he could catch a ferry that would take him into the burning cauldron. Once on a train, Leach didn't move far until the engine came to a halt; there was congestion down the line. Leach jumped down and caught up with another train that had begun to move toward the ferry slip. In this manner, he reached the dock only to find that no one was being allowed to cross the Bay to San Francisco. In a flash, Leach hunted up the division superintendent in charge of the ferries and was on the next boat to San Francisco.

Once the ferry got underway, Leach went to the top deck to survey the situation. He wanted to see where the fires were burning in relation to the Mint, located on the northwest corner of Fifth and Mission, a block south of Market Street, the main thoroughfare of the city that ran southwesterly from the ferry building. What he saw was at once both frightening and awesome. Flames leaping high were visible all along the front of the city facing the Bay with the devastation centered in the wholesale, financial, and retail districts downtown. As the ferry neared its destination, Leach could now see the horrible impact of the fires in detail. Buildings and houses in the path of the fire were going down as if they were constructed of cardboard. First little puffs of white smoke would appear, coming out of the crevices of a structure. Next black smoke would envelop the whole building for an instant. Then, in a *coup de grâce*, flames would leap out seemingly from everywhere and the building would disappear. Still there was hope. Leach could not determine how far inland the fires had advanced; the Mint might yet be safe.

After the ferry docked, Leach walked out into a sea of fleeing refugees. Moving against the flow of people embarking, Leach saw that both sides of Market Street were ablaze. He first moved south, the most direct detour to the Mint; but these streets were burning too. Overhead, when the sun was visible at all in the dense black smoke, it appeared as an angry red orb. He then fought his way back north among the firefighters who were pumping the only water to be had, from the Bay, in an effort to save the docks. Going two or three blocks to the north he found he could skirt the fires. He worked his way to Union Square, noting that well-constructed buildings had survived the quake while poorly constructed frame structures were in a shambles, much like Oakland. There was just one big difference. In San Francisco the water and gas mains were hopelessly broken, a fatal combination.

From Union Square, Leach used Powell to reach Market, just slightly to the west of Fifth Street. Here he had his first encounter with the military. Without waiting for proper authority, the soldiers had been ordered from their barracks at the Presidio to help wherever possible. They had been posted along Market Street to keep people from going back into the districts to the south where the destruction and fires to that

This photo taken the day of the earthquake at the corner of California and Front streets, one and a half blocks north of Market Street, shows both the rubble from the quake and the subsequent fires. This is the inferno that Frank Leach had to fight through to get to the San Francisco Mint from the ferry terminal.

point were the most severe. Leach needed to break through their cordon to get to the Mint, barely a block away. Stopped immediately and physically pushed back; Leach found himself unable to rationalize with the soldier. The man's orders were that absolutely no one was to pass. Leach was angered by this soldier's mindless adherence to orders issued without first-hand knowledge. People were being prevented from going into their places of businesses to salvage what they could well in advance of the fires. Furthermore, the soldiers were under orders to shoot to kill any looters.[4] Why not clear out a store in advance of the flames? The goods inside would do nobody any good once the fire consumed them. The surreal situation in which Leach seemed now trapped angered him.

Leach worked his way toward Mason and tried to cross a second time, only to be stopped again. This time a nearby policeman recognized him, ignored the soldier, and escorted him across Market and down Fifth to the Mint. Leach found the Mint to be at the edge of the fire zone. Buildings directly opposite on Fifth had already burned. Another branch of the fire had swept Mission Street, again on the opposite side to the Mint. Now all was quiet at the front steps of the Mint.

Had Frank Leach arrived a little earlier, he would have been aghast at the sight. Women from the nearby Tenderloin District's red-light section had somehow decided to gather at the steps of the Mint. The evacuation had been gradual, allowing the women time to put on their finest. Some were in their new spring hats while others carried birdcages and jewel boxes. As they gathered with their male handlers, the mood of these women varied from gaiety to doom. Then a restaurant proprietor, well known to the women, came up the street with a wagonload of liquor and champagne that he was trying to save. The crowd closed around him, and he got no farther. Bottles of champagne were quickly consumed. Dancing started. More champagne was drunk. Then all propriety was thrown to the wind. The newspapers would report that an orgy developed on the steps of the Mint, stopped only by the bayonets and clubs of the soldiers and police shoving the revelers to safety as the fire approached along Mission Street.[5]

While escaping that first wave of fire, the Mint was far from safe. Surveying the situation, Leach could see that the Fifth Street fire and the Mission Street fire were going to converge along Fifth Street. A roaring inferno would then result, isolating the Mint and cutting off any possibility of outside assistance. Escape at that point would be problematic at best. If the Mint succumbed to this fire, anyone inside would be incinerated.

While Leach could see the fires, he really knew nothing of them. One had started a block from the Mint in an old boarding house. A stove had been started to cook breakfast and was upset by the earthquake. Had the hydrants been useable, this fire could easily have been put out. It was not, and its convergence with other flames eventually would produce what became known as the "Ham and Eggs" fire, the most vicious of the fires spawned that day by the earthquake. Frank Leach and the Mint were in the heart of this greatest of the conflagrations.

Leach found forty-seven employees inside. What he didn't know at the time was that many more had tried to reach the Mint but had been stopped by the soldiers and police. Whatever their fears for the safety of their homes and family, the employees had willingly put them aside to defend the Mint. In addition, Leach found a squad of ten soldiers commanded by a lieutenant who had been ordered to guard the place. The only real damage suffered to this point was to the two large stacks above the refinery that were cracked through a few feet above the roof. The men had already fought off the first fires. In the process they had removed everything flammable from the roof and thrown it down into the interior courtyard. Workmen had just replaced the wooden water tanks on the roof, leaving scraps of lumber strewn about. In addition, material from the old water tanks had been cut into firewood and dumped in the courtyard as part of the reconstruction effort. Now the courtyard was essentially fuel for the approaching flames.

Frank Leach knew he had little time; the worst was yet to come. He ordered all flammable material removed from openings in the walls from the north and west sides of the building. Everything moveable such as furniture was shifted to the south side. The steel shutters on the lower floors had been sufficient with the earlier fire as it passed on the south side of Mission. Now people had piled up bedding and furniture along the walls of the building, thinking it would be safe there. There was no time to remove these doomed household goods; Leach would just have to hope for the best.

The superintendent went up to the roof at one o'clock to survey the situation. It looked bad; by his reckoning, steel shutters would not save the building this time. A mass of flames was sweeping down on the Mint from Market Street. The fire had indeed crossed Mission to the west, moved northwesterly toward Market and then turned east toward the Mint. It had joined forces with the fires around the Emporium Building as if seeking reinforcements before making the ultimate assault on the Mint structure. Flames were reaching 200 and 300 feet into the air. Like some giant, horrible monster, it had circled its prey, building up a sufficient fury to now close in for the kill.

Leach divided his men and some of the soldiers and their lieutenant into groups and posted them to each floor and the interior courtyard. Hawes, captain of the watchmen, had the third floor. McLaughlin, superintendent of machinery, and Kennedy, former Oakland fire chief, were in charge of the roof. Kennedy's experience would prove to be a godsend if the going got tough, as expected, on the roof. Leach initially positioned himself in the basement. As Leach divvied up his manpower, he again encountered unbending military orders. A portion of the soldiers must guard the vaults that contained some $300,000,000 in gold coin and bullion. Never mind who would carry the gold away in this raging inferno.

Leach and his men were not helpless in the face of the onrushing flames. Some two or three years previously, he had decided to have the building piped and equipped with fire hydrants and hose, installed at suitable intervals on each floor, in case of an interior fire. The last of the hydrants had just been placed in service ten days previously. More importantly, the Mint had its own independent water supply. An artesian well had been drilled in the inner courtyard as part of the original construction of the building. This well was coupled with the strong pump in the boiler room to complete the fire suppression system. There had been just one problem with the system that morning. The pump connections were badly broken by the earthquake. In a repair that normally would have been very time consuming, Leach's engineer, Brady, now had the piping system serviceable.

All was ready. The pump in the boiler room would enable Leach to force a stream of water to any point on the roof. There were also the two large water tanks on the roof that, when filled, provided enough pressure for two hose streams at the basement floor. However, there was not enough water pressure to support hoses on the intervening levels. A bucket brigade would be necessary where there were no hoses. By now it was apparent to all that escape from the building, should the fire overwhelm them, was unlikely. Leach had a plan to evacuate the building but said nothing of it. He would take the men out onto the street to the burned-out section south of the building in hopes of riding out the heat generated from the ring of fire. It was a flimsy plan, and he knew it.

Frank Leach had barely placed his men at their stations when a shower of red-hot cinders, big and small, fell upon the roof. The weakest point was the tar and gravel hip roof section above the refinery. Along with the rest of the roof, this section had originally been sheathed in copper. However, over the years, this copper had gradually deteriorated due to the acid fumes from the refinery, necessitating its replacement with the much less fire-resistant material. Here also were located the damaged twin stacks from which bricks and plaster would peel off from time to time to add to the woes of the firefighters. As the fire neared, the cinders began to fall like hail stones in a storm. Their size ranged from a walnut to a man's hat in diameter. They formed a molten drift two feet thick in places where they piled together against a twenty-foot section of the building's protruding firewall. The men immediately turned their hose to wherever fires broke out on the roof and concentrated on keeping the tarred section wetted down at all costs.

Initially, Leach posted himself just inside from the courtyard. Upon seeing a soldier struggle with the water placement from one of the hoses, he went outside to show the man how to get the most efficient water stream. When he retreated, his hat and clothes were scorched from the heat of the fire. There still was a problem—one hose could not cover the entire courtyard. Engineer Brady came to the rescue by improvising an extra length of hose that turned the tide. With the remaining basement hose, the men now were faced with the fire coming in behind the iron shutters, fueled by the household items stacked against the exterior wall. Blinding smoke poured in from the smoldering bedding as well. The heat was so terrific that the shutters glowed cherry red; but still the men persevered.

As the shower of cinders played out, Frank Leach went up to the third floor, the most vulnerable. The buildings across the alley from the Mint were now burning. The Mint's granite and sandstone exterior began to flake from the heat. Each flake as it popped off the surface of the building would produce an explosive sound, much like cannon fire. In addition, the floors of the Mint were shaking from buildings tumbling to the ground in the wake of the fire.

Driven by the fierce heat, the situation was becoming critical. In complete desperation, Leach pulled the hose from the roof with its better head of pressure to fight the battle on the third floor. If he lost here, he was defeated. He was betting that he could stop the fire with the help of seventy-five feet of one-inch hose, little more than a garden hose! He initially placed the hose in the refinery where the floor was awash in diluted sulfuric acid. The glass in the windows of this room began to melt, allowing the flames and heat to pour through the open window frames and forcing the men to retreat. Now, with the added hose and buckets, a team would rush into a room holding their breath. They would put water down on the flames as long as they could stand it. Then they would retreat, and another team would take their place. Leach manned the hose with the men. Faces and hands were blistered from the intense heat. In this manner they rotated from room to room. Just as the men began to make progress, a billow of dense black smoke rolled into the building. It was suffocating, pushing the men away from the north side of the third floor and allowing the fire there to burn at will. Frank Leach had a sinking feeling that all was lost. The men with him looked at each other, wondering if the streets outside were passable and knowing the answer to that question. In desperation, and needing fresh air, Leach threw open a window on the east side of the third floor.

Just as the fight now appeared lost, the buildings adjacent to the Mint on the north side collapsed. With them went the platform from which the fire had been attacking the third floor. Now, without realizing it, Leach had created a cross draft with the open window on the east side. Just as quickly as it had come, the dense smoke retreated from the building. Leach immediately led the attack to retake the north end of the third floor. As they began to once again make headway against the fire, a desperate call came from the roof. The hose was badly needed again.

All through this onslaught, relying on Chief Kennedy's experience, the men on the roof had fought bravely. They had crouched behind the water tanks and chimneys, fighting to keep the fire off themselves and the hose as well as the roof. Now, without the use of their hose, the tar roof above the refinery was on fire. Also, the sub-roof under the copper sheathing where the cinders had drifted was in danger of burning through. Leach made a decision; the roof would have to wait. He had to control the fire on the third floor, or all was lost.

The area around the San Francisco Mint was reduced to rubble by the fires that swept the city after the devastating earthquake. The "Granite Lady," as the structure was affectionately known by San Franciscans, is scarred and scorched but still standing.

Leach and his crew fought on, standing in ankle deep diluted sulfuric acid and water. Finally, the fire's intensity eased, allowing the bucket brigade to handle the third floor alone. Leach then shifted the hose to the roof, where the men used axes to tear out the burning tar roof. Now able to propel water from the hose onto the burning sub roof beneath, the men quickly brought the situation to a satisfactory close.[6] Leach's decision to ignore the roof had been based upon the premise that the copper sheathed portion would burn much slower and that he had time before the situation above became irreversible. It was a gamble that proved correct, but just barely; the roof over the refinery had effectively been day-lighted. It was extremely close, but the battle had been won.[7]

It was now between four and five in the afternoon. Leach posted the men in watches. He ordered that steam be maintained in the boiler so that water pressure could be quickly gotten up should the need arise. Hoses and buckets were placed at perceived weak points in the building. Then, Leach let those he could spare go home to see what was left of their families and belongings. For Leach, the next job was to find his way back through the fire to the ferry building. He must get to a telegraph to notify Treasury that the Mint was still standing and the vaults, full of gold, unharmed.

When Frank Leach stepped into the street, he was shocked. Just a few hours earlier, buildings around the Mint were still standing. Now, all was desolation and smoking rubble. Nothing remained but the Mint. The street was a tangle of trolley wires, poles, and debris from the buildings. The cobblestones were hot to the touch, and the air was stifling to breathe. Eerily, there was not a human being in sight. His detour again led north of Market Street. The distance was much farther this time because of the advancing fire line. Leach saw the evacuation of Chinatown, chaos unto itself. The soldiers were using dynamite on structures in an attempt to form a new line of defense that the fire could not jump. It was a kaleidoscope of unbelievable sights for a man who had just spent the afternoon facing almost certain death defending the Mint. Not knowing whether the ferry building even still existed, Leach stumbled forward. This time, there were no soldiers to block his way. To his relief as he approached the dock area, he could see the building still stood. Along with the thousands of homeless refugees, Frank Leach boarded a ferry to Oakland. Like all the others now, he was numb from what he had been through.

When he disembarked, Leach headed immediately for the telegraph office. As could be expected, confusion reigned there. Leach as a government official had priority. He went to the head of the line and wired George Roberts in Washington that the Mint in San Francisco had been saved. Up to that time, no one in Washington had any idea of the extent of the damage. Reports were both horrific and fragmentary. Leach's wire was one bit of good news in an otherwise sea of disaster. To be on the safe side, Frank Leach, in a shaky hand, also scribbled out a note to Roberts. "Our boys made one of the wonderful fights in saving the Mint building. I don't see how it was done, courage and determination I guess it must have been." Along the way to the telegraph office, he had bought a newspaper. It wasn't even his old paper! The headlines screamed out: "San Francisco Doomed." He threw the extra edition into the envelope with the note, mailed them and headed home. It was past 9:30 in the evening, and he was dog-tired. As he walked home, flames from San Francisco illuminated the night sky in Oakland as if it were twilight.

When Frank Leach arrived at the ferry building in San Francisco early the next morning, it was almost deserted, a stark contrast to the previous day's pandemonium. He found a policeman and asked if he could reach the Mint on foot. The man was pessimistic; the fire was burning north and south of the ferry building along the Bay. A passerby overheard the conversation and volunteered that two parties had made it to the ferry building that morning along Market Street. However, falling walls from a burned-out building had killed one of their number.

The initial going was tough; the smoke rapidly enveloped him so that he could barely see or breathe. Rubble was everywhere and in a couple of places, he had to crawl on all fours to get over the fallen ruins. Any kind of an aftershock would bring the teetering walls, the burned-out shells of the buildings that had lined San Francisco's main thoroughfare, down on his head. Luckily conditions eased as he approached Fifth Street. Now, as he made his way forward, he noticed the awful silence that had settled over the burned-out ruins. When the superintendent turned the corner onto Fifth Street, his heart thrilled at what he saw. Amidst the blacks and grays of the surrounding rubble, the red, white, and blue of the American flag blazed forth from a makeshift flagstaff from the front gable of the San Francisco Mint.

Once inside the building, Leach encountered a problem. The squad of soldiers had remained over night to stand watch. One or two of them had found some whiskey and gotten drunk. Fearing trouble, the officer in charge had ordered the doorman not to let the men outside. Now one of the drunks was threatening to shoot the doorman if he did not let him go out. In Leach's words, "it was an ugly situation." Leach talked the soldier down, sent for the sergeant in charge and dismissed the troops. This kind of protection he did not need, no matter how much gold was in the vaults.

With the Mint safely secured, the work at hand centered on reestablishing a financial system and restoring confidence in the area banks. Every bank had burned. While they had fireproof vaults, it would be many weeks before the vaults cooled sufficiently to open.[8] Included with the banks was the Sub-Treasury through which funds were transferred into and out of the region. Without the Sub-Treasury, there was no effective way to transfer funds into the devastated area. Assessing the situation, Leach on Friday advised the secretary of the Treasury that the Mint could accommodate the Sub-Treasury. Authorization was prompt in coming.

On Saturday, Leach requested of the Treasury Department the free and prompt transfer of funds through the Mint against deposits held by the area banks in New York City. Again authorization came, and the privilege was extended to individuals as well. Leach was also seeking permission to cash checks for the War and Navy Departments in the region. He would even go so far as to advance money to the commandant of the Mare Island Navy Yard to help meet the payroll.

By Sunday all but four of Leach's employees were accounted for; however, a lot of them had no home left. He was faced with the reality of providing accommodations for his men within the Mint building. He turned to the army for what cots, bedding, and supplies they could provide and purchased the rest of the needed supplies in Oakland. It was obvious to him that subsistence for the employees was going to be a long-term situation. Meanwhile, his electrician, James Marshall, had ingeniously converted a large motor into a generator so that he had electricity for lights Saturday night. Lighting was also provided around the outside of the building where the homeless were gathering. His permanent furnaces being down for lack of gas, he next requisitioned portable coke cupelling furnaces so that he would be able to receive and assay deposits of bullion. Frank Leech intended to be open for business on Monday morning, and he was. The army signal corps had even run a wire to the building, connecting him to the rest of the world. His four missing employees reported in as well. In addition, he had his engineer run a water line to the outside of the Mint for the refugees who had now formed a sort of tent city around the building. He even had some of the comforts of home; two enterprising barbers had set up shop on the front steps of the Mint.

Frank Leach made himself available to the press on that Monday, April 23, with quotes both succinct and positive. The Mint was virtually unharmed. The men had been at their posts since Wednesday, the day of the earthquake. There was an ample supply of money in the Mint's vaults. In fact, there was more money than San Francisco needed. The secretary of the Treasury had instructed Leach to turn over money to the banking institutions whenever needed. Leach had talked to the area bankers, and they were all anxious to have money transferred promptly. Leach was only awaiting the establishment of some sort of financial accounting system by the commercial and banking interests.[9] Anyone reading his quotes could not help but conclude that the banks were both solvent and stable, and recovery was just a matter of time.

Even with that support, the banks delayed, fearing a run on their institutions by a panicked civilian population in an effort to obtain cash for food and shelter. A delegation of bankers came to Leach for help on Wednesday. Without the use of their vaults, the bankers wanted Leach to debit against their credits at the Mint for funds that could be drawn by their clients. This request was beyond him; he was no banker and had not the manpower to keep the ledgers necessary to support such an operation. After much discussion, he proposed a central bank or clearinghouse made up of all the San Francisco banks be set up within the Mint. From the moneys in the vault, Mint funds would provide the initial capitalization of this combined banking operation.[10] The banks agreed and were to request permission to establish such from the secretary of the Treasury. By Friday of that week, April 27, Leach could not determine the status of that request, but he had a bigger problem.

As early as the Monday after the quake struck, the city had put crews into the burned-out areas with virtually no training to dynamite the unstable walls that were still standing.[11] Leach observed that the dynamiters worked on the principle that if a small amount of dynamite was good, a large amount was even better. One of his men skilled in the use of dynamite observed that he could have removed all the walls standing on Market Street with the powder these inexperienced men used on just one building. Blasting from as far away as Seventh and Market damaged the Mint. Pieces of iron from blasts a quarter-mile away were landing in the courtyard, and the signal corps telegraph wire had to be abandoned. Before it was over, no windowpane in the building remained completely intact. The fate of the stacks over the refinery that had been in question was now sealed; they would have to come down.

In response to the problem, Leach offered to supply men experienced in the use of dynamite, but the offer was ignored. He protested to the mayor that produced a non-meeting the following morning. However, from that meeting, Leach learned that the Emporium Building was to be demolished that very day. In frustration, he immediately turned to General Funston, the officer in charge of the regular army troops deployed in the city. Funston sent a colonel to meet with him. It was now near noon, and the dynamite crew was approaching the Emporium. The area blasting had become so heavy that the Mint building suffered some kind of injury from every blast, halting its repair work. Leach tried to explain to the colonel his predicament, but the man was disbelieving, stating that there was no danger and the work was in competent hands. At this point, a blast a quarter-mile away rained debris down upon the building and the two men, putting the discussion at an end. The colonel stopped the demolition of the Emporium as well as all blasting in the vicinity of the Mint.

The issue of whether the banks would establish a clearing-house bank at the Mint was settled in the headlines of the *San Francisco Chronicle* on Sunday morning, April 29.[12] The paper announced that the banks would begin collectively disbursing funds at the Mint on Tuesday, May 1.[13] The bankers had never contacted the Treasury Department for permission. Leach got formal notification from them on Monday, April 30, to the effect that the clearing-house operation would open for business the next day.

At 9 o'clock on May 1, a line of people waiting to withdraw their deposits had formed at the main entrance to the Mint. Would there be a run on this makeshift banking association when it was scheduled to open at 11 o'clock? The setup was hardly one to instill confidence. Situated in the Mint cashier's office, tellers and officials were crammed into the now tight quarters. Nailed to the jamb of the door was a narrow piece of rough board with the black letters "Clearing-House Bank." The time for the operation to commence arrived, and still the doors did not open. By now the line stretched into Fifth Street and around the corner onto Mission. Leach and his men were still laboring to bring two and a half million dollars in gold and silver from the vaults to the cashier's office.

At 11:30 all was ready, and the depositors were escorted into the building in groups of twenty past armed guards stationed in the corridors leading to the cashier's office. Withdrawals were restricted to $500 per customer.[14] All that day the tellers kept busy paying depositors; but, on Wednesday the rate of withdrawal fell significantly. On Thursday the rate had slowed to a trickle. In the three days, some $500,000 had been withdrawn.[15] There would be no run on the banks, an event Leach had never felt was going to happen in the first place. Perhaps realizing the awkward position into which they had put Leach, the bankers sent a resolution of thanks to Secretary Shaw for the use of the Mint on May 10.

There remained one more significant action for the superintendent. The Selby Smelting and Lead Company was possibly the distributor of the greatest amount of cash of any business in the region.[16] Leach asked permission on May 1 for Selby to set up a temporary office within the Mint, expecting that they would need it no more than three or four weeks. Selby could in this manner resume purchases of bullion from the mines. Leach then promised that the Mint would take delivery from the company of their finished product immediately. It was an efficient and quick way to pump cash into the crippled regional economy that funneled into San Francisco. Shaw was resistant, initially not wanting to show such favoritism to a private company. However, his concerns were overcome, with Selby receiving permission on May 3.[17]

The San Francisco Mint was now truly open for business. However, these myriad activities were all temporary. On May 23 the clearing-house operation closed, and the banks in San Francisco opened for business on their own. With the removal of this activity, business at the Mint returned to as near normal as could be expected.[18]

Frank Leach had done as much as any one human being could to ease the pain of this great catastrophe. However, the chaos extended far beyond the cinders and charred remains of this great financial center of the Pacific Coast. Total losses were estimated at the time to be a staggering $350 million to $500 million. There would be worldwide implications from a loss of this magnitude.

As the initial financial losses became known, stocks dropped across the board on both the New York and London exchanges. In the two weeks following the earthquake, particularly hard hit were railroads, off 15 percent and insurance companies, off as much as 30 percent.

Relief funds were drawn not only from across the United States but from England, France, Germany, and the Netherlands. These countries collectively sent $50 million with Great Britain alone contributing $20 million. However, looming largest were potential insurance claims from the catastrophe. Much of San Francisco's insurance underwriting protection was provided by foreign concerns. British firms had provided about half of the city's fire insurance policies and faced losses of as much as $50 million. For some domestic insurance companies, the situation was even worse. Fireman's Fund Insurance with assets of $4.5 million faced claim losses of $11.5 million.

Faced with financially crippling claims, some underwriters imposed lengthy delays in payouts while others discounted claims, insisting that earthquake related fire damage was not covered in their policies. The Hamburg-Bremen Insurance Company imposed a 25 percent discount on all claims. Only six companies fully honored their obligations.

To fund these payments, every insurance company was forced to liquidate significant investments, further depressing markets. It also prompted a major flow of gold from London to the United States in support of claims settlements. By September 1906, Great Britain's gold stocks had declined by 14 percent, the largest outflow to be experienced in the first decade of the twentieth century for the British, creating problems for the Bank of England.

The East Coast was not immune to this gold flow to San Francisco. With fall, came the annual outflow of money from New York to the agricultural regions of the country to fund the harvest of a bumper crop. As a result, by winter 1906–07 a capital shortage developed in New York, causing interest rates to increase. As the year 1907 began, there was a growing concern among the upper echelons of the New York financial institutions, foremost among them being J. P. Morgan & Company.[19] Would there be enough money available to fund America's continued economic expansion or would there be a serious economic reversal?

Chapter 56

Racing Against Death

As his focus shifted from the Franklin Medal back to the gold coins design, Augustus Saint-Gaudens was sicker than he wanted the world to know. In early May 1906 when Stanford White and Charles McKim wanted to visit him, he put them off, saying that the mud season was worse than normal that year.[1] However, he could not put off the gold coins design; work needed to resume, no matter his condition.

Gus quickly finished the sketches that laid out the composition and arrangement of the design devices. In his weakened state, he delegated the modeling to his assistant Henry Hering. Although he knew that Hering would be sadly at sea if left on his own, Saint-Gaudens considered him an admirable workman who could create excellently what was laid before him to do.[2]

Once again Gus seemed to cause a stir at Treasury when he wrote to update Secretary Shaw on May 23 that the reverse was almost complete and the obverse was proceeding nicely. Now, he was asking permission to use Roman numerals for the date. He also wanted to make a plaster cast of the existing twenty-dollar gold piece that would reveal precisely the relief presently being achieved.[3] By inference, Saint-Gaudens was going to adapt his design first to this largest of the gold coins. Shaw was against Roman numerals but told Gus he would take it up with Roosevelt.[4] Roosevelt promptly overrode his secretary of the Treasury.[5]

It was an upbeat Saint-Gaudens that reported to the president on May 29 that the reverse model was done. However, before showing it to Roosevelt, he wished to have reductions made at different reliefs that would take some additional time. In the meantime, the sculptor would continue work on the obverse so that no time would be lost. Saint-Gaudens was also sending Hering to the Philadelphia Mint to obtain additional details necessary to complete the project. His closing comment to Roosevelt had a certain chill to it. "If you succeed in getting the best of the polite Mr. Barber down there, or the others in charge, you will have done a greater work than putting through the Panama Canal. Nevertheless, I shall stick at it, even unto death." [6]

Did Saint-Gaudens have a premonition about the gravity of his illness? His son, Homer, wrote his father-in-law that Gus was a very sick man. The doctors were no longer optimistic about his long-term prognosis. Homer was beginning to fear that his father would not survive to yearend.[7]

Feeling that his design for the gold coins was to the point of fine-tuning, Saint-Gaudens shifted his creative work to the one-cent piece. He wrote to George Roberts on June 16, his first direct communication with anyone at the Bureau of the Mint since taking on the redesign commission, to ask if there would be a problem resurrecting a version of the flying eagle design that had been used for a short period in the late 1850s on the newly created small-sized cent.[8] Roberts wrote back that there was no problem using some form of the old design.[9]

If the president had missed the offhand comment about Gus's health in the previous letter, Gus's letter of June 28 from New York was much more direct. He was in the hands of the doctors until the beginning of August. Gus would let Roosevelt know when his presidential persuasion might be needed at the Mint.[10]

Sick or not, Saint-Gaudens now began maneuvering to cut Barber out of engraving the dies. In an undated note that summer, Gus asked Watson Gilder to come see him. The standing eagle side of the design was done, and he wanted Gilder to help with having at least the dies cut abroad. "A word in someone's ear (meaning Roosevelt's) from you would settle it."[11] Anticipating gaining that permission, Gus had sent the reverse model to France on June 10 to have the reductions prepared at three differing reliefs.[12]

Saint-Gaudens first envisioned a standing eagle for the reverse of the gold coins design. He sent his model to Paris for reduction in the summer of 1906, seeking the best possible reduction. This reduction was part of the package shown to President Roosevelt on September 10, 1906.

Roosevelt wrote again on July 30 for an update. Unable to leave his room for days at a time[13] and frustrated with the slowness of his recovery,[14] Saint-Gaudens had Homer answer on August 2. Homer was not willing to discuss the cancer and told the president that Saint-Gaudens was sick with sciatica. Through the clear eyes of Homer's young wife, Cottie, the sculptor seemed to be dying by inches.[15]

Homer went on to say that the studio work was done. Experimental reductions were being carried out in Paris. It was the only place where the reductions could be given their proper relief. Homer expected the reductions for the reverse of the gold coins to be back by the end of the month. Then if considered advisable, the model for the obverse in the studio could be sent to Paris where the dies could be properly made unless there was some difficulty with striking American coins with French dies. However, if the president wished, Homer could bring the models to Oyster Bay immediately for his review.[16]

First, Theodore wrote back to Homer not to concern himself with the delay. It was a kinder and gentler Roosevelt who was now aware that Saint-Gaudens was seriously ill, wishing him a speedy recovery. The president would postpone action on the design effort until the following March 1907, after the Fifty-Ninth Congress had adjourned.[17] The family's public denial of Gus's terminal illness had had the unintended effect of misleading Theodore Roosevelt. In fact, they were also keeping the gravity of the situation from the sculptor himself for fear that he could not stand the shock.[18] Time was of the essence and neither the president nor Saint-Gaudens realized it.

When the reverse reductions returned from Paris, Homer met with the president at his Sagamore Hill home on September 10,[19] also bringing the plaster models for the obverse of the gold coins and both sides of the one-cent piece. There is no written record of the meeting, how much discussion was had, or if the son was even capable of holding his own with the president. Only Roosevelt's subsequent communication with Secretary Shaw gave an indication.

This model (in the negative) of a Winged Liberty was intended as the obverse for the gold coins design in the package presented to President Roosevelt on September 10, 1906. Liberty sports a feather headdress that Roosevelt had successfully advocated for previously with Saint-Gaudens.

This Flying Eagle model was intended by Saint-Gaudens to be used as the obverse of the one-cent design. However, when President Roosevelt saw this design in the September 10 1906 package, he insisted it be used for the reverse of the gold coins design.

President Roosevelt anticipated difficulty with the Mint people over relief. Clearly Hering's meeting in Philadelphia that summer had not gone well. Barber was quoted as saying they could not make cuts deep enough in the die to achieve the relief Saint-Gaudens wanted. Saint-Gaudens had then directed the same question to Tiffany and Gorham. George Kunz of Tiffany & Company stated they could make cuts deep enough in the die without difficulty at a single stroke. At this point Roosevelt took off the kid gloves.

> All I want to know from Mr. Barber is how long it will take to make them, and the cost, and if there is likely to be a long delay and seemingly too much expense, I shall want him to communicate with Messrs. Buck [Gorham] and Kunz [Tiffany]. But if he has to communicate with them, I should regard it as rather a black eye for the Mint and a confession of inferiority on their part to Tiffany and Gorham.[20]

This letter exploded with the impact of a bombshell at Treasury. Shaw wanted Barber to proceed with the work at once.[21] The engraver was rushed to Washington for a meeting on September 25 with Roberts.[22,23] High relief remained an issue, needing a practical test to determine its feasibility. It would take six weeks to prepare the hubs and first two sets of dies. Everyone at the Mint would cooperate in this test. The Mint's coin presses and all their other equipment were modern and up to date, but those presses might not have the capability to strike the desired relief. If either Tiffany & Company or Gorham had developed coin presses better suited to high relief, Mint personnel would not hesitate in seeking their help.[24]

Maybe the coin presses were up to date, but the Hill reducing machine certainly was not, being almost forty years old. Efforts to replace this machine had ended in failure in June 1906 with Roberts cancelling the contract.[25]

Roosevelt forwarded Roberts's letter to Gus. He put the sculptor in a tight spot. Now that he had the Mint's attention, how soon could Saint-Gaudens get models to them for a test?[26] Foreclosed was any attempt to have the dies cut outside the Mint. On October 6, Homer Saint-Gaudens communicated Saint-Gaudens's fallback position to Roosevelt. Gus was insisting upon "a machine as is to be had in Paris" and asking the president's help.[27] Again the president came at the Mint.[28] Barber found himself writing the justification for the purchase of a new Janvier reducing lathe on October 8. In fact, Barber had had discussions with Deitsch Brothers in the past, and at that time they had been willing to give the Mint a machine at cost.[29]

Roberts immediately wrote Saint-Gaudens on October 10 to update him on the proposed purchase. Saint-Gaudens should forward the 5-3/8-inch model of the standing eagle to the Philadelphia Mint so that Charles Barber could take up work on it.[30]

Now Gus needed to update Roberts on the latest design changes. Roosevelt had taken a liking to Gus's flying eagle design for the one-cent piece. However, the president, using a flawed legal interpretation, had assumed the coinage statutes precluded its use on the penny. Wanting to preserve the design, Roosevelt had proposed using it for the reverse of the gold coins design. The standing eagle design was now orphaned. Homer's luncheon meeting with the president was the only opportunity for this switch to have occurred. Thus, the son, besides foreclosing the option of using the Paris artisans, had ceded artistic control to the president. That was something that could not have pleased the father and explains why Homer never subsequently revealed the events of the September 10, 1906, meeting in any detail. The sculptor must start over on the obverse as well. In reality, the meeting between Homer and the president now became a complete nightmare for Augustus Saint-Gaudens.

This setback could not have come at a more unfortunate time for Gus. He was laid up in bed, seeing no one and unable to visit the studio even for a short time. The treatments over the summer in combination with the surgery the preceding spring had been unable to stop the resurging cancer. To help with Gus's discomfort, a sleep aid, bromidia, was prescribed. Homer's mother-in-law, who was staying with the family at the time, feared that the dosage was particularly strong but did not want to cross Mrs. Saint-Gaudens.[31]

Gussie had another burden that she was unwilling to share with her husband. Work at the studio without Gus's participation had slowed. The studio and its staff of assistants required $1,000 a week to operate. If Gus could not resume his supervisory duties, Augusta was seriously considering layoffs.[32] Over the years, Gussie had grown to hate the staff. She saw Gus getting high prices for his work but spending it all on assistants.[33] With the backlog of commissions, shuttering would eliminate future cash flow while generating liabilities from previous progress payments on the unfinished work. For once, Augusta turned her back on her economizing ways, seeking instead a loan from one of Gus's clients.[34]

On November 6, George Roberts left for an extended trip to the Pacific Coast. However, before leaving, he failed to explain to Barber that the model Saint-Gaudens had sent was only for the standing eagle reverse and that Barber's work would be "experimental." On the day of Roberts's departure, Barber wrote in answer that Saint-Gaudens had indeed supplied only the eagle side of the coin. He had completed his work from that model. He could do nothing more until he had the model for the other side.[35] On the next day, Robert Preston, once again serving as acting director, wrote Barber, suggesting that he inform Saint-Gaudens that he was waiting for the obverse model.[36] Neither of these two men was going to communicate directly with Saint-Gaudens. That task fell to Secretary Shaw who queried Saint-Gaudens on November 10 as to the status of the model for the Liberty side of the twenty-dollar gold piece.[37]

Puzzled, Homer Saint-Gaudens replied on November 14 that the other models in the larger sizes were not ready due to his father's illness. He repeated that the reduction on which Barber had worked was experimental to test their machinery. He also attached a copy of the letter of explanation to Director Roberts from October 10 in support.[38]

Barber, seeing this correspondence, on November 20 rebutted that he stood ready to take the models chosen by the president in eleven- to fourteen-inch diameters (as required by the Hill reducing machine) and make the required reductions. He rightly took issue with experimenting with a one-sided design that was not going to be used. The only experiment, of any use, would have to be made from designs ultimately to be struck.[39]

That was Barber's official response; his unofficial letter of protest went to Preston on November 26. He was just as sure that the relief of the standing eagle design would never coin as he was that the sun would rise each morning. "I think our friend is

Charles Barber in his later years as engraver at the Philadelphia Mint.

playing a game as he did when you and John G. [Carlisle] had to call him down, and that he is not anxious to show his hand, he possibly thought we would say we cannot coin your work and that would end the matter." Barber closed by saying he was just simply desirous that Preston understand why nothing was being done at Philadelphia so that "when the patience of all folks in Washington is exhausted, the wrath shall not descend upon us."[40]

Did Barber have an ulterior motive for making these comments? Sometime in 1906, he had set to work with George Morgan's help on a competing design for the twenty-dollar gold piece.[41] With the exception of the placement of the motto "E Pluribus Unum" in raised letters on the coin's edge, his work plowed no new ground. The obverse bore a striking resemblance to his Liberty as depicted on the obverse of the subsidiary silver coinage. The reverse resurrected his standing figure of Columbia that had been rejected early in design project of 1891.[42] It would not do to bring this work out in competition with Saint-Gaudens; however, if the sculptor had no viable design, the way would be clear for Barber.

This 1906 pattern double eagle (J-1773) was executed by Charles Barber, probably in late fall when he expressed the belief that Saint-Gaudens did not have a workable design. The obverse design featured a head of Liberty, not unlike his image for the subsidiary silver coins. The reverse borrowed the design from his rejected initial pattern (J-1766) for the subsidiary silver coinage.

With George Roberts's return, affairs at the Mint resumed a more even keel. The Mint director wrote George Kunz at Tiffany; he wanted to see what could be done using a forming die to pre-strike each planchet before gaining the final impression from the regular die. He believed the beauty of the resulting piece would be worth the slight additional expense. However, Roberts remained concerned about metal loss from abrasion and whether the Mint could maintain satisfactory execution of the design in the striking process when mass producing the coins.[43]

On December 8, Gus wrote to Roberts saying the models were ready. He asked if the Mint wanted the plaster models shellacked. Shellacking sealed the plaster surface making it suitable for producing an intermediate bronze cast. Augusta signed this letter.[44] Roberts replied that he was hopeful that a forming die to pre-strike each planchet would be successful. The Mint would work on the problem after receiving both the obverse and reverse models. He asked that Gus be patient, as the Mint was attempting something that had not been done before.[45]

Now the correspondence resumed between the president and Saint-Gaudens. Roosevelt's note was polite but adamant, when could he have the new models.[46] For once, Saint-Gaudens was prepared.

Just before Christmas 1906, a severely ill Augustus Saint-Gaudens sent this first model to Theodore Roosevelt at the White House. It would produce the ultra-high relief double eagle. Gone was the feather headdress; Saint-Gaudens had unilaterally rejected the president's wishes in this matter. Combined with the elimination of Liberty's wings, the new look was cleaner and allowed for an increased emphasis upon the rays of the sun in the field.

By late that fall 1906, Henry Hering had returned to Cornish from his New York City studio to rework the gold coins design for Saint-Gaudens.[47] Liberty, patterned after the Sherman Angel, had lost her wings and headdress. President or not, the headdress was a distraction. In Liberty's right hand was a torch, a concept borrowed from the rejected reverse of Saint-Gaudens's World's Columbian Exposition Award Medal. In the left field was a silhouette of the United States Capitol, Saint-Gaudens's quiet salute to the ongoing efforts of the 1902 plan for the nation's Capital. The reverse was the flying eagle originally intended for the one-cent piece. This was no ordinary eagle; the wings of the Angel of Victory might be gone from the obverse, but they were not forgotten. They now graced a majestic eagle in full flight on the reverse.

With anxiety, Gus shipped the large plasters to Theodore on December 14.[48] Roosevelt responded on December 20, 1906.

> These models are simply immense—if such a slang way of talking is permissible in reference to giving a modern nation one coinage at least which should be as good as the ancient Greeks. I have instructed the director of the Mint that these dies are to be reproduced just as quickly as possible and just as they are. It is simply splendid. I suppose I shall be impeached for it in Congress, but I shall regard that as a very cheap payment! [49]

Roosevelt immediately sent the models to the director of the Mint who took the opportunity to personally deliver them to Philadelphia so that he could have another chat with Barber.[50] On Christmas day 1906, Theodore Roosevelt and Augustus Saint-Gaudens had every reason to be optimistic that the end of their project was now in sight.

Chapter 57
Twice a Failure

President Roosevelt knew Saint-Gaudens' gold coin model was not going to be practical for standard coinage. Yet he told Roberts, "I want for once at least to have had this nation, the great republic of the West, with its extraordinary facility of industrial, commercial and mechanical expression, do something in the way of artistic expression that shall rank with the best work of the kind that has ever been seen."[1] Likewise, Roberts thought the design beautiful and considered that its ultimate execution for general circulation would be a mark of distinction during his service at the Bureau of the Mint.

Again, Henry Hering drew the difficult duty of dealing with Charles Barber. When Hering wrote of this experience in 1949, the last year of his life, he recollected meeting George Roberts and Charles Barber in Philadelphia that week following Christmas, 1906. He brought models with him that had been cast after the first set sent to Roosevelt and now in Roberts' hands. He knew the model would meet resistance and had told Saint-Gaudens that it would not work. Gus had lightly responded that Hering could do as he pleased because "Teddy and I are behind you."

The tone of the meeting with Charles Barber had not dimmed in Hering's memory. When Barber saw the models, his ability to envision how a design would strike caused him to reject them out of hand. No modern mint could produce a coin for general circulation from these models with their extremely high relief. Hering informed Barber that he wanted to start from the highest relief possible and work backward, experimenting to find an acceptable level of relief. Barber, after much discussion, acceded to Hering's request to prepare dies from this model.[2] He really had no choice.

Hering got his two cents' worth in with Barber as well. When Barber showed him the reduction of the standing eagle model done the previous fall, Hering informed him that it was a pretty poor reduction and he thought that Barber could do better. Hering asked about the reducing lathe that Barber had used on the standing eagle model. Barber showed Hering the old machine but was not forthcoming about the recently installed Janvier machine.[3] After the meeting, Hering complained to Saint-Gaudens, "They take me for a kid. I can talk to these fellows about it but they are liable to run me down."

Immediately there were delays. Roberts, unhappy with the situation, wanted to know why the use of the new reducing machine would not shorten the time required.[4] Barber was then forced to admit that he did not know how to use the Janvier reducing lathe. He complained that the person sent to Philadelphia to set up the machine and provide training had stayed for only a day and a half. Barber wanted Roberts to have the man return to conduct additional training and to make the paraffin reductions from the Saint-Gaudens' design for the twenty-dollar gold piece.[5]

Roberts approved Barber's request. Deitsch Brothers sent Henri Weil to the Mint from January 3 through the 8 where he made two full-sized plaster casts of the Saint-Gaudens models, paraffin reductions and two plaster casts of these reductions.[6] Barber was pleased as Weil displayed, in his opinion, an excellent knowledge of the machine and its capabilities.[7] However, Weil performed no work that would have demonstrated to Barber how to raise or lower the relief with the Janvier machine. Here Weil's work on the Saint-Gaudens models sat for the remainder of January.

As events in Philadelphia slowed to a snail's pace, Roberts turned for advice to Frank Leach in San Francisco, who had seen the standing eagle design. In Leach's opinion, the standing eagle had not been a faithful representation of the national bird since its legs were entirely too long. "This design inclines one to the impression of a crane in masquerade wearing pantaloons and a cutaway coat." Now seeing Saint-Gaudens' latest design with the flying eagle, Leach was pleased, yet he had his doubts about its popularity. However, he would not speak for the public, as one never knew how these things might be received.

Design aside, Leach wanted to help in striking this high relief coin. While Roberts was on the Pacific Coast the preceding November, Leach had told the director that he thought he could put the planchets in optimum shape for striking high relief by manipulating the milling machine. Upon receiving Roberts' latest letter, he had had the pressman make an experiment that confirmed it would be easier and less expensive than a forming die, though additional experiments would be necessary. He also observed that the high relief portion of the design must be contained within a certain radius of the center, away from the margin of the coin. When the dies were finalized, Leach wanted an opportunity to try his approach with the milling machine. He stood ready to help Roberts in any way.[8]

Hering returned to Philadelphia during the week of February 10 and joined Charles Barber in the pressroom. [9] Using a medal press with a hydraulic pressure of 150 tons, the first blow was struck on the gold planchet.[10] The resulting impression showed little more than half of the design elements. It was only after seven blows that all the details of the die emerged.[11] Before each striking, the coin underwent an annealing process. The coin was heated red hot and then cooled in a diluted solution of nitric acid. This process removed the copper alloy on the surface of the coin, leaving a thin film of pure, malleable gold.[12] The trial ended when the dies failed. The result, termed ultra high relief and more medal than coin, was entirely unsuitable for general coinage.

The ultra high relief version of the double eagle struck from the first model.

Saint-Gaudens had followed all of his basic rules for a successful composition. He used the simple verticals formed by the folds in Liberty's skirt to impart a sense of tallness and beauty to the figure.[13] The acute angles of the folds at the base of the skirt as well as Liberty's hair blowing in the wind gave an overall feeling of motion.[14] In the background, rays emanated from a sun rising on Liberty's right with the Capitol in silhouette on the left. In a theme from the Washington Inauguration Centennial Medal, 46 stars for the states of the Union encircled the coin's rim.[15] Saint-Gaudens would admonish his students and assistants, "Remember that your background is your atmosphere, and part of the composition, and that the composition should extend from edge to edge of the frame."[16] On the reverse, the flying eagle was adorned with a style of feathers that was unique to Saint-Gaudens. A sunburst in low relief radiated in the background. The fields on both sides of the coin were kept clean by placing the motto, "E Pluribus Unum" on the edge of the coin. There was one question concerning his composition. Saint-Gaudens felt that a full face in a medallion was too much for the gods.[17] Now he was violating his own rule with a full frontal standing figure that had never been employed on an American coin. He was not one for technical explanations, composing more often than not based on intuition. If pressed, he would simply say that the face was frontal because that was what was meant to be.[18]

A second production experiment was then undertaken, using a planchet the size of a ten-dollar gold piece, expecting that the extreme relief would be easier to strike on the smaller area. To meet the gold content requirements, the thickness of the planchet was increased to approximately the size of a checker. It was subsequently discovered that the 1890 revisions to the coinage statutes fixed the diameter for all coins, making this experimental gold coin illegal.[19]

The second model for the double eagle still exhibited too much relief. However, when this relief was reduced mechanically by the Janvier machine there was potential that a third model would be successful.

Roberts now asked that Saint-Gaudens in his next modification include a well-rounded rim that would better withstand abrasion.[20] Expecting a successful conclusion with the next set of models, Roberts on February 23, 1907 ordered Superintendent Landis at the Philadelphia Mint not to place any of the double eagles of the old design for 1907 in circulation.[21] Only minor coinages of double eagles had taken place in 1905 and 1906 at Philadelphia so that this order effectively extended for a third year a halt to their coinage. Instead the emphasis would be on converting gold bullion and foreign gold coins received in New York into bars at the New York Assay Office.

At this same time, a changing of the guard was underway at the Treasury Department. Secretary Leslie Shaw resigned effective March 4th.[22] [23] Roosevelt chose George B. Cortelyou as Shaw's replacement.

On March 12, Gus sent Roberts plaster casts of the second model. While the basic design concept was unchanged, there were modifications and enhancements. A fold was added to Liberty's skirt to further emphasize the beauty and sense of motion of the figure and to smooth the transition from the high relief of the central figure to the surrounding field. The Capitol silhouette was made more prominent and Liberty's torch was slimmed down. This second model would result in a coin artistically superior to the ultra high relief version.

So it seemed that steady, if slow, progress was now being made on the gold coins design. Yet this was misleading. Witter Bynner, a professional writer who was a friend and former classmate of Homer's at Harvard, was spending the winter at Cornish.[24] He arrived in mid-January and set up a work area for himself in the studio. The second day there, Bynner found Saint-Gaudens looking so ill he lost his composure and Gus saw it. He described Saint-Gaudens' face as pinched and grey, his hands as long, thin with little bones as limp as spaghetti. There were hot water bottles between the knees and the shins. The touching of one toe to another was torture to his nerves. In such pain, Gus had great difficulty holding onto a thought.

Bynner went on to say that Saint-Gaudens had been having setbacks. The sculptor thought that his family and the doctors were drugging him, but the family said the sculptor was on very few drugs. Gus believed that he was mortally ill and not being told.[25]

Throughout the fall and early winter Saint-Gaudens had been given morphine as a painkiller. Morphine dependency in combination with the large dosages of bromidia had proved lethal. A cycle of pain followed by morphine followed by sleep took over his need to eat. Malnutrition led to a vitamin deficiency that in turn caused the neuropathy. The doctors had recognized the symptoms and eliminated the morphine in October. In January they had taken away the bromidia. Thus by the end of January, Saint-Gaudens, as Witter Bynner described him, was in a living hell from the withdrawal of these medications.

Nikh-Eiphnh **plaster cast for the uniface medal.**

Victory–Peace **obverse model for the one-cent piece.**

Victory–Peace **model modified with Indian headdress.**

In February lumps were discovered in Saint-Gaudens's rectum and the pain treatment had to be resumed.[26] To concentrate on the gold coins design took a will of iron.

In spite of the pain, Saint-Gaudens now proceeded to rework his one-cent model, eliminating the eagle.[27] The finished work bore an exact resemblance to his earlier uniface medal *Nikh–Eiphnh* or *Victory–Peace*. That medal in turn had been taken directly from his *Head of Victory*. Gus really had no choice in the matter. Given his greatly weakened physical state, he had to turn to a design that was tried and acceptable in his eyes. Over Liberty's head, he symbolically arranged thirteen stars in an arc.

Saint-Gaudens sent the completed models to the President on February 5.[28] Up came the Indian headdress issue, with Gus again resistant.[29] Roosevelt's affinity for all things Western was unwavering. With a letter to Gus on February 8, Theodore pleaded his case, asking for just one coin with the headdress. This time Saint-Gaudens conceded the point to President Roosevelt.

On February 18 with the "revised" one-cent model in hand, the President pretty much preempted the decision in regard to the feather headdress. He did not see why the country should not have a conventional headdress of purely American type for the Liberty figure.[30] The approved one-cent models went to the Mint on March 12, 1907, in the same package as the second model for the double eagle.

Saint-Gaudens gradually warmed to the idea of the feather headdress.[31] Gus wrote the President that he was pleased with the results; and now he wanted to see how this head would look in place of the proposed standing Liberty on the double eagle. His fear now was that the standing Liberty design did not "tell" enough in contrast to the eagle on the other side. He was sure, however, that this would not be the case using the head of Liberty with the feathered headdress and asked the President's permission to have a trial strike using this Liberty paired with the flying eagle reverse.[32] Writing on March 14, Roosevelt quickly encouraged Saint-Gaudens. [33]

With the warmer weather of the approaching spring had come some improvement in Gus's condition.[34] His mind was clear and active and he could put about two hours daily into his work.[35] He had once advised a friend that work could be of some comfort in the presence of the great and awful mystery of death.[36]

A single pattern double eagle was struck at Philadelphia pairing Liberty in feathered headdress with the flying eagle reverse.

Still there was no real progress on the second model for the double eagle. Charles Barber could not delegate the reduction work as he had the first time. He found himself unable to make a reduction from the models and complained that the soft plaster that Saint-Gaudens had used hampered the reduction process. It was at this point that Roberts was forced to reveal to Saint-Gaudens that it was not Barber who actually made the reductions from the first model.[37,38]

Lost in this back and forth, Saint-Gaudens had missed an opportunity. Roberts had inadvertently opened the door for Gus to suggest the Mint again use Henri Weil. Perhaps it was the illness; maybe it was the disputed bill from Deitsch Brothers on the Franklin Medal. However, there was no doubt that Weil would have provided a much better reduction and been able to accurately vary the relief.

On April 12 the Mint received Saint-Gaudens's bronze casting of his second model.[39] Roberts cautioned the sculptor he could not assume that no additional modifications of the design or models would be required until the Mint had made a test of the hubs in process.[40] The next day a surly Barber answered an inquiry by Roberts that it was impossible for him to state when the hubs from the second model would be ready. He was working day and night.[41]

All was not well with the Mint people. Barber's technical knowledge told him that this second model was almost as unacceptable as the first. Bluntly, Barber had told Hering that he wanted nothing to do with it.[42] With Barber's observations in hand, Roberts now began contacting mint officials in Britain and France. He had to have substantiating facts on his side if he was going to convince the President of the impracticality of striking high relief coins. However, no useful prompt reply came out of either country.

Roberts also turned to Frank Leach, forwarding to him an ultra high relief double eagle. Leach's reply revealed the Mint's concerns. A heavier rim was imperative. No part of the relief must rise above the rim; otherwise the coins would not stack, making them unacceptable to bankers. Leach was not concerned about counterfeiting, in particular the practice of sweating to reduce the coin's gold content. He also dismissed the concern that the coin would gather dirt. Finally, Roberts asked Leach to comment upon the public's acceptance of the design. Leach would never personally like the flying eagle of the reverse. The man had a hard time balancing his real-world knowledge of eagles with Saint-Gaudens' artistic interpretations. However, he did have a valid point when he said the design was bad for the "peculiarities of the piece." By this, he meant it would prove difficult to strike fully when the obverse design was matched with that of the reverse. Leach was the first person in this project to verbalize the potential pitfalls of Saint-Gaudens' design. He did, however, regard the coin as a beautiful piece of work.

Meanwhile in Cornish, Gus seemed a little better. He was able to take in bread and milk without indigestion.

May in Washington and Philadelphia is without fail a beautiful month. The cold has receded. The weather is mild; the flowers are blooming and the trees are bringing forth their foliage. Even in Cornish, winter has released its icy grip. Yet, in all three locations, May 1907 brought forth none of this optimism when it came to the redesign of the gold coins and the one-cent piece.

Charles Barber kicked off events in a May 4 letter to Philadelphia Mint Superintendent John Landis. The dies were completed and he had attempted to strike some pieces that he was enclosing for examination. He had subjected the planchets to 150 tons of pressure, the practical limit of endurance for a die with the diameter of a twenty-dollar gold piece. He had encountered immediate difficulties. The convexity of the die was so pronounced in order to yield the desired high relief that the pressure of the medal press was in effect concentrated upon a much smaller area. The resulting die wear was excessive with one of the dies sinking or losing its convexity.[43] The conclusion from these disappointing tests was that the reliefs of both the first and second models was quite similar. What changes Saint-Gaudens had made to the design to facilitate striking a high relief had fallen short.

Eight pieces were sent for Roberts' inspection.[44] When on May 6 Roosevelt had his secretary inquire of Cortelyou on the progress of the double eagle, Mint personnel were ready.[45] In their view, significant changes were going to be required in order for this coin project to be successful. Roberts spelled out the details of the test results to Saint-Gaudens and enclosed the eight trial strikes.

The results were clearly unsatisfactory and went far towards convincing Roberts that a radical modification of the designs would be required. While a single blow accomplished much, subsequent blows just simply did not produce commensurate results. Roberts felt that the relief must be reduced and strongly wanted Saint-Gaudens to come to the Mint. He could not possibly have had any idea of Gus's failing health.[46]

It was a discouraged, almost defeated Theodore Roosevelt who wrote to Gus on May 8. Of course he could have a few hundreds of these beautiful coins made, but they would be merely souvenirs and medals, and not part of the true coinage of the country, his primary objective. In a handwritten note at the bottom of the page, a more upbeat Roosevelt said he believed that either a slightly altered or low relief or possibly a profile figure of Liberty might yet produce a coinable design.[47]

Chapter 58
Chaos Reigns

The gold coin project now hung in the balance. Gus knew there was not time to start over with a standing Liberty in profile. However, he did offer Roosevelt a fallback position if all else failed. He would substitute the head of Liberty with the feather headdress for the obverse. If the idea appealed to Roosevelt, he would refine the modeling of the head from the pattern piece to bring it to scale with the eagle. Meanwhile Hering would go to Philadelphia.[1] Roosevelt responded, telling Saint-Gaudens to move forward with refinement of the Liberty in headdress and to send Hering to the White House after his meeting at the Philadelphia Mint.[2]

As this letter exchange was transpiring, there was a softening of opposition at the Philadelphia Mint. Superintendent Landis, essentially a bystander up to this point, wrote to Roberts, subtly casting doubt on Barber's opinion that the design was unworkable. By asking for permission to strike the coin with a one-fifth reduction in relief, he effectively undercut the engraver's position and supported the position of Roosevelt and Saint-Gaudens. This lowering of the relief could be accomplished with the Janvier lathe. Landis closed with the prescient observation that he very much regretted the exclusion of the motto "In God We Trust."[3] This communication was out of character for Landis whom Roberts had considered replacing the prior year.

On May 17 Hering was at the Mint along with Roberts and a manufacturing superintendent from Tiffany & Company. Roberts wanted the Tiffany man there to confirm the opinions of the Mint for Saint-Gaudens and Roosevelt.[4] They examined both the standing Liberty and Liberty in headdress reductions. They also inspected the reduction made at Landis's suggestion. Nothing was revealed as to the coinability of this last modification. That a third model would be needed could be inferred from Gus's subsequent note to Landis. He asked for lead impressions of the standing Liberty and Liberty with feather headdress models as well as an impression or cast of Barber's lower relief reduction of the standing Liberty.[5] Those lead impressions would reveal that Barber had not mastered the ability to reduce relief mechanically with the Janvier machine. His reduction from the second model had lost much detail that he had then attempted to restore by hand directly on the hub. From Philadelphia, Hering went to the White House the next day to give Roosevelt a full progress report.[6]

Faced with the inevitable reduction in relief for the next set of models, Gus tried one more time May 23 to sway the President to his thinking for the twenty-dollar gold piece. He had looked over his models and to his mind the standing eagle was a better match than the flying eagle for the twenty-dollar gold piece. It was more in scale with the standing Liberty on the obverse side. It eliminated the use of the sunburst on both sides of the coin. It was a more dignified presentation of the national bird. Finally, substituting this design would take no additional time and might be more favorable for striking up in the coin press. Saint-Gaudens was making one last plea to return to the designs closest to his original concept, but he would once again defer to the President. Yet what was behind Saint-Gaudens's saying that there would be no delay? In the sculptor's mind Roosevelt had rejected his original standing eagle design. What modifications would Gus have made to sway the President? The answer, based upon a resin model at the Philadelphia Mint, is that Saint-Gaudens had replaced his standing eagle with Weinman's eagle from the reverse of the inaugural medal. Yet the sculptor held back on forwarding this model to the President, waiting for some encouragement in that direction.

Roosevelt, without responding to Saint-Gaudens's latest recommendation, asked Roberts to meet with him on May 25 to discuss Gus's new position on the gold coins design. Roberts supported Saint-Gaudens's views, advocating the standing Liberty in combination with the standing eagle as the primary design for use on the twenty-dollar gold piece. Theodore stood firm. He wanted the full figure of Liberty in combination with the flying eagle reverse. Having been briefed by Hering the previous week on the probable success of a 20% reduction in relief, there was no moving him. The President agreed that the relief should be reduced to a degree that would make it practical without further experiments. This was to be "the last word on the subject."[7]

The last-minute modification put forth by Saint-Gaudens for the reverse of the double eagle. However, the sculptor did not forward this model to the president for his consideration.

Gus readily accepted the President's decision. He promised models to follow in two reliefs; one in a form that Henry Hering believed would be practical and another in ordinary flat, coin relief. Once again the parties involved thought that decisions had been made that would bring the project to a satisfactory conclusion.

That was not all that came out of that meeting of Roberts and the president. The Mint director had previously reported to Saint-Gaudens the outcome of a meeting with Roosevelt at the White House on Saturday, March 22, 1907,[8] that had left the sculptor puzzled. Roberts had stated, "The obverse of the one-cent design is now wanting" with a view to the use upon a gold coin.[9] In the May 25 meeting, when Roosevelt rejected Saint-Gaudens's recommendation of the pairing of the standing Liberty with the standing eagle, the President threw out a compromise. He was willing to use Liberty in the feather headdress in combination with the standing eagle for a ten-dollar gold piece. Gus had never considered this pairing. Left open was whether this design would also be applied to the smaller gold coins, although Roberts expected that it would.[10] It certainly was a better fit on the smaller diameter five-dollar and two-and-a-half dollar gold coins.

During the first week of June, Gus sent models to the Mint for the obverse and reverse of the ten-dollar gold coin. The adaptation had not been difficult, centering primarily on the inscriptions. The date on the obverse model was in Roman numerals. Saint-Gaudens had set the relief to what Charles Barber had told Henry Hering could probably be struck. If the models did not strike up successfully, Barber had assured Hering that the relief could be lowered very simply on the Janvier reducing machine.[11] Saint-Gaudens added that models in coin relief would follow.

Charles Barber was cornered again. His lack of proficiency in reducing the relief would be there for all to see. Defensively he sat down and penned another of his letters, saying Saint-Gaudens was mistaken. Barber had never said anything other than standard coin relief was acceptable. The current models sent were not coin relief although Barber would not unconditionally call them unacceptable as he had with previous models. He also strongly took issue with the statement that the Janvier machine could adequately reduce the model in both size and relief. Defensively, Barber claimed the machine lost design details when used to reduce relief. Finally, Barber raised the issue of Roman numerals versus Arabic; Roman numerals were too cumbersome for certain dates. Roberts in turn conveyed Barber's objections to Saint-Gaudens on June 18. Responding, Gus confirmed he was willing to use Arabic numbers on the ten-dollar gold piece and forwarded a new model on June 24.[12] The next day Saint-Gaudens again wrote Roberts that, after consulting with Hering, he did not believe the problem of loss of the finer details during the reduction process would occur. Enhanced sharpness of the design elements compared to the standing eagle model reduced in Paris would be enough to overcome the problem.[13]

During June activity at Cornish slowed down. Hering was inexplicably away for ten days. Concurrently Gus went into decline.[14] Then, another snag developed. The annual Philadelphia Mint maintenance shutdown scheduled for July had been advanced to June 22 to accommodate tours for an Elks convention starting on July 15.[15]

Essentially six weeks were going to pass with little or nothing accomplished from the Mint's standpoint on the design project

When the Mint came back into operation, Barber completed hubs for the new ten-dollar gold piece design. Two new gold coins were put in Roberts's hands, and he forwarded one to Cortelyou on July 22. Work was not quite complete. Lacking the necessary segmented collars, the 46 stars representing the states of the Union were not yet on the edge of the coin as intended. Roberts was not happy with the new coin. Its finish was smooth without the sharply cut details that he had desired to guard against counterfeiting. Herein lay a conflict. One of Gus's basic tenets was that the outline of the face must not be too sharply cut against the background so as to give a look of having been shaved off and pasted against the field.[16] Roberts did state that he felt the relief was now perfectly feasible to coin but there was a defect on the reverse. The standing eagle was a shade too high compared to the rim. Two coins, when placed back to back, would rock, clearly an unacceptable situation.[17] There was also a curiosity about these coins; they did not bear Saint-Gaudens's initials. He always placed his initials on his medallic work. The reality was that this design was as much Roosevelt's as it was his.

Saint-Gaudens, from the very beginning of the project, knew that the rim of the coin had to be higher than its design elements. His model would never have left Cornish with this defect, no matter how sick the man. Barber, preparing the hubs, had reduced the relief from the models as much as the lathe would allow.[18] The problem had to be somewhere in Barber's work. Still there was more; the sharp triangular bullet points that Saint-Gaudens used before and after the legends on the reverse model were reduced in some cases to mere blobs. On the obverse, the points of the stars were fuzzy and weak. If nothing else, this episode corroborated Hering's observations concerning Barber's inexperience with the Janvier reducing machine.[19] Sick or not, Gus asked the Mint director on that same July 22 for the results obtained from the new ten-dollar gold coin dies.[20] Roberts complied immediately, forwarding his remaining strike of the new gold coin.

Once again, Theodore Roosevelt weighed in on the coin designs. Cortelyou had forwarded the ten-dollar gold coin he had received from Roberts to the president. Roosevelt liked the smooth finish. He recognized the Mint's concern over counterfeiting but asked if a few thousand pieces could be struck and then the rest struck in sharp detail, consistent with existing practice.[21] The ten-dollar gold piece was very near fruition.

Now a blow to the project came from an unexpected quarter. On July 8, George Roberts announced his resignation as director of the Mint.[22] He had a lucrative offer to become president of the Commercial National Bank in Chicago.[23] Roosevelt would certainly miss Roberts and appointed him to the 1909 Assay Commission.[24]

George Roberts wound up his term as Mint director with a letter to Secretary Cortelyou. He addressed President Roosevelt's desire to have a special issue of the first model ultra high relief twenty-dollar gold pieces, saying there was no law prohibiting this action. He suggested that several hundred pieces, enough to eliminate any numismatic premium, be coined and distributed only after the regular issue of the new Saint-Gaudens design in low relief for the twenty-dollar gold piece was generally available.[25] Cortelyou kicked this letter to Roosevelt who agreed. Handwritten at the end of Roosevelt's response, he stated that this design should be preserved as the work of a great American artist.[26]

Roberts, with this approval in hand, ordered new dies to replace the ones broken in February to facilitate a limited production run of ultra high relief double eagles. He also paid into Treasury forty dollars in compensation for taking with him the two surviving double eagles from the February trial.

Keeping the pressure on, Theodore Roosevelt from the summer White House at Oyster Bay sent requests for updates with maddening frequency to Cortelyou.[27] The secretary's answers were vague. Roberts had promised Cortelyou that before he retired at the end of the month, he would visit Philadelphia and "give further attention to the matter" but that circle was never closed.[28]

Meanwhile July in Cornish was proving to be unseasonably hot, punctuated by rolling thunderstorms, causing Gus to suffer even more. He was having fevers of 104 degrees. Mercifully however the pain had abated.[29] Gus had worked in these last months on a bas-relief of Gussie holding a golden bowl from a special masque held in 1905. He never finished that portrait relief. On his last day of consciousness, he shooed off Witter Bynner, saying, "Go away. Don't look at me. It's too humiliating."

He slipped into a coma on August 2nd and died the following evening.[30] Roosevelt's design project for the gold coins was once more hanging in the balance.

Chapter 59
A Bad Time for a Bear Hunt

The day before the San Francisco earthquake was Pierpont Morgan's 69th birthday. He was now in semi-retirement, having delegated most of his business responsibilities to his son, J.P. "Jack" Morgan Jr.

The first strains in the American financial system appeared in the winter of 1906–07. A modest drop in the stock market reached serious proportions on March 14, 1907, with prices dropping 25 percent in a single day. Currency suddenly was needed by the brokerage houses to fund this sharp liquidation. Jack Morgan speculated that if gold began to flow out of England to fund this liquidation, the Bank of England would raise its discount rate to stop it. By the end of March, money in the United States was commanding such high interest rates that low-interest municipal bonds could not attract buyers.

Promptly, Treasury announced a deposit of $12 million with national banks in New York City to ease the tight money situation. Jack Morgan breathed a sigh of relief. This decisive action by Secretary Cortelyou, in office maybe two weeks, won the respect of Wall Street. No more would the lesser lights on the exchanges jokingly call him a mere stenographer, referring to his time as personal secretary to McKinley and Roosevelt.[1] In addition, New York financiers purchased £4 million (approximately $20 million) in gold on the London markets. Thereafter the markets eased in what would be called the silent crash.[2]

George Cortelyou enjoyed no honeymoon period when he replaced Leslie Shaw as secretary of the Treasury.

Then, the Bank of England imposed a "soft" prohibition on American finance bills. These finance bills, typically drawn in the summer, two or three months before the crop movement, were a crude way to play currency futures. Underpinning this speculation, American farmers had produced bumper harvests since 1902, driving larger swings that generated more profit to the currency speculators. In 1906, the British, facing a large drain in gold from the San Francisco earthquake insurance claims, found this speculation particularly harmful. In October of that year, the Bank of England had been forced to raise the discount rate steeply to 6 percent to preserve its gold stocks, risking the impairment of that country's domestic economy. In 1907 the Bank of England was determined not to allow a repeat.[3]

Without the customary borrowings from these finance bills, gold flowed out from New York City banks in June 1907 to fund normal seasonal trade balances. The British bankers were heartened that the Americans had met their gold obligations without seemingly any difficulty, and finance bills were again negotiated with unexpected ease.[4]

Gold exports were again required of the New York banks in July, and their gold reserves fell to the lowest point for that date since 1893. Conservative elements within the London money managers called for the U.S. money market to take care of itself.[5] Once again, finance bills were few in number.[6]

As July closed, the American banks in the major financial centers were faced with another looming problem. The time was rapidly approaching when money must flow into the interior of the country to fund the harvest. With a legitimate need for finance bills, the Americans again entered the British money market. Bills of this nature were met freely. However, bills of a speculative nature were placed at very high rates of interest.[7] Concurrently, the Bank of England preemptively raised its discount rate from 4 to 4-1/2 percent to avoid a repeat of 1906.[8]

Reflecting British unease, economic conditions showed signs of deterioration in the United States. Backlogs of business declined, and raw-material prices began to drop. New York City tried for a second time to place municipal bonds at a reasonable interest rate and failed. The city was faced with making layoffs and slow paying vendors.

A major stock market selloff occurred on August 10 and was attributed by President Roosevelt's opponents to the negative regulatory atmosphere within his administration. Roosevelt dismissed the market downturn, choosing to call it a market flurry rather than a full-blown panic. However, behind the scenes, Roosevelt ordered his attorney general, in the process of preparing an anti-trust suit against International Harvester, to hold off filing until communicating with him.[9]

By October 1, 1907, the American financial markets were straining to provide the liquidity necessary to fuel economic growth and meet the cash flow needs of ordinary commerce. Worse, the harvest had been a disappointment. Now the annual inflow of gold from crop sales to Europe was going to be reduced. As a result, an upset of any nature in the American financial markets was going to trigger grave repercussions.[10]

Augustus Heinze had made his fortune in Montana copper mining. However, his methods were ruthless, gaming the mining laws concerning ownership of the copper seams. Eventually Heinze butted heads with Amalgamated Copper, owned by Standard Oil. The end result was Amalgamated Copper buying out Heinze for $12 million in 1905. Fresh from this windfall, Heinze and his two brothers consolidated their remaining copper holdings into United Copper and brought their money to Wall Street. Here Heinze met Charles Morse, one of New York's most notorious bankers.

Branch banks being illegal, it was Morse who established the practice of chain-banking. Morse would buy a bank and then use that bank's assets as collateral to purchase shares in another bank. Over time Morse was able, in this manner, to create a pyramid of interlocking banking relationships.

Through Morse's influence, Heinze purchased Mercantile National Bank in New York, becoming its president in February 1907. Heinze and his two brothers then used their shares of United Copper as security to finance controlling positions in numerous additional banking concerns. United Copper shares were not listed on the New York Stock Exchange; instead, their value was established through the less reputable activity known as curb trading. In the early fall of 1907, the Heinzes began purchasing on margin large blocks of the United Copper's stock to prop up its price in a down market, thereby maintaining the value of their stock pledged as security for their banking acquisitions.

At this point, Augustus Heinze and Charles Morse were serving as directors in at least six national banks, 10 or 12 state banks, and five or six trust companies.[11] Still, it was a house built on sand. A dip in the United Copper stock price would cause the loans used to acquire their banking interests to be called.

Augustus Heinze's brother, Otto, noticed that the total shares of United Copper trading exceeded the number of issued and outstanding shares. This could only happen if certain brokers were loaning out shares purchased on margin by the brothers to traders who wanted to speculate in the stock, shorting it in anticipation of a market selloff. If the Heinzes called in their shares, the shorts holding the loaned shares would be squeezed. They would be forced to find United Copper shares on the open market to meet their obligations. Finding none available, they would have to buy at inflated prices or settle with the Heinze brothers directly. This was known as a "bear squeeze." Otto needed $1.5 million by his estimate to execute the squeeze but Augustus refused to advance.

Instead, Augustus set up a meeting with Charles Morse and Charles T. Barney, president of the Knickerbocker Trust Company. The needed cash was now $1.5 to $3 million. They also denied Otto. Meanwhile weakness in United Copper's price was driving margin calls from brokers on the brothers' existing holdings.

On Monday October 14, Otto Heinze decided to initiate the squeeze on his own, calling for the shares held by brokers. On Tuesday to his surprise all the shares materialized; he had been wrong. Then thousands of shares began to appear from the price rise that Monday's call had precipitated. The market for United Copper went to pieces.[12]

With Otto Heinze's debacle, the dominos started to fall. Immediately the directors of Mercantile National Bank insisted upon Augustus's "voluntary" resignation.[13] The burning question at the time was how far would the disease spread?

Mercantile National feared a run on the bank would result from the Heinze brothers interlocking failure. They approached the New York Clearing-House for support. On Friday morning the clearinghouse announced the bank was solvent and would open for business. A run on the bank developed anyway. Spelling wider problems, other banks with connections to Mercantile National were showing poor reserve positions.

Meanwhile the run was spreading. Depositors were already beginning to withdraw funds from banks owned by Charles Morse. On Sunday the clearinghouse ordered the immediate elimination of Augustus Heinze and Charles Morse from all banking interests in New York City. They also ruled that the two men must promptly repay any loans to their banks and that any evidence of "chain banking" would disqualify such banks or bankers from membership in the New York Clearing-House. This rapid intervention of the clearinghouse seemed to do the trick although Augustus Heinze was ruined. Optimism ruled on Monday morning, October 21, that quick action had prevented a crisis. It was not to be.

In 1907 there were three types of banks in the United States: national banks that were authorized to receive federal deposits and issue currency, state banks that were chartered by the various state legislatures, and private banks that ran the gamut from J.P. Morgan & Company to small shoebox operations that operated from the back rooms of a saloon. In addition, there had evolved a variant of the savings bank—a trust company. Trust companies invested in longer-term assets including direct ownership of stocks and paid higher interest rates than commercial or savings banks. In 1906, New York State had finally imposed a 15-percent reserve requirement on trust companies but only one third in cash on hand. Likewise, the rural national banks had similar reserve requirements. Money not required for cash on hand then moved to New York for investment. Thus, a financial upset in New York City would reverberate throughout the country.[14]

Trust companies were not allowed to be members of clearinghouse associations, given their higher risk profile. Therefore, they were forced to form relationships with individual large clearinghouse member banks to gain access to the clearinghouse. Knickerbocker Trust did business with the National Bank of Commerce in this manner. Though Knickerbocker was a large, well-regarded trust company, Charles Barney ran his banking operation without transparency.[15]

On Monday morning, rumors swirled that Barney might have been involved in the Heinze affair.[16] That afternoon the public learned that the Knickerbocker Trust board had asked Charles Barney to tender his resignation. Shortly after that, the National Bank of Commerce announced it would no longer act as clearinghouse agent for the trust company. Tuesday promised to be a very rough day.[17]

The previous week, Pierpont Morgan had remained disengaged lest his return to New York City arouse further fears over the banking crisis. By Thursday October 17, Morgan's closest advisors deemed the situation acute and felt he should return. Still Morgan waited until Saturday.

On Sunday Morgan assembled two teams. The first consisted of his close associates, George Baker of First National Bank and James Stillman of National City Bank. The second group consisted of his partner, George Perkins, Henry Davison, vice president of First National Bank, and Benjamin Strong, secretary of Bankers Trust. This last group was assigned to review the financial integrity of the New York Clearing-House banks and the trust companies. The banks proved in good shape. The trust companies were questionable. Through this review, Morgan got a picture of which entities should be allowed to fail. On that Sunday Charles Barney attempted to meet with Morgan. However, Morgan considered this man a speculator and not a gentleman; he refused to see Barney.[18]

The run on Knickerbocker Trust started the following Tuesday morning, October 22. The run on the downtown branch at 60 Broadway started slowly; maybe 50 depositors were in line at 10 o'clock when the paying tellers drew back their curtains. As the morning progressed, the line doubled into a great figure, 8 and care was taken by special officers to crowd everybody inside the building so as to prevent excitement of the general public outside.

As depositors stood in line for their money, Morgan sent Strong to review the Knickerbocker's books. All during the morning, Strong worked and at noon reported to Davison that the trust company was not solvent. Within two and a half hours the Knickerbocker had paid out $8 million in cash. At 12:30, two large checks arrived for cashing from two different banks totaling $2.5 million. They were paid and then all other activity was suspended.[19]

With the Knickerbocker failure, all available funds seemed to instantly dry up as banks and trust companies held onto their cash. This action had a detrimental impact on the stock exchanges as call money became practically impossible to obtain and stock prices slumped accordingly.

Pierpont Morgan had come to the rescue of the nation's finances during the Panic of 1893. Now in semi-retirement, he was going to have to do it again.

On Tuesday afternoon Morgan decided that Secretary Cortelyou should be summoned to New York City. Banks from around the country were rapidly pulling their reserves out of the New York banks, worsening an already bad liquidity crunch. Cortelyou took the afternoon train from Washington, arriving at nine that evening. Immediately Morgan, suffering from a monumental head cold, Stillman, Baker, and Perkins went to see him at his hotel. High on the list of topics to be discussed was the financial condition of the Trust Company of America.[20]

Theodore Roosevelt is shown departing St. Louis, having joined the Inland Waterways Commission on an inspection trip.

On October 1, President Roosevelt had boarded a steamer at Keokuk, Iowa, to join the Inland Waterways Commission midway through their inspection trip to inventory the nation's inland waterway resources. Roosevelt's party consisted of some 20 governors and Gifford Pinchot, conservationist and head of the Forest Service. Theodore disembarked at Memphis and proceeded on a two-week bear hunt in the canebrakes of the Tensas River bottoms in northeast Louisiana.[21]

The Roosevelt hunting party In the canebrakes of northeast Louisiana. To Roosevelt's left is his friend and former Rough Rider John Avery McIlhenny. His father was the originator of Tabasco Sauce.

Roosevelt returned to civilization without bagging a bear on Monday, October 21, at Vicksburg. He gave a short speech that afternoon advocating for an expanded levee system for the Mississippi River and then boarded a waiting special train at 3 p.m. for his return to Memphis. His train arrived shortly after midnight where he transferred for the journey east through Nashville and Chattanooga on his return to Washington.[22]

Roosevelt was scheduled to layover in Nashville on October 22 for four hours with a speech planned for the Ryman Auditorium. He arrived at Union Station promptly at 9 that morning. He boarded a horse-drawn carriage escorted by some 25 to 30 automobiles and Troop A of the Confederate Veteran Cavalry for a run down Broadway. The entourage turned at Eighth Avenue to pass through the business district lined with well wishers.[23] Old Glory, both large and small, was everywhere to be seen.[24]

By now Roosevelt was aware that there was trouble brewing in New York. Here was an opportunity for him to rail against the various financiers and businessmen as malefactors of great wealth and he took it. The president noted that there had been trouble in the stock market for which his policies were being blamed. He countered that his policies represented an effort to punish successful dishonesty. Roosevelt would protect with all his power honest property; he would protect honest men of wealth to the extent of his ability.[25] Had Roosevelt understood the gravity of the situation, a simple "no comment" would have instilled more confidence in the markets than what he said.

At Chattanooga the enthusiastic cheering of the crowd was so loud that Roosevelt could not be heard and gave up trying to speak. It was for the best. As the special train pulled out of Chattanooga and hurdled through the evening hours toward Washington, it was a journey every bit as important as that helter-skelter trip from the Adirondacks to Buffalo in September 1901. There, Theodore Roosevelt had taken control of the levers of power after McKinley's death. Now it was different but no less important. No president had ever stopped a financial panic at this advanced stage. The likelihood of a full-blown depression developing that would overshadow the successes of his presidency was almost certain.

Theodore Roosevelt was facing one of the most difficult decisions of his presidency. He must turn control of those levers of power, albeit temporarily, over to Pierpont Morgan, a man whose core values differed in fundamental ways from Roosevelt's. Yet there was common ground within these core values; both men, pragmatically, wanted what was best for their country and its people. Now Roosevelt must depend upon Morgan to do what he could not—stop the panic. It was the mark of a mature leader.

Around 2 a.m. on Wednesday, October 23, Benjamin Strong was rousted from bed and told to go to the Trust Company of America to assess its financial strength. Meanwhile Cortelyou would standby; he would provide what was hoped to be the final firewall to stem the panic.

As morning dawned, Morgan was so down from his head cold he seemed in a stupor. By one that afternoon, Strong had reached an opinion on the ailing trust company. He went to Morgan's library, the command center for the fight to stem the panic. Morgan asked, "Are we solvent?" He wanted no details, just yes or no. Baker and Stillman were in the room with Morgan. Strong stated that the withdrawals by depositors the day before had pretty much wiped out Trust Company of America's liquidity, but that the assets were such that the company remained solvent. Morgan said very little during the course of the 45-minute discussion as Strong disgorged the full details of his review. When Strong was finished, Morgan asked him if he thought the bankers would be justified in seeing the trust company through its troubles. Strong answered in the affirmative. Morgan turned to Stillman and Baker, "This is the place to stop the trouble then."

At 2:15 p.m., Trust Company of America was preparing to suspend. Morgan called for Trust Company of America to bring all their securities, and he would make loans against them. All told, $3 million was delivered directly to the company's vaults and they made it to closing.[26]

After dinner that evening, Morgan met with the presidents of the various trust companies. He told them he needed $10 million from them to stem the run by the next morning. No one was enthusiastic about letting go of cash. Morgan let the conversation exhaust itself, even dozing off from the effects of the head cold. Finally, he took control and polled each of the trust company presidents and secured $8.25 million. He then stated that First National, National City, and Hanover National would make up the difference. It was nearly midnight of October 23. That would be enough for Trust Company of America to weather another day in the continuing run of its depositors.[27]

Morgan knew that more was going to be needed; it was time to announce the support of the Treasury Department. On Thursday morning, October 24, George Cortelyou reported to the press that $25 million in Treasury funds would be deposited with selected national banks in New York City. From the minute the New York Sub-Treasury opened at 10 a.m. until it closed, it was the scene of frenetic activity. From all over the city, messengers arrived with leather satchels and suitcases to carry away money. Trucks heavily laden with bags and cases of gold coin drew away from the Sub-Treasury. There was substantial demand for subsidiary silver driven by depositors closing out their bank accounts to the last penny. Yet $10 million had to come from currency provided from Washington, small bills to again facilitate the closeouts.[28]

A panic is driven by fear. Yet here in New York, all Cortelyou could muster from his most important Sub-Treasury was something less than $15 million in gold coin. He had gold ingots aplenty, utterly useless in this case, but not gold coin. When divided among the various banks, this gold coin would certainly help but it was inadequate to snuff out the public fear and quell the run.

More troubling, Morgan had problems of a different but equally serious nature that Thursday. Call money on the New York Stock Exchange had become extremely expensive. In a panic, Ransom Thomas, president of the exchange, came to Morgan early that afternoon; he was going to have to close the exchange early that day. Morgan wouldn't have it; it would undo all his efforts of the past two days. Within minutes, Morgan had $23.5 million pledged from 14 banks that would form a money pool to support exchange transactions.

On Friday morning, October 25, George Perkins made early visits to Cortelyou, Stillman, Baker, and Morgan, the purpose of which was to reaffirm everyone's determination to save Trust Company of America and now, Lincoln Trust. At 10 a.m. the New York Stock Exchange opened for trading with fear pervading every trading desk. Prices quickly began to crater. The other trust companies were persisting in calling in their loans, causing a second shortage of money. Thomas asked Morgan to raise a second pool of cash. Morgan instead went himself to the offices of the New York Clearing-House to ask them to raise a pool of $15 million. This time the banks balked. Margin sales must be disallowed, and a partial pool would be provided that afternoon.

At the library that evening Morgan and his men acknowledged that they could not go on bailing out trust companies and forming money pools at the New York Stock Exchange. They needed to attack the psychology of the panic. They formed a committee to disseminate information about the financial rescue efforts and answer any inquiries that might arise. They went so far as to encourage sermons on that coming Sunday, cautioning people to act calmly and not to withdraw money and lock it up.[29]

On Saturday, October 26, Morgan received word that $3 million in gold was in route from London to New York. Large or small, any amount of gold coming his way was good news indeed. But there was bad news as well. Nearly 2,000 safe deposit boxes had been rented since Monday. People were doing as he feared, taking their money out of circulation and stuffing it under the mattress. With the dollar amount of currency issuable by Treasury and the national banks capped by law, there was no way to expand to offset that being removed from circulation and hoarded.

Morgan, Stillman, and Baker were now faced with the reality that they were going to have to create fiat money to help bridge the crisis. The New York Clearing-House must issue temporary loans to its members in the form of clearinghouse certificates. Their issuance was viewed as an act of desperation; but the three men had no choice. They authorized their 53 member banks to issue $100 million to be available on Monday, October 28, to meet short-term liquidity needs.

To counteract this negative turn of events and project confidence, the three men encouraged Cortelyou to return to Washington. They also requested that a letter President Roosevelt had written on October 24 be made available for publication. Addressed to Cortelyou, it struck a more appropriate, reassuring tone than his impromptu speech two days before in Nashville.

> I congratulate you upon the admirable way in which you have handled the present crisis. I congratulate also those conservative and substantial businessmen who in this crisis have acted with such wisdom and public spirit. . . .
>
> The action taken by you and by the businessmen in question has been of the utmost consequence and has secured opportunity for the calm consideration which must inevitably produce entire confidence in our business conditions.

The release of this letter from Washington went to pains to emphasize that Roosevelt was kept in constant contact with Cortelyou by long-distance telephone and that he had approved the policy of making further deposits of the public funds in the New York City depository banks to ease the strain on the nation's money supply.[30] Truth be told, without readily available gold coin there was little more either the president or the secretary of the Treasury could do.

These weekend efforts to soothe the nerves of the public had their desired effect. Trading on the New York Stock Exchange opened on Monday morning, October 28, without incident. In addition, the first shipments of gold expected from Great Britain, Argentina, France, and Australia began arriving. Yet there was still another hurdle facing Morgan.

On Sunday night a city official met with George Perkins. Unless New York City could raise $20 to $30 million by November 1, they would be insolvent. Tuesday, after a second meeting with the mayor and his staff, Morgan, at his desk in his library, drafted a three-page document committing J.P. Morgan & Company to $30 million of the city's revenue bonds. There would be no municipal default.[31]

For the remaining days of October, the financial system seemed to settle down and begin healing itself. It was only an illusion. Early on Sunday morning, November 2, Morgan called another emergency conference at his library. One of the largest brokerage houses, Moore & Schley, was teetering on the verge of collapse. The firm of Moore & Schley had borrowed $30 million from numerous banks, trust companies, and financial institutions in New York using its stock holdings of Tennessee Coal & Iron (TC&I) as collateral. These shares had not been immune to the overall collapse of stock prices. On Monday many of the banks would likely call in the Moore & Schley loans and most likely throw the market into a tailspin.

Morgan called in trusted staff from U.S. Steel and J.P. Morgan & Company to search for a solution. Next, he called a meeting of the U.S. Steel finance committee. At this point, U.S. Steel controlled 60 percent of the nation's steel production and had just finished the second most profitable quarter in its history. More importantly, the company had cash resources of $76 million.

TC&I was based in northern Alabama, holding reserves of coal and iron ore within 25 miles of its furnaces. In addition, it controlled deposits of dolomitic limestone and other raw materials necessary for the manufacture of steel. In short, this company held a competitive advantage over U. S. Steel in the Southern market.[32]

However, before Morgan could address this situation, he called the representatives of the trust companies to his library. He demanded a commitment from them to provide another pool of $25 million to be loaned to those in trouble from the runs. This time Morgan was taking no prisoners; he locked the doors to the library, retaining the only key, until the funds were committed. In essence he forced the trust companies to take care of themselves, leaving him free to deal with Moore & Schley.[33]

At 4:30 p.m. that Sunday, Morgan convened a meeting that included his key players and Elbert Gary and Henry Clay Frick from U.S. Steel management. Morgan wanted U.S. Steel to buy TC&I, yet he did not have the power to order it; he could only urge its consideration. Gary and Frick saw operational problems at TC&I and believed this acquisition would expose them to an antitrust lawsuit

Discussion went into the evening. A deal was structured with one contingency. Gary and Frick insisted President Roosevelt must agree to the acquisition.[34] Roosevelt would not be able to say yes or no, but he did control the general direction of the Justice Department where the power to delay the deal would cause it to unravel with untold market implications. Morgan reluctantly agreed.

At 10 p.m. Gary called William Loeb, Roosevelt's personal secretary, for an appointment as early as possible Monday morning. Loeb agreed. At midnight Gary and Frick departed on their special train to Washington. They needed to have the go-ahead by the opening bell of the New York Stock Exchange at 10 a.m.

The two men arrived at the White House at 8 a.m. Loeb firmly refused to allow the men to see Roosevelt. The president saw no one before 10 in the morning. Elbert Gary pleaded to no avail; there was a routine in the White House that was inviolate. At nine each morning, immediately after breakfast, Edith set aside an hour to herself. Theodore always made it a point not to conduct official business at this time. They would walk the grounds or sit in the second-floor library if the weather was inclement and talk of whatever was on their minds. Woe unto any staffer who was forced to interrupt them.[35]

Gary was beside himself when he spied James Garfield, secretary of the Interior. Yes, Garfield, holding sufficient rank to smother any wrath, would speak to Roosevelt as to the urgency of the meeting. The two men met President Roosevelt at 9:45 a.m. Attorney General Charles Bonaparte was out of town, so Roosevelt had Elihu Root, the former Wall Street attorney, at his side when Gary and Frick entered the meeting. At 10:15 Gary stepped out of the meeting to say that Roosevelt was reading the matter favorably. Finally, at 11 a.m., Gary had Roosevelt's full approval of the proposal. Given that both Gary and Frick believed the consequences of not doing the combination would be ruinous to the financial markets, Roosevelt answered that while he could not advise them to take the action proposed, he felt it no public duty of his to interpose any objection.[36]

With the acquisition of TC&I by U. S. Steel, the Panic of 1907 had been stopped. Ominously, by mid-November Treasury had only $5 million in ready cash left.[37] It had been a very near thing.

The British press summed up the situation perhaps better than anyone else. "The lesson of the crisis is not that American commercial honesty is less than that of other countries, but that the opportunities for successful dishonesty are more abundant and more tempting."[38]

On November 14, 1907, Charles Barney, stripped of his wealth and the prestige of his position at Knickerbocker Trust, committed suicide.

Once back in Washington Secretary Cortelyou ordered the immediate coinage at the Philadelphia Mint of $15 million in twenty-dollar gold pieces. That amounted to 750,000 pieces, and there would be more. Not since 1904 had double eagles been coined at Philadelphia at this rate. This would use about three-fifths of the bullion on hand at the Philadelphia Mint.[39] Two weeks into November, Mint workers were pulling overtime, straining to meet Cortelyou's orders for additional double eagles. The new British luxury liner, Lusitania, had just delivered $20 million in gold to New York City that would be converted into coin. These newly minted coins using the old Liberty Head design would be distributed throughout the Sub-Treasury network.[40]

What had happened to cause Cortelyou to come up so short of gold coin when he distributed the $25 million to the banks on October 24? George Roberts's virtual suspension of the coinage at Philadelphia of double eagles, the workhorse of the American financial system, on February 23, 1907, was made with the best of intentions. Roberts could not have anticipated that Charles Barber would slow walk the die preparation of the second Saint-Gaudens double eagle design through March, April, and into late May. Barber's overtly passive-aggressive action toward the Saint-Gaudens high-relief design was clearly unacceptable.

Yet George Roberts was not blameless in Barber's failure to execute the new design. He certainly could have insisted upon Barber returning Henri Weil to prepare dies from the second model at varying reliefs using the Janvier lathe. Roberts did not, going instead in the opposite direction, querying European mints about the feasibility of high-relief coinage in April.

Roberts compounded this misjudgment in his last days in office at the end of July. He advised Cortelyou that he had rejected a quote by the United States Express Company to move gold bullion from the West Coast to Philadelphia. He dismissed the exposure of having large amounts of gold at the San Francisco Mint and could not foresee a financial situation in the East that could not be met with the gold stocks at hand. He did concede that it was more desirable to have gold coins accumulated in the East but not at the expense of the transfer at what he deemed an exorbitant rate.[41] Thus all the gold accumulated at the San Francisco Mint would sit on the sidelines when the October panic hit.

By September, the United States treasurer had recognized a gold coin shortage in the East and requested an increase in production from the Bureau of the Mint. Instructions went out on the 18th to the Philadelphia Mint to begin striking 20-dollar gold pieces from the old design. Philadelphia was to have a go on this coinage until told otherwise.[42] However, even this order had no urgency attached to it; only 100,000 double eagles were struck there in the remaining days of September.[43] It was definitely too little, and it was definitely too late.

Finally, Theodore Roosevelt should share some of the blame. He insisted at the May meeting with Roberts that the standing Liberty obverse be paired with the flying eagle reverse in spite of the recommendation of both Saint-Gaudens and Roberts that the pairing of the standing Liberty with the standing eagle would coin better. Frank Leach had said this in so many words, and Charles Barber knew it but kept silent.

One can argue whether to place the blame on George Roberts for pausing the coining of double eagles in Philadelphia and not reducing their inventory at San Francisco or on Charles Barber for his animosity towards Saint-Gaudens. However, the fact remains that the Mint Service's failure to have sufficient quantities of doubles eagles available at New York City when they were needed in that chaotic last week in October was absolutely inexcusable.

The Panic of 1907 had been a very near tragedy. That it was not was through the efforts primarily of one man, Pierpont Morgan. The lack of gold coin at the New York Sub-Treasury had complicated matters but that shortage had been overcome. However, had Morgan failed, that lack of gold coin could certainly have been considered the straw that broke the camel's back.

Part 8

Beauty Is Truth, Truth Beauty—Keats

Chapter 60
FRANK LEACH

It was Friday, November 22, 1907. The day was cloudy and cold with some light rain that chilled to the bone. Thanksgiving was just around the corner as Frank Leach walked into the office of the president of the United States. While he had been sworn in as interim director of the Mint on October 1, he had not effectively taken over the office until the beginning of November. As such, he was hardly settled into his job, much less ready for a face-to-face encounter with an irate Theodore Roosevelt. It had been nearly four months since Saint-Gaudens had passed away. Yet from his first days in office, Leach had been dealing with the new gold coin designs. He was aware that this project had the attention of a number of prominent people in New York City and Boston, as well as the president himself.[1] Decisions had been made on the ten-dollar gold piece, but the twenty-dollar gold piece was still mired in problems.

Theodore lost no time in warming to his subject. From the very beginning of this project, his interest had been with the twenty-dollar gold piece. The project was languishing, and his patience was at an end. Saint-Gaudens was gone and his beautiful double-eagle design might never see the light of day.

Roosevelt would accept no more bureaucratic excuses. In Frank Leach's words, he set out what he wanted, the striking of the new twenty-dollar gold pieces. He went on to describe the problems and failures that had been encountered to date with the high relief design. Finally, he told Leach what he needed to accomplish. But it was much more colorful than that. Theodore would typically hammer his desk with his fist to emphasize his anger. He also had a habit of thrusting his head forward aggressively when making a point. He suggested, in Leach's tempered words, "some details of action of a drastic character."[2] That was an understatement. Roosevelt's anger and denunciations could be truly blasting when he turned on his full voltage, a tropic blaze of heat.[3] All of the frustration of almost three years of futile effort in dealing with the Mint came flooding out.

The news of Gus's death had profoundly saddened Theodore and Edith Roosevelt; they had lost a friend.[4] Edith was moved to write a personal note of condolence to Gussie lamenting that so much work seemed to be before the sculptor.[5]

Indeed, there was. Edith knew exactly where the gold coin design project stood. It was stopped dead in its tracks.

Storm clouds indicating trouble gathered almost at once. George Roberts, on his last day as Mint director, communicated to Cortelyou that his successor, Frank Leach, would not be ready to assume his post in Washington for an indefinite period. There had been difficulties finding his replacement at the San Francisco Mint. Roberts assured Cortelyou that the Mint would be in capable hands under Robert Preston. He went on to recommend that the gold coin designs be delayed until dies that fully met coinage standards were obtained.

Theodore Roosevelt was having no more such delays. In a letter on August 7, he demanded Cortelyou move forward with work on the ten-dollar gold piece. Moreover, the president wanted the Mint to move ahead with the dies for the new twenty-dollar gold piece just as they were. He added in frustration "there has been a certain cumbersomeness of mind and inability to do the speediest modern work" on this project. The Mint should get in touch with Saint-Gaudens's assistant, Henry Hering, to address any concerns. Roosevelt wanted both gold pieces issued by September 1.[6]

Roosevelt's order created a stir. Preston, not adequately up to speed after one week as acting director, queried Roberts as to the exact status of the project.[7] At the same time, Preston forwarded Roosevelt's letter to Philadelphia. He trusted that every effort would be made to expedite this coinage. Preston was passing the buck.

Charles Barber, on vacation at the beach in New Jersey, got the phone call. The engraver returned and made arrangements for the striking of new gold coins during the following week.[8] He would use the existing dies to strike the ten-dollar gold piece. Those dies had been waiting approval since July 22.

The double eagle was an entirely different matter. Barber was still waiting for a new model that would remove the objectionable high relief features. The engraver argued that the delays on the twenty-dollar gold piece were not the fault of the engraving department; they had worked nights and Sundays on the Saint-Gaudens designs. Until the Saint-Gaudens people supplied him with a model in low enough relief that could be reduced on the Janvier machine, his hands were tied. It would be utterly impossible to meet the September 1 deadline for the new twenty-dollar gold piece, even if the models were now in hand.[9]

Receiving this protest, Robert Preston asked Philadelphia Superintendent Landis to wire Homer Saint-Gaudens to inquire about the status of the third twenty-dollar gold coin model.[10] Homer replied that a finished model for the ten-dollar coin, one that had been promised with "flat relief" from the end of May, would be sent during the following week. He was silent on the status of the third model for the twenty-dollar gold coin.[11]

A second query brought forth that the new twenty-dollar model would be ready in one month.[12] Henry Hering was waiting for the results of the latest model for the ten-dollar coin, which was at a relief slightly lower than the French twenty-franc piece that Barber had assured Hering the Mint could produce. This relief was the lowest that Saint-Gaudens would have accepted. This second model for the ten-dollar gold piece would be ready in four days. Until the results on this coin were known, it would be fruitless to begin work on another twenty-dollar gold coin model.[13]

Roosevelt, unaware of this correspondence, wrote Cortelyou again on August 22. He would accept no additional delays. He wanted to know exactly when the new coins would be issued. He reminded Cortelyou that a few thousand of the ultra high relief coins were to be struck after the first of the regular issue twenty-dollar gold pieces. If there were delays, he was going to ask George Kunz from Tiffany & Company to take over the project.[14] That was tantamount to removal for Charles Barber. The president meant business.

Meanwhile, Barber, as if he were acting in a vacuum, on August 26 raised the issue of the lack of an acceptable edge on the existing ten-dollar model to Landis. When the coin was struck, the metal, not having a border area to flow into, would be forced between the die and the collar forming a fin or wire edge. He again brought up the stacking issue. However, Barber now no longer blamed Saint-Gaudens. It was due to the convexity of the die, which had a tendency to change during the tempering of the steel and in the striking process itself. His solution was to turn a border in the die. There would be a delay, but only a minor one. In his opinion the border did not detract from the artistic merits of the coin and added to its appearance.[15]

On August 27 Preston instructed the Mint to strike 500 of the ten-dollar gold pieces from the unaltered first model and the same quantity of twenty-dollar gold pieces. Cortelyou had ordered it done.[16] Preston would amend this order three days later to allow the medal press to be used in striking these coins. Barber was now faced with pressing into service the double eagle dies from the second model using the twenty percent reduction in relief that he had prepared in May. These coins were the first emission of what was to be known as the high-relief twenty-dollar gold piece.

Known as Wire Rim pieces, these ten-dollar gold pieces were struck to satisfy Roosevelt's order.

At the end of August, Augusta Saint-Gaudens entered the picture. She now conveyed Hering's second ten-dollar gold coin model to the Philadelphia Mint.

The model appeared to be quite satisfactory. A rim had been added, and the relief was now coinable.[17] Hering had completely eliminated the triangular bullet points on the reverse that Barber had been unable to accurately engrave. Both Preston and Landis pressed the engraver to complete these dies as soon as possible.[18] Barber expected this set of models to be satisfactory. [19] He even optimistically ventured that if the new twenty-dollar models arrived with the same relief, acceptable coinage dies could be made.[20]

Just prior to receiving this second ten-dollar gold coin model from the Saint-Gaudens Estate, Charles Barber completed his modifications, turning the border in the hub to correct the faults he originally raised on the first model. On August 27 he sent a strike from the modified hub to Preston. The raised stars adjacent to the rim still needed perfecting. Preston viewed this coin as superior to those now being struck and did not expect the president to object to this modification.[21]

Barber's modified version from the first model would ultimately go to the melting pot.

Meanwhile Preston was unwilling to wait for the preparation of dies from the second model for the ten-dollar gold coin and authorized coinage to commence from the Barber-modified dies from the first model.[22] Starting September 13, a total of 31,500 were struck on the coin presses. Another 50 were produced on the medal press.[23] Then production just as suddenly was halted on September 18.[24] The decision had come down to Preston that none would go into circulation until the new twenty-dollar gold pieces were ready, making their continued striking unnecessary.[25]

Shifting gears, on September 10, five of the high relief double eagles were delivered to Assistant Treasury Secretary J.H. Edwards.[26] Roosevelt's order had been met.

On September 11, Gussie reentered the picture. She informed Preston that work on the third set of models for the twenty-dollar gold coin had been ongoing for a month and two more weeks would be required.[27]

Meanwhile Charles Barber had completed the hub from the second model for the new ten-dollar coin. The coinability of this design was much improved. Details were much sharper, particularly the feather ends near the rim on the obverse. Also, the relief was virtually eliminated. On September 23, Augusta Saint-Gaudens relayed Hering's request that it would be well to see a sample striking of the ten-dollar gold piece from the second model. That request was ignored.[28]

The question now stood: use the modified first model or the second model for the new ten-dollar gold coin. Preston favored the second model that gave a well-detailed appearance. Theodore Roosevelt, with his limited striking of the first model accomplished, signed off October 3.[29] The production run of ten-dollar gold pieces from the modified first model would now sit in limbo during the October panic.

Struck using the second model, this ten-dollar gold piece entered circulation in November 1907. The combination of the head of Liberty and the standing eagle proved very adaptable for coinage.

Barber's rolled-edge variety from the first model was ordered to the melting pot on November 9. However, about 50 of these coins survived.[30] The 500 from the unmodified first model, known as the wire-rim variety, were held in abeyance. In December, Assistant Secretary Edwards ordered these gold pieces transferred to Treasury for the president. They were subsequently distributed to friends of Roosevelt and administration officials.[31] In retrospect, the whole situation in August and September had bordered on chaotic.

On Saturday, September 28, Hering appeared at the Philadelphia Mint with the third model for the twenty-dollar gold coin. In Hering's words, Barber rejected it out of hand. While it had the lowest relief, Barber insisted that it was still much too high. Hering was surprised at this rejection.[32] Nevertheless, Barber knew that he had no choice but to proceed.[33]

On October 10, Barber wrote Robert Preston giving numerous reasons why this third model would fail just as the previous two had. The engraver also took the opportunity to blow off some steam. He accused Saint-Gaudens of furnishing models without the least knowledge of minting coins. The result had been simply a failure and an unparalleled waste of time. Nevertheless, in Barber's opinion, the Mint was doing all that it could to solve the problem.

On October 22, Barber came back with the results of his work. The dies from the third model had been completed and trial strikes made with the coining press. Reducing the relief from the model with the Janvier lathe had, as expected, caused a considerable loss of detail. One specimen was forwarded to Washington and ended up in the hands of Edwards.[34] Barber recommended that he start with a model with much less relief so that such loss of detail on the figure of Liberty and the eagle would not occur with the reducing lathe. In addition, the modeling technique would have to eliminate all steep changes in relief in order to bring up the design with only one blow from the coin press.[35] Barber was asking for a fourth model for the twenty-dollar gold coin. This letter earned the engraver an immediate trip to Washington.[36]

Barber's line of reasoning was not the only one being put forth in Philadelphia. Coiner Rhine R. Freed had specific ideas to improve the coining characteristics of this third model. He suggested to Landis reducing the relief on the foot, knee, and chest of Liberty's figure. Metal flow requirements would then be lessened, allowing the other portions of the die to impress more sharply on the planchet.[37] This report was not forwarded to Preston.

The obverse of the third model (shown in the negative) exhibited lower relief, but in Charles Barber's opinion a fourth model would be needed.

The meeting in Washington on October 24 did not advance Barber's cause. Assistant Secretary Edwards, acting for Cortelyou in New York dealing with the panic, had a different reaction to the problems encountered. How many twenty-dollar gold pieces of the new design could be coined operating the existing medal presses around the clock? What would be the cost compared to that for the present design? How long before additional presses could be built? Edwards was feeling the pressure that week from the lack of double eagles in the New York Sub-Treasury.

Meanwhile Augusta Saint-Gaudens was again writing on October 25 to Preston, saying that she had received no reply to her inquiry as to the status of the design project. It was left to Superintendent Landis to convey to her that the models for the twenty-dollar gold coin still exhibited too great a relief, and a fourth model would be needed.[38]

This was the combination hornet's nest, three-ring circus, headless horse that greeted Frank Leach as he took over the directorship of the Mint. His immediate problem was that Assistant Secretary Edwards, needing gold coins from any source, had authorized the Mint to begin paying out the new ten-dollar gold pieces. However, the Mint had not started coining the new gold pieces based on the order to delay public release until the new twenty-dollar gold pieces were ready.[39] Still, enough working dies were on hand that Leach could order this coin into full production.

Gussie, now aware that the third model for the twenty-dollar gold piece was unsatisfactory, sensed trouble. The estate's attorney, Charles O. Brewster, requested a meeting in Philadelphia that included Frank Leach and Charles Barber. That was held November 14.[40]

For Leach, the education about the twenty-dollar gold piece was beginning. Hering had not seen a trial strike from the third model for the big gold coin. At the very least, he wanted to see plaster casts of the dies that Barber had prepared from the last model. In this manner Hering could determine if the lack of detail was an engraving problem or a coining issue.

Leach, in turn, wanted a fourth model from Hering. If Hering would exaggerate the detail in a certain manner, the resulting sharpness would not be lost in the reduction process, and the chances for a successful design were quite good. However, Hering wanted to wait until he could see the business strikes from the third model.[41,42] This added delay before a fourth model could be commenced did not suit Leach.

For his part, Brewster raised the issue of compensation. The work that the Saint-Gaudens Estate had been required to perform had far exceeded that contemplated in the original contract. Additional moneys should be considered for the estate to cover the expense of a fourth model.[43] Yet in spite of the outstanding issues, Brewster walked away from the meeting with a good impression of Leach.[44]

On November 16, Leach met with Charles Barber in Washington. They talked at length about how to make the third model work. The Mint director asked Barber to make another set of dies from this model. That work would take another two to three weeks. Leach also wanted to conduct some experiments with the coin presses to better determine the maximum pressure the dies would tolerate as well as the die life itself.

After his meeting with Barber, Leach wrote expectantly to Brewster asking when he could expect to receive the fourth model. Leach believed Hering had enough information, without waiting for the business strike from the third model, to ensure that a fourth model would be successful. Regarding additional compensation, there was no more money available at that time. Leach acknowledged that their request was justified and that there might be reconsideration at a later time.[45]

Brewster came back with a disheartening reply to the Mint director. Hering would require three weeks on the reverse model and seven weeks on the obverse model. In addition, Brewster stated Hering urgently needed the strike from the third model at full pressure from the coin presses. Hering was not going to shortcut the process as Leach wanted.

Brewster had another piece of bad news for Leach. A fourth model would cost from $500 to $1,000. Brewster did not see why Cortelyou could not join Leach in giving assurances that at least $7,500 in total would be paid to the estate at completion of the contract. Otherwise, he expected that Augusta would drop the work where it stood and file a claim at a later date for additional compensation.[46]

Thus, matters were threatening to escalate out of control for Frank Leach when William Loeb on November 20 conveyed President Roosevelt's query as to the whereabouts of the new twenty-dollar gold pieces to Cortelyou. They were a much more handsome coin than the new ten-dollar gold pieces, and he wanted them distributed at once if possible.[47] Frank Leach was on his way to the White House.

When George Roberts announced his retirement as director of the Mint, he had recommended Frank Leach as his successor.[48] In his opinion, Leach had the experience and the executive ability for the job. Cortelyou's unqualified endorsement came the next day, and Roosevelt promptly approved the recommendation.[49] In Roosevelt's words, he could not do otherwise than appoint Frank Leach. It would have been both unwise and improper to pass the man over. The job required a *special* ability.[50] That being said, as Frank Leach faced Roosevelt that cold, wet November day, he knew the honeymoon was over.

Once the fury that had overtaken Theodore Roosevelt had expended itself, Frank Leach told the president point blank that if he "did not have free rein in the matter he would not attempt the work." Leach asked for time to assess the situation. He would correct the problem, but he insisted that he be in charge. "All you want, Mr. President, is the production of the coin with the new design, is it not?" Leach asked. "Yes," Roosevelt answered. "Well that I promise you," Leach replied.

Frank Leach wasted no time. On that same Friday, by order of the president, he instructed the Mint to use every facility at its command to strike high-relief twenty-dollar gold pieces using the second model with its relief modified as Landis had suggested. Never mind that the Mint was straining to pump liquidity into the American financial markets. Never mind that in the previous week they had produced 50,000 twenty-dollar gold pieces of the old design in one day at Philadelphia in response to the monetary crisis. Never mind that the men were regularly staying well beyond their normal four o'clock quitting time.[51] It was Leach's intention to strike 5,000 or 6,000 of the new twenty-dollar gold pieces by the first week in December on the medal press to satisfy Theodore Roosevelt. Additional strikes of the ultra high relief coin were no longer under consideration. Meanwhile, Barber was ordered to rush completion of a second hub from Hering's third model for use in the standard coin presses.[52]

Leach revealed these decisions and a little more of the meeting with the president in a letter to Charles Brewster on November 23.[53] Brewster replied two days later, concurring with that decision but raised another point. The obverse of the third model plaster cast had been returned from the Mint. Was it necessary to destroy all the sharpness before making the reduction?[54] Leach was puzzled. Certainly no one at the Mint would have taken the liberty to alter the models. If current efforts ran into problems, he would consider calling in Henry Hering again.[55] Leach left immediately for Philadelphia.[56]

Meanwhile in Philadelphia, Charles Barber was pulling out all stops to comply with Frank Leach's directive. He put his people to work around the clock and on Sundays. For the second model, high relief coin, he needed another set of dies in order to start a second production line. That was no easy process. The die stock for these dies had to be cut to measure, trued up, and annealed to get the steel to flow into all the difficult and high points of the design when hubbed. Only Barber and his long-time assistant, George Morgan, had the skill to do this work.

The engraver wanted the twenty-dollar gold pieces struck in 1,000 coin lots. Given that multiple strikes were required for each completed coin, if one of the dies broke in mid-process, all would not be lost as a replacement die would almost certainly produce an unacceptable doubling effect. A collar would be added for the final strike to place the inscription, "E Pluribus Unum," on the edge.[57]

As if pulling a rabbit out of a hat, on December 2, Leach walked into Roosevelt's office with a trial strike of the Saint-Gaudens twenty-dollar gold piece from Barber's second go at the third model.[58] Of course the piece was low relief. Its tone was pale compared to the high-relief coins, which exhibited a true gold color as a result of their annealing process. Theodore was "delighted."[59] Acting under Leach's authority, Barber could now make the needed modifications to strike up the design on the coin presses.[60]

Leaving Roosevelt, Leach wrote to Brewster that same day, enclosing the new low relief coin for his review. If Brewster wished any of the features touched up, it could be done on the master dies. However, the lawyer must not delay, as every moment was precious. Pride exuded from the letter. However, Leach left the door open for a fourth model if the Saint-Gaudens people felt the coin could be improved. At the same time, he could not promise any additional compensation but felt he could gain approval after the financial crisis had passed.[61]

Production of the high relief twenty-dollar gold pieces continued, coupled with close inspection to throw out the defective pieces with excessive fins on the edges, until Leach had an occasion to bring Charles Barber to Washington. Leach believed the problem of striking high relief coins might be helped with pre-milled planchets that he had had prepared at the San Francisco Mint before arriving in Washington, D.C.[62] These pre-milled pieces showed some potential for rectifying the fin problem. Barber returned to Philadelphia where Mint personnel implemented a new design for a milling machine which, when placed in operation, eliminated the fin. It did this by thickening the edges of the planchet and producing a flat rim in advance of striking. Pieces struck prior to this changeover were known as wire rim and afterwards, as flat rim.

Artistically superior, the high relief twenty-dollar gold piece continues to command a premium above its numismatic value in the marketplace today.

Naturally, Barber was proud of this accomplishment, sending Leach two sample coins. This coin was and would remain the most beautiful American design to ever reach the general public. Barber was quick to point out to Leach that this modified process still required the same three blows from the medal press.[63] The engraver was careful, however, to remain mum about how long it now took to strike each coin, given the efficiencies learned.

This new issue was avidly sought. Justice Oliver Wendell Holmes wanted one.[64] James Ellsworth had an agent working to acquire this twenty-dollar gold piece and the ten-dollar example from the first model.[65] Even former Superintendent Bosbyshell wanted one.[66] A premium for this double eagle quickly developed that ranged from five to 15 dollars.[67] Over the years, this coin would continue to command sums far above other coins of comparable numismatic rarity.

Theodore was more than "delighted" over the new twenty-dollar gold piece. When Leach brought him the new low relief coin for his inspection, he immediately asked for twenty more of the high relief coins.[68] When Leach returned just before Christmas with high relief coins without the wire edge, Theodore confiscated them and wanted more.[69]

Even as the high relief gold pieces were being struck, production from the modified low relief dies of the third model was ready to be set in motion. On December 6 Leach gave authority to commence striking twenty-dollar gold pieces from the coin presses.[70] Still Barber balked at carrying out Leach's orders. Barber wrote Landis, questioning the legal status of the new twenty-dollar gold coin design. No formal declaration of approval had been given. All of his work had been of an experimental nature. No provision had been made in the engraving department to support a full-scale production of this coin. He needed authority to make the dies for the business strikes from the third model.[71] Leach was miffed. He replied that the formal declaration would be attended to at the proper time.[72]

Still, Leach had second thoughts and ordered Barber to come to Washington. They reviewed Hering's points and the issue of a fourth model for the better part of a day. Leach felt that it was possible with a new model to better bring up the background detail. However, that model must have a lower relief than the third model that had required adjustment mechanically with the Janvier machine. While the coin from the third model was now in production, Leach believed that the Mint was capable of producing a coin with a higher final relief than was presently being done.

Leach conveyed these thoughts to Charles Brewster. There was just one problem. Leach could not guarantee that the government would pay for another model. If the estate wished to improve the appearance of the coin, they would have to accept the burden of the expense at least temporarily.[73] Brewster, in turn, placed the issue of the fourth model to Augusta.[74] For Gussie, it was an issue of money, not art. There would be no fourth model.

On December 19 Frank Leach received official approval for the Saint-Gaudens design for the twenty-dollar gold coin. Likewise, he belatedly received approval for the ten-dollar coin, already released into circulation.[75] Production delays had been encountered after Leach's first authorization of December 6. This double eagle was both new to the pressmen and a very difficult piece to strike. There had also been initial troubles getting the lettering on the edges of the coins. However, by the weekend of December 15 that problem was overcome. Over the second half of December, the Mint was coining up to 25,000 of the new low relief twenty-dollar gold pieces a day.[76]

Frank Leach was not quite finished. On January 14, 1908, Augusta Saint-Gaudens wrote to Secretary Cortelyou asking for payment of $8,000. Her issue, the preparation of numerous models had pushed out-of-pocket expenses to $3,700.[77] In the end there was $6098 remaining in the account that funded the work. Leach recommended paying $6000.[78]

In conveying Augusta's reluctant acceptance of the government's offer for final settlement, Brewster made a subtle linkage. Had Leach been able to secure an ultra high relief twenty-dollar gold piece for Augusta Saint-Gaudens yet?[79] Either Leach missed the linkage or chose to ignore it, replying that it now looked doubtful.[80] There

On the low relief double eagle, Liberty's face had been noticeably flattened. The relief of Liberty's chest, knee, and foot was lowered in apparent recognition of the coiner's suggestions. Also some of the rich detail of Liberty's blouse at the bust line was lost. Most disappointing was the treatment of the sunrays. Hering had made the obverse rays sharper, more rounded. Likewise he had sharpened the rays on the reverse, resulting in a diminished appearance of the eagle.

had been three struck at yearend with one intended for the estate. However, it was discovered that President Roosevelt did not possess an ultra high relief coin and the Saint-Gaudens piece had been diverted to the president.

For Gussie, the frustration of the coins would not end; she was going to stand her ground on the ultra high relief double eagle. She took her case directly to Theodore Roosevelt. The answer was swift. Leach wrote Brewster that Augusta could obtain one ultra high relief double eagle for $20 plus 12 cents postage.[81] Thus, Gussie received her additional compensation through the back door.

Frank Leach, the man who singlehandedly bulled the Saint-Gaudens double eagle to fruition, was confirmed as director of the Mint on February 12, 1908.

Chapter 61
The Last Word

The twenty-dollar gold piece wasn't issued yet when the firestorm over the new designs erupted. Roosevelt had had misgivings about the omission of the motto "In God We Trust." The law was clear that he had the ability to omit the words on the new gold coins. However, he had never anticipated that leaving the motto off the coins would stir up such a public stink.

Diverse groups across all spectrums of society were quick in their denunciation. Overlooked was the fact that Congress had not mandated the incorporation of this motto onto the nation's coinage in the revised statutes of 1874. Nevertheless, Roosevelt was blamed; his tampering was perceived as unpatriotic and unchristian.[1]

This grass roots opposition was aided by those against the president for other reasons. The New York *Sun* had opposed Roosevelt at practically every turn in his political career. The *Wall Street Journal* was upset that the needs of the commercial interests had been ignored in the drive for high relief.[2]

More serious in Theodore's mind, his good friend Lyman Abbot, editor of the *Outlook*, was only lukewarm in support. Abbot acknowledged that the new ten-dollar gold coin was the more beautiful compared to the previous coins for the simplicity of its design, helped in part by the omission of the motto. However, the strength of the aesthetic reasons for removing the motto did not adequately compensate for the resulting public misunderstanding. Abbot felt that Roosevelt had shocked the people.[3]

Religious leaders hit the president from the pulpit. The most strident opponents declared that Roosevelt was an atheist.[4] The Episcopal Diocese of New York, in convention, passed a resolution seeking the restoration of the motto.[5] J.P. Morgan, while not attending, was reportedly very much worked up and actively seeking the resolution's passage.[6]

In turn, President Roosevelt sought support from his network of influential friends. Unfortunately, this support came only from the nation's intellectual leadership. It was narrow-based, which boded ill for the president.

Roosevelt addressed the issue head on in a letter to a clergyman on November 11, 1907. He pointed out that he was not required by law to include the motto on the new coins. Here, however, he faced the issue squarely. He stated that he would have included it if he felt its use on coinage warranted. He believed that the motto's inclusion on coins was irreverent and came very close to sacrilege.[7] He went on to say that in his lifetime, he had never heard anyone speak reverently of the motto. Instead, people would twist the phrase's meaning by saying such things as "In God we trust for the short weight." This last comment was a slam against the depreciated bullion value of the nation's silver coinage. He closed by saying that if Congress directed him to restore the motto, he would do it promptly.[8]

Congress reconvened on December 2, 1907. Constituents had already inundated their congressmen to do something about the issue, causing a stampede to introduce legislation restoring the motto.[9] Even old Thomas Platt could not resist piling on, presenting a supporting petition in the Senate.[10] Roosevelt, now definitely a lame duck, could not even restrain his own party. Worse, as this controversy was reaching the boiling stage, the Saint-Gaudens twenty-dollar gold coin had yet to be authorized. There was a real chance that Congress would act rashly, seeking to block its issue. Subsequently, one proposed piece of legislation restoring the motto did just that.[11] There was also the fact that the high relief coins were costly to mint which added fuel to the fire. Roosevelt even obliquely referred to the fact that House Speaker Joe Cannon or one of his minions had called him to task on this point.[12] Thus, Frank Leach had understood political pressures precluded waiting for a fourth model.

If Republicans in Congress were not going to stand by Theodore Roosevelt, they would give him a way out. A bill introduced by one of their own, Congressman J. Hampton Moore from Pennsylvania and a friend of the president, would provide that exit.[13] The Republican leadership knew that Roosevelt's dander was up over the issue, and they feared an emotion-driven veto. They pressed Moore to go to the White House to resolve the impasse. Moore likened this assignment to going to beard the lion in his den.[14]

There was a set protocol to visiting the president. Roosevelt received visitors between 10 a.m. and 1:30 p.m. For the first two hours, senators and representatives had entrée without going through Loeb for an appointment. Sometimes there would be a score of people waiting for the president in the Executive Office. Theodore would go from one to another making a circle of the room, sometimes half a dozen times, speaking rapidly and gesturing freely.[15]

The Executive Office was crowded that day. Roosevelt "was putting them through, senators, congressmen, and citizens in his usual whirlwind fashion." Moore broached the subject of the motto. The president's hackles rose immediately. He did not see the need for legislation to mandate its use on the nation's coinage. Moore argued that the Democrats were pressing the issue and the newspapers were picking up on the story. Roosevelt sneered. Then Moore blundered, starting to mention the *Sun*. Roosevelt lost his temper, but Moore stood his ground. The president had needlessly shocked the country with this action. More conversation ensued, and the president finally relented somewhat. While he felt the issue was "rot," there was potential to misconstrue his motives and stir up a sensation. Therefore, if the Senate and House passed such a law, he would not veto it. Moore had survived the lion's den.[16]

The fact was that Roosevelt had already conceded the issue in his own mind as early as February. In March Brewster had asked that the Saint-Gaudens estate be involved with the insertion of the motto "In God We Trust" into the gold coin designs. Leach wrote back that it never occurred to him that the estate would be interested in this matter. Wanting to avoid any delay once the legislation requiring this motto looked certain, Leach had submitted the necessary modifications to Roosevelt for approval the previous month.[17]

The president signed the bill into law on May 19, 1908. The motto was restored effective July 1. The issue quickly subsided and the beauty of the new designs by Saint-Gaudens became the intended focal point. Theodore had lost the battle over the motto in order to achieve the broader goal of acceptance of the new coins themselves.

When the coins were first issued in July 1908, Charles Barber had modified the reverse of the double eagle to place the motto in an arc above the sun.

As the motto issue boiled and moved to resolution, comments on the coins themselves began to be heard. However, it was obvious that the twenty-dollar gold piece far surpassed the ten-dollar gold piece in beauty. The ten-dollar coin came in for criticism of the Indian headdress.[18] The public failed to see the headdress as the unique American symbol of liberty as Theodore Roosevelt had. It mattered little how brilliantly Saint-Gaudens had treated that headdress. Reflective of the time, the *New York Times* claimed that a woman named Mary Cunningham had posed for some of the later work on the ten-dollar gold coin model. She was of Irish heritage and that would not do. Only a pure American should be on the coinage.[19] Likewise, the eagle on the reverse of the ten-dollar gold piece was both praised as bold and strutting and criticized for legs that seemed disproportionately large.

Frank Leach made the mistake of repeating to Roosevelt the criticism that on the twenty-dollar gold piece the eagle was flying stiff-legged. The Mint director just could not bring himself to like Saint-Gaudens's artistic eagles. Leach had no idea that Theodore was a naturalist at heart. His comment earned the Mint director a trip to the presidential woodshed. In this case, Roosevelt sent Leach to the Rock Creek Aviary.[20] Leach returned with a new respect for Theodore Roosevelt. Eagles did indeed fly with their talons extended in a stiff-legged style.

♛ ♛ ♛

Across the Atlantic, with spring 1908 on the horizon, an old man reached into his pocket. His head was crowned with an almost full mane of white hair; likewise, his face was accented with both a white mustache and goatee, quite dignified for the times. This individual as a newspaperman had recorded first-hand the metamorphosis of his country into a world power. Now he was in London in the final stages of a distinguished career, serving as the American ambassador to the Court of St. James. He pulled out the twenty-dollar gold piece that was carefully protected so that it would not become worn or scratched. He had insisted that Treasury Secretary Cortelyou give him a flawless example of this unusual gold coin.[21] Today he was showing it to another of his friends in the English government as a striking example of what the American government under Roosevelt's leadership could do. Few who saw the flashy coin with its stunning high relief failed to speak of it as the most beautiful coin they had ever seen. The old man agreed. After all, as he had uncharacteristically carried on to Cortelyou, he had been there at the beginning, had procured General Sherman's sitting for Saint-Gaudens.[22] He had even been sitting at the dinner table where Roosevelt challenged Saint-Gaudens to redesign America's coinage. Whitelaw Reid smiled at his English friend and carefully put the shimmering beauty back into his pocket.

♛ ♛ ♛

So, did these beautiful gold coins blunt the cause for silver? At least in the short term, it is hard to make that case. As Treasury Secretary Shaw pointed out to Roosevelt early in the process, most of the double eagles would go into bank vaults, seeing very little general circulation. On top of that fact, foot dragging first by Saint-Gaudens and then by Charles Barber had these coins being issued late in the game to impact the presidential election of 1908. In fact, the five-dollar gold piece, the gold coin of the workingman, had yet to be changed.

Still Theodore Roosevelt was right in one regard. William Jennings Bryan did gain the Democratic nomination in 1908. However, he chose not to make silver an issue of the campaign. Beyond the redesign of the gold coins there was another reason. Gold production worldwide was up. The grinding deflation in commodity prices that previous shortages of gold had brought about was in the past. Roosevelt's anointed successor, William Howard Taft, easily defeated Bryan in the general election.

Chapter 62

The Golden Era Begins

Like the stars of the great constellations in the sky, the new designs on American coinage that followed Theodore Roosevelt's introduction of the two Saint-Gaudens gold coin designs illuminated American commerce. Not only gold and silver but even bronze and nickel glittered in the hands of the American public. It was a glorious time for United States coinage and the art embodied in the images on these coins.

The first to follow was a design for the two lesser gold coins, the quarter eagle and half eagle. The Saint-Gaudens Liberty in feather headdress, thought to be the logical design for downsizing was cast aside, perhaps by initial criticism of the ten-dollar gold piece, in favor of the images on the twenty-dollar gold piece. However, it was quickly found that this design lost its beauty when scaled down to the smaller coins.

Once again President Roosevelt stirred the pot. An old friend, Sturgis Bigelow, believed it was possible to strike a coin with high relief that permitted stacking. He was waiting on models before approaching the president.[1] Impetuously, Roosevelt replied that he was extremely interested.[2] The man putting Bigelow's idea into a practical design and model was the Boston area sculptor and former Saint-Gaudens pupil at the Art Students League, Bela Lyon Pratt.

On April 2, 1908, Theodore Roosevelt sprang his little surprise on Frank Leach over a simple lunch, devoid of any ceremony.[3] Tellingly, Edith attended. Among others present was Bigelow. After lunch, Bigelow unveiled Pratt's new design for the smaller gold pieces. The novel idea was an incused relief design first employed by the ancient Egyptians. In other words, the design was cut intaglio, below the surface of the planchet, thus gaining greater relief without impairing the ability of the coins to stack.

Pratt's model was a faithful image of the head of an American Indian in full feathered headdress. That choice certainly played to Roosevelt's affinity for all things Western. The president ended the meeting by authorizing Leach to produce some trial pieces.[4]

As Leach left the White House, the plan was for Pratt to complete the obverse model of the Native American. Barber would be instructed to model the reverse based upon the ten-dollar gold coin in deference to Saint-Gaudens.[5] Pratt was more than pleased with this arrangement in spite of the fact that he was to receive only $300.[6]

The reverse model was another story. Charles Barber wanted nothing to do with preparing a standing eagle design in the incused style that would undoubtedly be compared to that of Saint-Gaudens. Leach then returned to Pratt and asked that he do the modeling. He told Pratt to take one of the new ten-dollar gold pieces for an idea of positioning. However, he might want to consider shortening the legs of the bird, if indeed that was to be his design, to improve and make more realistic its appearance.[7] Frank Leach would finally have his revenge on allegorical eagles.

On June 29, Pratt sent his models to the Philadelphia Mint. He innocently asked that they be followed literally in preparing the dies. If any changes were necessary, Leach should notify him. He also wanted to see the finished coin.[8] Leach assured Pratt that Barber would not take liberties or make changes unless the model was found to be inconsistent with acceptable coinage operations. In that case, Pratt would be promptly notified.[9]

At this point, Leach stepped out of the process for good reason. He had recommended to Secretary Cortelyou that the $270 million in gold coin and bars then at the San Francisco Mint be moved away from the coastline to a more secure location. Cortelyou had been immediately receptive, as had President Roosevelt. The necessary money had been expeditiously appropriated, and Leach went back to his old home to supervise this extraordinary movement of gold. The transfer was designed to attract as little attention as possible. The gold was actually transported by the railroad in horse cars normally used for expensive racehorses. It was shipped to the centrally located Denver Mint, which offered adequate storage in vaults equipped with up-to-date security. Two shipments per week commenced August 15.[10]

Leach returned to Washington in time to re-engage himself in the final stage of the Pratt design. The Mint director presented a pattern piece for Roosevelt's review. Changes would be needed; details needed sharpening and the relief strengthened.[11] Nevertheless, Roosevelt gave his conditional approval.[12] The original pattern was then sent to Bigelow; however, the man was traveling. By the time the pattern strike caught up to Bigelow, the Mint had completed work on the new dies that restored detail that had been lost in reducing the design from the model. It was the same old story. Barber still had not mastered the Janvier lathe.

Finally at the end of October, Pratt saw his first production strike from his now modified models. He was not at all happy with the retouching. He told Leach that he was shocked at the liberties taken by Barber.[13] It was too late; the new half and quarter eagle coins were already being released into circulation. However, there was an immediate problem that could not be fixed. Given equal masses of metal, the incused design called for a raised field resulting in a thinner coin when compared to a standard design raised over a recessed field. Thus, counting mixed quantities of the old and new designs using stacks of equal height in commercial establishments was impossible.

Pratt's designs for the quarter and half eagle gold coins shifted away from allegories for the first time on circulating American coins.

With only months left of his presidency, Roosevelt was not done; he still had the one-cent design to replace. Time was running out. Facts concerning the genesis of Roosevelt's final effort are lacking. Sometime in the summer of 1908 the president was sitting for Victor D. Brenner for the preparation of a Panama Canal service medal when the topic came up. Brenner, who had just finished a plaque of Lincoln, was enthusiastic to adapt this work to a coin design. The 100th anniversary of the birth of Lincoln was coming in 1909. Whether Brenner initiated the discussion or not, Roosevelt was receptive.[14]

On December 14, 1908, Brenner brought models to the White House.[15] From this point forward, Brenner would work within the system. For the obverse, Brenner had employed a version of his own Lincoln in profile. For the reverse he apparently submitted two alternatives straight from current French coinage. Brenner was fishing to provide designs for the subsidiary silver coinage. It took Leach to rein him in, saying they would concentrate on the one-cent piece. His current submittals for the reverse were unacceptable, and Brenner must come up with his own design.

In February 1909 the sculptor submitted models that reflected the Lincoln cent with the wheatear reverse. Of course, there would be issues when Barber saw the model. The engraver objected to Brenner's use of multiple radii when developing the field of the coin. The engraver wanted only one. Brenner stood his ground.

Brenner also stood his ground over review of Barber's reductions. When he saw the hubs that Barber had prepared, he was not pleased, particularly with the obverse. Barber in turn suggested that Brenner be allowed to supply his own hubs. After much posturing, Brenner went to Henri Weil at Deitsch Brothers.

Up to this point, the proposed Lincoln cent did not incorporate the motto "In God We Trust" as it was not required on minor coins in the law change of 1908. Leach was not happy over the design; the head was too near the rim resulting in difficulties striking up Lincoln's features. The Mint director had Barber recenter the

Lincoln profile. This resulted in an unseemly gap between the top of Lincoln's head and the coin's rim. Into this void went the motto. After one minor blow-up over the coin's thickness, which was causing it to jam in vending machines, the design was approved on July 14, 1909. Roosevelt was now gone but his coin redesign project was finally completed.

The obverse of the new one-cent piece would stand the test of time, remaining in use into the twenty-first century.

In May 1909 rumors surfaced that Leach was considering resigning, or rather, retiring. Friends were saying that Leach's wife was in ill health. Other sources revealed that Leach was being considered to be president of Peoples Water Company in Oakland.[16] In his autobiography Leach added further light on his reasons for resigning. He had struggled working under President Taft, whose management style was too easy going.[17] In addition, Taft was gradually rooting out the Roosevelt people. It was time for Leach to return home.

By 1911 George Roberts was back as director of the Mint. Treasury Secretary MacVeagh wanted a replacement for the Liberty Head nickel designed by Charles Barber. It seemed only natural for Roberts to turn to James Earle Fraser, the most accomplished of the former assistants of Augustus Saint-Gaudens.

As Fraser and Roberts started down this road, there was some concern within the Treasury Department that a competition be held. Fraser wanted no part of it. He argued that a competition tied the Mint to the particular design chosen with little or no chance to make subsequent modifications. Whereas Fraser proposed to work with the Mint and let the design evolve through modifications and improvements.

By September 1911, Fraser had moved well beyond where he should have, considering that he did not have a commission. With George Roberts's encouragement, he submitted to MacVeagh electrotypes for his various sketches. One was an obverse head of Abraham Lincoln, far superior to that by Brenner. However, his sketch of an American Indian with feathers from his scalp lock was the better composition. This design, combined with the buffalo Black Diamond on the reverse, made for a truly American coin. In January 1912, MacVeagh signed off.

Yet there were complications in the summer of 1912. A premature announcement that Treasury was considering a change in the nickel's design brought forth objections from the vending industry. One man, Clarence Hobbs, of Hobbs Company and the American Stamp and Ticket Vending Machine Company, would be a thorn in Fraser's side right up to adoption of the new design.

Meanwhile MacVeagh had an issue of his own. He wanted President Taft's approval for the new design. MacVeagh brought letters of recommendation to Taft in September. The president wanted to see the "thing." MacVeagh embarrassingly had not brought Fraser's models with him. Ultimately, MacVeagh arranged to accompany Fraser to meet Taft at the White House. As the two men waited to see the president, they heard gales of laughter coming from the president's office. The loudest was Taft's.[18] It unnerved Fraser. Having had an intimate inside look at the high-energy Roosevelt White House while he modeled the president, the sculptor was not prepared for the informal approach of this president. Regardless, Taft's approval was gained.

With the presidential hurdle cleared, MacVeagh had no problem putting the vending machine issue to rest. He urged Roberts to give Fraser final approval for his designs. Now it was time for the hubs to be prepared. Charles Barber, facing higher relief than he wanted and an unfamiliar design, once again wanted nothing to do with this function. Consequently, Fraser retained Henri Weil to do the work.

The issues with Hobbs prolonged the process into February 1913. Taft had lost the election and the Democrats would take office on March 4. MacVeagh was not going to share credit for the new nickel design. He overrode Hobbs's objections and the new coins were issued on Inauguration Day.

Just after the release of the new nickel, James Earle Fraser wed Laura Gardin. She had been his student at the Art Students League from 1907 to 1910.[19] She was an accomplished sculptor in her own right. When they left the church, the newlyweds took a bus to go to the Metropolitan Museum of Art, their favorite haunt. Jimmie gave a quarter to the conductor and in change received his first buffalo nickel. The Frasers were elated.[20]

That elation did not last long. Charles Barber had been afraid from the design's inception of counterfeiting. Fraser had placed the coin's denomination on the raised ground upon which the buffalo was standing, the highest point on the reverse. It became evident to Barber that even the slightest wear would be enough to obliterate the inscription. He even went so far as to gild a coin to test whether it could be passed as a five-dollar gold piece. Fraser approved Barber's solution, recessing the area where the inscription had been placed, sheltering it from virtually any wear. Now the buffalo appeared to be standing upon a plain. It was the other action of Barber, of which Fraser was unaware, that crossed the line. Barber polished out all of the texture in the fields of the reverse, giving it a smooth finish. However, no one called his hand, and the change was allowed to stand.[21]

Type 1, with the denomination in relief

Type 2, with the denomination incused

Fraser's design is shown with the two reverses. The raised mound design would be replaced with a recessed area to protect the coin's denomination from any wear.

Regardless of the polishing, this nickel over the following century would become an American icon. James Earle Fraser had easily cleared the bar set by Augustus Saint-Gaudens.

In 1915 San Francisco celebrated the opening of the Panama Canal as well as that city's rebirth from the earthquake with the great Panama Pacific International Exposition. Plans called for four commemorative coins, a half dollar in silver and a dollar, quarter eagle, and fifty-dollar piece or quintuple eagle struck in gold by the Mint. The fifty-dollar gold piece was reminiscent of the assay office coins from the gold rush and would be in both round and octagonal form.

At that point, George Roberts was still at the helm of the Mint. Recognizing his position as a Republican under a Democratic secretary of the Treasury, Roberts had recommended going in advance to the Commission of Fine Arts, which had been established by Congress in 1910 and charged to advise in matters of art and national symbols.[22] Secretary William Gibbs McAdoo approved, and the commission designated four sculptors to design the pieces.[23] The sketches were submitted, and McAdoo, at the urging of Assistant Secretary William Malburn, rejected all four.[24] Immediately upon the rejections, Barber was instructed to begin preparing alternatives.[25]

Only after much prodding did the Treasury Department give their objections, and these only for the one-dollar and fifty-dollar gold pieces.[26] Time was of the essence; given the likelihood that Charles Barber would provide alternative designs.

Charles Keck, a former Saint-Gaudens assistant, redesigned his one-dollar gold piece with excellent results, given its small diameter. Robert Aitken, designer of the fifty-dollar gold piece, only modified his, addressing Treasury's objections specifically. Ironically it was Henri Weil again who assisted Aitken in making his bronze reductions.[27] Treasury had then accepted these changes and substituted work by Morgan and Barber for the other two pieces.

The commission chairman at the time, Daniel Chester French, was upset but could effectively do nothing.[28] However, one good thing had come from the process. Robert Aitken, taking Minerva from the California state seal and pairing her with the owl, sacred to the goddess, on the reverse, had designed a spectacular piece, particularly in its octagonal form.

The 1915 Panama-Pacific International Exposition commemorative coins: half dollar, gold dollar, quarter eagle, and fifty-dollar gold pieces.

1915 Panama Pacific Exposition official poster showing Hercules parting the continents, symbolic of the canal, with the skyline of the exposition in the background.

1915 Panama Pacific Exposition Award Medal designed by John Flanagan.

1915 Panama Pacific Exposition Official Medal designed by Robert Aitken, a San Francisco native. HK 399

As 1915 drew to a close, Treasury Secretary McAdoo chose to treat the coinage law as a mandate to change designs every 25 years. As a result, the three Barber-designed subsidiary silver coins were up for replacement in 1916. On December 3, 1915, Mint Director Robert Woolley, President Wilson's replacement for Roberts, met with the Commission of Fine Arts. He brought along Charles Barber. Before going outside for designs, he wanted the commission to review some designs that Barber had developed. It was the Mint's intent to use three different designs this time around. The commission formed a committee that rejected Barber's sketches and recommended Adolph Weinman, Hermon MacNeil, and Albin Polasek. prepare sketches for the coins.[29]

It was the committee's intent that each artist be asked to devote his work to one coin. When Woolley interviewed the artists at the end of December in New York City, they came away with differing ideas of what was being asked of them. One thing was clear, they were being asked to submit several designs that could be used for one, two, or even three of the coins. In effect it would be a competition. The Mint director would discuss resulting designs with the Commission of Fine Arts. That was a fine distinction. He was not going to seek the approval of the commission.[30]

By the end of February 1916, the three artists had submitted about two-dozen designs for consideration. Woolley informed the commission that there were six designs that he and McAdoo liked: five by Weinman and one by MacNeil. It was Woolley's intent to combine one of Weinman's designs with the single approved work of MacNeil for the quarter. Weinman would get the dime and half dollar. Woolley carefully pointed out that Treasury had made these selections. The Commission of Fine Arts was welcome to look at what was done, but that there would be no formal submission to the commission.[31]

In March, Herbert Adams, holding the sculpture chair on the commission, met Woolley in New York and recommended that MacNeil be given an opportunity to design a reverse to pair with his approved obverse.[32] Woolley accepted Adams's guidance, and the work now was in the hands of Weinman and MacNeil. Afterwards, Adams groused that it seemed the Mint's approach was to make the Commission of Fine Arts almost irrelevant.[33]

Both men submitted their models close to the deadline. Weinman's dime design consisted of a head of Liberty with a winged cap on the obverse. The reverse design featured a fasces, symbolic of unity, the nation's strength. Weinman's half dollar obverse featured a full-length figure of Liberty enveloped in folds of the national flag. On the reverse, an eagle perched on a high mountain crag.[34]

MacNeil's design for the quarter was intended to typify the awakening interest of the country in its own defense. On the obverse of the quarter, a full-figured Liberty was shown in a front view, head turned to the left, one breast exposed, stepping forward to the gateway of the country. The reverse depicted an eagle in full flight sweeping across the coin.

In July 1916, Weinman forwarded new bronze intermediate reductions made by Henri Weil for the dime to the Mint. The sculptor was staying on top of the process. In a letter to Secretary McAdoo, Weinman complained that the dies made from the first set of models for the dime were weak, the relief being less than his models called for. He requested that McAdoo instruct Barber to use the strongest possible relief for both his coins.[35]

McAdoo approved the new dime design on August 10, 1916. [36] At this point a problem developed from a not unexpected source. The vending industry had requested some of the new dimes to test in their machines. Clarence Hobbs was in the mix again. This time he had an ally in American Telephone and Telegraph that operated 60,000 to 70,000 pay phones where the dimes were found to easily jam.

Concurrently, the Bureau of the Mint acquired a new director, F. J. H. von Engelken. Woolley had resigned to work in President Wilson's reelection campaign. With the election at hand, McAdoo was all over this potentially embarrassing situation. He even considered having Barber take over the design process. However, the engraver would require six to eight months to complete the project and with expectations of new designs, that was an unacceptable delay.[37] The inscription of "Liberty" on the obverse was moved to accommodate Hobbs, and the rim was rounded with the relief lowered slightly to eliminate a possible fin that would cause jamming in the pay phones. The end result was the delay of issuance of the new dimes until October.

The head of Liberty is meant to be simple yet firm and forceful. The fasces fully surrounded by an olive branch is meant to symbolize peace.

Meanwhile Weinman had made progress on the 50-cent piece. After consultation at Philadelphia, he had reduced the figure of Liberty on the obverse and rearranged the inscriptions. Still, there remained problems with the uneven rim thickness. Barber tried a beaded border.[38] That move required a reduction in the size of the design devices on both sides. Weinman kept quiet. Von Engelken opted Weinman's way and authorized production from the sculptor's last models without the beaded border.

Throughout this process little was heard from Hermon MacNeil. The sculptor modified both his obverse and his reverse during the summer months. Dolphins had been added to either side at the base of the gate on the obverse. He learned from Barber that the quarter would be minted from these last designs that McAdoo had approved.[39,40]

It was a naïve MacNeil who wrote to Philadelphia Superintendent Joyce on January 6, 1917, saying that he saw in the newspapers that the new quarter was being issued. He hoped that the last models had been workable. Having heard nothing, he presumed that this was indeed true. He would like to see the new coins.[41] Was he in for a surprise when this happened?

The full figure of Liberty strides toward the dawn of a new day carrying branches of laurel and oak, symbolic of civil and military glory. Liberty's right hand is outstretched in bestowal of the spirit of freedom to America. On the reverse, the eagle is fearless in spirit and conscious of its power; and a mountain pine sapling, symbolic of America, springs from a rift in the rock.

The Mint had discarded the approved second design and used a modification from his first submittal for the obverse. The reverse was only a resemblance of his original work. MacNeil immediately went to the Mint where he saw the many variations that had been tried and discarded. He was frustrated at having been shut out of the process, since he himself had tried some of these variations in arriving at his final designs. Still, more could be done to improve the design. The figure of Liberty needed

Liberty's left arm is upraised and bears a shield in the attitude of protection from which the covering is being withdrawn. In the second version Liberty's chest is covered in chain mail, suitable for the mood of the country, now at war.

to be reworked to bring it more in line with the second model. This and other changes were absolutely essential. On the reverse the eagle needed badly to be raised in the field.[42] Overall MacNeil seemed surprisingly restrained in his communication with von Engelken over the liberty taken with his design.

While understanding, MacNeil was not folding his tent; he brought Herbert Adams back into the equation. Adams was a strong advocate, stating that it was unacceptable that the Mint had made changes without consulting MacNeil. To von Engelken's credit, he knew he was in the wrong ordering Joyce to tell Barber to keep his objections to himself.[43] That admonition was really not necessary; Charles Barber died February 18, 1917. MacNeil then began working directly with George Morgan, still the assistant engraver. When the enabling legislation passed on July 9, 1917, a modified design was placed into circulation, and MacNeil's ordeal was over.

In spite of wartime restrictions, Congress in April 1918 authorized a commemorative half dollar to celebrate the Illinois Centennial.[44] This was George Morgan's first effort as engraver. Portrayed on the obverse was a deeply introspective young Lincoln. The reverse, designed by assistant engraver John Sinnock, portrayed the Illinois state seal. This was George Morgan's first design of an obverse for legal tender coinage since his dollar of 1878. It is clearly his finest work and his signature piece as the Mint's engraver. Newly appointed assistant engraver John Sinnock executed the reverse design.[45]

Morgan's obverse image was taken from Andrew O'Connor's heroic monument in Springfield, Illinois.

Chapter 63

Fixing an International Nuisance

A. Piatt Andrew, Frank Leach's replacement as director of the Mint, knew little more than that coins were round! Andrew was an authority on financial matters, being a professor of economics at Harvard.[1] He was appointed on the recommendation of Massachusetts Senators Lodge and Crane. The Mint slot was a placeholder to get Andrew into the government. Margaret Kelly, Director Roberts's personal secretary and then a clerk for Leach, would handle the day-to-day affairs of the Mint.[2] Andrew's real role was assistant secretary of the National Monetary Commission that had required a leave of absence from Harvard and a move to Washington.

Once Theodore Roosevelt had understood the full import of the events surrounding the Panic of 1907, he had pressed the leaders of the House and Senate to pass a currency bill in the next session of Congress that convened in December 1907. The result was the introduction of a bill in the House by Edward Vreeland, chairman of the Committee on Banking and Currency, and a second one in the Senate by Nelson Aldrich, chairman of the Committee on Finance. The problem was that neither of these two powerful Republican politicians could convince the members of the other chamber to accept their bill so that both bills wound up in a conference committee to resolve the differences.

The Mint director's slot was a placeholder to get A. Piatt Andrew into the government. His expertise was economics.

The Republican conferees met in caucus to hammer out a compromise, effectively excluding the Democratic conferees and raising their ire. Representative Carter Glass from Virginia, a member of the House Committee on Banking and Finance, pronounced the compromise 50 percent House infamy and 50 percent Senate infamy. Dissatisfaction spurred a move in the Senate to mount a filibuster that cut across party lines.

The bill provided for National Currency Associations with authority to issue through their members additional circulating currency of $500 million. In all but name, these associations were little more than local clearinghouses. However, that name had grown since John Sherman's time to have bad connotations in Congress, particularly among Silver Democrats. As security for this additional currency issue, any member bank could deposit with the association various financial instruments beyond U.S. bonds. In addition, the bill called for a tax on this additional currency, when issued, to ensure its short-term nature and prevent serving as fuel for inflation. The bill acknowledged the fact that this fix was temporary until something more permanent could be developed through a sunset provision of June 30, 1914. To facilitate finding a long-term solution, the bill established a National Currency Commission to inquire into and report to Congress changes necessary in the U.S. monetary system or in the laws relating to banking and currency.[3]

With passage in question, President Roosevelt began calling senators and representatives to come see him in unusual numbers, urging them to support the bill.[4] Speaker Joe Cannon shoved this compromise bill through the House on May 27. The real fireworks were in the Senate where a small group of senators led by Robert La Follette of Wisconsin staged a filibuster. La Follette spoke for 18 hours, going into the early morning of May 30. However, the effort was in vain; his group was too small to sustain the filibuster. The bill passed with Roosevelt signing it into law that evening. The Senate then promptly adjourned.[5] It would be up to Taft to craft a permanent solution.

Membership in the National Currency Commission that Piatt Andrew went to work for was limited to members of Congress, the thinking being that they would be the ones most influential in promoting enactment of any recommendations. Even the bankers were excluded. Senator Aldrich was the chair. Subsequently, matters dragged through the first half of the Taft Administration and attrition resulted in only one-third of the commission members still retaining their seats in Congress.[6]

Compounding the problem, there was a lack of direction from the Taft Administration. Treasury Secretary Franklin MacVeagh had no real banking background. He had been a wholesale grocer in Chicago. His only exposure to banking had been as a director of the Commercial National Bank in Chicago. When George Roberts resigned as director of the Mint in 1907, he subsequently assumed the presidency of this bank. MacVeagh's appointment defied logic given that Taft had to be aware that Roosevelt, being a lame duck, had only gotten a band-aid fix on currency out of Congress in 1908 and that heavy lifting remained to be done on the issue of a central bank. Something badly needed to be done.

In a first hint that something was afoot, A. Piatt Andrew moved over to be assistant secretary of the Treasury on June 3, 1910.[7] Then George Roberts lost his job when his bank was acquired in Chicago. MacVeagh brought him back to be director of the Mint on September 14.[8] Now there were two advocates for a central bank within the Taft Administration.

In November 1910 a secret meeting took place at the ultra exclusive Jekyll Island Club off the coast of Georgia. In fact, it was so secret that its existence was not revealed until 1916. It was rumored that Pierpont Morgan handled the arrangements for the meeting as he was a member of the club, but he did not attend. He did not have to; he was well represented by the people who were there. Senator Aldrich issued invitations to A. Piatt Andrew; Arthur Shelton, Aldrich's private secretary; Henry Davison, a senior partner at J.P. Morgan & Company; Frank Vanderlip successor to James Stillman as president of National City Bank and Paul Warburg, a partner at Kuhn, Loeb & Company.

It took more than a week of long hours to hammer out a plan acceptable to all. Vanderlip in his autobiography recalled it as the most intense time in his professional career. Their plan called for a national reserve association consisting of a central bank with 15 branches across the country. Each branch would be governed by boards of directors elected by the member banks in that district with larger banks getting more votes. The branches would be responsible for holding the reserves of their member banks, issuing currency, rediscounting commercial paper from another branch, transferring balances between branches, and check clearing and collection. The national body would set discount rates for the system as a whole and buy and sell securities. In this manner they hoped to smooth out the short-term interest rate fluctuations that were driven by such factors as crop harvests.

Upon concluding, Aldrich fell ill before he could translate his notes into a final report. Vanderlip brought Ben Strong, another banker highly regarded by Morgan from the days of the 1907 financial panic, to Washington, and the two men drafted what would be known as the Aldrich Plan when it was released in 1911.[9]

In stumping for the adoption of legislation based upon the plan, Frank Vanderlip said: "The whole world is united in agreement that we have about the worst system of banking that there is anywhere in existence. It makes us . . . an international nuisance."[10] However, support was not unanimous. Former Treasury Secretary Shaw opposed the plan. The executive committee of the proposed national reserve association would be based in Washington. The boards of the branches, controlled by the larger banks, would elect this governing committee. While the president would appoint the governor of the association, he could not remove that individual without cause.[11] Shaw had a point that this plan was a boon for large banks and a lightning rod for progressive opposition.

There was urgency in this work. The third session of the Sixty-First Congress convened on December 5, 1910, and would adjourn at the expiration of this Congress on March 3, 1911. Just as crucial, Senator Aldrich was retiring at the end of this session. In the previous November elections, the Republicans had lost control of the House of Representatives in the upcoming Congress. If a central bank were to be established, it needed to happen within this time period, as the upcoming 1912 presidential election would surely result in a stalemate in the next Congress.

Yet President Taft hesitated, choosing instead to confer at the White House with a number of leading bankers on the currency question. Quietly Pierpont Morgan came to Washington, accompanied by his daughter and son-in-law, on Friday, January 13, 1911, staying at the Arlington Hotel. No one knew why Morgan was there. Speculation connected his presence with the possibility that the National Currency Commission was reaching a point of making a final report to Congress and that Morgan was being consulted.[12] For whatever the reason that Morgan came to Washington, results were not forthcoming. Faced with the lack of consensus support for the plan, Taft let the issue drift. A golden opportunity for Republicans had been squandered.

The Republicans convened their convention in Chicago in mid-June 1912. Taft had opposition. Theodore Roosevelt had been unhappy with what he perceived as Taft's failure to adequately build upon his administration's progressive policies. The two men had fought it out in the primaries where Roosevelt gained an advantage. However, Taft had the support of the Republican Party bosses, giving him a decided edge at the convention. Delegate credential disputes went one-sidedly in Taft's favor, and he gained the nomination on the first ballot.

Within the platform the Republicans approved at the convention was a plank on banking legislation. It called for measures that would prevent the recurrence of money panics and financial disturbances and that would promote the prosperity of business and the welfare of labor by producing constant employment.[13] It had absolutely no substance.

The Democrats held their convention in Baltimore in late June. By that point, it was an accepted fact that Theodore Roosevelt would bolt the Republican Party, running a third-party campaign. William Jennings Bryan, although a three-time loser for the Democrats, still exerted considerable influence. Early on, Bryan announced that he might veto the party platform if it did not suit him. Within the influential New York delegation, there was opposition to a central bank as well as fear that a small group of financiers or politicians would control the banks of the country.[14]

The final platform declared for a strong banking and currency law, reforming existing conditions. It declared for legislation establishing greater security for bank depositors. Like the Republicans, the Democrats did not really know what they wanted. However, they knew what they were against. Their platform specifically opposed the Aldrich Plan or any form of central bank.[15]

On the forty-sixth ballot the Democrats gave their nomination to the moderately liberal Woodrow Wilson. This nomination sealed the fate for Theodore Roosevelt's Progressive Bull Moose Party. No progressive Democrats would defect to the former president. Thus, Roosevelt's candidacy brought on a disastrous defeat for the Republicans. Taft was third in the popular vote, and the party lost control by a wide margin in both houses of Congress. Even Nicholas Longworth, Roosevelt's son-in-law, lost his "safe" seat in Cincinnati. For the first time since before the Civil War, Democrats controlled both the executive and legislative branches of the federal government.

Carter Glass, still smarting from the Democrats' abject defeat at the hands of Aldrich and Vreeland in 1908, worked relentlessly through the summer and fall of 1912 with Parker Willis, the advisor to the House Committee on Banking and Finance, to devise a currency and banking plan. The day after Christmas, 1912, they met with Wilson to unveil their recommendation. It divided the country into numerous regions controlled by reserve banks that would hold member banks' mandated reserves, perform various banking functions, and issue currency against commercial paper and a gold reserve of 33-1/3 percent. Wilson liked the concept but wanted a central board to control and coordinate the regional reserve banks.[16]

President Wilson wasted no time in exploiting his electoral victory, calling Congress into special session on April 7, 1913, for the purpose of addressing first tariff and then banking legislation. Consequently, Carter Glass put his currency legislation on hold. However, all was not well with Glass's plan; Bryan opposed it from his position as secretary of State. He thought it gave the bankers too much power and was determined to give government a larger role within the proposed system.

What Bryan really wanted was a more sophisticated version of his "Free Silver" campaign. National bank notes would be retired and replaced with a supply of paper money issued at the initiative of public officials and backed only by the government's promise to pay. Signing on as a supporter of Bryan's plan was Oklahoma Senator Robert Owen, chair of the newly created Senate Committee on Banking and Currency.

Bankers immediately opened fire with four leading bankers meeting with Wilson, Glass, Owen and Treasury Secretary William Gibbs McAdoo. Important revisions were made for a gradual retiring of national bank notes. Authority of the proposed Federal Reserve Board over discount rates would be diluted. A Federal advisory council would be created, consisting of bankers to serve as a liaison between the regional Federal Reserve Banks and the Federal Reserve Board.

The bill was jointly introduced in the House and Senate on August 29, 1913. It was perfunctorily approved in the House the following month. The Senate was another story. Three Democratic senators on the Committee on Banking and Finance consistently sided with the Republican opposition. Hearings extended through September and into October. The committee then went into executive session. On November 20, the committee reported a disagreement to the full Senate. Wanting a decision before Christmas, the Democratic caucus modified the bill slightly to ensure full party support and decided to hold the Senate in session well into the night each day until the bill was passed.

The Republicans kept the debate open until the week before Christmas. Elihu Root, now a senator from New York, scored one not-inconsequential victory. The bill called for a gold reserve of 33-1/3 percent for the currency to be issued. Root argued that this requirement was not stiff enough and would ultimately lead to too much currency being issued, creating an inflationary environment. The Democrats compromised it out, raising the reserve requirement to 40 percent.[17] Finally, the Senate passed its version of the bill on December 20, and it went to conference for reconciliation with the House bill. The version out of conference passed both houses on December 23. At 6:02 that evening, President Wilson with a flourish and four gold pens signed the Federal Reserve into existence.[18]

The law established a Federal Reserve Board based in Washington. This board consisted of five members appointed by the president and subject to confirmation by the Senate. To aid implementation the currency provisions of the Aldrich Vreeland Act of 1908 were extended. The Federal Reserve Board was given the power to issue Federal Reserve Notes. These notes were to be obligations of the United States receivable for all taxes, customs, and public dues and redeemable in gold at the Treasury.

Furthermore, this board was mandated to divide the United States into at least eight districts but not more than 12 with one regional Federal Reserve Bank for each district. The national banks within each district were required to subscribe to the capital stock of their regional Federal Reserve Bank equal to 6 percent of their paid-in capital and capital surplus. One half of this amount, payable in gold or gold certificates, was due within six months and the other half was subject to call. Other banks and trust companies could participate in this stock subscription, provided they met all the requirements of a national bank.

Each regional Federal Reserve Bank would have a nine-member board. The stockholding banks would choose three members, and shareholders would choose another three from within the district that were engaged in commerce, agriculture, or industrial activity. The Federal Reserve Board would designate the remaining three members. Each regional Federal Reserve Bank was required to pay a 6 percent dividend and distribute other profits.

Each regional bank was restricted to doing business only with its member banks and the conduct of certain open market operations such as the purchase and sale of gold, government or municipal bonds, and certain bills of exchange. The regional Federal Reserve Banks were empowered to buy commercial paper from their member banks that were seeking to convert assets into Federal Reserve Notes, advanced by and at discount rates to be set by the regional Federal Reserve Bank, subject to review and determination by the Federal Reserve Board. In this manner, by raising or lowering the discount rate, the Federal Reserve Banks in association with the Federal Reserve Board could control the amount of currency in circulation and seek to either stimulate or restrain economic growth.

Each regional Federal Reserve Bank was required to maintain a specified reserve against Federal Reserve Notes it issued as well as a 40 percent gold reserve. If the gold reserve fell behind the currency issued, a heavy tax was to be imposed by the federal government.

None of the existing forms of currency except national bank notes, scheduled to be gradually withdrawn, would be disturbed under the new law.

With a stable central banking system in place, American coins, and in particular gold coins, were in a position at the peak of the American monetary pyramid. The strength of the American financial system rested upon these gold coins.

Chapter 64

The Great War and the Return of the Silver Dollar

As the second decade of the 20th century played out, gold coinage at the three mints continued at high levels, particularly the half eagle. This five-dollar gold piece was the workhorse of the gold coins in everyday commerce.

All this changed in late July 1914 as Europe slipped into war. Both sides in this escalating conflict, led by the English, moved rapidly to liquidate their holdings in American stocks and bonds. Treasury Secretary William Gibbs McAdoo was forced to exert drastic influence on Wall Street to prevent a precipitous loss of gold and a financial panic that would have rivaled 1893. He also invoked the emergency currency provisions of the Aldrich-Vreeland Act as a backstop. As a result, the New York Stock Exchange halted trading on July 31, 1914, and did not reopen until November 28, 1914. Even then, stocks and bonds were not allowed to price below their close on July 30, 1914. It was not until April 1, 1915, that all trading was allowed without price floors. Likewise, gold coinage slackened in 1915 and fell precipitously in 1916. Only the San Francisco Mint struck gold coins that last year in support of the local economy.

Woodrow Wilson narrowly won a second term in the presidential election of 1916 on the theme, "He kept us out of war." Not quite three weeks after the election, the Mint announced that gold coinage was being suspended. The stated reason given by the Mint director was the need to strike subsidiary silver coinage to meet high demand. If the new designs for the quarter and half dollar were not ready, coinage of the old Barber design would continue to be struck.[1] This line of reasoning seemed a stretch. British action in regard to gold coinage gave a better indication of what was afoot at the Mint. In September 1916, that government outlawed the melting of gold coins for jewelry.[2] The American Mint Service was preparing for war in spite of the sloganeering.

During the Great War, the Mint Service produced significant quantities of minor and subsidiary silver coins. At the same time, the federal government hoarded gold bullion that accumulated from war material sales to the Allies. However, there was one notable exception to what was otherwise almost routine activity at the mints: The Pittman Act of April 22, 1918.

The story opened in early 1918 when the German government launched a propaganda campaign against the English in India. The colonial government in India had over many years worked to have the general population accept paper currency backed by silver rupees. With the onset of war in 1914, British demand for Indian materials escalated, exacerbating the need for paper rupees to support the expanding colonial economy.[3] A German-fueled rumor that the British could not redeem these silver certificates started a run on the colonial redemption agencies located throughout India. If the British failed to redeem this paper currency, a revolt was likely that would either split India away from Great Britain or require a diversion of troops from the Western Front to reestablish order in the colony.

There was only one place where the British Government could acquire the needed silver bullion quickly: the silver dollars sitting in the United States Treasury vaults. Senator Key Pittman from Nevada introduced the administration's bill to satisfy the British ambassador's request. Literally at the speed of lightning, this bill was introduced on April 22, 1918, and enacted into law that same day.[4] It called for the conversion of up to 350 million silver dollars into bullion and their sale or use for subsidiary silver coinage. It then directed the purchase of domestic silver subsequently for the recoinage of a like number of silver dollars that would support a replacement of the withdrawn Silver Certificates due to the original melting. The act also stipulated that the Silver Certificates to be removed from circulation be replaced with Federal Reserve Notes. The sales price to the British was set at the advantageous rate of $1 per fine troy ounce. Even at this rate, the intrinsic value of the silver dollar, which contained .773 troy ounces of silver, was only 77.3 cents, resulting in negative seigniorage.[5] Likewise the act provided for the purchase of silver for the replacement dollars at $1 per fine troy ounce. Ultimately 270 million standard silver dollars were converted to bullion by the Mint, with 259 million going to Great Britain.[6]

At the end of the Great War upon the Armistice of November 11, 1918, silver prices remained higher than the purchase provisions provided for in the Pittman Act. The silver price bubble did not burst until 1920. At that point Treasury acquired the necessary silver, and required the old Morgan Dollar be resurrected for coinage in 1921. Yet there was no master die remaining to support renewed minting. While Mint director, Piatt Andrew had ordered all dies from obsolete or retired designs destroyed in 1910. Thus engraver George Morgan found himself with the chore of recreating his own design for a new master die.

After waiting in the shadows for forty years, George Morgan finally became engraver upon Charles Barber's death in 1917.

Others had a different idea as to how these replacement silver dollars should appear. The American Numismatic Association began lobbying Congress at the end of 1920 to issue a circulating silver dollar commemorating the peace. This move was a bit premature; the United States and Germany would not conclude a separate peace agreement until July 2, 1921. Ultimately, legislation calling for a commemorative Peace dollar with an appropriate design was introduced on May 9, 1921.

At this point, the Commission of Fine Arts entered the picture. Charles Moore and James Earle Fraser met with Mint Director Raymond Baker on May 26. Baker wanted a design that was distinctly American, while commemorating the Great War and subsequent peace. He wanted to leave the matter of securing the design up to the commission. Moore noted that the designs called for in the legislation might conflict with existing laws. Baker's reply was to quote the existing statutes for coin designs.[7]

With another coin design project likely, the Commission of Fine Arts now moved to reinforce their standing with the Mint. The Wilson Administration had turned a tin ear to the arts.[8] Now with President Warren Harding, there was hope for something better. On July 22, 1921, the president issued an executive order extending the Commission's authority to include review of coin designs.[9] Immediately, Charles Moore related to Baker their resolve to retain the head of Liberty on the obverse while trying for a really fine head. In regard to the reverse, they asked whether the present law would allow them to consider anything other than an eagle and solicited Baker's suggestions for a new design.[10]

On the heels of Moore's communication to Baker, a move was made to advance the enabling legislation by having it placed on the House's Unanimous Consent calendar. When the title of the bill was read before the House on August 1, there was one objection and the bill died.[11] Here the matter sat for the remainder of the summer and into the fall.

Fraser and Director Baker met on November 12 to talk the matter over. The decision was made to seek designs under the authority of the 1890 act that provided for the replacement of the Morgan Dollar design at any time. Baker would leave it up to the commission as to the mechanics of obtaining sketches. Reductions of the chosen models and dies would be made at the Mint.[12]

The commission moved rapidly, desiring that the issuance of the coin commence in the year that peace had been formally reached with Germany. Fraser along with Herbert Adams and Daniel Chester French would judge the sketches.[13,14] Eight artists were asked, not later than December 12, to submit proposals: Robert Aitken, Chester Beach, Victor D. Brenner, Anthony de Francisci, John Flanagan, Henry Hering, Hermon MacNeil, and Adolph Weinman.[15]

On December 14 the commission notified Baker that the obverse and reverse designs of Anthony de Francisci had been chosen. De Francisci was a former pupil of James Earle Fraser and had worked for Weinman and MacNeil.[16] It appears that all three men on the jury were particularly taken by de Francisci's head of Liberty. Afterwards, Moore said he was particularly happy over the head; it was exactly what he had been longing for and expecting for some time to see realized.[17] What the three men saw was a rendition strikingly similar to Saint-Gaudens's aborted one-cent design that ended up on the ten-dollar gold piece with the Indian headdress. After the meeting, Fraser gave de Francisci his cast of Saint-Gaudens's Head of Victory from which to make improvements upon his model before submitting it to the director of the Mint for approval.[18] For the reverse, de Francisci had submitted two models from which the committee chose the naturalistic standing eagle on a mountain crag facing a rising sun, the dawn of a new era. The rejected option showed an eagle tearing at a sword representing disarmament.

George Morgan was required to cut the broken sword, viewed as signifying defeat, out of the hub.

Now, the rush was on to make the production deadline. Somewhere in the process a broken sword was added to the standing eagle model. Moore told Fraser on December 20 that Baker was depending upon him and de Francisci to get a perfect coin. Baker would back the two men all the way at Philadelphia.[19] That same day, with the necessary approvals in hand, a beaming Director Baker went public with the new designs.[20] The broken sword was explained as representing the likely outcome of the ongoing arms conference. Then the firestorm hit. A broken sword symbolized only one thing in the public's mind: Defeat. It had to go.

There is little doubt of the origin of the new silver dollar design: Compare the Peace dollar with Saint-Gaudens's one-cent model without feather headdress (which served as a basis for the ten-dollar gold piece) and with the double eagle model for the reverse of the Roosevelt Inaugural Medal.

The coin that reached the public bearing the date 1921 was in high relief. This silver dollar design approximated what Saint-Gaudens's ten-dollar gold piece would have looked like without a headdress, paired with the eagle from the Roosevelt inaugural medal. Of course, it was still de Francisci's work but Fraser's influence is there. One is left to wonder if Fraser and Moore had influenced the design process in a manner that resulted in a coin that approximated Saint-Gaudens's ten-dollar gold piece stripped of Roosevelt's involvement and the allegorical eagle.

Unfortunately, this high relief coin was a one-year issue. Die life was entirely unacceptable. Given the volume of silver that the Mint had to monetize in 1922, it was an untenable situation. In fact, subsidiary silver coinage was eliminated entirely in 1922 to facilitate the mass coinage of these replacement dollars, needed foremost for the reissue of silver certificates. Fraser and de Francisci tried, but in the end, the design finished the rest of its life in standard coin relief. The Mint completed its recoinage as required by the Pittman Act in 1928 and promptly suspended coinage of the Peace dollar.

Chapter 65

The Nicest Birthday Present Ever

The 1920s brought the United States to the forefront of the world order of nations, easily surpassing the exhausted and depleted economies of Europe. Its economy had evolved from that in the first years of the century, prior to the Great War. No longer did a majority of Americans work on the farm or as skilled craftsmen. The commercialization of new consumer technologies, including the radio and labor-saving appliances like the washing machine and vacuum sweeper, brought new manufacturing jobs to the major cities. In addition, commercial aviation spread its fledgling wings. Affordable automobiles for the middle class suddenly became reality with Henry Ford's innovation of the assembly line. Cars and household appliances quickly became a necessity of life. If the cash wasn't there to buy these innovations, easy credit bridged the gap.

After a mild recession, the American economy grew at a blistering annual rate of 7 percent in this great transformation from 1922 to 1927. With such prosperity, the Republican-dominated government adopted a laissez-faire approach to business regulation. President Coolidge was quoted in 1927 as saying, "The business of America is business." This was the environment within which the Roaring Twenties made their mark on American culture; financial panics seemed like phenomena of the past. Reflecting this unbridled optimism, the stock market experienced one long, steep, uninterrupted climb. In turn, the prospect of easy and instant wealth led to a broader participation in stock ownership outside of Wall Street and widespread use of margin buying.[1] As was the case in the Panic of 1907, a downturn in this environment could lead to disastrous consequences.

In this veritable Roaring Twenties Garden of Eden, commemorative coins authorized by Congress flourished. At the forefront was the body of work by Jimmie and Laura Fraser. James Earle Fraser's best standalone work was the 1925 Norse-American Centennial medal.[2] The Norse piece, free from inscription requirements of legal tender United States coinage, was struck in bronze, silver, and a few pieces in gold. It was remarkable for its clean fields and simple yet artistic portrayals of Vikings. However, by far the zenith of commemorative coin designs from this period was the Oregon Trail Memorial half dollar, a collaboration of the Frasers. Laura sketched the obverse and Jimmie, the reverse, while Laura prepared both models. This half dollar would be struck intermittently from 1926 to 1939.[3]

The 1925 Norse-American Centennial medal demonstrated the consummate skill of James Earle Fraser in coin art.

The team of Jimmie and Laura Fraser reached a pinnacle in 1926 with their Oregon Trail half dollar.

The resumption after the Great War of gold coinage of the United States reflected the increased economic activity but changed in a fundamental way. The mintage of quarter eagles resumed in 1925, but these coins were never a factor in daily commercial transactions due to their awkward denomination of two and a half dollars. The issuing of five-dollar gold pieces did not resume until 1929, and most of these pieces were never released into circulation. The coining of ten-dollar gold pieces, though resumed in 1920, was sporadic over the decade. It was the double eagle that drove postwar American gold coinage.

Starting with 1920, the twenty-dollar gold piece was issued every year of the decade. However, mintages ramped up significantly in 1924 to 10.3 million pieces from the three mints. Double eagles minted in 1925 totaled 9.5 million. Coinage slacked somewhat in the next two years and then ramped up to 8.8 million in 1928. These coins for the most part never went into circulation; they went into bank reserve holdings. Given that Federal Reserve notes could be issued at a multiplier of 2-1/2 times each dollar in gold held in reserve, the mintage of these double eagles was like pouring an accelerant on the already overheated economy.

The Dow Jones Industrial Average (DJIA) hit an all-time high on September 3, 1929, at 381.17. Secretary of the Treasury Andrew Mellon, in office through three Republican administrations, was quoted as stating American investors were acting as if the price of securities would infinitely advance. Great Britain's chancellor of the exchequer described the American stock market as a perfect orgy of speculation. The inevitable selling started on Thursday, October 24, 1929. Bankers stepped in on that Friday to staunch the bleeding only to be overwhelmed on the following Monday and Tuesday. At the market close on October 28, the DJIA stood at 230.07. Margin calls crushed the individual investor and in turn saddled the banks and brokerage houses behind these loans with a bundle of bad debts. The DJIA would not exceed its peak of September 3 until 1954. The never-ending economic expansion was clearly over.

With tax revenues falling and a clamor for protection of domestic industry, Congress passed the Smoot-Hawley Tariff on June 17, 1930. It was a major mistake. It taxed the consumer and invited retaliatory tariffs from America's trading partners. For industries driven by incremental profits from high-volume assembly-line production, this tariff cut into their international markets, decreasing sales and increasing unit costs. At the same time, an ever-shrinking domestic sales base would not support price increases to absorb the higher unit costs. It was a recipe for disaster.

Matters worsened in 1931 as the economies in Europe, greatly weakened by the destruction and loss of manpower from the Great War, began to crack under the pressure from the downturn. In response, the New York Federal Reserve Bank loaned $150 million in gold to European central banks without regard to the concomitant shrinkage this action would force upon circulating Federal Reserve notes. Meanwhile, the Federal Reserve Board kept interest rates high to defend the dollar internationally when they should have lowered them to stimulate the economy. National banks in the United States, faced with falling loan demand from these high interest rates in a down economy, began exchanging their idle Federal Reserve notes for gold. This shrinking currency base in turn brought on a disastrous round of deflation.

In Europe, the Bank of England, after suffering speculative attacks on the pound sterling, "temporarily" abandoned the gold standard on September 19, 1931. Germany and Austria did likewise. In spite of these actions, there was reluctance in Congress to abandon the gold standard and float the dollar as the British had done with the pound sterling.

After grossly mismanaging the economic collapse, Republicans were not just turned out of office in 1932; they were wiped out. Theodore Roosevelt's cousin Franklin, having followed in his predecessor's footsteps as a New York state legislator, assistant secretary of the Navy, and governor of New York, was now president. The comparison ended right there; the one was direct and in-your-face to get results, and the other was much more nuanced in achieving his goals.

Inaugurated on March 4, 1933, Franklin Roosevelt lost no time in making sweeping economic policy changes as part of his "New Deal" to revive the nation and dig out of the depression. In fairness to Roosevelt, he inherited a full-blown crisis that required instant action upon taking the oath of office.

The trouble began in February when gold withdrawals from the banks reached epidemic proportions. Right into January, gold imports had exceeded exports, but the situation turned drastically in the opposite direction over the next 30 days, largely due to exports to London, fueled by exchange speculation. On March 1, the Bank of England held more gold than at any time since the country had "temporarily" gone off the gold standard.

As the outward flow accelerated, Congress initiated debate on the subject. The public picked up on speculation in this debate that the United States might go off the gold standard. That concern led to widespread withdrawals of gold and currency from the banks, reaching an unacceptable level and producing a banking crisis in Detroit. Reacting to the local situation, the Michigan governor at the end of February declared a bank holiday in the state. Nationally, the withdrawals accelerated as the Hoover Administration approached its last days. President Hoover actually approached Franklin Roosevelt before the inauguration, offering to declare a national bank holiday with Roosevelt's accord. Roosevelt, powerless at this point, refused to proceed in this manner. So when the president-elect took office, several of the regional Federal Reserve banks, including New York City, were dangerously close to breaking the 40 percent gold reserve requirement for their Federal Reserve Notes.[4]

On the Sunday following the inauguration at 11 p.m., President Roosevelt issued a bank proclamation. He blamed the withdrawal of gold and currency from American banks on hoarding. Compounding the problem, foreign speculation was adding to the severe drain on the nation's stock of gold. As a result, he declared the country to be in a national emergency. Under the provisions of the Wartime Act of October 6, 1917, he was prohibiting any transactions in foreign exchange and the export, hoarding, or melting of gold and silver coin, bullion, and currency. In order to fully assess the emergency, Roosevelt declared a national bank holiday, starting the following morning and extending through Thursday, March 9.[5] Questions immediately arose that caused Secretary of the Treasury William Woodin to state that the country was still on the gold standard. It was ridiculous and misleading to say otherwise.[6]

Although the bank runs quickly ebbed, Roosevelt wanted total control of the gold. On April 5, 1933, the president issued an executive order that stated a national emergency still existed and set out in detail the government's prohibition against hoarding. All persons were required on or before May 1 to deliver to a regional Federal Reserve Bank or member bank all gold coin, gold bullion, or gold certificates held or coming into their possession before April 28. Failure to do so would result in a severe fine, prison time, or both. Holders of such gold or gold-equivalent currency would receive lawful money in return. The order exempted gold holdings of $100 or less, gold coins of numismatic value, and gold bullion necessary for use in industry.

The *New York Times* critically observed that gold coin and certificates in circulation or held by foreign banks were at their lowest point since 1928 with the exception of 1930. Since February, there had been a large return of gold coin to the regional Federal Reserve banks. The president, in spite of this favorable trend, evidently desired to speed up the process.[7] The paper reported in a separate article that $433 million in gold coin and gold certificates had been voluntarily turned in without any direct demand by the government.[8] This fact made no difference; Roosevelt had recalled the gold coin. He had accomplished by a questionable executive order what the Silverites and William Jennings Bryan with his figurative cross of gold had not.

In this whirlwind, the mint was caught. They had already coined 445,000 double eagles for 1933 but had not released them. Given that the New York Federal Reserve Bank was so terribly short of gold, it argues that someone high in the Hoover Administration knew that gold recall was or should have been a serious consideration. These coins went to the melting pot. Well, almost all of them. A couple handfuls went out the back door. Since they had not been monetized with the subsequent exception of

Franklin Roosevelt signed the Gold Reserve Act into law on his fifty-second birthday.

one coin, they were and remain illegal to own, and the mint has been on a witch hunt ever since to recover them.

January 30, 1934, was Franklin Roosevelt's fifty-secnd birthday. In his office in the presence of Missy LeHand, his personal secretary, Secretary of the Treasury Robert Morganthau, the fifteen members of the White House press corps, and a few other friends and officials, he signed into law the Gold Reserve Act. While this act ratified his executive order recalling gold, it went much further. Under its authority, Roosevelt would arbitrarily raise the price of gold from $20.67 to $35 per fine troy ounce, thereby devaluing the dollar by an equivalent amount. The profits, never mind that they were noncash, would fund a $2 billion Exchange Stabilization Fund to defend the dollar on foreign exchanges. It also pulled all gold held by the regional Federal Reserve banks into the Treasury, abrogated all gold clauses in contracts and prohibited the mint from striking gold coins for domestic use. After affixing his signature, Franklin Roosevelt beamed at the reporters saying this was the nicest birthday present he ever had.[9]

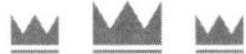

Ironically, the silver dollar now was the lone survivor with an unlimited legal tender. Under the Thomas Amendment to the Agricultural Adjustment Act of May 12, 1933, President Roosevelt was authorized for a period of five months to accept silver on payments of war debts at a maximum price of 50 cents per fine troy ounce with total amounts accepted limited to $200 million. Silver certificates were to be issued against the silver received and silver dollars coined to the extent necessary to meet any consequent redemption demands at Treasury. This action resulted in limited coinages of Peace dollars in 1934 and 1935.

Gold's reign was over, cut short by yet another financial crisis.

Chapter 66
The Bitter End

The Silver Purchase Act of June 18, 1934, instructed the secretary of the Treasury to purchase silver domestically and internationally until the market reached a value of $1.29 per fine troy ounce, equivalent to the face value of the standard silver dollar, or until the monetary value of Treasury's silver stock reached one-third of the value of its gold stock. All Silver Certificates issued for the purchase of such silver were redeemable at Treasury for silver dollars.[1] This act was further augmented by an executive order on August 9 that mandated the sale of all silver bullion in the United States at a price of 49.5 cents per fine troy ounce, well above market prices. Silver not used for coinage would be held in stockpiles.[2]

President Roosevelt's objective through the Silver Purchase Act was to pump up silver prices, further inflating the American economy. Somebody forgot to tell Roosevelt that a variation of this idea had been tried before and did not work. Even with control of the gold, all this policy did was to fill the government's coffers with unwanted silver bullion.

During the early 1960s demand for silver began mounting, pushing the price of this metal against the $1.29 per fine troy ounce price cap of the Silver Purchase Act. Previously the federal government had been able to maintain this cap by releasing silver from government stockpiles in times of tight supply. However, these stockpiles were rapidly being depleted as production of subsidiary silver coins was increased to meet growing demand in commerce coupled with a slowing in the velocity of transactions due to ever-widening applications for vending machines.

Government projections anticipated silver stockpiles would be exhausted by 1968, leaving silver prices to rise unfettered above $1.29, at which point the Silver Purchase Act prohibited government purchases of the metal. Congress responded by repealing the Silver Purchase Act on June 4, 1963, effective in March 1964. Until that deadline, Silver Certificates could be redeemed for bullion or silver dollars from the federal government.

In early 1964, anticipating a need for additional silver dollars, the Treasury Department included in its appropriation request funds for the minting of 150 million of the big shiny coins. In a speech, Mint Director Eva Adams opposed this appropriation. The House Committee on Appropriations promptly removed the request in the belief that there was a serious shortage of subsidiary silver coins and a diversion to strike silver dollars would be counterproductive.[3] As a result, the Nevada gaming houses and other users of silver dollars in the West began to accumulate the coin from existing stocks for their operations. Much to their surprise the silver dollars received from the Treasury Department contained some Morgan and Peace dollars carrying a numismatic premium mixed with a few of the old Seated Liberty design.[4]

It was only a matter of time until word leaked out of potential riches to be had at the coin window at the Treasury Department in Washington. At the start of 1963, Treasury still held 94 million silver dollars. The ensuing great Treasury raid peaked in mid-March 1964. Daily, a long line of collectors, speculators, and hoarders snaked out of the Treasury building onto Pennsylvania Avenue. They carted off to waiting cars and trucks countless bags of silver dollars, each containing 1,000 coins and weighing 60 pounds. One individual alone bought 35 bags![5] On Wednesday, March 25, with only 3 million silver dollars remaining in Treasury's vaults, Secretary Dillon called a halt.[6]

The emptying of Treasury's vaults only spurred the Western senators to greater efforts to restart minting silver dollars. They successfully inserted an amendment for $600,000 to mint 45 million silver dollars into the House's appropriations bill, which President Johnson signed into law on August 3, 1964. The law specified the date 1964 and use of the Peace dollar design.[7] Coinage started on May 12, 1965, at the Denver Mint. A numismatic premium developed in advance of the release of these coins, making their ultimate circulation in commercial channels doubtful. However, the silver dollars were withheld because by now the Mint had a serious problem with silver coinage.

The need to address silver in the subsidiary coinage reached a crisis point when on June 3, 1965, President Johnson sent a message to Congress requesting a change in the metal content of these coins. World use of silver was so far above annual production that it was only a matter of a short time before the price of silver reached the point that these coins would go to the melting pot of speculators as fast as they were minted. The proposed new surface of the dime and quarter would be composed of an alloy, 75 percent copper and 25 percent nickel bonded to a core of pure copper. The half dollar would have a surface alloy that was 80 percent silver and 20 percent copper bonded to a core of copper and silver such that the overall coin had a silver fineness of 400 (40 percent). Ultimately the half dollar would lose its remaining silver in 1971. This legislation steam-rolled through Congress. Silver coinage dated 1964 would continue to be minted until first the quarter and then the half dollar and dime, in the new composition, were coined in sufficient quantities bearing the date 1965 to support being placed in circulation. Almost immediately, subsidiary silver coins disappeared by the bagful, going either to bulk sales or the melting pot. The law placed a five-year ban on coinage of silver dollars, resulting in the 316,076 Peace dollars from 1964 going to the melting pot.[8] As with the 1933 double eagles, there have been rumors that a few coins survived. The melting process was in bulk with no exact count for reconciliation purposes.

Today, the quarter bears the brunt of American coin needs. With its clad composition, it has no meaningful intrinsic value. It is worth whatever goods and services it can purchase. Over the years, inflation has steadily chipped away at the value of its purchasing power. Vending machines take paper currency. The once ubiquitous pay phone is extinct. In addition, the credit card has gradually eaten into the domain of coins, even for parking meters. Today, metal detectors are everywhere there is a crowd: sporting events, airports, and government buildings, even at the headquarters of the United States Mint. Loose coins in a pocket now are more nuisance than necessity. Thus, the golden reign of coins that went into decline with President Franklin Roosevelt's recall of gold has reached a nadir that will only be reversed if larger denominations are substituted for paper currency. It was a glorious ride while it lasted!

EPILOGUE

As a member of the Citizens Coinage Advisory Committee (CCAC) charged with the review and critique of all coin and medal designs at the U.S. Mint, I remember Mint staff addressing the 100th anniversary of the Weinman and MacNeil subsidiary silver designs. They would be coined in gold. I asked why they weren't being done in silver. That is when I learned the Mint now has unlimited authority to issue gold coins but not silver coins. I knew it was a great opportunity lost and vowed that the Peace dollar would not suffer the same fate.

I started on a preliminary basis with Representative Andy Barr and his staff. I go back a long way with his family and was an early supporter in his first unsuccessful run for Congress. I teased him afterward that, through my CCAC appointment, I got to Washington before he did. Funny for me but it was not very funny for him. He made it the next time, and at the beginning of 2017, he was named chair of the House subcommittee with Mint oversight responsibility. I quickly met with his staff and Joe Pinder, then on the permanent staff of the Committee on Finance to discuss the idea of reissuing the Peace dollar in 2021. The idea was favorably received, but in legislative terms, 2021 was an eon away.

Fast forward to early fall 2018 and Tom Uram and I were both under consideration to chair the CCAC. I did not get it, but it made no difference. The members of the CCAC are a collegial group, and Tom is my good friend. We both shared the goal of pushing for a Peace dollar coin. In addition, Tom struck upon the idea of doing the Morgan dollar as well. Now, we needed to get it done.

The 116th Congress convened on January 3, 2019. It took us until early March to get a meeting with Mint Director David Ryder. Without the Mint's approval, this project was going nowhere. Our plan was to introduce legislation authorizing the two silver dollars as commemorative coins for 2021. By rule, Congress limits commemorative coin legislation to two programs per year. If two programs received approval in front of us, we were dead in the water.

The meeting with Ryder went well; he gave us the green light from the Mint's perspective while reminding us that the Mint was prohibited by law from lobbying Congress. Immediately after the meeting, I texted Andy Barr and asked for a meeting. He could give me ten minutes that afternoon. I carried in my pocket that day an 1878 Morgan dollar from the Carson City Mint and a high relief 1921 Peace dollar. I showed them to Representative Barr as I pitched the legislation. He was all in but there was a problem. The Democrats had won control of the House in the mid-term elections. Andy was no longer even on the subcommittee with Mint oversight.

However, he knew Representative Emanuel Cleaver, the new chair. Support was forthcoming.

Next came the decisions regarding allocation of the surcharges from the commemorative program that went to charitable organizations. Our intention originally was to name the American Numismatic Association and earmark the funds for numismatic education. The World War I Museum is situated in Cleaver's district, and he was on its board of directors. We split the surcharge. Then we received feedback that Director Ryder wanted to involve the Carson City Mint Museum. As part of that package, Representative Mark Amodei, representing the district within which the museum is situated, came on board.

All this maneuvering stretched into June. By then several other commemorative coin proposals were well out in front of us. We finally got all the necessary signoffs, and the bill was introduced on July 16, 2019. At that point, Ryder wished Tom and me good luck; we both understood that to mean the Mint was limited in what support could be provided.

It takes 290 cosponsors to release a commemorative coin bill from committee for a House vote. By September, it was obvious to me that we were never going to get the needed cosponsors. Tom and I were two people without an organization behind us to get those endorsements. To have a fighting chance, an organization needs a Washington presence to pass a commemorative coin bill.

My reaction was to ask the Mint to draft a bill that would authorize the two silver dollars straight up without any ties to commemorative coinage. However, Representative Barr was not ready to quit with the bill, working that fall to gain supporters on the House floor. Meanwhile Tom and I continued to work the few congressmen we knew in support of his efforts.

Our work was for naught when at the end of October, Director Ryder, at a numismatic forum, called for a gold version of the Morgan silver dollar. Tom and I had no advance warning. At that time, I had ten years in service on the CCAC. Over time I had come to describe the Mint as a black box. The CCAC had input through our critiques of designs but were restricted beyond that function. I knew there were naysayers within the hierarchy of the Mint regarding Tom's and my belief that these silver dollars would be a blockbuster in the marketplace. We had at the start proposed moving a coin press from the Denver Mint to the old Carson City Mint for a special striking as part of the program. That had been killed internally as too risky. Now one thing was definite; this bill was hanging by a thread at best.

By Christmas, two other bills had passed the House and Senate. Andy asked for a meeting and came to my home to talk about the situation. Three hours later, he was on board. His only stipulation was that Director Ryder must commit to the project. After the first of the year, he and Amodei met with Ryder, and the decision was made to draft a new bill. There was one key change from the draft legislation I had requested in September; there would be no termination in the authority to strike the dollar coins. In addition, Amodei was pressing for some type of recognition of the former Carson City and New Orleans Mints that struck the Morgan dollar. Ryder resolved this issue through the use of privy marks on some of the dollars that would be struck at Philadelphia. While the game plan was now set, time was short. This Congress would adjourn on December 17, 2020.

Then COVID hit and the federal government went remote. At the CCAC telephonic administrative meeting on March 10, Ryder was optimistic about the silver dollar legislation in his report. He went on to state that the Mint had done an economic analysis of the bill, and it generated $30 million for the organization. He was meeting with Treasury Secretary Mnuchin the following week to seek Treasury Department support. The bill, HR.6192, was introduced on Wednesday, March 11.

All Ryder would ever say about his meeting at Treasury was that it was "difficult." There was also the matter of a financial assessment of the bill by the Office of Management and Budget. At the next remote CCAC meeting on April 14, Director Ryder reported that the silver dollar legislation had received favorable comment from both Democrats and Republicans. Jennifer Warren, director of legislative and intergovernmental affairs at the Mint, was explaining the bill on the Hill and getting a positive reception. Ryder was still optimistic. The revenue numbers were good and projected for a timeframe when they would be most needed at the Mint. Ryder was focused here on the imminent runoff of the America the Beautiful Quarter program. However, the bad news was that Congress had adjourned due to COVID and would not reconvene until May 4.

After Congress reconvened, an effort was geared up to find a senator to introduce the bill in that chamber. We hit a brick wall; all our approaches fell flat. On June 2, I kicked it up a notch, calling Jimmy Hayes. Jimmy is a retired congressman from Lafayette, Louisiana, and a serious numismatist. Our friendship had formed over the years as we each had interests in the medallic work of Augustus Saint-Gaudens. Hayes at the very onset of this effort had agreed to be "of counsel" to me. Now he told me to have somebody get in touch with Senator Mike Enzi. While he was retiring at the end of this Congress, his involvement with the Sacagawea dollar legislation might make him favorable to these silver dollars as well. Hayes gave me two other observations. If Senator Enzi took this project, he would not just introduce the bill and let it sit, something that I had learned happens all too often. Also, Enzi maintained a good staff.

The next day, Matt Jackson, Andy Barr's staffer working this legislation, made the call to Enzi's office. They had questions; that was good, nobody else had even shown that much interest. The senator's staff reached out directly to Warren at the Mint. She met with them and "convinced" them it was a good bill. Jackson relayed to me on June 12 that Senator Enzi would introduce the bill the following week. First he needed to enlist a Democrat to introduce the bill with him.

On July 7, Warren sent word to Tom that she had been in contact with Senator Enzi's office, working with Conroy Stout, his legislative aid. She had told Stout that Tom and I had worked the bill on the House side, and we would be able to assist him. That was all the introduction I needed. In an email, I filled in Stout on our efforts to date and that it was retired Representative Hayes who first suggested Senator Enzi, the two men having been friends during their time in Congress together.

Emails quickly morphed into phone calls. I learned that Stout always tried to pick up the Mint bills within Enzi's office because his great grandfather and grandfather had been coin collectors. For me that was a relief; I quickly learned that Stout knew way more than the basics about numismatics. However, the conundrum still remained; we needed a Democrat to cosponsor.

On Monday, July 23, the logjam broke both in the House and Senate. Jackson told me the HR.6192 had been paired with Democratic Representative Barbara Lee's HR.1923, Women's History and 19th Amendment Centennial Quarter Dollar Coin Program. The two bills, one Democratic and one Republican, would be brought up for Unanimous Consent together and passed the following Monday. I would never know what involvement the Mint had in this pairing but it was crucial to the bill's success.

When the Lee bill was originally introduced on March 27, 2019, it called for commemorating the 19th Amendment with the issuance of a series of quarters, bearing designs emblematic of the accomplishments and contributions of a prominent woman in this field from each state, the District of Columbia, and each territory. Senators Cortez Masto and Deb Fischer had introduced a companion bill in the Senate on August 1, 2019.

Now renamed The Circulating Collectible Coin Redesign Act of 2020, the Lee bill modified its original proposal and added those that had been advocated by Director Ryder at the Mint. There would be quarters through 2025 depicting prominent American women. A coinage program was included for the Semiquincentennial in 2026. A final series of quarters and half dollars for 2027–2030 would honor American youth sports and the Paralympics.

At this same point, Stout called me to relate that Senator Masto would be the Democrat with Enzi on Senate Bill S.4326. There was a caveat in my view that arose from this pairing in the two houses of Congress. The companion bill violated both of Jimmy Hayes's basic rules; it was neither short nor simple.

On the morning of the Monday appointed to seek Unanimous Consent, the two bills were pulled from the House agenda. According to Jackson, the recent changes in the Lee bill had caused revenue projection issues that the sponsors needed to fix. Without knowledge of the exact workings, I understood enough to know that HR.6192 was stalled until this issue was fixed and probably would not make the House agenda again until its members returned from summer break, after Labor Day. The real problem was that the Congressional Budget Office, which evaluated all the bills for financial impact, was totally wrapped up with scoring proposals for another round of COVID stimuli.

Labor Day was late in 2020, falling on September 7. That week came and went. Much to my frustration, so did the following week. Jackson bore the brunt of my impatience and short emails. Yet neither of us could do anything to speed up the process.

The CCAC met telephonically on Tuesday of the third week that the House was back in session. In the administrative meeting, Director Ryder was still positive that the legislation was going to happen. He mentioned that he had had a conversation with the chief financial officer of the Congressional Budget Office. He said no more, but I could fill in the blanks. The director was pushing or perhaps shoving as hard as he legally could. The next morning, as I was finishing my coffee and preparing for the final session of the CCAC meeting, Tom called. The bill had passed the House the previous evening.

The time lost in the House now compressed the time available for passage in the Senate. Adding to my worries on that Thursday, September 24, Warren called Tom and told him the two of us should start pushing for cosponsors in the Senate. I spent Friday spinning my wheels and getting nowhere.

On Saturday, I called Jimmy Hayes, really only looking to tell him that the Mint had been successful getting the bill out of the ditch in the House. After talking a bit about Saint-Gaudens, Jimmy chided me for not calling him on Friday. My comment was that I had simply run out of energy. He told me that Senator Enzi and his wife had called, and they had had a long conversation. Had Hayes known, he would have pushed Enzi to get the Senate bill out for a vote under Unanimous Consent. He and I talked some more, and then Jimmy volunteered to call the senator back to discuss the bill.

On the following Monday, I talked with Stout, and he stated that the Senate had passed a rule that no coin bills would come to the floor under Unanimous Consent rules. If the intent was to duplicate the House approach, pairing Enzi with Masto's bill, amended to reflect HR.1923 in its final form, that effort was absolutely dead. We needed 67 cosponsors to get S.4326 out of the Committee on Banking, Housing and Urban Affairs and up for a vote. I questioned how firm that rule was. It was firm according to Stout. The odds of success in the Senate just got a whole lot longer.

As if on cue, Donald Scarinci, our colleague from the CCAC, entered the picture. Tom had repeatedly called and emailed him in August to make an approach to his friend, Senator Robert Menendez, to cosponsor S.4326 to no avail. We waited, but still nothing on that front. I sent an email that was almost desperate in tone on October 14. I knew gaining Menendez's support was not low-hanging fruit, but we needed broad bipartisan support. Without Scarinci's help, I worried that we would fail to get this bill passed. After sending the email, I told Stout that either I had just accomplished something, or I had accomplished nothing. I got a heartening response later that day. Scarinci had already spoken to Menendez and would follow up. On October 24, Scarinci came through with the co-sponsorship of Senator Menendez.

The other key to our efforts was Pennsylvania Senator Toomey. Tom had met him at a campaign rally in Pittsburgh the prior year, seeking support for the earlier bill. Toomey had been negative; he did not support coin bills. When he questioned why Tom was approaching him, Tom's answer was to the point: the Philadelphia Mint. Toomey softened his stance, and Tom closed the conversation by giving him a 1921 Morgan silver dollar. Toomey looked it over and put it in his pocket. Tom also had close contacts within Toomey's staff that he had worked. On October 26 Tom's hard work came to fruition, Toomey broke from his past practice and agreed to cosponsor the bill. We now had two key members from the Committee on Banking, Housing and Urban Affairs on board.

Yet nothing happened; all eyes were on the looming presidential election. The election came and went. When President Trump failed to concede, the turmoil of the election simply continued unabated. That left only one logical approach; get the bill out of committee under Unanimous Consent rules as had been done in the House of Representatives.

In frustration, I asked Conroy Stout: "Why wouldn't Senator Crapo want to push this bill?" Crapo was chair of the banking committee. Stout told me that he had researched for precedents to justify the release of this coin bill and had found four instances, although not the strongest in terms of supporting the effort. Still, it was a disappointment when I learned at the Mint CCAC administrative briefing prior to the public meeting of November 17 that Senator Crapo was still refusing to move the bill. He would release the bill if it gained the required cosponsors, but he would not take the initiative to push the bill in order to surmount that hurdle.

The Thanksgiving recess came and went. I talked to Jimmy Hayes once more only to hear what I already knew: Unanimous Consent was the way to go. I did learn early the next week that Senator Enzi was on the floor of the Senate actively working this bill. Yet while I kept Jimmy in the loop, I was careful not to tread upon the relationship that he had with Enzi. If Jimmy was going to talk to Enzi, I knew it had to be on his own terms. It was tough for me after all this time to sit on the sidelines unable to lend a hand. The simple fact was that the action had moved above my pay grade.

The first positive news came on Friday, December 4. Senator Enzi had convinced Senator Crapo the night before to cosponsor the bill. When Stout told me in a text, I was elated. After acknowledging the good news, I knew I had to ask the question; still I waited a good five minutes to savor the small victory before sending a new text back to Stout. Did this mean that Crapo was now willing to consider letting the bill out under Unanimous Consent rules? Of course not, we still needed the 67 cosponsors.

It was now two weeks until the 116th Congress closed its doors for good. On Sunday, I updated Andy Barr and asked for advice. He came back with a solution; it seemed a long shot to me. The omnibus spending bill was still pending in the Senate. Get Senator Enzi to push to have the silver dollar bill folded into this package as a "pay for" item. I passed it on to Stout. We had nothing to lose; maybe some mud would stick to the wall.

Monday, December 6, came and went with nothing. On Tuesday morning I sent Stout a text, asking, with some fear, where things stood. Stout replied that, surprisingly, they were not in a bad position; he wanted a conference call at 2:00 that afternoon with Tom and me. On that call we learned that Senator Enzi had convinced Senator Crapo to allow a hotline. In this action HR.6192 would be brought directly to the Senate floor and if there were no objections, it would be passed. If all went well, Stout thought the bill might pass by Friday. I was beside myself, simply ecstatic. Then it sank in. I must wait, and the longer it took, the less time was available to remedy any objection and still the bill must get the necessary floor time to pass.

What a hotline really means is that the original House bill would be brought up in a "Cloakroom Meeting" held separately by both political parties. These cloakrooms are an entity unto themselves. It is where the senators hang out when not required on the floor. There is permanent staff assigned in support. In effect these cloakrooms are a cross between a wheelhouse and an officers' wardroom for the Democrats and Republicans in the Senate. Staff will notify each senator of any bill being hotlined. If there are no holds placed by any senator, then the bill is cleared for consideration by the whole Senate to be passed under Unanimous Consent. These holds can be arbitrary and capricious, even vicious. I was well aware of the Peace dollar's fate under Unanimous Consent rules in 1921.

Of course, nothing seemed to happen. I held my breath into the weekend. Monday of the last week the Senate was scheduled to be in session came and went. On

Tuesday I could not stand it any longer; I asked Stout for an update. Stout did not have one. He knew the bill came up in the Republican cloakroom the preceding Tuesday. However, the Democrats did not bring it up in their cloakroom until Thursday, thus the reason for yet another delay. Stout did not know how long after the bill came up in the meetings that senators had to place a hold. The time was arbitrary and varied. I turned to Masto's assistant. She knew that no holds had come out of the Democrats. I felt buoyed by that information.

All I had to do was look at the calendar. We were assured of time only through Friday to get this bill on the floor. All Stout could say was that he was hopeful. There was nothing Wednesday. Thursday, I did not ask for an update. It was better to pretend I was an ostrich and stick my head into the sand. In this case it at least was safer that way. Suddenly, a senator placed a hold on the companion Lee bill. Stout and Warren swung into action, inserting an amendment addressing the objection and that bill was back on track a couple hours later. What next?

The text came Thursday night at 7:30. The bill had passed. It had only taken 52 seconds during the day's wrap-up.

The Constitution provides that legislation enacted by both houses of Congress become law after ten days without a presidential signature unless Congress adjourns. In the case of adjournment, the president must sign the legislation within ten days, or it is deemed to be pocket vetoed. The Constitution explicitly excludes Sundays from being considered in that timeline. My problem was I could not find out whether legal holidays were excluded and when the ten-day count commenced.

On the positive side, Congress did not adjourn the week before Christmas as originally anticipated. Instead, a circus-like atmosphere developed over the defense spending bill and a third COVID stimulus bill. Meanwhile I counted days on my fingers. The good news in this mess was that Speaker Pelosi was not going to adjourn the 116th Congress until the morning of January 3 when the new Congress convened at noon. She wanted to prevent President Trump from making interim appointments that would be valid until the adjournment of the next Congress. As a result, I thought the silver dollar bill was home free and could become law without the president's signature.

Still, I worried; I could not find Andy Barr to get any update. Tom worked his contacts and got the answer. The ten-day period did not start until the bill was delivered to the White House. That was December 24, a full week after it had passed Congress. That meant a presidential signature was going to be required for the bill to become law. While of little comfort, there were 50 bills on Trump's desk awaiting his signature.

Now I had reason to worry again. I could see from the newspaper reports that Trump was in Georgia on Monday, January 4, campaigning for the Republican senatorial candidates in a last-ditch effort before the special runoff election the next day. I could forget Monday.

Tuesday morning, January 5, on a short vacation, I went for a long walk in the Smokey Mountains with my wife. There was nothing I could do about the situation in Washington anyway. About halfway through, my phone buzzed. Surprisingly, given my remote location, I had a text. Conroy Stout informed me that President Trump had signed the bill that morning. It was now officially known as Public Law 116-286.

In my personal triumph, I knew there was one unanswered question. I waited until February 3 to call Jimmy Hayes. Deep down I had suspected that he had helped somehow in the Senate. He had been coy in our conversation at Christmastime after the Senate passage. I suspected that something had happened, and now I pressed my friend. He told me that he had known Crapo when the senator was in the House with him. He also knew that one of Crapo's good friends was a major coin collector. Jimmy called Crapo about the bill, and then had Crapo's coin-collector friend call as well. Coupled with Senator Enzi's persistence, Crapo then agreed to the hotline.

The Morgan and Peace dollars struck under the authority of PL 116-286.

The market reception for these silver dollars was tremendous. The dollar coins were offered for sale in groups of two over three ordering periods. The order window in each instance maxed out and closed within 20 minutes. Mike Enzi never saw the coins; he died in a biking accident on July 26, 2021. Ultimately, collectors would purchase more than one million of these silver dollars in an overwhelming market response. And thus the Morgan and Peace dollars returned—a final encore from "when coins were king."

January 13, 2023
The Hermitage Hotel
Nashville, Tennessee

ACKNOWLEDGMENTS

My previous historical works all had a start point and an end point before I set out to tell their stories. I certainly had a start point for this book as well. It is the sequel to my second book, *Philadelphia Strikes Gold*. It picks up in the United States Senate as William Gwin, facing a political career cut short by the coming Civil War, moves to split Nevada away from Utah Territory. His action will place the Comstock Lode firmly in the hands of San Francisco financiers. What follows is a colorful story of when coins dominated American politics.

I originally intended to end the story with Franklin Roosevelt's recall of gold coins in 1933. It did not turn out the way I planned. As I began researching material for the book, I also began a quest to coin Peace dollars in 2021 in celebration of the 100th anniversary of the implementation of this design. It was a logical next step to include the iconic Morgan dollar in the celebration as the idea matured and gathered support. With the enactment of the authorizing legislation on January 5, 2021, I suddenly had the end point of my book. It was the celebration of that time when coins were king.

My research for this book was done almost entirely online. However, there are key people who were essential to my efforts. Nancy Oliver and Rich Kelly played an outsized role in supporting my efforts to tell the story from San Francisco. Their biography of Joseph Breck Harmstead served as the glue that held the storyline together in San Francisco. However, they were more to me, helping when my research hit a dead end as it did from time to time. Rich was also kind enough to serve as a first reader of my draft chapters. Also invaluable to me was Lexie Paulson, who served as my on-the-ground researcher in San Francisco. She gave me much of the material for the story of George Pinney. For the story in Washington, D.C., I am indebted to the Newman Numismatic Portal at Washington University in St. Louis, Missouri. I extend my gratitude to the researchers who have contributed material from Treasury Department records at the National Archives and Records Administration to this portal. Also, Christine Jacobson of the Houghton Library at Harvard University was very helpful pulling together the images of Theodore Roosevelt. Finally, there is Pam Scot, who has helped with all three of my books.

There are four published works that also deserve special acknowledgment by me: William Bierly's *In God We Trust*, Richard Zacks's *Island of Vice*, William Jett Lauck's *The Causes of the Panic of 1893*, and Robert F. Bruner and Sean D. Carr's *The Panic of 1907 Lessons Learned from the Market's Perfect Storm*. Each provided important insights at specific places in the story.

I also want to recognize Dr. Michael Richman for being both a friend and a patient teacher as I progressed from a coin collector to a numismatist knowledgeable in the fine arts. Finally, there is my friendship with Jeff and Mary Lynn Garrett. I can't thank them enough for their support through the years.

About the Author

Michael F. Moran has been a numismatist since childhood, when his grandfather got him started collecting Indian Head pennies. He fell in love with the art of Augustus Saint-Gaudens in 1960, and spent the summer's lawn-mowing income on one of the artist's $20 gold pieces.

Moran holds a bachelor's degree in civil engineering and a master's in industrial administration from Purdue University. He has spent a business career in corporate mergers and acquisitions in the energy fields and now serves as a managing partner in several diverse businesses.

Since leaving his corporate life, Moran has embarked on a numismatic writing career. His accolades include the American Numismatic Association's Heath Literary Award for an article on the San Francisco earthquake, the Professional Numismatists Guild's Robert Friedberg Award for *Striking Change,* and the Numismatic Literary Guild Award for best U.S. coin book for *1849: Philadelphia Strikes Gold.* Moran is currently serving his fourth term on the Citizens Coinage Advisory Committee at the United States Mint, reviewing and critiquing the designs for all the Mint's coins and medals. In addition, he partnered with Tom Uram to spearhead the drive for Congressional authorization to allow the Mint to again strike Morgan and Peace silver dollars in 2021.

Besides his numismatic pursuits, Moran is active in the Congressionally chartered Theodore Roosevelt Association. He presently serves on the executive committee and is the association's treasurer. He also chairs the finance committee and the development committee.

Moran resides with his wife, Dee Dee, in Lexington, Kentucky.

Notes and Bibliography

Please use the QR code to view the endnotes and bibliography for this volume.

Index

Aldrich-Vreeland Act, 476–478
Allison, William Boyd, 167–168, 298
aluminum, 311, 312
Anderson, Harriette Eugenia, 339, 397–398
Andrew, A. Piatt, 476, 484
Angel of Victory, 182, 249, 272, 338, 353–355, 373, 397, 399, 420, 427, 486
Anglo-California Bank, 151, 173–174, 179, 186, 209–210
arrastras, 3
Arthur, Chester, 196, 206, 223, 226–227

Babcox, Jefferson, 96, 127
Badlands, 229, 257–260
Bank Crowd, 16, 17
Bank of California, 13–15, 18, 20, 29–31, 95, 106, 111, 113
  failure of, 174–176
Bank of England, 295, 435–436, 490–491
Barber, Charles, 139–140, 190–192, 274–280, 284–288, 290, 292–293, 304–306, 309–310, 315, 317–319, 323–324, 348–351, 385, 392–393, 415, 417–419, 422–424, 428–429, 430–433, 446–447, 450–457, 458, 463, 465–466, 468, 472–473, 475
Barber, William, 90, 93, 120–121, 139–142, 192
bimetallic standard, 54, 67, 135, 161, 266–270, 295, 329, 329
  international, 167, 297–298, 331–332
Birdsall, Lewis, 8
Blaine, James G., 133, 136, 194–196, 205–207, 231, 237, 251–252, 262, 297
Bland Allison Act, 170, 180, 186, 245, 267–269
Bland, Richard, 160–161, 167
bonanza, 3, 77–78, 81, 99
Boutwell, George, 30, 58
branch mints, 51–52, 170, 180, 344–345
Brenner, Victor D., 466–467
Broderick, Senator David, 9
Browne, J. Ross, 3–4, 9, 11
Bryan, William Jennings, 332, 334, 335–336, 463, 480
Burchard, Horatio, 189, 239–240, 265
Burnham, Daniel, 283, 365, 369

Cameron, Donald, 136–137, 183–185, 189, 195–196, 215, 249, 255, 265, 269–271, 316, 341
Cameron, Elizabeth Sherman, 182–186, 248, 271–272, 341, 354–355, 383
Cannon, Joe, 137, 365, 369, 382, 461, 478
Carlisle, John G., 298–299, 304, 308–309, 312–313, 316–321, 325–326, 331, 374
Carr, Bill, 87–88, 149, 153
Carson City Mint, 52, 128, 241, 266, 312, 497–498
Centennial Exposition, 139–140, 146–147
central bank, 479
Central Pacific Railroad, 18, 20, 31
Cheeseman, David W., 11, 19, 29–30
Civil Service Commission, 215–216, 262, 271, 325–326, 331
civil service reform, 194, 196, 214–216, 230, 237, 264, 325–326, 339, 343
Civil War, 26–27, 47, 166, 295, 312, 347
clearinghouse, 168, 187, 223, 296, 300, 412–413, 438–439, 443–444, 477
Cleveland, Grover, 228–231, 237, 245–246, 298–300, 321, 326, 331, 343
Cochran, J, 97, 130, 153
Cochran, Joe, 30
Coinage Act of 1873, 70–73, 90, 222, 244, 329
coinage charge, 35–36, 52, 57, 60–63, 66, 71–73, 117–118, 123
commemorative coins, 283, 284–288, 485, 489
  Columbian half dollar, 283–288, 303
  Columbian quarter dollar, 303
  Illinois Centennial, 475
  Lafayette Memorial, 348–351
  Panama Pacific International Exposition, 469–470
  so-called dollars, 141
Commission of Fine Arts, 469, 472, 485
Comstock, Henry, 3–4
Comstock Lode, 4–5, 6
  discovery of, 3–4
  expansion of, 77
  struggle for control of, 15–17
Conkling, Roscoe, 136, 204–207, 226–227
Conness, Joseph, 33, 39
Consolidated Virginia, 80–81, 99–100, 108, 110
copper-nickel coinage, 47–50, 57, 59–61, 64–66, 68, 71, 217–218, 495–496

Cortelyou, George, 370, 376, 379, 425, 433–434, 435, 440, 443–444, 446–447, 455, 465
Crown Point Mine, 76–79, 80

Davis, Martin, 210–213
de Francisci, Anthony, 486–487
Dodge, Henry, 208–210
Donohoe, Joseph, 14
Donohoe, Ralston & Company, 4
double eagle, 9, 22, 42, 126, 274, 425, 446–447, 454, 458–459, 463, 490, 492

earthquake, 39–40, 403–406, 436, 469
Eckfeldt, John, 8–9, 10, 10, 98, 104–105
Ellsworth, James, 284–288, 315, 382, 457

Fair, James, 79–80, 99–100
Farragut statue, 198–204
Federal Reserve, 481–482, 490–492
Federal Reserve Notes, 481–482, 484, 491
Felton, Charles, 18–19, 29, 127
financial panic, 483
  of 1873, 73–74, 115–116
  of 1893, 294, 299–300, 320, 329
  of 1907, 435–440, 442–447, 453, 476
  or 1873, 161
  Great Depression, 489–490
  San Francisco earthquake, 410
Fisk, Jim, 29
five-dollar gold, 190, 219–220, 463, 468, 483, 489
fractional currency, 47, 50, 116–117, 122–123, 125, 134, 137, 138
Fraser, James Earle, 353, 362–364, 467–469, 486, 489
Fraser, Laura Gardin, 468, 489
free silver, 224, 247, 267–269, 296–297, 300, 330–332, 336, 480
Fry, J.D., 15

Gage, Lyman, 283, 343
Gap Nickel Mine, 49
Garfield, James, 194–196, 204–207, 446
Gilder, Richard Watson, 202–204, 221, 230–231, 237, 243–244, 258, 260–261, 264, 273–277, 307, 317–320, 360–361, 367, 371, 383–384, 415
Glover, John, 177–179, 181
Gold certificates, 299, 347, 481, 491–493
gold standard, 26–27, 115, 194, 245, 297, 313, 329–332, 346, 376, 482
  end of, 493
  international, 54–55, 69, 74, 101, 161, 484, 490–491
Gould and Curry Mine, 13, 14, 80

Gould, Jay, 29, 228
greenbacks, 27, 116, 118, 167, 295–297
Gwin, Senator William, 2, 5–6, 7–8

Hale & Norcross, 23–24
half eagle, 54–56, 464, 466
Haraszthy, Augustin, 8, 9–10, 153
hard money, 74
Harmstead, Joseph, 7–8, 9, 10–11, 30, 38, 41–43, 85–87, 94–96, 98, 105, 127, 154, 210, 214, 243
Harrison, Benjamin, 238, 255–256, 266–269, 295–296
Harrison, Russell, 238–241, 262–265
Hayes, Rutherford B., 133, 136, 137, 168, 226–227
Hayward, Alvinza, 23, 77–78, 179
Hempstead, Charles, 10
Hering, Henry, 353, 360, 414–415, 420, 422–423, 428, 431–433, 450–456
Hewston, John, 8, 9, 10

"In God We Trust," 48–49, 60, 73, 142–143, 273–275, 396, 430, 460–462, 466–467
Janvier lathe, 393, 417, 423, 431–433, 446, 450, 453, 465
Jones, John Percival, 24, 76–80, 102–103, 119–120, 122, 161, 298, 329
JP Morgan & Company, 379, 413, 438, 444–445

Kelley, Judge, 192
Kelley, William, 56–57, 64–65
Kelly, Eugene, 14, 33
Kimball, James P., 240–244, 264–265

LaGrange, Hugh, 173–175, 177
LaGrange, Oscar Hugh, 40–42, 60, 82–85, 88–89, 94–95, 96, 104, 108–110, 112, 124–129, 130–132, 149–149, 153–154, 155–159
Leach, Frank, 342–343, 402, 423, 428, 449–450, 454–459, 462–463, 465–467
ledge, 3
Leech, Edward, 90, 130, 265, 273–278, 284–286, 290–291, 303–306
Lees, James, 14
Linderman, Henry, 31, 33, 37, 53, 58, 62–63, 67–68, 69, 72–73, 90–94, 97–98, 100–101, 104–105, 108–110, 111–112, 119–122, 122–123, 124, 138–145, 149–151, 154, 159, 162–164, 170–172, 173–181
lode, 3
Lodge, Henry Cabot, 230–231, 330, 336–337
Low, F.F., 19, 150–151, 153–155, 157, 166, 173–174, 178–179, 186, 210

MacNeil, Hermon, 361, 472–475, 497
McAdoo, William Gibbs, 469, 472, 483
McKim, Charles, 328, 358–359, 365–366, 368–372, 381–382
McKinley Act, 295, 297
McKinley, William, 329–330, 333, 336–338, 363–364
medals, 276, 361–362, 489
- Benjamin Franklin, 385, 393–395, 396–397, 399–401
- Centennial Internation Exposition, 140–144
- Pan-American Exposition, 363–364
- Panama Canal service, 466
- Roosevelt Inaugural, 386–391
- Washington Inauguration Centennial, 242, 260–263
- World's Columbian Exposition, 290–293, 307–320, 323, 348, 420

Millet, Frank, 350, 386–387
Mills, Ogden, 14, 17, 81, 101–102
Mint technology, 108, 108–109, 344–345, 392–393, 417, 423, 431, 453, 465
Morgan dollar, 171, 497–504
Morgan tomb, 232–236, 351
Morgan, Edwin, 35, 55–57, 147, 198–202, 232–234, 232–234
Morgan, George, 143–145, 162–163, 219, 287, 350, 419, 456, 470, 475, 484
Morgan, J.P., 321, 377–379, 382, 435, 439–440, 442–447, 461, 478–479

national bank, 29, 116–117, 347, 438, 481, 490
National Bank Notes, 27, 186–187, 266, 480–481
National Banking Act, 299–300
National Currency Commission, 477–478
National Silver Committee, 267–269
Nevada Bank, 104, 166
New Orleans Mint, 7, 210–213
New York Stock Exchange, 73, 443–445, 483
nickel coins, 49–51, 57, 59, 65, 218–219, 467–469
nickel metal, 49–50, 57, 217

Ophir Gold & Silver Mining Company, 4–5, 13
Ophir Mine, 13–14, 4, 13, 80, 101–102, 107–108
Oriental Bank of London, 31, 32, 95, 101, 108

Pacific Company, 5
Pacific Refinery and Bullion Exchange Co, 125
Palmer, Bertha, 303–306
Pan-American Exposition, 360–361, 363
Panama Canal, 469
Panama Pacific International Exposition, 469
patronage system, 8, 61, 87, 204–206, 213–214, 252, 256, 265, 267, 312, 326, 331, 342–343
pattern coins, 48, 51, 90–94, 120–121, 140–143, 142, 162–164, 170, 190–191, 217–218, 219–220, 242, 278–280, 278–280, 284–288, 304–306, 349–350, 419, 427, 430, 465
Peace dollar, 485–487, 493, 497–504
Peddle, Caroline, 303–307
Pendleton, George, 214–216
Pinney, George, 83–85, 89, 97–98, 103–104, 112–113, 148–150, 152–154, 156–158
Pittman Act of 1918, 484, 487
Platt, Thomas, 206–207, 215, 252, 256, 264, 297, 330–331, 337–338, 360, 461
Pollock Commission, 97–98
Pollock, James, 47–49, 60
porphyry, 4, 76
Pratt, Bela Lyon, 464–466
Preston, Robert, 90, 188–190, 211–213, 244, 284, 308–311, 314–315, 317–321, 323, 343, 418–419, 450–454

Ralston, Billy, 2, 4–5, 12–16, 17–19, 23–25, 29–31, 32–34, 36–37, 61–63, 67, 81, 94–95, 100, 106, 110–111
Ralston, James Alpheus, 15, 16
Ralston, William, 174–176
refining contracts, 33–37, 62–63, 66–67, 73, 78, 84, 95, 124–125, 177
refining process, 32–33, 108–109, 124, 344–345
- legislation, 33–34, 35–36

relief, 454–457
Resumption Act of 1875, 122, 133, 165, 184–185, 312-313
Roberts, George, 343–345, 348–349, 385, 392, 418, 425, 428–429, 433–434, 446–447, 450, 467, 469
Roosevelt, Edith Carow, 225, 257–259, 271–272, 361, 365–366, 367–371, 380, 382–383, 386–387, 390–391, 399, 450
Roosevelt, Franklin Delano, 491–493, 494
Roosevelt, Theodore, 225–231, 257–260, 262–264, 302–303, 324–328, 329–330, 332, 333–334, 335–338, 360–362, 363–365, 367–370, 376–380, 383–385, 395–396, 397–398, 416, 420–421, 422, 430, 433–434, 436, 441–442, 445–447, 449, 456, 460–463, 464–465, 476–478, 479–780
Root, Elihu, 258, 366, 374, 378, 382–383, 395–397, 399–401, 446, 481

Saint-Gaudens, Augusta "Gussie," 198–203, 234, 352, 354–356, 400, 418, 420, 450, 452, 454–455, 458–459

Saint-Gaudens, Augustus, 146–147, 198, 231–236, 250–254, 260–261, 272, 274–280, 282, 289–293, 303, 306–308, 309–311, 313–321, 322–324, 328, 334–335, 338–339, 353–357, 358, 371–375, 381, 422, 430, 499
coinage of, 383–385, 387, 392, 395–396, 397–398, 414–421, 424–425, 427, 460–463, 464–465, 487
illness of, 352–353, 356–358, 393, 395, 399–401, 414–416, 418, 425–427, 433–434
Saint-Gaudens, Louis, 202, 276, 353, 385, 393–395
San Francisco Assaying and Refining Works, 32, 34, 36–37, 95, 104, 111–112, 158, 174
San Francisco Chronicle, 79–80, 127, 149–150, 152–157, 155–157, 159, 173–174, 176–177, 412
San Francisco Mint, 38–39, 42–45, 108–109, 124–125, 342
corruption at, 82–87, 94–95, 149, 173–177
earthquake, 45, 403–410
first, 7, 8, 9
Sargent, Aaron, 36–37, 52, 87–88, 149, 159, 186, 342
Schmolz, William, 11
seigniorage, 66, 117, 123, 135, 346, 484
Sharon, William, 15–18, 23, 77–78, 101–103, 111
Shaw Memorial, 232, 289–293, 307, 318, 324, 334–335, 338–339, 360
Shaw, Leslie, 383, 385, 392, 398, 425, 463
Sherman, John, 30, 54–55, 70–72, 115–118, 134–135, 137, 138, 160–162, 181, 184–187, 226, 267–270, 297, 298, 347
presidential runs by, 133–134, 193–196, 231, 251–252
as treasury secretary, 164
Sherman Monument, 338–339, 353–356, 358, 363, 371–375
Sherman Silver Purchase Act, 270, 295, 336, 346
repeal of, 298–300, 312
Sherman, William Tecumseh, 138, 183–184, 252–254, 272, 374
Silver Certificates, 169, 187, 222–223, 247, 266, 295–296, 298, 347, 484, 493, 494
silver dollars, 123, 134, 136–137, 222–223, 245, 322–323, 331, 484, 493
legislation concerning, 59–61, 64–67
remonetized, 160–161, 165, 168–170
Silver Kings, 99, 106, 124–125
silver movement, 74
Silver Purchase Act, 494
silver standard, 161, 300
Slocum, Riley, 10–11
Snowden, A. Loudon, 188–189, 192, 217
Snyder, Jacob, 11
specie payments, 27–29, 116, 187, 313
resumption of, 55, 74, 124, 133–135
stamping mills, 16
Stella, 190
Stevens, Robert, 11
Stewart, William, 246, 329
Stewart, William Morris, 5, 30, 35–36, 61, 101–102, 153
stock market, 29, 73, 111, 435–436, 442, 490
Sutro, Adolph, 16

Taft, William Howard, 463, 467–468, 479–480
Tammany Hall, 230, 327
tariffs, 251, 266–267, 269, 294–295, 296–297, 312, 329, 480, 490
ten-dollar gold coins, 126, 490
Saint-Gaudens, 432–433, 449–455, 458
Thacher, John Boyd, 290–293, 307, 316
Tiffany & Company, 244, 261, 309–310, 388–390, 397, 400–401, 417, 430, 451
trade dollars, 65–66, 69–70, 71, 90–94, 100–101, 123, 134–135, 136–137, 165
demonetization, 223
suspension of, 178
Treasury Commission, 150, 195
Treasury Notes, 267–270, 295–296, 299, 346–347
trust company, 438–440, 442–443, 445, 481
twenty-cent piece, 119–122
twenty-dollar gold coins, 22, 126, 446, 490
Saint-Gaudens, 430–434, 449–459

U.S. Steel, 377, 445–446
Union Mill and Mining Company, 16–17
Union Pacific Railroad, 20, 65
Union Party, 18
United States Notes, 194, 346

variety coins, 171–172
vein, 3
vending machine, 467–468, 473, 495–496
Virginia and Truckee Railroad, 17
Virginia City, Nevada, 3–4

Warner, Olin, 284–288
Weil, Henri, 388, 390, 394–395, 423, 428, 466, 468, 470, 472
Weinman, Adolph, 388–390, 472–474, 497
Wilson, Woodrow, 480–481, 483
World's Columbian Exposition, 282, 288, 290, 301–303, 313–314

Yellow Jacket Mine, 24–25, 78